International Sources of Electronic Commerce Regulation

edited by

Thomas Hoeren and Jochen Stauder

Arbeitsberichte zum Informations-,
Telekommunikations- und Medienrecht

Herausgegeben von
Thomas Hoeren und Bernd Holznagel

Institut für Informations-, Telekommunikations-
und Medienrecht (ITM)
der Westfälischen Wilhelms-Universität

Band 8

LIT

International Sources of Electronic Commerce Regulation

edited by

Thomas Hoeren and Jochen Stauder

LIT

2., erweiterte Auflage 2003

Bibliographic information published by Die Deutsche Bibliothek
Die Deutsche Bibliothek lists this publication in the Deutsche
Nationalbibliografie; detailed bibliographic data are available in the
Internet at http://dnb.ddb.de.

ISBN 3-8258-5514-7

© LIT VERLAG Münster   2003
Grevener Str./Fresnostr. 2   48159 Münster
Tel. 0251-23 50 91   Fax 0251-23 19 72
e-Mail: lit@lit-verlag.de   http://www.lit-verlag.de

Distributed in North America by:

Transaction Publishers
New Brunswick (U.S.A.) and London (U.K.)

Transaction Publishers   Tel.: (732) 445 - 2280
Rutgers University   Fax: (732) 445 - 3138
35 Berrue Circle   for orders (U. S. only):
Piscataway, NJ 08854   toll free (888) 999 - 6778

Electronic Commerce Regulation

Textbook on International and European Sources

Edited by

Prof. Dr. Thomas Hoeren

and

Jochen Stauder

Contents

1. Domain Names / Trademarks *1*

    First Council Directive 89/104/EEC of 21 December 1988 to approximate the laws of the Member States relating to trade marks 1

    ICANN - Private Uniform Domain Name Dispute Resolution Policy 9

    ICANN - Rules for Uniform Domain Name Dispute Resolution Policy 14

    Policy and Rules for .biz Domain Names 22

    Policy and Rules for .info Domain Names 41

    Anticybersquatting Consumer Protection Act 52

2. Intellectual Property Rights *59*

a) International and US Law *59*

    Berne Convention for the Protection of Literary and Artistic Works 59

    Agreement on Trade Related Aspects of Intellectual Property Rights (TRIPs) 85

    WIPO Copyright Treaty 110

    WIPO Performances and Phonograms Treaty 115

    Digital Millennium Copyright Act 122

b) European Law *161*

    Council Directive 91/250/EEC of 14 May 1991 on the legal protection of computer programs 161

    Council Directive 92/100/EEC of 19 November 1992 on rental right and lending right and on certain rights related to copyright in the field of intellectual property 167

    Council Directive 93/83/EEC of 27 September 1993 on the coordination of certain rules concerning copyright and rights related to copyright applicable to satellite broadcasting and cable retransmission 174

    Council Directive 93/98/EEC of 29 October 1993 harmonizing the term of protection of copyright and certain related rights 183

    Commission Regulation (EC) No 240/96 of 31 January 1996 on the application of Article 85 (3) of the Treaty to certain categories of technology transfer agreements 189

    Directive 96/9/EC of the European Parliament and of the Council of 11 March 1996 on the legal protection of databases 203

    Directive 2001/29/EC of the European Parliament and of the Council of 22 May 2001 on the harmonisation of certain aspects of copyright and related rights in the information society 213

    Council Regulation (EC) No 6/2002 of 12 December 2001 on Community Designs 227

3. Electronic Payments *260*

    Commission Recommendation 97/489/EC of 30 July 1997 concerning transactions by electronic payment instruments and in particular the relationship between issuer and holder 260

    Directive 2000/12/EC of the European Parliament and of the Council of 20 March 2000 relating to the taking up and pursuit of the business of credit institutions 267

    Directive 2000/28/EC of the European Parliament and of the Council of 18 September 2000 amending Directive 2000/12/EC relating to the taking up and pursuit of the business of credit institutions 318

Directive 2000/46/EC of the European Parliament and of the Council of 18 September 2000 on the taking up, pursuit of and prudential supervision of the business of electronic money institutions 320

4. E-Contracting..326

UNCITRAL Model Law on Electronic Commerce 326

UNCITRAL Model Law on Electronic Signatures 333

International League for Competition Law - Code of Conduct in Regard to Fair Competition in Electronic Commerce..337

Directive 98/34/EC of the European Parliament and of the Council of 22 June 1998 laying down a procedure for the provision of information in the field of technical standards and regulations ...344

Directive 98/48/EC of the European Parliament and of the Council of 20 July 1998 amending Directive 98/34/EC laying down a procedure for the provision of information in the field of technical standards and regulations 355

Directive 1999/93/EC of the European Parliament and of the Council of 13 December 1999 on a Community framework for electronic signatures 365

Directive 2000/31/EC of the European Parliament and of the Council of 8 June 2000 on certain legal aspects of information society services, in particular electronic commerce, in the Internal Market 375

5. Consumer Protection 394

Directive 97/7/EC of the European Parliament and of the Council of 20 May 1997 on the protection of consumers in respect of distance contracts 394

Directive 2002/65/EC of the European Parliament and of the Council of 23 September 2002 concerning the distance marketing of consumer financial services and amending Council Directive 90/619/EEC and Directives 97/7/EC and 98/27/EC 404

Recommendation of the OECD Council concerning Guidelines for Consumer Protection in the Context of Electronic Commerce 416

6. Data Protection 423

Directive 95/46/EC of the European Parliament and of the Council of 24 October 1995 on the protection of individuals with regard to the processing of personal data and on the free movement of such data 423

Directive 97/66/EC of the European Parliament and of the Council of 15 December 1997 concerning the processing of personal data and the protection of privacy in the telecommunications sector...445

7. Other Regulations 454

Directive 98/84/EC of the European Parliament and of the Council of 20 November 1998 on the legal protection of services based on, or consisting of, conditional access 454

Council Regulation (EC) No 44/2001 of 22 December 2000 on jurisdiction and the recognition and enforcement of judgments in civil and commercial matters..459

Child Online Protection Act 483

1. Domain Names / Trademarks

FIRST COUNCIL DIRECTIVE 89/104/EEC
OF 21 DECEMBER 1988
TO APPROXIMATE THE LAWS OF THE MEMBER STATES RELATING TO TRADE MARKS

(Official Journal L 040, 11/02/1989, p.0001)

THE COUNCIL OF THE EUROPEAN COMMUNITIES,

Having regard to the Treaty establishing the European Economic Community, and in particular Article 100a thereof,
Having regard to the proposal from the Commission[1],
In cooperation with the European Parliament[2],
Having regard to the opinion of the Economic and Social Committee[3],

(1) Whereas the trade mark laws at present applicable in the Member States contain disparities which may impede the free movement of goods and freedom to provide services and may distort competition within the common market; whereas it is therefore necessary, in view of the establishment and functioning of the internal market, to approximate the laws of Member States;

(2) Whereas it is important not to disregard the solutions and advantages which the Community trade mark system may afford to undertakings wishing to acquire trade marks;

(3) Whereas it does not appear to be necessary at present to undertake full-scale approximation of the trade mark laws of the Member States and it will be sufficient if approximation is limited to those national provisions of law which most directly affect the functioning of the internal market;

(4) Whereas the Directive does not deprive the Member States of the right to continue to protect trademarks acquired through use but takes them into account only in regard to the relationship between them and trade marks acquired by registration;

(5) Whereas Member States also remain free to fix the provisions of procedure concerning the registration, the revocation and the invalidity of trade marks acquired by registration; whereas they can, for example, determine the form of trade mark registration and invalidity procedures, decide whether earlier rights should be invoked either in the registration procedure or in the invalidity procedure or in both and, if they allow earlier rights to be invoked in the registration procedure, have an opposition procedure or an ex officio examination procedure or both; whereas Member States remain free to determine the effects of revocation or invalidity of trade marks;

(6) Whereas this Directive does not exclude the application to trade marks of provisions of law of the Member States other than trade mark law, such as the provisions relating to unfair competition, civil liability or consumer protection;

(7) Whereas attainment of the objectives at which this approximation of laws is aiming requires that the conditions for obtaining and continuing to hold a registered trade mark are, in general, identical in all Member States; whereas, to this end, it is necessary to list examples of

---
[1] OJ No C 351, 31. 12. 1980, p. 1 and OJ No C 351, 31. 12. 1985, p. 4.
[2] OJ No C 307, 14. 11. 1983, p. 66 and OJ No C 309, 5. 12. 1988.
[3] OJ No C 310, 30. 11. 1981, p. 22.

signs which may constitute a trade mark, provided that such signs are capable of distinguishing the goods or services of one undertaking from those of other undertakings; whereas the grounds for refusal or invalidity concerning the trade mark itself, for example, the absence of any distinctive character, or concerning conflicts between the trade mark and earlier rights, are to be listed in an exhaustive manner, even if some of these grounds are listed as an option for the Member States which will therefore be able to maintain or introduce those grounds in their legislation; whereas Member States will be able to maintain or introduce into their legislation grounds of refusal or invalidity linked to conditions for obtaining and continuing to hold a trade mark for which there is no provision of approximation, concerning, for example, the eligibility for the grant of a trade mark, the renewal of the trade mark or rules on fees, or related to the non-compliance with procedural rules;

(8) Whereas in order to reduce the total number of trade marks registered and protected in the Community and, consequently, the number of conflicts which arise between them, it is essential to require that registered trade marks must actually be used or, if not used, be subject to revocation; whereas it is necessary to provide that a trade mark cannot be invalidated on the basis of the existence of a non-used earlier trade mark, while the Member States remain free to apply the same principle in respect of the registration of a trade mark or to provide that a trade mark may not be successfully invoked in infringement proceedings if it is established as a result of a plea that the trade mark could be revoked; whereas in all these cases it is up to the Member States to establish the applicable rules of procedure;

(9) Whereas it is fundamental, in order to facilitate the free circulation of goods and services, to ensure that henceforth registered trade marks enjoy the same protection under the legal systems of all the Member States; whereas this should however not prevent the Member States from granting at their option extensive protection to those trade marks which have a reputation;

(10) Whereas the protection afforded by the registered trade mark, the function of which is in particular to guarantee the trade mark as an indication of origin, is absolute in the case of identity between the mark and the sign and goods or services; whereas the protection applies also in case of similarity between the mark and the sign and the goods or services; whereas it is indispensable to give an interpretation of the concept of similarity in relation to the likelihood of confusion; whereas the likelihood of confusion, the appreciation of which depends on numerous elements and, in particular, on the recognition of the trade mark on the market, of the association which can be made with the used or registered sign, of the degree of similarity between the trade mark and the sign and between the goods or services identified, constitutes the specific condition for such protection; whereas the ways in which likelihood of confusion may be established, and in particular the onus of proof, are a matter for national Procedural rules which are not prejudiced by the Directive;

(11) Whereas it is important, for reasons of legal certainty and without inequitably prejudicing the interests of a proprietor of an earlier trade mark, to Provide that the latter may no longer request a declaration of invalidity nor may he oppose the use of a trade mark subsequent to his own of which he has knowingly tolerated the use for a substantial length of time, unless the application for the subsequent trade mark was made in bad faith:

(12) Whereas all Member States of the Community are bound by the Paris Convention for the Protection of Industrial Property; whereas it is necessary that the provisions of this Directive are entirely consistent with those of the Paris Convention; whereas the obligations of the Member States resulting from this Convention are not affected by this Directive; whereas, where appropriate, the second subparagraph of Article 234 of the Treaty is applicable,

HAS ADOPTED THIS DIRECTIVE:

Trademark Directive (89/104/EEC)

Article 1 - Scope

This Directive shall apply to every trade mark in respect of goods or services which is the subject of registration or of an application in a Member State for registration as an individual trade mark, a collective mark or a guarantee or certification mark, or which is the subject of a registration or an application for registration in the Benelux Trade Mark Office or of an international registration having effect in a Member State.

Article 2 - Signs of which a trade mark may consist

A trade mark may consist of any sign capable of being represented graphically, particularly words, including personal names, designs, letters, numerals, the shape of goods or of their packaging, provided that such signs are capable of distinguishing the goods or services of one undertaking from those of other undertakings.

Article 3 - Grounds for refusal or invalidity

1. the following shall not be registered or if registered shall be liable to be declared invalid:
(a) signs which cannot constitute a trade mark;
(b) trade marks which are devoid of any distinctive character;
(c) trade marks which consist exclusively of signs or indications which may serve, in trade, to designate the kind, quality, quantity, intended purpose, value, geographical origin, or the time of production of the goods or of rendering of the service, or other characteristics of the goods;
(d) trade marks which consist exclusively of signs or indications which have become customary in the current language or in the bona fide and established practices of the trade;
(e) signs which consist exclusively of:
- the shape which results from the nature of the goods themselves, or
- the shape of goods which is necessary to obtain a technical result, or
- the shape which gives substantial value to the goods;
(f) trade marks which are contrary to public policy or to accepted principles of morality;
(g) trade marks which are of such a nature as to deceive the public, for instance as to the nature, quality or geographical origin of the goods or service;
(h) trade marks which have not been authorized by the competent authorities and are to be refused or invalidated pursuant to Article 6 ter of the Paris Convention for the Protection of Industrial Property, hereinafter referred to as the 'Paris Convention'.
2. Any Member State may provide that a trade mark shall not be registered or, if registered, shall be liable to be declared invalid where and to the extent that:
(a) the use of that trade mark may be prohibited pursuant to provisions of law other than trade mark law of the Member State concerned or of the Community;
(b) the trade mark covers a sign of high symbolic value, in particular a religious symbol;
(c) the trade mark includes badges, emblems and escutcheons other than those covered by Article 6 ter of the Paris Convention and which are of Public interest, unless the consent of the appropriate authorities to its registration has been given in conformity with the legislation of the Member State;
(d) the application for registration of the trade mark was made in bad faith by the applicant.
3. A trade mark shall not be refused registration or be declared invalid in accordance with paragraph 1 (b), (c) or (d) if, before the date of application for registration and following the use which has been made of it, it has acquired a distinctive character. Any Member State may in addition provide that this provision shall also apply where the distinctive character was acquired after the date of application for registration or after the date of registration.
4. Any Member State may provide that, by derogation from the preceding paragraphs, the grounds of refusal of registration or invalidity in force in that State prior to the date on

which the provisions necessary to comply with this Directive enter into force, shall apply to trade marks for which application has been made prior to that date.

Article 4 - Further grounds for refusal or invalidity concerning conflicts with earlier rights

1. A trade mark shall not be registered or, if registered, shall be liable to be declared invalid:
   (a) if it is identical with an earlier trade mark, and the goods or services for which the trade mark is applied for or is registered are identical with the goods or services for which the earlier trade mark is protected;
   (b) if because of its identity with, or similarity to, the earlier trade mark and the identity or similarity of the goods or services covered by the trade marks, there exists a likelihood of confusion on the part of the public, which includes the likelihood of association with the earlier trade mark.
2. 'Earlier trade marks' within the meaning of paragraph 1 means:
   (a) trade marks of the following kinds with a date of application for registration which is earlier than the date of application for registration of the trade mark, taking account, where appropriate, of the priorities claimed in respect of those trade marks;
   (i) Community trade marks;
   (ii) trade marks registered in the Member State or, in the case of Belgium, Luxembourg or the Netherlands, at the Benelux Trade Mark Office;
   (iii) trade marks registered under international arrangements which have effect in the Member State;
   (b) Community trade marks which validly claim seniority, in accordance with the Regulation on the Community trade mark, from a trade mark referred to in (a) (ii) and (iii), even when the latter trade mark has been surrendered or allowed to lapse;
   (c) applications for the trade marks referred to in (a) and (b), subject to their registration;
   (d) trade marks which, on the date of application for registration of the trade mark, or, where appropriate, of the priority claimed in respect of the application for registration of the trade mark, are well known in a Member State, in the sense in which the words 'well known' are used in Article 6 bis of the Paris Convention.
3. A trade mark shall furthermore not be registered or, if registered, shall be liable to be declared invalid if it is identical with, or similar to, an earlier Community trade mark within the meaning of paragraph 2 and is to be, or has been, registered for goods or services which are not similar to those for which the earlier Community trade mark is registered, where the earlier Community trade mark has a reputation in the Community and where the use of the later trade mark without due cause would take unfair advantage of, or be detrimental to, the distinctive character or the repute of the earlier Community trade mark.
4. Any Member State may furthermore provide that a trade mark shall not be registered or, if registered, shall be liable to be declared invalid where, and to the extent that:
   (a) the trade mark is identical with, or similar to, an earlier national trade mark within the meaning of paragraph 2 and is to he, or has been, registered for goods or services which are not similar to those for which the earlier trade mark is registered, where the earlier trade mark has a reputation in the Member State concerned and where the use of the later trade mark without due cause would take unfair advantage of, or be detrimental to, the distinctive character or the repute of the earlier trade mark;
   (b) rights to a non-registered trade mark or to another sign used in the course of trade were acquired prior to the date of application for registration of the subsequent trade mark, or the date of the priority claimed for the application for registration of the subsequent trade mark and that non-registered trade mark or other sign confers on its proprietor the right to prohibit the use of a subsequent trade mark;
   (c) the use of the trade mark may be prohibited by virtue of an earlier right other than the rights referred to in paragraphs 2 and 4 (b) and in particular:

(i) a right to a name;
(ii) a right of personal portrayal:
(iii) a copyright;
(iv) an industrial property right;
(d) the trade mark is identical with, or similar to, an earlier collective trade mark conferring a right which expired within a period of a maximum of three years preceding application;
(e) the trade mark is identical with, or similar to, an earlier guarantee or certification mark conferring a right which expired within a period preceding application the length of which is fixed by the Member State;
(f) the trade mark is identical with, or similar to, an earlier trade mark which was registered for identical or similar goods or services and conferred on them a right which has expired for failure to renew within a period of a maximum of two years preceding application, unless the proprietor of the earlier trade mark gave his agreement for the registration of the later mark or did not use his trade mark;
(g) the trade mark is liable to be confused with a mark which was in use abroad on the filing date of the application and which is still in use there, provided that at the date of the application the applicant was acting in bad faith
5. The Member States may permit that in appropriate circumstances registration need not be refused or the trade mark need not be declared invalid where the proprietor of the earlier trade mark or other earlier right consents to the registration of the later trade mark.
6. Any Member State may provide that, by derogation from paragraphs 1 to S, the grounds for refusal of registration or invalidity in force in that State prior to the date on which the provisions necessary to comply with this Directive enter into force, shall apply to trade marks for which application has been made prior to that date.

Article 5 - Rights conferred by a trade mark

1. The registered trade mark shall confer on the proprietor exclusive rights therein. The proprietor shall be entitled to prevent all third parties not having his consent from using in the course of trade:
(a) any sign which is identical with the trade mark in relation to goods or services which are identical with those for which the trade mark is registered;
(b) any sign where, because of its identity with, or similarity to, the trade mark and the identity or similarity of the goods or services covered by the trade mark and the sign, there exists a likelihood of confusion on the part of the public, which includes the likelihood of association between the sign and the trade mark.
2. Any Member State may also provide that the proprietor shall be entitled to prevent all third parties not having his consent from using in the course of trade any sign which is identical with, or similar to, the trade mark in relation to goods or services which are not similar to those for which the trade mark is registered, where the latter has a reputation in the Member State and where use of that sign without due cause takes unfair advantage of, or is detrimental to, the distinctive character or the repute of the trade mark.
3. The following, inter alia, may be prohibited under paragraphs 1 and 2:
(a) affixing the sign to the goods or to the packaging thereof;
(b) offering the goods, or putting them on the market or stocking them for these purposes under that sign, or offering or supplying services thereunder;
(c) importing or exporting the goods under the sign;
(d) using the sign on business papers and in advertising.
4. Where, under the law of the Member State, the use of a sign under the conditions referred to in 1 (b) or 2 could not be prohibited before the date on which the provisions necessary to comply with this Directive entered into force in the Member State concerned, the rights conferred by the trade mark may not be relied on to prevent the continued use of the sign.

5. Paragraphs 1 to 4 shall not affect provisions in any Member State relating to the protection against the use of a sign other than for the purposes of distinguishing goods or services, where use of that sign without due cause takes unfair advantage of, or is detrimental to, the distinctive character or the repute of the trade mark

Article 6 - Limitation of the effects of a trade mark

1. The trade mark shall not entitle the proprietor to prohibit a third party from using, in the course of trade,
   (a) his own name or address;
   (b) indications concerning the kind, quality, quantity, intended purpose, value, geographical origin, the time of production of goods or of rendering of the service, or other characteristics of goods or services;
   (c) the trade mark where it is necessary to indicate the intended purpose of a product or service, in particular as accessories or spare parts;
   provided he uses them in accordance with honest practices in industrial or commercial matters
2. The trade mark shall not entitle the proprietor to prohibit a third party from using, in the course of trade, an earlier right which only applies in a particular locality if that right is recognized by the laws of the Member State in question and within the limits of the territory in which it is recognized.

Article 7 - Exhaustion of the rights conferred by a trade mark

1. The trade mark shall not entitle the proprietor to prohibit its use in relation to goods which have been put on the market in the Community under that trade mark by the proprietor or with his consent.
2. Paragraph 1 shall not apply where there exist legitimate reasons for the proprietor to oppose further commercialization of the goods, especially where the condition of the goods is changed or impaired after they have been put on the market.

Article 8 - Licensing

1. A trade mark may be licensed for some or all of the goods or services for which it is registered and for the whole or part of the Member State concerned. A license may be exclusive or non-exclusive.
2. The proprietor of a trade mark may invoke the rights conferred by that trade mark against a licensee who contravenes any provision in his licensing contract with regard to its duration, the form covered by the registration in which the trade mark may be used, the scope of the goods or services for which the licence is granted, the territory in which the trade mark may be affixed, or the quality of the goods manufactured or of the services provided by the licensee.

Article 9 - Limitation in consequence of acquiescence

1. Where, in a Member State, the proprietor of an earlier trade mark as referred to in Article 4 (2) has acquiesced, for a period of five successive years, in the use of a later trade mark registered in that Member State while being aware of such use, he shall no longer be entitled on the basis of the earlier trade mark either to apply for a declaration that the later trade mark is invalid or to oppose the use of the later trade mark in respect of the goods or services for which the later trade mark has been used, unless registration of the later trade mark was applied for in bad faith.
2. Any Member State may provide that paragraph 1 shall apply mutatis mutandis to the proprietor of an earlier trade mark referred to in Article 4 (4) (a) or an other earlier right referred to in Article 4 (4) (b) or (c).

3. In the cases referred to in paragraphs 1 and 2, the proprietor of a later registered trade mark shall not be entitled to oppose the use of the earlier right, even though that right may no longer be invoked against the later trade mark.

Article 10 - Use of trade marks

1. If, within a period of five years following the date of the completion of the registration procedure, the proprietor has not put the trade mark to genuine use in the Member State in connection with the goods or services in respect of which it is registered, or if such use has been suspended during an uninterrupted period of five years, the trade mark shall be subject to the sanctions provided for in this Directive, unless there are proper reasons for non-use.
2. The following shall also constitute use within the meaning of paragraph 1:
(a) use of the trade mark in a form differing in elements which do not alter the distinctive character of the mark in the form in which it was registered;
(b) affixing of the trade mark to goods or to the packaging thereof in the Member State concerned solely for export purposes.
3. Use of the trade mark with the consent of the proprietor or by any person who has authority to use a collective mark or a guarantee or certification mark shall be deemed to constitute use by the proprietor.
4. In relation to trade marks registered before the date on which the provisions necessary to comply with this Directive enter into force in the Member State concerned:
(a) where a provision in force prior to that date attaches sanctions to non-use of a trade mark during an uninterrupted period, the relevant period of five years mentioned in paragraph 1 shall be deemed to have begun to run at the same time as any period of non-use which is already running at that date;
(b) where there is no use provision in force prior to that date, the periods of five years mentioned in paragraph 1 shall be deemed to run from that date at the earliest.

Article 11 - Sanctions for non use of a trade mark in legal or administrative proceedings

1. A trade mark may not be declared invalid on the ground that there is an earlier conflicting trade mark if the latter does not fulfil the requirements of use set out in Article 10 (1), (2) and (3) or in Article 10 (4), as the case may be.
2. Any Member State may provide that registration of a trade mark may not be refused on the ground that there is an earlier conflicting trade mark if the latter does not fulfil the requirements of use set out in Article 10 (1), (2) and (3) or in Article 10 (4), as the case may be.
3. Without prejudice to the application of Article 12, where a counter-claim for revocation is made, any Member State may provide that a trade mark may not be successfully invoked in infringement proceedings if it is established as a result of a plea that the trade mark could be revoked pursuant to Article 12 (1).
4. If the earlier trade mark has been used in relation to part only of the goods or services for which it is registered, it shall, for purposes of applying paragraphs 1, 2 and 3, be deemed to be registered in respect only of that part of the goods or services.

Article 12 - Grounds for revocation

1. A trade mark shall be liable to revocation if, within a continuous period of five years, it has not been put to genuine use in the Member State in connection with the goods or services in respect of which it is registered, and there are no proper reasons for non-use; however, no person may claim that the proprietor's rights in a trade mark should be revoked where, during the interval between expiry of the five-year period and filing of the application for revocation, genuine use of the trade mark has been started or resumed; the commencement

or resumption of use within a period of three months preceding the filing of the application for revocation which began at the earliest on expiry of the continuous period of five years of non-use, shall, however, be disregarded where preparations for the commencement or resumption occur only after the proprietor becomes aware that the application for revocation may be filed.

2. A trade mark shall also be liable to revocation if, after the date on which it was registered,
(a) in consequence of acts or inactivity of the proprietor, it has become the common name in the trade for a product or service in respect of which it is registered;
(b) in consequence of the use made of it by the proprietor of the trade mark or with his consent in respect of the goods or services for which it is registered, it is liable to mislead the public, particularly as to the nature, quality or geographical origin of those goods or services.

Article 13 - Grounds for refusal or revocation or invalidity relating to only some of the goods or services

Where grounds for refusal of registration or for revocation or invalidity of a trade mark exist in respect of only some of the goods or services for which that trade mark has been applied for or registered, refusal of registration or revocation or invalidity shall cover those goods or services only.

Article 14 - Establishment a posteriori of invalidity or revocation of a trade mark

Where the seniority of an earlier trade mark which has been surrendered or allowed to lapse, is claimed for a Community trade mark, the invalidity or revocation of the earlier trade mark may be established a posteriori

Article 15 - Special provisions in respect of collective marks, guarantee marks and certification marks

1. Without prejudice to Article 4, Member States whose laws authorize the registration of collective marks or of guarantee or certification marks may provide that such marks shall not be registered, or shall be revoked or declared invalid, on grounds additional to those specified in Articles 3 and 12 where the function of those marks so requires.
2. By way of derogation from Article 3 (1) (c), Member States may provide that signs or indications which may serve, in trade, to designate the geographical origin of the goods or services may constitute collective, guarantee or certification marks. Such a mark does not entitle the proprietor to prohibit a third party from using in the course of trade such signs or indications, provided he uses them in accordance with honest practices in industrial or commercial matters; in particular, such a mark may not be invoked against a third party who is entitled to use a geographical name

Article 16 - National provisions to be adopted pursuant to this Directive

1. The Member States shall bring into force the laws, regulations and administrative provisions necessary to comply with this Directive not later than 28 December 1991 They shall immediately inform the Commission thereof.
2. Acting on a proposal from the Commission, the Council, acting by qualified majority, may defer the date referred to in paragraph 1 until 31 December 1992 at the latest.
3. Member States shall communicate to the Commission the text of the main provisions of national law which they adopt in the field governed by this Directive.

Article 17 - Addressees

This Directive is addressed to the Member States.

ICANN - PRIVATE UNIFORM DOMAIN NAME DISPUTE RESOLUTION POLICY

Policy Adopted: August 26, 1999
Implementation Documents Approved: October 24, 1999

(Source: http://www.icann.org/udrp/udrp.htm)

Notes:
1. This policy is now in effect. See www.icann.org/udrp/udrp-schedule.htm for the implementation schedule.
2. This policy has been adopted by all accredited domain-name registrars for domain names ending in .com, .net, and .org. It has also been adopted by certain managers of country-code top-level domains (e.g., .nu, .tv, . ws).
3. The policy is between the registrar (or other registration authority in the case of a country-code top-level domain) and its customer (the domain-name holder or registrant). Thus, the policy uses "we" and "our" to refer to the registrar and it uses "you" and "your" to refer to the domain-name holder.

Uniform Domain Name Dispute Resolution Policy

1. Purpose

This Uniform Domain Name Dispute Resolution Policy (the "Policy") has been adopted by the Internet Corporation for Assigned Names and Numbers ("ICANN"), is incorporated by reference into your Registration Agreement, and sets forth the terms and conditions in connection with a dispute between you and any party other than us (the registrar) over the registration and use of an Internet domain name registered by you. Proceedings under Paragraph 4 of this Policy will be conducted according to the Rules for Uniform Domain Name Dispute Resolution Policy (the "Rules of Procedure"), which are available at www.icann.org/udrp/udrp-rules-24oct99.htm, and the selected administrative-dispute-resolution service provider's supplemental rules.

2. Your Representations

By applying to register a domain name, or by asking us to maintain or renew a domain name registration, you hereby represent and warrant to us that (a) the statements that you made in your Registration Agreement are complete and accurate; (b) to your knowledge, the registration of the domain name will not infringe upon or otherwise violate the rights of any third party; (c) you are not registering the domain name for an unlawful purpose; and (d) you will not knowingly use the domain name in violation of any applicable laws or regulations. It is your responsibility to determine whether your domain name registration infringes or violates someone else's rights.

3. Cancellations, Transfers, and Changes

We will cancel, transfer or otherwise make changes to domain name registrations under the following circumstances:

(a) subject to the provisions of Paragraph 8, our receipt of written or appropriate electronic instructions from you or your authorized agent to take such action;

(b) our receipt of an order from a court or arbitral tribunal, in each case of competent jurisdiction, requiring such action; and/or

ICANN - UDRP Policy

(c) our receipt of a decision of an Administrative Panel requiring such action in any administrative proceeding to which you were a party and which was conducted under this Policy or a later version of this Policy adopted by ICANN. (See Paragraph 4 (i) and (k) below.)

We may also cancel, transfer or otherwise make changes to a domain name registration in accordance with the terms of your Registration Agreement or other legal requirements.

4. Mandatory Administrative Proceeding

This Paragraph sets forth the type of disputes for which you are required to submit to a mandatory administrative proceeding. These proceedings will be conducted before one of the administrative-dispute-resolution service providers listed at www.icann.org/udrp/approved-providers.htm (each, a "Provider").

(a) Applicable Disputes

You are required to submit to a mandatory administrative proceeding in the event that a third party (a "complainant") asserts to the applicable Provider, in compliance with the Rules of Procedure, that
(i) your domain name is identical or confusingly similar to a trademark or service mark in which the complainant has rights; and
(ii) you have no rights or legitimate interests in respect of the domain name; and
(iii) your domain name has been registered and is being used in bad faith.
In the administrative proceeding, the complainant must prove that each of these three elements are present.

(b) Evidence of Registration and Use in Bad Faith

For the purposes of Paragraph 4(a)(iii), the following circumstances, in particular but without limitation, if found by the Panel to be present, shall be evidence of the registration and use of a domain name in bad faith:
(i) circumstances indicating that you have registered or you have acquired the domain name primarily for the purpose of selling, renting, or otherwise transferring the domain name registration to the complainant who is the owner of the trademark or service mark or to a competitor of that complainant, for valuable consideration in excess of your documented out-of-pocket costs directly related to the domain name; or
(ii) you have registered the domain name in order to prevent the owner of the trademark or service mark from reflecting the mark in a corresponding domain name, provided that you have engaged in a pattern of such conduct; or
(iii) you have registered the domain name primarily for the purpose of disrupting the business of a competitor; or
(iv) by using the domain name, you have intentionally attempted to attract, for commercial gain, Internet users to your web site or other on-line location, by creating a likelihood of confusion with the complainant's mark as to the source, sponsorship, affiliation, or endorsement of your web site or location or of a product or service on your web site or location.

(c) How to Demonstrate Your Rights to and Legitimate Interests in the Domain Name in Responding to a Complaint

When you receive a complaint, you should refer to Paragraph 5 of the Rules of Procedure in determining how your response should be prepared. Any of the following circumstances, in particular but without limitation, if found by the Panel to be proved based on its evaluation of all evidence presented, shall demonstrate your rights or legitimate interests to the domain name for purposes of Paragraph 4(a)(ii):

(i) before any notice to you of the dispute, your use of, or demonstrable preparations to use, the domain name or a name corresponding to the domain name in connection with a bona fide offering of goods or services; or
(ii) you (as an individual, business, or other organization) have been commonly known by the domain name, even if you have acquired no trademark or service mark rights; or
(iii) you are making a legitimate noncommercial or fair use of the domain name, without intent for commercial gain to misleadingly divert consumers or to tarnish the trademark or service mark at issue.

(d) Selection of Provider
The complainant shall select the Provider from among those approved by ICANN by submitting the complaint to that Provider. The selected Provider will administer the proceeding, except in cases of consolidation as described in Paragraph 4(f).

(e) Initiation of Proceeding and Process and Appointment of Administrative Panel
The Rules of Procedure state the process for initiating and conducting a proceeding and for appointing the panel that will decide the dispute (the "Administrative Panel").

(f) Consolidation
In the event of multiple disputes between you and a complainant, either you or the complainant may petition to consolidate the disputes before a single Administrative Panel. This petition shall be made to the first Administrative Panel appointed to hear a pending dispute between the parties. This Administrative Panel may consolidate before it any or all such disputes in its sole discretion, provided that the disputes being consolidated are governed by this Policy or a later version of this Policy adopted by ICANN.

(g) Fees
All fees charged by a Provider in connection with any dispute before an Administrative Panel pursuant to this Policy shall be paid by the complainant, except in cases where you elect to expand the Administrative Panel from one to three panelists as provided in Paragraph 5 (b)(iv) of the Rules of Procedure, in which case all fees will be split evenly by you and the complainant.

(h) Our Involvement in Administrative Proceedings
We do not, and will not, participate in the administration or conduct of any proceeding before an Administrative Panel. In addition, we will not be liable as a result of any decisions rendered by the Administrative Panel.

(i) Remedies
The remedies available to a complainant pursuant to any proceeding before an Administrative Panel shall be limited to requiring the cancellation of your domain name or the transfer of your domain name registration to the complainant.

(j) Notification and Publication
The Provider shall notify us of any decision made by an Administrative Panel with respect to a domain name you have registered with us. All decisions under this Policy will be published in full over the Internet, except when an Administrative Panel determines in an exceptional case to redact portions of its decision.

(k) Availability of Court Proceedings
The mandatory administrative proceeding requirements set forth in Paragraph 4 shall not prevent either you or the complainant from submitting the dispute to a court of competent jurisdiction for

ICANN - UDRP Policy

independent resolution before such mandatory administrative proceeding is commenced or after such proceeding is concluded. If an Administrative Panel decides that your domain name registration should be cancelled or transferred, we will wait ten (10) business days (as observed in the location of our principal office) after we are informed by the applicable Provider of the Administrative Panel's decision before implementing that decision. We will then implement the decision unless we have received from you during that ten (10) business day period official documentation (such as a copy of a complaint, file-stamped by the clerk of the court) that you have commenced a lawsuit against the complainant in a jurisdiction to which the complainant has submitted under Paragraph 3(b)(xiii) of the Rules of Procedure. (In general, that jurisdiction is either the location of our principal office or of your address as shown in our Whois database. See Paragraphs 1 and 3(b)(xiii) of the Rules of Procedure for details.) If we receive such documentation within the ten (10) business day period, we will not implement the Administrative Panel's decision, and we will take no further action, until we receive (i) evidence satisfactory to us of a resolution between the parties; (ii) evidence satisfactory to us that your lawsuit has been dismissed or withdrawn; or (iii) a copy of an order from such court dismissing your lawsuit or ordering that you do not have the right to continue to use your domain name.

5. All Other Disputes and Litigation

All other disputes between you and any party other than us regarding your domain name registration that are not brought pursuant to the mandatory administrative proceeding provisions of Paragraph 4 shall be resolved between you and such other party through any court, arbitration or other proceeding that may be available.

6. Our Involvement in Disputes

We will not participate in any way in any dispute between you and any party other than us regarding the registration and use of your domain name. You shall not name us as a party or otherwise include us in any such proceeding. In the event that we are named as a party in any such proceeding, we reserve the right to raise any and all defenses deemed appropriate, and to take any other action necessary to defend ourselves.

7. Maintaining the Status Quo

We will not cancel, transfer, activate, deactivate, or otherwise change the status of any domain name registration under this Policy except as provided in Paragraph 3 above.

8. Transfers During a Dispute

(a) Transfers of a Domain Name to a New Holder

You may not transfer your domain name registration to another holder (i) during a pending administrative proceeding brought pursuant to Paragraph 4 or for a period of fifteen (15) business days (as observed in the location of our principal place of business) after such proceeding is concluded; or (ii) during a pending court proceeding or arbitration commenced regarding your domain name unless the party to whom the domain name registration is being transferred agrees, in writing, to be bound by the decision of the court or arbitrator. We reserve the right to cancel any transfer of a domain name registration to another holder that is made in violation of this subparagraph.

(b) Changing Registrar

You may not transfer your domain name registration to another registrar during a pending administrative proceeding brought pursuant to Paragraph 4 or for a period of fifteen (15) business days (as observed in the location of our principal place of business) after such proceeding is concluded. You may transfer administration of your domain name registration to another registrar during a pending court action or arbitration, provided that the domain name you have registered with us shall continue to be subject to the proceedings commenced against you in accordance with the terms of this Policy. In the event that you transfer a domain name registration to us during the pendency of a court action or arbitration, such dispute shall remain subject to the domain name dispute policy of the registrar from which the domain name registration was transferred.

9. Policy Modifications

We reserve the right to modify this Policy at any time with the permission of ICANN. We will post our revised Policy at ##<URL> at least thirty (30) calendar days before it becomes effective. Unless this Policy has already been invoked by the submission of a complaint to a Provider, in which event the version of the Policy in effect at the time it was invoked will apply to you until the dispute is over, all such changes will be binding upon you with respect to any domain name registration dispute, whether the dispute arose before, on or after the effective date of our change. In the event that you object to a change in this Policy, your sole remedy is to cancel your domain name registration with us, provided that you will not be entitled to a refund of any fees you paid to us. The revised Policy will apply to you until you cancel your domain name registration.

ICANN - RULES FOR UNIFORM DOMAIN NAME DISPUTE RESOLUTION POLICY

(the "Rules")
Approved by ICANN on October 24, 1999

(Source: http://www.icann.org/udrp/udrp.htm)

Administrative proceedings for the resolution of disputes under the Uniform Dispute Resolution Policy adopted by ICANN shall be governed by these Rules and also the Supplemental Rules of the Provider administering the proceedings, as posted on its web site.

1. Definitions

In these Rules:

Complainant means the party initiating a complaint concerning a domain-name registration.
ICANN refers to the Internet Corporation for Assigned Names and Numbers.
Mutual Jurisdiction means a court jurisdiction at the location of either (a) the principal office of the Registrar (provided the domain-name holder has submitted in its Registration Agreement to that jurisdiction for court adjudication of disputes concerning or arising from the use of the domain name) or (b) the domain-name holder's address as shown for the registration of the domain name in Registrar's Whois database at the time the complaint is submitted to the Provider.
Panel means an administrative panel appointed by a Provider to decide a complaint concerning a domain-name registration.
Panelist means an individual appointed by a Provider to be a member of a Panel.
Party means a Complainant or a Respondent.
Policy means the Uniform Domain Name Dispute Resolution Policy that is incorporated by reference and made a part of the Registration Agreement.
Provider means a dispute-resolution service provider approved by ICANN. A list of such Providers appears at www.icann.org/udrp/approved-providers.htm.
Registrar means the entity with which the Respondent has registered a domain name that is the subject of a complaint.
Registration Agreement means the agreement between a Registrar and a domain-name holder.
Respondent means the holder of a domain-name registration against which a complaint is initiated.
Reverse Domain Name Hijacking means using the Policy in bad faith to attempt to deprive a registered domain-name holder of a domain name.
Supplemental Rules means the rules adopted by the Provider administering a proceeding to supplement these Rules. Supplemental Rules shall not be inconsistent with the Policy or these Rules and shall cover such topics as fees, word and page limits and guidelines, the means for communicating with the Provider and the Panel, and the form of cover sheets.

2. Communications

(a) When forwarding a complaint to the Respondent, it shall be the Provider's responsibility to employ reasonably available means calculated to achieve actual notice to Respondent. Achieving actual notice, or employing the following measures to do so, shall discharge this responsibility:

(i) sending the complaint to all postal-mail and facsimile addresses (A) shown in the domain name's registration data in Registrar's Whois database for the registered domain-name holder, the technical contact, and the administrative contact and (B) supplied by Registrar to the Provider for the registration's billing contact; and

(ii) sending the complaint in electronic form (including annexes to the extent available in that form) by e-mail to:
  (A) the e-mail addresses for those technical, administrative, and billing contacts;
  (B) postmaster@<the contested domain name>; and
  (C) if the domain name (or "www." followed by the domain name) resolves to an active web page (other than a generic page the Provider concludes is maintained by a registrar or ISP for parking domain-names registered by multiple domain-name holders), any e-mail address shown or e-mail links on that web page; and

(iii) sending the complaint to any address the Respondent has notified the Provider it prefers and, to the extent practicable, to all other addresses provided to the Provider by Complainant under Paragraph 3(b)(v).

(b) Except as provided in Paragraph 2(a), any written communication to Complainant or Respondent provided for under these Rules shall be made by the preferred means stated by the Complainant or Respondent, respectively (see Paragraphs 3(b)(iii) and 5(b)(iii)), or in the absence of such specification

(i) by telecopy or facsimile transmission, with a confirmation of transmission; or
(ii) by postal or courier service, postage pre-paid and return receipt requested; or
(iii) electronically via the Internet, provided a record of its transmission is available.

(c) Any communication to the Provider or the Panel shall be made by the means and in the manner (including number of copies) stated in the Provider's Supplemental Rules.

(d) Communications shall be made in the language prescribed in Paragraph 11. E-mail communications should, if practicable, be sent in plaintext.

(e) Either Party may update its contact details by notifying the Provider and the Registrar.

(f) Except as otherwise provided in these Rules, or decided by a Panel, all communications provided for under these Rules shall be deemed to have been made:

(i) if delivered by telecopy or facsimile transmission, on the date shown on the confirmation of transmission; or
(ii) if by postal or courier service, on the date marked on the receipt; or
(iii) if via the Internet, on the date that the communication was transmitted, provided that the date of transmission is verifiable.

(g) Except as otherwise provided in these Rules, all time periods calculated under these Rules to begin when a communication is made shall begin to run on the earliest date that the communication is deemed to have been made in

(h) Any communication by
(i) Panel to any Party shall be copied to the Provider and to the other Party;
(ii) the Provider to any Party shall be copied to the other Party; and
(iii) a Party shall be copied to the other Party, the Panel and the Provider, as the case may be.

(i) It shall be the responsibility of the sender to retain records of the fact and circumstances of sending, which shall be available for inspection by affected parties and for reporting purposes.

(j) In the event a Party sending a communication receives notification of non-delivery of the communication, the Party shall promptly notify the Panel (or, if no Panel is yet appointed, the Provider) of the circumstances of the notification. Further proceedings concerning the communication and any response shall be as directed by the Panel (or the Provider).

3. The Complaint

(a) Any person or entity may initiate an administrative proceeding by submitting a complaint in accordance with the Policy and these Rules to any Provider approved by ICANN. (Due to capacity constraints or for other reasons, a Provider's ability to accept complaints may be

suspended at times. In that event, the Provider shall refuse the submission. The person or entity may submit the complaint to another Provider.)
(b) The complaint shall be submitted in hard copy and (except to the extent not available for annexes) in electronic form and shall:
(i) Request that the complaint be submitted for decision in accordance
(ii) Provide the name, postal and e-mail addresses, and the telephone and telefax numbers of the Complainant and of any representative authorized to act for the Complainant in the administrative proceeding;
(iii) Specify a preferred method for communications directed to the Complainant in the administrative proceeding (including person to be contacted, medium, and address information) for each of (A) electronic-only material and (B) material including hard copy;
(iv) Designate whether Complainant elects to have the dispute decided by a single-member or a three-member Panel and, in the event Complainant elects a three-member Panel, provide the names and contact details of three candidates to serve as one of the Panelists (these candidates may be drawn from any ICANN-approved Provider's list of panelists);
(v) Provide the name of the Respondent (domain-name holder) and all information (including any postal and e-mail addresses and telephone and telefax numbers) known to Complainant regarding how to contact Respondent or any representative of Respondent, including contact information based on pre-complaint dealings, in sufficient detail to allow the Provider to send the complaint as described in Paragraph 2(a);
(vi) Specify the domain name(s) that is/are the subject of the complaint;
(vii) Identify the Registrar(s) with whom the domain name(s) is/are registered at the time the complaint is filed;
(viii) Specify the trademark(s) or service mark(s) on which the complaint is based and, for each mark, describe the goods or services, if any, with which the mark is used (Complainant may also separately describe other goods and services with which it intends, at the time the complaint is submitted, to use the mark in the future.);
(ix) Describe, in accordance with the Policy, the grounds on which the complaint is made including, in particular,
  (1) the manner in which the domain name(s) is/are identical or confusingly similar to a trademark or service mark in which the Complainant has rights; and
  (2) why the Respondent (domain-name holder) should be considered as having no rights or legitimate interests in respect of the domain name(s) that is/are the subject of the complaint; and
  (3) why the domain name(s) should be considered as having been registered and being used in bad faith (The description should, for elements (2) and (3), discuss any aspects of Paragraphs 4(b) and 4(c) of the Policy that are applicable. The description shall comply with any word or page limit set forth in the Provider's Supplemental Rules.);
(x) Specify, in accordance with the Policy, the remedies sought;
(xi) Identify any other legal proceedings that have been commenced or terminated in connection with or relating to any of the domain name(s) that are the subject of the complaint;
(xii) State that a copy of the complaint, together with the cover sheet as prescribed by the Provider's Supplemental Rules, has been sent or transmitted to the Respondent (domain-name holder), in accordance with
(xiii) State that Complainant will submit, with respect to any challenges to a decision in the administrative proceeding cancelling or transferring the domain name, to the jurisdiction of the courts in at least one specified Mutual Jurisdiction;
(xiv) Conclude with the following statement followed by the signature of the Complainant or its authorized representative: "Complainant agrees that its claims and remedies concerning the registration of the domain name, the dispute, or the dispute's resolution shall be solely against the domain-name holder and waives all such claims and remedies against (a) the

dispute-resolution provider and panelists, except in the case of deliberate wrongdoing, (b) the registrar, (c) the registry administrator, and (d) the Internet Corporation for Assigned Names and Numbers, as well as their directors, officers, employees, and agents." "Complainant certifies that the information contained in this Complaint is to the best of Complainant's knowledge complete and accurate, that this Complaint is not being presented for any improper purpose, such as to harass, and that the assertions in this Complaint are warranted under these Rules and under applicable law, as it now exists or as it may be extended by a good-faith and

(xv) Annex any documentary or other evidence, including a copy of the Policy applicable to the domain name(s) in dispute and any trademark or service mark registration upon which the complaint relies, together with a schedule indexing such evidence.

(c) The complaint may relate to more than one domain name, provided that the domain names are registered by the same domain-name holder.

4. Notification of Complaint

(a) The Provider shall review the complaint for administrative compliance with the Policy and these Rules and, if in compliance, shall forward the complaint (together with the explanatory cover sheet prescribed by the Provider's Supplemental Rules) to the Respondent, in the manner prescribed by Paragraph 2(a), within three (3) calendar days following receipt of the fees to be paid by the Complainant in accordance with Paragraph 19.

(b) If the Provider finds the complaint to be administratively deficient, it shall promptly notify the Complainant and the Respondent of the nature of the deficiencies identified. The Complainant shall have five (5) calendar days within which to correct any such deficiencies, after which the administrative proceeding will be deemed withdrawn without prejudice to submission of a different complaint by Complainant.

(c) The date of commencement of the administrative proceeding shall be the date on which the Provider completes its responsibilities under Paragraph 2(a) in connection with forwarding the Complaint to the Respondent.

(d) The Provider shall immediately notify the Complainant, the Respondent, the concerned Registrar(s), and ICANN of the date of commencement of the administrative proceeding.

5. The Response

(a) Within twenty (20) days of the date of commencement of the administrative proceeding the Respondent shall submit a response to the Provider.

(b) The response shall be submitted in hard copy and (except to the extent not available for annexes) in electronic form and shall:

(i) Respond specifically to the statements and allegations contained in the complaint and include any and all bases for the Respondent (domain-name holder) to retain registration and use of the disputed domain name (This portion of the response shall comply with any word or page limit set forth in the Provider's Supplemental Rules.);

(ii) Provide the name, postal and e-mail addresses, and the telephone and telefax numbers of the Respondent (domain-name holder) and of any representative authorized to act for the Respondent in the administrative proceeding;

(iii) Specify a preferred method for communications directed to the Respondent in the administrative proceeding (including person to be contacted, medium, and address information) for each of (A) electronic-only material and (B) material including hard copy;

(iv) If Complainant has elected a single-member panel in the Complaint (see Paragraph 3(b)(iv)), state whether Respondent elects instead to have the dispute decided by a three-member panel;

(v) If either Complainant or Respondent elects a three-member Panel, provide the names and contact details of three candidates to serve as one of the Panelists (these candidates may be drawn from any ICANN-approved Provider's list of panelists);
(vi) Identify any other legal proceedings that have been commenced or terminated in connection with or relating to any of the domain name(s) that are the subject of the complaint;
(vii) State that a copy of the response has been sent or transmitted to the Complainant, in accordance with Paragraph 2(b); and
(viii) Conclude with the following statement followed by the signature of the Respondent or its authorized representative: "Respondent certifies that the information contained in this Response is to the best of Respondent's knowledge complete and accurate, that this Response is not being presented for any improper purpose, such as to harass, and that the assertions in this Response are warranted under these Rules and under applicable law, as it now exists or as it may be extended by a good-faith and reasonable argument."; and
(ix) Annex any documentary or other evidence upon which the Respondent relies, together with a schedule indexing such documents.
(c) If Complainant has elected to have the dispute decided by a single-member Panel and Respondent elects a three-member Panel, Respondent shall be required to pay one-half of the applicable fee for a three-member Panel as set forth in the Provider's Supplemental Rules. This payment shall be made together with the submission of the response to the Provider. In the event that the required payment is not made, the dispute shall be decided by a single-member Panel.
(d) At the request of the Respondent, the Provider may, in exceptional cases, extend the period of time for the filing of the response. The period may also be extended by written stipulation between the Parties, provided the stipulation is approved by the Provider.
(e) If a Respondent does not submit a response, in the absence of exceptional circumstances, the Panel shall decide the dispute based upon the complaint.

6. Appointment of the Panel and Timing of Decision

(a) Each Provider shall maintain and publish a publicly available list of panelists and their qualifications.
(b) If neither the Complainant nor the Respondent has elected a three-member Panel (Paragraphs 3(b)(iv) and 5(b)(iv)), the Provider shall appoint, within five (5) calendar days following receipt of the response by the Provider, or the lapse of the time period for the submission thereof, a single Panelist from its list of panelists. The fees for a single-member Panel shall be paid entirely by the Complainant.
(c) If either the Complainant or the Respondent elects to have the dispute decided by a three-member Panel, the Provider shall appoint three Panelists in accordance with the procedures identified in Paragraph 6(e). The fees for a three-member Panel shall be paid in their entirety by the Complainant, except where the election for a three-member Panel was made by the Respondent, in which case the applicable fees shall be shared equally between the Parties.
(d) Unless it has already elected a three-member Panel, the Complainant shall submit to the Provider, within five (5) calendar days of communication of a response in which the Respondent elects a three-member Panel, the names and contact details of three candidates to serve as one of the Panelists. These candidates may be drawn from any ICANN-approved Provider's list of panelists.
(e) In the event that either the Complainant or the Respondent elects a three-member Panel, the Provider shall endeavor to appoint one Panelist from the list of candidates provided by each of the Complainant and the Respondent. In the event the Provider is unable within five (5) calendar days to secure the appointment of a Panelist on its customary terms from either Party's list of candidates, the Provider shall make that appointment from its list of panelists. The third Panelist shall be appointed by the Provider from a list of five candidates submitted

by the Provider to the Parties, the Provider's selection from among the five being made in a manner that reasonably balances the preferences of both Parties, as they may specify to the Provider within five (5) calendar days of the Provider's submission of the five-candidate list to the Parties.
(f) Once the entire Panel is appointed, the Provider shall notify the Parties of the Panelists appointed and the date by which, absent exceptional circumstances, the Panel shall forward its decision on the complaint to the Provider.

7. Impartiality and Independence

A Panelist shall be impartial and independent and shall have, before accepting appointment, disclosed to the Provider any circumstances giving rise to justifiable doubt as to the Panelist's impartiality or independence. If, at any stage during the administrative proceeding, new circumstances arise that could give rise to justifiable doubt as to the impartiality or independence of the Panelist, that Panelist shall promptly disclose such circumstances to the Provider. In such event, the Provider shall have the discretion to appoint a substitute Panelist.

8. Communication Between Parties and the Panel

No Party or anyone acting on its behalf may have any unilateral communication with the Panel. All communications between a Party and the Panel or the Provider shall be made to a case administrator appointed by the Provider in the manner prescribed in the Provider's Supplemental Rules.

9. Transmission of the File to the Panel

The Provider shall forward the file to the Panel as soon as the Panelist is appointed in the case of a Panel consisting of a single member, or as soon as the last Panelist is appointed in the case of a three-member Panel.

10. General Powers of the Panel

(a) The Panel shall conduct the administrative proceeding in such manner as it considers appropriate in accordance with the Policy and these Rules.
(b) In all cases, the Panel shall ensure that the Parties are treated with equality and that each Party is given a fair opportunity to present its case.
(c) The Panel shall ensure that the administrative proceeding takes place with due expedition. It may, at the request of a Party or on its own motion, extend, in exceptional cases, a period of time fixed by these Rules or by the Panel.
(d) The Panel shall determine the admissibility, relevance, materiality and weight of the evidence.
(e) A Panel shall decide a request by a Party to consolidate multiple domain name disputes in accordance with the Policy and these Rules.

11. Language of Proceedings

(a) Unless otherwise agreed by the Parties, or specified otherwise in the Registration Agreement, the language of the administrative proceeding shall be the language of the Registration Agreement, subject to the authority of the Panel to determine otherwise, having regard to the circumstances of the administrative proceeding.
(b) The Panel may order that any documents submitted in languages other than the language of the administrative proceeding be accompanied by a translation in whole or in part into the language of the administrative proceeding.

12. Further Statements

In addition to the complaint and the response, the Panel may request, in its sole discretion, further statements or documents from either of the Parties.

13. In-Person Hearings

There shall be no in-person hearings (including hearings by teleconference, videoconference, and web conference), unless the Panel determines, in its sole discretion and as an exceptional matter, that such a hearing is necessary for deciding the complaint.

14. Default

(a) In the event that a Party, in the absence of exceptional circumstances, does not comply with any of the time periods established by these Rules or the Panel, the Panel shall proceed to a decision on the complaint.

(b) If a Party, in the absence of exceptional circumstances, does not comply with any provision of, or requirement under, these Rules or any request from the Panel, the Panel shall draw such inferences therefrom as it considers appropriate.

15. Panel Decisions

(a) A Panel shall decide a complaint on the basis of the statements and documents submitted and in accordance with the Policy, these Rules and any rules and principles of law that it deems applicable.

(b) In the absence of exceptional circumstances, the Panel shall forward its decision on the complaint to the Provider within fourteen (14) days of its appointment pursuant to Paragraph 6.

(c) In the case of a three-member Panel, the Panel's decision shall be made by a majority.

(d) The Panel's decision shall be in writing, provide the reasons on which it is based, indicate the date on which it was rendered and identify the name(s) of the Panelist(s).

(e) Panel decisions and dissenting opinions shall normally comply with the guidelines as to length set forth in the Provider's Supplemental Rules. Any dissenting opinion shall accompany the majority decision. If the Panel concludes that the dispute is not within the scope of Paragraph 4(a) of the Policy, it shall so state. If after considering the submissions the Panel finds that the complaint was brought in bad faith, for example in an attempt at Reverse Domain Name Hijacking or was brought primarily to harass the domain-name holder, the Panel shall declare in its decision that the complaint was brought in bad faith and constitutes an abuse of the administrative proceeding.

16. Communication of Decision to Parties

(a) Within three (3) calendar days after receiving the decision from the Panel, the Provider shall communicate the full text of the decision to each Party, the concerned Registrar(s), and ICANN. The concerned Registrar(s) shall immediately communicate to each Party, the Provider, and ICANN the date for the implementation of the decision in accordance with the Policy.

(b) Except if the Panel determines otherwise (see Paragraph 4(j) of the Policy), the Provider shall publish the full decision and the date of its implementation on a publicly accessible web site. In any event, the portion of any decision determining a complaint to have been brought in bad faith (see Paragraph 15(e) of these Rules) shall be published.

17. Settlement or Other Grounds for Termination

(a) If, before the Panel's decision, the Parties agree on a settlement, the Panel shall terminate the administrative proceeding.
(b) If, before the Panel's decision is made, it becomes unnecessary or impossible to continue the administrative proceeding for any reason, the Panel shall terminate the administrative proceeding, unless a Party raises justifiable grounds for objection within a period of time to be determined by the Panel.

18. Effect of Court Proceedings

(a) In the event of any legal proceedings initiated prior to or during an administrative proceeding in respect of a domain-name dispute that is the subject of the complaint, the Panel shall have the discretion to decide whether to suspend or terminate the administrative proceeding, or to proceed to a decision.
(b) In the event that a Party initiates any legal proceedings during the pendency of an administrative proceeding in respect of a domain-name dispute that is the subject of the complaint, it shall promptly notify the Panel and the Provider. See Paragraph 8 above.

19. Fees

(a) The Complainant shall pay to the Provider an initial fixed fee, in accordance with the Provider's Supplemental Rules, within the time and in the amount required. A Respondent electing under Paragraph 5(b)(iv) to have the dispute decided by a three-member Panel, rather than the single-member Panel elected by the Complainant, shall pay the Provider one-half the fixed fee for a three-member Panel. See Paragraph 5(c). In all other cases, the Complainant shall bear all of the Provider's fees, except as prescribed under Paragraph 19(d). Upon appointment of the Panel, the Provider shall refund the appropriate portion, if any, of the initial fee to the Complainant, as specified in the Provider's Supplemental Rules.
(b) No action shall be taken by the Provider on a complaint until it has received from Complainant the initial fee in accordance with Paragraph 19(a).
(c) If the Provider has not received the fee within ten (10) calendar days of receiving the complaint, the complaint shall be deemed withdrawn and the administrative proceeding terminated.
(d) In exceptional circumstances, for example in the event an in-person hearing is held, the Provider shall request the Parties for the payment of additional fees, which shall be established in agreement with the Parties and the Panel.

20. Exclusion of Liability

Except in the case of deliberate wrongdoing, neither the Provider nor a Panelist shall be liable to a Party for any act or omission in connection with any administrative proceeding under these Rules.

21. Amendments

The version of these Rules in effect at the time of the submission of the complaint to the Provider shall apply to the administrative proceeding commenced thereby. These Rules may not be amended without the express written approval of ICANN.

POLICY AND RULES FOR .BIZ DOMAIN NAMES

Restrictions Dispute Resolution Policy (RDRP)

1. Purpose.

This Restrictions Dispute Resolution Policy (the "RDRP") is incorporated by reference into your .BIZ Registration Agreement. It sets out the terms and conditions that will apply in the event of a dispute between you (as the registrant) and a third party other than us (as the registrar) or the registry administrator for the .BIZ toplevel domain over the registration or use of your domain name in violation of the .BIZ Registration Restrictions (available at www.icann.org/tlds/agreements/biz/registry-agmt-appl-18apr01.htm).
Proceedings under Paragraph 4 of the RDRP will be conducted according to the Supplemental Rules for Restrictions Dispute Resolution Policy (the "Supplemental RDRP Rules"), which are available below, and the selected administrative dispute resolution service provider's supplemental rules.

2. Your Representations.

By applying to register a domain name, or by asking us to maintain or renew a domain name registration, you hereby represent and warrant to us that
(a) the statements that you made in your Registration Agreement are complete and accurate;
(b) to your knowledge, the registration of the domain name will not infringe upon or otherwise violate the rights of any third party;
(c) you are not registering the domain name for an unlawful purpose;
(d) you will not knowingly use the domain name in violation of any applicable laws or regulations;
(e) your domain name registration does not and will not violate the terms and conditions of the .BIZ Registration Restrictions. It is your responsibility to determine whether your domain name registration infringes or violates someone else's rights. It is also your responsibility to determine whether your domain name registration violates the .BIZ Registration Restrictions.

3. Cancellations, Transfers and Changes.

We will cancel, transfer or otherwise make changes to domain name registrations under the following circumstances:
- subject to the provisions of Paragraph 8, our receipt of written or appropriate electronic instructions from you or your authorized agent to take such action;
- our receipt of an order from a court or arbitral tribunal, in each case of competent jurisdiction, requiring such action; and/or
- our receipt of a decision of an Administrative Panel requiring such action in any administrative proceeding to which you were a party and which was conducted under the RDRP or a later version of the RDRP adopted by ICANN.

We may also cancel, transfer or otherwise make changes to a domain name registration in accordance with the terms of your .BIZ Registration Agreement, ICANN policy, or other legal requirements.

4. Mandatory Administrative Proceeding.

This Paragraph sets forth the type of disputes for which you are required to submit to a mandatory administrative proceeding. These proceedings will be conducted before one of the administrative

dispute resolution service providers listed at www.icann.org/udrp/approved-providers.htm (each, a "Provider").
a. Applicable Disputes.
In addition to the grounds set out in Paragraph 4(a) of the UDRP, you will also be required to submit to a mandatory administrative proceeding in the event that a complainant asserts to a Provider that your domain is not being or will not be used primarily for a bona fide business or commercial purpose. In the administrative proceeding, the complainant will bear the burden of proving that the above elements is present. A complaint under the RDRP will not be considered valid if based exclusively on the alleged non-use of your domain name.
b. Bona Fide Business or Commercial Use.
"Bona fide business or commercial use" shall mean the bona fide use or bona fide intent to use the domain name or any content software, materials, graphics or other information thereon, to permit Internet users to access one or more host computers through the DNS:
  i.   to exchange goods, services, or property of any kind; or
  ii. in the ordinary course of trade or business; or
  iii. to facilitate the exchange of goods, services, information, or property of any kind or the ordinary course of trade or business.
c. Not a Bona Fide Business or Commercial Use.
Registering a domain name solely for the purposes identified below shall not constitute a "bona fide business or commercial use" of that domain name:
  a. selling, trading or leasing the domain name for compensation, or
  b. the unsolicited offering to sell, trade or lease the domain name for compensation.
  c. For illustration purposes, the following shall not constitute a "bona fide business or commercial use" of a domain name:
     i. Using or intending to use the domain name exclusively for personal, noncommercial purposes; or
     ii. Using or intending to use the domain name exclusively for the expression of noncommercial ideas (e.g., registering exclusively to criticize or otherwise express an opinion on the products or services of ABC company, with no other intended business or commercial purpose).
d. Selection of Provider.
The complainant shall select the Provider from among those approved by ICANN by submitting the complaint to that Provider. The selected Provider will administer the proceeding, except in cases of consolidation as described in Paragraph 4(f).
e. Initiation of Proceeding and Process and Appointment of Administrative Panel.
The Supplemental RDRP Rules state the process for initiating and conducting a proceeding and for appointing the panel that will decide the dispute (the "Administrative Panel").
f. Consolidation.
In the event of multiple disputes between you and a complainant, either you or the complainant may petition to consolidate the disputes before a single Administrative Panel. This petition shall be made to the first Administrative Panel appointed to hear a pending dispute between the parties. This Administrative Panel may consolidate before it any or all such disputes in its sole discretion, provided that the disputes being consolidated are governed by the RDRP or another dispute resolution policy adopted by ICANN.
g. Fees.
All fees charged by a Provider in connection with any dispute before an Administrative Panel pursuant to the RDRP shall be paid by the complainant, except in cases where you elect to expand the Administrative Panel from one to three panelists as provided in the Supplemental RDRP Rules, in which case all fees will be split evenly by you and the complainant.
h. Our Involvement in Administrative Proceedings.

We do not, and will not, participate in the administration or conduct of any proceeding before an Administrative Panel. In addition, we will not be liable as a result of any decisions rendered by the Administrative Panel.

i. Remedies.

The remedies available to a complainant pursuant to any proceeding before an Administrative Panel shall be limited to requiring the cancellation of your domain name or the transfer of your domain name registration to the complainant.

j. Notification and Publication.

The Provider shall notify us of any decision made by an Administrative Panel with respect to a domain name you have registered with us. All decisions under the RDRP will be published in full over the Internet, except when an Administrative Panel determines in an exceptional case to redact portions of its decision.

k. Availability of Court Proceedings.

The mandatory administrative proceeding requirements set forth in Paragraph 4 shall not prevent either you or the complainant from submitting the dispute to a court of competent jurisdiction for independent resolution before such mandatory administrative proceeding is commenced or after such proceeding is concluded. If an Administrative Panel decides that your domain name registration should be canceled or transferred, we will wait ten (10) business days (as observed in the location of our principal office) after we are informed by the applicable Provider of the Administrative Panel's decision before implementing that decision. We will then implement the decision unless we have received from you during that ten (10) business day period official documentation (such as a copy of a complaint, file-stamped by the clerk of the court) that you have commenced a lawsuit against the complainant in a jurisdiction to which the complainant has submitted under the Supplemental RDRP Rules. (In general, that jurisdiction is either the location of our principal office or of your address as shown in our Whois database.) If we receive such documentation within the ten (10) business day period, we will not implement the Administrative Panel's decision, and we will take no further action, until we receive

    (i)   evidence satisfactory to us of a resolution between the parties;

    (ii)   evidence satisfactory to us that your lawsuit has been dismissed or withdrawn; or

    (iii) a copy of an order from such court dismissing your lawsuit or ordering that you do not have the right to continue to use your domain name.

5. All Other Disputes and Litigation.

All other disputes between you and any party other than us regarding your domain name registration that are not brought pursuant to the mandatory administrative proceeding provisions of Paragraph 4 shall be resolved between you and such other party through any court, arbitration or other proceeding that may be available.

6. Our Involvement in Disputes.

We will not participate in any way in any dispute between you and any party other than us regarding the registration and use of your domain name. You shall not name us as a party or otherwise include us in any such proceeding. In the event that we are named as a party in any such proceeding, we reserve the right to raise any and all defenses deemed appropriate, and to take any other action necessary to defend ourselves.

7. Maintaining the Status Quo.

We will not cancel, transfer, activate, deactivate, or otherwise change the status of any domain name registration under the RDRP except as provided in Paragraph 3 above.

8. Transfers During a Dispute.

a. Transfers of a Domain Name to a New Holder.
   You may not transfer your domain name registration to another holder
   (i) during a pending administrative proceeding brought pursuant to Paragraph 4 or for a period of fifteen (15) business days (as observed in the location of our principal place of business) after such proceeding is concluded; or
   (ii) during a pending court proceeding or arbitration commenced regarding your domain name unless the party to whom the domain name registration is being transferred agrees, in writing, to be bound by the decision of the court or arbitrator. We reserve the right to cancel any transfer of a domain name registration to another holder that is made in violation of this subparagraph.

b. Changing Registrars.
   You may not transfer your domain name registration to another registrar during a pending administrative proceeding brought pursuant to Paragraph 4 or for a period of fifteen (15) business days (as observed in the location of our principal place of business) after such proceeding is concluded. You may transfer administration of your domain name registration to another registrar during a pending court action or arbitration, provided that the domain name you have registered with us shall continue to be subject to the proceedings commenced against you in accordance with the terms of the RDRP. In the event that you transfer a domain name registration to us during the pendency of a court action or arbitration, such dispute shall remain subject to the domain name dispute policy of the registrar from which the domain name registration was transferred.

9. Policy Modifications.

We reserve the right to modify the RDRP at any time with the permission of ICANN. We will post the revised RDRP at (http://www.neulevel.biz/ardp/docs/rdrp.html) at least thirty (30) calendar days before it becomes effective. Unless this version of the RDRP has already been invoked by the submission of a complaint to a Provider, in which event the version of the RDRP in effect at the time it was invoked will apply to you until the dispute is over, all such changes will be binding upon you with respect to any domain name registration dispute, whether the dispute arose before, on or after the effective date of our change. In the event that you object to a change in this version of the RDRP, your sole remedy is to cancel your domain name registration with us, provided that you will not be entitled to a refund of any fees you paid to us. The revised RDRP will apply to you until you cancel your domain name registration.

SUPPLEMENTAL RULES FOR RESTRICTIONS DISPUTE RESOLUTION POLICY

1. Purpose.

Administrative proceedings for the resolution of disputes under the Restrictions Dispute Resolution Policy ("RDRP"); shall be governed by the Rules for Uniform Domain Name Dispute Resolution Policy ("UDRP Rules"; www.icann.org/udrp/udrp-rules-24oct99.htm) as supplemented or modified by these Supplemental Rules for Restrictions Dispute Resolution Policy (the "Supplemental RDRP Rules") and any supplemental rules of the dispute resolution service provider administering the proceedings.

2. Definitions.

Defined terms in the UDRP Rules shall have the same meaning in these Supplemental RDRP Rules, subject to the following:
a. Complaint based on UDRP and RDRP.
 If a complaint is based on the UDRP and the RDRP, the term "Policy" shall refer to the Uniform Domain Name Dispute Resolution Policy ("UDRP") and the RDRP, and the term "Rules" shall refer to the UDRP Rules as supplemented or modified by these Supplemental RDRP Rules.
b. Complaint based on the RDRP alone.
 If a complaint is based on the RDRP alone, the term "Policy" shall refer to the RDRP, and the term "Rules" shall refer to the UDRP Rules as supplemented or modified by these Supplemental RDRP Rules.

3. RDRP Grounds.

A complaint pursuant to the RDRP (whether or not also based on the UDRP) shall describe, in accordance with Paragraph 4(a)-(c), the grounds on which the complaint is made including, in particular, the extent to which the domain name is not being or will not be used primarily for a bona fide business or commercial purpose.

Start-up Trademark Opposition Policy and Rules for .BIZ

(As adopted by NeuLevel, Inc. and approved by ICANN on May 11, 2001)

1. Start-up Trademark Opposition Policy.
This policy is followed by all ICANN Accredited Registrars. The Policy, is made a part of the ICANN-Accredited Registrarregistrant agreement. Registry Operator has begun the process of contacting potential dispute providers and will announce these providers in the near future.

2. Rules for Start-Up Trademark Opposition Policy.
These rules are followed by all dispute-resolution service providers, with supplementation by each provider's supplemental rules. The rules are set forth below. Registry Operator has begun the process of contacting potential dispute providers and will announce these providers in the near future.

START-UP TRADEMARK OPPOSITION POLICY FOR .BIZ
(Revised 9/19/01)

1. Purpose.

This Start-up Trademark Opposition Policy (the "Policy") is incorporated by reference into the .BIZ Registration Agreement. It sets forth the terms and conditions in connection with a dispute between you (as the registrant) and any party other than us (as the registrar) or the registry administrator for the .BIZ top-level domain (the "Registry") over the registration or use of an Internet domain name registered by you that is subject to the Intellectual Property Claim Service ("IP Claim Service").

The IP Claim Service is a service introduced by the Registry Operator to notify a trademark or service mark holder ("Claimant") that a second-level domain name has been registered in which that Claimant claims intellectual property rights. In order to benefit from the IP Claim Service, a Claimant was required to submit a Intellectual Property Claim Form ("IP Claim Form") for the .BIZ domain name matching the exact alphanumeric string contained in the trade or service mark in which that Claimant has rights. Neither the Registry Operator nor we verified whether the IP Claim Form information provided by a Claimant is accurate. Neither the Registry Operator nor we provide any warranties or guarantees in respect of that information. No restriction wasplaced on the number of Claimants that could file a IP Claim Form for a given domain name. Accordingly, in some cases, there are multiple Claimants for a single domain name. If your domain name identically matches a trade or service mark string specified in a IP Claim Form, any Claimant that filed such a IP Claim Form will be notified of this fact. The notification will provide the relevant details of your registration, including your contact details. In accordance with this Policy and the Rules, those Claimants will have the right to challenge your domain name registration, subject to the challenge priority established by the Registry Operator. Proceedings under Paragraph 4 of this Policy will be conducted according to the Rules for Start-up Trademark Opposition Policy (the "Rules"), which are available at below, and the selected administrative dispute resolution service provider's supplemental rules.

2. Your Representations.

By applying to register a domain name in the start-up period, you hereby represent and warrant to us that

(a) the statements that you made in your .BIZ Registration Agreement are complete and accurate;
(b) to your knowledge, the domain name will not infringe upon or otherwise violate the rights of any third party;
(c) you are not registering the domain name for an unlawful purpose; and
(d) you will not knowingly use the domain name in violation of any applicable laws or regulations. It is your responsibility to determine whether your domain name registration infringes or violates someone else's rights.

3. Cancellations, Transfers, and Changes.

We will cancel, transfer or otherwise make changes to a domain name registration that is subject to this Policy under the following circumstances:

a. Subject to the provisions of Paragraph 8, our receipt of written or appropriate electronic instructions from you or your authorized agent to take such action, and there are no further Claimants with respect to your domain name(s); and/or
b. Our receipt of an order from a court or arbitral tribunal, in each case of competent jurisdiction, requiring such action; and/or
c. Our receipt of a decision of an Administrative Panel requiring such action in any administrative proceeding to which you were a party and which was conducted under this Policy or a later version of this Policy adopted by ICANN.

We may also cancel, transfer or otherwise make changes to a domain name registration in accordance with the terms of the .BIZ Registration Agreement, ICANN Policy, or other legal requirements.

4. Mandatory Administrative Proceeding.

This Paragraph sets forth the type of disputes for which you are required to submit to a mandatory administrative proceeding. These proceedings will be conducted before one of the administrative dispute resolution service providers listed at www.icann.org/udrp/approvedproviders.htm (each, a "Provider").

a. Applicable Disputes.

You are required to submit to a mandatory administrative proceeding in the event that a Complainant asserts to the applicable Provider, in compliance with the Rules, that:

i. Your domain name is identical to a trademark or service mark in which the Complainant has rights; and
ii. You have no rights or legitimate interests in respect of the domain name; and
iii. Your domain name has been registered or is being used in bad faith.

In the administrative proceeding, the Complainant must prove that each of these three elements is present.

b. Evidence of Registration or Use in Bad Faith.

For the purposes of Paragraph 4(a)(iii), the following circumstances, in particular but without limitation, if found by the Panel to be present, shall be considered evidence of the registration or use of a domain name in bad faith:

i. Circumstances indicating that you have registered the domain name primarily for the purpose of selling, renting, or otherwise transferring the domain name registration to the Complainant or to a competitor of the Complainant, for valuable consideration in excess of your documented out-of-pocket costs directly related to the domain name; or
ii. You have registered the domain name in order to prevent the Complainant from reflecting the mark in a corresponding domain name; or
iii. You have registered the domain name primarily for the purpose of disrupting the business of a competitor; or

iv. By using the domain name, you have intentionally attempted to attract, for commercial gain, Internet users to your web site or other on-line location, by creating a likelihood of confusion with the Complainant's mark as to the source, sponsorship, affiliation, or endorsement of your web site or location or of a product or service on your web site or location.

c. How to Demonstrate Your Rights to and Legitimate Interests in the Domain Name in Responding to a Complaint.

When you receive a complaint, ou should refer to the Rules to determine how your response should be repared. Any of the following circumstances, in particular but without limitation, if found by the Panel to be proved based on its evaluation of all evidence presented, shall demonstrate your rights or legitimate interests to the domain name for purposes of Paragraph 4(a)(ii):

i. You are the owner or beneficiary of a trade or service mark that is identical to the domain name; or
ii. Before any notice to you of the dispute, your use of, or demonstrable preparations to use, the domain name or a name corresponding to the domain name in connection with a bona fide offering of goods or services; or
iii. You (as an individual, business, or other organization) have been commonly known by the domain name, even if you have acquired no trademark or service mark rights.

d. Selection of Provider.

The Claimant shall select the Provider from among those approved by ICANN and electing to offer STOP dispute resolution services, by submitting the complaint to that Provider. The selected Provider will administer the proceeding, except in cases of consolidation as described in Paragraph 4(f). A list of STOP Providers can be found at: http://www.neulevel.biz/stop_overview/stop_overview.html.

e. Initiation of Proceeding and Process and Appointment of Administrative Panel.

All disputes will be decided by a single Panelist, who shall be appointed by the Provider. The Rules state the process for initiating and conducting a proceeding and for appointing the Sole Panelist that will decide the dispute (the "Administrative Panel").

f. Consolidation.

In the event of multiple disputes between you and a Complainant, either you or the Complainant may petition to consolidate the disputes before a single Administrative Panel. This petition shall be made to the first Administrative Panel appointed to hear a pending dispute between the parties. This Administrative Panel may consolidate before it any or all such disputes in its sole discretion, provided that the disputes being consolidated are governed by this Policy or another dispute resolution policy adopted by ICANN, and the Complainant has priority to challenge you under the STOP Policy and Rules.

g. Fees.

All fees charged by a Provider in connection with any dispute before an Administrative Panel pursuant to this Policy shall be paid by the Complainant.

h. Our Involvement in Administrative Proceedings.

We do not, and will not, participate in the administration or conduct of any proceeding before an Administrative Panel. In addition, we will not be liable as a result of any decisions rendered by an Administrative Panel.

i. Remedies.

The remedies available to a Complainant pursuant to any proceeding before an Administrative Panel shall be limited to requiring the transfer of your domain name registration to the Complainant.

j. Notification and Publication.

The Provider shall notify us and the Registry Operator of any decision made by an Administrative Panel with respect to a domain name you have registered with us. All

k. Implementation of the Administrative Panel's Decision.

decisions under this Policy will be published in full over the Internet, except when an Administrative Panel determines in an exceptional case to redact portions of its decision.

If an Administrative Panel decides that your domain name registration should be transferred, we will wait ten (10) business days (as observed in the location of our principal office) after we are informed by the applicable Provider of the Administrative Panel's decision before implementing that decision. We will then implement the decision unless we have received from you during that ten (10) business day period official documentation (such as a copy of a complaint, filestamped by the clerk of the court) that you have commenced a lawsuit against the Complainant in a jurisdiction to which the Complainant has submitted under Paragraph 3 of the Rules (In general, that jurisdiction is either the location of our principal office or of your address as shown in our Whois database.) If we receive such documentation within the ten (10) business day period, we will not implement the Administrative Panel's decision, and we will take no further action, until we receive
(i) evidence satisfactory to us of a resolution between the parties;
(ii) evidence satisfactory to us that your lawsuit has been dismissed or withdrawn; or
(iii) a copy of an order from such court dismissing your lawsuit or ordering that you do not have the right to continue to use your domain name.

l. Multiple Challenges.
   i. Your domain name may be the subject of multiple challenges by Claimants. In such event, the Registry Operator will be responsible for establishing the challenge priority among multiple Claimants on a randomized basis.
   ii. In the event that there is more than one Claimant, the Administrative Panel shall decide, in light of its findings in respect of each of the elements identified in Paragraph 4(a), whether any further challenges shall be permitted in respect of your domain name under this Policy by using the following criteria:
      1. In the event that the Complainant demonstrates that:
         a. it has legitimate rights to the domain name,
         b. you have no legitimate rights, and
         c. you have either registered the domain name in bad faith or used the domain name in bad faith, and the Respondent fails to demonstrate that it has legitimate rights to the domain name, the Panel will find in favor of the Complainant, award the domain name to the Complainant, and decide that no subsequent challenges under this Policy against the domain name(s) that is/are the subject of the Panel's decision shall be permitted.
      2. In the event that you demonstrate that you have legitimate rights to the domain name, the Panel will dismiss the complaint, and decide that no subsequent challenges under this Policy against the domain name(s) that is/are the subject of the Panel's decision shall be permitted.
      3. In the event that you do not, or are unable to, demonstrate legitimate rights to the domain name(s), and the Complainant is unable to demonstrate either
         (a) it has legitimate rights, or
         (b) the domain name(s) was/were registered in bad faith, the Panel will dismiss the complaint, and decide that subsequent challenges under this Policy against the domain name(s) that is/are subject of the Panel's decision shall be permitted. Such challenges under this Policy, however, may not be brought by the same Complainant.

5. All Other Disputes and Litigation.

All other disputes between you and any party other than us or the Registry Operator regarding your domain name registration that are not brought pursuant to the mandatory administrative proceeding provisions of Paragraph 4 shall be resolved between you and such other party through any court, arbitration or other proceeding that may be available, or the Uniform Domain Name Dispute Resolution Policy, as supplemented by the Registration Restrictions Dispute Resolution Criteria. Proceedings under the the Uniform Domain Name Dispute Resolution Policy, whether or not supplemented by the Registration Restrictions Dispute Resolution Criteria, shall not be brought against a domain name, as long as this domain name is, or can be, subject to an administrative proceeding under the Policy.

6. Our Involvement in Disputes.

We will not participate in any way in any dispute between you and any party other than us regarding the registration and use of your domain name. You shall not name us as a party or otherwise include us in any such proceeding. In the event that we are named as a party in any such proceeding, we reserve the right to raise any and all defenses deemed appropriate, and to take any other action necessary to defend ourselves.

7. Maintaining the Status Quo.

We will not cancel, transfer, activate, de-activate, or otherwise change the status of any domain name registration subject to this Policy, except as provided in Paragraph 3 above.

8. Transfers During a Dispute.

a. Transfers of a Domain Name to a New Holder.
You may not transfer a domain name registration that is subject to this Policy to another holder until all pending or prospective challenges pursuant to this Policy have been resolved, except that a transfer may be made to the Complainant in a pending administrative proceeding (e.g., in the event of a settlement of the dispute), provided that there are no further Claimants with respect to your domain name.

b. Changing Registrars.
You may not transfer a domain name registration that is subject to this Policy to another registrar until all pending or prospective challenges pursuant to this Policy have been resolved.

9. Policy Modifications.

The Registry Operator reserves the right to modify this Policy at any time with the permission of ICANN. We will post the revised Policy at http://www.neulevel.biz/ardp/docs/stop.html at least fifteen (15) calendar days before it becomes effective. Unless this Policy has already been invoked by the submission of a complaint to a Provider, in which event the version of the Policy in effect at the time it was invoked will apply to you until the dispute is over, all such changes will be binding upon you with respect to any domain name registration dispute, whether the dispute arose before, on or after the effective date of the change. In the event that you object to a change in this Policy, your sole remedy is to cancel your domain name registration with us, provided that you will not be entitled to a refund of any fees you paid to us. The revised Policy will apply to you until you cancel your domain name registration.

RULES FOR START-UP TRADEMARK OPPOSTION POLICY
(Revised 9/19/01)

Administrative proceedings for the resolution of disputes pursuant to the Start-up Trademark Opposition Policy shall be governed by these Rules and any Supplemental Rules of the dispute resolution service provider administering the proceedings, as posted at its web site.

Start-up Trademark Opposition Policy and Rules for .BIZ Domains

1. Definitions

In these Rules:
- **Case Ticket Number** means the number assigned by Registry Operator to Claimants that register its intent to file a complaint with a Provider.
- **Claimant** means a trademark or service mark holder that submitted an Intellectual Property Claim Form ("IP Claim Form") for a .BIZ domain name under the Intellectual Property Claim Service ("IP Claim Service").
- **Complainant** means a Claimant that has initiated an administrative proceeding under the Start-up Trademark Opposition Policy against a domain name registration that is subject to the IP Claim Service.
- **ICANN** refers to the Internet Corporation for Assigned Names and Numbers.
- **Mutual Jurisdiction** means a court jurisdiction at the location of either (a) the principal office of the Registrar of the domain name in question, or (b) the domain name holder's address, as shown for the registration of the domain name in the Registrar's Whois database at the time a complaint is submitted to a Provider.
- **Panel** means the sole panelist appointed by a Provider to decide a complaint pursuant to the Policy.
- **Party** means a Complainant or a Respondent.
- **Policy** means the Start-up Trademark Opposition Policy that is incorporated by reference and made a part of the Registration Agreement.
- **Provider** means a dispute resolution service provider approved by ICANN. A list of such Providers appears at http://www.icann.org/udrp/approvedproviders.htm.
- **Registrar** means the entity with which the Respondent has registered a domain name that is the subject of a complaint.
- **Registration Agreement** means the agreement between a Registrar and a domain name holder.
- **Registry Operator** means the registry operator for the .BIZ top-level domain.
- **Respondent** means the holder of a domain name registration against which a complaint is initiated.
- **Reverse Domain Name Hijacking** means using the Policy in bad faith to attempt to deprive a registered domain name holder of a domain name.
- **Supplemental Rules** means the rules adopted by the Provider administering a proceeding to supplement these Rules. Supplemental Rules shall not be inconsistent with the Policy or these Rules.

2. Communications

a. Any written communication to the Complainant or the Respondent required under these Rules shall be made by the means specified by the Complainant or the Respondent, respectively, or in the absence of such specification:
   i. By facsimile with a confirmation of transmission; or
   ii. By postal or courier service, postage pre-paid and return receipt requested; and/or
   iii. Electronically via the Internet, provided a record of its transmission is available.
b. Any communication to the Provider or the Panel shall be made in accordance with the Provider's Supplemental Rules.
c. All communications shall be made in the language prescribed in Paragraph 11.
d. Either Party may update its contact details by notifying the other Party, the Provider and the Registrar.
e. Except as otherwise provided in these Rules, or decided by a Panel, all communications provided for under these Rules shall be deemed to have been made:
   i. If delivered by facsimile transmission, on the date shown on the confirmation of transmission; or

- ii. If by postal or courier service, on the date marked on the receipt; or
- iii. If via the Internet, on the date that the communication was transmitted, provided that the date of transmission is verifiable.
- f. Except as otherwise provided in these Rules, all time periods calculated under these Rules shall begin to run on the earliest date that the communication is deemed to have been made in accordance with Paragraph 2(e).
- g. Except as otherwise provided in these Rules, any communication by:
  - i. A Panel to any Party shall be copied to the Provider and to the other Party;
  - ii. The Provider, following the commencement of an administrative proceeding pursuant to Paragraph 4(c), to any Party shall be copied to the other Party; and
  - iii. A Party shall be copied to the other Party, the Panel and the Provider, as the case may be.
- h. It shall be the responsibility of the sender to retain records of the fact and circumstances of sending, which shall be available for inspection by affected parties and for reporting purposes.
- i. In the event that a Party sending a communication receives notification of nondelivery of the communication, that Party shall promptly notify the Provider of the circumstances of the notification.

3. The Complaint

- a. A Complainant shall initiate an administrative proceeding under this Policy by:
  - i. Registering with the Registry Operator, its intent to submit a complaint to a Provider. By registering the submission of its complaint with Registry Operator, the Complainant shall be given a Case Ticket Number; AND
  - ii. Submitting its complaint to the Provider of its choice within twenty (20) calendar days of being notified by the Registry Operator of its challenge priority in accordance with the Rules and Policy; and

  If the Complainant fails to submit its complaint to a Provider or to complete its registration with the Registry Operator by the specified deadline, it shall be deemed to have forfeited its right to challenge the domain name registration under this Policy. In any event, a Complainant shall as soon as possible after receiving notification of its challenge priority advise the Registry Operator in writing of its election not to challenge the domain name registration under this Policy.
- b. The complaint shall be submitted in hard copy (with annexes) and in electronic form (without annexes).
- c. The complaint shall:
  - i. Request that the complaint be submitted for decision in accordance with the Policy and Rules and describe why the domain name registration should be considered subject to the Policy;
  - ii. Provide the full name, postal and e-mail addresses, and the telephone and telefax numbers of the Complainant and of any representative authorized to act for the Complainant in the administrative proceeding;
  - iii. Provide the Registry Account Number, the Case Ticket Number and the Challenge Priority Number provided by the Registry Operator;
  - iv. Specify a preferred method for communications to the Complainant in the administrative proceeding (including person to be contacted, medium, and address information) for each of (A) electronic-only material and (B) material including hard copy;
  - v. Provide the full name of the Respondent and, if different from the contact details available in the Whois database for the domain name, provide all information known

to the Complainant regarding how to contact the Respondent or any representative of the Respondent, including contact information based on pre-complaint dealings;
vi. Specify the domain name(s) that is/are the subject of the complaint;
vii. Identify the Registrar(s) with whom the domain name(s) is/are registered at the time the complaint is filed;
viii. Specify the trademark(s) or service mark(s) on which the complaint is based and, for each mark, describe the goods or services, if any, with which the mark is used (the Complainant may also separately describe other goods and services for which it intends, at the time the complaint is submitted, to use the mark in the future);
ix. Describe, in accordance with the Policy, the grounds on which the complaint is made including, in particular,
   (1) the extent to which the domain name(s) is/are identical to a trademark or service mark in which the Complainant has rights; and
   (2) why the Respondent should be considered as having no rights or legitimate interests in respect of the domain name(s) that is/are the subject of the complaint; and
   (3) why the domain name(s) should be considered as having been registered or used in bad faith. This portion of the complaint shall comply with any word or page limit set forth in the Provider's Supplemental Rules;
x. Identify any other proceedings that have been commenced or terminated in connection with or relating to any of the domain name(s) that is/are the subject of the complaint, including any such proceedings under this Policy;
xi. State that a copy of the complaint, together with the cover sheet as prescribed by the Provider's Supplemental Rules, has been sent or transmitted to the Respondent (domain-name holder), in accordance with Paragraph 2(a);
xii. Identify the Mutual Jurisdiction to which the Complainant(s) will submit, with respect to any challenges to a decision in the administrative proceeding to transfer the domain name, as follows:
"The Complainant hereby designates [identify precisely the court jurisdiction] as the Mutual Jurisdiction, for the purposes of any challenges to a decision in the administrative proceeding to cancel or transfer the domain name."
xiii. Conclude with the following statement followed by the signature of the Complainant or its authorized representative:
"Complainant agrees that its claims and remedies concerning the registration of the domain name, the dispute, or the dispute's resolution shall be solely against the domain name holder and waives all such claims and remedies against (a) the dispute resolution service provider and the Administrative Panelist, except in the case of deliberate wrongdoing, (b) the registrar, (c) the Registry Operator, and (d) the Internet Corporation for Assigned Names and Numbers, as well as their directors, officers, employees, and agents."
"Complainant certifies that the information contained in this Complaint is to the best of Complainant's knowledge complete and accurate, that this Complaint is not being presented for any improper purpose, such as to harass, and that the assertions in this Complaint are warranted under the Start-up Trademark Opposition Policy, the Rules for Start-up Trademark Opposition Policy and under applicable law, as it now exists or as it may be extended by a good-faith and reasonable argument."; and
xiv. Annex any documentary or other evidence, including any trademark or service mark registration upon which the complaint relies and a schedule indexing such evidence.

d. The complaint may relate to more than one domain name, provided that the domain names are registered by the same domain name holder and the Complainant has an equal challenge priority in respect of each domain name that is the subject of the complaint.

4. Notification of Complaint

a. The Provider shall review the complaint for formal compliance with the Policy and the Rules. If the complaint is found to be in compliance, the Provider shall notify the Respondent, in the manner prescribed in Paragraph 2(a). For the purposes of notifying the complaint, the Provider shall not be required to use any contact details other than those available in the Whois database for the domain name(s) in dispute.
b. If the Provider finds the complaint to be formally deficient, it shall promptly notify the Complainant of the nature of the deficiencies identified. The Complainant shall have five (5) calendar days within which to correct any such deficiencies, after which the administrative proceeding will be deemed terminated and the Complainant shall be deemed to have forfeited its right to challenge the domain name registration under this Policy.
c. The date of commencement of the administrative proceeding shall be the date the complaint is notified by the Provider to the Respondent.
d. The Provider shall immediately notify the Complainant, the Respondent, the Registry Operator and ICANN of the date of commencement of the administrative proceeding.

5. The Response

a. Within twenty (20) calendar days of the date of commencement of the administrative proceeding the Respondent shall submit a response to the Provider.
b. The response shall be submitted in hard copy (with annexes) and in electronic form (without annexes).
c. The response shall:
   i. Specifically respond to the statements and allegations contained in the complaint and include any and all bases for the Respondent to retain registration and use of the disputed domain name(s). This portion of the response shall comply with any word or page limit set forth in the Provider's Supplemental Rules;
   ii. Provide the name, postal and e-mail addresses, and the telephone and telefax numbers of the Respondent and of any representative authorized to act for the Respondent in the administrative proceeding;
   iii. Specify a preferred method for communications directed to the Respondent in the administrative proceeding (including person to be contacted, medium, and address information) for each of (A) electroniconly material and (B) material including hard copy;
   iv. Identify any other proceedings that have been commenced or terminated in connection with or relating to any of the domain name(s) that is/are the subject of the complaint, including any such proceedings under the Policy;
   v. State that a copy of the response has been sent or transmitted to the Complainant, in accordance with Paragraph 2(a); and
   vi. Conclude with the following statement followed by the signature of the Respondent or its authorized representative:
      "Respondent certifies that the information contained in this Response is to the best of Respondent's knowledge complete and accurate, that this Response is not being presented forany improper purpose and that the assertions in this Response are warranted under the Start-up Trademark Opposition Policy, the Rules for Start-up Trademark Opposition Policy and under applicable law, as it now exists or as it may be extended by a good-faith and reasonableargument."; and

vii. Annex any documentary or other evidence upon which the Respondent relies, together with a schedule indexing such documents.
d. At the request of the Respondent, the Provider may, in exceptional cases, extend the period of time for the filing of the response. The period may also be extended by written stipulation between the Parties, provided the stipulation is approved by the Provider.
e. If a Respondent does not submit a response, in the absence of exceptional circumstances, the Panel shall decide the dispute based upon the complaint.
f. Where, in accordance with Paragraph 4(l)(ii) of the Policy, a subsequent challenge has been brought in respect of a domain name registration, a Respondent that has already submitted a response, shall be entitled to rely on such response and, subject to the time limits specified in Paragraph 5(a), to supplement any previously submitted response.

6. Appointment of the Panel and Timing of Decision

a. Each Provider shall maintain and publish a publicly available list of panelists and their qualifications.
b. The Provider shall appoint a single Panelist from its published list, taking into consideration such factors as the nationalities of the parties and the circumstances of the dispute.
c. Once the Panel is appointed, the Provider shall notify the Parties of the Panelist appointed and the date by which, absent exceptional circumstances, the Panel shall forward its decision on the complaint to the Provider.

7. Impartiality and Independence

The Panelist shall be impartial and independent and shall have, before accepting appointment, disclosed to the Provider any circumstances giving rise to justifiable doubt as to the Panelist's impartiality or independence. If, at any stage during the administrative proceeding, new circumstances arise that could give rise to justifiable doubt as to the impartiality or independence of the Panelist, that Panelist shall promptly disclose such circumstances to the Provider. In such event, the Provider shall have the discretion to appoint a substitute Panelist in accordance with Paragraph 6.

8. Communication Between Parties and the Panel

No Party or anyone acting on its behalf may have any unilateral communication with the Panel. All communications between a Party and the Panel or the Provider shall be made to a case administrator appointed by the Provider in the manner prescribed in the Provider's Supplemental Rules.

9. Transmission of the File to the Panel

The Provider shall forward the case file as soon as the Administrative Panel is appointed.

10. General Powers of the Panel

a. The Panel shall conduct the administrative proceeding in such manner as it considers appropriate in accordance with the Policy and the Rules.
b. In all cases, the Panel shall ensure that the Parties are treated with equality and that each Party is given a fair opportunity to present its case.
c. The Panel shall ensure that the administrative proceeding takes place with due expedition. It may, at the request of a Party or on its own motion, extend, in exceptional cases, a period of time fixed by the Rules or by the Panel.
d. The Panel shall determine the admissibility, relevance, materiality and weight of the evidence.

e. A Panel shall decide a request by a Party to consolidate multiple domain name disputes in accordance with the Policy and the Rules.

11. Language of Proceedings

a. Unless otherwise agreed by the Parties, or specified otherwise in the Registration Agreement, the language of the administrative proceeding shall be the language of the Registration Agreement, subject to the authority of the Provider or the Panel, as the case may be, to determine otherwise, having regard to the circumstances of the administrative proceeding.
b. The Panel may order that any documents submitted in languages other than the language of the administrative proceeding be accompanied by a translation in whole or in part into the language of the administrative proceeding.

12. Further Statements

In addition to the complaint and the response, the Panel may request, in its sole discretion, further statements or documents from either of the Parties.

13. In-Person Hearings

There shall be no in-person hearings (including hearings by teleconference, videoconference, and web conference), unless the Panel determines, in its sole discretion and as an exceptional matter, that such a hearing is necessary for deciding the complaint.

14. Default

a. In the event that a Party, in the absence of exceptional circumstances, does not comply with any of the time periods established by the Rules or the Panel, the Panel shall proceed to a decision on the complaint.
b. If a Party, in the absence of exceptional circumstances, does not comply with any provision of, or requirement under, the Rules or any request from the Panel, the Panel shall draw such inferences therefrom as it considers appropriate.

15. Panel Decisions

a. A Panel shall decide a complaint on the basis of the statements and documents submitted and in accordance with the Policy, these Rules and any rules and principles of law that it deems applicable.
b. In the absence of exceptional circumstances, the Panel shall forward its decision on the complaint to the Provider within fourteen (14) calendar days of its appointment.
c. The Panel's decision shall be in writing, provide the reasons on which it is based, indicate the date on which it was rendered and identify the name of the Panelist.
d. If the Panel concludes that the dispute is not within the scope of Paragraph 4(a) of the Policy, it shall so state. If after considering the submissions the Panel finds that the complaint was brought in an attempt at Reverse Domain Name Hijacking the Panel shall state its findings to this effect in its decision.
e. Multiple Challenges. In the event that there are multiple Claimants, each Panel shall specify in its decision whether any subsequent challenges against the domain name(s) that is/are the subject of the Panel's decision shall be permitted by using the following criteria:
    i. In the event that the Complainant demonstrates that:
        a. it has legitimate rights to the domain name,
        b. the Registrant has no legitimate rights, and
        c. the Registrant registered the domain name in bad faith or used the domain name in bad faith,

and the Respondent fails to demonstrate that it has legitimate rights to the domain name, the Panel will find in favor of the Complainant, award the domain name to the Complainant, and decide that no subsequent challenges under this Policy against the domain name(s) that is/are the subject of the Panel's decision shall be permitted.

ii. In the event that the Respondent demonstrates that it has legitimate rights to the domain name, the Panel will dismiss the complaint, and decide that no subsequent challenges under this Policy against the domain name(s) that is/are the subject of the Panel's decision shall be permitted.

iii. In the event that the Respondent does not, or is unable to, demonstrate legitimate rights to the domain name(s), and the Complainant is unable to demonstrate either (a) it has legitimate rights, or (b) the domain name(s) was/were registered in bad faith, the Panel will dismiss the complaint, and decide that subsequent challenges under this Policy against the domain name(s) that is/are subject of the Panel's decision shall be permitted. Such challenges under this Policy, however, may not be brought by, or on behalf of, the same Complainant.

16. Communication of Decision to Parties

a. Within three (3) business days (as observed at the Provider's principal place of business) after receiving the decision from the Panel, the Provider shall endeavour to communicate the full text of the decision to each Party, the Registry Operator and ICANN.

b. In the event of a determination in favor of the Complainant, the Registry Operator shall immediately communicate to each Party the date for the implementation of the decision in accordance with the Policy and any action required by the Parties in connection therewith.

c. Except if the Panel determines otherwise, the Provider shall publish the full decision and the date of its implementation on a publicly accessible web site. In any event, the portion of any decision determining a complaint to have been brought in bad faith shall be published.

d. In the event of multiple Complainants, the Registry shall be responsible for communicating the Panel's decision to all Complainants, including specifying whether a further challenge has been authorized by the Panel.

17. Settlement or Other Grounds for Termination

a. Settlements between Complainants and Respondents shall only be allowed if the domain name registration that is subject to the Policy has no other pending or prospective challenges pursuant to the Policy.

b. If the conditions in paragraph (a) above are present, and the Complainant notifies the Provider or the Panel that the Parties have agreed on a settlement, the Provider or the Panel, as the case may be, shall suspend or terminate the administrative proceeding.

c. If, it becomes unnecessary or impossible to continue the administrative proceeding for any other reason, the Provider or Panel, as the case may be, shall terminate the administrative proceeding, unless a Party raises justifiable grounds for objection within a period of time to be determined by the Provider or Panel.

18. Fees

a. The Complainant shall pay to the Provider an initial fixed fee, in accordance with the Provider's Supplemental Rules, within the time and in the amount required.

b. The Provider shall be under no obligation to take any action on a complaint until it has received from the Complainant the initial fee in accordance with Paragraph 18(a).

c. If the Provider has not received the fee within ten (10) calendar days of receiving the complaint, the Provider shall have the discretion to terminate the administrative proceeding

and the Complainant shall be deemed to have forfeited its right to challenge the domain name registration pursuant to the Policy.
d. In exceptional circumstances, the Provider shall be entitled to request payment of additional fees.

19. Exclusion of Liability

Except in the case of deliberate wrongdoing, neither the Provider nor a Panelist shall be liable to a Party for any act or omission in connection with any administrative proceeding under the Policy and the Rules.

20. Amendments

The version of these Rules in effect at the time of the submission of the complaint to the Provider shall apply to the administrative proceeding commenced thereby. These Rules may not be amended without the express written approval of ICANN.

STOP For Multiple Claimants

When multiple IP Claims are submitted for the same domain name, each applicant for a domain name that is in conflict with an IP Claim will be notified via e-mail of all of the IP Claims submitted for that domain name.

The following is a summary of the STOP process if there are multiple Claimants:

1. In the event of multiple Claims for the same domain name, the multiple Claims will be randomized by the Registry to determine the order in which the IP Claimants can elect to enter the Start-up Trademark Opposition Policy (STOP) proceeding. This list of priorities will be made known to all of the IP Claimants when they are notified of who successfully registered the domain name. The IP Claimant in the "first priority" position will have 20 calendar days, once notified of who got the registration, to file a STOP complaint in accordance with the STOP Rules. If the first Claimant does not file within 20 calendar days, then the second Claimant will have 20 days from then to file.
2. In the event that the first Claimant files a complaint and wins—i.e., it has shown that (a) it has legitimate rights to the domain name, (b) the Registrant has no legitimate rights, and (c) the Registrant registered the domain name in bad faith or used the domain name in bad faith—then the dispute panel will find for the first Claimant, award the domain name to the first Claimant and no further STOP proceedings will commence.
3. In the event that the Registrant demonstrates before a dispute panel that it has legitimate rights to the domain name, it will win the STOP proceeding and be allowed to keep the name. In addition, no further Claimants will be allowed to invoke STOP proceeding because the Registrant has shown that it has legitimate rights to the domain name. However, nothing prevents any other Claimant from bringing a UDRP action against the Registrant if the Claimant can show the necessary elements of a UDRP action.
4. In the event that the Registrant cannot show legitimate rights and the first Claimant cannot show that either (a) it has legitimate rights, or (b) the domain name was not registered in bad faith, then the second Claimant will be allowed to submit its STOP action to any ICANN-accredited dispute-resolution provider and the process begins again.

Note: Although there is only a 30-day hold period for any domain name that is subject to an IP Claim (i.e., the domain name will resolve on the 31st day), a Registry lock will be in place until the STOP process has been completed. During this lock period, although a domain name will resolve, no changes in ownership or transfers will be allowed.

POLICY AND RULES FOR .INFO DOMAIN NAMES

.Info Sunrise Challenge Policy
(Revised)

[This revised version of the Policy was posted November 20, 2001, persuant to the Policy Modification provisions (see paragraph 7), and after approval by ICANN.]

1. Purpose.

This Sunrise Registration Challenge Policy (the "Policy") has been adopted by Afilias. The Policy applies to domain names originally created during the Sunrise Registration Period, which began on July 25, 2001 and ended on August 31, 2001, including any subsequent transfers of such names under this policy. It is incorporated by reference into the <.info> Registration Agreement (the "Registration Agreement"). It sets forth the terms and conditions in connection with a dispute between you (as the registrant) and any party other than us (as the registrar) or the registry operator for the <.info> top-level domain (the "Registry") regarding the compliance of your registration of a second-level domain name (the "Domain Name") with the sunrise registration conditions set forth in the Registration Agreement. However, the Registry reserves the right to bring, after the conclusion of the Sunrise Challenge Period, a Challenge of Last Resort in connection with Sunrise registrations appearing to be made in violation of the sunrise registration conditions.

Proceedings under Paragraph 4 of this Policy will be conducted according to the Rules for Sunrise Registration Challenge Policy (the "Rules"), which are available at http://www.afilias.info .

2. Your Representations.

By applying to register a Domain Name in accordance with the Sunrise registration conditions of the Registration Agreement, you hereby represent and warrant to us that
(a) the statements that you made in your Registration Agreement are complete and accurate;
(b) the registration of the Domain Name complies with the sunrise registration conditions set forth in the Registration Agreement;
(c) to your knowledge, the Domain Name will not infringe upon or otherwise violate the rights of any third party;
(d) you are not registering the Domain Name for an unlawful purpose; and
(e) you will not knowingly use the Domain Name in violation of any applicable laws or regulations. It is your responsibility to determine whether your Domain Name registration infringes or violates someone else's rights.

3. Cancellations, Transfers, and Changes.

We will cancel, transfer or otherwise make changes to a domain name registration that is subject to this Policy under the following circumstances:
a. subject to the provisions of Paragraph 6, our receipt of written or appropriate electronic instructions from you or your authorized agent to take such action; and/or
b. our receipt of an order from a court or arbitral tribunal, in each case of competent jurisdiction, requiring such action; and/or
c. our receipt of a decision requiring such action in any administrative proceeding to which you were a party and which was conducted under this Policy or a later version of this Policy adopted by Afilias.

We may also cancel, transfer or otherwise make changes to a domain name registration in accordance with the terms of the Registration Agreement or other legal requirements.

4. Mandatory Administrative Proceeding.

This Paragraph sets forth the type of disputes for which you are required to submit to a mandatory administrative proceeding. These proceedings will be administered by the World Intellectual Property Organization Arbitration and Mediation Center (the "Center").

a. **Applicable Disputes.**

You are required to submit to a mandatory administrative proceeding in the event that a third party (the "Challenger") asserts to the Center, in compliance with the Rules, that:

(i) at the time of your registration of the Domain Name, no current (non-expired) trademark or service mark registration was issued in your name;[1] or

(ii) the Domain Name is not identical to the textual or word elements of the trademark or service mark registration on which the registration of your Domain Name is based;[2] or

(iii) the trademark or service mark registration on which the registration of your Domain Name is based is not of national effect;[3] or

(iv) the trademark or service mark registration on which the registration of your Domain Name was based did not issue prior to October 2, 2000.

All challenges under this Policy (except the Challenge of Last Resort) must be submitted to the Center not later than one hundred and twenty (120) days after the conclusion of the Sunrise Registration Period, which is 23:59 UTC, December 26, 2001.

b. **Challenger's Compliance with the Sunrise Registration Conditions.**

A Challenger seeking transfer of the Domain Name is required to demonstrate, as part of the administrative proceeding and as a condition for such transfer, the Challenger's compliance with the Sunrise registration conditions.

c. **How to Demonstrate Compliance with the Sunrise Registration Conditions.**

To demonstrate compliance with the Sunrise registration conditions, a Party must submit, as further specified in the Rules, an original or a certified copy of a trademark or service mark certificate establishing that:

(i) at the time of the registration of the Domain Name, a trademark or service mark was registered in the name of the Party, and was current (non-expired), as evidenced by the date(s) set forth in the certificate itself;[4] and

(ii) the textual or word elements of the trademark or service mark registration are identical to the Domain Name;[5] and

(iii) the trademark or service mark registration is of national effect;[6] and

(iv) the trademark or service mark registration was issued prior to October 2, 2000.

d. **Multiple Challenges.**

In the event more than one challenge is submitted to the Center regarding the same Domain Name, all such challenges will be queued in accordance with the date and time they were received by the Center. The first challenge to be filed will be granted priority, provided the Center is satisfied that the Challenger concerned paid the Challenger's fee in accordance with the Rules. Priority Challenge / Priority Challenger refers to a Challenge that has been given notice that it has priority under this Paragraph. Any further Challenges in the queue will be dealt with in accordance with the provision of subparagraph 4.e.

e. **Decision.**

---

[1] A registration in the supplemental register of the United States Patent and Trademark Office does not qualify as such registration.

[2] Identity will be deemed to exist also where there is a space between the textual or word elements of the mark (e.g., service mark) and a hyphen is used or the elements are combined in the Domain Name (e.g., service-mark.info or servicemark.info). In all other respects, the Domain Name must be identical to the textual or word elements of the mark.

[3] For instance, European Community Trademarks meet the condition of national effect, but United States state trademarks or service marks do not.

[4] Reference is made to footnote 1.

[5] Reference is made to footnote 2.

[6] Reference is made to footnote 3.

The challenge will be decided upon by the Center as set out in Subparagraphs (i)-(v) below. The Center's determination of whether the Sunrise registration conditions set forth in Paragraph 4(c) are met will be based solely on a prima facie examination of any trademark or service mark certificates submitted in relation to the information contained in the relevant Afilias Whois database. The Center's decision is of an administrative nature and shall be final. The Center shall not be required to state reasons for its decision.

(i) If the Center finds that you have registered the Domain Name in compliance with the sunrise registration conditions set forth in the Registration Agreement, the Center will dismiss the Priority Challenge, as well as all other challenges in the queue, if any.

(ii) If the Center is unable to find that you have registered the Domain Name in compliance with the sunrise registration conditions set forth in the Registration Agreement, the Priority Challenge will be granted[7]. If the Priority Challenger has requested transfer, this will be subject to a decision by the Center that the challenge complies with the sunrise registration conditions set forth in Paragraph 4(c), failing which Subparagraph (iii) shall apply.

(iii) If a prevailing Priority Challenger sought a cancellation or if neither Party established compliance with the sunrise registration conditions set forth in Paragraph 4(c), or if the Center is informed by the Registry that a prevailing Priority Challenger, who sought a transfer and established compliance with the sunrise registration conditions set forth in Paragraph 4(c), has failed to register the Domain Name in its name by the end of the time period stipulated in Paragraph 4(l) of this Policy, the Center shall proceed to the next Challenger in the queue, if any, seeking transfer of the Domain Name. Such Challenger shall be granted the opportunity to register the Domain Name in its name, only if such Challenger has submitted a challenge which is in formal compliance with the Policy and the Rules, the Center is satisfied that the Challenger has paid the Challenger's fee in accordance with the Rules and decides that such challenge complies with the sunrise registration conditions set forth in Paragraph 4(c). (Any such registration by a Successful Challenger will be subject to the Sunrise Registration Policy.) This procedure will be repeated until the Domain Name has been registered in the name of a Challenger in the queue, if any, or until there are no Challengers in the queue.

(iv) If, upon the expiry of the Sunrise Challenge Period there are no Challengers in the queue, the Domain Name will be made available at a later date in accordance with the Registry's procedures.

(v) As soon as a Domain Name has been registered in the name of a Challenger in accordance with the previous provisions of this Paragraph, the Registry will notify the Center thereof and any remaining challenges will be deemed terminated and no subsequent challenges allowed.

f. **Initiation of Proceeding.**
The Rules state the process for initiating and conducting a proceeding under this Policy.

g. **Consolidation.**
A challenge may not relate to more than one Domain Name. In the event a Challenger under this Policy submitted more than one challenge against you, either you or the Challenger may petition the Center to consolidate such disputes. The Center may consolidate before it any or all such disputes in its sole discretion, provided that the disputes being consolidated are governed by this Policy.

h. **Fees.**

---

[7] The Center will be unable to find that you have registered the Domain Name in compliance with the sunrise registration conditions set forth in the Registration Agreement if inter alia you fail to pay the Respondent's fee referred to in Paragraph 4(h) of this Policy.

In accordance with the Rules, the submission of a challenge under this Policy (subject to any other arrangements that may apply to the submission of Challenges of Last Resort filed by the Registry), as well as the submission of a response thereto, is subject to the payment of, respectively, a Challenger's fee and a Respondent's fee in the amount of USD 295, subject to the provisions of Rules, Paragraph 13. All payments are to be made by credit card. If a challenge is submitted, but the Challenger's fee is not paid in accordance with the Rules, the challenge will be dismissed on the basis of the Challenger's failure to pay its fee. If the Respondent's fee is not paid in accordance with the Rules, the challenge will be granted on the basis of the Respondent's failure to pay its fee, provided the challenge is in formal compliance with the Policy and Rules. If the Challenger has requested transfer of the Domain Name, that transfer will be subject to the Center's decision that the challenge complies with the Sunrise registration conditions set forth in Paragraph 4(c). The Rules describe the circumstances under which either the Challenger or the Respondent will be entitled to a reimbursement of the fees paid.

i. **Our Involvement in Administrative Proceedings.**
We do not, and will not, participate in the administration or conduct of any proceeding before the Center under this Policy. In addition, we will not be liable as a result of any decisions rendered by the Center. The Registry reserves the right to bring, after the conclusion of the Sunrise Challenge Period, a Challenge of Last Resort, as set forth in Paragraph 1.

j. **Remedies.**
The remedies available to a Challenger shall be limited to requiring the cancellation of your Domain Name registration or the transfer of your Domain Name registration to the Challenger.

k. **Notification.**
The Center shall notify any decision made under this Policy with respect to a Domain Name you have registered with us in accordance with the Rules.

l. **Implementation of the Decision.**
The Center will notify its decision to the Registry for implementation. If the Center decides that the domain name be transferred to the Challenger, it shall provide the Challenger with an authorization code generated by the Registry which will allow the Challenger to register the Domain Name in its name, and update all WHOIS information, at the registrar of its choice, within 30 days of the date on which the notification of the authorization code is sent to the Challenger, in accordance with and subject to the Sunrise registration conditions set forth in the Registration Agreement. The Challenger must update all WHOIS information to be in compliance with the original Sunrise terms pertaining to the transferred Domain Name within the above-mentioned 30 day time period.

m. **Request for Information.**
Afilias reserves the right to request and verify information under Paragraph 4(c) of this Policy directly from any party at any time.

5. Maintaining the Status Quo.

Except as may be required by other policies or legal requirements, we will not cancel, transfer, activate, deactivate, or otherwise change the status of any Domain Name registration subject to this Policy, except as provided in Paragraph 3 and 4 above and 6 below.

6. Transfers During a Dispute.

a. **Transfers of a Domain Name to a New Holder.**
You may not transfer your Domain Name registration that is subject to this Policy to another holder until all challenges brought pursuant to this Policy in relation to this Domain Name have been resolved, except that a transfer may be made to the Priority Challenger in a

pending administrative proceeding under this Policy (e.g., in the event of a settlement of the dispute), provided that the Center decides that the challenge complies with the Sunrise registration conditions set forth in Paragraph 4(c). Any registration pursuant to such transfer will be subject the sunrise registration conditions set forth in the Registration Agreement.

b. **Changing Registrars.**

You may not transfer your Domain Name registration that is subject to this Policy to another registrar until all challenges pursuant to this Policy have been resolved.

7. Policy Modifications.

Afilias reserves the right to modify this Policy at any time with the permission of ICANN. We will post the revised Policy at http://www.afilias.info at least fifteen (15) days before it becomes effective. Unless this Policy has already been invoked by the submission of a challenge to the Center, in which event the version of the Policy in effect at the time it was invoked will apply to you until the dispute is over, all such changes will be binding upon you with respect to any Domain Name registration dispute, whether the dispute arose before, on or after the effective date of the change. In the event that you object to a change in this Policy, your sole remedy is to cancel your Domain Name registration with us, provided that you will not be entitled to a refund of any fees you paid to us. The revised Policy will apply to you until you cancel your Domain Name registration.

Sunrise Challenge Rules
(Revised)

[This revised version of the Policy was posted November 20, 2001, persuant to the Rules (see paragraph 15), and after approval by ICANN.]

Administrative proceedings for the resolution of disputes pursuant to the revised Sunrise Registration Challenge Policy adopted by Afilias shall be governed by these Rules.

1. Definitions

In these Rules:
- **Center** refers to the World Intellectual Property Organization Arbitration and Mediation Center.
- **Challenger** means a party which is challenging a domain name registration under the Sunrise Registration Challenge Policy.
- **Challenge of Last Resort** refers to a challenge initiated by the Registry after the conclusion of the Sunrise Challenge Period in connection with Sunrise registrations made in violation of the Sunrise registration conditions.
- **ICANN** refers to the Internet Corporation for Assigned Names and Numbers.
- **Party** means a Challenger or a Respondent.
- **Policy** means the Sunrise Registration Challenge Policy that is incorporated by reference and made a part of the Registration Agreement.
- **Priority Challenge / Priority Challenger** refers to a Challenge that has been given notice that it has priority under Paragraph 4 of the Policy.
- **Registrar** means the entity with which the Respondent has registered a domain name that is the subject of a challenge.
- **Registration Agreement** means the agreement between a Registrar and a domain name holder.
- **Registry** means the registry operator for the <.info> top-level domain.

- **Respondent** means the holder of a domain name registration against which a challenge is initiated.

2. Communications

(a) Except as otherwise provided in these Rules, any communication required under these Rules shall be made by electronic mail via the Internet.
(b) For the purposes of any communications to the Center, the following addresses should be used:
- (i) electronic mail: see http://arbiter.wipo.int/domains/
- (ii) facsimile transmission: see http://arbiter.wipo.int/domains/
- (iii) postal or courier service:
  WIPO Arbitration and Mediation Center
  34 chemin des Colombettes
  1211 Geneva 20
  Switzerland
(c) All communications shall be made in the language prescribed in Paragraph 6.
(d) Either Party may update its contact details by notifying the other Party, the Center, the Registrar and the Registry.
(e) Except as otherwise provided in these Rules, all communications provided for under these Rules shall be deemed to have been made:
- (i) if via the Internet, on the date that the communication was transmitted, provided that the date of transmission is verifiable; or
- (ii) if by postal or courier service, on the date of mailing marked on the receipt; or
- (iii) if delivered by facsimile transmission, on the date shown on the confirmation of transmission.
(f) Except as otherwise provided in these Rules, all time periods calculated under these Rules shall commence on the earliest date that the communication is deemed to have been made in accordance with Paragraph 2(e).
(g) Except as otherwise provided in these Rules, any communication by
- (i) the Center, following the commencement of an administrative proceeding pursuant to Paragraph 4(c), to any Party shall be copied to the other Party; and
- (ii) a Party shall be copied to the other Party and the Center.
(h) It shall be the responsibility of the sender to retain records of the fact and circumstances of sending, which shall be available for inspection by affected parties and for reporting purposes.
(i) In the event that a Party sending a communication receives notification of non-delivery of the communication, that Party shall promptly notify the Center of the circumstances of the notification.
(j) When a paper submission is to be made to the Center by a Party, it shall be submitted in three (3) sets, including the original of such submission.

3. The Challenge

(a) Any person or entity may initiate an administrative proceeding by submitting a challenge to the Center in accordance with the Policy and Rules.
(b) The challenge shall be submitted in electronic form via the Internet using the Model Challenge Form made available by the Center.
(c) The challenge shall:
- (i) Request that the challenge be submitted for decision in accordance with the Policy and Rules and describe why the Domain Name registration should be considered subject to the Policy;

Policy and Rules for .INFO Domain Names

(ii) Provide the full name, postal and e-mail addresses, and the telephone and telefax numbers of the Challenger and of any representative authorized to act for the Challenger in the administrative proceeding;
(iii) Provide complete bank account details of the Challenger for purposes of any reimbursement of fees in accordance with Paragraph 13;
(iv) Provide the full name of the Respondent and, if different from the contact details available in the Whois database for the Domain Name, provide all information known to the Challenger regarding how to contact the Respondent or any representative of the Respondent, including contact information based on pre-challenge dealings;
(v) Specify the Domain Name that is the subject of the challenge;
(vi) Identify the Registrar with whom the Domain Name is registered at the time the challenge is filed;
(vii) Describe, in accordance with the Policy, the grounds on which the challenge is made including, in particular, why the Domain Name that is the subject of the dispute should be considered to have been registered in violation of the Sunrise registration conditions set forth in the Registration Agreement with specific reference to Policy, Paragraph 4 (a):
   (1) at the time of the Respondent's registration of the Domain Name, no current (non-expired) trademark or service mark registration was issued in the Respondent's name; or
   (2) the Domain Name is not identical to the textual or word elements of the trademark or service mark registration on which the registration of the Respondent's Domain Name is based; or
   (3) the trademark or service mark registration on which the registration of the Respondent's Domain Name is based is not of national effect; or
   (4) the trademark or service mark registration on which the registration of the Respondent's Domain Name was based did not issue prior to October 2, 2000.
   In addition, Challengers requesting transfer of the disputed Domain Name shall also specify any and all bases for such transfer with specific reference to Policy, Paragraph (4)(c).
   The above description should not exceed 2000 words;
(viii) Specify, in accordance with the Policy, the remedies sought, i.e. transfer or cancellation of the Domain Name registration;
(ix) Identify any other proceedings that have been commenced or terminated in connection with or relating to the domain name that is the subject of the challenge;
(x) State that a copy of the challenge, together with the coversheet set out in Annex A hereto, has been sent or transmitted to the Respondent, the Registrar and the Registry;
(xi) Include the following statement (for Challengers seeking transfer of the Domain Name):
"Challenger certifies that the trademark or service mark forming the basis of this challenge and potential registration of the Domain Name in question was issued prior to October 2, 2000 and was current (non-expired) at the time of the registration of the Domain Name.";
(xii) Include the following statement (for all Challengers):
"Challenger agrees that its claims and remedies concerning the registration of the domain name, the dispute, or the dispute's resolution shall be solely against the domain name holder and waives all such claims and remedies against (a) the Center, (b) the Registrar, (c) the Registry, and (d) ICANN, as well as their directors, officers, employees, and agents.
Challenger certifies that the information contained in this challenge is to the best of Challenger's knowledge complete and accurate, that this challenge is not being

presented for any improper purpose, such as to harass, and that the assertions in this challenge are warranted under the Sunrise Registration Challenge Policy, the Rules for Sunrise Registration Challenge Policy and under applicable law, as it now exists or as it may be extended by good-faith and reasonable argument."

(xiii) Specify the credit card (American Express, Visa or MasterCard), together with the name of the cardholder as it appears on the card, the card number and the card expiration date for purposes of payment of the Challenger's fee in accordance with Paragraph 13 (a).

(d) The challenge may not relate to more than one Domain Name.

(e) Challengers seeking transfer of the Domain Name, shall submit to the Center the originals or certified copies of any trademark or service mark certificates required to be submitted under Paragraph 4(c) of the Policy within sixty (60) days of the commencement of the administrative proceeding, or, as the case may be, within 60 days of the notification of the opportunity to register the Domain Name in accordance with Policy, Paragraph 4(e)(iii).

4. Notification of Challenge

(a) The Center shall review the Priority Challenge for formal compliance with the Policy and the Rules. If the priority challenge is found to be in compliance with the Policy and the Rules and the Center is satisfied that the Challenger's fee has been paid in accordance with Paragraph 13 (a), the Center shall notify the Priority Challenge to the Respondent by sending it to the e-mail addresses and telefax numbers of the administrative contact for the Domain Name, as shown in the Whois database at the time of the notification of the Priority Challenge by the Center to the Respondent. In addition, the Center shall notify the Priority Challenge to the e-mail addresses and telefax numbers of the Respondent, or of any representative of the Respondent, as provided by the Priority Challenger in accordance with Paragraph 3 (c) (iv).

(b) If the Center finds the Priority Challenge to be formally deficient, it shall promptly notify the Priority Challenger of the nature of the deficiencies identified. The Priority Challenger shall have ten (10) days after such notification within which to correct any such deficiencies, after which the administrative proceeding will be deemed terminated without prejudice to the submission of another challenge by the Challenger.

(c) The date of commencement of the administrative proceeding shall be the date the Priority Challenge is notified by the Center to the Respondent.

(d) The Center shall notify the Priority Challenger, the Respondent, the Registrar, and the Registry of the date of commencement of the administrative proceeding.

(e) If the Priority Challenger fails to remedy any deficiencies identified by the Center within the time period provided for in Paragraph 4 (b), the Center shall notify the Priority Challenger, the Respondent, the Registrar and the Registry of the deemed termination of the challenge and the fee of USD 295 paid by the Challenger pursuant to Paragraph 13 (a) of the Rules shall be deemed forfeited.

5. The Response

(a) Within ten (10) days of the date of commencement of the administrative proceeding, the Respondent shall specify the credit card (American Express, Visa or MasterCard), together with the name of the cardholder as it appears on the card, the card number and the card expiration date for purposes of payment of the Respondent's fee in accordance with Paragraph 13 (b).

(b) Within sixty (60) days of the date of commencement of the administrative proceeding the Respondent shall submit a response to the Center.

(c) The response shall be submitted in hard copy (with annexes) by postal or courier service (postage pre-paid and return receipt requested) and in electronic form (without annexes) via the Internet using the Model Response Form made available by the Center.
(d) The response shall:
(i) Annex the originals or certified copies of any trademark or service mark certificates required to be submitted by the Respondent under Paragraph 4(b) of the Policy and respond specifically to the statements and allegations contained in the complaint and include any and all bases for the Respondent to retain registration of the disputed Domain Name with specific reference to Policy, Paragraph (4) (c). Such description should not exceed 2000 words;
(ii) Provide the name, postal and e-mail addresses, and the telephone and telefax numbers of the Respondent and of any representative authorized to act for the Respondent in the administrative proceeding;
(iii) Provide complete bank account details of the Respondent for purposes of any reimbursement of fees paid by the Respondent in accordance with Paragraph 13 (c);
(iv) Identify any other proceedings that have been commenced or terminated in connection with or relating to the Domain Name that is the subject of the challenge;
(v) Include the following statement:
"Respondent certifies that the trademark or service mark forming the basis for the registration of the domain name was issued prior to October 2, 2000 and was current (non-expired) at the time of the registration of the domain name";
(vi) Include the following statement followed by the signature of the Respondent or its authorized representative:
"Respondent certifies that the information contained in this Response is to the best of Respondent's knowledge complete and accurate, that this Response is not being presented for any improper purpose and that the assertions in this Response are warranted under the Sunrise Registration Challenge Policy, the Rules for Sunrise Registration Challenge Policy and under applicable law, as it now exists or as it may be extended by good-faith and reasonable argument."
(e) At the request of the Respondent, the Center may, in exceptional cases, extend the period of time for the filing of the response.
(f) If a Respondent does not pay the Respondent's fee in accordance with Paragraph 13 (b) or does not submit a response, the Respondent shall be deemed to have defaulted and the remedy sought by the Priority Challenger will be granted. If the Priority Challenger has requested transfer, the transfer will be subject to a decision by the Center that the challenge complies with the Sunrise registration conditions set forth in Policy, Paragraph 4 (c), failing which Policy, Paragraph 4 (e)(iii) shall apply.

6. Language of Proceedings

(a) Unless otherwise agreed by the Center in exceptional circumstances, the language of the administrative proceeding shall be English.
(b) Any trademark or service mark certificates in a language other than English, submitted by the Challenger in accordance with Paragraph 3(e) or the Respondent in accordance with Paragraph 5 (d)(i), must be accompanied by a certified translation into English.

7. Further Statements

Unless otherwise requested or agreed by the Center in exceptional circumstances, no further statements or documents from either of the Parties are to be submitted.

8. In-Person Hearings

There shall be no in-person hearings.

9. Default

(a) In the event that a Respondent does not comply with any of the time periods established by the Rules or the Center, the Center, unless it finds exceptional circumstances apply, shall proceed to a decision on the challenge.

(b) If a Party, in the absence of exceptional circumstances, does not comply with any provision of, or requirement under, the Rules or any request from the Center, the Center may draw such inferences therefrom and may undertake such procedural steps as it considers appropriate.

10. Center Decisions

(a) The Center's decision of whether the Sunrise registration conditions set forth in Paragraph 4(c) of the Policy are met will be based solely on a prima facie examination of any trademark or service mark certificates submitted in relation to the information contained in the relevant Afilias Whois database. The Center's decision is of an administrative nature and shall be final. The Center shall not be required to state reasons for its decision.

(b) The Center will use reasonable efforts to decide upon a challenge within twenty (20) days (as observed at the Center's place of business) of the receipt of all submissions to be made under the Policy and the Rules or of the expiry of the deadline for such submissions. The Center will also use reasonable effort to decide any Challenge of Last Resort as soon as possible under the circumstances.

(c) The Center, in its sole discretion, may prior to rendering the decision, consult relevant intellectual property offices in the context of reaching its determination.

11. Communication of Decision

(a) The Center shall communicate the decision to each Party, the Registrar, and the Registry.

(b) If the Center decides that the Domain Name be transferred to the Challenger in accordance with Policy, Paragraph 4, it shall provide the Challenger with an authorization code generated by the Registry which will allow the Challenger to register the Domain Name in its name and to update all Challenger Whois information, at the Registrar of its choice, within 30 days of the date on which the notification of the authorization is sent to the Challenger, in accordance with the Sunrise registration conditions of the Registration Agreement.

(c) In case of multiple challenges, the Center will issue the relevant notifications in accordance with Paragraph 4 (e) of the Policy.

12. Settlement or Other Grounds for Termination

(a) If the Challenger notifies the Center that the Parties have agreed on a settlement, the Center may suspend or terminate the administrative proceeding, subject to any conditions that may apply under Policy, Paragraph 6(a).

(b) If it becomes unnecessary or impossible to continue the administrative proceeding for any other reason, the Center shall terminate the administrative proceeding.

(c) In case of a termination of the administrative proceeding in accordance with (b), any fees paid by the Parties in accordance with Paragraph 13 shall be deemed forfeited.

13. Fees

(a) The filing of a challenge is subject to the payment of a Challenger's fee in the amount of USD 295, comprising of a non-refundable fee of USD 75 and a refundable fee of USD 220. This fee is to be paid by credit card at the time of the submission of the challenge in accordance with Paragraph 3 (c)(xii). If the Center is not satisfied that the Challenger's fee has been paid within 15 days of the filing of the challenge, the Center will dismiss the challenge on the basis of the Challenger's failure to pay the Challenger's fee. In case of multiple challenges, Paragraph 4 (e) of the Policy shall apply and the credit card of a Non-Priority Challenger will be debited only in the amount of the non-refundable fee of USD 75. Other arrangements may apply to the submission of Challenges of Last Resort filed by the Registry.

(b) The filing of a response is subject to the payment of a Respondent's fee in the amount of USD 295. This fee is to be paid by credit card within ten (10) days of the date of commencement of the administrative proceeding in accordance with Paragraph 5 (a). If the Respondent fails to provide the credit card information for the payment of the Respondent's fee within ten days of the date of commencement of the administrative proceeding, the Center will send a reminder to the Respondent requiring it to submit such payment within ten (10) further days. If the Center is not satisfied that the Respondent's fee has been paid within this period, the challenge will be granted on the basis of the Respondent's failure to pay its fee. If the Priority Challenger has requested transfer, this will be subject to a decision by the Center that the challenge complies with the sunrise registration conditions set forth in Policy Paragraph 4(c), failing which Policy, Paragraph 4 (e)(iii) shall apply.

(c) If a Respondent pays the Respondent's fee and establishes that the domain name subject to the dispute has been registered in compliance with the sunrise registration conditions set forth in the Registration Agreement, the Center will reimburse the Respondent's fee.

(d) If a Respondent pays the Respondent's fee but fails to establish that the Domain Name subject to the dispute has been registered in compliance with the Sunrise registration conditions set forth in the Registration Agreement, the Center will reimburse the Challenger's fee, subject to the withholding of the non-refundable fee in the amount of USD 75.

(e) If a challenge other than a Priority Challenge is dismissed by the Center in accordance with Paragraph 4 (e) (i) or (v) of the Policy, the Center shall retain only a non-refundable fee in the amount of USD 75 as referred to in (a).

(f) Under no other circumstances will a Challenger's fee or a Respondent's fee be reimbursed by the Center.

14. Exclusion of Liability

The Center and any intellectual property office consulted by the Center shall not be liable to a Party for any act or omission in connection with any administrative proceeding under the Policy and the Rules.

15. Amendments

The version of these Rules in effect at the time of the submission of the challenge to the Center shall apply to the administrative proceeding commenced thereby. The Registry reserves the right to modify the Rules at any time.

ANTICYBERSQUATTING CONSUMER PROTECTION ACT

S. 1948 - Intellectual Property and Communications Omnibus Reform Act,
incorporated in [H.R. 3194], Public Law Number 106-113
enacted on November 29, 1999
(Source: http://thomas.loc.gov)

A bill
to amend the provisions of title 17, United States Code, and the Communications Act of 1934, relating to copyright licensing and carriage of broadcast signals by satellite.

TITLE III -- Trademark Cyberpiracy Prevention

Sec. 3001: Short Title; References.

(a) **Short title**- This title may be cited as the *'Anticybersquatting Consumer Protection Act'*.
(b) **References to the Trademark Act of 1946**- Any reference in this title to the Trademark Act of 1946 shall be a reference to the Act entitled 'An Act to provide for the registration and protection of trademarks used in commerce, to carry out the provisions of certain international conventions, and for other purposes', approved July 5, 1946 (15 U.S.C. 1051 et seq.).

Sec. 3002: Cyberpiracy Prevention.

(a) **In general**- Section 43 of the Trademark Act of 1946 (15 U.S.C. 1125) is amended by inserting at the end the following:

"[(d)] (1)
(A) A person shall be liable in a civil action by the owner of a mark, including a personal name which is protected as a mark under this section, if, without regard to the goods or services of the parties, that person
(i) has a bad faith intent to profit from that mark, including a personal name which is protected as a mark under this section; and
(ii) registers, traffics in, or uses a domain name that
  (I) in the case of a mark that is distinctive at the time of registration of the domain name, is identical or confusingly similar to that mark;
  (II) in the case of a famous mark that is famous at the time of registration of the domain name, is identical or confusingly similar to or dilutive of that mark; or
  (III) is a trademark, word, or name protected by reason of section 706 of title 18, United States Code, or section 220506 of title 36, United States Code.

(B)
(i) In determining whether a person has a bad faith intent described under subparagraph (A), a court may consider factors such as, but not limited to
  (I) the trademark or other intellectual property rights of the person, if any, in the domain name;

(II) the extent to which the domain name consists of the legal name of the person or a name that is otherwise commonly used to identify that person;

(III) the person's prior use, if any, of the domain name in connection with the bona fide offering of any goods or services;

(IV) the person's bona fide noncommercial or fair use of the mark in a site accessible under the domain name;

(V) the person's intent to divert consumers from the mark owner's online location to a site accessible under the domain name that could harm the goodwill represented by the mark, either for commercial gain or with the intent to tarnish or disparage the mark, by creating a likelihood of confusion as to the source, sponsorship, affiliation, or endorsement of the site;

(VI) the person's offer to transfer, sell, or otherwise assign the domain name to the mark owner or any third party for financial gain without having used, or having an intent to use, the domain name in the bona fide offering of any goods or services, or the person's prior conduct indicating a pattern of such conduct;

(VII) the person's provision of material and misleading false contact information when applying for the registration of the domain name, the person's intentional failure to maintain accurate contact information, or the person's prior conduct indicating a pattern of such conduct;

(VIII) the person's registration or acquisition of multiple domain names which the person knows are identical or confusingly similar to marks of others that are distinctive at the time of registration of such domain names, or dilutive of famous marks of others that are famous at the time of registration of such domain names, without regard to the goods or services of the parties; and

(IX) the extent to which the mark incorporated in the person's domain name registration is or is not distinctive and famous within the meaning of subsection (c)(1) of section 43.

(ii) Bad faith intent described under subparagraph (A) shall not be found in any case in which the court determines that the person believed and had reasonable grounds to believe that the use of the domain name was a fair use or otherwise lawful.

(C) In any civil action involving the registration, trafficking, or use of a domain name under this paragraph, a court may order the forfeiture or cancellation of the domain name or the transfer of the domain name to the owner of the mark.

(D) A person shall be liable for using a domain name under subparagraph (A) only if that person is the domain name registrant or that registrant's authorized licensee.

(E) As used in this paragraph, the term 'traffics in' refers to transactions that include, but are not limited to, sales, purchases, loans, pledges, licenses, exchanges of currency, and any other transfer for consideration or receipt in exchange for consideration.

[(d)] (2)

(A) The owner of a mark may file an in rem civil action against a domain name in the judicial district in which the domain name registrar, domain name registry, or other domain name authority that registered or assigned the domain name is located if
(i) the domain name violates any right of the owner of a mark registered in the Patent and Trademark Office, or protected under subsection (a) or (c); and
(ii) the court finds that the owner
   (I) is not able to obtain in personam jurisdiction over a person who would have been a defendant in a civil action under paragraph (1); or
   (II) through due diligence was not able to find a person who would have been a defendant in a civil action under paragraph (1) by
      (aa) sending a notice of the alleged violation and intent to proceed under this paragraph to the registrant of the domain name at the postal and e-mail address provided by the registrant to the registrar; and
      (bb) publishing notice of the action as the court may direct promptly after filing the action.

(B) The actions under subparagraph (A)(ii) shall constitute service of process.

(C) In an in rem action under this paragraph, a domain name shall be deemed to have its situs in the judicial district in which
(i) the domain name registrar, registry, or other domain name authority that registered or assigned the domain name is located; or
(ii) documents sufficient to establish control and authority regarding the disposition of the registration and use of the domain name are deposited with the court.

(D)
(i) The remedies in an in rem action under this paragraph shall be limited to a court order for the forfeiture or cancellation of the domain name or the transfer of the domain name to the owner of the mark. Upon receipt of written notification of a filed, stamped copy of a complaint filed by the owner of a mark in a United States district court under this paragraph, the domain name registrar, domain name registry, or other domain name authority shall
   (I) expeditiously deposit with the court documents sufficient to establish the court's control and authority regarding the disposition of the registration and use of the domain name to the court; and
   (II) not transfer, suspend, or otherwise modify the domain name during the pendency of the action, except upon order of the court.
(ii) The domain name registrar or registry or other domain name authority shall not be liable for injunctive or monetary relief under this paragraph except in the case of bad faith or reckless disregard, which includes a willful failure to comply with any such court order.

[(d)] (3)

The civil action established under paragraph (1) and the in rem action established under paragraph (2), and any remedy available under either such action, shall be in addition to any other civil action or remedy otherwise applicable.

[(d)] (4)
The in rem jurisdiction established under paragraph (2) shall be in addition to any other jurisdiction that otherwise exists, whether in rem or in personam."

(b) Cyberpiracy Protections for Individuals-

(1) **In general-**

    (A) **Civil Liability-** Any person who registers a domain name that consists of the name of another living person, or a name substantially and confusingly similar thereto, without that person's consent, with the specific intent to profit from such name by selling the domain name for financial gain to that person or any third party, shall be liable in a civil action by such person.

    (B) **Exception-** A person who in good faith registers a domain name consisting of the name of another living person, or a name substantially and confusingly similar thereto, shall not be liable under this paragraph if such name is used in, affiliated with, or related to a work of authorship protected under title 17, United States Code, including a work made for hire as defined in section 101 of title 17, United States Code, and if the person registering the domain name is the copyright owner or licensee of the work, the person intends to sell the domain name in conjunction with the lawful exploitation of the work, and such registration is not prohibited by a contract between the registrant and the named person. The exception under this subparagraph shall apply only to a civil action brought under paragraph (1) and shall in no manner limit the protections afforded under the Trademark Act of 1946 (15 U.S.C. 1051 et seq.) or other provision of Federal or State law.

(2) **Remedies-** In any civil action brought under paragraph (1), a court may award injunctive relief, including the forfeiture or cancellation of the domain name or the transfer of the domain name to the plaintiff. The court may also, in its discretion, award costs and attorneys fees to the prevailing party.

(3) **Definition-** In this subsection, the term 'domain name' has the meaning given that term in section 45 of the Trademark Act of 1946 (15 U.S.C. 1127).

(4) **Effective date-** This subsection shall apply to domain names registered on or after the date of the enactment of this Act.

Sec. 3003: Damages and Remedies.

(a) **Remedies in Cases of Domain Name Piracy-**

(1) **Injunctions-** Section 34(a) of the Trademark Act of 1946 (15 U.S.C. 1116(a)) is amended in the first sentence by striking '(a) or (c)' and inserting '(a), (c), or (d)'.

(2) Damages- Section 35(a) of the Trademark Act of 1946 (15 U.S.C. 1117(a)) is amended in the first sentence by inserting ', (c), or (d)' after 'section 43(a)'.

(b) Statutory damages- Section 35 of the Trademark Act of 1946 (15 U.S.C. 1117) is amended by adding at the end the following:

"(d) In a case involving a violation of section 43(d)(1), the plaintiff may elect, at any time before final judgment is rendered by the trial court, to recover, instead of actual damages and profits, an award of statutory damages in the amount of not less than $1,000 and not more than $100,000 per domain name, as the court considers just."

Sec. 3004: Limitation on Liability.

Section 32(2) of the Trademark Act of 1946 (15 U.S.C. 1114) is amended

(1) in the matter preceding subparagraph (A) by striking 'under section 43(a)' and inserting 'under section 43(a) or (d)'; and

(2) by redesignating subparagraph (D) as subparagraph (E) and inserting after subparagraph (C) the following:

"(D)
- (i)
  - (I) A domain name registrar, a domain name registry, or other domain name registration authority that takes any action described under clause (ii) affecting a domain name shall not be liable for monetary relief or, except as provided in subclause (II), for injunctive relief, to any person for such action, regardless of whether the domain name is finally determined to infringe or dilute the mark.
  - (II) A domain name registrar, domain name registry, or other domain name registration authority described in subclause (I) may be subject to injunctive relief only if such registrar, registry, or other registration authority has
    - (aa) not expeditiously deposited with a court, in which an action has been filed regarding the disposition of the domain name, documents sufficient for the court to establish the court's control and authority regarding the disposition of the registration and use of the domain name;
    - (bb) transferred, suspended, or otherwise modified the domain name during the pendency of the action, except upon order of the court; or
    - (cc) willfully failed to comply with any such court order.
- (ii) An action referred to under clause (i)(I) is any action of refusing to register, removing from registration, transferring, temporarily disabling, or permanently cancelling a domain name
  - (I) in compliance with a court order under section 43(d); or
  - (II) in the implementation of a reasonable policy by such registrar, registry, or authority prohibiting the registration of a domain name that is identical to, confusingly similar to, or dilutive of another's mark.
- (iii) A domain name registrar, a domain name registry, or other domain name registration authority shall not be liable for damages under this section for the registration or maintenance of a domain name for another absent a showing of bad faith intent to profit from such registration or maintenance of the domain name.

(iv) If a registrar, registry, or other registration authority takes an action described under clause (ii) based on a knowing and material misrepresentation by any other person that a domain name is identical to, confusingly similar to, or dilutive of a mark, the person making the knowing and material misrepresentation shall be liable for any damages, including costs and attorney's fees, incurred by the domain name registrant as a result of such action. The court may also grant injunctive relief to the domain name registrant, including the reactivation of the domain name or the transfer of the domain name to the domain name registrant.

(v) A domain name registrant whose domain name has been suspended, disabled, or transferred under a policy described under clause (ii)(II) may, upon notice to the mark owner, file a civil action to establish that the registration or use of the domain name by such registrant is not unlawful under this Act. The court may grant injunctive relief to the domain name registrant, including the reactivation of the domain name or transfer of the domain name to the domain name registrant."

Sec. 3005: Definitions.

Section 45 of the Trademark Act of 1946 (15 U.S.C. 1127) is amended by inserting after the undesignated paragraph defining the term 'counterfeit' the following:

"The term '**domain name**' means any alphanumeric designation which is registered with or assigned by any domain name registrar, domain name registry, or other domain name registration authority as part of an electronic address on the Internet. The term '**Internet**' has the meaning given that term in section 230(f)(1) of the Communications Act of 1934 (47 U.S.C. 230(f)(1))."

Sec. 3006: Study on Abusive Domain Name Registrations Involving Personal Names.

(a) **In general-** Not later than 180 days after the date of the enactment of this Act, the Secretary of Commerce, in consultation with the Patent and Trademark Office and the Federal Election Commission, shall conduct a study and report to Congress with recommendations on guidelines and procedures for resolving disputes involving the registration or use by a person of a domain name that includes the personal name of another person, in whole or in part, or a name confusingly similar thereto, including consideration of and recommendations for

(1) protecting personal names from registration by another person as a second level domain name for purposes of selling or otherwise transferring such domain name to such other person or any third party for financial gain;

(2) protecting individuals from bad faith uses of their personal names as second level domain names by others with malicious intent to harm the reputation of the individual or the goodwill associated with that individual's name;

(3) protecting consumers from the registration and use of domain names that include personal names in the second level domain in manners which are intended or are likely to confuse or deceive the public as to the affiliation, connection, or association of the domain name registrant, or a site accessible under the domain name, with such other person, or as to the origin, sponsorship, or approval of the goods, services, or commercial activities of the domain name registrant;

(4) protecting the public from registration of domain names that include the personal names of government officials, official candidates, and potential official candidates for Federal, State, or local political office in the United States, and the use of such domain names in a manner that disrupts the electoral process or the public's ability to access accurate and reliable information regarding such individuals;

(5) existing remedies, whether under State law or otherwise, and the extent to which such remedies are sufficient to address the considerations described in paragraphs (1) through (4); and

(6) the guidelines, procedures, and policies of the Internet Corporation for assigned Names and Numbers and the extent to which they address the considerations described in paragraphs (1) through (4).

(b) **Guidelines and Procedures**- The Secretary of Commerce shall, under its Memorandum of Understanding with the Internet Corporation for Assigned Names and Numbers, collaborate to develop guidelines and procedures for resolving disputes involving the registration or use by a person of a domain name that includes the personal name of another person, in whole or in part, or a name confusingly similar thereto.

Sec. 3007: Historic Preservation.

[...]

Sec. 3008: Savings Clause.

Nothing in this title shall affect any defense available to a defendant under the Trademark Act of 1946 (including any defense under section 43(c)(4) of such Act or relating to fair use) or a person's right of free speech or expression under the first amendment of the United States Constitution.

Sec. 3009: Technical and Conforming Amendments.

Chapter 85 of title 28, United States Code, is amended as follows:
(1) Section 1338 of title 28, United States Codes, is amended
(A) in the section heading by striking 'trade-marks' and inserting 'trademarks';
(B) in subsection (a) by striking 'trade-marks' and inserting 'trademarks'; and
(C) in subsection (b) by striking 'trade-mark' and inserting 'trademark'.
(2) The item relating to section 1338 in the table of sections for chapter 85 of title 28, United States Code, is amended by striking 'trade-marks' and inserting 'trademarks'.

Sec. 3010: Effective Date.

Sections 3002(a), 3003, 3004, 3005, and 3008 of this title shall apply to all domain names registered before, on, or after the date of the enactment of this Act, except that damages under subsection (a) or (d) of section 35 of the Trademark Act of 1946 (15 U.S.C. 1117), as amended by section 3003 of this title, shall not be available with respect to the registration, trafficking, or use of a domain name that occurs before the date of the enactment of this Act.

2. Intellectual Property Rights

a) International and US Law

BERNE CONVENTION FOR THE PROTECTION OF LITERARY AND ARTISTIC WORKS

(http://www.wipo.int/treaties/ip/berne/index.html)

Berne Convention
for the Protection of Literary and Artistic Works
of September 9, 1886,
completed at PARIS on May 4, 1896,
revised at BERLIN on November 13, 1908,
completed at BERNE on March 20, 1914,
revised at ROME on June 2, 1928,
at BRUSSELS on June 26, 1948,
at STOCKHOLM on July 14, 1967,
and at PARIS on July 24, 1971,
and amended on September 28, 1979

The countries of the Union, being equally animated by the desire to protect, in as effective and uniform a manner as possible, the rights of authors in their literary and artistic works,

Recognizing the importance of the work of the Revision Conference held at Stockholm in 1967,

Have resolved to revise the Act adopted by the Stockholm Conference, while maintaining without change Articles 1 to 20 and 22 to 26 of that Act.

Consequently, the undersigned Plenipotentiaries, having presented their full powers, recognized as in good and due form, have agreed as follows:

Article 1 - [Establishment of a Union][1]

The countries to which this Convention applies constitute a Union for the protection of the rights of authors in their literary and artistic works.

Article 2 - [Protected Works: 1. "Literary and artistic works"; 2. Possible requirement of fixation; 3. Derivative works; 4. Official texts; 5. Collections; 6. Obligation to protect; beneficiaries of protection; 7. Works of applied art and industrial designs; 8. News]

(1) The expression "literary and artistic works" shall include every production in the literary, scientific and artistic domain, whatever may be the mode or form of its expression, such as books, pamphlets and other writings; lectures, addresses, sermons and other works of the

---

[1] Each Article and the Appendix have been given titles to facilitate their identification. There are no titles in the signed (English) text.

same nature; dramatic or dramatico-musical works; choreographic works and entertainments in dumb show; musical compositions with or without words; cinematographic works to which are assimilated works expressed by a process analogous to cinematography; works of drawing, painting, architecture, sculpture, engraving and lithography; photographic works to which are assimilated works expressed by a process analogous to photography; works of applied art; illustrations, maps, plans, sketches and three-dimensional works relative to geography, topography, architecture or science.

(2) It shall, however, be a matter for legislation in the countries of the Union to prescribe that works in general or any specified categories of works shall not be protected unless they have been fixed in some material form.

(3) Translations, adaptations, arrangements of music and other alterations of a literary or artistic work shall be protected as original works without prejudice to the copyright in the original work.

(4) It shall be a matter for legislation in the countries of the Union to determine the protection to be granted to official texts of a legislative, administrative and legal nature, and to official translations of such texts.

(5) Collections of literary or artistic works such as encyclopaedias and anthologies which, by reason of the selection and arrangement of their contents, constitute intellectual creations shall be protected as such, without prejudice to the copyright in each of the works forming part of such collections.

(6) The works mentioned in this Article shall enjoy protection in all countries of the Union. This protection shall operate for the benefit of the author and his successors in title.

(7) Subject to the provisions of Article 7(4) of this Convention, it shall be a matter for legislation in the countries of the Union to determine the extent of the application of their laws to works of applied art and industrial designs and models, as well as the conditions under which such works, designs and models shall be protected. Works protected in the country of origin solely as designs and models shall be entitled in another country of the Union only to such special protection as is granted in that country to designs and models; however, if no such special protection is granted in that country, such works shall be protected as artistic works.

(8) The protection of this Convention shall not apply to news of the day or to miscellaneous facts having the character of mere items of press information.

Article 2bis - [Possible Limitation of Protection of Certain Works: 1. Certain speeches; 2. Certain uses of lectures and addresses; 3. Right to make collections of such works]

(1) It shall be a matter for legislation in the countries of the Union to exclude, wholly or in part, from the protection provided by the preceding Article political speeches and speeches delivered in the course of legal proceedings.

(2) It shall also be a matter for legislation in the countries of the Union to determine the conditions under which lectures, addresses and other works of the same nature which are delivered in public may be reproduced by the press, broadcast, communicated to the public by wire and made the subject of public communication as envisaged in Article 11bis(1) of this Convention, when such use is justified by the informatory purpose.

(3) Nevertheless, the author shall enjoy the exclusive right of making a collection of his works mentioned in the preceding paragraphs.

Article 3 - [Criteria of Eligibility for Protection: 1. Nationality of author; place of publication of work; 2. Residence of author; 3. "Published" works; 4. "Simultaneously published" works]

(1) The protection of this Convention shall apply to:

(a) authors who are nationals of one of the countries of the Union, for their works, whether published or not;
(b) authors who are not nationals of one of the countries of the Union, for their works first published in one of those countries, or simultaneously in a country outside the Union and in a country of the Union.
(2) Authors who are not nationals of one of the countries of the Union but who have their habitual residence in one of them shall, for the purposes of this Convention, be assimilated to nationals of that country.
(3) The expression "published works" means works published with the consent of their authors, whatever may be the means of manufacture of the copies, provided that the availability of such copies has been such as to satisfy the reasonable requirements of the public, having regard to the nature of the work. The performance of a dramatic, dramatico-musical, cinematographic or musical work, the public recitation of a literary work, the communication by wire or the broadcasting of literary or artistic works, the exhibition of a work of art and the construction of a work of architecture shall not constitute publication.
(4) A work shall be considered as having been published simultaneously in several countries if it has been published in two or more countries within thirty days of its first publication.

Article 4 - [Criteria of Eligibility for Protection of Cinematographic Works, Works of Architecture and Certain Artistic Works]

The protection of this Convention shall apply, even if the conditions of Article 3 are not fulfilled, to:
(a) authors of cinematographic works the maker of which has his headquarters or habitual residence in one of the countries of the Union;
(b) authors of works of architecture erected in a country of the Union or of other artistic works incorporated in a building or other structure located in a country of the Union.

Article 5 - [Rights Guaranteed: 1. and 2. Outside the country of origin; 3. In the country of origin; 4. "Country of origin"]

(1) Authors shall enjoy, in respect of works for which they are protected under this Convention, in countries of the Union other than the country of origin, the rights which their respective laws do now or may hereafter grant to their nationals, as well as the rights specially granted by this Convention.
(2) The enjoyment and the exercise of these rights shall not be subject to any formality; such enjoyment and such exercise shall be independent of the existence of protection in the country of origin of the work. Consequently, apart from the provisions of this Convention, the extent of protection, as well as the means of redress afforded to the author to protect his rights, shall be governed exclusively by the laws of the country where protection is claimed.
(3) Protection in the country of origin is governed by domestic law. However, when the author is not a national of the country of origin of the work for which he is protected under this Convention, he shall enjoy in that country the same rights as national authors.
(4) The country of origin shall be considered to be:
(a) in the case of works first published in a country of the Union, that country; in the case of works published simultaneously in several countries of the Union which grant different terms of protection, the country whose legislation grants the shortest term of protection;
(b) in the case of works published simultaneously in a country outside the Union and in a country of the Union, the latter country;
(c) in the case of unpublished works or of works first published in a country outside the Union, without simultaneous publication in a country of the Union, the country of the Union of which the author is a national, provided that:

(i) when these are cinematographic works the maker of which has his headquarters or his habitual residence in a country of the Union, the country of origin shall be that country, and
(ii) when these are works of architecture erected in a country of the Union or other artistic works incorporated in a building or other structure located in a country of the Union, the country of origin shall be that country.

Article 6 - [Possible Restriction of Protection in Respect of Certain Works of Nationals of Certain Countries Outside the Union: 1. In the country of the first publication and in other countries; 2. No retroactivity; 3. Notice]

(1) Where any country outside the Union fails to protect in an adequate manner the works of authors who are nationals of one of the countries of the Union, the latter country may restrict the protection given to the works of authors who are, at the date of the first publication thereof, nationals of the other country and are not habitually resident in one of the countries of the Union. If the country of first publication avails itself of this right, the other countries of the Union shall not be required to grant to works thus subjected to special treatment a wider protection than that granted to them in the country of first publication.
(2) No restrictions introduced by virtue of the preceding paragraph shall affect the rights which an author may have acquired in respect of a work published in a country of the Union before such restrictions were put into force.
(3) The countries of the Union which restrict the grant of copyright in accordance with this Article shall give notice thereof to the Director General of the World Intellectual Property Organization (hereinafter designated as "the Director General") by a written declaration specifying the countries in regard to which protection is restricted, and the restrictions to which rights of authors who are nationals of those countries are subjected. The Director General shall immediately communicate this declaration to all the countries of the Union.

Article 6bis - [Moral Rights: 1. To claim authorship; to object to certain modifications and other derogatory actions; 2. After the author's death; 3. Means of redress]

(1) Independently of the author's economic rights, and even after the transfer of the said rights, the author shall have the right to claim authorship of the work and to object to any distortion, mutilation or other modification of, or other derogatory action in relation to, the said work, which would be prejudicial to his honor or reputation.
(2) The rights granted to the author in accordance with the preceding paragraph shall, after his death, be maintained, at least until the expiry of the economic rights, and shall be exercisable by the persons or institutions authorized by the legislation of the country where protection is claimed. However, those countries whose legislation, at the moment of their ratification of or accession to this Act, does not provide for the protection after the death of the author of all the rights set out in the preceding paragraph may provide that some of these rights may, after his death, cease to be maintained.
(3) The means of redress for safeguarding the rights granted by this Article shall be governed by the legislation of the country where protection is claimed.

Article 7 - [Term of Protection: 1. Generally; 2. For cinematographic works; 3. For anonymous and pseudonymous works; 4. For photographic works and works of applied art; 5. Starting date of computation; 6. Longer terms; 7. Shorter terms; 8. Applicable law; "comparison" of terms]

(1) The term of protection granted by this Convention shall be the life of the author and fifty years after his death.
(2) However, in the case of cinematographic works, the countries of the Union may provide that the term of protection shall expire fifty years after the work has been made available to the

public with the consent of the author, or, failing such an event within fifty years from the making of such a work, fifty years after the making.
(3) In the case of anonymous or pseudonymous works, the term of protection granted by this Convention shall expire fifty years after the work has been lawfully made available to the public. However, when the pseudonym adopted by the author leaves no doubt as to his identity, the term of protection shall be that provided in paragraph (1). If the author of an anonymous or pseudonymous work discloses his identity during the above-mentioned period, the term of protection applicable shall be that provided in paragraph (1). The countries of the Union shall not be required to protect anonymous or pseudonymous works in respect of which it is reasonable to presume that their author has been dead for fifty years.
(4) It shall be a matter for legislation in the countries of the Union to determine the term of protection of photographic works and that of works of applied art in so far as they are protected as artistic works; however, this term shall last at least until the end of a period of twenty-five years from the making of such a work.
(5) The term of protection subsequent to the death of the author and the terms provided by paragraphs (2), (3) and (4) shall run from the date of death or of the event referred to in those paragraphs, but such terms shall always be deemed to begin on the first of January of the year following the death or such event.
(6) The countries of the Union may grant a term of protection in excess of those provided by the preceding paragraphs.
(7) Those countries of the Union bound by the Rome Act of this Convention which grant, in their national legislation in force at the time of signature of the present Act, shorter terms of protection than those provided for in the preceding paragraphs shall have the right to maintain such terms when ratifying or acceding to the present Act.
(8) In any case, the term shall be governed by the legislation of the country where protection is claimed; however, unless the legislation of that country otherwise provides, the term shall not exceed the term fixed in the country of origin of the work.

Article 7bis - [Term of Protection for Works of Joint Authorship]

The provisions of the preceding Article shall also apply in the case of a work of joint authorship, provided that the terms measured from the death of the author shall be calculated from the death of the last surviving author.

Article 8 - [Right of Translation]

Authors of literary and artistic works protected by this Convention shall enjoy the exclusive right of making and of authorizing the translation of their works throughout the term of protection of their rights in the original works.

Article 9 - [Right of Reproduction: 1. Generally; 2. Possible exceptions; 3. Sound and visual recordings]

(1) Authors of literary and artistic works protected by this Convention shall have the exclusive right of authorizing the reproduction of these works, in any manner or form.
(2) It shall be a matter for legislation in the countries of the Union to permit the reproduction of such works in certain special cases, provided that such reproduction does not conflict with a normal exploitation of the work and does not unreasonably prejudice the legitimate interests of the author.
(3) Any sound or visual recording shall be considered as a reproduction for the purposes of this Convention.

Article 10 - [Certain Free Uses of Works: 1. Quotations; 2. Illustrations for teaching; 3. Indication of source and author]

(1) It shall be permissible to make quotations from a work which has already been lawfully made available to the public, provided that their making is compatible with fair practice, and their extent does not exceed that justified by the purpose, including quotations from newspaper articles and periodicals in the form of press summaries.

(2) It shall be a matter for legislation in the countries of the Union, and for special agreements existing or to be concluded between them, to permit the utilization, to the extent justified by the purpose, of literary or artistic works by way of illustration in publications, broadcasts or sound or visual recordings for teaching, provided such utilization is compatible with fair practice.

(3) Where use is made of works in accordance with the preceding paragraphs of this Article, mention shall be made of the source, and of the name of the author if it appears thereon.

Article 10bis - [Further Possible Free Uses of Works: 1. Of certain articles and broadcast works; 2. Of works seen or heard in connection with current events]

(1) It shall be a matter for legislation in the countries of the Union to permit the reproduction by the press, the broadcasting or the communication to the public by wire of articles published in newspapers or periodicals on current economic, political or religious topics, and of broadcast works of the same character, in cases in which the reproduction, broadcasting or such communication thereof is not expressly reserved. Nevertheless, the source must always be clearly indicated; the legal consequences of a breach of this obligation shall be determined by the legislation of the country where protection is claimed.

(2) It shall also be a matter for legislation in the countries of the Union to determine the conditions under which, for the purpose of reporting current events by means of photography, cinematography, broadcasting or communication to the public by wire, literary or artistic works seen or heard in the course of the event may, to the extent justified by the informatory purpose, be reproduced and made available to the public.

Article 11 - [Certain Rights in Dramatic and Musical Works: 1. Right of public performance and of communication to the public of a performance; 2. In respect of translations]

(1) Authors of dramatic, dramatico-musical and musical works shall enjoy the exclusive right of authorizing:
(i) the public performance of their works, including such public performance by any means or process;
(ii) any communication to the public of the performance of their works.

(2) Authors of dramatic or dramatico-musical works shall enjoy, during the full term of their rights in the original works, the same rights with respect to translations thereof.

Article 11bis - [Broadcasting and Related Rights: 1. Broadcasting and other wireless communications, public communication of broadcast by wire or rebroadcast, public communication of broadcast by loudspeaker or analogous instruments; 2. Compulsory licenses; 3. Recording; ephemeral recordings]

(1) Authors of literary and artistic works shall enjoy the exclusive right of authorizing:
(i) the broadcasting of their works or the communication thereof to the public by any other means of wireless diffusion of signs, sounds or images;
(ii) any communication to the public by wire or by rebroadcasting of the broadcast of the work, when this communication is made by an organization other than the original one;
(iii) the public communication by loudspeaker or any other analogous instrument transmitting, by signs, sounds or images, the broadcast of the work.

(2) It shall be a matter for legislation in the countries of the Union to determine the conditions under which the rights mentioned in the preceding paragraph may be exercised, but these conditions shall apply only in the countries where they have been prescribed. They shall not in any circumstances be prejudicial to the moral rights of the author, nor to his right to obtain equitable remuneration which, in the absence of agreement, shall be fixed by competent authority.
(3) In the absence of any contrary stipulation, permission granted in accordance with paragraph (1) of this Article shall not imply permission to record, by means of instruments recording sounds or images, the work broadcast. It shall, however, be a matter for legislation in the countries of the Union to determine the regulations for ephemeral recordings made by a broadcasting organization by means of its own facilities and used for its own broadcasts. The preservation of these recordings in official archives may, on the ground of their exceptional documentary character, be authorized by such legislation.

Article 11ter - [Certain Rights in Literary Works: 1. Right of public recitation and of communication to the public of a recitation; 2. In respect of translations]

(1) Authors of literary works shall enjoy the exclusive right of authorizing:
(i) the public recitation of their works, including such public recitation by any means or process;
(ii) any communication to the public of the recitation of their works.
(2) Authors of literary works shall enjoy, during the full term of their rights in the original works, the same rights with respect to translations thereof.

Article 12 - [Right of Adaptation, Arrangement and Other Alteration]

Authors of literary or artistic works shall enjoy the exclusive right of authorizing adaptations, arrangements and other alterations of their works.

Article 13 - [Possible Limitation of the Right of Recording of Musical Works and Any Words Pertaining Thereto: 1. Compulsory licenses; 2. Transitory measures; 3. Seizure on importation of copies made without the author's permission]

(1) Each country of the Union may impose for itself reservations and conditions on the exclusive right granted to the author of a musical work and to the author of any words, the recording of which together with the musical work has already been authorized by the latter, to authorize the sound recording of that musical work, together with such words, if any; but all such reservations and conditions shall apply only in the countries which have imposed them and shall not, in any circumstances, be prejudicial to the rights of these authors to obtain equitable remuneration which, in the absence of agreement, shall be fixed by competent authority.
(2) Recordings of musical works made in a country of the Union in accordance with Article 13(3) of the Conventions signed at Rome on June 2, 1928, and at Brussels on June 26, 1948, may be reproduced in that country without the permission of the author of the musical work until a date two years after that country becomes bound by this Act.
(3) Recordings made in accordance with paragraphs (1) and (2) of this Article and imported without permission from the parties concerned into a country where they are treated as infringing recordings shall be liable to seizure.

Article 14 - [Cinematographic and Related Rights: 1. Cinematographic adaptation and reproduction; distribution; public performance and public communication by wire of works thus adapted or reproduced; 2. Adaptation of cinematographic productions; 3. No compulsory licenses]

(1) Authors of literary or artistic works shall have the exclusive right of authorizing:
 (i) the cinematographic adaptation and reproduction of these works, and the distribution of the works thus adapted or reproduced;
 (ii) the public performance and communication to the public by wire of the works thus adapted or reproduced.
(2) The adaptation into any other artistic form of a cinematographic production derived from literary or artistic works shall, without prejudice to the authorization of the author of the cinematographic production, remain subject to the authorization of the authors of the original works.
(3) The provisions of Article 13(1) shall not apply.

Article 14bis - [Special Provisions Concerning Cinematographic Works: 1. Assimilation to "original" works; 2. Ownership; limitation of certain rights of certain contributors; 3. Certain other contributors]

(1) Without prejudice to the copyright in any work which may have been adapted or reproduced, a cinematographic work shall be protected as an original work. The owner of copyright in a cinematographic work shall enjoy the same rights as the author of an original work, including the rights referred to in the preceding Article.
(2)
(a) Ownership of copyright in a cinematographic work shall be a matter for legislation in the country where protection is claimed.
(b) However, in the countries of the Union which, by legislation, include among the owners of copyright in a cinematographic work authors who have brought contributions to the making of the work, such authors, if they have undertaken to bring such contributions, may not, in the absence of any contrary or special stipulation, object to the reproduction, distribution, public performance, communication to the public by wire, broadcasting or any other communication to the public, or to the subtitling or dubbing of texts, of the work.
(c) The question whether or not the form of the undertaking referred to above should, for the application of the preceding subparagraph (b), be in a written agreement or a written act of the same effect shall be a matter for the legislation of the country where the maker of the cinematographic work has his headquarters or habitual residence. However, it shall be a matter for the legislation of the country of the Union where protection is claimed to provide that the said undertaking shall be in a written agreement or a written act of the same effect. The countries whose legislation so provides shall notify the Director General by means of a written declaration, which will be immediately communicated by him to all the other countries of the Union.
(d) By "contrary or special stipulation" is meant any restrictive condition which is relevant to the aforesaid undertaking.
(3) Unless the national legislation provides to the contrary, the provisions of paragraph (2)(b) above shall not be applicable to authors of scenarios, dialogues and musical works created for the making of the cinematographic work, or to the principal director thereof. However, those countries of the Union whose legislation does not contain rules providing for the application of the said paragraph (2)(b) to such director shall notify the Director General by means of a written declaration, which will be immediately communicated by him to all the other countries of the Union.

Article 14ter - ["Droit de suite" in Works of Art and Manuscripts: 1. Right to an interest in resales; 2. Applicable law; 3. Procedure]

(1) The author, or after his death the persons or institutions authorized by national legislation, shall, with respect to original works of art and original manuscripts of writers and composers, enjoy the inalienable right to an interest in any sale of the work subsequent to the first transfer by the author of the work.
(2) The protection provided by the preceding paragraph may be claimed in a country of the Union only if legislation in the country to which the author belongs so permits, and to the extent permitted by the country where this protection is claimed.
(3) The procedure for collection and the amounts shall be matters for determination by national legislation.

Article 15 - [Right to Enforce Protected Rights: 1. Where author's name is indicated or where pseudonym leaves no doubt as to author's identity; 2. In the case of cinematographic works; 3. In the case of anonymous and pseudonymous works; 4. In the case of certain unpublished works of unknown authorship]

(1) In order that the author of a literary or artistic work protected by this Convention shall, in the absence of proof to the contrary, be regarded as such, and consequently be entitled to institute infringement proceedings in the countries of the Union, it shall be sufficient for his name to appear on the work in the usual manner. This paragraph shall be applicable even if this name is a pseudonym, where the pseudonym adopted by the author leaves no doubt as to his identity.
(2) The person or body corporate whose name appears on a cinematographic work in the usual manner shall, in the absence of proof to the contrary, be presumed to be the maker of the said work.
(3) In the case of anonymous and pseudonymous works, other than those referred to in paragraph (1) above, the publisher whose name appears on the work shall, in the absence of proof to the contrary, be deemed to represent the author, and in this capacity he shall be entitled to protect and enforce the author's rights. The provisions of this paragraph shall cease to apply when the author reveals his identity and establishes his claim to authorship of the work.
(4)
(a) In the case of unpublished works where the identity of the author is unknown, but where there is every ground to presume that he is a national of a country of the Union, it shall be a matter for legislation in that country to designate the competent authority which shall represent the author and shall be entitled to protect and enforce his rights in the countries of the Union.
(b) Countries of the Union which make such designation under the terms of this provision shall notify the Director General by means of a written declaration giving full information concerning the authority thus designated. The Director General shall at once communicate this declaration to all other countries of the Union.

Article 16 - [Infringing Copies: 1. Seizure; 2. Seizure on importation; 3. Applicable law]

(1) Infringing copies of a work shall be liable to seizure in any country of the Union where the work enjoys legal protection.
(2) The provisions of the preceding paragraph shall also apply to reproductions coming from a country where the work is not protected, or has ceased to be protected.
(3) The seizure shall take place in accordance with the legislation of each country.

Article 17 - [Possibility of Control of Circulation, Presentation and Exhibition of Works]

The provisions of this Convention cannot in any way affect the right of the Government of each country of the Union to permit, to control, or to prohibit, by legislation or regulation, the circulation, presentation, or exhibition of any work or production in regard to which the competent authority may find it necessary to exercise that right.

Article 18 - [Works Existing on Convention's Entry Into Force: 1. Protectable where protection not yet expired in country of origin; 2. Non-protectable where protection already expired in country where it is claimed; 3. Application of these principles; 4. Special cases]

(1) This Convention shall apply to all works which, at the moment of its coming into force, have not yet fallen into the public domain in the country of origin through the expiry of the term of protection.
(2) If, however, through the expiry of the term of protection which was previously granted, a work has fallen into the public domain of the country where protection is claimed, that work shall not be protected anew.
(3) The application of this principle shall be subject to any provisions contained in special conventions to that effect existing or to be concluded between countries of the Union. In the absence of such provisions, the respective countries shall determine, each in so far as it is concerned, the conditions of application of this principle.
(4) The preceding provisions shall also apply in the case of new accessions to the Union and to cases in which protection is extended by the application of Article 7 or by the abandonment of reservations.

Article 19 - [Protection Greater than Resulting from Convention]

The provisions of this Convention shall not preclude the making of a claim to the benefit of any greater protection which may be granted by legislation in a country of the Union.

Article 20 - [Special Agreements Among Countries of the Union]

The Governments of the countries of the Union reserve the right to enter into special agreements among themselves, in so far as such agreements grant to authors more extensive rights than those granted by the Convention, or contain other provisions not contrary to this Convention. The provisions of existing agreements which satisfy these conditions shall remain applicable.

Article 21 - [Special Provisions Regarding Developing Countries: 1. Reference to Appendix; 2. Appendix part of Act]

(1) Special provisions regarding developing countries are included in the Appendix.
(2) Subject to the provisions of Article 28(1)(b), the Appendix forms an integral part of this Act.

Article 22 - [Assembly: 1. Constitution and composition; 2. Tasks; 3. Quorum, voting, observers; 4. Convocation; 5. Rules of procedure]

(1)
(a) The Union shall have an Assembly consisting of those countries of the Union which are bound by Articles 22 to 26.
(b) The Government of each country shall be represented by one delegate, who may be assisted by alternate delegates, advisors, and experts.
(c) The expenses of each delegation shall be borne by the Government which has appointed it.
(2)
(a) The Assembly shall:

(i) deal with all matters concerning the maintenance and development of the Union and the implementation of this Convention;
(ii) give directions concerning the preparation for conferences of revision to the International Bureau of Intellectual Property (hereinafter designated as "the International Bureau") referred to in the Convention Establishing the World Intellectual Property Organization (hereinafter designated as "the Organization"), due account being taken of any comments made by those countries of the Union which are not bound by Articles 22 to 26;
(iii) review and approve the reports and activities of the Director General of the Organization concerning the Union, and give him all necessary instructions concerning matters within the competence of the Union;
(iv) elect the members of the Executive Committee of the Assembly;
(v) review and approve the reports and activities of its Executive Committee, and give instructions to such Committee;
(vi) determine the program and adopt the biennial budget of the Union, and approve its final accounts;
(vii) adopt the financial regulations of the Union;
(viii) establish such committees of experts and working groups as may be necessary for the work of the Union;
(ix) determine which countries not members of the Union and which intergovernmental and international non-governmental organizations shall be admitted to its meetings as observers;
(x) adopt amendments to Articles 22 to 26;
(xi) take any other appropriate action designed to further the objectives of the Union;
(xii) exercise such other functions as are appropriate under this Convention;
(xiii) subject to its acceptance, exercise such rights as are given to it in the Convention establishing the Organization.

(b) With respect to matters which are of interest also to other Unions administered by the Organization, the Assembly shall make its decisions after having heard the advice of the Coordination Committee of the Organization.

(3)
(a) Each country member of the Assembly shall have one vote.
(b) One-half of the countries members of the Assembly shall constitute a quorum.
(c) Notwithstanding the provisions of subparagraph (b), if, in any session, the number of countries represented is less than one-half but equal to or more than one-third of the countries members of the Assembly, the Assembly may make decisions but, with the exception of decisions concerning its own procedure, all such decisions shall take effect only if the following conditions are fulfilled. The International Bureau shall communicate the said decisions to the countries members of the Assembly which were not represented and shall invite them to express in writing their vote or abstention within a period of three months from the date of the communication. If, at the expiration of this period, the number of countries having thus expressed their vote or abstention attains the number of countries which was lacking for attaining the quorum in the session itself, such decisions shall take effect provided that at the same time the required majority still obtains.
(d) Subject to the provisions of Article 26(2), the decisions of the Assembly shall require two-thirds of the votes cast.
(e) Abstentions shall not be considered as votes.
(f) A delegate may represent, and vote in the name of, one country only.
(g) Countries of the Union not members of the Assembly shall be admitted to its meetings as observers.

(4)

(a) The Assembly shall meet once in every second calendar year in ordinary session upon convocation by the Director General and, in the absence of exceptional circumstances, during the same period and at the same place as the General Assembly of the Organization.
(b) The Assembly shall meet in extraordinary session upon convocation by the Director General, at the request of the Executive Committee or at the request of one-fourth of the countries members of the Assembly.
(5) The Assembly shall adopt its own rules of procedure.

Article 23 - [Executive Committee: 1. Constitution; 2. Composition; 3. Number of members; 4. Geographical distribution; special agreements; 5. Term, limits of re-eligibility, rules of election; 6. Tasks; 7. Convocation; 8. Quorum, voting; 9. Observers; 10. Rules of procedure]

(1) The Assembly shall have an Executive Committee.
(2)
(a) The Executive Committee shall consist of countries elected by the Assembly from among countries members of the Assembly. Furthermore, the country on whose territory the Organization has its headquarters shall, subject to the provisions of Article 25(7)(b), have an ex officio seat on the Committee.
(b) The Government of each country member of the Executive Committee shall be represented by one delegate, who may be assisted by alternate delegates, advisors, and experts.
(c) The expenses of each delegation shall be borne by the Government which has appointed it.
(3) The number of countries members of the Executive Committee shall correspond to one-fourth of the number of countries members of the Assembly. In establishing the number of seats to be filled, remainders after division by four shall be disregarded.
(4) In electing the members of the Executive Committee, the Assembly shall have due regard to an equitable geographical distribution and to the need for countries party to the Special Agreements which might be established in relation with the Union to be among the countries constituting the Executive Committee.
(5)
(a) Each member of the Executive Committee shall serve from the close of the session of the Assembly which elected it to the close of the next ordinary session of the Assembly.
(b) Members of the Executive Committee may be re-elected, but not more than two-thirds of them.
(c) The Assembly shall establish the details of the rules governing the election and possible re-election of the members of the Executive Committee.
(6)
(a) The Executive Committee shall:
(i) prepare the draft agenda of the Assembly;
(ii) submit proposals to the Assembly respecting the draft program and biennial budget of the Union prepared by the Director General;
(iii) [deleted]
(iv) submit, with appropriate comments, to the Assembly the periodical reports of the Director General and the yearly audit reports on the accounts;
(v) in accordance with the decisions of the Assembly and having regard to circumstances arising between two ordinary sessions of the Assembly, take all necessary measures to ensure the execution of the program of the Union by the Director General;
(vi) perform such other functions as are allocated to it under this Convention.
(b) With respect to matters which are of interest also to other Unions administered by the Organization, the Executive Committee shall make its decisions after having heard the advice of the Coordination Committee of the Organization.
(7)

(a) The Executive Committee shall meet once a year in ordinary session upon convocation by the Director General, preferably during the same period and at the same place as the Coordination Committee of the Organization.
(b) The Executive Committee shall meet in extraordinary session upon convocation by the Director General, either on his own initiative, or at the request of its Chairman or one-fourth of its members.

(8)
(a) Each country member of the Executive Committee shall have one vote.
(b) One-half of the members of the Executive Committee shall constitute a quorum.
(c) Decisions shall be made by a simple majority of the votes cast.
(d) Abstentions shall not be considered as votes.
(e) A delegate may represent, and vote in the name of, one country only.

(9) Countries of the Union not members of the Executive Committee shall be admitted to its meetings as observers.
(10) The Executive Committee shall adopt its own rules of procedure.

Article 24 - [International Bureau: 1. Tasks in general, Director General; 2. General information; 3. Periodical; 4. Information to countries; 5. Studies and services; 6. Participation in meetings; 7. Conferences of revision; 8. Other tasks]

(1)
(a) The administrative tasks with respect to the Union shall be performed by the International Bureau, which is a continuation of the Bureau of the Union united with the Bureau of the Union established by the International Convention for the Protection of Industrial Property.
(b) In particular, the International Bureau shall provide the secretariat of the various organs of the Union.
(c) The Director General of the Organization shall be the chief executive of the Union and shall represent the Union.

(2) The International Bureau shall assemble and publish information concerning the protection of copyright. Each country of the Union shall promptly communicate to the International Bureau all new laws and official texts concerning the protection of copyright.
(3) The International Bureau shall publish a monthly periodical.
(4) The International Bureau shall, on request, furnish information to any country of the Union on matters concerning the protection of copyright.
(5) The International Bureau shall conduct studies, and shall provide services, designed to facilitate the protection of copyright.
(6) The Director General and any staff member designated by him shall participate, without the right to vote, in all meetings of the Assembly, the Executive Committee and any other committee of experts or working group. The Director General, or a staff member designated by him, shall be ex officio secretary of these bodies.

(7)
(a) The International Bureau shall, in accordance with the directions of the Assembly and in cooperation with the Executive Committee, make the preparations for the conferences of revision of the provisions of the Convention other than Articles 22 to 26.
(b) The International Bureau may consult with intergovernmental and international non-governmental organizations concerning preparations for conferences of revision.
(c) The Director General and persons designated by him shall take part, without the right to vote, in the discussions at these conferences.

(8) The International Bureau shall carry out any other tasks assigned to it.

Article 25 - [**Finances: 1.** Budget; **2.** Coordination with other Unions; **3.** Resources; **4.** Contributions; possible extension of previous budget; **5.** Fees and charges; **6.** Working capital fund; **7.** Advances by host Government; **8.** Auditing of accounts]

(1)
(a) The Union shall have a budget.
(b) The budget of the Union shall include the income and expenses proper to the Union, its contribution to the budget of expenses common to the Unions, and, where applicable, the sum made available to the budget of the Conference of the Organization.
(c) Expenses not attributable exclusively to the Union but also to one or more other Unions administered by the Organization shall be considered as expenses common to the Unions. The share of the Union in such common expenses shall be in proportion to the interest the Union has in them.
(2) The budget of the Union shall be established with due regard to the requirements of coordination with the budgets of the other Unions administered by the Organization.
(3) The budget of the Union shall be financed from the following sources:
(i) contributions of the countries of the Union;
(ii) fees and charges due for services performed by the International Bureau in relation to the Union;
(iii) sale of, or royalties on, the publications of the International Bureau concerning the Union;
(iv) gifts, bequests, and subventions;
(v) rents, interests, and other miscellaneous income.

(4)
(a) For the purpose of establishing its contribution towards the budget, each country of the Union shall belong to a class, and shall pay its annual contributions on the basis of a number of units fixed as follows:
Class I 25
Class II 20
Class III 15
Class IV 10
Class V 5
Class VI 3
Class VII 1
(b) Unless it has already done so, each country shall indicate, concurrently with depositing its instrument of ratification or accession, the class to which it wishes to belong. Any country may change class. If it chooses a lower class, the country must announce it to the Assembly at one of its ordinary sessions. Any such change shall take effect at the beginning of the calendar year following the session.
(c) The annual contribution of each country shall be an amount in the same proportion to the total sum to be contributed to the annual budget of the Union by all countries as the number of its units is to the total of the units of all contributing countries.
(d) Contributions shall become due on the first of January of each year.
(e) A country which is in arrears in the payment of its contributions shall have no vote in any of the organs of the Union of which it is a member if the amount of its arrears equals or exceeds the amount of the contributions due from it for the preceding two full years. However, any organ of the Union may allow such a country to continue to exercise its vote in that organ if, and as long as, it is satisfied that the delay in payment is due to exceptional and unavoidable circumstances.
(f) If the budget is not adopted before the beginning of a new financial period, it shall be at the same level as the budget of the previous year, in accordance with the financial regulations.

(5) The amount of the fees and charges due for services rendered by the International Bureau in relation to the Union shall be established, and shall be reported to the Assembly and the Executive Committee, by the Director General.

(6)
(a) The Union shall have a working capital fund which shall be constituted by a single payment made by each country of the Union. If the fund becomes insufficient, an increase shall be decided by the Assembly.
(b) The amount of the initial payment of each country to the said fund or of its participation in the increase thereof shall be a proportion of the contribution of that country for the year in which the fund is established or the increase decided.
(c) The proportion and the terms of payment shall be fixed by the Assembly on the proposal of the Director General and after it has heard the advice of the Coordination Committee of the Organization.

(7)
(a) In the headquarters agreement concluded with the country on the territory of which the Organization has its headquarters, it shall be provided that, whenever the working capital fund is insufficient, such country shall grant advances. The amount of these advances and the conditions on which they are granted shall be the subject of separate agreements, in each case, between such country and the Organization. As long as it remains under the obligation to grant advances, such country shall have an ex officio seat on the Executive Committee.
(b) The country referred to in subparagraph (a) and the Organization shall each have the right to denounce the obligation to grant advances, by written notification. Denunciation shall take effect three years after the end of the year in which it has been notified.

(8) The auditing of the accounts shall be effected by one or more of the countries of the Union or by external auditors, as provided in the financial regulations. They shall be designated, with their agreement, by the Assembly.

Article 26 - [Amendments: 1. Provisions susceptible of amendment by the Assembly; proposals; 2. Adoption; 3. Entry into force]

(1) Proposals for the amendment of Articles 22, 23, 24, 25, and the present Article, may be initiated by any country member of the Assembly, by the Executive Committee, or by the Director General. Such proposals shall be communicated by the Director General to the member countries of the Assembly at least six months in advance of their consideration by the Assembly.

(2) Amendments to the Articles referred to in paragraph (1) shall be adopted by the Assembly. Adoption shall require three-fourths of the votes cast, provided that any amendment of Article 22, and of the present paragraph, shall require four-fifths of the votes cast.

(3) Any amendment to the Articles referred to in paragraph (1) shall enter into force one month after written notifications of acceptance, effected in accordance with their respective constitutional processes, have been received by the Director General from three-fourths of the countries members of the Assembly at the time it adopted the amendment. Any amendment to the said Articles thus accepted shall bind all the countries which are members of the Assembly at the time the amendment enters into force, or which become members thereof at a subsequent date, provided that any amendment increasing the financial obligations of countries of the Union shall bind only those countries which have notified their acceptance of such amendment.

Article 27 - [Revision: 1. Objective; 2. Conferences; 3. Adoption]

(1) This Convention shall be submitted to revision with a view to the introduction of amendments designed to improve the system of the Union.

(2) For this purpose, conferences shall be held successively in one of the countries of the Union among the delegates of the said countries.
(3) Subject to the provisions of Article 26 which apply to the amendment of Articles 22 to 26, any revision of this Act, including the Appendix, shall require the unanimity of the votes cast.

Article 28 - [Acceptance and Entry Into Force of Act for Countries of the Union: 1. Ratification, accession; possibility of excluding certain provisions; withdrawal of exclusion; 2. Entry into force of Articles 1 to 21 and Appendix; 3. Entry into force of Articles 22 to 38]

(1)
(a) Any country of the Union which has signed this Act may ratify it, and, if it has not signed it, may accede to it. Instruments of ratification or accession shall be deposited with the Director General.
(b) Any country of the Union may declare in its instrument of ratification or accession that its ratification or accession shall not apply to Articles 1 to 21 and the Appendix, provided that, if such country has previously made a declaration under Article VI(1) of the Appendix, then it may declare in the said instrument only that its ratification or accession shall not apply to Articles 1 to 20.
(c) Any country of the Union which, in accordance with subparagraph (b), has excluded provisions therein referred to from the effects of its ratification or accession may at any later time declare that it extends the effects of its ratification or accession to those provisions. Such declaration shall be deposited with the Director General.

(2)
(a) Articles 1 to 21 and the Appendix shall enter into force three months after both of the following two conditions are fulfilled:
(i) at least five countries of the Union have ratified or acceded to this Act without making a declaration under paragraph (1)(b),
(ii) France, Spain, the United Kingdom of Great Britain and Northern Ireland, and the United States of America, have become bound by the Universal Copyright Convention as revised at Paris on July 24, 1971.
(b) The entry into force referred to in subparagraph (a) shall apply to those countries of the Union which, at least three months before the said entry into force, have deposited instruments of ratification or accession not containing a declaration under paragraph (1)(b).
(c) With respect to any country of the Union not covered by subparagraph (b) and which ratifies or accedes to this Act without making a declaration under paragraph (1)(b), Articles 1 to 21 and the Appendix shall enter into force three months after the date on which the Director General has notified the deposit of the relevant instrument of ratification or accession, unless a subsequent date has been indicated in the instrument deposited. In the latter case, Articles 1 to 21 and the Appendix shall enter into force with respect to that country on the date thus indicated.
(d) The provisions of subparagraphs (a) to (c) do not affect the application of Article VI of the Appendix.
(3) With respect to any country of the Union which ratifies or accedes to this Act with or without a declaration made under paragraph (1)(b), Articles 22 to 38 shall enter into force three months after the date on which the Director General has notified the deposit of the relevant instrument of ratification or accession, unless a subsequent date has been indicated in the instrument deposited. In the latter case, Articles 22 to 38 shall enter into force with respect to that country on the date thus indicated.

Article 29 - [Acceptance and Entry Into Force for Countries Outside the Union: 1. Accession; 2. Entry into force]

(1) Any country outside the Union may accede to this Act and thereby become party to this Convention and a member of the Union. Instruments of accession shall be deposited with the Director General.

(2)

(a) Subject to subparagraph (b), this Convention shall enter into force with respect to any country outside the Union three months after the date on which the Director General has notified the deposit of its instrument of accession, unless a subsequent date has been indicated in the instrument deposited. In the latter case, this Convention shall enter into force with respect to that country on the date thus indicated.

(b) If the entry into force according to subparagraph (a) precedes the entry into force of Articles 1 to 21 and the Appendix according to Article 28(2)(a), the said country shall, in the meantime, be bound, instead of by Articles 1 to 21 and the Appendix, by Articles 1 to 20 of the Brussels Act of this Convention.

Article 29bis - [Effect of Acceptance of Act for the Purposes of Article 14(2) of the WIPO Convention]

Ratification of or accession to this Act by any country not bound by Articles 22 to 38 of the Stockholm Act of this Convention shall, for the sole purposes of Article 14(2) of the Convention establishing the Organization, amount to ratification of or accession to the said Stockholm Act with the limitation set forth in Article 28(1)(b)(i) thereof.

Article 30 - [Reservations: 1. Limits of possibility of making reservations; 2. Earlier reservations; reservation as to the right of translation; withdrawal of reservation]

(1) Subject to the exceptions permitted by paragraph (2) of this Article, by Article 28(1)(b), by Article 33(2), and by the Appendix, ratification or accession shall automatically entail acceptance of all the provisions and admission to all the advantages of this Convention.

(2)

(a) Any country of the Union ratifying or acceding to this Act may, subject to Article V(2) of the Appendix, retain the benefit of the reservations it has previously formulated on condition that it makes a declaration to that effect at the time of the deposit of its instrument of ratification or accession.

(b) Any country outside the Union may declare, in acceding to this Convention and subject to Article V(2) of the Appendix, that it intends to substitute, temporarily at least, for Article 8 of this Act concerning the right of translation, the provisions of Article 5 of the Union Convention of 1886, as completed at Paris in 1896, on the clear understanding that the said provisions are applicable only to translations into a language in general use in the said country. Subject to Article I(6)(b) of the Appendix, any country has the right to apply, in relation to the right of translation of works whose country of origin is a country availing itself of such a reservation, a protection which is equivalent to the protection granted by the latter country.

(c) Any country may withdraw such reservations at any time by notification addressed to the Director General.

Article 31 - [Applicability to Certain Territories: 1. Declaration; 2. Withdrawal of declaration; 3. Effective date; 4. Acceptance of factual situations not implied]

(1) Any country may declare in its instrument of ratification or accession, or may inform the Director General by written notification at any time thereafter, that this Convention shall be

applicable to all or part of those territories, designated in the declaration or notification, for the external relations of which it is responsible.
(2) Any country which has made such a declaration or given such a notification may, at any time, notify the Director General that this Convention shall cease to be applicable to all or part of such territories.
(3)
(a) Any declaration made under paragraph (1) shall take effect on the same date as the ratification or accession in which it was included, and any notification given under that paragraph shall take effect three months after its notification by the Director General.
(b) Any notification given under paragraph (2) shall take effect twelve months after its receipt by the Director General.
(4) This Article shall in no way be understood as implying the recognition or tacit acceptance by a country of the Union of the factual situation concerning a territory to which this Convention is made applicable by another country of the Union by virtue of a declaration under paragraph (1).

Article 32 - [Applicability of this Act and of Earlier Acts: 1. As between countries already members of the Union; 2. As between a country becoming a member of the Union and other countries members of the Union; 3. Applicability of the Appendix in Certain Relations]

(1) This Act shall, as regards relations between the countries of the Union, and to the extent that it applies, replace the Berne Convention of September 9, 1886, and the subsequent Acts of revision. The Acts previously in force shall continue to be applicable, in their entirety or to the extent that this Act does not replace them by virtue of the preceding sentence, in relations with countries of the Union which do not ratify or accede to this Act.
(2) Countries outside the Union which become party to this Act shall, subject to paragraph (3), apply it with respect to any country of the Union not bound by this Act or which, although bound by this Act, has made a declaration pursuant to Article 28(1)(b). Such countries recognize that the said country of the Union, in its relations with them:
(i) may apply the provisions of the most recent Act by which it is bound, and
(ii) subject to Article I(6) of the Appendix, has the right to adapt the protection to the level provided for by this Act.
(3) Any country which has availed itself of any of the faculties provided for in the Appendix may apply the provisions of the Appendix relating to the faculty or faculties of which it has availed itself in its relations with any other country of the Union which is not bound by this Act, provided that the latter country has accepted the application of the said provisions.

Article 33 - [Disputes: 1. Jurisdiction of the International Court of Justice; 2. Reservation as to such jurisdiction; 3. Withdrawal of reservation]

(1) Any dispute between two or more countries of the Union concerning the interpretation or application of this Convention, not settled by negotiation, may, by any one of the countries concerned, be brought before the International Court of Justice by application in conformity with the Statute of the Court, unless the countries concerned agree on some other method of settlement. The country bringing the dispute before the Court shall inform the International Bureau; the International Bureau shall bring the matter to the attention of the other countries of the Union.
(2) Each country may, at the time it signs this Act or deposits its instrument of ratification or accession, declare that it does not consider itself bound by the provisions of paragraph (1). With regard to any dispute between such country and any other country of the Union, the provisions of paragraph (1) shall not apply.
(3) Any country having made a declaration in accordance with the provisions of paragraph (2) may, at any time, withdraw its declaration by notification addressed to the Director General.

Article 34 - [Closing of Certain Earlier Provisions: 1. Of earlier Acts; 2. Of the Protocol to the Stockholm Act]

(1) Subject to Article 29bis no country may ratify or accede to earlier Acts of this Convention once Articles 1 to 21 and the Appendix have entered into force.
(2) Once Articles 1 to 21 and the Appendix have entered into force, no country may make a declaration under Article 5 of the Protocol Regarding Developing Countries attached to the Stockholm Act.

Article 35 - [Duration of the Convention; Denunciation: 1. Unlimited duration; 2. Possibility of denunciation; 3. Effective date of denunciation; 4. Moratorium on denunciation]

(1) This Convention shall remain in force without limitation as to time.
(2) Any country may denounce this Act by notification addressed to the Director General. Such denunciation shall constitute also denunciation of all earlier Acts and shall affect only the country making it, the Convention remaining in full force and effect as regards the other countries of the Union.
(3) Denunciation shall take effect one year after the day on which the Director General has received the notification.
(4) The right of denunciation provided by this Article shall not be exercised by any country before the expiration of five years from the date upon which it becomes a member of the Union.

Article 36 - [Application of the Convention: 1. Obligation to adopt the necessary measures; 2. Time from which obligation exists]

(1) Any country party to this Convention undertakes to adopt, in accordance with its constitution, the measures necessary to ensure the application of this Convention.
(2) It is understood that, at the time a country becomes bound by this Convention, it will be in a position under its domestic law to give effect to the provisions of this Convention.

Article 37 - [Final Clauses: 1. Languages of the Act; 2. Signature; 3. Certified copies; 4. Registration; 5. Notifications]

(1)
(a) This Act shall be signed in a single copy in the French and English languages and, subject to paragraph (2), shall be deposited with the Director General.
(b) Official texts shall be established by the Director General, after consultation with the interested Governments, in the Arabic, German, Italian, Portuguese and Spanish languages, and such other languages as the Assembly may designate.
(c) In case of differences of opinion on the interpretation of the various texts, the French text shall prevail.
(2) This Act shall remain open for signature until January 31, 1972. Until that date, the copy referred to in paragraph (1)(a) shall be deposited with the Government of the French Republic.
(3) The Director General shall certify and transmit two copies of the signed text of this Act to the Governments of all countries of the Union and, on request, to the Government of any other country.
(4) The Director General shall register this Act with the Secretariat of the United Nations.
(5) The Director General shall notify the Governments of all countries of the Union of signatures, deposits of instruments of ratification or accession and any declarations included in such instruments or made pursuant to Articles 28(1)(c), 30(2)(a) and (b), and 33(2), entry into force of any provisions of this Act, notifications of denunciation, and notifications pursuant to Articles 30(2)(c), 31(1) and (2), 33(3), and 38(1), as well as the Appendix.

Article 38 - [Transitory Provisions: 1. Exercise of the "five-year privilege"; 2. Bureau of the Union, Director of the Bureau; 3. Succession of Bureau of the Union]

(1) Countries of the Union which have not ratified or acceded to this Act and which are not bound by Articles 22 to 26 of the Stockholm Act of this Convention may, until April 26, 1975, exercise, if they so desire, the rights provided under the said Articles as if they were bound by them. Any country desiring to exercise such rights shall give written notification to this effect to the Director General; this notification shall be effective on the date of its receipt. Such countries shall be deemed to be members of the Assembly until the said date.

(2) As long as all the countries of the Union have not become Members of the Organization, the International Bureau of the Organization shall also function as the Bureau of the Union, and the Director General as the Director of the said Bureau.

(3) Once all the countries of the Union have become Members of the Organization, the rights, obligations, and property, of the Bureau of the Union shall devolve on the International Bureau of the Organization.

APPENDIX
[SPECIAL PROVISIONS REGARDING DEVELOPING COUNTRIES]

Article I

[Faculties Open to Developing Countries: 1. Availability of certain faculties; declaration: 2. Duration of effect of declaration, 3. Cessation of developing country status; 4. Existing stocks of copies; 5. Declarations concerning certain territories; 6. Limits of reciprocity]

(1) Any country regarded as a developing country in conformity with the established practice of the General Assembly of the United Nations which ratifies or accedes to this Act, of which this Appendix forms an integral part, and which, having regard to its economic situation and its social or cultural needs, does not consider itself immediately in a position to make provision for the protection of all the rights as provided for in this Act, may, by a notification deposited with the Director General at the time of depositing its instrument of ratification or accession or, subject to Article V(1)(c), at any time thereafter, declare that it will avail itself of the faculty provided for in Article II, or of the faculty provided for in Article III, or of both of those faculties. It may, instead of availing itself of the faculty provided for in Article II, make a declaration according to Article V(1)(a).

(2)

(a) Any declaration under paragraph (1) notified before the expiration of the period of ten years from the entry into force of Articles 1 to 21 and this Appendix according to Article 28(2) shall be effective until the expiration of the said period. Any such declaration may be renewed in whole or in part for periods of ten years each by a notification deposited with the Director General not more than fifteen months and not less than three months before the expiration of the ten-year period then running.

(b) Any declaration under paragraph (1) notified after the expiration of the period of ten years from the entry into force of Articles 1 to 21 and this Appendix according to Article 28(2) shall be effective until the expiration of the ten-year period then running. Any such declaration may be renewed as provided for in the second sentence of subparagraph (a).

(3) Any country of the Union which has ceased to be regarded as a developing country as referred to in paragraph (1) shall no longer be entitled to renew its declaration as provided in paragraph (2), and, whether or not it formally withdraws its declaration, such country shall be precluded from availing itself of the faculties referred to in paragraph (1) from the expiration of the ten-year period then running or from the expiration of a period of three

years after it has ceased to be regarded as a developing country, whichever period expires later.
(4) Where, at the time when the declaration made under paragraph (1) or (2) ceases to be effective, there are copies in stock which were made under a license granted by virtue of this Appendix, such copies may continue to be distributed until their stock is exhausted.
(5) Any country which is bound by the provisions of this Act and which has deposited a declaration or a notification in accordance with Article 31(1) with respect to the application of this Act to a particular territory, the situation of which can be regarded as analogous to that of the countries referred to in paragraph (1), may, in respect of such territory, make the declaration referred to in paragraph (1) and the notification of renewal referred to in paragraph (2). As long as such declaration or notification remains in effect, the provisions of this Appendix shall be applicable to the territory in respect of which it was made.
(6)
(a) The fact that a country avails itself of any of the faculties referred to in paragraph (1) does not permit another country to give less protection to works of which the country of origin is the former country than it is obliged to grant under Articles 1 to 20.
(b) The right to apply reciprocal treatment provided for in Article 30(2)(b), second sentence, shall not, until the date on which the period applicable under Article I(3) expires, be exercised in respect of works the country of origin of which is a country which has made a declaration according to Article V(1)(a).

Article II

[Limitations on the Right of Translation: 1. Licenses grantable by competent authority; 2. to 4. Conditions allowing the grant of such licenses; 5. Purposes for which licenses may be granted; 6. Termination of licenses; 7. Works composed mainly of illustrations; 8. Works withdrawn from circulation; 9. Licenses for broadcasting organizations]

(1) Any country which has declared that it will avail itself of the faculty provided for in this Article shall be entitled, so far as works published in printed or analogous forms of reproduction are concerned, to substitute for the exclusive right of translation provided for in Article 8 a system of non-exclusive and non-transferable licenses, granted by the competent authority under the following conditions and subject to Article IV.
(2)
(a) Subject to paragraph (3), if, after the expiration of a period of three years, or of any longer period determined by the national legislation of the said country, commencing on the date of the first publication of the work, a translation of such work has not been published in a language in general use in that country by the owner of the right of translation, or with his authorization, any national of such country may obtain a license to make a translation of the work in the said language and publish the translation in printed or analogous forms of reproduction.
(b) A license under the conditions provided for in this Article may also be granted if all the editions of the translation published in the language concerned are out of print.
(3)
(a) In the case of translations into a language which is not in general use in one or more developed countries which are members of the Union, a period of one year shall be substituted for the period of three years referred to in paragraph (2)(a).
(b) Any country referred to in paragraph (1) may, with the unanimous agreement of the developed countries which are members of the Union and in which the same language is in general use, substitute, in the case of translations into that language, for the period of three years referred to in paragraph (2)(a) a shorter period as determined by such agreement but not less than one year. However, the provisions of the foregoing sentence shall not apply

where the language in question is English, French or Spanish. The Director General shall be notified of any such agreement by the Governments which have concluded it.

(4)
- (a) No license obtainable after three years shall be granted under this Article until a further period of six months has elapsed, and no license obtainable after one year shall be granted under this Article until a further period of nine months has elapsed

    (i) from the date on which the applicant complies with the requirements mentioned in Article IV(1), or

    (ii) where the identity or the address of the owner of the right of translation is unknown, from the date on which the applicant sends, as provided for in Article IV(2), copies of his application submitted to the authority competent to grant the license.

- (b) If, during the said period of six or nine months, a translation in the language in respect of which the application was made is published by the owner of the right of translation or with his authorization, no license under this Article shall be granted.

(5) Any license under this Article shall be granted only for the purpose of teaching, scholarship or research.

(6) If a translation of a work is published by the owner of the right of translation or with his authorization at a price reasonably related to that normally charged in the country for comparable works, any license granted under this Article shall terminate if such translation is in the same language and with substantially the same content as the translation published under the license. Any copies already made before the license terminates may continue to be distributed until their stock is exhausted.

(7) For works which are composed mainly of illustrations, a license to make and publish a translation of the text and to reproduce and publish the illustrations may be granted only if the conditions of Article III are also fulfilled.

(8) No license shall be granted under this Article when the author has withdrawn from circulation all copies of his work.

(9)
- (a) A license to make a translation of a work which has been published in printed or analogous forms of reproduction may also be granted to any broadcasting organization having its headquarters in a country referred to in paragraph (1), upon an application made to the competent authority of that country by the said organization, provided that all of the following conditions are met:

    (i) the translation is made from a copy made and acquired in accordance with the laws of the said country;

    (ii) the translation is only for use in broadcasts intended exclusively for teaching or for the dissemination of the results of specialized technical or scientific research to experts in a particular profession;

    (iii) the translation is used exclusively for the purposes referred to in condition (ii) through broadcasts made lawfully and intended for recipients on the territory of the said country, including broadcasts made through the medium of sound or visual recordings lawfully and exclusively made for the purpose of such broadcasts;

    (iv) all uses made of the translation are without any commercial purpose.

- (b) Sound or visual recordings of a translation which was made by a broadcasting organization under a license granted by virtue of this paragraph may, for the purposes and subject to the conditions referred to in subparagraph (a) and with the agreement of that organization, also be used by any other broadcasting organization having its headquarters in the country whose competent authority granted the license in question.

- (c) Provided that all of the criteria and conditions set out in subparagraph (a) are met, a license may also be granted to a broadcasting organization to translate any text incorporated in an

audio-visual fixation where such fixation was itself prepared and published for the sole purpose of being used in connection with systematic instructional activities.
(d) Subject to subparagraphs (a) to (c), the provisions of the preceding paragraphs shall apply to the grant and exercise of any license granted under this paragraph.

Article III

[Limitation on the Right of Reproduction: 1. Licenses grantable bycompetent authority; 2. to 5. Conditions allowing the grant of suchlicenses; 6. Termination of licenses; 7. Works to which this Articleapplies]

(1) Any country which has declared that it will avail itself of the faculty provided for in this Article shall be entitled to substitute for the exclusive right of reproduction provided for in Article 9 a system of non-exclusive and non-transferable licenses, granted by the competent authority under the following conditions and subject to Article IV.

(2)
(a) If, in relation to a work to which this Article applies by virtue of paragraph (7), after the expiration of
(i) the relevant period specified in paragraph (3), commencing on the date of first publication of a particular edition of the work, or
(ii) any longer period determined by national legislation of the country referred to in paragraph (1), commencing on the same date,copies of such edition have not been distributed in that country to the general public or in connection with systematic instructional activities, by the owner of the right of reproduction or with his authorization, at a price reasonably related to that normally charged in the country for comparable works, any national of such country may obtain a license to reproduce and publish such edition at that or a lower price for use in connection with systematic instructional activities.

(b) A license to reproduce and publish an edition which has been distributed as described in subparagraph (a) may also be granted under the conditions provided for in this Article if, after the expiration of the applicable period, no authorized copies of that edition have been on sale for a period of six months in the country concerned to the general public or in connection with systematic instructional activities at a price reasonably related to that normally charged in the country for comparable works.

(3) The period referred to in paragraph (2)(a)(i) shall be five years, except that
(i) for works of the natural and physical sciences, including mathematics, and of technology, the period shall be three years;
(ii) for works of fiction, poetry, drama and music, and for art books, the period shall be seven years.

(4)
(a) No license obtainable after three years shall be granted under this Article until a period of six months has elapsed
(i) from the date on which the applicant complies with the requirements mentioned in Article IV(1), or
(ii) where the identity or the address of the owner of the right of reproduction is unknown, from the date on which the applicant sends, as provided for in Article IV(2), copies of his application submitted to the authority competent to grant the license.

(b) Where licenses are obtainable after other periods and Article IV(2) is applicable, no license shall be granted until a period of three months has elapsed from the date of the dispatch of the copies of the application.

(c) If, during the period of six or three months referred to in subparagraphs (a) and (b), a distribution as described in paragraph (2)(a) has taken place, no license shall be granted under this Article.

(d) No license shall be granted if the author has withdrawn from circulation all copies of the edition for the reproduction and publication of which the license has been applied for.
(5) A license to reproduce and publish a translation of a work shall not be granted under this Article in the following cases:
(i) where the translation was not published by the owner of the right of translation or with his authorization, or
(ii) where the translation is not in a language in general use in the country in which the license is applied for.
(6) If copies of an edition of a work are distributed in the country referred to in paragraph (1) to the general public or in connection with systematic instructional activities, by the owner of the right of reproduction or with his authorization, at a price reasonably related to that normally charged in the country for comparable works, any license granted under this Article shall terminate if such edition is in the same language and with substantially the same content as the edition which was published under the said license. Any copies already made before the license terminates may continue to be distributed until their stock is exhausted.
(7)
(a) Subject to subparagraph (b), the works to which this Article applies shall be limited to works published in printed or analogous forms of reproduction.
(b) This Article shall also apply to the reproduction in audio-visual form of lawfully made audio-visual fixations including any protected works incorporated therein and to the translation of any incorporated text into a language in general use in the country in which the license is applied for, always provided that the audio-visual fixations in question were prepared and published for the sole purpose of being used in connection with systematic instructional activities.

Article IV

[Provisions Common to Licenses Under Articles II and III: 1 and 2. Procedure; 3. Indication of author and title of work; 4. Exportation of copies; 5. Notice; 6. Compensation]

(1) A license under Article II or Article III may be granted only if the applicant, in accordance with the procedure of the country concerned, establishes either that he has requested, and has been denied, authorization by the owner of the right to make and publish the translation or to reproduce and publish the edition, as the case may be, or that, after due diligence on his part, he was unable to find the owner of the right. At the same time as making the request, the applicant shall inform any national or international information center referred to in paragraph (2).
(2) If the owner of the right cannot be found, the applicant for a license shall send, by registered airmail, copies of his application, submitted to the authority competent to grant the license, to the publisher whose name appears on the work and to any national or international information center which may have been designated, in a notification to that effect deposited with the Director General, by the Government of the country in which the publisher is believed to have his principal place of business.
(3) The name of the author shall be indicated on all copies of the translation or reproduction published under a license granted under Article II or Article III. The title of the work shall appear on all such copies. In the case of a translation, the original title of the work shall appear in any case on all the said copies.
(4)
(a) No license granted under Article II or Article III shall extend to the export of copies, and any such license shall be valid only for publication of the translation or of the reproduction, as the case may be, in the territory of the country in which it has been applied for.

(b) For the purposes of subparagraph (a), the notion of export shall include the sending of copies from any territory to the country which, in respect of that territory, has made a declaration under Article I(5).
(c) Where a governmental or other public entity of a country which has granted a license to make a translation under Article II into a language other than English, French or Spanish sends copies of a translation published under such license to another country, such sending of copies shall not, for the purposes of subparagraph (a), be considered to constitute export if all of the following conditions are met:
(i) the recipients are individuals who are nationals of the country whose competent authority has granted the license, or organizations grouping such individuals;
(ii) the copies are to be used only for the purpose of teaching, scholarship or research;
(iii) the sending of the copies and their subsequent distribution to recipients is without any commercial purpose; and
(iv) the country to which the copies have been sent has agreed with the country whose competent authority has granted the license to allow the receipt, or distribution, or both, and the Director General has been notified of the agreement by the Government of the country in which the license has been granted.
(5) All copies published under a license granted by virtue of Article II or Article III shall bear a notice in the appropriate language stating that the copies are available for distribution only in the country or territory to which the said license applies.
(6)
(a) Due provision shall be made at the national level to ensure
(i) that the license provides, in favour of the owner of the right of translation or of reproduction, as the case may be, for just compensation that is consistent with standards of royalties normally operating on licenses freely negotiated between persons in the two countries concerned, and
(ii) payment and transmittal of the compensation: should national currency regulations intervene, the competent authority shall make all efforts, by the use of international machinery, to ensure transmittal in internationally convertible currency or its equivalent.
(b) Due provision shall be made by national legislation to ensure a correct translation of the work, or an accurate reproduction of the particular edition, as the case may be.

Article V

[Alternative Possibility for Limitation of the Right of Translation: 1. Regime provided for under the 1886 and 1896 Acts; 2. No possibility of change to regime under Article II; 3. Time limit for choosing the alternative possibility]

(1)
(a) Any country entitled to make a declaration that it will avail itself of the faculty provided for in Article II may, instead, at the time of ratifying or acceding to this Act:
(i) if it is a country to which Article 30(2)(a) applies, make a declaration under that provision as far as the right of translation is concerned;
(ii) if it is a country to which Article 30(2)(a) does not apply, and even if it is not a country outside the Union, make a declaration as provided for in Article 30(2)(b), first sentence.
(b) In the case of a country which ceases to be regarded as a developing country as referred to in Article I(1), a declaration made according to this paragraph shall be effective until the date on which the period applicable under Article I(3) expires.
(c) Any country which has made a declaration according to this paragraph may not subsequently avail itself of the faculty provided for in Article II even if it withdraws the said declaration.

(2) Subject to paragraph (3), any country which has availed itself of the faculty provided for in Article II may not subsequently make a declaration according to paragraph (1).
(3) Any country which has ceased to be regarded as a developing country as referred to in Article I(1) may, not later than two years prior to the expiration of the period applicable under Article I(3), make a declaration to the effect provided for in Article 30(2)(b), first sentence, notwithstanding the fact that it is not a country outside the Union. Such declaration shall take effect at the date on which the period applicable under Article I(3) expires.

Article VI

[Possibilities of applying, or admitting the application of, certainprovisions of the Appendix before becoming bound by it: 1. Declaration; 2. Depository and effective date of declaration]

(1) Any country of the Union may declare, as from the date of this Act, and at any time before becoming bound by Articles 1 to 21 and this Appendix:

(i) if it is a country which, were it bound by Articles 1 to 21 and this Appendix, would be entitled to avail itself of the faculties referred to in Article I(1), that it will apply the provisions of Article II or of Article III or of both to works whose country of origin is a country which, pursuant to (ii) below, admits the application of those Articles to such works, or which is bound by Articles 1 to 21 and this Appendix; such declaration may, instead of referring to Article II, refer to Article V;

(ii) that it admits the application of this Appendix to works of which it is the country of origin by countries which have made a declaration under (i) above or a notification under Article I.

(2) Any declaration made under paragraph (1) shall be in writing and shall be deposited with the Director General. The declaration shall become effective from the date of its deposit.

AGREEMENT ON TRADE RELATED ASPECTS OF INTELLECTUAL PROPERTY RIGHTS (TRIPS)

Date: 15/04/1994
(Source: http://www.wto.org)

Members,

Desiring to reduce distortions and impediments to international trade, and taking into account the need to promote effective and adequate protection of intellectual property rights, and to ensure that measures and procedures to enforce intellectual property rights do not themselves become barriers to legitimate trade;

Recognizing, to this end, the need for new rules and disciplines concerning:
(a) the applicability of the basic principles of GATT 1994 and of relevant international intellectual property agreements or conventions;
(b) the provision of adequate standards and principles concerning the availability, scope and use of trade-related intellectual property rights;
(c) the provision of effective and appropriate means for the enforcement of trade-related intellectual property rights, taking into account differences in national legal systems;
(d) the provision of effective and expeditious procedures for the multilateral prevention and settlement of disputes between governments; and
(e) transitional arrangements aiming at the fullest participation in the results of the negotiations;

Recognizing the need for a multilateral framework of principles, rules and disciplines dealing with international trade in counterfeit goods;

Recognizing that intellectual property rights are private rights;

Recognizing the underlying public policy objectives of national systems for the protection of intellectual property, including developmental and technological objectives;

Recognizing also the special needs of the least-developed country Members in respect of maximum flexibility in the domestic implementation of laws and regulations in order to enable them to create a sound and viable technological base;

Emphasizing the importance of reducing tensions by reaching strengthened commitments to resolve disputes on trade-related intellectual property issues through multilateral procedures;

Desiring to establish a mutually supportive relationship between the WTO and the World Intellectual Property Organization (referred to in this Agreement as "WIPO") as well as other relevant international organizations;

Hereby agree as follows:

PART I - GENERAL PROVISIONS AND BASIC PRINCIPLES

Article 1 - Nature and Scope of Obligations

1. Members shall give effect to the provisions of this Agreement. Members may, but shall not be obliged to, implement in their law more extensive protection than is required by this Agreement, provided that such protection does not contravene the provisions of this Agreement. Members shall be free to determine the appropriate method of implementing the provisions of this Agreement within their own legal system and practice.
2. For the purposes of this Agreement, the term "intellectual property" refers to all categories of intellectual property that are the subject of Sections 1 through 7 of Part II.
3. Members shall accord the treatment provided for in this Agreement to the nationals of other Members.[1] In respect of the relevant intellectual property right, the nationals of other Members shall be understood as those natural or legal persons that would meet the criteria for eligibility for protection provided for in the Paris Convention (1967), the Berne Convention (1971), the Rome Convention and the Treaty on Intellectual Property in Respect of Integrated Circuits, were all Members of the WTO members of those conventions.[2] Any Member availing itself of the possibilities provided in paragraph 3 of Article 5 or paragraph 2 of Article 6 of the Rome Convention shall make a notification as foreseen in those provisions to the Council for Trade-Related Aspects of Intellectual Property Rights (the "Council for TRIPS").

Article 2 - Intellectual Property Conventions

1. In respect of Parts II, III and IV of this Agreement, Members shall comply with Articles 1 through 12, and Article 19, of the Paris Convention (1967).
2. Nothing in Parts I to IV of this Agreement shall derogate from existing obligations that Members may have to each other under the Paris Convention, the Berne Convention, the Rome Convention and the Treaty on Intellectual Property in Respect of Integrated Circuits.

Article 3 - National Treatment

1. Each Member shall accord to the nationals of other Members treatment no less favourable than that it accords to its own nationals with regard to the protection[3] of intellectual property, subject to the exceptions already provided in, respectively, the Paris Convention (1967), the Berne Convention (1971), the Rome Convention or the Treaty on Intellectual Property in Respect of Integrated Circuits. In respect of performers, producers of phonograms and broadcasting organizations, this obligation only applies in respect of the rights provided under this Agreement. Any Member availing itself of the possibilities provided in Article 6 of the Berne Convention (1971) or paragraph 1(b) of Article 16 of the Rome Convention shall make a notification as foreseen in those provisions to the Council for TRIPS.

---

[1] When "nationals" are referred to in this Agreement, they shall be deemed, in the case of a separate customs territory Member of the WTO, to mean persons, natural or legal, who are domiciled or who have a real and effective industrial or commercial establishment in that customs territory.

[2] In this Agreement, "Paris Convention" refers to the Paris Convention for the Protection of Industrial Property; "Paris Convention (1967)" refers to the Stockholm Act of this Convention of 14 July 1967. "Berne Convention" refers to the Berne Convention for the Protection of Literary and Artistic Works; "Berne Convention (1971)" refers to the Paris Act of this Convention of 24 July 1971. "Rome Convention" refers to the International Convention for the Protection of Performers, Producers of Phonograms and Broadcasting Organizations, adopted at Rome on 26 October 1961. "Treaty on Intellectual Property in Respect of Integrated Circuits" (IPIC Treaty) refers to the Treaty on Intellectual Property in Respect of Integrated Circuits, adopted at Washington on 26 May 1989. "WTO Agreement" refers to the Agreement Establishing the WTO.

[3] For the purposes of Articles 3 and 4, "protection" shall include matters affecting the availability, acquisition, scope, maintenance and enforcement of intellectual property rights as well as those matters affecting the use of intellectual property rights specifically addressed in this Agreement.

2. Members may avail themselves of the exceptions permitted under paragraph 1 in relation to judicial and administrative procedures, including the designation of an address for service or the appointment of an agent within the jurisdiction of a Member, only where such exceptions are necessary to secure compliance with laws and regulations which are not inconsistent with the provisions of this Agreement and where such practices are not applied in a manner which would constitute a disguised restriction on trade.

Article 4 - Most-Favoured-Nation Treatment

With regard to the protection of intellectual property, any advantage, favour, privilege or immunity granted by a Member to the nationals of any other country shall be accorded immediately and unconditionally to the nationals of all other Members. Exempted from this obligation are any advantage, favour, privilege or immunity accorded by a Member:
(a) deriving from international agreements on judicial assistance or law enforcement of a general nature and not particularly confined to the protection of intellectual property;
(b) granted in accordance with the provisions of the Berne Convention (1971) or the Rome Convention authorizing that the treatment accorded be a function not of national treatment but of the treatment accorded in another country;
(c) in respect of the rights of performers, producers of phonograms and broadcasting organizations not provided under this Agreement;
(d) deriving from international agreements related to the protection of intellectual property which entered into force prior to the entry into force of the WTO Agreement, provided that such agreements are notified to the Council for TRIPS and do not constitute an arbitrary or unjustifiable discrimination against nationals of other Members.

Article 5 - Multilateral Agreements on Acquisition or Maintenance of Protection

The obligations under Articles 3 and 4 do not apply to procedures provided in multilateral agreements concluded under the auspices of WIPO relating to the acquisition or maintenance of intellectual property rights.

Article 6 - Exhaustion

For the purposes of dispute settlement under this Agreement, subject to the provisions of Articles 3 and 4 nothing in this Agreement shall be used to address the issue of the exhaustion of intellectual property rights.

Article 7 - Objectives

The protection and enforcement of intellectual property rights should contribute to the promotion of technological innovation and to the transfer and dissemination of technology, to the mutual advantage of producers and users of technological knowledge and in a manner conducive to social and economic welfare, and to a balance of rights and obligations.

Article 8 - Principles

1. Members may, in formulating or amending their laws and regulations, adopt measures necessary to protect public health and nutrition, and to promote the public interest in sectors of vital importance to their socio-economic and technological development, provided that such measures are consistent with the provisions of this Agreement.
2. Appropriate measures, provided that they are consistent with the provisions of this Agreement, may be needed to prevent the abuse of intellectual property rights by right holders or the resort to practices which unreasonably restrain trade or adversely affect the international transfer of technology.

PART II - STANDARDS CONCERNING THE AVAILABILITY, SCOPE AND USE OF INTELLECTUAL PROPERTY RIGHTS

SECTION 1: COPYRIGHT AND RELATED RIGHTS

Article 9 - Relation to the Berne Convention

1. Members shall comply with Articles 1 through 21 of the Berne Convention (1971) and the Appendix thereto. However, Members shall not have rights or obligations under this Agreement in respect of the rights conferred under Article 6*bis* of that Convention or of the rights derived therefrom.
2. Copyright protection shall extend to expressions and not to ideas, procedures, methods of operation or mathematical concepts as such.

Article 10 - Computer Programs and Compilations of Data

1. Computer programs, whether in source or object code, shall be protected as literary works under the Berne Convention (1971).
2. Compilations of data or other material, whether in machine readable or other form, which by reason of the selection or arrangement of their contents constitute intellectual creations shall be protected as such. Such protection, which shall not extend to the data or material itself, shall be without prejudice to any copyright subsisting in the data or material itself.

Article 11 - Rental Rights

In respect of at least computer programs and cinematographic works, a Member shall provide authors and their successors in title the right to authorize or to prohibit the commercial rental to the public of originals or copies of their copyright works. A Member shall be excepted from this obligation in respect of cinematographic works unless such rental has led to widespread copying of such works which is materially impairing the exclusive right of reproduction conferred in that Member on authors and their successors in title. In respect of computer programs, this obligation does not apply to rentals where the program itself is not the essential object of the rental.

Article 12 - Term of Protection

Whenever the term of protection of a work, other than a photographic work or a work of applied art, is calculated on a basis other than the life of a natural person, such term shall be no less than 50 years from the end of the calendar year of authorized publication, or, failing such authorized publication within 50 years from the making of the work, 50 years from the end of the calendar year of making.

Article 13 - Limitations and Exceptions

Members shall confine limitations or exceptions to exclusive rights to certain special cases which do not conflict with a normal exploitation of the work and do not unreasonably prejudice the legitimate interests of the right holder.

Article 14 - Protection of Performers, Producers of Phonograms (Sound Recordings) and Broadcasting Organizations

1. In respect of a fixation of their performance on a phonogram, performers shall have the possibility of preventing the following acts when undertaken without their authorization: the fixation of their unfixed performance and the reproduction of such fixation. Performers shall

also have the possibility of preventing the following acts when undertaken without their authorization: the broadcasting by wireless means and the communication to the public of their live performance.

2. Producers of phonograms shall enjoy the right to authorize or prohibit the direct or indirect reproduction of their phonograms.

3. Broadcasting organizations shall have the right to prohibit the following acts when undertaken without their authorization: the fixation, the reproduction of fixations, and the rebroadcasting by wireless means of broadcasts, as well as the communication to the public of television broadcasts of the same. Where Members do not grant such rights to broadcasting organizations, they shall provide owners of copyright in the subject matter of broadcasts with the possibility of preventing the above acts, subject to the provisions of the Berne Convention (1971).

4. The provisions of Article 11 in respect of computer programs shall apply *mutatis mutandis* to producers of phonograms and any other right holders in phonograms as determined in a Member's law. If on 15 April 1994 a Member has in force a system of equitable remuneration of right holders in respect of the rental of phonograms, it may maintain such system provided that the commercial rental of phonograms is not giving rise to the material impairment of the exclusive rights of reproduction of right holders.

5. The term of the protection available under this Agreement to performers and producers of phonograms shall last at least until the end of a period of 50 years computed from the end of the calendar year in which the fixation was made or the performance took place. The term of protection granted pursuant to paragraph 3 shall last for at least 20 years from the end of the calendar year in which the broadcast took place.

6. Any Member may, in relation to the rights conferred under paragraphs 1, 2 and 3, provide for conditions, limitations, exceptions and reservations to the extent permitted by the Rome Convention. However, the provisions of Article 18 of the Berne Convention (1971) shall also apply, *mutatis mutandis*, to the rights of performers and producers of phonograms in phonograms.

SECTION 2: TRADEMARKS

Article 15 - Protectable Subject Matter

1. Any sign, or any combination of signs, capable of distinguishing the goods or services of one undertaking from those of other undertakings, shall be capable of constituting a trademark. Such signs, in particular words including personal names, letters, numerals, figurative elements and combinations of colours as well as any combination of such signs, shall be eligible for registration as trademarks. Where signs are not inherently capable of distinguishing the relevant goods or services, Members may make registrability depend on distinctiveness acquired through use. Members may require, as a condition of registration, that signs be visually perceptible.

2. Paragraph 1 shall not be understood to prevent a Member from denying registration of a trademark on other grounds, provided that they do not derogate from the provisions of the Paris Convention (1967).

3. Members may make registrability depend on use. However, actual use of a trademark shall not be a condition for filing an application for registration. An application shall not be refused solely on the ground that intended use has not taken place before the expiry of a period of three years from the date of application.

4. The nature of the goods or services to which a trademark is to be applied shall in no case form an obstacle to registration of the trademark.

5. Members shall publish each trademark either before it is registered or promptly after it is registered and shall afford a reasonable opportunity for petitions to cancel the registration. In addition, Members may afford an opportunity for the registration of a trademark to be opposed.

Article 16 - Rights Conferred

1. The owner of a registered trademark shall have the exclusive right to prevent all third parties not having the owner's consent from using in the course of trade identical or similar signs for goods or services which are identical or similar to those in respect of which the trademark is registered where such use would result in a likelihood of confusion. In case of the use of an identical sign for identical goods or services, a likelihood of confusion shall be presumed. The rights described above shall not prejudice any existing prior rights, nor shall they affect the possibility of Members making rights available on the basis of use.
2. Article 6*bis* of the Paris Convention (1967) shall apply, *mutatis mutandis*, to services. In determining whether a trademark is well-known, Members shall take account of the knowledge of the trademark in the relevant sector of the public, including knowledge in the Member concerned which has been obtained as a result of the promotion of the trademark.
3. Article 6*bis* of the Paris Convention (1967) shall apply, *mutatis mutandis*, to goods or services which are not similar to those in respect of which a trademark is registered, provided that use of that trademark in relation to those goods or services would indicate a connection between those goods or services and the owner of the registered trademark and provided that the interests of the owner of the registered trademark are likely to be damaged by such use.

Article 17 - Exceptions

Members may provide limited exceptions to the rights conferred by a trademark, such as fair use of descriptive terms, provided that such exceptions take account of the legitimate interests of the owner of the trademark and of third parties.

Article 18 - Term of Protection

Initial registration, and each renewal of registration, of a trademark shall be for a term of no less than seven years. The registration of a trademark shall be renewable indefinitely.

Article 19 - Requirement of Use

1. If use is required to maintain a registration, the registration may be cancelled only after an uninterrupted period of at least three years of non-use, unless valid reasons based on the existence of obstacles to such use are shown by the trademark owner. Circumstances arising independently of the will of the owner of the trademark which constitute an obstacle to the use of the trademark, such as import restrictions on or other government requirements for goods or services protected by the trademark, shall be recognized as valid reasons for non-use.
2. When subject to the control of its owner, use of a trademark by another person shall be recognized as use of the trademark for the purpose of maintaining the registration.

Article 20 - Other Requirements

The use of a trademark in the course of trade shall not be unjustifiably encumbered by special requirements, such as use with another trademark, use in a special form or use in a manner detrimental to its capability to distinguish the goods or services of one undertaking from those of other undertakings. This will not preclude a requirement prescribing the use of the trademark identifying the undertaking producing the goods or services along with, but without linking it to, the trademark distinguishing the specific goods or services in question of that undertaking.

Article 21 - Licensing and Assignment

Members may determine conditions on the licensing and assignment of trademarks, it being understood that the compulsory licensing of trademarks shall not be permitted and that the owner of a registered trademark shall have the right to assign the trademark with or without the transfer of the business to which the trademark belongs.

SECTION 3: GEOGRAPHICAL INDICATIONS

Article 22 - Protection of Geographical Indications

1. Geographical indications are, for the purposes of this Agreement, indications which identify a good as originating in the territory of a Member, or a region or locality in that territory, where a given quality, reputation or other characteristic of the good is essentially attributable to its geographical origin.
2. In respect of geographical indications, Members shall provide the legal means for interested parties to prevent:
(a) the use of any means in the designation or presentation of a good that indicates or suggests that the good in question originates in a geographical area other than the true place of origin in a manner which misleads the public as to the geographical origin of the good;
(b) any use which constitutes an act of unfair competition within the meaning of Article 10*bis* of the Paris Convention (1967).
3. A Member shall, *ex officio* if its legislation so permits or at the request of an interested party, refuse or invalidate the registration of a trademark which contains or consists of a geographical indication with respect to goods not originating in the territory indicated, if use of the indication in the trademark for such goods in that Member is of such a nature as to mislead the public as to the true place of origin.
4. The protection under paragraphs 1, 2 and 3 shall be applicable against a geographical indication which, although literally true as to the territory, region or locality in which the goods originate, falsely represents to the public that the goods originate in another territory.

Article 23 - Additional Protection for Geographical Indications for Wines and Spirits

1. Each Member shall provide the legal means for interested parties to prevent use of a geographical indication identifying wines for wines not originating in the place indicated by the geographical indication in question or identifying spirits for spirits not originating in the place indicated by the geographical indication in question, even where the true origin of the goods is indicated or the geographical indication is used in translation or accompanied by expressions such as "kind", "type", "style", "imitation" or the like.[4]
2. The registration of a trademark for wines which contains or consists of a geographical indication identifying wines or for spirits which contains or consists of a geographical indication identifying spirits shall be refused or invalidated, *ex officio* if a Member's legislation so permits or at the request of an interested party, with respect to such wines or spirits not having this origin.
3. In the case of homonymous geographical indications for wines, protection shall be accorded to each indication, subject to the provisions of paragraph 4 of Article 22. Each Member shall determine the practical conditions under which the homonymous indications in question will

---

[4] Notwithstanding the first sentence of Article 42, Members may, with respect to these obligations, instead provide for enforcement by administrative action.

be differentiated from each other, taking into account the need to ensure equitable treatment of the producers concerned and that consumers are not misled.
4. In order to facilitate the protection of geographical indications for wines, negotiations shall be undertaken in the Council for TRIPS concerning the establishment of a multilateral system of notification and registration of geographical indications for wines eligible for protection in those Members participating in the system.

Article 24 - International Negotiations; Exceptions

1. Members agree to enter into negotiations aimed at increasing the protection of individual geographical indications under Article 23. The provisions of paragraphs 4 through 8 below shall not be used by a Member to refuse to conduct negotiations or to conclude bilateral or multilateral agreements. In the context of such negotiations, Members shall be willing to consider the continued applicability of these provisions to individual geographical indications whose use was the subject of such negotiations.
2. The Council for TRIPS shall keep under review the application of the provisions of this Section; the first such review shall take place within two years of the entry into force of the WTO Agreement. Any matter affecting the compliance with the obligations under these provisions may be drawn to the attention of the Council, which, at the request of a Member, shall consult with any Member or Members in respect of such matter in respect of which it has not been possible to find a satisfactory solution through bilateral or plurilateral consultations between the Members concerned. The Council shall take such action as may be agreed to facilitate the operation and further the objectives of this Section.
3. In implementing this Section, a Member shall not diminish the protection of geographical indications that existed in that Member immediately prior to the date of entry into force of the WTO Agreement.
4. Nothing in this Section shall require a Member to prevent continued and similar use of a particular geographical indication of another Member identifying wines or spirits in connection with goods or services by any of its nationals or domiciliaries who have used that geographical indication in a continuous manner with regard to the same or related goods or services in the territory of that Member either (*a*) for at least 10 years preceding 15 April 1994 or (*b*) in good faith preceding that date.
5. Where a trademark has been applied for or registered in good faith, or where rights to a trademark have been acquired through use in good faith either:
(a) before the date of application of these provisions in that Member as defined in Part VI; or
(b) before the geographical indication is protected in its country of origin;
measures adopted to implement this Section shall not prejudice eligibility for or the validity of the registration of a trademark, or the right to use a trademark, on the basis that such a trademark is identical with, or similar to, a geographical indication.
6. Nothing in this Section shall require a Member to apply its provisions in respect of a geographical indication of any other Member with respect to goods or services for which the relevant indication is identical with the term customary in common language as the common name for such goods or services in the territory of that Member. Nothing in this Section shall require a Member to apply its provisions in respect of a geographical indication of any other Member with respect to products of the vine for which the relevant indication is identical with the customary name of a grape variety existing in the territory of that Member as of the date of entry into force of the WTO Agreement.
7. A Member may provide that any request made under this Section in connection with the use or registration of a trademark must be presented within five years after the adverse use of the protected indication has become generally known in that Member or after the date of registration of the trademark in that Member provided that the trademark has been published by that date, if such date is earlier than the date on which the adverse use became generally

known in that Member, provided that the geographical indication is not used or registered in bad faith.
8. The provisions of this Section shall in no way prejudice the right of any person to use, in the course of trade, that person's name or the name of that person's predecessor in business, except where such name is used in such a manner as to mislead the public.
9. There shall be no obligation under this Agreement to protect geographical indications which are not or cease to be protected in their country of origin, or which have fallen into disuse in that country.

SECTION 4: INDUSTRIAL DESIGNS

Article 25 - Requirements for Protection

1. Members shall provide for the protection of independently created industrial designs that are new or original. Members may provide that designs are not new or original if they do not significantly differ from known designs or combinations of known design features. Members may provide that such protection shall not extend to designs dictated essentially by technical or functional considerations.
2. Each Member shall ensure that requirements for securing protection for textile designs, in particular in regard to any cost, examination or publication, do not unreasonably impair the opportunity to seek and obtain such protection. Members shall be free to meet this obligation through industrial design law or through copyright law.

Article 26 - Protection

1. The owner of a protected industrial design shall have the right to prevent third parties not having the owner's consent from making, selling or importing articles bearing or embodying a design which is a copy, or substantially a copy, of the protected design, when such acts are undertaken for commercial purposes.
2. Members may provide limited exceptions to the protection of industrial designs, provided that such exceptions do not unreasonably conflict with the normal exploitation of protected industrial designs and do not unreasonably prejudice the legitimate interests of the owner of the protected design, taking account of the legitimate interests of third parties.
3. The duration of protection available shall amount to at least 10 years.

SECTION 5: PATENTS

Article 27 - Patentable Subject Matter

1. Subject to the provisions of paragraphs 2 and 3, patents shall be available for any inventions, whether products or processes, in all fields of technology, provided that they are new, involve an inventive step and are capable of industrial application.[5] Subject to paragraph 4 of Article 65, paragraph 8 of Article 70 and paragraph 3 of this Article, patents shall be available and patent rights enjoyable without discrimination as to the place of invention, the field of technology and whether products are imported or locally produced.
2. Members may exclude from patentability inventions, the prevention within their territory of the commercial exploitation of which is necessary to protect *ordre public* or morality, including to protect human, animal or plant life or health or to avoid serious prejudice to the

---

[5] For the purposes of this Article, the terms "inventive step" and "capable of industrial application" may be deemed by a Member to be synonymous with the terms "non-obvious" and "useful" respectively.

environment, provided that such exclusion is not made merely because the exploitation is prohibited by their law.
3. Members may also exclude from patentability:
(a) diagnostic, therapeutic and surgical methods for the treatment of humans or animals;
(b) plants and animals other than micro-organisms, and essentially biological processes for the production of plants or animals other than non-biological and microbiological processes. However, Members shall provide for the protection of plant varieties either by patents or by an effective *sui generis* system or by any combination thereof. The provisions of this subparagraph shall be reviewed four years after the date of entry into force of the WTO Agreement.

Article 28 - Rights Conferred

1. A patent shall confer on its owner the following exclusive rights:
(a) where the subject matter of a patent is a product, to prevent third parties not having the owner's consent from the acts of: making, using, offering for sale, selling, or importing[6] for these purposes that product;
(b) where the subject matter of a patent is a process, to prevent third parties not having the owner's consent from the act of using the process, and from the acts of: using, offering for sale, selling, or importing for these purposes at least the product obtained directly by that process.
2. Patent owners shall also have the right to assign, or transfer by succession, the patent and to conclude licensing contracts.

Article 29 - Conditions on Patent Applicants

1. Members shall require that an applicant for a patent shall disclose the invention in a manner sufficiently clear and complete for the invention to be carried out by a person skilled in the art and may require the applicant to indicate the best mode for carrying out the invention known to the inventor at the filing date or, where priority is claimed, at the priority date of the application.
2. Members may require an applicant for a patent to provide information concerning the applicant's corresponding foreign applications and grants.

Article 30 - Exceptions to Rights Conferred

Members may provide limited exceptions to the exclusive rights conferred by a patent, provided that such exceptions do not unreasonably conflict with a normal exploitation of the patent and do not unreasonably prejudice the legitimate interests of the patent owner, taking account of the legitimate interests of third parties.

Article 31 - Other Use Without Authorization of the Right Holder

Where the law of a Member allows for other use[7] of the subject matter of a patent without the authorization of the right holder, including use by the government or third parties authorized by the government, the following provisions shall be respected:
(a) authorization of such use shall be considered on its individual merits;
(b) such use may only be permitted if, prior to such use, the proposed user has made efforts to obtain authorization from the right holder on reasonable commercial terms and conditions and that such efforts have not been successful within a reasonable period of time. This

---

[6] This right, like all other rights conferred under this Agreement in respect of the use, sale, importation or other distribution of goods, is subject to the provisions of Article 6.

[7] "Other use" refers to use other than that allowed under Article 30.

requirement may be waived by a Member in the case of a national emergency or other circumstances of extreme urgency or in cases of public non-commercial use. In situations of national emergency or other circumstances of extreme urgency, the right holder shall, nevertheless, be notified as soon as reasonably practicable. In the case of public non-commercial use, where the government or contractor, without making a patent search, knows or has demonstrable grounds to know that a valid patent is or will be used by or for the government, the right holder shall be informed promptly;

(c) the scope and duration of such use shall be limited to the purpose for which it was authorized, and in the case of semi-conductor technology shall only be for public non-commercial use or to remedy a practice determined after judicial or administrative process to be anti-competitive;

(d) such use shall be non-exclusive;

(e) such use shall be non-assignable, except with that part of the enterprise or goodwill which enjoys such use;

(f) any such use shall be authorized predominantly for the supply of the domestic market of the Member authorizing such use;

(g) authorization for such use shall be liable, subject to adequate protection of the legitimate interests of the persons so authorized, to be terminated if and when the circumstances which led to it cease to exist and are unlikely to recur. The competent authority shall have the authority to review, upon motivated request, the continued existence of these circumstances;

(h) the right holder shall be paid adequate remuneration in the circumstances of each case, taking into account the economic value of the authorization;

(i) the legal validity of any decision relating to the authorization of such use shall be subject to judicial review or other independent review by a distinct higher authority in that Member;

(j) any decision relating to the remuneration provided in respect of such use shall be subject to judicial review or other independent review by a distinct higher authority in that Member;

(k) Members are not obliged to apply the conditions set forth in subparagraphs (b) and (f) where such use is permitted to remedy a practice determined after judicial or administrative process to be anti-competitive. The need to correct anti-competitive practices may be taken into account in determining the amount of remuneration in such cases. Competent authorities shall have the authority to refuse termination of authorization if and when the conditions which led to such authorization are likely to recur;

(l) where such use is authorized to permit the exploitation of a patent ("the second patent") which cannot be exploited without infringing another patent ("the first patent"), the following additional conditions shall apply:

  (i) the invention claimed in the second patent shall involve an important technical advance of considerable economic significance in relation to the invention claimed in the first patent;

  (ii) the owner of the first patent shall be entitled to a cross-licence on reasonable terms to use the invention claimed in the second patent; and

  (iii) the use authorized in respect of the first patent shall be non-assignable except with the assignment of the second patent.

Article 32 - Revocation/Forfeiture

An opportunity for judicial review of any decision to revoke or forfeit a patent shall be available.

Article 33 - Term of Protection

The term of protection available shall not end before the expiration of a period of twenty years counted from the filing date.[8]

Article 34 - Process Patents: Burden of Proof

1. For the purposes of civil proceedings in respect of the infringement of the rights of the owner referred to in paragraph 1(b) of Article 28, if the subject matter of a patent is a process for obtaining a product, the judicial authorities shall have the authority to order the defendant to prove that the process to obtain an identical product is different from the patented process. Therefore, Members shall provide, in at least one of the following circumstances, that any identical product when produced without the consent of the patent owner shall, in the absence of proof to the contrary, be deemed to have been obtained by the patented process:
   (a) if the product obtained by the patented process is new;
   (b) if there is a substantial likelihood that the identical product was made by the process and the owner of the patent has been unable through reasonable efforts to determine the process actually used.
2. Any Member shall be free to provide that the burden of proof indicated in paragraph 1 shall be on the alleged infringer only if the condition referred to in subparagraph (a) is fulfilled or only if the condition referred to in subparagraph (b) is fulfilled.
3. In the adduction of proof to the contrary, the legitimate interests of defendants in protecting their manufacturing and business secrets shall be taken into account.

SECTION 6: LAYOUT-DESIGNS (TOPOGRAPHIES) OF INTEGRATED CIRCUITS

Article 35 - Relation to the IPIC Treaty

Members agree to provide protection to the layout-designs (topographies) of integrated circuits (referred to in this Agreement as "layout-designs") in accordance with Articles 2 through 7 (other than paragraph 3 of Article 6), Article 12 and paragraph 3 of Article 16 of the Treaty on Intellectual Property in Respect of Integrated Circuits and, in addition, to comply with the following provisions.

Article 36 - Scope of the Protection

Subject to the provisions of paragraph 1 of Article 37, Members shall consider unlawful the following acts if performed without the authorization of the right holder:[9] importing, selling, or otherwise distributing for commercial purposes a protected layout-design, an integrated circuit in which a protected layout-design is incorporated, or an article incorporating such an integrated circuit only in so far as it continues to contain an unlawfully reproduced layout-design.

Article 37 - Acts Not Requiring the Authorization of the Right Holder

1. Notwithstanding Article 36, no Member shall consider unlawful the performance of any of the acts referred to in that Article in respect of an integrated circuit incorporating an unlawfully reproduced layout-design or any article incorporating such an integrated circuit where the person performing or ordering such acts did not know and had no reasonable

---

[8] It is understood that those Members which do not have a system of original grant may provide that the term of protection shall be computed from the filing date in the system of original grant.

[9] The term "right holder" in this Section shall be understood as having the same meaning as the term "holder of the right" in the IPIC Treaty.

ground to know, when acquiring the integrated circuit or article incorporating such an integrated circuit, that it incorporated an unlawfully reproduced layout-design. Members shall provide that, after the time that such person has received sufficient notice that the layout-design was unlawfully reproduced, that person may perform any of the acts with respect to the stock on hand or ordered before such time, but shall be liable to pay to the right holder a sum equivalent to a reasonable royalty such as would be payable under a freely negotiated licence in respect of such a layout-design.

2. The conditions set out in subparagraphs (a) through (k) of Article 31 shall apply *mutatis mutandis* in the event of any non-voluntary licensing of a layout-design or of its use by or for the government without the authorization of the right holder.

Article 38 - Term of Protection

1. In Members requiring registration as a condition of protection, the term of protection of layout-designs shall not end before the expiration of a period of 10 years counted from the date of filing an application for registration or from the first commercial exploitation wherever in the world it occurs.
2. In Members not requiring registration as a condition for protection, layout-designs shall be protected for a term of no less than 10 years from the date of the first commercial exploitation wherever in the world it occurs.
3. Notwithstanding paragraphs 1 and 2, a Member may provide that protection shall lapse 15 years after the creation of the layout-design.

SECTION 7: PROTECTION OF UNDISCLOSED INFORMATION

Article 39

1. In the course of ensuring effective protection against unfair competition as provided in Article 10*bis* of the Paris Convention (1967), Members shall protect undisclosed information in accordance with paragraph 2 and data submitted to governments or governmental agencies in accordance with paragraph 3.
2. Natural and legal persons shall have the possibility of preventing information lawfully within their control from being disclosed to, acquired by, or used by others without their consent in a manner contrary to honest commercial practices[10] so long as such information:
(a) is secret in the sense that it is not, as a body or in the precise configuration and assembly of its components, generally known among or readily accessible to persons within the circles that normally deal with the kind of information in question;
(b) has commercial value because it is secret; and
(c) has been subject to reasonable steps under the circumstances, by the person lawfully in control of the information, to keep it secret.
3. Members, when requiring, as a condition of approving the marketing of pharmaceutical or of agricultural chemical products which utilize new chemical entities, the submission of undisclosed test or other data, the origination of which involves a considerable effort, shall protect such data against unfair commercial use. In addition, Members shall protect such data against disclosure, except where necessary to protect the public, or unless steps are taken to ensure that the data are protected against unfair commercial use.

---

[10] For the purpose of this provision, "a manner contrary to honest commercial practices" shall mean at least practices such as breach of contract, breach of confidence and inducement to breach, and includes the acquisition of undisclosed information by third parties who knew, or were grossly negligent in failing to know, that such practices were involved in the acquisition.

SECTION 8: CONTROL OF ANTI-COMPETITIVE PRACTICES IN CONTRACTUAL LICENCES

Article 40

1. Members agree that some licensing practices or conditions pertaining to intellectual property rights which restrain competition may have adverse effects on trade and may impede the transfer and dissemination of technology.
2. Nothing in this Agreement shall prevent Members from specifying in their legislation licensing practices or conditions that may in particular cases constitute an abuse of intellectual property rights having an adverse effect on competition in the relevant market. As provided above, a Member may adopt, consistently with the other provisions of this Agreement, appropriate measures to prevent or control such practices, which may include for example exclusive grantback conditions, conditions preventing challenges to validity and coercive package licensing, in the light of the relevant laws and regulations of that Member.
3. Each Member shall enter, upon request, into consultations with any other Member which has cause to believe that an intellectual property right owner that is a national or domiciliary of the Member to which the request for consultations has been addressed is undertaking practices in violation of the requesting Member's laws and regulations on the subject matter of this Section, and which wishes to secure compliance with such legislation, without prejudice to any action under the law and to the full freedom of an ultimate decision of either Member. The Member addressed shall accord full and sympathetic consideration to, and shall afford adequate opportunity for, consultations with the requesting Member, and shall cooperate through supply of publicly available non-confidential information of relevance to the matter in question and of other information available to the Member, subject to domestic law and to the conclusion of mutually satisfactory agreements concerning the safeguarding of its confidentiality by the requesting Member.
4. A Member whose nationals or domiciliaries are subject to proceedings in another Member concerning alleged violation of that other Member's laws and regulations on the subject matter of this Section shall, upon request, be granted an opportunity for consultations by the other Member under the same conditions as those foreseen in paragraph 3.

PART III - ENFORCEMENT OF INTELLECTUAL PROPERTY RIGHTS

SECTION 1: GENERAL OBLIGATIONS

Article 41

1. Members shall ensure that enforcement procedures as specified in this Part are available under their law so as to permit effective action against any act of infringement of intellectual property rights covered by this Agreement, including expeditious remedies to prevent infringements and remedies which constitute a deterrent to further infringements. These procedures shall be applied in such a manner as to avoid the creation of barriers to legitimate trade and to provide for safeguards against their abuse.
2. Procedures concerning the enforcement of intellectual property rights shall be fair and equitable. They shall not be unnecessarily complicated or costly, or entail unreasonable time-limits or unwarranted delays.
3. Decisions on the merits of a case shall preferably be in writing and reasoned. They shall be made available at least to the parties to the proceeding without undue delay. Decisions on the merits of a case shall be based only on evidence in respect of which parties were offered the opportunity to be heard.

4. Parties to a proceeding shall have an opportunity for review by a judicial authority of final administrative decisions and, subject to jurisdictional provisions in a Member's law concerning the importance of a case, of at least the legal aspects of initial judicial decisions on the merits of a case. However, there shall be no obligation to provide an opportunity for review of acquittals in criminal cases.
5. It is understood that this Part does not create any obligation to put in place a judicial system for the enforcement of intellectual property rights distinct from that for the enforcement of law in general, nor does it affect the capacity of Members to enforce their law in general. Nothing in this Part creates any obligation with respect to the distribution of resources as between enforcement of intellectual property rights and the enforcement of law in general.

SECTION 2: CIVIL AND ADMINISTRATIVE PROCEDURES AND REMEDIES

Article 42 - Fair and Equitable Procedures

Members shall make available to right holders[11] civil judicial procedures concerning the enforcement of any intellectual property right covered by this Agreement. Defendants shall have the right to written notice which is timely and contains sufficient detail, including the basis of the claims. Parties shall be allowed to be represented by independent legal counsel, and procedures shall not impose overly burdensome requirements concerning mandatory personal appearances. All parties to such procedures shall be duly entitled to substantiate their claims and to present all relevant evidence. The procedure shall provide a means to identify and protect confidential information, unless this would be contrary to existing constitutional requirements.

Article 43 - Evidence

1. The judicial authorities shall have the authority, where a party has presented reasonably available evidence sufficient to support its claims and has specified evidence relevant to substantiation of its claims which lies in the control of the opposing party, to order that this evidence be produced by the opposing party, subject in appropriate cases to conditions which ensure the protection of confidential information.
2. In cases in which a party to a proceeding voluntarily and without good reason refuses access to, or otherwise does not provide necessary information within a reasonable period, or significantly impedes a procedure relating to an enforcement action, a Member may accord judicial authorities the authority to make preliminary and final determinations, affirmative or negative, on the basis of the information presented to them, including the complaint or the allegation presented by the party adversely affected by the denial of access to information, subject to providing the parties an opportunity to be heard on the allegations or evidence.

Article 44 - Injunctions

1. The judicial authorities shall have the authority to order a party to desist from an infringement, *inter alia* to prevent the entry into the channels of commerce in their jurisdiction of imported goods that involve the infringement of an intellectual property right, immediately after customs clearance of such goods. Members are not obliged to accord such authority in respect of protected subject matter acquired or ordered by a person prior to knowing or having reasonable grounds to know that dealing in such subject matter would entail the infringement of an intellectual property right.
2. Notwithstanding the other provisions of this Part and provided that the provisions of Part II specifically addressing use by governments, or by third parties authorized by a government,

---

[11] For the purpose of this Part, the term "right holder" includes federations and associations having legal standing to assert such rights.

without the authorization of the right holder are complied with, Members may limit the remedies available against such use to payment of remuneration in accordance with subparagraph (h) of Article 31. In other cases, the remedies under this Part shall apply or, where these remedies are inconsistent with a Member's law, declaratory judgments and adequate compensation shall be available.

Article 45 - Damages

1. The judicial authorities shall have the authority to order the infringer to pay the right holder damages adequate to compensate for the injury the right holder has suffered because of an infringement of that person's intellectual property right by an infringer who knowingly, or with reasonable grounds to know, engaged in infringing activity.
2. The judicial authorities shall also have the authority to order the infringer to pay the right holder expenses, which may include appropriate attorney's fees. In appropriate cases, Members may authorize the judicial authorities to order recovery of profits and/or payment of pre-established damages even where the infringer did not knowingly, or with reasonable grounds to know, engage in infringing activity.

Article 46 - Other Remedies

In order to create an effective deterrent to infringement, the judicial authorities shall have the authority to order that goods that they have found to be infringing be, without compensation of any sort, disposed of outside the channels of commerce in such a manner as to avoid any harm caused to the right holder, or, unless this would be contrary to existing constitutional requirements, destroyed. The judicial authorities shall also have the authority to order that materials and implements the predominant use of which has been in the creation of the infringing goods be, without compensation of any sort, disposed of outside the channels of commerce in such a manner as to minimize the risks of further infringements. In considering such requests, the need for proportionality between the seriousness of the infringement and the remedies ordered as well as the interests of third parties shall be taken into account. In regard to counterfeit trademark goods, the simple removal of the trademark unlawfully affixed shall not be sufficient, other than in exceptional cases, to permit release of the goods into the channels of commerce.

Article 47 - Right of Information

Members may provide that the judicial authorities shall have the authority, unless this would be out of proportion to the seriousness of the infringement, to order the infringer to inform the right holder of the identity of third persons involved in the production and distribution of the infringing goods or services and of their channels of distribution.

Article 48 - Indemnification of the Defendant

1. The judicial authorities shall have the authority to order a party at whose request measures were taken and who has abused enforcement procedures to provide to a party wrongfully enjoined or restrained adequate compensation for the injury suffered because of such abuse. The judicial authorities shall also have the authority to order the applicant to pay the defendant expenses, which may include appropriate attorney's fees.
2. In respect of the administration of any law pertaining to the protection or enforcement of intellectual property rights, Members shall only exempt both public authorities and officials from liability to appropriate remedial measures where actions are taken or intended in good faith in the course of the administration of that law.

Article 49 - Administrative Procedures

To the extent that any civil remedy can be ordered as a result of administrative procedures on the merits of a case, such procedures shall conform to principles equivalent in substance to those set forth in this Section.

SECTION 3: PROVISIONAL MEASURES

Article 50

1. The judicial authorities shall have the authority to order prompt and effective provisional measures:
   (a) to prevent an infringement of any intellectual property right from occurring, and in particular to prevent the entry into the channels of commerce in their jurisdiction of goods, including imported goods immediately after customs clearance;
   (b) to preserve relevant evidence in regard to the alleged infringement.
2. The judicial authorities shall have the authority to adopt provisional measures *inaudita altera parte* where appropriate, in particular where any delay is likely to cause irreparable harm to the right holder, or where there is a demonstrable risk of evidence being destroyed.
3. The judicial authorities shall have the authority to require the applicant to provide any reasonably available evidence in order to satisfy themselves with a sufficient degree of certainty that the applicant is the right holder and that the applicant's right is being infringed or that such infringement is imminent, and to order the applicant to provide a security or equivalent assurance sufficient to protect the defendant and to prevent abuse.
4. Where provisional measures have been adopted *inaudita altera parte*, the parties affected shall be given notice, without delay after the execution of the measures at the latest. A review, including a right to be heard, shall take place upon request of the defendant with a view to deciding, within a reasonable period after the notification of the measures, whether these measures shall be modified, revoked or confirmed.
5. The applicant may be required to supply other information necessary for the identification of the goods concerned by the authority that will execute the provisional measures.
6. Without prejudice to paragraph 4, provisional measures taken on the basis of paragraphs 1 and 2 shall, upon request by the defendant, be revoked or otherwise cease to have effect, if proceedings leading to a decision on the merits of the case are not initiated within a reasonable period, to be determined by the judicial authority ordering the measures where a Member's law so permits or, in the absence of such a determination, not to exceed 20 working days or 31 calendar days, whichever is the longer.
7. Where the provisional measures are revoked or where they lapse due to any act or omission by the applicant, or where it is subsequently found that there has been no infringement or threat of infringement of an intellectual property right, the judicial authorities shall have the authority to order the applicant, upon request of the defendant, to provide the defendant appropriate compensation for any injury caused by these measures.
8. To the extent that any provisional measure can be ordered as a result of administrative procedures, such procedures shall conform to principles equivalent in substance to those set forth in this Section.

SECTION 4: SPECIAL REQUIREMENTS RELATED TO BORDER MEASURES[12]

Article 51 - Suspension of Release by Customs Authorities

Members shall, in conformity with the provisions set out below, adopt procedures[13] to enable a right holder, who has valid grounds for suspecting that the importation of counterfeit trademark or pirated copyright goods[14] may take place, to lodge an application in writing with competent authorities, administrative or judicial, for the suspension by the customs authorities of the release into free circulation of such goods. Members may enable such an application to be made in respect of goods which involve other infringements of intellectual property rights, provided that the requirements of this Section are met. Members may also provide for corresponding procedures concerning the suspension by the customs authorities of the release of infringing goods destined for exportation from their territories.

Article 52 - Application

Any right holder initiating the procedures under Article 51 shall be required to provide adequate evidence to satisfy the competent authorities that, under the laws of the country of importation, there is *prima facie* an infringement of the right holder's intellectual property right and to supply a sufficiently detailed description of the goods to make them readily recognizable by the customs authorities. The competent authorities shall inform the applicant within a reasonable period whether they have accepted the application and, where determined by the competent authorities, the period for which the customs authorities will take action.

Article 53 - Security or Equivalent Assurance

1. The competent authorities shall have the authority to require an applicant to provide a security or equivalent assurance sufficient to protect the defendant and the competent authorities and to prevent abuse. Such security or equivalent assurance shall not unreasonably deter recourse to these procedures.
2. Where pursuant to an application under this Section the release of goods involving industrial designs, patents, layout-designs or undisclosed information into free circulation has been suspended by customs authorities on the basis of a decision other than by a judicial or other independent authority, and the period provided for in Article 55 has expired without the granting of provisional relief by the duly empowered authority, and provided that all other conditions for importation have been complied with, the owner, importer, or consignee of such goods shall be entitled to their release on the posting of a security in an amount sufficient to protect the right holder for any infringement. Payment of such security shall not prejudice any other remedy available to the right holder, it being understood that the security shall be released if the right holder fails to pursue the right of action within a reasonable period of time.

---

[12] Where a Member has dismantled substantially all controls over movement of goods across its border with another Member with which it forms part of a customs union, it shall not be required to apply the provisions of this Section at that border.

[13] It is understood that there shall be no obligation to apply such procedures to imports of goods put on the market in another country by or with the consent of the right holder, or to goods in transit.

[14] For the purposes of this Agreement:
(a) "counterfeit trademark goods" shall mean any goods, including packaging, bearing without authorization a trademark which is identical to the trademark validly registered in respect of such goods, or which cannot be distinguished in its essential aspects from such a trademark, and which thereby infringes the rights of the owner of the trademark in question under the law of the country of importation;
(b) "pirated copyright goods" shall mean any goods which are copies made without the consent of the right holder or person duly authorized by the right holder in the country of production and which are made directly or indirectly from an article where the making of that copy would have constituted an infringement of a copyright or a related right under the law of the country of importation.

Article 54 - Notice of Suspension

The importer and the applicant shall be promptly notified of the suspension of the release of goods according to Article 51.

Article 55 - Duration of Suspension

If, within a period not exceeding 10 working days after the applicant has been served notice of the suspension, the customs authorities have not been informed that proceedings leading to a decision on the merits of the case have been initiated by a party other than the defendant, or that the duly empowered authority has taken provisional measures prolonging the suspension of the release of the goods, the goods shall be released, provided that all other conditions for importation or exportation have been complied with; in appropriate cases, this time-limit may be extended by another 10 working days. If proceedings leading to a decision on the merits of the case have been initiated, a review, including a right to be heard, shall take place upon request of the defendant with a view to deciding, within a reasonable period, whether these measures shall be modified, revoked or confirmed. Notwithstanding the above, where the suspension of the release of goods is carried out or continued in accordance with a provisional judicial measure, the provisions of paragraph 6 of Article 50 shall apply.

Article 56 - Indemnification of the Importer and of the Owner of the Goods

Relevant authorities shall have the authority to order the applicant to pay the importer, the consignee and the owner of the goods appropriate compensation for any injury caused to them through the wrongful detention of goods or through the detention of goods released pursuant to Article 55.

Article 57 - Right of Inspection and Information

Without prejudice to the protection of confidential information, Members shall provide the competent authorities the authority to give the right holder sufficient opportunity to have any goods detained by the customs authorities inspected in order to substantiate the right holder's claims. The competent authorities shall also have authority to give the importer an equivalent opportunity to have any such goods inspected. Where a positive determination has been made on the merits of a case, Members may provide the competent authorities the authority to inform the right holder of the names and addresses of the consignor, the importer and the consignee and of the quantity of the goods in question.

Article 58 - Ex Officio Action

Where Members require competent authorities to act upon their own initiative and to suspend the release of goods in respect of which they have acquired *prima facie* evidence that an intellectual property right is being infringed:
(a) the competent authorities may at any time seek from the right holder any information that may assist them to exercise these powers;
(b) the importer and the right holder shall be promptly notified of the suspension. Where the importer has lodged an appeal against the suspension with the competent authorities, the suspension shall be subject to the conditions, *mutatis mutandis*, set out at Article 55;
(c) Members shall only exempt both public authorities and officials from liability to appropriate remedial measures where actions are taken or intended in good faith.

Article 59 - Remedies

Without prejudice to other rights of action open to the right holder and subject to the right of the defendant to seek review by a judicial authority, competent authorities shall have the authority to order the destruction or disposal of infringing goods in accordance with the principles set out in Article 46. In regard to counterfeit trademark goods, the authorities shall not allow the re-exportation of the infringing goods in an unaltered state or subject them to a different customs procedure, other than in exceptional circumstances.

Article 60 - De Minimis Imports

Members may exclude from the application of the above provisions small quantities of goods of a non-commercial nature contained in travellers' personal luggage or sent in small consignments.

SECTION 5: CRIMINAL PROCEDURES

Article 61

Members shall provide for criminal procedures and penalties to be applied at least in cases of wilful trademark counterfeiting or copyright piracy on a commercial scale. Remedies available shall include imprisonment and/or monetary fines sufficient to provide a deterrent, consistently with the level of penalties applied for crimes of a corresponding gravity. In appropriate cases, remedies available shall also include the seizure, forfeiture and destruction of the infringing goods and of any materials and implements the predominant use of which has been in the commission of the offence. Members may provide for criminal procedures and penalties to be applied in other cases of infringement of intellectual property rights, in particular where they are committed wilfully and on a commercial scale.

PART IV - ACQUISITION AND MAINTENANCE OF INTELLECTUAL PROPERTY RIGHTS AND RELATED *INTER-PARTES* PROCEDURES

Article 62

1. Members may require, as a condition of the acquisition or maintenance of the intellectual property rights provided for under Sections 2 through 6 of Part II, compliance with reasonable procedures and formalities. Such procedures and formalities shall be consistent with the provisions of this Agreement.
2. Where the acquisition of an intellectual property right is subject to the right being granted or registered, Members shall ensure that the procedures for grant or registration, subject to compliance with the substantive conditions for acquisition of the right, permit the granting or registration of the right within a reasonable period of time so as to avoid unwarranted curtailment of the period of protection.
3. Article 4 of the Paris Convention (1967) shall apply *mutatis mutandis* to service marks.
4. Procedures concerning the acquisition or maintenance of intellectual property rights and, where a Member's law provides for such procedures, administrative revocation and *inter partes* procedures such as opposition, revocation and cancellation, shall be governed by the general principles set out in paragraphs 2 and 3 of Article 41.
5. Final administrative decisions in any of the procedures referred to under paragraph 4 shall be subject to review by a judicial or quasi-judicial authority. However, there shall be no obligation to provide an opportunity for such review of decisions in cases of unsuccessful opposition or administrative revocation, provided that the grounds for such procedures can be the subject of invalidation procedures.

PART V - DISPUTE PREVENTION AND SETTLEMENT

Article 63 - Transparency

1. Laws and regulations, and final judicial decisions and administrative rulings of general application, made effective by a Member pertaining to the subject matter of this Agreement (the availability, scope, acquisition, enforcement and prevention of the abuse of intellectual property rights) shall be published, or where such publication is not practicable made publicly available, in a national language, in such a manner as to enable governments and right holders to become acquainted with them. Agreements concerning the subject matter of this Agreement which are in force between the government or a governmental agency of a Member and the government or a governmental agency of another Member shall also be published.
2. Members shall notify the laws and regulations referred to in paragraph 1 to the Council for TRIPS in order to assist that Council in its review of the operation of this Agreement. The Council shall attempt to minimize the burden on Members in carrying out this obligation and may decide to waive the obligation to notify such laws and regulations directly to the Council if consultations with WIPO on the establishment of a common register containing these laws and regulations are successful. The Council shall also consider in this connection any action required regarding notifications pursuant to the obligations under this Agreement stemming from the provisions of Article 6*ter* of the Paris Convention (1967).
3. Each Member shall be prepared to supply, in response to a written request from another Member, information of the sort referred to in paragraph 1. A Member, having reason to believe that a specific judicial decision or administrative ruling or bilateral agreement in the area of intellectual property rights affects its rights under this Agreement, may also request in writing to be given access to or be informed in sufficient detail of such specific judicial decisions or administrative rulings or bilateral agreements.
4. Nothing in paragraphs 1, 2 and 3 shall require Members to disclose confidential information which would impede law enforcement or otherwise be contrary to the public interest or would prejudice the legitimate commercial interests of particular enterprises, public or private.

Article 64 - Dispute Settlement

1. The provisions of Articles XXII and XXIII of GATT 1994 as elaborated and applied by the Dispute Settlement Understanding shall apply to consultations and the settlement of disputes under this Agreement except as otherwise specifically provided herein.
2. Subparagraphs 1(b) and 1(c) of Article XXIII of GATT 1994 shall not apply to the settlement of disputes under this Agreement for a period of five years from the date of entry into force of the WTO Agreement.
3. During the time period referred to in paragraph 2, the Council for TRIPS shall examine the scope and modalities for complaints of the type provided for under subparagraphs 1(b) and 1(c) of Article XXIII of GATT 1994 made pursuant to this Agreement, and submit its recommendations to the Ministerial Conference for approval. Any decision of the Ministerial Conference to approve such recommendations or to extend the period in paragraph 2 shall be made only by consensus, and approved recommendations shall be effective for all Members without further formal acceptance process.

PART VI - TRANSITIONAL ARRANGEMENTS

Article 65 - Transitional Arrangements

1. Subject to the provisions of paragraphs 2, 3 and 4, no Member shall be obliged to apply the provisions of this Agreement before the expiry of a general period of one year following the date of entry into force of the WTO Agreement.
2. A developing country Member is entitled to delay for a further period of four years the date of application, as defined in paragraph 1, of the provisions of this Agreement other than Articles 3, 4 and 5.
3. Any other Member which is in the process of transformation from a centrally-planned into a market, free-enterprise economy and which is undertaking structural reform of its intellectual property system and facing special problems in the preparation and implementation of intellectual property laws and regulations, may also benefit from a period of delay as foreseen in paragraph 2.
4. To the extent that a developing country Member is obliged by this Agreement to extend product patent protection to areas of technology not so protectable in its territory on the general date of application of this Agreement for that Member, as defined in paragraph 2, it may delay the application of the provisions on product patents of Section 5 of Part II to such areas of technology for an additional period of five years.
5. A Member availing itself of a transitional period under paragraphs 1, 2, 3 or 4 shall ensure that any changes in its laws, regulations and practice made during that period do not result in a lesser degree of consistency with the provisions of this Agreement.

Article 66 - Least-Developed Country Members

1. In view of the special needs and requirements of least-developed country Members, their economic, financial and administrative constraints, and their need for flexibility to create a viable technological base, such Members shall not be required to apply the provisions of this Agreement, other than Articles 3, 4 and 5, for a period of 10 years from the date of application as defined under paragraph 1 of Article 65. The Council for TRIPS shall, upon duly motivated request by a least-developed country Member, accord extensions of this period.
2. Developed country Members shall provide incentives to enterprises and institutions in their territories for the purpose of promoting and encouraging technology transfer to least-developed country Members in order to enable them to create a sound and viable technological base.

Article 67 - Technical Cooperation

In order to facilitate the implementation of this Agreement, developed country Members shall provide, on request and on mutually agreed terms and conditions, technical and financial cooperation in favour of developing and least-developed country Members. Such cooperation shall include assistance in the preparation of laws and regulations on the protection and enforcement of intellectual property rights as well as on the prevention of their abuse, and shall include support regarding the establishment or reinforcement of domestic offices and agencies relevant to these matters, including the training of personnel.

PART VII - INSTITUTIONAL ARRANGEMENTS; FINAL PROVISIONS

Article 68 - Council for Trade-Related Aspects of Intellectual Property Rights

The Council for TRIPS shall monitor the operation of this Agreement and, in particular, Members' compliance with their obligations hereunder, and shall afford Members the opportunity of consulting on matters relating to the trade-related aspects of intellectual property rights. It shall carry out such other responsibilities as assigned to it by the Members, and it shall, in particular, provide any assistance requested by them in the context of dispute settlement procedures. In carrying out its functions, the Council for TRIPS may consult with and seek information from any source it deems appropriate. In consultation with WIPO, the Council shall seek to establish, within one year of its first meeting, appropriate arrangements for cooperation with bodies of that Organization.

Article 69 - International Cooperation

Members agree to cooperate with each other with a view to eliminating international trade in goods infringing intellectual property rights. For this purpose, they shall establish and notify contact points in their administrations and be ready to exchange information on trade in infringing goods. They shall, in particular, promote the exchange of information and cooperation between customs authorities with regard to trade in counterfeit trademark goods and pirated copyright goods.

Article 70 - Protection of Existing Subject Matter

1. This Agreement does not give rise to obligations in respect of acts which occurred before the date of application of the Agreement for the Member in question.
2. Except as otherwise provided for in this Agreement, this Agreement gives rise to obligations in respect of all subject matter existing at the date of application of this Agreement for the Member in question, and which is protected in that Member on the said date, or which meets or comes subsequently to meet the criteria for protection under the terms of this Agreement. In respect of this paragraph and paragraphs 3 and 4, copyright obligations with respect to existing works shall be solely determined under Article 18 of the Berne Convention (1971), and obligations with respect to the rights of producers of phonograms and performers in existing phonograms shall be determined solely under Article 18 of the Berne Convention (1971) as made applicable under paragraph 6 of Article 14 of this Agreement.
3. There shall be no obligation to restore protection to subject matter which on the date of application of this Agreement for the Member in question has fallen into the public domain.
4. In respect of any acts in respect of specific objects embodying protected subject matter which become infringing under the terms of legislation in conformity with this Agreement, and which were commenced, or in respect of which a significant investment was made, before the date of acceptance of the WTO Agreement by that Member, any Member may provide for a limitation of the remedies available to the right holder as to the continued performance of such acts after the date of application of this Agreement for that Member. In such cases the Member shall, however, at least provide for the payment of equitable remuneration.
5. A Member is not obliged to apply the provisions of Article 11 and of paragraph 4 of Article 14 with respect to originals or copies purchased prior to the date of application of this Agreement for that Member.
6. Members shall not be required to apply Article 31, or the requirement in paragraph 1 of Article 27 that patent rights shall be enjoyable without discrimination as to the field of technology, to use without the authorization of the right holder where authorization for such use was granted by the government before the date this Agreement became known.

7. In the case of intellectual property rights for which protection is conditional upon registration, applications for protection which are pending on the date of application of this Agreement for the Member in question shall be permitted to be amended to claim any enhanced protection provided under the provisions of this Agreement. Such amendments shall not include new matter.
8. Where a Member does not make available as of the date of entry into force of the WTO Agreement patent protection for pharmaceutical and agricultural chemical products commensurate with its obligations under Article 27, that Member shall:
(a) notwithstanding the provisions of Part VI, provide as from the date of entry into force of the WTO Agreement a means by which applications for patents for such inventions can be filed;
(b) apply to these applications, as of the date of application of this Agreement, the criteria for patentability as laid down in this Agreement as if those criteria were being applied on the date of filing in that Member or, where priority is available and claimed, the priority date of the application; and
(c) provide patent protection in accordance with this Agreement as from the grant of the patent and for the remainder of the patent term, counted from the filing date in accordance with Article 33 of this Agreement, for those of these applications that meet the criteria for protection referred to in subparagraph (b).
9. Where a product is the subject of a patent application in a Member in accordance with paragraph 8(a), exclusive marketing rights shall be granted, notwithstanding the provisions of Part VI, for a period of five years after obtaining marketing approval in that Member or until a product patent is granted or rejected in that Member, whichever period is shorter, provided that, subsequent to the entry into force of the WTO Agreement, a patent application has been filed and a patent granted for that product in another Member and marketing approval obtained in such other Member.

Article 71 - Review and Amendment

1. The Council for TRIPS shall review the implementation of this Agreement after the expiration of the transitional period referred to in paragraph 2 of Article 65. The Council shall, having regard to the experience gained in its implementation, review it two years after that date, and at identical intervals thereafter. The Council may also undertake reviews in the light of any relevant new developments which might warrant modification or amendment of this Agreement.
2. Amendments merely serving the purpose of adjusting to higher levels of protection of intellectual property rights achieved, and in force, in other multilateral agreements and accepted under those agreements by all Members of the WTO may be referred to the Ministerial Conference for action in accordance with paragraph 6 of Article X of the WTO Agreement on the basis of a consensus proposal from the Council for TRIPS.

Article 72 - Reservations

Reservations may not be entered in respect of any of the provisions of this Agreement without the consent of the other Members.

Article 73 - Security Exceptions

Nothing in this Agreement shall be construed:
(a) to require a Member to furnish any information the disclosure of which it considers contrary to its essential security interests; or
(b) to prevent a Member from taking any action which it considers necessary for the protection of its essential security interests;
 (i) relating to fissionable materials or the materials from which they are derived;

(ii) relating to the traffic in arms, ammunition and implements of war and to such traffic in other goods and materials as is carried on directly or indirectly for the purpose of supplying a military establishment;
   (iii) taken in time of war or other emergency in international relations; or
(c) to prevent a Member from taking any action in pursuance of its obligations under the United Nations Charter for the maintenance of international peace and security.

WIPO COPYRIGHT TREATY

adopted by the Diplomatic Conference on December 20, 1996

(Source: http://www.wipo.org/clea/en/index.html)

Preamble

The Contracting Parties,

Desiring to develop and maintain the protection of the rights of authors in their literary and artistic works in a manner as effective and uniform as possible,

Recognizing the need to introduce new international rules and clarify the interpretation of certain existing rules in order to provide adequate solutions to the questions raised by new economic, social, cultural and technological developments,

Recognizing the profound impact of the development and convergence of information and communication technologies on the creation and use of literary and artistic works,

Emphasizing the outstanding significance of copyright protection as an incentive for literary and artistic creation,

Recognizing the need to maintain a balance between the rights of authors and the larger public interest, particularly education, research and access to information, as reflected in the Berne Convention,

Have agreed as follows:

Article 1 - Relation to the Berne Convention

(1) This Treaty is a special agreement within the meaning of Article 20 of the Berne Convention for the Protection of Literary and Artistic Works, as regards Contracting Parties that are countries of the Union established by that Convention. This Treaty shall not have any connection with treaties other than the Berne Convention, nor shall it prejudice any rights and obligations under any other treaties.

(2) Nothing in this Treaty shall derogate from existing obligations that Contracting Parties have to each other under the Berne Convention for the Protection of Literary and Artistic Works.

(3) Hereinafter, "Berne Convention" shall refer to the Paris Act of July 24, 1971 of the Berne Convention for the Protection of Literary and Artistic Works.

(4) Contracting Parties shall comply with Articles 1 to 21 and the Appendix of the Berne Convention.

Article 2 - Scope of Copyright Protection

Copyright protection extends to expressions and not to ideas, procedures, methods of operation or mathematical concepts as such.

Article 3 - Application of Articles 2 to 6 of the Berne Convention

Contracting Parties shall apply mutatis mutandis the provisions of Articles 2 to 6 of the Berne Convention in respect of the protection provided for in this Treaty.

Article 4 - Computer Programs

Computer programs are protected as literary works within the meaning of Article 2 of the Berne Convention. Such protection applies to computer programs, whatever may be the mode or form of their expression.

Article 5 - Compilations of Data (Databases)

Compilations of data or other material, in any form, which by reason of the selection or arrangement of their contents constitute intellectual creations, are protected as such. This protection does not extend to the data or the material itself and is without prejudice to any copyright subsisting in the data or material contained in the compilation.

Article 6 - Right of Distribution

(1) Authors of literary and artistic works shall enjoy the exclusive right of authorizing the making available to the public of the original and copies of their works through sale or other transfer of ownership.
(2) Nothing in this Treaty shall affect the freedom of Contracting Parties to determine the conditions, if any, under which the exhaustion of the right in paragraph (1) applies after the first sale or other transfer of ownership of the original or a copy of the work with the authorization of the author.

Article 7 - Right of Rental

(1) Authors of:
(i) computer programs;
(ii) cinematographic works; and
(iii) works embodied in phonograms as determined in the national law of Contracting Parties,
shall enjoy the exclusive right of authorizing commercial rental to the public of the originals or copies of their works.
(2) Paragraph (1) shall not apply:
(i) in the case of computer programs where the program itself is not the essential object of the rental; and
(ii) in the case of cinematographic works, unless such commercial rental has led to widespread copying of such works materially impairing the exclusive right of reproduction.
(3) Notwithstanding the provisions of paragraph (1), a Contracting Party that, on April 15, 1994, had and continues to have in force a system of equitable remuneration of authors for the rental of copies of their works embodied in phonograms may maintain that system provided that the commercial rental of works embodied in phonograms is not giving rise to the material impairment of the exclusive rights of reproduction of authors.

Article 8 - Right of Communication to the Public

Without prejudice to the provisions of Articles 11(1)(ii), 11bis(1)(i) and (ii), 11ter(1)(ii), 14(1)(ii) and 14bis(1) of the Berne Convention, authors of literary and artistic works shall enjoy the exclusive right of authorizing any communication to the public of their works, by wire or wireless means, including the making available to the public of their works in such a way that members of the public may access these works from a place and at a time individually chosen by them.

Article 9 - Duration of the Protection of Photographic Works

In respect of photographic works, the Contracting Parties shall not apply the provisions of Article 7(4) of the Berne Convention.

Article 10 - Limitations and Exceptions

(1) Contracting Parties may, in their national legislation, provide for limitations of or exceptions to the rights granted to authors of literary and artistic works under this Treaty in certain special cases that do not conflict with a normal exploitation of the work and do not unreasonably prejudice the legitimate interests of the author.

(2) Contracting Parties shall, when applying the Berne Convention, confine any limitations of or exceptions to rights provided for therein to certain special cases that do not conflict with a normal exploitation of the work and do not unreasonably prejudice the legitimate interests of the author.

Article 11 - Obligations concerning Technological Measures

Contracting Parties shall provide adequate legal protection and effective legal remedies against the circumvention of effective technological measures that are used by authors in connection with the exercise of their rights under this Treaty or the Berne Convention and that restrict acts, in respect of their works, which are not authorized by the authors concerned or permitted by law.

Article 12 - Obligations concerning Rights Management Information

1. Contracting Parties shall provide adequate and effective legal remedies against any person knowingly performing any of the following acts knowing or, with respect to civil remedies having reasonable grounds to know, that it will induce, enable, facilitate or conceal an infringement of any right covered by this Treaty or the Berne Convention:
(i) to remove or alter any electronic rights management information without authority;
(ii) to distribute, import for distribution, broadcast or communicate to the public, without authority, works or copies of works knowing that electronic rights management information has been removed or altered without authority.

2. As used in this Article, "rights management information" means information which identifies the work, the author of the work, the owner of any right in the work, or information about the terms and conditions of use of the work, and any numbers or codes that represent such information, when any of these items of information is attached to a copy of a work or appears in connection with the communication of a work to the public.

Article 13 - Application in Time

Contracting Parties shall apply the provisions of Article 18 of the Berne Convention to all protection provided for in this Treaty.

Article 14 - Provisions on Enforcement of Rights

(1) Contracting Parties undertake to adopt, in accordance with their legal systems, the measures necessary to ensure the application of this Treaty.

(2) Contracting Parties shall ensure that enforcement procedures are available under their law so as to permit effective action against any act of infringement of rights covered by this Treaty, including expeditious remedies to prevent infringements and remedies which constitute a deterrent to further infringements.

Article 15 - Assembly

(1)
(a) The Contracting Parties shall have an Assembly.
(b) Each Contracting Party shall be represented by one delegate who may be assisted by alternate delegates, advisors and experts.

(c) The expenses of each delegation shall be borne by the Contracting Party that has appointed the delegation. The Assembly may ask the World Intellectual Property Organization (hereinafter referred to as "WIPO") to grant financial assistance to facilitate the participation of delegations of Contracting Parties that are regarded as developing countries in conformity with the established practice of the General Assembly of the United Nations or that are countries in transition to a market economy.

(2)
(a) The Assembly shall deal with matters concerning the maintenance and development of this Treaty and the application and operation of this Treaty.
(b) The Assembly shall perform the function allocated to it under Article 17(2) in respect of the admission of certain intergovernmental organizations to become party to this Treaty.
(c) The Assembly shall decide the convocation of any diplomatic conference for the revision of this Treaty and give the necessary instructions to the Director General of WIPO for the preparation of such diplomatic conference.

(3)
(a) Each Contracting Party that is a State shall have one vote and shall vote only in its own name.
(b) Any Contracting Party that is an intergovernmental organization may participate in the vote, in place of its Member States, with a number of votes equal to the number of its Member States which are party to this Treaty. No such intergovernmental organization shall participate in the vote if any one of its Member States exercises its right to vote and vice versa.

(4) The Assembly shall meet in ordinary session once every two years upon convocation by the Director General of WIPO.

(5) The Assembly shall establish its own rules of procedure, including the convocation of extraordinary sessions, the requirements of a quorum and, subject to the provisions of this Treaty, the required majority for various kinds of decisions.

Article 16 - International Bureau

The International Bureau of WIPO shall perform the administrative tasks concerning the Treaty.

Article 17 - Eligibility for Becoming Party to the Treaty

(1) Any Member State of WIPO may become party to this Treaty.
(2) The Assembly may decide to admit any intergovernmental organization to become party to this Treaty which declares that it is competent in respect of, and has its own legislation binding on all its Member States on, matters covered by this Treaty and that it has been duly authorized, in accordance with its internal procedures, to become party to this Treaty.
(3) The European Community, having made the declaration referred to in the preceding paragraph in the Diplomatic Conference that has adopted this Treaty, may become party to this Treaty.

Article 18 - Rights and Obligations under the Treaty

Subject to any specific provisions to the contrary in this Treaty, each Contracting Party shall enjoy all of the rights and assume all of the obligations under this Treaty.

Article 19 - Signature of the Treaty

This Treaty shall be open for signature until December 31, 1997, by any Member State of WIPO and by the European Community.

Article 20 - Entry into Force of the Treaty

This Treaty shall enter into force three months after 30 instruments of ratification or accession by States have been deposited with the Director General of WIPO.

Article 21 - Effective Date of Becoming Party to the Treaty

This Treaty shall bind
(i) the 30 States referred to in Article 20, from the date on which this Treaty has entered into force;
(ii) each other State from the expiration of three months from the date on which the State has deposited its instrument with the Director General of WIPO;
(iii) the European Community, from the expiration of three months after the deposit of its instrument of ratification or accession if such instrument has been deposited after the entry into force of this Treaty according to Article 20, or, three months after the entry into force of this Treaty if such instrument has been deposited before the entry into force of this Treaty;
(iv) any other intergovernmental organization that is admitted to become party to this Treaty, from the expiration of three months after the deposit of its instrument of accession.

Article 22 - No Reservations to the Treaty

No reservation to this Treaty shall be admitted.

Article 23 - Denunciation of the Treaty

This Treaty may be denounced by any Contracting Party by notification addressed to the Director General of WIPO. Any denunciation shall take effect one year from the date on which the Director General of WIPO received the notification.

Article 24 - Languages of the Treaty

(1) This Treaty is signed in a single original in English, Arabic, Chinese, French, Russian and Spanish languages, the versions in all these languages being equally authentic.
(2) An official text in any language other than those referred to in paragraph (1) shall be established by the Director General of WIPO on the request of an interested party, after consultation with all the interested parties. For the purposes of this paragraph, "interested party" means any Member State of WIPO whose official language, or one of whose official languages, is involved and the European Community, and any other intergovernmental organization that may become party to this Treaty, if one of its official languages is involved.

Article 25 - Depositary

The Director General of WIPO is the depositary of this Treaty.

WIPO PERFORMANCES AND PHONOGRAMS TREATY

Adopted by the Diplomatic Conference on December 20, 1996

(Source: http://www.wipo.org/clea/en/index.html)

Preamble

The Contracting Parties,

Desiring to develop and maintain the protection of the rights of performers and producers of phonograms in a manner as effective and uniform as possible,
Recognizing the need to introduce new international rules in order to provide adequate solutions to the questions raised by economic, social, cultural and technological developments,
Recognizing the profound impact of the development and convergence of information and communication technologies on the production and use of performances and phonograms,
Recognizing the need to maintain a balance between the rights of the performers and producers of phonograms and the larger public interest, particularly education, research and access to information,

Have agreed as follows:

CHAPTER I: GENERAL PROVISIONS

Article 1 - Relation to Other Conventions

(1) Nothing in this Treaty shall derogate from existing obligations that Contracting Parties have to each other under the International Convention for the Protection of Performers, Producers of Phonograms and Broadcasting Organizations done in Rome, October 26, 1961 (hereinafter the "Rome Convention").
(2) Protection granted under this Treaty shall leave intact and shall in no way affect the protection of copyright in literary and artistic works. Consequently, no provision of this Treaty may be interpreted as prejudicing such protection.
(3) This Treaty shall not have any connection with, nor shall it prejudice any rights and obligations under, any other treaties.

Article 2 - Definitions

For the purposes of this Treaty:
(a) "performers" are actors, singers, musicians, dancers, and other persons who act, sing, deliver, declaim, play in, interpret, or otherwise perform literary or artistic works or expressions of folklore;
(b) "phonogram" means the fixation of the sounds of a performance or of other sounds, or of a representation of sounds other than in the form of a fixation incorporated in a cinematographic or other audiovisual work;
(c) "fixation" means the embodiment of sounds, or of the representations thereof, from which they can be perceived, reproduced or communicated through a device;
(d) "producer of a phonogram" means the person, or the legal entity, who or which takes the initiative and has the responsibility for the first fixation of the sounds of a performance or other sounds, or the representations of sounds;

(e) "publication" of a fixed performance or a phonogram means the offering of copies of the fixed performance or the phonogram to the public, with the consent of the rightholder, and provided that copies are offered to the public in reasonable quantity;
(f) "broadcasting" means the transmission by wireless means for public reception of sounds or of images and sounds or of the representations thereof; such transmission by satellite is also "broadcasting"; transmission of encrypted signals is "broadcasting" where the means for decrypting are provided to the public by the broadcasting organization or with its consent;
(g) "communication to the public" of a performance or a phonogram means the transmission to the public by any medium, otherwise than by broadcasting, of sounds of a performance or the sounds or the representations of sounds fixed in a phonogram. For the purposes of Article 15, "communication to the public" includes making the sounds or representations of sounds fixed in a phonogram audible to the public.

Article 3 - Beneficiaries of Protection under this Treaty

(1) Contracting Parties shall accord the protection provided under this Treaty to the performers and producers of phonograms who are nationals of other Contracting Parties.
(2) The nationals of other Contracting Parties shall be understood to be those performers or producers of phonograms who would meet the criteria for eligibility for protection provided under the Rome Convention, were all the Contracting Parties to this Treaty Contracting States of that Convention. In respect of these criteria of eligibility, Contracting Parties shall apply the relevant definitions in Article 2 of this Treaty.
(3) Any Contracting Party availing itself of the possibilities provided in Article 5(3) of the Rome Conventions or, for the purposes of Article 5 of the same Convention, Article thereof 17 shall make a notification as foreseen in those provisions to the Director General of the World Intellectual Property Organization (WIPO).

Article 4 - National Treatment

(1) Each Contracting Party shall accord to nationals of other Contracting Parties, as defined in Article 3(2), the treatment it accords to its own nationals with regard to the exclusive rights specifically granted in this Treaty and to the right to equitable remuneration provided for in Article 15 of this Treaty.
(2) The obligation provided for in paragraph (1) does not apply to the extent that another Contracting Party makes use of the reservations permitted by Article 15(3) of this Treaty.

CHAPTER II: RIGHTS OF PERFORMERS

Article 5 - Moral Rights of Performers

(1) Independently of a performer's economic rights, and even after the transfer of those rights, the performer shall, as regards his live aural performances or perfomances fixed in phonograms have the right to claim to be identified as the performer of his performances, except where omission is dictated by the manner of the use of the performance, and to object to any distortion, mutilation or other modification of his performances that would be prejudicial to his reputation.
(2) The rights granted to a performer in accordance with paragraph (1) shall, after his death, be maintained, at least until the expiry of the economic rights, and shall be exercisable by the persons or institutions authorized by the legislation of the Contracting Party where protection is claimed. However, those Contracting Parties whose legislation, at the moment of their ratification of or accession to this Treaty, does not provide for protection after the death of the performer of all rights set out in the preceding paragraph may provide that some of these rights will, after his death, cease to be maintained.

(3) The means of redress for safeguarding the rights granted under this Article shall be governed by the legislation of the Contracting Party where protection is claimed.

Article 6 - Economic Rights of Performers in their Unfixed Performances

Performers shall enjoy the exclusive right of authorizing, as regards their performances:
(i) the broadcasting and communication to the public of their unfixed performances except where the performance is already a broadcast performance; and
(ii) the fixation of their unfixed performances.

Article 7 - Right of Reproduction

Performers shall enjoy the exclusive right of authorizing the direct or indirect reproduction of their performances fixed in phonograms, in any manner or form.

Article 8 - Right of Distribution

(1) Performers shall enjoy the exclusive right of authorizing the making available to the public of the original and copies of their performances fixed in phonograms through sale or other transfer of ownership.
(2) Nothing in this Treaty shall affect the freedom of Contracting Parties to determine the conditions, if any, under which the exhaustion of the right in paragraph (1) applies after the first sale or other transfer of ownership of the original or a copy of the fixed performance with the authorization of the performer.

Article 9 - Right of Rental

(1) Performers shall enjoy the exclusive right of authorizing the commercial rental to the public of the original and copies of their performances fixed in phonograms as determined in the national law of Contracting Parties, even after distribution of them by, or pursuant to, authorization by the performer.
(2) Notwithstanding the provisions of paragraph (1), a Contracting Party that, on April 15, 1994, had and continues to have in force a system of equitable remuneration of performers for the rental of copies of their performances fixed in phonograms, may maintain that system provided that the commercial rental of phonograms is not giving rise to the material impairment of the exclusive rights of reproduction of performers.

Article 10 - Right of Making Available of Fixed Performances

Performers shall enjoy the exclusive right of authorizing the making available to the public of their performances fixed in phonograms, by wire or wireless means, in such a way that members of the public may access them from a place and at a time individually chosen by them.

CHAPTER III: RIGHTS OF PRODUCERS OF PHONOGRAMS

Article 11 - Right of Reproduction

Producers of phonograms shall enjoy the exclusive right of authorizing the direct or indirect reproduction of their phonograms, in any manner or form.

Article 12 - Right of Distribution

(1) Producers of phonograms shall enjoy the exclusive right of authorizing the making available to the public of the original and copies of their phonograms through sale or other transfer of ownership.

(2) Nothing in this Treaty shall affect the freedom of Contracting Parties to determine the conditions, if any, under which the exhaustion of the right in paragraph (1) applies after the first sale or transfer of ownership of the original or a copy of the phonogram with the authorization of the producer of phonograms.

Article 13 - Right of Rental

(1) Producers of phonograms shall enjoy the exclusive right of authorizing the commercial rental to the public of the original and copies of their phonograms, even after distribution of them by or pursuant to authorization by the producer.
(2) Notwithstanding the provisions of paragraph (1), a Contracting Party that, on April 15, 1994, had and continues to have in force a system of equitable remuneration of producers of phonograms for the rental of copies of their phonograms, may maintain that system provided that the commercial rental of phonograms is not giving rise to the material impairment of the exclusive rights of reproduction of producers of phonograms.

Article 14 - Right of Making Available of Phonograms

Producers of phonograms shall enjoy the exclusive right of authorizing the making available to the public of their phonograms, by wire or wireless means, in such a way that members of the public may access them from a place and at a time individually chosen by them.

CHAPTER IV: COMMON PROVISIONS

Article 15 - Right to Remuneration for Broadcasting and Communication to the Public

(1) Performers and producers of phonograms shall enjoy the right to a single equitable remuneration for the direct or indirect use of phonograms published for commercial purposes for broadcasting or for any communication to the public.
(2) Contracting Parties may establish in their national legislation that the single equitable remuneration shall be claimed from the user by the performer or by the producer of a phonogram or by both. Contracting Parties may enact national legislation that, in the absence of an agreement between the performer and the producer of a phonogram, sets the terms according to which performers and producers of phonograms shall share the single equitable remuneration.
(3) Any Contracting Party may in a notification deposited with the Director General of WIPO, declare that it will apply the provisions of paragraph (1) only in respect of certain uses, or that it will limit their application in some other way, or that it will not apply these provisions at all.
(4) For the purposes of this Article, phonograms made available to the to the public by wire or wireless means in such a way that members of the public may access them from a place and at a time individually chosen by them shall be considered as if they had been published for commercial purposes.

Article 16 - Limitations and Exceptions

(1) Contracting Parties may, in their national legislation, provide for the same kinds of limitations or exceptions with regard to the protection of performers and producers of phonograms as they provide for, in their national legislation, in connection with the protection of copyright in literary and artistic works.
(2) Contracting Parties shall confine any limitations of or exceptions to rights provided for in this Treaty to certain special cases which do not conflict with a normal exploitation of the performance or phonogram and do not unreasonably prejudice the legitimate interests of the performer or of the producer of phonograms.

Article 17 - Term of Protection

(1) The term of protection to be granted to performers under this Treaty shall last, at least, until the end of a period of 50 years computed from the end of the year in which the performance was fixed in a phonogram.
(2) The term of protection to be granted to producers of phonograms under this Treaty shall last, at least, until the end of a period of 50 years computed from the end of the year in which the phonogram was published, or failing such publication within 50 years from fixation of the phonogram, 50 years from the end of the year in which the fixation was made.

Article 18 - Obligations concerning Technological Measures

Contracting Parties shall provide adequate legal protection and effective legal remedies against the circumvention of effective technological measures that are used by performers or producers of phonograms in connection with the exercise of their rights under this Treaty and that restrict acts, in respect of their performances or phonograms, which are not authorized by the performers or the producers of phonograms concerned or permitted by law.

Article 19 - Obligations concerning Rights Management Information

(1) Contracting Parties shall provide adequate and effective legal remedies against any person knowingly performing any of the following acts knowing or, with respect to civil remedies, having reasonable grounds to know that it will induce, enable, facilitate or conceal an infringement of any right covered by this Treaty:
(i) to remove or alter any electronic rights management information without authority;
(ii) to distribute, import for distribution, broadcast, communicate or make available to the public, without authority, performances, copies of fixed performances or phonograms knowing that electronic rights management information has been removed or altered without authority.
(2) As used in this Article, "rights management information" means information which identifies the performer, the performance of the performer, the producer of the phonogram, the phonogram, the owner of any right in the performance or phonogram, or information about the terms and conditions of use of the performance or phonogram, and any numbers or codes that represent such information, when any of these items of information is attached to a copy of a fixed performance or a phonogram or appears in connection with the communication or making available of a fixed performance or a phonogram to the public.

Article 20 - Formalities

The enjoyment and exercise of the rights provided for in this Treaty shall not be subject to any formality.

Article 21 - Reservations

Subject to the provisions of Article 15(3), no reservations to this Treaty shall be permitted.

Article 22 - Application in Time

(1) Contracting Parties shall apply the provisions of Article 18 of the Berne Convention, *mutatis mutandis*, to the rights of performers and producers of phonograms provided for in this Treaty.
(2) Notwithstanding paragraph (1), a Contracting Party may limit the application of Article 5 of this Treaty to performances which occurred after the entry into force of this Treaty for that Party.

Article 23 - Provisions on Enforcement of Rights

(1) Contracting Parties undertake to adopt, in accordance with their legal systems, the measures necessary to ensure the application of this Treaty.
(2) Contracting Parties shall ensure that enforcement procedures are available under their law so as to permit effective action against any act of infringement of rights covered by this Treaty, including expeditious remedies to prevent infringements and remedies which constitute a deterrent to further infringements.

CHAPTER V: ADMINISTRATIVE AND FINAL CLAUSES

Article 24 - Assembly

(1)
(a) The Contracting Parties shall have an Assembly.
(b) Each Contracting Party shall be represented by one delegate who may be assisted by alternate delegates, advisors and experts.
(c) The expenses of each delegation shall be borne by the Contracting Party that has appointed the delegation. The Assembly may ask WIPO to grant financial assistance to facilitate the participation of delegations of Contracting Parties that are regarded as developing countries in conformity with the established practice of the General Assembly of the United Nations or that are countries in transition to a market economy.

(2)
(a) The Assembly shall deal with matters concerning the maintenance and development of this Treaty and the application and operation of this Treaty.
(b) The Assembly shall perform the function allocated to it under Article 26(2) in respect of the admission of certain intergovernmental organizations to become party to this Treaty.
(c) The Assembly shall decide the convocation of any diplomatic conference for the revision of this Treaty and give the necessary instructions to the Director General of WIPO for the preparation of such diplomatic conference.

(3)
(a) Each Contracting Party that is a State shall have one vote and shall vote only in its own name.
(b) Any Contracting Party that is an intergovernmental organization may participate in the vote, in place of its Member States, with a number of votes equal to the number of its Member States which are party to this Treaty. No such intergovernmental organization shall participate in the vote if any one of its Member States exercises its right to vote and vice versa.

(4) The Assembly shall meet in ordinary session once every two years upon convocation by the Director General of WIPO.
(5) The Assembly shall establish its own rules of procedure, including the convocation of extraordinary sessions, the requirements of a quorum and, subject to the provisions of this Treaty, the required majority for various kinds of decisions.

Article 25 - International Bureau

The International Bureau of WIPO shall perform the administrative tasks concerning the Treaty.

Article 26 - Eligibility for Becoming Party to the Treaty

(1) Any Member State of WIPO may become party to this Treaty.
(2) The Assembly may decide to admit any intergovernmental organization to become party to this Treaty which declares that it is competent in respect of, and has its own legislation

binding on all its Member States on, matters covered by this Treaty and that it has been duly authorized, in accordance with its internal procedures, to become party to this Treaty.
(3) The European Community, having made the declaration referred to in the preceding paragraph in the Diplomatic Conference that has adopted this Treaty, may become party to this Treaty.

Article 27 - Rights and Obligations under the Treaty

Subject to any specific provisions to the contrary in this Treaty, each Contracting Party shall enjoy all of the rights and assume all of the obligations under this Treaty.

Article 28 - Signature of the Treaty

This Treaty shall be open for signature until December 31, 1997, by any Member State of WIPO and by the European Community.

Article 29 - Entry into Force of the Treaty

This Treaty shall enter into force three months after 30 instruments of ratification or accession by States have been deposited with the Director General of WIPO.

Article 30 - Effective Date of Becoming Party to the Treaty

This Treaty shall bind
(i) the 30 States referred to in Article 29, from the date on which this Treaty has entered into force;
(ii) each other State from the expiration of three months from the date on which the State has deposited its instrument with the Director General of WIPO;
(iii) the European Community, from the expiration of three months after the deposit of its instrument of ratification or accession if such instrument has been deposited after the entry into force of this Treaty according to Article 29, or, three months after the entry into force of this Treaty if such instrument has been deposited before the entry into force of this Treaty;
(iv) any other intergovernmental organization that is admitted to become party to this Treaty, from the expiration of three months after the deposit of its instrument of accession.

Article 31 - Denunciation of the Treaty

This Treaty may be denounced by any Contracting Party by notification addressed to the Director General of WIPO. Any denunciation shall take effect one year from the date on which the Director General of WIPO received the notification.

Article 32 - Languages of the Treaty

(1) This Treaty is signed in a single original in English, Arabic, Chinese, French, Russian and Spanish languages, the versions in all these languages being equally authentic.
(2) An official text in any language other than those referred to in paragraph (1) shall be established by the Director General of WIPO on the request of an interested party, after consultation with all the interested parties. For the purposes of this paragraph, "interested party" means any Member State of WIPO whose official language, or one of whose official languages, is involved and the European Community, and any other intergovernmental organization that may become party to this Treaty, if one of its official languages is involved.

Article 33 - Depositary

The Director General of WIPO is the depositary of this Treaty.

DIGITAL MILLENNIUM COPYRIGHT ACT

[H.R. 2281] Public Law Number 105-304,
(Source: http://thomas.loc.gov)

A bill
to amend title 17, United States Code, to implement the World Intellectual Property Organization Copyright Treaty and Performances and Phonograms Treaty, and for other purposes.

October, 28th, 1998

SECTION 1. SHORT TITLE.
This Act may be cited as the "Digital Millennium Copyright Act".

SECTION. 2. TABLE OF CONTENTS.

TITLE I - WIPO TREATIES IMPLEMENTATION
Sec. 101. Short title.
Sec. 102. Technical amendments.
Sec. 103. Copyright protection systems and copyright management information.
Sec. 104. Evaluation of impact of copyright law and amendments on electronic commerce and technological development.
Sec. 105. Effective date.

TITLE II - ONLINE COPYRIGHT INFRINGEMENT LIABILITY LIMITATION
Sec. 201. Short title.
Sec. 202. Limitations on liability for copyright infringement.
Sec. 203. Effective date.

TITLE III - COMPUTER MAINTENANCE OR REPAIR COPYRIGHT EXEMPTION
Sec. 301. Short title.
Sec. 302. Limitations on exclusive rights; computer programs.

TITLE IV - MISCELLANEOUS PROVISIONS
Sec. 401. Provisions Relating to the Commissioner of Patents and Trademarks and the Register of Copyrights.
Sec. 402. Ephemeral recordings.
Sec. 403. Limitations on exclusive rights; distance education.
Sec. 404. Exemption for libraries and archives.
Sec. 405. Scope of exclusive rights in sound recordings; ephemeral recordings.
Sec. 406. Assumption of contractual obligations related to transfers of rights in motion pictures.
Sec. 407. Effective date.

TITLE V - PROTECTION OF CERTAIN ORIGINAL DESIGNS
Sec. 501. Short title.
[...]

TITLE I - WIPO TREATIES IMPLEMENTATION

Sec. 101: Short Title.

This title may be cited as the "WIPO Copyright and Performances and Phonograms Treaties Implementation Act of 1998".

Sec. 102: Technical Amendments.

Definitions- Section 101 of title 17, United States Code, is amended
(1) by striking the definition of "Berne Convention work";
(2) in the definition of "The 'country of origin' of a Berne Convention work"
  (A) by striking "The 'country of origin' of a Berne Convention work, for purposes of section 411, is the United States if" and inserting "For purposes of section 411, a work is a 'United States work' only if";
  (B) in paragraph (1)
    (i) in subparagraph (B) by striking "nation or nations adhering to the Berne Convention" and inserting "treaty party or parties";
    (ii) in subparagraph (C) by striking "does not adhere to the Berne Convention" and inserting "is not a treaty party"; and
    (iii) in subparagraph (D) by striking "does not adhere to the Berne Convention" and inserting "is not a treaty party"; and
  (C) in the matter following paragraph (3) by striking "For the purposes of section 411, the 'country of origin' of any other Berne Convention work is not the United States.";
(3) by inserting after the definition of "fixed" the following: "The 'Geneva Phonograms Convention' is the Convention for the Protection of Producers of Phonograms Against Unauthorized Duplication of Their Phonograms, concluded at Geneva, Switzerland, on October 29, 1971.";
(4) by inserting after the definition of "including" the following:
"An 'international agreement' is--
  (1) the Universal Copyright Convention;
  (2) the Geneva Phonograms Convention;
  (3) the Berne Convention;
  (4) the WTO Agreement;
  (5) the WIPO Copyright Treaty;
  (6) the WIPO Performances and Phonograms Treaty; and
  (7) any other copyright treaty to which the United States is a party";
(5) by inserting after the definition of "transmit" the following: "A 'treaty party' is a country or intergovernmental organization other than the United States that is a party to an international agreement.";
(6) by inserting after the definition of "widow" the following: "The 'WIPO Copyright Treaty' is the WIPO Copyright Treaty concluded at Geneva, Switzerland, on December 20, 1996.";
(7) by inserting after the definition of "The 'WIPO Copyright Treaty' " the following: "The 'WIPO Performances and Phonograms Treaty' is the WIPO Performances and Phonograms Treaty concluded at Geneva, Switzerland, on December 20, 1996."; and
(8) by inserting after the definition of "work made for hire" the following: "The terms 'WTO Agreement' and 'WTO member country' have the meanings given those terms in paragraphs (9) and (10), respectively, of section 2 of the Uruguay Round Agreements Act.".

(a) Subject Matter of Copyright; National Origin.--

Section 104 of title 17, United States Code, is amended

(1) in subsection (b)--
- (A) in paragraph (1) by striking "foreign nation that is a party to a copyright treaty to which the United States is also a party" and inserting "treaty party";
- (B) in paragraph (2) by striking "party to the Universal Copyright Convention" and inserting "treaty party";
- (C) by redesignating paragraph (5) as paragraph (6);
- (D) by redesignating paragraph (3) as paragraph (5) and inserting it after paragraph (4);
- (E) by inserting after paragraph (2) the following: "(3) the work is a sound recording that was first fixed in a treaty party; or";
- (F) in paragraph (4) by striking "Berne Convention work" and inserting "pictorial, graphic, or sculptural work that is incorporated in a building or other structure, or an architectural work that is embodied in a building and the building or structure is located in the United States or a treaty party"; and
- (G) by inserting after paragraph (6), as so redesignated, the following: "For purposes of paragraph (2), a work that is published in the United States or a treaty party within 30 days after publication in a foreign nation that is not a treaty party shall be considered to be first published in the United States or such treaty party, as the case may be."; and

(2) by adding at the end the following new subsection: "(d) EFFECT OF PHONOGRAMS TREATIES.--Notwithstanding the provisions of subsection (b), no works other than sound recordings shall be eligible for protection under this title solely by virtue of the adherence of the United States to the Geneva Phonograms Convention or the WIPO Performances and Phonograms Treaty.".

(b) Copyright in Restored Works.--

Section 104A(h) of title 17, United States Code, is amended

(1) in paragraph (1), by striking subparagraphs (A) and (B) and inserting the following:
"(A) a nation adhering to the Berne Convention;
"(B) WTO member country;
"(C) a nation adhering to the WIPO Copyright Treaty;
"(D) a nation adhering to the WIPO Performances and Phonograms Treaty; or
"(E) subject to a Presidential proclamation under subsection (g).";

(2) by amending paragraph (3) to read as follows:
"(3) The term 'eligible country' means a nation, other than the United States, that--
"(A) becomes a WTO member country after the date of the enactment of the Uruguay Round Agreements Act;
"(B) on such date of enactment is, or after such date of enactment becomes, a nation adhering to the Berne Convention;
"(C) adheres to the WIPO Copyright Treaty;
"(D) adheres to the WIPO Performances and Phonograms Treaty; or
"(E) after such date of enactment becomes subject to a proclamation under subsection (g).";

(3) in paragraph (6)--
- (A) in subparagraph (C)(iii) by striking "and" after the semicolon;
- (B) at the end of subparagraph (D) by striking the period and inserting "; and"; and
- (C) by adding after subparagraph (D) the following: "(E) if the source country for the work is an eligible country solely by virtue of its adherence to the WIPO Performances and Phonograms Treaty, is a sound recording.";

(4) in paragraph (8)(B)(i)--
- (A) by inserting "of which" before "the majority"; and
- (B) by striking "of eligible countries"; and

(5) by striking paragraph (9).

(c) Registration and Infringement Actions.--

Section 411(a) of title 17, United States Code, is amended in the first sentence
(1) by striking "actions for infringement of copyright in Berne Convention works whose country of origin is not the United States and"; and
(2) by inserting "United States" after "no action for infringement of the copyright in any".

(d) Statute of Limitations.--

Section 507(a) of title 17, United State Code, is amended by striking "No" and inserting "Except as expressly provided otherwise in this title, no".

Sec. 103: Copyright Protection Systems and Copyright Management Information

(a) In General.--

Title 17, United States Code is amended by adding at the end the following new chapter:

"CHAPTER 12--Copyright Protection and Management Systems

"Sec.
"1201: Circumvention of copyright protection systems
"1202: Integrity of copyright management information
"1203: Civil remedies
"1204: Criminal offenses and penalties
"1205: Savings clause

"Sec. 1201: Circumvention of Copyright Protection Systems

"(a) Violations Regarding Circumvention of Technological Measures.-
"(1)

"(A) No person shall circumvent a technological measure that effectively controls access to a work protected under this title. The prohibition contained in the preceding sentence shall take effect at the end of the 2-year period beginning on the date of the enactment of this chapter.

"(B) The prohibition contained in subparagraph (A) shall not apply to persons who are users of a copyrighted work which is in a particular class of works, if such persons are, or are likely to be in the succeeding 3-year period, adversely affected by virtue of such prohibition in their ability to make noninfringing uses of that particular class of works under this title, as determined under subparagraph (C).

"(C) During the 2-year period described in subparagraph (A), and during each succeeding 3-year period, the Librarian of Congress, upon the recommendation of the Register of Copyrights, who shall consult with the Assistant Secretary for Communications and Information of the Department of Commerce and report and comment on his or her views in making such recommendation, shall make the determination in a rulemaking proceeding on the record for purposes of subparagraph (B) of whether persons who are users of a copyrighted work are, or are likely to be in the succeeding 3-year period, adversely affected by the prohibition under subparagraph (A) in their ability to make noninfringing uses under this title of a particular class of copyrighted works. In conducting such rulemaking, the Librarian shall examine-

"(i) the availability for use of copyrighted works;

"(ii) the availability for use of works for nonprofit archival, preservation, and educational purposes;

"(iii) the impact that the prohibition on the circumvention of technological measures applied to copyrighted works has on criticism, comment, news reporting, teaching, scholarship, or research;

"(iv) the effect of circumvention of technological measures on the market for or value of copyrighted works; and

"(v) such other factors as the Librarian considers appropriate.

"(D) The Librarian shall publish any class of copyrighted works for which the Librarian has determined, pursuant to the rulemaking conducted under subparagraph (C), that noninfringing uses by persons who are users of a copyrighted work are, or are likely to be, adversely affected, and the prohibition contained in subparagraph (A) shall not apply to such users with respect to such class of works for the ensuing 3-year period.

"(E) Neither the exception under subparagraph (B) from the applicability of the prohibition contained in subparagraph (A), nor any determination made in a rulemaking conducted under subparagraph (C), may be used as a defense in any action to enforce any provision of this title other than this paragraph.

"(2) No person shall manufacture, import, offer to the public, provide, or otherwise traffic in any technology, product, service, device, component, or part thereof, that--

"(A) is primarily designed or produced for the purpose of circumventing a technological measure that effectively controls access to a work protected under this title;

"(B) has only limited commercially significant purpose or use other than to circumvent a technological measure that effectively controls access to a work protected under this title; or

"(C) is marketed by that person or another acting in concert with that person with that person's knowledge for use in circumventing a technological measure that effectively controls access to a work protected under this title.

"(3) As used in this subsection--

"(A) to 'circumvent a technological measure' means to descramble a scrambled work, to decrypt an encrypted work, or otherwise to avoid, bypass, remove, deactivate, or impair a technological measure, without the authority of the copyright owner; and

"(B) a technological measure 'effectively controls access to a work' if the measure, in the ordinary course of its operation, requires the application of information, or a process or a treatment, with the authority of the copyright owner, to gain access to the work.

"(b) Additional Violations.--

"(1) No person shall manufacture, import, offer to the public, provide, or otherwise traffic in any technology, product, service, device, component, or part thereof, that

"(A) is primarily designed or produced for the purpose of circumventing protection afforded by a technological measure that effectively protects a right of a copyright owner under this title in a work or a portion thereof;

"(B) has only limited commercially significant purpose or use other than to circumvent protection afforded by a technological measure that effectively protects a right of a copyright owner under this title in a work or a portion thereof; or

"(C) is marketed by that person or another acting in concert with that person with that person's knowledge for use in circumventing protection afforded by a technological measure that effectively protects a right of a copyright owner under this title in a work or a portion thereof.

"(2) As used in this subsection

"(A) to 'circumvent protection afforded by a technological measure' means avoiding, bypassing, removing, deactivating, or otherwise impairing a technological measure; and

"(B) a technological measure 'effectively protects a right of a copyright owner under this title' if the measure, in the ordinary course of its operation, prevents, restricts, or otherwise limits the exercise of a right of a copyright owner under this title.

"(c) Other Rights, etc., not Affected.--

"(1) Nothing in this section shall affect rights, remedies, limitations, or defenses to copyright infringement, including fair use, under this title.

"(2) Nothing in this section shall enlarge or diminish vicarious or contributory liability for copyright infringement in connection with any technology, product, service, device, component, or part thereof.

"(3) Nothing in this section shall require that the design of, or design and selection of parts and components for, a consumer electronics, telecommunications, or computing product provide for a response to any particular technological measure, so long as such part or component, or the product in which such part or component is integrated, does not otherwise fall within the prohibitions of subsection (a)(2) or (b)(1).

"(4) Nothing in this section shall enlarge or diminish any rights of free speech or the press for activities using consumer electronics, telecommunications, or computing products.

"(d) Exemption for Nonprofit Libraries, Archives, and Educational Institutions.--

"(1) A nonprofit library, archives, or educational institution which gains access to a commercially exploited copyrighted work solely in order to make a good faith determination of whether to acquire a copy of that work for the sole purpose of engaging in conduct permitted under this title shall not be in violation of subsection (a)(1)(A). A copy of a work to which access has been gained under this paragraph

"(A) may not be retained longer than necessary to make such good faith determination; and

"(B) not be used for any other purpose.

"(2) The exemption made available under paragraph (1) shall only apply with respect to a work when an identical copy of that work is not reasonably available in another form.

"(3) A nonprofit library, archives, or educational institution that willfully for the purpose of commercial advantage or financial gain violates paragraph (1)

"(A) shall, for the first offense, be subject to the civil remedies under section 1203; and

"(B) shall, for repeated or subsequent offenses, in addition to the civil remedies under section 1203, forfeit the exemption provided under paragraph (1).

"(4) This subsection may not be used as a defense to a claim under subsection (a)(2) or (b), nor may this subsection permit a nonprofit library, archives, or educational institution to manufacture, import, offer to the public, provide, or otherwise traffic in any technology, product, service, component, or part thereof, which circumvents a technological measure.

"(5) In order for a library or archives to qualify for the exemption under this subsection, the collections of that library or archives shall be

"(A) open to the public; or

"(B) available not only to researchers affiliated with the library or archives or with the institution of which it is a part, but also to other persons doing research in a specialized field.

"(e) Law Enforcement, Intelligence, and Other Government Activities.--

This section does not prohibit any lawfully authorized investigative, protective, information security, or intelligence activity of an officer, agent, or employee of the United States, a State, or a political subdivision of a State, or a person acting pursuant to a contract with the United States, a State, or a political subdivision of a State. For purposes of this subsection, the term 'information security' means activities carried out in order to identify and address the vulnerabilities of a government computer, computer system, or computer network.

"(f) Reverse Engineering.--

"(1) Notwithstanding the provisions of subsection (a)(1)(A), a person who has lawfully obtained the right to use a copy of a computer program may circumvent a technological measure that effectively controls access to a particular portion of that program for the sole purpose of identifying and analyzing those elements of the program that are necessary to achieve interoperability of an independently created computer program with other programs, and that have not previously been readily available to the person engaging in the circumvention, to the extent any such acts of identification and analysis do not constitute infringement under this title.

"(2) Notwithstanding the provisions of subsections (a)(2) and (b), a person may develop and employ technological means to circumvent a technological measure, or to circumvent protection afforded by a technological measure, in order to enable the identification and analysis under paragraph (1), or for the purpose of enabling interoperability of an independently created computer program with other programs, if such means are necessary to achieve such interoperability, to the extent that doing so does not constitute infringement under this title.

"(3) The information acquired through the acts permitted under paragraph (1), and the means permitted under paragraph (2), may be made available to others if the person referred to in paragraph or (2), as the case may be, provides such information or means solely for the purpose of enabling interoperability of an independently created computer program with other programs, and to the extent that doing so does not constitute infringement under this title or violate applicable law other than this section.

"(4) For purposes of this subsection, the term 'interoperability' means the ability of computer programs to exchange information, and of such programs mutually to use the information which has been exchanged.

"(g) Encryption Research.--

"(1) DEFINITIONS.--

For purposes of this subsection--

"(A) the term 'encryption research' means activities necessary to identify and analyze flaws and vulnerabilities of encryption technologies applied to copyrighted works, if these activities are conducted to advance the state of knowledge in the field of encryption technology or to assist in the development of encryption products; and

"(B) the term 'encryption technology' means the scrambling and descrambling of information using mathematical formulas or algorithms.

"(2) PERMISSIBLE ACTS OF ENCRYPTION RESEARCH.--

Notwithstanding the provisions of subsection (a)(1)(A), it is not a violation of that subsection for a person to circumvent a technological measure as applied to a copy, phonorecord, performance, or display of a published work in the course of an act of good faith encryption research if--

"(A) the person lawfully obtained the encrypted copy, phonorecord, performance, or display of the published work;

"(B) such act is necessary to conduct such encryption research;

"(C) the person made a good faith effort to obtain authorization before the circumvention; and

"(D) such act does not constitute infringement under this title or a violation of applicable law other than this section, including section 1030 of title 18 and those provisions of title 18 amended by the Computer Fraud and Abuse Act of 1986.

"(3) FACTORS IN DETERMINING EXEMPTION.--

In determining whether a person qualifies for the exemption under paragraph (2), the factors to be considered shall include--

"(A) whether the information derived from the encryption research was disseminated, and if so, whether it was disseminated in a manner reasonably calculated to advance the state of knowledge or development of encryption technology, versus whether it was disseminated in a manner that facilitates infringement under this title or a violation of applicable law other than this section, including a violation of privacy or breach of security;

"(B) whether the person is engaged in a legitimate course of study, is employed, or is appropriately trained or experienced, in the field of encryption technology; and

"(C) whether the person provides the copyright owner of the work to which the technological measure is applied with notice of the findings and documentation of the research, and the time when such notice is provided.

"(4) USE OF TECHNOLOGICAL MEANS FOR RESEARCH ACTIVITIES.--
Notwithstanding the provisions of subsection (a)(2), it is not a violation of that subsection for a person to--

"(A) develop and employ technological means to circumvent a technological measure for the sole purpose of that person performing the acts of good faith encryption research described in paragraph (2); and

"(B) provide the technological means to another person with whom he or she is working collaboratively for the purpose of conducting the acts of good faith encryption research described in paragraph (2) or for the purpose of having that other person verify his or her acts of good faith encryption research described in paragraph (2).

"(5) REPORT TO CONGRESS.--
Not later than 1 year after the date of the enactment of this chapter, the Register of Copyrights and the Assistant Secretary for Communications and Information of the Department of Commerce shall jointly report to the Congress on the effect this subsection has had on--

"(A) encryption research and the development of encryption technology;

"(B) the adequacy and effectiveness of technological measures designed to protect copyrighted works; and

"(C) protection of copyright owners against the unauthorized access to their encrypted copyrighted works.

The report shall include legislative recommendations, if any.

"(h) Exceptions Regarding Minors.--
In applying subsection (a) to a component or part, the court may consider the necessity for its intended and actual incorporation in a technology, product, service, or device, which--

"(1) does not itself violate the provisions of this title; and

"(2) has the sole purpose to prevent the access of minors to material on the Internet.

"(i) Protection of Personally Identifying Information.--
"(1) CIRCUMVENTION PERMITTED.--
Notwithstanding the provisions of subsection (a)(1)(A), it is not a violation of that subsection for a person to circumvent a technological measure that effectively controls access to a work protected under this title, if--

"(A) the technological measure, or the work it protects, contains the capability of collecting or disseminating personally identifying information reflecting the online activities of a natural person who seeks to gain access to the work protected;

"(B) in the normal course of its operation, the technological measure, or the work it protects, collects or disseminates personally identifying information about the person who seeks to gain access to the work protected, without providing conspicuous notice of such collection or dissemination to such person, and without providing such person with the capability to prevent or restrict such collection or dissemination;

"(C) the act of circumvention has the sole effect of identifying and disabling the capability described in subparagraph (A), and has no other effect on the ability of any person to gain access to any work; and

"(D) the act of circumvention is carried out solely for the purpose of preventing the collection or dissemination of personally identifying information about a natural person who seeks to gain access to the work protected, and is not in violation of any other law.

"(2) INAPPLICABILITY TO CERTAIN TECHNOLOGICAL MEASURES--

This subsection does not apply to a technological measure, or a work it protects, that does not collect or disseminate personally identifying information and that is disclosed to a user as not having or using such capability.

"(j) Security Testing.--

"(1) DEFINITION.--

For purposes of this subsection, the term 'security testing' means accessing a computer, computer system, or computer network, solely for the purpose of good faith testing, investigating, or correcting, a security flaw or vulnerability, with the authorization of the owner or operator of such computer, computer system, or computer network.

"(2) PERMISSIBLE ACTS OF SECURITY TESTING. --

Notwithstanding the provisions of subsection (a)(1)(A), it is not a violation of that subsection for a person to engage in an act of security testing, if such act does not constitute infringement under this title or a violation of applicable law other than this section, including section 1030 of title 18 and those provisions of title 18 amended by the Computer Fraud and Abuse Act of 1986.

"(3) FACTORS IN DETERMINING EXEMPTION.--

In determining whether a person qualifies for the exemption under paragraph (2), the factors to be considered shall include--

"(A) whether the information derived from the security testing was used solely to promote the security of the owner or operator of such computer, computer system or computer network, or shared directly with the developer of such computer, computer system, or computer network; and

"(B) whether the information derived from the security testing was used or maintained in a manner that does not facilitate infringement under this title or a violation of applicable law other than this section, including a violation of privacy or breach of security.

"(4) USE OF TECHNOLOGICAL MEANS FOR SECURITY TESTING--

Notwithstanding the provisions of subsection (a)(2), it is not a violation of that subsection for a person to develop, produce, distribute or employ technological means for the sole purpose of performing the acts of security testing described in subsection (2), provided such technological means does not otherwise violate section (a)(2).

"(k) Certain Analog Devices and Certain Technological Measures.-

"(1) CERTAIN ANALOG DEVICES.--

"(A) Effective 18 months after the date of the enactment of this chapter, no person shall manufacture, import, offer to the public, provide or otherwise traffic in any--

"(i) VHS format analog video cassette recorder unless such recorder conforms to the automatic gain control copy control technology;

"(ii) 8mm format analog video cassette camcorder unless such camcorder conforms to the automatic gain control technology;

"(iii) Beta format analog video cassette recorder, unless such recorder conforms to the automatic gain control copy control technology, except that this requirement shall not apply until there are 1,000 Beta format analog video cassette recorders sold in the United States in any one calendar year after the date of the enactment of this chapter;

"(iv) 8mm format analog video cassette recorder that is not an analog video cassette camcorder, unless such recorder conforms to the automatic gain control copy control technology, except that this requirement shall not apply until there are 20,000 such recorders sold in the United States in any one calendar year after the date of the enactment of this chapter; or

"(v) analog video cassette recorder that records using an NTSC format video input and that is not otherwise covered under clauses (i) through (iv), unless such device conforms to the automatic gain control copy control technology.

"(B) Effective on the date of the enactment of this chapter, no person shall manufacture, import, offer to the public, provide or otherwise traffic in--

"(i) any VHS format analog video cassette recorder or any 8mm format analog video cassette recorder if the design of the model of such recorder has been modified after such date of enactment so that a model of recorder that previously conformed to the automatic gain control copy control technology no longer conforms to such technology; or

"(ii) any VHS format analog video cassette recorder, or any 8mm format analog video cassette recorder that is not an 8mm analog video cassette camcorder, if the design of the model of such recorder has been modified after such date of enactment so that a model of recorder that previously conformed to the four-line colorstripe copy control technology no longer conforms to such technology.

Manufacturers that have not previously manufactured or sold a VHS format analog video cassette recorder, or an 8mm format analog cassette recorder, shall be required to conform to the four-line colorstripe copy control technology in the initial model of any such recorder manufactured after the date of the enactment of this chapter, and thereafter to continue conforming to the four-line colorstripe copy control technology. For purposes of this subparagraph, an analog video cassette recorder 'conforms to' the four-line colorstripe copy control technology if it records a signal that, when played back by the playback function of that recorder in the normal viewing mode, exhibits, on a reference display device, a display containing distracting visible lines through portions of the viewable picture.

"(2) CERTAIN ENCODING RESTRICTIONS.--

No person shall apply the automatic gain control copy control technology or colorstripe copy control technology to prevent or limit consumer copying except such copying--

"(A) of a single transmission, or specified group of transmissions, of live events or of audiovisual works for which a member of the public has exercised choice in selecting the transmissions, including the content of the transmissions or the time of receipt of such transmissions, or both, and as to which such member is charged a separate fee for each such transmission or specified group of transmissions;

"(B) from a copy of a transmission of a live event or an audiovisual work if such transmission is provided by a channel or service where payment is made by a member of the public for such channel or service in the form of a subscription fee that entitles the member of the public to receive all of the programming contained in such channel or service;

"(C) from a physical medium containing one or more prerecorded audiovisual works; or

"(D) from a copy of a transmission described in subparagraph (A) or from a copy made from a physical medium described in subparagraph (C).

In the event that a transmission meets both the conditions set forth in subparagraph (A) and those set forth in subparagraph (B), the transmission shall be treated as a transmission described in subparagraph (A).

"(3) INAPPLICABILITY.--

This subsection shall not--

"(A) require any analog video cassette camcorder to conform to the automatic gain control copy control technology with respect to any video signal received through a camera lens;

"(B) apply to the manufacture, importation, offer for sale, provision of, or other trafficking in, any professional analog video cassette recorder; or

"(C) apply to the offer for sale or provision of, or other trafficking in, any previously owned analog video cassette recorder, if such recorder was legally manufactured and sold when new and not subsequently modified in violation of paragraph (1)(B).

"(4) DEFINITIONS.--

For purposes of this subsection:

"(A) An 'analog video cassette recorder' means a device that records, or a device that includes a function that records, on electromagnetic tape in an analog format the electronic impulses produced by the video and audio portions of a television program, motion picture, or other form of audiovisual work.

"(B) An 'analog video cassette camcorder' means an analog video cassette recorder that contains a recording function that operates through a camera lens and through a video input that may be connected with a television or other video playback device.

"(C) An analog video cassette recorder 'conforms' to the automatic gain control copy control technology if it--

"(i) detects one or more of the elements of such technology and does not record the motion picture or transmission protected by such technology; or

"(ii) records a signal that, when played back, exhibits a meaningfully distorted or degraded display.

"(D) The term 'professional analog video cassette recorder' means an analog video cassette recorder that is designed, manufactured, marketed, and intended for use by a person who regularly employs such a device for a lawful business or industrial use, including making, performing, displaying, distributing, or transmitting copies of motion pictures on a commercial scale.

"(E) The terms 'VHS format,' '8mm format,' 'Beta format,' 'automatic gain control copy control technology,' 'colorstripe copy control technology,' 'four-line version of the colorstripe copy control technology,' and 'NTSC' have the meanings that are commonly understood in the consumer electronics and motion picture industries as of the date of the enactment of this chapter.

"(5) VIOLATIONS.--

Any violation of paragraph (1) of this subsection shall be treated as a violation of subsection (b)(1) of this section. Any violation of paragraph (2) of this subsection shall be deemed an 'act of circumvention' for the purposes of section 1203(c)(3)(A) of this chapter.

"Sec. 1202. Integrity of Copyright Management Information

"(a) False Copyright Management Information.--

No person shall knowingly and with the intent to induce, enable, facilitate, or conceal infringement--

"(1) provide copyright management information that is false, or

"(2) distribute or import for distribution copyright management information that is false.

"(b) Removal or Alteration of Copyright Management Information.--

No person shall, without the authority of the copyright owner or the law--

"(1) intentionally remove or alter any copyright management information,

"(2) distribute or import for distribution copyright management information knowing that the copyright management information has been removed or altered without authority of the copyright owner or the law, or

"(3) distribute, import for distribution, or publicly perform works, copies of works, or phonorecords, knowing that copyright management information has been removed or altered without authority of the copyright owner or the law,

knowing, or, with respect to civil remedies under section 1203, having reasonable grounds to know, that it will induce, enable, facilitate, or conceal an infringement of any right under this title.

"(c) Definition.--

As used in this section, the term 'copyright management information' means any of the following information conveyed in connection with copies or phonorecords of a work or performances or displays of a work, including in digital form, except that such term does not include any personally identifying information about a user of a work or of a copy, phonorecord, performance, or display of a work:

"(1) The title and other information identifying the work, including the information set forth on a notice of copyright.

"(2) The name of, and other identifying information about, the author of a work.

"(3) The name of, and other identifying information about, the copyright owner of the work, including the information set forth in a notice of copyright.

"(4) With the exception of public performances of works by radio and television broadcast stations, the name of, and other identifying information about, a performer whose performance is fixed in a work other than an audiovisual work.

"(5) With the exception of public performances of works by radio and television broadcast stations, in the case of an audiovisual work, the name of, and other identifying information about, a writer, performer, or director who is credited in the audiovisual work.

"(6) Terms and conditions for use of the work.

"(7) Identifying numbers or symbols referring to such information or links to such information.

"(8) Such other information as the Register of Copyrights may prescribe by regulation, except that the Register of Copyrights may not require the provision of any information concerning the user of a copyrighted work.

"(d) Law Enforcement, Intelligence, and Other Government Activities.--

This section does not prohibit any lawfully authorized investigative, protective, information security, or intelligence activity of an officer, agent, or employee of the United States, a State, or a political subdivision of a State, or a person acting pursuant to a contract with the United States, a State, or a political subdivision of a State. For purposes of this subsection, the term 'information security' means activities carried out in order to identify and address the vulnerabilities of a government computer, computer system, or computer network.

"(e) Limitations on Liability.--

"(1) ANALOG TRANSMISSIONS.--

In the case of an analog transmission, a person who is making transmissions in its capacity as a broadcast station, or as a cable system, or someone who provides programming to such station or system, shall not be liable for a violation of subsection (b) if--

"(A) avoiding the activity that constitutes such violation is not technically feasible or would create an undue financial hardship on such person; and

"(B) such person did not intend, by engaging in such activity, to induce, enable, facilitate, or conceal infringement of a right under this title.

"(2) DIGITAL TRANSMISSIONS.--

"(A) If a digital transmission standard for the placement of copyright management information for a category of works is set in a voluntary, consensus standard-setting process involving a representative cross-section of broadcast stations or cable systems and copyright owners of a category of works that are intended for public performance by such stations or systems, a person identified in paragraph (1) shall not be liable for a violation of subsection (b) with respect to the particular copyright management information addressed by such standard if--

"(i) the placement of such information by someone other than such person is not in accordance with such standard; and

"(ii) the activity that constitutes such violation is not intended to induce, enable, facilitate, or conceal infringement of a right under this title.

"(B) Until a digital transmission standard has been set pursuant to subparagraph (A) with respect to the placement of copyright management information for a category or works, a person identified in paragraph (1) shall not be liable for a violation of subsection (b) with respect to such copyright management information, if the activity that constitutes such violation is not intended to induce, enable, facilitate, or conceal infringement of a right under this title, and if--

"(i) the transmission of such information by such person would result in a perceptible visual or aural degradation of the digital signal; or

"(ii) the transmission of such information by such person would conflict with--

"(I) an applicable government regulation relating to transmission of information in a digital signal;

"(II) an applicable industry-wide standard relating to the transmission of information in a digital signal that was adopted by a voluntary consensus standards body prior to the effective date of this chapter; or

"(III) an applicable industry-wide standard relating to the transmission of information in a digital signal that was adopted in a voluntary, consensus standards-setting process open to participation by a representative cross-section of broadcast stations or cable systems and copyright owners of a category of works that are intended for public performance by such stations or systems.

"(3) DEFINITIONS.--

As used in this subsection--

"(A) the term 'broadcast station' has the meaning given that term in section 3 of the Communications Act of 1934 (47 U.S.C. 153)); and

"(B) the term 'cable system' has the meaning given that term in section 602 of the Communications Act of 1934 (47 U.S.C. 522)).

"Sec. 1203. Civil Remedies

"(a) Civil Actions.--

Any person injured by a violation of section 1201 or 1202 may bring a civil action in an appropriate United States district court for such violation.

"(b) Powers of the Court.--

In an action brought under subsection (a), the court--

"(1) may grant temporary and permanent injunctions on such terms as it deems reasonable to prevent or restrain a violation, but in no event shall impose a prior restraint on free speech or the press protected under the 1st amendment to the Constitution;

"(2) at any time while an action is pending, may order the impounding, on such terms as it deems reasonable, of any device or product that is in the custody or control of the alleged violator and that the court has reasonable cause to believe was involved in a violation;

"(3) may award damages under subsection (c);

"(4) in its discretion may allow the recovery of costs by or against any party other than the United States or an officer thereof;

"(5) in its discretion may award reasonable attorney's fees to the prevailing party; and

"(6) may, as part of a final judgment or decree finding a violation, order the remedial modification or the destruction of any device or product involved in the violation that is in the custody or control of the violator or has been impounded under paragraph (2).

"(c) Award of Damages.--

"(1) IN GENERAL.--

Except as otherwise provided in this title, a person committing a violation of section 1201 or 1202 is liable for either--

"(A) the actual damages and any additional profits of the violator, as provided in paragraph (2), or

"(B) statutory damages, as provided in paragraph (3).

"(2) ACTUAL DAMAGES.--

The court shall award to the complaining party the actual damages suffered by the party as a result of the violation, and any profits of the violator that are attributable to the violation and are not taken into account in computing the actual damages, if the complaining party elects such damages at any time before final judgment is entered.

"(3) STATUTORY DAMAGES.--

"(A) At any time before final judgment is entered, a complaining party may elect to recover an award of statutory damages for each violation of section 1201 in the sum of not less than $200 or more than $2,500 per act of circumvention, device, product, component, offer, or performance of service, as the court considers just.

"(B) At any time before final judgment is entered, a complaining party may elect to recover an award of statutory damages for each violation of section 1202 in the sum of not less than $2,500 or more than $25,000.

"(4) REPEATED VIOLATIONS.--

In any case in which the injured party sustains the burden of proving, and the court finds, that a person has violated section 1201 or 1202 within three years after a final judgment was entered against the person for another such violation, the court may increase the award of damages up to triple the amount that would otherwise be awarded, as the court considers just.

"(5) INNOCENT VIOLATIONS.--

"(A) IN GENERAL.-- The court in its discretion may reduce or remit the total award of damages in any case in which the violator sustains the burden of proving, and the court finds, that the violator was not aware and had no reason to believe that its acts constituted a violation.

"(B) NONPROFIT LIBRARY, ARCHIVES, OR EDUCATIONAL INSTITUTIONS.--In the case of a nonprofit library, archives, or educational institution, the court shall remit damages in any case in which the library, archives, or educational institution sustains the burden of proving, and the court finds, that the library, archives, or educational institution was not aware and had no reason to believe that its acts constituted a violation.

"Sec. 1204. Criminal Offenses and Penalties

"(a) In General.--

Any person who violates section 1201 or 1202 willfully and for purposes of commercial advantage or private financial gain--

"(1) shall be fined not more than $500,000 or imprisoned for not more than 5 years, or both, for the first offense; and

"(2) shall be fined not more than $1,000,000 or imprisoned for not more than 10 years, or both, for any subsequent offense.

"(b) Limitation for Nonprofit Library, Archives, or Educational Institution.--

Subsection (a) shall not apply to a nonprofit library, archives, or educational institution.

"(c) Statute of Limitations.--

No criminal proceeding shall be brought under this section unless such proceeding is commenced within five years after the cause of action arose.

"Sec. 1205. Savings Clause

"Nothing in this chapter abrogates, diminishes, or weakens the provisions of, nor provides any defense or element of mitigation in a criminal prosecution or civil action under, any Federal or State law that prevents the violation of the privacy of an individual in connection with the individual's use of the Internet.".

(b) Conforming Amendment.--

The table of chapters for title 17, United States Code, is amended by adding after the item relating to chapter 11 the following:
"12. Copyright Protection and Management Systems 1201".

Sec. 104: Evaluation of Impact of Copyright Law and Amendments on Electronic Commerce and Technological Development.

(a) Evaluation by the Register of Copyrights and the Assistant Secretary for Communications and Information.--

The Register of Copyrights and the Assistant Secretary for Communications and Information of the Department of Commerce shall jointly evaluate--
(1) the effects of the amendments made by this title and the development of electronic commerce and associated technology on the operation of sections 109 and 117 of title 17, United States Code; and
(2) the relationship between existing and emergent technology and the operation of sections 109 and 117 of title 17, United States Code.

(b) Report to Congress.--

The Register of Copyrights and the Assistant Secretary for Communications and Information of the Department of Commerce shall, not later than 24 months after the date of the enactment of this Act, submit to the Congress a joint report on the evaluation conducted under subsection (a), including any legislative recommendations the Register and the Assistant Secretary may have.

Sec. 105: Effective Date.

(a)   In General.--

Except as otherwise provided in this title, this title and the amendments made by this title shall take effect on the date of the enactment of this Act.

(b)   Amendments Relating to Certain International Agreements.--

(1) The following shall take effect upon the entry into force of the WIPO Copyright Treaty with respect to the United States:
   (A) Paragraph (5) of the definition of "international agreement" contained in section 101 of title 17, United States Code, as amended by section 102(a)(4) of this Act.
   (B) The amendment made by section 102(a)(6) of this Act.
   (C) Subparagraph (C) of section 104A(h)(1) of title 17, United States Code, as amended by section 102(c)(1) of this Act.
   (D) Subparagraph (C) of section 104A(h)(3) of title 17, United States Code, as amended by section 102(c)(2) of this Act.

(2) The following shall take effect upon the entry into force of the WIPO Performances and Phonograms Treaty with respect to the United States:
- (A) Paragraph (6) of the definition of "international agreement" contained in section 101 of title 17, United States Code, as amended by section 102(a)(4) of this Act.
- (B) The amendment made by section 102(a)(7) of this Act.
- (C) The amendment made by section 102(b)(2) of this Act.
- (D) Subparagraph (D) of section 104A(h)(1) of title 17, United States Code, as amended by section 102(c)(1) of this Act.
- (E) Subparagraph (D) of section 104A(h)(3) of title 17, United States Code, as amended by section 102(c)(2) of this Act.
- (F) The amendments made by section 102(c)(3) of this Act.

TITLE II - ONLINE COPYRIGHT INFRINGEMENT LIABILITY LIMITATION

Sec. 201: Short Title.

This title may be cited as the "Online Copyright Infringement Liability Limitation Act".

Sec. 202: Limitations on Liability for Copyright Infringement.

(a) In General.--

Chapter 5 of title 17, United States Code, is amended by adding after section 511 the following new section:

"Sec. 512. Limitations on Liability Relating to Material Online

"(a) Transitory Digital Network Communications.--

A service provider shall not be liable for monetary relief, or, except as provided in subsection (j), for injunctive or other equitable relief, for infringement of copyright by reason of the provider's transmitting, routing, or providing connections for, material through a system or network controlled or operated by or for the service provider, or by reason of the intermediate and transient storage of that material in the course of such transmitting, routing, or providing connections, if--

"(1) the transmission of the material was initiated by or at the direction of a person other than the service provider;

"(2) the transmission, routing, provision of connections, or storage is carried out through an automatic technical process without selection of the material by the service provider;

"(3) the service provider does not select the recipients of the material except as an automatic response to the request of another person;

"(4) no copy of the material made by the service provider in the course of such intermediate or transient storage is maintained on the system or network in a manner ordinarily accessible to anyone other than anticipated recipients, and no such copy is maintained on the system or network in a manner ordinarily accessible to such anticipated recipients for a longer period than is reasonably necessary for the transmission, routing, or provision of connections; and

"(5) the material is transmitted through the system or network without modification of its content.

"(b) System Caching.--

"(1) LIMITATION ON LIABILITY.--

Digitial Millenium Copyright Act (DMCA)

A service provider shall not be liable for monetary relief, or, except as provided in subsection (j), for injunctive or other equitable relief, for infringement of copyright by reason of the intermediate and temporary storage of material on a system or network controlled or operated by or for the service provider in a case in which--
"(A) the material is made available online by a person other than the service provider,
"(B) the material is transmitted from the person described in subparagraph (A) through the system or network to a person other than the person described in subparagraph (A) at the direction of that other person, and
"(C) the storage is carried out through an automatic technical process for the purpose of making the material available to users of the system or network who, after the material is transmitted as described in subparagraph (B), request access to the material from the person described in subparagraph (A),
if the conditions set forth in paragraph (2) are met.
"(2) CONDITIONS.--
The conditions referred to in paragraph (1) are that--
"(A) the material described in paragraph (1) is transmitted to the subsequent users described in paragraph (1)(C) without modification to its content from the manner in which the material was transmitted from the person described in paragraph (1)(A);
"(B) the service provider described in paragraph (1) complies with rules concerning the refreshing, reloading, or other updating of the material when specified by the person making the material available online in accordance with a generally accepted industry standard data communications protocol for the system or network through which that person makes the material available, except that this subparagraph applies only if those rules are not used by the person described in paragraph (1)(A) to prevent or unreasonably impair the intermediate storage to which this subsection applies;
"(C) the service provider does not interfere with the ability of technology associated with the material to return to the person described in paragraph (1)(A) the information that would have been available to that person if the material had been obtained by the subsequent users described in paragraph (1)(C) directly from that person, except that this subparagraph applies only if that technology--
"(i) does not significantly interfere with the performance of the provider's system or network or with the intermediate storage of the material;
"(ii) is consistent with generally accepted industry standard communications protocols; and
"(iii) does not extract information from the provider's system or network other than the information that would have been available to the person described in paragraph (1)(A) if the subsequent users had gained access to the material directly from that person;
"(D) if the person described in paragraph (1)(A) has in effect a condition that a person must meet prior to having access to the material, such as a condition based on payment of a fee or provision of a password or other information, the service provider permits access to the stored material in significant part only to users of its system or network that have met those conditions and only in accordance with those conditions; and
"(E) if the person described in paragraph (1)(A) makes that material available online without the authorization of the copyright owner of the material, the service provider responds expeditiously to remove, or disable access to, the material that is claimed to be infringing upon notification of claimed infringement as described in subsection (c)(3), except that this subparagraph applies only if--
"(i) the material has previously been removed from the originating site or access to it has been disabled, or a court has ordered that the material be removed from the originating site or that access to the material on the originating site be disabled; and

Digitial Millenium Copyright Act (DMCA)

"(ii) the party giving the notification includes in the notification a statement confirming that the material has been removed from the originating site or access to it has been disabled or that a court has ordered that the material be removed from the originating site or that access to the material on the originating site be disabled.

"(c) Information Residing on Systems or Networks at Direction of Users.--

"(1) IN GENERAL.--
A service provider shall not be liable for monetary relief, or, except as provided in subsection (j), for injunctive or other equitable relief, for infringement of copyright by reason of the storage at the direction of a user of material that resides on a system or network controlled or operated by or for the service provider, if the service provider--

"(A)
"(i) does not have actual knowledge that the material or an activity using the material on the system or network is infringing;
"(ii) in the absence of such actual knowledge, is not aware of facts or circumstances from which infringing activity is apparent; or
"(iii) upon obtaining such knowledge or awareness, acts expeditiously to remove, or disable access to, the material;
"(B) does not receive a financial benefit directly attributable to the infringing activity, in a case in which the service provider has the right and ability to control such activity; and
"(C) upon notification of claimed infringement as described in paragraph (3), responds expeditiously to remove, or disable access to, the material that is claimed to be infringing or to be the subject of infringing activity.

"(2) DESIGNATED AGENT.--
The limitations on liability established in this subsection apply to a service provider only if the service provider has designated an agent to receive notifications of claimed infringement described in paragraph (3), by making available through its service, including on its website in a location accessible to the public, and by providing to the Copyright Office, substantially the following information:

"(A) the name, address, phone number, and electronic mail address of the agent.
"(B) other contact information which the Register of Copyrights may deem appropriate.

The Register of Copyrights shall maintain a current directory of agents available to the public for inspection, including through the Internet, in both electronic and hard copy formats, and may require payment of a fee by service providers to cover the costs of maintaining the directory.

"(3) ELEMENTS OF NOTIFICATION.--

"(A) To be effective under this subsection, a notification of claimed infringement must be a written communication provided to the designated agent of a service provider that includes substantially the following:

"(i) A physical or electronic signature of a person authorized to act on behalf of the owner of an exclusive right that is allegedly infringed.
"(ii) Identification of the copyrighted work claimed to have been infringed, or, if multiple copyrighted works at a single online site are covered by a single notification, a representative list of such works at that site.
"(iii) Identification of the material that is claimed to be infringing or to be the subject of infringing activity and that is to be removed or access to which is to be disabled, and information reasonably sufficient to permit the service provider to locate the material.
"(iv) Information reasonably sufficient to permit the service provider to contact the complaining party, such as an address, telephone number, and, if available, an electronic mail address at which the complaining party may be contacted.

"(v) A statement that the complaining party has a good faith belief that use of the material in the manner complained of is not authorized by the copyright owner, its agent, or the law.

"(vi) A statement that the information in the notification is accurate, and under penalty of perjury, that the complaining party is authorized to act on behalf of the owner of an exclusive right that is allegedly infringed.

"(B) "(i) Subject to clause (ii), a notification from a copyright owner or from a person authorized to act on behalf of the copyright owner that fails to comply substantially with the provisions of subparagraph (A) shall not be considered under paragraph (1)(A) in determining whether a service provider has actual knowledge or is aware of facts or circumstances from which infringing activity is apparent.

"(ii) In a case in which the notification that is provided to the service provider's designated agent fails to comply substantially with all the provisions of subparagraph (A) but substantially complies with clauses (ii), (iii), and (iv) of subparagraph (A), clause (i) of this subparagraph applies only if the service provider promptly attempts to contact the person making the notification or takes other reasonable steps to assist in the receipt of notification that substantially complies with all the provisions of subparagraph (A).

"(d) Information Location Tools.--

A service provider shall not be liable for monetary relief, or, except as provided in subsection (j), for injunctive or other equitable relief, for infringement of copyright by reason of the provider referring or linking users to an online location containing infringing material or infringing activity, by using information location tools, including a directory, index, reference, pointer, or hypertext link, if the service provider--

"(1)

"(A) does not have actual knowledge that the material or activity is infringing;

"(B) in the absence of such actual knowledge, is not aware of facts or circumstances from which infringing activity is apparent; or

"(C) upon obtaining such knowledge or awareness, acts expeditiously to remove, or disable access to, the material;

"(2) does not receive a financial benefit directly attributable to the infringing activity, in a case in which the service provider has the right and ability to control such activity; and

"(3) upon notification of claimed infringement as described in subsection (c)(3), responds expeditiously to remove, or disable access to, the material that is claimed to be infringing or to be the subject of infringing activity, except that, for purposes of this paragraph, the information described in subsection (c)(3)(A)(iii) shall be identification of the reference or link, to material or activity claimed to be infringing, that is to be removed or access to which is to be disabled, and information reasonably sufficient to permit the service provider to locate that reference or link.

"(e) Limitation on Liability of Nonprofit Educational Institutions.--

"(1) When a public or other nonprofit institution of higher education is a service provider, and when a faculty member or graduate student who is an employee of such institution is performing a teaching or research function, for the purposes of subsections (a) and (b) such faculty member or graduate student shall be considered to be a person other than the institution, and for the purposes of subsections (c) and (d) such faculty member's or graduate student's knowledge or awareness of his or her infringing activities shall not be attributed to the institution, if--

"(A) such faculty member's or graduate student's infringing activities do not involve the provision of online access to instructional materials that are or were required or recommended, within the preceding 3-year period, for a course taught at the institution by such faculty member or graduate student;

"(B) the institution has not, within the preceding 3-year period, received more than 2 notifications described in subsection (c)(3) of claimed infringement by such faculty member or graduate student, and such notifications of claimed infringement were not actionable under subsection (f); and

"(C) the institution provides to all users of its system or network informational materials that accurately describe, and promote compliance with, the laws of the United States relating to copyright.

"(2) INJUNCTIONS.-- For the purposes of this subsection, the limitations on injunctive relief contained in subsections (j)(2) and (j)(3), but not those in (j)(1), shall apply.

"(f) Misrepresentations.--

Any person who knowingly materially misrepresents under this section--
"(1) that material or activity is infringing, or
"(2) that material or activity was removed or disabled by mistake or misidentification,

shall be liable for any damages, including costs and attorneys' fees, incurred by the alleged infringer, by any copyright owner or copyright owner's authorized licensee, or by a service provider, who is injured by such misrepresentation, as the result of the service provider relying upon such misrepresentation in removing or disabling access to the material or activity claimed to be infringing, or in replacing the removed material or ceasing to disable access to it.

"(g) Replacement of Removed or Disabled Material and Limitation on Other Liability.--

"(1) NO LIABILITY FOR TAKING DOWN GENERALLY.-- Subject to paragraph (2), a service provider shall not be liable to any person for any claim based on the service provider's good faith disabling of access to, or removal of, material or activity claimed to be infringing or based on facts or circumstances from which infringing activity is apparent, regardless of whether the material or activity is ultimately determined to be infringing.

"(2) EXCEPTION.-- Paragraph (1) shall not apply with respect to material residing at the direction of a subscriber of the service provider on a system or network controlled or operated by or for the service provider that is removed, or to which access is disabled by the service provider, pursuant to a notice provided under subsection (c)(1)(C), unless the service provider--

"(A) takes reasonable steps promptly to notify the subscriber that it has removed or disabled access to the material;

"(B) upon receipt of a counter notification described in paragraph (3), promptly provides the person who provided the notification under subsection (c)(1)(C) with a copy of the counter notification, and informs that person that it will replace the removed material or cease disabling access to it in 10 business days; and

"(C) replaces the removed material and ceases disabling access to it not less than 10, nor more than 14, business days following receipt of the counter notice, unless its designated agent first receives notice from the person who submitted the notification under subsection (c)(1)(C) that such person has filed an action seeking a court order to restrain the subscriber from engaging in infringing activity relating to the material on the service provider's system or network.

"(3) CONTENTS OF COUNTER NOTIFICATION.-- To be effective under this subsection, a counter notification must be a written communication provided to the service provider's designated agent that includes substantially the following:

"(A) A physical or electronic signature of the subscriber.

Digitial Millenium Copyright Act (DMCA)

"(B) Identification of the material that has been removed or to which access has been disabled and the location at which the material appeared before it was removed or access to it was disabled.

"(C) A statement under penalty of perjury that the subscriber has a good faith belief that the material was removed or disabled as a result of mistake or misidentification of the material to be removed or disabled.

"(D) The subscriber's name, address, and telephone number, and a statement that the subscriber consents to the jurisdiction of Federal District Court for the judicial district in which the address is located, or if the subscriber's address is outside of the United States, for any judicial district in which the service provider may be found, and that the subscriber will accept service of process from the person who provided notification under subsection (c)(1)(C) or an agent of such person.

"(4) LIMITATION ON OTHER LIABILITY.-- A service provider's compliance with paragraph (2) shall not subject the service provider to liability for copyright infringement with respect to the material identified in the notice provided under subsection (c)(1)(C).

"**(h) Subpoena to Identify Infringer.--**

"(1) REQUEST.-- A copyright owner or a person authorized to act on the owner's behalf may request the clerk of any United States district court to issue a subpoena to a service provider for identification of an alleged infringer in accordance with this subsection.

"(2) CONTENTS OF REQUEST.-- The request may be made by filing with the clerk--

"(A) a copy of a notification described in subsection (c)(3)(A);

"(B) a proposed subpoena; and

"(C) a sworn declaration to the effect that the purpose for which the subpoena is sought is to obtain the identity of an alleged infringer and that such information will only be used for the purpose of protecting rights under this title.

"(3) CONTENTS OF SUBPOENA.-- The subpoena shall authorize and order the service provider receiving the notification and the subpoena to expeditiously disclose to the copyright owner or person authorized by the copyright owner information sufficient to identify the alleged infringer of the material described in the notification to the extent such information is available to the service provider.

"(4) BASIS FOR GRANTING SUBPOENA.-- If the notification filed satisfies the provisions of subsection (c)(3)(A), the proposed subpoena is in proper form, and the accompanying declaration is properly executed, the clerk shall expeditiously issue and sign the proposed subpoena and return it to the requester for delivery to the service provider.

"(5) ACTIONS OF SERVICE PROVIDER RECEIVING SUBPOENA.-- Upon receipt of the issued subpoena, either accompanying or subsequent to the receipt of a notification described in subsection (c)(3)(A), the service provider shall expeditiously disclose to the copyright owner or person authorized by the copyright owner the information required by the subpoena, notwithstanding any other provision of law and regardless of whether the service provider responds to the notification.

"(6) RULES APPLICABLE TO SUBPOENA.-- Unless otherwise provided by this section or by applicable rules of the court, the procedure for issuance and delivery of the subpoena, and the remedies for noncompliance with the subpoena, shall be governed to the greatest extent practicable by those provisions of the Federal Rules of Civil Procedure governing the issuance, service, and enforcement of a subpoena duces tecum.

"**(i) Conditions for Eligibility.--**

"(1) ACCOMMODATION OF TECHNOLOGY.-- The limitations on liability established by this section shall apply to a service provider only if the service provider--

"(A) has adopted and reasonably implemented, and informs subscribers and account holders of the service provider's system or network of, a policy that provides for the termination in appropriate circumstances of subscribers and account holders of the service provider's system or network who are repeat infringers; and

"(B) accommodates and does not interfere with standard technical measures.

"(2) DEFINITION.-- As used in this subsection, the term 'standard technical measures' means technical measures that are used by copyright owners to identify or protect copyrighted works and--

"(A) have been developed pursuant to a broad consensus of copyright owners and service providers in an open, fair, voluntary, multi-industry standards process;

"(B) are available to any person on reasonable and nondiscriminatory terms; and

"(C) do not impose substantial costs on service providers or substantial burdens on their systems or networks.

"(j) Injunctions.--

The following rules shall apply in the case of any application for an injunction under section 502 against a service provider that is not subject to monetary remedies under this section:

"(1) SCOPE OF RELIEF.--

"(A) With respect to conduct other than that which qualifies for the limitation on remedies set forth in subsection (a), the court may grant injunctive relief with respect to a service provider only in one or more of the following forms:

"(i) An order restraining the service provider from providing access to infringing material or activity residing at a particular online site on the provider's system or network.

"(ii) An order restraining the service provider from providing access to a subscriber or account holder of the service provider's system or network who is engaging in infringing activity and is identified in the order, by terminating the accounts of the subscriber or account holder that are specified in the order.

"(iii) Such other injunctive relief as the court may consider necessary to prevent or restrain infringement of copyrighted material specified in the order of the court at a particular online location, if such relief is the least burdensome to the service provider among the forms of relief comparably effective for that purpose.

"(B) If the service provider qualifies for the limitation on remedies described in subsection (a), the court may only grant injunctive relief in one or both of the following forms:

"(i) An order restraining the service provider from providing access to a subscriber or account holder of the service provider's system or network who is using the provider's service to engage in infringing activity and is identified in the order, by terminating the accounts of the subscriber or account holder that are specified in the order.

"(ii) An order restraining the service provider from providing access, by taking reasonable steps specified in the order to block access, to a specific, identified, online location outside the United States.

"(2) CONSIDERATIONS.-- The court, in considering the relevant criteria for injunctive relief under applicable law, shall consider--

"(A) whether such an injunction, either alone or in combination with other such injunctions issued against the same service provider under this subsection, would significantly burden either the provider or the operation of the provider's system or network;

"(B) the magnitude of the harm likely to be suffered by the copyright owner in the digital network environment if steps are not taken to prevent or restrain the infringement;

"(C) whether implementation of such an injunction would be technically feasible and effective, and would not interfere with access to noninfringing material at other online locations; and

"(D) whether other less burdensome and comparably effective means of preventing or restraining access to the infringing material are available.

"(3) NOTICE AND EX PARTE ORDERS.-- Injunctive relief under this subsection shall be available only after notice to the service provider and an opportunity for the service provider to appear are provided, except for orders ensuring the preservation of evidence or other orders having no material adverse effect on the operation of the service provider's communications network.

"**(k) Definitions.--**

"(1) SERVICE PROVIDER.--

"(A) As used in subsection (a), the term 'service provider' means an entity offering the transmission, routing, or providing of connections for digital online communications, between or among points specified by a user, of material of the user's choosing, without modification to the content of the material as sent or received.

"(B) As used in this section, other than subsection (a), the term 'service provider' means a provider of online services or network access, or the operator of facilities therefor, and includes an entity described in subparagraph (A).

"(2) MONETARY RELIEF.--

As used in this section, the term 'monetary relief' means damages, costs, attorneys' fees, and any other form of monetary payment.

"**(l) Other Defenses not Affected.--**

The failure of a service provider's conduct to qualify for limitation of liability under this section shall not bear adversely upon the consideration of a defense by the service provider that the service provider's conduct is not infringing under this title or any other defense.

"**(m) Protection of Privacy.--**

Nothing in this section shall be construed to condition the applicability of subsections (a) through (d) on--

"(1) a service provider monitoring its service or affirmatively seeking facts indicating infringing activity, except to the extent consistent with a standard technical measure complying with the provisions of subsection (i); or

"(2) a service provider gaining access to, removing, or disabling access to material in cases in which such conduct is prohibited by law.

"**(n) Construction.--**

Subsections (a), (b), (c), and (d) describe separate and distinct functions for purposes of applying this section. Whether a service provider qualifies for the limitation on liability in any one of those subsections shall be based solely on the criteria in that subsection, and shall not affect a determination of whether that service provider qualifies for the limitations on liability under any other such subsection.".

(b) Conforming Amendment.--

The table of sections for chapter 5 of title 17, United States Code, is amended by adding at the end the following:

"512. Limitations on liability relating to material online.".

Digitial Millenium Copyright Act (DMCA)

Sec. 203: Effective Date.

This title and the amendments made by this title shall take effect on the date of the enactment of this Act.

TITLE III - COMPUTER MAINTENANCE OR REPAIR COPYRIGHT EXEMPTION

Sec. 301: Short Title.

This title may be cited as the "Computer Maintenance Competition Assurance Act".

Sec. 302: Limitations on Exclusive Rights; Computer Programs.

Section 117 of title 17, United States Code, is amended--
(1) by striking "Notwithstanding" and inserting the following:

"**(a) Making of Additional Copy or Adaptation by Owner of Copy**.--Notwithstanding";

(2) by striking "Any exact" and inserting the following:

"**(b) Lease, Sale, or Other Transfer of Additional Copy or Adaptation**.--Any exact"; and

(3) by adding at the end the following:

"**(c) Machine Maintenance or Repair.**--Notwithstanding the provisions of section 106, it is not an infringement for the owner or lessee of a machine to make or authorize the making of a copy of a computer program if such copy is made solely by virtue of the activation of a machine that lawfully contains an authorized copy of the computer program, for purposes only of maintenance or repair of that machine, if--

"(1) such new copy is used in no other manner and is destroyed immediately after the maintenance or repair is completed; and

"(2) with respect to any computer program or part thereof that is not necessary for that machine to be activated, such program or part thereof is not accessed or used other than to make such new copy by virtue of the activation of the machine.

"**(d) Definitions**.--For purposes of this section--

"(1) the 'maintenance' of a machine is the servicing of the machine in order to make it work in accordance with its original specifications and any changes to those specifications authorized for that machine; and

"(2) the 'repair' of a machine is the restoring of the machine to the state of working in accordance with its original specifications and any changes to those specifications authorized for that machine.".

TITLE IV - MISCELLANEOUS PROVISIONS

Sec. 401: Provisions Relating to the Commissioner of Patents and Trademarks and the Register of Copyrights

(a) Compensation.--

(1) Section 3(d) of title 35, United States Code, is amended by striking "prescribed by law for Assistant Secretaries of Commerce" and inserting "in effect for level III of the Executive Schedule under section 5314 of title 5, United States Code".
(2) Section 701(e) of title 17, United States Code, is amended--
 (A) by striking "IV" and inserting "III"; and
 (B) by striking "5315" and inserting "5314".
(3) Section 5314 of title 5, United States Code, is amended by adding at the end the following: "Assistant Secretary of Commerce and Commissioner of Patents and Trademarks. Register of Copyrights.".

(b) Clarification of Authority of the Copyright Office.--

Section 701 of title 17, United States Code, is amended--
(1) by redesignating subsections (b) through (e) as subsections (c) through (f), respectively; and
(2) by inserting after subsection (a) the following:
"(b) In addition to the functions and duties set out elsewhere in this chapter, the Register of Copyrights shall perform the following functions:
"(1) Advise Congress on national and international issues relating to copyright, other matters arising under this title, and related matters.
"(2) Provide information and assistance to Federal departments and agencies and the Judiciary on national and international issues relating to copyright, other matters arising under this title, and related matters.
"(3) Participate in meetings of international intergovernmental organizations and meetings with foreign government officials relating to copyright, other matters arising under this title, and related matters, including as a member of United States delegations as authorized by the appropriate Executive branch authority.
"(4) Conduct studies and programs regarding copyright, other matters arising under this title, and related matters, the administration of the Copyright Office, or any function vested in the Copyright Office by law, including educational programs conducted cooperatively with foreign intellectual property offices and international intergovernmental organizations.
"(5) Perform such other functions as Congress may direct, or as may be appropriate in furtherance of the functions and duties specifically set forth in this title."

Sec. 402: Ephemeral Recordings.

Section 112(a) of title 17, United States Code, is amended--
(1) by redesignating paragraphs (1), (2), and (3) as subparagraphs (A), (B), and (C), respectively;
(2) by inserting "(1)" after "(a)";
(3) by inserting after "under a license" the following: ", including a statutory license under section 114(f),";
(4) by inserting after "114(a)," the following: "or for a transmitting organization that is a broadcast radio or television station licensed as such by the Federal Communications Commission and that makes a broadcast transmission of a performance of a sound recording in a digital format on a nonsubscription basis,"; and
(5) by adding at the end the following:
"(2) In a case in which a transmitting organization entitled to make a copy or phonorecord under paragraph (1) in connection with the transmission to the public of a performance or display of a

work is prevented from making such copy or phonorecord by reason of the application by the copyright owner of technical measures that prevent the reproduction of the work, the copyright owner shall make available to the transmitting organization the necessary means for permitting the making of such copy or phonorecord as permitted under that paragraph, if it is technologically feasible and economically reasonable for the copyright owner to do so. If the copyright owner fails to do so in a timely manner in light of the transmitting organization's reasonable business requirements, the transmitting organization shall not be liable for a violation of section 1201(a)(1) of this title for engaging in such activities as are necessary to make such copies or phonorecords as permitted under paragraph (1) of this subsection.".

Sec. 403: Limitations on Exclusive Rights; Distance Education.

(a) Recommendations by Register of Copyrights.--

Not later than 6 months after the date of the enactment of this Act, the Register of Copyrights, after consultation with representatives of copyright owners, nonprofit educational institutions, and nonprofit libraries and archives, shall submit to the Congress recommendations on how to promote distance education through digital technologies, including interactive digital networks, while maintaining an appropriate balance between the rights of copyright owners and the needs of users of copyrighted works. Such recommendations shall include any legislation the Register of Copyrights considers appropriate to achieve the objective described in the preceding sentence.

(b) Factors.--

In formulating recommendations under subsection (a), the Register of Copyrights shall consider--
(1) the need for an exemption from exclusive rights of copyright owners for distance education through digital networks;
(2) the categories of works to be included under any distance education exemption;
(3) the extent of appropriate quantitative limitations on the portions of works that may be used under any distance education exemption;
(4) the parties who should be entitled to the benefits of any distance education exemption;
(5) the parties who should be designated as eligible recipients of distance education materials under any distance education exemption;
(6) whether and what types of technological measures can or should be employed to safeguard against unauthorized access to, and use or retention of, copyrighted materials as a condition of eligibility for any distance education exemption, including, in light of developing technological capabilities, the exemption set out in section 110(2) of title 17, United States Code;
(7) the extent to which the availability of licenses for the use of copyrighted works in distance education through interactive digital networks should be considered in assessing eligibility for any distance education exemption; and (8) such other issues relating to distance education through interactive digital networks that the Register considers appropriate.

Sec. 404: Exemption for Libraries and Archives.

Section 108 of title 17, United States Code, is amended--
(1) in subsection (a)--
    (A) by striking "Notwithstanding" and inserting "Except as otherwise provided in this title and notwithstanding";
    (B) by inserting after "no more than one copy or phonorecord of a work" the following: ", except as provided in subsections (b) and (c)"; and

(C) in paragraph (3) by inserting after "copyright" the following: "that appears on the copy or phonorecord that is reproduced under the provisions of this section, or includes a legend stating that the work may be protected by copyright if no such notice can be found on the copy or phonorecord that is reproduced under the provisions of this section";
(2) in subsection (b)--
    (A) by striking "a copy or phonorecord" and inserting "three copies or phonorecords";
    (B) by striking "in facsimile form"; and
    (C) by striking "if the copy or phonorecord reproduced is currently in the collections of the library or archives." and inserting "if--
    "(1) the copy or phonorecord reproduced is currently in the collections of the library or archives; and
    "(2) any such copy or phonorecord that is reproduced in digital format is not otherwise distributed in that format and is not made available to the public in that format outside the premises of the library or archives."; and
(3) in subsection (c)--
    (A) by striking "a copy or phonorecord" and inserting "three copies or phonorecords";
    (B) by striking "in facsimile form";
    (C) by inserting "or if the existing format in which the work is stored has become obsolete," after "stolen,"; and
    (D) by striking "if the library or archives has, after a reasonable effort, determined that an unused replacement cannot be obtained at a fair price." and inserting "if--
    "(1) the library or archives has, after a reasonable effort, determined that an unused replacement cannot be obtained at a fair price;
    "(2) any such copy or phonorecord that is reproduced in digital format is not made available to the public in that format outside the premises of the library or archives in lawful possession of such copy."; and
    (E) by adding at the end the following: "For purposes of this subsection, a format shall be considered obsolete if the machine or device necessary to render perceptible a work stored in that format is no longer manufactured or is no longer reasonably available in the commercial marketplace.".

Sec. 405: Scope of Exclusive Rights in Sound Recordings; Ephemeral Recordings.

(a) Scope of Exclusive Rights in Sound Recordings.--

Section 114 of title 17, United States Code, is amended as follows:
(1) Subsection (d) is amended--
    (A) in paragraph (1) by striking subparagraph (A) and inserting the following: "(A) a nonsubscription broadcast transmission;"; and
    (B) by amending paragraph (2) to read as follows:
"(1) STATUTORY LICENSING OF CERTAIN TRANSMISSIONS.-- The performance of a sound recording publicly by means of a subscription digital audio transmission not exempt under paragraph (1), an eligible nonsubscription transmission, or a transmission not exempt under paragraph (1) that is made by a pre-existing satellite digital audio radio service shall be subject to statutory licensing, in accordance with subsection (f) if--
    "(A)
        "(i) the transmission is not part of an interactive service;
        "(ii) except in the case of a transmission to a business establishment, the transmitting entity does not automatically and intentionally cause any device receiving the transmission to switch from one program channel to another; and

"(iii) except as provided in section 1002(e), the transmission of the sound recording is accompanied, if technically feasible, by the information encoded in that sound recording, if any, by or under the authority of the copyright owner of that sound recording, that identifies the title of the sound recording, the featured recording artist who performs on the sound recording, and related information, including information concerning the underlying musical work and its writer;

"(B) in the case of a subscription transmission not exempt under paragraph (1) that is made by a preexisting subscription service in the same transmission medium used by such service on July 31, 1998, or in the case of a transmission not exempt under paragraph (1) that is made by a preexisting satellite digital audio radio service--

"(i) the transmission does not exceed the sound recording performance complement; and

"(ii) the transmitting entity does not cause to be published by means of an advance program schedule or prior announcement the titles of the specific sound recordings or phonorecords embodying such sound recordings to be transmitted; and

"(C) in the case of an eligible nonsubscription transmission or a subscription transmission not exempt under paragraph (1) that is made by a new subscription service or by a preexisting subscription service other than in the same transmission medium used by such service on July 31, 1998--

"(i) the transmission does not exceed the sound recording performance complement, except that this requirement shall not apply in the case of a retransmission of a broadcast transmission if the retransmission is made by a transmitting entity that does not have the right or ability to control the programming of the broadcast station making the broadcast transmission, unless--

"(I) the broadcast station makes broadcast transmissions--

"(aa) in digital format that regularly exceed the sound recording performance complement; or

"(bb) in analog format, a substantial portion of which, on a weekly basis, exceed the sound recording performance complement; and

"(II) the sound recording copyright owner or its representative has notified the transmitting entity in writing that broadcast transmissions of the copyright owner's sound recordings exceed the sound recording performance complement as provided in this clause;

"(ii) the transmitting entity does not cause to be published, or induce or facilitate the publication, by means of an advance program schedule or prior announcement, the titles of the specific sound recordings to be transmitted, the phonorecords embodying such sound recordings, or, other than for illustrative purposes, the names of the featured recording artists, except that this clause does not disqualify a transmitting entity that makes a prior announcement that a particular artist will be featured within an unspecified future time period, and in the case of a retransmission of a broadcast transmission by a transmitting entity that does not have the right or ability to control the programming of the broadcast transmission, the requirement of this clause shall not apply to a prior oral announcement by the broadcast station, or to an advance program schedule published, induced, or facilitated by the broadcast station, if the transmitting entity does not have actual knowledge and has not received written notice from the copyright owner or its representative that the broadcast station publishes or induces or facilitates the publication of such advance program schedule, or if such advance program schedule is a schedule of classical music programming published by the broadcast station in the same manner as published by that broadcast station on or before September 30, 1998;

"(iii) the transmission--

"(I) is not part of an archived program of less than 5 hours duration;

"(II) is not part of an archived program of 5 hours or greater in duration that is made available for a period exceeding 2 weeks;

"(III) is not part of a continuous program which is of less than 3 hours duration; or

"(IV) is not part of an identifiable program in which performances of sound recordings are ren- dered in a predetermined order, other than an archived or continuous program, that is transmitted at--

"(aa) more than 3 times in any 2-week period that have been publicly announced in advance, in the case of a program of less than 1 hour in duration, or

"(bb) more than 4 times in any 2-week period that have been publicly announced in advance, in the case of a program of 1 hour or more in duration,

except that the requirement of this subclause shall not apply in the case of a retransmission of a broadcast transmission by a transmitting entity that does not have the right or ability to control the programming of the broadcast transmission, unless the transmitting entity is given notice in writing by the copyright owner of the sound recording that the broadcast station makes broadcast transmissions that regularly violate such requirement;

"(iv) the transmitting entity does not knowingly perform the sound recording, as part of a service that offers transmissions of visual images contemporaneously with transmissions of sound recordings, in a manner that is likely to cause confusion, to cause mistake, or to deceive, as to the affiliation, connection, or association of the copyright owner or featured recording artist with the transmitting entity or a particular product or service advertised by the transmitting entity, or as to the origin, sponsorship, or approval by the copyright owner or featured recording artist of the activities of the transmitting entity other than the performance of the sound recording itself;

"(v) the transmitting entity cooperates to prevent, to the extent feasible without imposing substantial costs or burdens, a transmission recipient or any other person or entity from automatically scanning the transmitting entity's transmissions alone or together with transmissions by other transmitting entities in order to select a particular sound recording to be transmitted to the transmission recipient, except that the requirement of this clause shall not apply to a satellite digital audio service that is in operation, or that is licensed by the Federal Communications Commission, on or before July 31, 1998;

"(vi) the transmitting entity takes no affirmative steps to cause or induce the making of a phonorecord by the transmission recipient, and if the technology used by the transmitting entity enables the transmitting entity to limit the making by the transmission recipient of phonorecords of the transmission directly in a digital format, the transmitting entity sets such technology to limit such making of phonorecords to the extent permitted by such technology;

"(vii) phonorecords of the sound recording have been distributed to the public under the authority of the copyright owner or the copyright owner authorizes the transmitting entity to transmit the sound recording, and the transmitting entity makes the transmission from a phonorecord lawfully made under the authority of the copyright owner, except that the requirement of this clause shall not apply to a retransmission of a broadcast transmission by a transmitting entity that does not have the right or ability to control the programming of the broadcast transmission, unless the transmitting entity is given notice in writing by the copyright owner of the sound recording that the broadcast station makes broadcast transmissions that regularly violate such requirement;

"(viii) the transmitting entity accommodates and does not interfere with the transmission of technical measures that are widely used by sound recording copyright owners to identify or protect copyrighted works, and that are technically feasible of being transmitted by the transmitting entity without imposing substantial costs on the transmitting entity or resulting in perceptible aural or visual degradation of the digital signal, except that the requirement of this clause shall not apply to a satellite digital audio service that is in operation, or that is licensed under the authority of the Federal Communications Commission, on or before July 31, 1998, to the extent that such service has designed, developed, or made commitments to procure equipment or technology that is not compatible with such technical measures before such technical measures are widely adopted by sound recording copyright owners; and

"(ix) the transmitting entity identifies in textual data the sound recording during, but not before, the time it is performed, including the title of the sound recording, the title of the phonorecord embodying such sound recording, if any, and the featured recording artist, in a manner to permit it to be displayed to the transmission recipient by the device or technology intended for receiving the service provided by the transmitting entity, except that the obligation in this clause shall not take effect until 1 year after the date of the enactment of the Digital Millennium Copyright Act and shall not apply in the case of a retransmission of a broadcast transmission by a transmitting entity that does not have the right or ability to control the programming of the broadcast transmission, or in the case in which devices or technology intended for receiving the service provided by the transmitting entity that have the capability to display such textual data are not common in the marketplace.".

(2) Subsection (f) is amended--
   (A) in the subsection heading by striking "NONEXEMPT SUBSCRIPTION" and inserting "CERTAIN NONEXEMPT";
   (B) in paragraph (1)--
      (i) in the first sentence--
         (I) by striking "(1) No" and inserting "(1)(A) No";
         (II) by striking "the activities" and inserting "subscription transmissions by preexisting subscription services and transmissions by preexisting satellite digital audio radio services"; and
         (III) by striking "2000" and inserting "2001"; and
      (ii) by amending the third sentence to read as follows: "Any copyright owners of sound recordings, preexisting subscription services, or preexisting satellite digital audio radio services may submit to the Librarian of Congress licenses covering such subscription transmissions with respect to such sound recordings."; and
   (C) by striking paragraphs (2), (3), (4), and (5) and inserting the following:

"(B) In the absence of license agreements negotiated under subparagraph (A), during the 60-day period commencing 6 months after publication of the notice specified in subparagraph (A), and upon the filing of a petition in accordance with section 803(a)(1), the Librarian of Congress shall, pursuant to chapter 8, convene a copyright arbitration royalty panel to determine and publish in the Federal Register a schedule of rates and terms which, subject to paragraph (3), shall be binding on all copyright owners of sound recordings and entities performing sound recordings affected by this paragraph. In establishing rates and terms for preexisting subscription services and preexisting satellite digital audio radio services, in addition to the objectives set forth in section 801(b)(1), the copyright arbitration royalty panel may consider the rates and terms for comparable types of subscription digital audio transmission services and comparable circumstances under voluntary license agreements negotiated as provided in subparagraph (A).

"(C)

"(i) Publication of a notice of the initiation of voluntary negotiation proceedings as specified in subparagraph (A) shall be repeated, in accordance with regulations that the Librarian of Congress shall prescribe--

"(I) no later than 30 days after a petition is filed by any copyright owners of sound recordings, any preexisting subscription services, or any preexisting satellite digital audio radio services indicating that a new type of subscription digital audio transmission service on which sound recordings are performed is or is about to become operational; and

"(II) in the first week of January, 2001, and at 5-year intervals thereafter.

"(ii) The procedures specified in subparagraph (B) shall be repeated, in accordance with regulations that the Librarian of Congress shall prescribe, upon filing of a petition in accordance with section 803(a)(1) during a 60-day period commencing--

"(I) 6 months after publication of a notice of the initiation of voluntary negotiation proceedings under subparagraph (A) pursuant to a petition under clause (i)(I) of this subparagraph; or

"(II) on July 1, 2001, and at 5-year intervals thereafter.

"(iii) The procedures specified in subparagraph (B) shall be concluded in accordance with section 802.

"(2)

"(A) No later than 30 days after the date of the enactment of the Digital Millennium Copyright Act, the Librarian of Congress shall cause notice to be published in the Federal Register of the initiation of voluntary negotiation proceedings for the purpose of determining reasonable terms and rates of royalty payments for public performances of sound recordings by means of eligible nonsubscription transmissions and transmissions by new subscription services specified by subsection (d)(2) during the period beginning on the date of the enactment of such Act and ending on December 31, 2000, or such other date as the parties may agree. Such rates and terms shall distinguish among the different types of eligible nonsubscription transmission services and new subscription services then in operation and shall include a minimum fee for each such type of service. Any copyright owners of sound recordings or any entities performing sound recordings affected by this paragraph may submit to the Librarian of Congress licenses covering such eligible nonsubscription transmissions and new subscription services with respect to such sound recordings. The parties to each negotiation proceeding shall bear their own costs.

"(B) In the absence of license agreements negotiated under subparagraph (A), during the 60-day period commencing 6 months after publication of the notice specified in subparagraph (A), and upon the filing of a petition in accordance with section 803(a)(1), the Librarian of Congress shall, pursuant to chapter 8, convene a copyright arbitration royalty panel to determine and publish in the Federal Register a schedule of rates and terms which, subject to paragraph (3), shall be binding on all copyright owners of sound recordings and entities performing sound recordings affected by this paragraph during the period beginning on the date of the enactment of the Digital Millennium Copyright Act and ending on December 31, 2000, or such other date as the parties may agree. Such rates and terms shall distinguish among the different types of eligible nonsubscription transmission services then in operation and shall include a minimum fee for each such type of service, such differences to be based on criteria including, but not limited to, the quantity and nature of the use of sound recordings and the degree to which use of the service may substitute for or may promote the purchase of phonorecords by consumers. In establishing rates and terms for transmissions by eligible nonsubscription services and new subscription services, the copyright arbitration royalty panel shall establish rates and terms that most clearly represent the rates and terms that would have been negotiated in the marketplace between a willing buyer and a willing seller. In determining such rates and terms, the copyright arbitration royalty panel shall base its decision on economic, competitive and programming information presented by the parties, including--

"(i) whether use of the service may substitute for or may promote the sales of phonorecords or otherwise may interfere with or may enhance the sound recording copyright owner's other streams of revenue from its sound recordings; and

"(ii) the relative roles of the copyright owner and the transmitting entity in the copyrighted work and the service made available to the public with respect to relative creative contribution, technological contribution, capital investment, cost, and risk.

In establishing such rates and terms, the copyright arbitration royalty panel may consider the rates and terms for comparable types of digital audio transmission services and comparable circumstances under voluntary license agreements negotiated under subparagraph (A).

"(C)

"(i) Publication of a notice of the initiation of voluntary negotiation proceedings as specified in subparagraph (A) shall be repeated in accordance with regulations that the Librarian of Congress shall prescribe--

"(I) no later than 30 days after a petition is filed by any copyright owners of sound recordings or any eligible nonsubscription service or new subscription service indicating that a new type of eligible nonsubscription service or new subscription service on which sound recordings are performed is or is about to become operational; and

"(II) in the first week of January 2000, and at 2-year intervals thereafter, except to the extent that different years for the repeating of such proceedings may be determined in accordance with subparagraph (A).

"(ii) The procedures specified in subparagraph (B) shall be repeated, in accordance with regulations that the Librarian of Congress shall prescribe, upon filing of a petition in accordance with section 803(a)(1) during a 60-day period commencing--

"(I) 6 months after publication of a notice of the initiation of voluntary negotiation proceedings under subparagraph (A) pursuant to a petition under clause (i)(I); or

"(II) on July 1, 2000, and at 2-year intervals thereafter, except to the extent that different years for the repeating of such proceedings may be determined in accordance with subparagraph (A).

"(iii) The procedures specified in subparagraph (B) shall be concluded in accordance with section 802.

"(3) License agreements voluntarily negotiated at any time between 1 or more copyright owners of sound recordings and 1 or more entities performing sound recordings shall be given effect in lieu of any determination by a copyright arbitration royalty panel or decision by the Librarian of Congress.

"(4)

"(A) The Librarian of Congress shall also establish requirements by which copyright owners may receive reasonable notice of the use of their sound recordings under this section, and under which records of such use shall be kept and made available by entities performing sound recordings.

"(B) Any person who wishes to perform a sound recording publicly by means of a transmission eligible for statutory licensing under this subsection may do so without infringing the exclusive right of the copyright owner of the sound recording--

"(i) by complying with such notice requirements as the Librarian of Congress shall prescribe by regulation and by paying royalty fees in accordance with this subsection; or

"(ii) if such royalty fees have not been set, by agreeing to pay such royalty fees as shall be determined in accordance with this subsection.

"(C) Any royalty payments in arrears shall be made on or before the twentieth day of the month next succeeding the month in which the royalty fees are set.".

(3) Subsection (g) is amended--
    (A) in the subsection heading by striking "SUBSCRIPTION";
    (B) in paragraph (1) in the matter preceding subparagraph (A), by striking "subscription transmission licensed" and inserting "transmission licensed under a statutory license";
    (C) in subparagraphs (A) and (B) by striking "subscription"; and
    (D) in paragraph (2) by striking "subscription".
(4) Subsection (j) is amended--
    (A) by striking paragraphs (4) and (9) and redesignating paragraphs (2), (3), (5), (6), (7), and (8) as paragraphs (3), (5), (9), (12), (13), and (14), respectively;
    (B) by inserting after paragraph (1) the following:
"(2) An 'archived program' is a predetermined program that is available repeatedly on the demand of the transmission recipient and that is performed in the same order from the beginning, except that an archived program shall not include a recorded event or broadcast transmission that makes no more than an incidental use of sound recordings, as long as such recorded event or broadcast transmission does not contain an entire sound recording or feature a particular sound recording.";
    (C) by inserting after paragraph (3), as so redesignated, the following:
"(4) A 'continuous program' is a predetermined program that is continuously performed in the same order and that is accessed at a point in the program that is beyond the control of the transmission recipient.";
    (D) by inserting after paragraph (5), as so redesignated, the following:
"(6) An 'eligible nonsubscription transmission' is a noninteractive nonsubscription digital audio transmission not exempt under subsection (d)(1) that is made as part of a service that provides audio programming consisting, in whole or in part, of performances of sound recordings, including retransmissions of broadcast transmissions, if the primary purpose of the service is to provide to the public such audio or other entertainment programming, and the primary purpose of the service is not to sell, advertise, or promote particular products or services other than sound recordings, live concerts, or other music related events.

"(7) An 'interactive service' is one that enables a member of the public to receive a transmission of a program specially created for the recipient, or on request, a transmission of a particular sound recording, whether or not as part of a program, which is selected by or on behalf of the recipient. The ability of individuals to request that particular sound recordings be performed for reception by the public at large, or in the case of a subscription service, by all subscribers of the service, does not make a service interactive, if the programming on each channel of the service does not substantially consist of sound recordings that are performed within 1 hour of the request or at a time designated by either the transmitting entity or the individual making such request. If an entity offers both interactive and noninteractive services (either concurrently or at different times), the noninteractive component shall not be treated as part of an interactive service.

"(8) A 'new subscription service' is a service that performs sound recordings by means of noninteractive subscription digital audio transmissions and that is not a preexisting subscription service or a preexisting satellite digital audio radio service.";
    (E) by inserting after paragraph (9), as so redesignated, the following:

"(10) A 'preexisting satellite digital audio radio service' is a subscription satellite digital audio radio service provided pursuant to a satellite digital audio radio service license issued by the Federal Communications Commission on or before July 31, 1998, and any renewal of such license to the extent of the scope of the original license, and may include a limited number of sample channels representative of the subscription service that are made available on a nonsubscription basis in order to promote the subscription service.

"(11) A 'preexisting subscription service' is a service that performs sound recordings by means of noninteractive audio only subscription digital audio transmissions, which was in existence and was making such transmissions to the public for a fee on or before July 31, 1998, and may include a limited number of sample channels representative of the subscription service that are made available on a nonsubscription basis in order to promote the subscription service."; and

(F) by adding at the end the following:

"(15) A 'transmission' is either an initial transmission or a retransmission.".

(5) The amendment made by paragraph (2)(B)(i)(III) of this subsection shall be deemed to have been enacted as part of the Digital Performance Right in Sound Recordings Act of 1995, and the publication of notice of proceedings under section 114(f)(1) of title 17, United States Code, as in effect upon the effective date of that Act, for the determination of royalty payments shall be deemed to have been made for the period beginning on the effective date of that Act and ending on December 1, 2001.

(6) The amendments made by this subsection do not annul, limit, or otherwise impair the rights that are preserved by section 114 of title 17, United States Code, including the rights preserved by subsections (c), (d)(4), and (i) of such section.

(b) Ephemeral Recordings.--

Section 112 of title 17, United States Code, is amended--
(1) by redesignating subsection (e) as subsection (f); and
(2) by inserting after subsection (d) the following:

"**(e) Statutory License.--**

"(1) A transmitting organization entitled to transmit to the public a performance of a sound recording under the limitation on exclusive rights specified by section 114(d)(1)(C)(iv) or under a statutory license in accordance with section 114(f) is entitled to a statutory license, under the conditions specified by this subsection, to make no more than 1 phonorecord of the sound recording (unless the terms and conditions of the statutory license allow for more), if the following conditions are satisfied:

"(A) The phonorecord is retained and used solely by the transmitting organization that made it, and no further phonorecords are reproduced from it.

"(B) The phonorecord is used solely for the transmitting organization's own transmissions originating in the United States under a statutory license in accordance with section 114(f) or the limitation on exclusive rights specified by section 114(d)(1)(C)(iv).

"(C) Unless preserved exclusively for purposes of archival preservation, the phonorecord is destroyed within 6 months from the date the sound recording was first transmitted to the public using the phonorecord.

"(D) Phonorecords of the sound recording have been distributed to the public under the authority of the copyright owner or the copyright owner authorizes the transmitting entity to transmit the sound recording, and the transmitting entity makes the phonorecord under this subsection from a phonorecord lawfully made and acquired under the authority of the copyright owner.

"(3) Notwithstanding any provision of the antitrust laws, any copyright owners of sound recordings and any transmitting organizations entitled to a statutory license under this subsection may negotiate and agree upon royalty rates and license terms and conditions for making phonorecords of such sound recordings under this section and the proportionate division of fees paid among copyright owners, and may designate common agents to negotiate, agree to, pay, or receive such royalty payments.

"(4) No later than 30 days after the date of the enactment of the Digital Millennium Copyright Act, the Librarian of Congress shall cause notice to be published in the Federal Register of the initiation of voluntary negotiation proceedings for the purpose of determining reasonable terms and rates of royalty payments for the activities specified by paragraph (2) of this subsection during the period beginning on the date of the enactment of such Act and ending on December 31, 2000, or such other date as the parties may agree. Such rates shall include a minimum fee for each type of service offered by transmitting organizations. Any copyright owners of sound recordings or any transmitting organizations entitled to a statutory license under this subsection may submit to the Librarian of Congress licenses covering such activities with respect to such sound recordings. The parties to each negotiation proceeding shall bear their own costs.

"(5) In the absence of license agreements negotiated under paragraph (3), during the 60-day period commencing 6 months after publication of the notice specified in paragraph (4), and upon the filing of a petition in accordance with section 803(a)(1), the Librarian of Congress shall, pursuant to chapter 8, convene a copyright arbitration royalty panel to determine and publish in the Federal Register a schedule of reasonable rates and terms which, subject to paragraph (6), shall be binding on all copyright owners of sound recordings and transmitting organizations entitled to a statutory license under this subsection during the period beginning on the date of the enactment of the Digital Millennium Copyright Act and ending on December 31, 2000, or such other date as the parties may agree. Such rates shall include a minimum fee for each type of service offered by transmitting organizations. The copyright arbitration royalty panel shall establish rates that most clearly represent the fees that would have been negotiated in the marketplace between a willing buyer and a willing seller. In determining such rates and terms, the copyright arbitration royalty panel shall base its decision on economic, competitive, and programming information presented by the parties, including--

"(A) whether use of the service may substitute for or may promote the sales of phonorecords or otherwise interferes with or enhances the copyright owner's traditional streams of revenue; and

"(B) the relative roles of the copyright owner and the transmitting organization in the copyrighted work and the service made available to the public with respect to relative creative contribution, technological contribution, capital investment, cost, and risk.

In establishing such rates and terms, the copyright arbitration royalty panel may consider the rates and terms under voluntary license agreements negotiated as provided in paragraphs (3) and (4). The Librarian of Congress shall also establish requirements by which copyright owners may receive reasonable notice of the use of their sound recordings under this section, and under which records of such use shall be kept and made available by transmitting organizations entitled to obtain a statutory license under this subsection.

"(6) License agreements voluntarily negotiated at any time between 1 or more copyright owners of sound recordings and 1 or more transmitting organizations entitled to obtain a statutory license under this subsection shall be given effect in lieu of any determination by a copyright arbitration royalty panel or decision by the Librarian of Congress.

"(7) Publication of a notice of the initiation of voluntary negotiation proceedings as specified in paragraph (4) shall be repeated, in accordance with regulations that the Librarian of Congress shall prescribe, in the first week of January 2000, and at 2-year intervals thereafter, except to the extent that different years for the repeating of such proceedings may be determined in accordance with paragraph (4). The procedures specified in paragraph (5) shall be repeated, in accordance with regulations that the Librarian of Congress shall prescribe, upon filing of a petition in accordance with section 803(a)(1), during a 60-day period commencing on July 1, 2000, and at 2-year intervals thereafter, except to the extent that different years for the repeating of such proceedings may be determined in accordance with paragraph (4). The procedures specified in paragraph (5) shall be concluded in accordance with section 802.

"(8)

"(A) Any person who wishes to make a phonorecord of a sound recording under a statutory license in accordance with this subsection may do so without infringing the exclusive right of the copyright owner of the sound recording under section 106(1)--

"(i) by complying with such notice requirements as the Librarian of Congress shall prescribe by regulation and by paying royalty fees in accordance with this subsection; or

"(ii) if such royalty fees have not been set, by agreeing to pay such royalty fees as shall be determined in accordance with this subsection.

"(B) Any royalty payments in arrears shall be made on or before the 20th day of the month next succeeding the month in which the royalty fees are set.

"(9) If a transmitting organization entitled to make a phonorecord under this subsection is prevented from making such phonorecord by reason of the application by the copyright owner of technical measures that prevent the reproduction of the sound recording, the copyright owner shall make available to the transmitting organization the necessary means for permitting the making of such phonorecord as permitted under this subsection, if it is technologically feasible and economically reasonable for the copyright owner to do so. If the copyright owner fails to do so in a timely manner in light of the transmitting organization's reasonable business requirements, the transmitting organization shall not be liable for a violation of section 1201(a)(1) of this title for engaging in such activities as are necessary to make such phonorecords as permitted under this subsection.

"(10) Nothing in this subsection annuls, limits, impairs, or otherwise affects in any way the existence or value of any of the exclusive rights of the copyright owners in a sound recording, except as otherwise provided in this subsection, or in a musical work, including the exclusive rights to reproduce and distribute a sound recording or musical work, including by means of a digital phonorecord delivery, under section 106(1), 106(3), and 115, and the right to perform publicly a sound recording or musical work, including by means of a digital audio transmission, under sections 106(4) and 106(6).".

(c) Scope of Section 112(A) of Title 17 not Affected.--

Nothing in this section or the amendments made by this section shall affect the scope of section 112(a) of title 17, United States Code, or the entitlement of any person to an exemption thereunder.

(d) Procedural Amendments to Chapter 8.--

Section 802 of title 17, United States Code, is amended--
(1) in subsection (f)--
    (A) in the first sentence by striking "60" and inserting "90"; and
    (B) in the third sentence by striking "that 60-day period" and inserting "an additional 30-day period"; and
(2) in subsection (g) by inserting after the second sentence the following: "When this title provides that the royalty rates or terms that were previously in effect are to expire on a specified date, any adjustment by the Librarian of those rates or terms shall be effective as of the day following the date of expiration of the rates or terms that were previously in effect, even if the Librarian's decision is rendered on a later date.".

(e) Conforming Amendments.--

(1) Section 801(b)(1) of title 17, United States Code, is amended in the second sentence by striking "sections 114, 115, and 116" and inserting "sections 114(f)(1)(B), 115, and 116".
(2) Section 802(c) of title 17, United States Code, is amended by striking "section 111, 114, 116, or 119, any person entitled to a compulsory license" and inserting "section 111, 112, 114, 116, or 119, any transmitting organization entitled to a statutory license under section 112(f), any person entitled to a statutory license".
(3) Section 802(g) of title 17, United States Code, is amended by striking "sections 111, 114" and inserting "sections 111, 112, 114".
(4) Section 802(h)(2) of title 17, United States Code, is amended by striking "section 111, 114" and inserting "section 111, 112, 114".
(5) Section 803(a)(1) of title 17, United States Code, is amended by striking "sections 114, 115" and inserting "sections 112, 114, 115".
(6) Section 803(a)(5) of title 17, United States Code, is amended--
   (A) by striking "section 114" and inserting "section 112 or 114"; and
   (B) by striking "that section" and inserting "those sections".

Sec. 406: Assumption of Contractual Obligations Related to Transfers of Rights in Motion Pictures.

(a) In General.--

Part VI of title 28, United States Code, is amended by adding at the end the following new chapter:

"CHAPTER 180--Assumption of Certain Contractual Obligations

"Sec. 4001: Assumption of contractual obligations related to transfers of rights in motion pictures.

"(a) Assumption of Obligations.--

"(1) In the case of a transfer of copyright ownership under United States law in a motion picture (as the terms 'transfer of copyright ownership' and 'motion picture' are defined in section 101 of title 17) that is produced subject to 1 or more collective bargaining agreements negotiated under the laws of the United States, if the transfer is executed on or after the effective date of this chapter and is not limited to public performance rights, the transfer instrument shall be deemed to incorporate the assumption agreements applicable to the copyright ownership being transferred that are required by the applicable collective bargaining agreement, and the transferee shall be subject to the obligations under each such assumption agreement to make residual payments and provide related notices, accruing after the effective date of the transfer and applicable to the exploitation of the rights transferred, and any remedies under each such assumption agreement for breach of those obligations, as those obligations and remedies are set forth in the applicable collective bargaining agreement, if--
   "(A) the transferee knows or has reason to know at the time of the transfer that such collective bargaining agreement was or will be applicable to the motion picture; or
   "(B) in the event of a court order confirming an arbitration award against the transferor under the collective bargaining agreement, the transferor does not have the financial ability to satisfy the award within 90 days after the order is issued.
"(2) For purposes of paragraph (1)(A), 'knows or has reason to know' means any of the following:
   "(A) Actual knowledge that the collective bargaining agreement was or will be applicable to the motion picture.

"(B)

"(i) Constructive knowledge that the collective bargaining agreement was or will be applicable to the motion picture, arising from recordation of a document pertaining to copyright in the motion picture under section 205 of title 17 or from publication, at a site available to the public online that is operated by the relevant union, of information that identifies the motion picture as subject to a collective bargaining agreement with that union, if the site permits commercially reasonable verification of the date on which the information was available for access.

"(ii) Clause (i) applies only if the transfer referred to in subsection (a)(1) occurs--

"(I) after the motion picture is completed, or

"(II) before the motion picture is completed and--

"(aa) within 18 months before the filing of an application for copyright registration for the motion picture under section 408 of title 17, or

"(bb) if no such application is filed, within 18 months before the first publication of the motion picture in the United States.

"(C) Awareness of other facts and circumstances pertaining to a particular transfer from which it is apparent that the collective bargaining agreement was or will be applicable to the motion picture.

"(b) Scope of Exclusion of Transfers of Public Performance Rights.--

For purposes of this section, the exclusion under subsection (a) of transfers of copyright ownership in a motion picture that are limited to public performance rights includes transfers to a terrestrial broadcast station, cable system, or programmer to the extent that the station, system, or programmer is functioning as an exhibitor of the motion picture, either by exhibiting the motion picture on its own network, system, service, or station, or by initiating the transmission of an exhibition that is carried on another network, system, service, or station. When a terrestrial broadcast station, cable system, or programmer, or other transferee, is also functioning otherwise as a distributor or as a producer of the motion picture, the public performance exclusion does not affect any obligations imposed on the transferee to the extent that it is engaging in such functions.

"(c) Exclusion for Grants of Security Interests.--

Subsection (a) shall not apply to--

"(1) a transfer of copyright ownership consisting solely of a mortgage, hypothecation, or other security interest; or

"(2) a subsequent transfer of the copyright ownership secured by the security interest described in paragraph (1) by or under the authority of the secured party, including a transfer through the exercise of the secured party's rights or remedies as a secured party, or by a subsequent transferee. The exclusion under this subsection shall not affect any rights or remedies under law or contract.

"(d) Deferral Pending Resolution of Bona Fide Dispute.--

A transferee on which obligations are imposed under subsection (a) by virtue of paragraph (1) of that subsection may elect to defer performance of such obligations that are subject to a bona fide dispute between a union and a prior transferor until that dispute is resolved, except that such deferral shall not stay accrual of any union claims due under an applicable collective bargaining agreement.

"(e) Scope of Obligations Determined by Private Agreement.--

Nothing in this section shall expand or diminish the rights, obligations, or remedies of any person under the collective bargaining agreements or assumption agreements referred to in this section.

"(f) Failure to Notify.--

If the transferor under subsection (a) fails to notify the transferee under subsection (a) of applicable collective bargaining obligations before the execution of the transfer instrument, and subsection (a) is made applicable to the transferee solely by virtue of subsection (a)(1)(B), the transferor shall be liable to the transferee for any damages suffered by the transferee as a result of the failure to notify.

"(g) Determination of Disputes and Claims.--

Any dispute concerning the application of subsections (a) through (f) shall be determined by an action in United States district court, and the court in its discretion may allow the recovery of full costs by or against any party and may also award a reasonable attorney's fee to the prevailing party as part of the costs.

"(h) Study.--

The Comptroller General, in consultation with the Register of Copyrights, shall conduct a study of the conditions in the motion picture industry that gave rise to this section, and the impact of this section on the motion picture industry. The Comptroller General shall report the findings of the study to the Congress within 2 years after the effective date of this chapter.".

(b) Conforming Amendment.--

The table of chapters for part VI of title 28, United States Code, is amended by adding at the end the following:
"180. Assumption of Certain Contractual Obligations .... 4001".

Sec. 407: Effective Date.

Except as otherwise provided in this title, this title and the amendments made by this title shall take effect on the date of the enactment of this Act.

TITLE V - PROTECTION OF CERTAIN ORIGINAL DESIGNS

Sec. 501: Short Title.

This Act may be referred to as the "Vessel Hull Design Protection Act".

[...]

b) European Law

COUNCIL DIRECTIVE 91/250/EEC
OF 14 MAY 1991
ON THE LEGAL PROTECTION OF COMPUTER PROGRAMS

(Official Journal L 122, 17/05/1991, p. 0042)

THE COUNCIL OF THE EUROPEAN COMMUNITIES,

Having regard to the Treaty establishing the European Economic Community and in particular Article 100a thereof,
Having regard to the proposal from the Commission,[1]
In cooperation with the European Parliament,[2]
Having regard to the opinion of the Economic and Social Committee[3],

(1) Whereas computer programs are at present not clearly protected in all Member States by existing legislation and such protection, where it exists, has different attributes;
(2) Whereas the development of computer programs requires the investment of considerable human, technical and financial resources while computer programs can be copied at a fraction of the cost needed to develop them independently;
(3) Whereas computer programs are playing an increasingly important role in a broad range of industries and computer program technology can accordingly be considered as being of fundamental importance for the Community's industrial development;
(4) Whereas certain differences in the legal protection of computer programs offered by the laws of the Member States have direct and negative effects on the functioning of the common market as regards computer programs and such differences could well become greater as Member States introduce new legislation on this subject;
(5) Whereas existing differences having such effects need to be removed and new ones prevented from arising, while differences not adversely affecting the functioning of the common market to a substantial degree need not be removed or prevented from arising;
(6) Whereas the Community's legal framework on the protection of computer programs can accordingly in the first instance be limited to establishing that Member States should accord protection to computer programs under copyright law as literary works and, further, to establishing who and what should be protected, the exclusive rights on which protected persons should be able to rely in order to authorize or prohibit certain acts and for how long the protection should apply;
(7) Whereas, for the purpose of this Directive, the term 'computer program' shall include programs in any form, including those which are incorporated into hardware; whereas this term also includes preparatory design work leading to the development of a computer program provided that the nature of the preparatory work is such that a computer program can result from it at a later stage;
(8) Whereas, in respect of the criteria to be applied in determining whether or not a computer program is an original work, no tests as to the qualitative or aesthetic merits of the program should be applied;

---

[1] OJ No C 91, 12. 4. 1989, p. 4; and OJ No C 320, 20. 12. 1990, p. 22.
[2] OJ No C 231, 17. 9. 1990, p. 78; and Decision of 17 April 1991 (not yet published in the Official Journal).
[3] OJ No C 329, 30. 12. 1989, p. 4.

(9) Whereas the Community is fully committed to the promotion of international standardization;
(10) Whereas the function of a computer program is to communicate and work together with other components of a computer system and with users and, for this purpose, a logical and, where appropriate, physical interconnection and interaction is required to permit all elements of software and hardware to work with other software and hardware and with users in all the ways in which they are intended to function;
(11) Whereas the parts of the program which provide for such interconnection and interaction between elements of software and hardware are generally known as 'interfaces';
(12) Whereas this functional interconnection and interaction is generally known as 'interoperability'; whereas such interoperability can be defined as the ability to exchange information and mutually to use the information which has been exchanged;
(13) Whereas, for the avoidance of doubt, it has to be made clear that only the expression of a computer program is protected and that ideas and principles which underlie any element of a program, including those which underlie its interfaces, are not protected by copyright under this Directive;
(14) Whereas, in accordance with this principle of copyright, to the extent that logic, algorithms and programming languages comprise ideas and principles, those ideas and principles are not protected under this Directive;
(15) Whereas, in accordance with the legislation and jurisprudence of the Member States and the international copyright conventions, the expression of those ideas and principles is to be protected by copyright;
(16) Whereas, for the purposes of this Directive, the term 'rental' means the making available for use, for a limited period of time and for profit-making purposes, of a computer program or a copy thereof; whereas this term does not include public lending, which, accordingly, remains outside the scope of this Directive;
(17) Whereas the exclusive rights of the author to prevent the unauthorized reproduction of his work have to be subject to a limited exception in the case of a computer program to allow the reproduction technically necessary for the use of that program by the lawful acquirer;
(18) Whereas this means that the acts of loading and running necessary for the use of a copy of a program which has been lawfully acquired, and the act of correction of its errors, may not be prohibited by contract; whereas, in the absence of specific contractual provisions, including when a copy of the program has been sold, any other act necessary for the use of the copy of a program may be performed in accordance with its intended purpose by a lawful acquirer of that copy;
(19) Whereas a person having a right to use a computer program should not be prevented from performing acts necessary to observe, study or test the functioning of the program, provided that these acts do not infringe the copyright in the program;
(20) Whereas the unauthorized reproduction, translation, adaptation or transformation of the form of the code in which a copy of a computer program has been made available constitutes an infringement of the exclusive rights of the author;
(21) Whereas, nevertheless, circumstances may exist when such a reproduction of the code and translation of its form within the meaning of Article 4 (a) and (b) are indispensable to obtain the necessary information to achieve the interoperability of an independently created program with other programs;
(22) Whereas it has therefore to be considered that in these limited circumstances only, performance of the acts of reproduction and translation by or on behalf of a person having a right to use a copy of the program is legitimate and compatible with fair practice and must therefore be deemed not to require the authorization of the rightholder;
(23) Whereas an objective of this exception is to make it possible to connect all components of a computer system, including those of different manufacturers, so that they can work together;

(24) Whereas such an exception to the author's exclusive rights may not be used in a way which prejudices the legitimate interests of the rightholder or which conflicts with a normal exploitation of the program;
(25) Whereas, in order to remain in accordance with the provisions of the Berne Convention for the Protection of Literary and Artistic Works, the term of protection should be the life of the author and fifty years from the first of January of the year following the year of his death or, in the case of an anonymous or pseudonymous work, 50 years from the first of January of the year following the year in which the work is first published;
(26) Whereas protection of computer programs under copyright laws should be without prejudice to the application, in appropriate cases, of other forms of protection; whereas, however, any contractual provisions contrary to Article 6 or to the exceptions provided for in Article 5 (2) and (3) should be null and void;
(27) Whereas the provisions of this Directive are without prejudice to the application of the competition rules under Articles 85 and 86 of the Treaty if a dominant supplier refuses to make information available which is necessary for interoperability as defined in this Directive;
(28) Whereas the provisions of this Directive should be without prejudice to specific requirements of Community law already enacted in respect of the publication of interfaces in the telecommunications sector or Council Decisions relating to standardization in the field of information technology and telecommunication;
(29) Whereas this Directive does not affect derogations provided for under national legislation in accordance with the Berne Convention on points not covered by this Directive,

HAS ADOPTED THIS DIRECTIVE:

Article 1 - Object of protection

1. In accordance with the provisions of this Directive, Member States shall protect computer programs, by copyright, as literary works within the meaning of the Berne Convention for the Protection of Literary and Artistic Works. For the purposes of this Directive, the term 'computer programs' shall include their preparatory design material.
2. Protection in accordance with this Directive shall apply to the expression in any form of a computer program. Ideas and principles which underlie any element of a computer program, including those which underlie its interfaces, are not protected by copyright under this Directive.
3. A computer program shall be protected if it is original in the sense that it is the author's own intellectual creation. No other criteria shall be applied to determine its eligibility for protection.

Article 2 - Authorship of computer programs

1. The author of a computer program shall be the natural person or group of natural persons who has created the program or, where the legislation of the Member State permits, the legal person designated as the rightholder by that legislation. Where collective works are recognized by the legislation of a Member State, the person considered by the legislation of the Member State to have created the work shall be deemed to be its author.
2. In respect of a computer program created by a group of natural persons jointly, the exclusive rights shall be owned jointly.
3. Where a computer program is created by an employee in the execution of his duties or following the instructions given by his employer, the employer exclusively shall be entitled to exercise all economic rights in the program so created, unless otherwise provided by contract.

Article 3 - Beneficiaries of protection

Protection shall be granted to all natural or legal persons eligible under national copyright legislation as applied to literary works.

Article 4 - Restricted Acts

Subject to the provisions of Articles 5 and 6, the exclusive rights of the rightholder within the meaning of Article 2, shall include the right to do or to authorize:
(a) the permanent or temporary reproduction of a computer program by any means and in any form, in part or in whole. Insofar as loading, displaying, running, transmission or storage of the computer program necessitate such reproduction, such acts shall be subject to authorization by the rightholder;
(b) the translation, adaptation, arrangement and any other alteration of a computer program and the reproduction of the results thereof, without prejudice to the rights of the person who alters the program;
(c) any form of distribution to the public, including the rental, of the original computer program or of copies thereof. The first sale in the Community of a copy of a program by the rightholder or with his consent shall exhaust the distribution right within the Community of that copy, with the exception of the right to control further rental of the program or a copy thereof.

Article 5 - Exceptions to the restricted acts

1. In the absence of specific contractual provisions, the acts referred to in Article 4 (a) and (b) shall not require authorization by the rightholder where they are necessary for the use of the computer program by the lawful acquirer in accordance with its intended purpose, including for error correction.
2. The making of a back-up copy by a person having a right to use the computer program may not be prevented by contract insofar as it is necessary for that use.
3. The person having a right to use a copy of a computer program shall be entitled, without the authorization of the rightholder, to observe, study or test the functioning of the program in order to determine the ideas and principles which underlie any element of the program if he does so while performing any of the acts of loading, displaying, running, transmitting or storing the program which he is entitled to do.

Article 6 - Decompilation

1. The authorization of the rightholder shall not be required where reproduction of the code and translation of its form within the meaning of Article 4 (a) and (b) are indispensable to obtain the information necessary to achieve the interoperability of an independently created computer program with other programs, provided that the following conditions are met:
(a) these acts are performed by the licensee or by another person having a right to use a copy of a program, or on their behalf by a person authorized to do so;
(b) the information necessary to achieve interoperability has not previously been readily available to the persons referred to in subparagraph (a); and
(c) these acts are confined to the parts of the original program which are necessary to achieve interoperability.
2. The provisions of paragraph 1 shall not permit the information obtained through its application:
(a) to be used for goals other than to achieve the interoperability of the independently created computer program;
(b) to be given to others, except when necessary for the interoperability of the independently created computer program; or

(c) to be used for the development, production or marketing of a computer program substantially similar in its expression, or for any other act which infringes copyright.
3. In accordance with the provisions of the Berne Convention for the protection of Literary and Artistic Works, the provisions of this Article may not be interpreted in such a way as to allow its application to be used in a manner which unreasonably prejudices the right holder's legitimate interests or conflicts with a normal exploitation of the computer program.

Article 7 - Special measures of protection

1. Without prejudice to the provisions of Articles 4, 5 and 6, Member States shall provide, in accordance with their national legislation, appropriate remedies against a person committing any of the acts listed in subparagraphs (a), (b) and (c) below:
(a) any act of putting into circulation a copy of a computer program knowing, or having reason to believe, that it is an infringing copy;
(b) the possession, for commercial purposes, of a copy of a computer program knowing, or having reason to believe, that it is an infringing copy;
(c) any act of putting into circulation, or the possession for commercial purposes of, any means the sole intended purpose of which is to facilitate the unauthorized removal or circumvention of any technical device which may have been applied to protect a computer program.
2. Any infringing copy of a computer program shall be liable to seizure in accordance with the legislation of the Member State concerned.
3. Member States may provide for the seizure of any means referred to in paragraph 1 (c).

Article 8 - Term of protection

1. Protection shall be granted for the life of the author and for fifty years after his death or after the death of the last surviving author; where the computer program is an anonymous or pseudonymous work, or where a legal person is designated as the author by national legislation in accordance with Article 2 (1), the term of protection shall be fifty years from the time that the computer program is first lawfully made available to the public. The term of protection shall be deemed to begin on the first of January of the year following the abovementioned events.
2. Member States which already have a term of protection longer than that provided for in paragraph 1 are allowed to maintain their present term until such time as the term of protection for copyright works is harmonized by Community law in a more general way.

Article 9 - Continued application of other legal provisions

1. The provisions of this Directive shall be without prejudice to any other legal provisions such as those concerning patent rights, trade-marks, unfair competition, trade secrets, protection of semi-conductor products or the law of contract. Any contractual provisions contrary to Article 6 or to the exceptions provided for in Article 5 (2) and (3) shall be null and void.
2. The provisions of this Directive shall apply also to programs created before 1 January 1993 without prejudice to any acts concluded and rights acquired before that date.

Article 10 - Final provisions

1. Member States shall bring into force the laws, regulations and administrative provisions necessary to comply with this Directive before 1 January 1993.
When Member States adopt these measures, the latter shall contain a reference to this Directive or shall be accompanied by such reference on the occasion of their official publication. The methods of making such a reference shall be laid down by the Member States.

2. Member States shall communicate to the Commission the provisions of national law which they adopt in the field governed by this Directive.

Article 11 - Addressees

This Directive is addressed to the Member States.

COUNCIL DIRECTIVE 92/100/EEC
OF 19 NOVEMBER 1992
ON RENTAL RIGHT AND LENDING RIGHT AND ON CERTAIN RIGHTS RELATED TO COPYRIGHT IN THE FIELD OF INTELLECTUAL PROPERTY

(Official Journal L 346, 27/11/1992, p. 0061 – 0066)

THE COUNCIL OF THE EUROPEAN COMMUNITIES,

Having regard to the Treaty establishing the European Economic Community, and in particular Articles 57 (2), 66 and 100a thereof,
Having regard to the proposal from the Commission[1],
In cooperation with the European Parliament[2],
Having regard to the opinion of the Economic and Social Committee[3],

(1) Whereas differences exist in the legal protection provided by the laws and practices of the Member States for copyright works and subject matter of related rights protection as regards rental and lending; whereas such differences are sources of barriers to trade and distortions of competition which impede the achievement and proper functioning of the internal market;
(2) Whereas such differences in legal protection could well become greater as Member States adopt new and different legislation or as national case-law interpreting such legislation develops differently;
(3) Whereas such differences should therefore be eliminated in accordance with the objective of introducing an area without internal frontiers as set out in Article 8a of the Treaty so as to institute, pursuant to Article 3 (f) of the Treaty, a system ensuring that competition in the common market is not distorted;
(4) Whereas rental and lending of copyright works and the subject matter of related rights protection is playing an increasingly important role in particular for authors, performers and producers of phonograms and films; whereas piracy is becoming an increasing threat;
(5) Whereas the adequate protection of copyright works and subject matter of related rights protection by rental and lending rights as well as the protection of the subject matter of related rights protection by the fixation right, reproduction right, distribution right, right to broadcast and communication to the public can accordingly be considered as being of fundamental importance for the Community's economic and cultural development;
(6) Whereas copyright and related rights protection must adapt to new economic developments such as new forms of exploitation;
(7) Whereas the creative and artistic work of authors and performers necessitates an adequate income as a basis for further creative and artistic work, and the investments required particularly for the production of phonograms and films are especially high and risky; whereas the possibility for securing that income and recouping that investment can only effectively be guaranteed through adequate legal protection of the rightholders concerned;
(8) Whereas these creative, artistic and entrepreneurial activities are, to a large extent, activities of self-employed persons; whereas the pursuit of such activities must be made easier by providing a harmonized legal protection within the Community;

---

[1] OJ No C 53, 28. 2. 1991, p. 35 and OJ No C 128, 20. 5. 1992, p. 8.
[2] OJ No C 67, 16. 3. 1992, p. 92 and Decision of 28 October 1992 (not yet published in the Official Journal).
[3] OJ No C 269, 14. 10. 1991, p. 54.

(9) Whereas, to the extent that these activities principally constitute services, their provision must equally be facilitated by the establishment in the Community of a harmonized legal framework;

(10) Whereas the legislation of the Member States should be approximated in such a way so as not to conflict with the international conventions on which many Member States' copyright and related rights laws are based;

(11) Whereas the Community's legal framework on the rental right and lending right and on certain rights related to copyright can be limited to establishing that Member States provide rights with respect to rental and lending for certain groups of rightholders and further to establishing the rights of fixation, reproduction, distribution, broadcasting and communication to the public for certain groups of rightholders in the field of related rights protection;

(12) Whereas it is necessary to define the concepts of rental and lending for the purposes of this Directive;

(13) Whereas it is desirable, with a view to clarity, to exclude from rental and lending within the meaning of this Directive certain forms of making available, as for instance making available phonograms or films (cinematographic or audiovisual works or moving images, whether or not accompanied by sound) for the purpose of public performance or broadcasting, making available for the purpose of exhibition, or making available for on-the-spot reference use; whereas lending within the meaning of this Directive does not include making available between establishments which are accessible to the public;

(14) Whereas, where lending by an establishment accessible to the public gives rise to a payment the amount of which does not go beyond what is necessary to cover the operating costs of the establishment, there is no direct or indirect economic or commercial advantage within the meaning of this Directive;

(15) Whereas it is necessary to introduce arrangements ensuring that an unwaivable equitable remuneration is obtained by authors and performers who must retain the possibility to entrust the administration of this right to collecting societies representing them;

(16) Whereas the equitable remuneration may be paid on the basis of one or several payments an any time on or after the conclusion of the contract;

(17) Whereas the equitable remuneration must take account of the importance of the contribution of the authors and performers concerned to the phonogram or film;

(18) Whereas it is also necessary to protect the rights at least of authors as regards public lending by providing for specific arrangements; whereas, however, any measures based on Article 5 of this Directive have to comply with Community law, in particular with Article 7 of the Treaty;

(19) Whereas the provisions of Chapter II do not prevent Member States from extending the presumption set out in Article 2 (5) to the exclusive rights included in that chapter; whereas furthermore the provisions of Chapter II do not prevent Member States from providing for a rebuttable presumption of the authorization of exploitation in respect of the exclusive rights of performers provided for in those articles, in so far as such presumption is compatible with the International Convention for the Protection of Performers, Producers of Phonograms and Broadcasting Organizations (hereinafter referred to as the Rome Convention);

(20) Whereas Member States may provide for more far-reaching protection for owners of rights related to copyright than that required by Article 8 of this Directive;

(21) Whereas the harmonized rental and lending rights and the harmonized protection in the field of rights related to copyright should not be exercised in a way which constitutes a disguised restriction on trade between Member States or in a way which is contrary to the rule of media exploitation chronology, as recognized in the Judgment handed down in Société Cinéthèque v. FNCF[4],

---

[4] Cases 60/84 and 61/84, ECR 1985, p. 2605.

HAS ADOPTED THIS DIRECTIVE:

CHAPTER I: RENTAL AND LENDING RIGHT

Article 1 - Object of harmonization

1. In accordance with the provisions of this Chapter, Member States shall provide, subject to Article 5, a right to authorize or prohibit the rental and lending of originals and copies of copyright works, and other subject matter as set out in Article 2 (1).
2. For the purposes of this Directive, 'rental' means making available for use, for a limited period of time and for direct or indirect economic or commercial advantage.
3. For the purposes of this Directive, 'lending' means making available for use, for a limited period of time and not for direct or indirect economic or commercial advantage, when it is made through establishments which are accessible to the public.
4. The rights referred to in paragraph 1 shall not be exhausted by any sale or other act of distribution of originals and copies of copyright works and other subject matter as set out in Article 2 (1).

Article 2 - Rightholders and subject matter of rental and lending right

1. The exclusive right to authorize or prohibit rental and lending shall belong:
- to the author in respect of the original and copies of his work,
- to the performer in respect of fixations of his performance,
- to the phonogram producer in respect of his phonograms, and
- to the producer of the first fixation of a film in respect of the original and copies of his film.

For the purposes of this Directive, the term 'film' shall designate a cinematographic or audiovisual work or moving images, whether or not accompanied by sound.

2. For the purposes of this Directive the principal director of a cinematographic or audiovisual work shall be considered as its author or one of its authors. Member States may provide for others to be considered as its co-authors.
3. This Directive does not cover rental and lending rights in relation to buildings and to works of applied art.
4. The rights referred to in paragraph 1 may be transferred, assigned or subjet to the granting of contractual licences.
5. Without prejudice to paragraph 7, when a contract concerning film production is concluded, individually or collectively, by performers with a film producer, the performer covered by this contract shall be presumed, subject to contractual clauses to the contrary, to have transferred his rental right, subject to Article 4.
6. Member States may provide for a similar presumption as set out in paragraph 5 with respect to authors.
7. Member States may provide that the signing of a contract concluded between a performer and a film producer concerning the production of a film has the effect of authorizing rental, provided that such contract provides for an equitable remuneration within the meaning of Article 4. Member States may also provide that this paragraph shall apply mutatis mutandis to the rights included in Chapter II.

Article 3 - Rental of computer programs

This Directive shall be without prejudice to Article 4 (c) of Council Directive 91/250/EEC of 14 May 1991 on the legal protection of computer programs[5].

Article 4 - Unwaivable right to equitable remuneration

1. Where an author or performer has transferred or assigned his rental right concerning a phonogram or an original or copy of a film to a phonogram or film producer, that author or performer shall retain the right to obtain an equitable remuneration for the rental.
2. The right to obtain an equitable remuneration for rental cannot be waived by authors or performers.
3. The administration of this right to obtain an equitable remuneration may be entrusted to collecting societies representing authors or performers.
4. Member States may regulate whether and to what extent administration by collecting societies of the right to obtain an equitable remuneration may be imposed, as well as the question from whom this remuneration may be claimed or collected.

Article 5 - Derogation from the exclusive public lending right

1. Member States may derogate from the exclusive right provided for in Article 1 in respect of public lending, provided that at least authors obtain a remuneration for such lending. Member States shall be free to determine this remuneration taking account of their cultural promotion objectives.
2. When Member States do not apply the exclusive lending right provided for in Article 1 as regards phonograms, films and computer programs, they shall introduce, at least for authors, a remuneration.
3. Member States may exempt certain categories of establishments from the payment of the remuneration referred to in paragraphs 1 and 2.
4. The Commission, in cooperation with the Member States, shall draw up before 1 July 1997 a report on public lending in the Community. It shall forward this report to the European Parliament and to the Council.

CHAPTER II: RIGHTS RELATED TO COPYRIGHT

Article 6 - Fixation right

1. Member States shall provide for performers the exclusive right to authorize or prohibit the fixation of their performances.
2. Member States shall provide for broadcasting organizations the exclusive right to authorize or prohibit the fixation of their broadcasts, whether these broadcasts are transmitted by wire or over the air, including by cable or satellite.
3. A cable distributor shall not have the right provided for in paragraph 2 where it merely retransmits by cable the broadcasts of broadcasting organizations.

Article 7 - Reproduction right

1. Member States shall provide the exclusive right to authorize or prohibit the direct or indirect reproduction:
- for performers, of fixations of their performances,
- for phonogram producers, of their phonograms,

---

[5] OJ No L 122, 17. 5. 1991, p. 42.

- for producers of the first fixations of films, in respect of the original and copies of their films, and
- for broadcasting organizations, of fixations of their broadcasts, as set out in Article 6 (2).
2. The reproduction right referred to in paragraph 1 may be transferred, assigned or subject to the granting of contractual licences.

Article 8 - Broadcasting and communication to the public

1. Member States shall provide for performers the exclusive right to authorize or prohibit the broadcasting by wireless means and the communication to the public of their performances, except where the performance is itself already a broadcast performance or is made from a fixation.
2. Member States shall provide a right in order to ensure that a single equitable remuneration is paid by the user, if a phonogram published for commercial purposes, or a reproduction of such phonogram, is used for broadcasting by wireless means or for any communication to the public, and to ensure that this remuneration is shared between the relevant performers and phonogram producers. Member States may, in the absence of agreement between the performers and phonogram producers, lay down the conditions as to the sharing of this remuneration between them.
3. Member States shall provide for broadcasting organizations the exclusive right to authorize or prohibit the rebroadcasting of their broadcasts by wireless means, as well as the communication to the public of their broadcasts if such communication is made in places accessible to the public against payment of an entrance fee.

Article 9 - Distribution right

1. Member States shall provide
- for performers, in respect of fixations of their performances,
- for phonogram producers, in respect of their phonograms,
- for producers of the first fixations of films, in respect of the original and copies of their films,
- for broadcasting organizations, in respect of fixations of their broadcast as set out in Article 6 (2),

the exclusive right to make available these objects, including copies thereof, to the public by sale or otherwise, hereafter referred to as the 'distribution right'.
2. The distribution right shall not be exhausted within the Community in respect of an object as referred to in paragraph 1, except where the first sale in the Community of that object is made by the rightholder or with his consent.
3. The distribution right shall be without prejudice to the specific provisions of Chapter I, in particular Article 1 (4).
4. The distribution right may be transferred, assigned or subject to the granting of contractual licences.

Article 10 - Limitations to rights

1. Member States may provide for limitations to the rights referred to in Chapter II in respect of:
(a) private use;
(b) use of short excerpts in connection with the reporting of current events;
(c) ephemeral fixation by a broadcasting organization by means of its own facilities and for its own broadcasts;
(d) use solely for the purposes of teaching or scientific research.

2. Irrespective of paragraph 1, any Member State may provide for the same kinds of limitations with regard to the protection of performers, producers of phonograms, broadcasting organizations and of producers of the first fixations of films, as it provides for in connection with the protection of copyright in literary and artistic works. However, compulsory licences may be provided for only to the extent to which they are compatible with the Rome Convention.
3. Paragraph 1 (a) shall be without prejudice to any existing or future legislation on remuneration for reproduction for private use.

CHAPTER III: DURATION

Article 11 - Duration of authors' rights

Without prejudice to further harmonization, the authors' rights referred to in this Directive shall not expire before the end of the term provided by the Berne Convention for the Protection of Literary and Artistic Works.

Article 12 - Duration of related rights

Without prejudice to further harmonization, the rights referred to in this Directive of performers, phonogram producers and broadcasting organizations shall not expire before the end of the respective terms provided by the Rome Convention. The rights referred to in this Directive for producers of the first fixations of films shall not expire before the end of a period of 20 years computed from the end of the year in which the fixation was made.

CHAPTER IV: COMMON PROVISIONS

Article 13 - Application in time

1. This Directive shall apply in respect of all copyright works, performances, phonograms, broadcasts and first fixations of films referred to in this Directive which are, on 1 July 1994, still protected by the legislation of the Member States in the field of copyright and related rights or meet the criteria for protection under the provisions of this Directive on that date.
2. This Directive shall apply without prejudice to any acts of exploitation performed before 1 July 1994.
3. Member States may provide that the rightholders are deemed to have given their authorization to the rental or lending of an object referred to in Article 2 (1) which is proven to have been made available to third parties for this purpose or to have been acquired before 1 July 1994. However, in particular where such an object is a digital recording, Member States may provide that rightholders shall have a right to obtain an adequate remuneration for the rental or lending of that object.
4. Member States need not apply the provisions of Article 2 (2) to cinematographic or audiovisual works created before 1 July 1994.
5. Member States may determine the date as from which the Article 2 (2) shall apply, provided that date is no later than 1 July 1997.
6. This Directive shall, without prejudice to paragraph 3 and subject to paragraphs 8 and 9, not affect any contracts concluded before the date of its adoption.
7. Member States may provide, subject to the provisions of paragraphs 8 and 9, that when rightholders who acquire new rights under the national provisions adopted in implementation of this Directive have, before 1 July 1994, given their consent for exploitation, they shall be presumed to have transferred the new exclusive rights.

8. Member States may determine the date as from which the unwaivable right to an equitable remuneration referred to in Article 4 exists, provided that that date is no later than 1 July 1997.
9. For contracts concluded before 1 July 1994, the unwaivable right to an equitable remuneration provided for in Article 4 shall apply only where authors or performers or those representing them have submitted a request to that effect before 1 January 1997. In the absence of agreement between rightholders concerning the level of remuneration, Member States may fix the level of equitable remuneration.

Article 14 - Relation between copyright and related rights

Protection of copyright-related rights under this Directive shall leave intact and shall in no way affect the protection of copyright.

Article 15 - Final provisions

1. Member States shall bring into force the laws, regulations and administrative provisions necessary to comply with this Directive not later than 1 July 1994. They shall forthwith inform the Commission thereof.
   When Member States adopt these measures, they shall contain a reference to this Directive or shall be accompanied by such reference at the time of their official publication. The methods of making such a reference shall be laid down by the Member States.
2. Member States shall communicate to the Commission the main provisions of domestic law which they adopt in the field covered by this Directive.

Article 16 - Addressees

This Directive is addressed to the Member States.

COUNCIL DIRECTIVE 93/83/EEC
OF 27 SEPTEMBER 1993
ON THE COORDINATION OF CERTAIN RULES CONCERNING COPYRIGHT AND RIGHTS RELATED TO COPYRIGHT APPLICABLE TO SATELLITE BROADCASTING AND CABLE RETRANSMISSION

(Official Journal L 248, 06/10/1993, p. 0015)

THE COUNCIL OF THE EUROPEAN COMMUNITIES,

Having regard to the Treaty establishing the European Economic Community, and in particular Articles 57 (2) and 66 thereof,
Having regard to the proposal from the Commission,[1]
In cooperation with the European Parliament,[2]
Having regard to the opinion of the Economic and Social Committee[3],

(1) Whereas the objectives of the Community as laid down in the Treaty include establishing an ever closer union among the peoples of Europe, fostering closer relations between the States belonging to the Community and ensuring the economic and social progress of the Community countries by common action to eliminate the barriers which divide Europe;

(2) Whereas, to that end, the Treaty provides for the establishment of a common market and an area without internal frontiers; whereas measures to achieve this include the abolition of obstacles to the free movement of services and the institution of a system ensuring that competition in the common market is not distorted; whereas, to that end, the Council may adopt directives for the coordination of the provisions laid down by law, regulation or administrative action in Member States concerning the taking up and pursuit of activities as self-employed persons;

(3) Whereas broadcasts transmitted across frontiers within the Community, in particular by satellite and cable, are one of the most important ways of pursuing these Community objectives, which are at the same time political, economic, social, cultural and legal;

(4) Whereas the Council has already adopted Directive 89/552/EEC of 3 October 1989 on the coordination of certain provisions laid down by law, regulation or administrative action in Member States concerning the pursuit of television broadcasting activities,[4] which makes provision for the promotion of the distribution and production of European television programmes and for advertising and sponsorship, the protection of minors and the right of reply;

(5) Whereas, however, the achievement of these objectives in respect of cross-border satellite broadcasting and the cable retransmission of programmes from other Member States is currently still obstructed by a series of differences between national rules of copyright and some degree of legal uncertainty; whereas this means that holders of rights are exposed to the threat of seeing their works exploited without payment of remuneration or that the individual holders of exclusive rights in various Member States block the exploitation of their rights; whereas the legal uncertainty in particular constitutes a direct obstacle in the free circulation of programmes within the Community;

(6) Whereas a distinction is currently drawn for copyright purposes between communication to the public by direct satellite and communication to the public by communications satellite;

---

[1] OJ No C 255, 1. 10. 1991, p. 3 and OJ No C 25, 28. 1. 1993, p. 43.
[2] OJ No C 305, 23. 11. 1992, p. 129 and OJ No C 255, 20. 9. 1993.
[3] OJ No C 98, 21. 4. 1992, p. 44.
[4] OJ No L 298, 17. 10. 1989, p. 23.

Satellite and Cable Directive (93/83/EEC)

whereas, since individual reception is possible and affordable nowadays with both types of satellite, there is no longer any justification for this differing legal treatment;
(7) Whereas the free broadcasting of programmes is further impeded by the current legal uncertainty over whether broadcasting by a satellite whose signals can be received directly affects the rights in the country of transmission only or in all countries of reception together; whereas, since communications satellites and direct satellites are treated alike for copyright purposes, this legal uncertainty now affects almost all programmes broadcast in the Community by satellite;
(8) Whereas, furthermore, legal certainty, which is a prerequisite for the free movement of broadcasts within the Community, is missing where programmes transmitted across frontiers are fed into and retransmitted through cable networks;
(9) Whereas the development of the acquisition of rights on a contractual basis by authorization is already making a vigorous contribution to the creation of the desired European audiovisual area; whereas the continuation of such contractual agreements should be ensured and their smooth application in practice should be promoted wherever possible;
(10) Whereas at present cable operators in particular cannot be sure that they have actually acquired all the programme rights covered by such an agreement;
(11) Whereas, lastly, parties in different Member States are not all similarly bound by obligations which prevent them from refusing without valid reason to negotiate on the acquisition of the rights necessary for cable distribution or allowing such negotiations to fail;
(12) Whereas the legal framework for the creation of a single audiovisual area laid down in Directive 89/552/EEC must, therefore, be supplemented with reference to copyright;
(13) Whereas, therefore, an end should be put to the differences of treatment of the transmission of programmes by communications satellite which exist in the Member States, so that the vital distinction throughout the Community becomes whether works and other protected subject matter are communicated to the public; whereas this will also ensure equal treatment of the suppliers of cross-border broadcasts, regardless of whether they use a direct broadcasting satellite or a communications satellite;
(14) Whereas the legal uncertainty regarding the rights to be acquired which impedes cross-border satellite broadcasting should be overcome by defining the notion of communication to the public by satellite at a Community level; whereas this definition should at the same time specify where the act of communication takes place; whereas such a definition is necessary to avoid the cumulative application of several national laws to one single act of broadcasting; whereas communication to the public by satellite occurs only when, and in the Member State where, the programme-carrying signals are introduced under the control and responsibility of the broadcasting organization into an uninterrupted chain of communication leading to the satellite and down towards the earth; whereas normal technical procedures relating to the programme-carrying signals should not be considered as interruptions to the chain of broadcasting;
(15) Whereas the acquisition on a contractual basis of exclusive broadcasting rights should comply with any legislation on copyright and rights related to copyright in the Member State in which communication to the public by satellite occurs;
(16) Whereas the principle of contractual freedom on which this Directive is based will make it possible to continue limiting the exploitation of these rights, especially as far as certain technical means of transmission or certain language versions are concerned;
(17) Whereas, in arriving at the amount of the payment to be made for the rights acquired, the parties should take account of all aspects of the broadcast, such as the actual audience, the potential audience and the language version;
(18) Whereas the application of the country-of-origin principle contained in this Directive could pose a problem with regard to existing contracts; whereas this Directive should provide for a period of five years for existing contracts to be adapted, where necessary, in the light of the

Directive; whereas the said country-of-origin principle should not, therefore, apply to existing contracts which expire before 1 January 2000; whereas if by that date parties still have an interest in the contract, the same parties should be entitled to renegotiate the conditions of the contract;

(19) Whereas existing international co-production agreements must be interpreted in the light of the economic purpose and scope envisaged by the parties upon signature; whereas in the past international co-production agreements have often not expressly and specifically addressed communication to the public by satellite within the meaning of this Directive a particular form of exploitation; whereas the underlying philosophy of many existing international co-production agreements is that the rights in the co-production are exercised separately and independently by each co-producer, by dividing the exploitation rights between them along territorial lines; whereas, as a general rule, in the situation where a communication to the public by satellite authorized by one co-producer would prejudice the value of the exploitation rights of another co-producer, the interpretation of such an existing agreement would normally suggest that the latter co-producer would have to give his consent to the authorization, by the former co-producer, of the communication to the public by satellite; whereas the language exclusivity of the latter co-producer will be prejudiced where the language version or versions of the communication to the public, including where the version is dubbed or subtitled, coincide(s) with the language or the languages widely understood in the territory allotted by the agreement to the latter co-producer; whereas the notion of exclusivity should be understood in a wider sense where the communication to the public by satellite concerns a work which consists merely of images and contains no dialogue or subtitles; whereas a clear rule is necessary in cases where the international co-production agreement does not expressly regulate the division of rights in the specific case of communication to the public by satellite within the meaning of this Directive;

(20) Whereas communications to the public by satellite from non-member countries will under certain conditions be deemed to occur within a Member State of the Community;

(21) Whereas it is necessary to ensure that protection for authors, performers, producers of phonograms and broadcasting organizations is accorded in all Member States and that this protection is not subject to a statutory licence system; whereas only in this way is it possible to ensure that any difference in the level of protection within the common market will not create distortions of competition;

(22) Whereas the advent of new technologies is likely to have an impact on both the quality and the quantity of the exploitation of works and other subject matter;

(23) Whereas in the light of these developments the level of protection granted pursuant to this Directive to all rightholders in the areas covered by this Directive should remain under consideration;

(24) Whereas the harmonization of legislation envisaged in this Directive entails the harmonization of the provisions ensuring a high level of protection of authors, performers, phonogram producers and broadcasting organizations; whereas this harmonization should not allow a broadcasting organization to take advantage of differences in levels of protection by relocating activities, to the detriment of audiovisual productions;

(25) Whereas the protection provided for rights related to copyright should be aligned on that contained in Council Directive 92/100/EEC of 19 November 1992 on rental right and lending right and on certain rights related to copyright in the field of intellectual property[5] for the purposes of communication to the public by satellite; whereas, in particular, this will ensure that performers and phonogram producers are guaranteed an appropriate remuneration for the communication to the public by satellite of their performances or phonograms;

---

[5] OJ No L 346, 27. 11. 1992, p. 61.

(26) Whereas the provisions of Article 4 do not prevent Member States from extending the presumption set out in Article 2 (5) of Directive 92/100/EEC to the exclusive rights referred to in Article 4; whereas, furthermore, the provisions of Article 4 do not prevent Member States from providing for a rebuttable presumption of the authorization of exploitation in respect of the exclusive rights of performers referred to in that Article, in so far as such presumption is compatible with the International Convention for the Protection of Performers, Producers of Phonograms and Broadcasting Organizations;

(27) Whereas the cable retransmission of programmes from other Member States is an act subject to copyright and, as the case may be, rights related to copyright; whereas the cable operator must, therefore, obtain the authorization from every holder of rights in each part of the programme retransmitted; whereas, pursuant to this Directive, the authorizations should be granted contractually unless a temporary exception is provided for in the case of existing legal licence schemes;

(28) Whereas, in order to ensure that the smooth operation of contractual arrangements is not called into question by the intervention of outsiders holding rights in individual parts of the programme, provision should be made, through the obligation to have recourse to a collecting society, for the exclusive collective exercise of the authorization right to the extent that this is required by the special features of cable retransmission; whereas the authorization right as such remains intact and only the exercise of this right is regulated to some extent, so that the right to authorize a cable retransmission can still be assigned; whereas this Directive does not affect the exercise of moral rights;

(29) Whereas the exemption provided for in Article 10 should not limit the choice of holders of rights to transfer their rights to a collecting society and thereby have a direct share in the remuneration paid by the cable distributor for cable retransmission;

(30) Whereas contractual arrangements regarding the authorization of cable retransmission should be promoted by additional measures; whereas a party seeking the conclusion of a general contract should, for its part, be obliged to submit collective proposals for an agreement; whereas, furthermore, any party shall be entitled, at any moment, to call upon the assistance of impartial mediators whose task is to assist negotiations and who may submit proposals; whereas any such proposals and any opposition thereto should be served on the parties concerned in accordance with the applicable rules concerning the service of legal documents, in particular as set out in existing international conventions; whereas, finally, it is necessary to ensure that the negotiations are not blocked without valid justification or that individual holders are not prevented without valid justification from taking part in the negotiations; whereas none of these measures for the promotion of the acquisition of rights calls into question the contractual nature of the acquisition of cable retransmission rights;

(31) Whereas for a transitional period Member States should be allowed to retain existing bodies with jurisdiction in their territory over cases where the right to retransmit a programme by cable to the public has been unreasonably refused or offered on unreasonable terms by a broadcasting organization; whereas it is understood that the right of parties concerned to be heard by the body should be guaranteed and that the existence of the body should not prevent the parties concerned from having normal access to the courts;

(32) Whereas, however, Community rules are not needed to deal with all of those matters, the effects of which perhaps with some commercially insignificant exceptions, are felt only inside the borders of a single Member State;

(33) Whereas minimum rules should be laid down in order to establish and guarantee free and uninterrupted cross-border broadcasting by satellite and simultaneous, unaltered cable retransmission of programmes broadcast from other Member States, on an essentially contractual basis;

(34) Whereas this Directive should not prejudice further harmonization in the field of copyright and rights related to copyright and the collective administration of such rights; whereas the

possibility for Member States to regulate the activities of collecting societies should not prejudice the freedom of contractual negotiation of the rights provided for in this Directive, on the understanding that such negotiation takes place within the framework of general or specific national rules with regard to competition law or the prevention of abuse of monopolies;

(35) Whereas it should, therefore, be for the Member States to supplement the general provisions needed to achieve the objectives of this Directive by taking legislative and administrative measures in their domestic law, provided that these do not run counter to the objectives of this Directive and are compatible with Community law;

(36) Whereas this Directive does not affect the applicability of the competition rules in Articles 85 and 86 of the Treaty,

HAS ADOPTED THIS DIRECTIVE:

CHAPTER I: DEFINITIONS

Article 1 - Definitions

1. For the purpose of this Directive, 'satellite' means any satellite operating on frequency bands which, under telecommunications law, are reserved for the broadcast of signals for reception by the public or which are reserved for closed, point-to-point communication. In the latter case, however, the circumstances in which individual reception of the signals takes place must be comparable to those which apply in the first case.

2.
(a) For the purpose of this Directive, 'communication to the public by satellite' means the act of introducing, under the control and responsibility of the broadcasting organization, the programme-carrying signals intended for reception by the public into an uninterrupted chain of communication leading to the satellite and down towards the earth.
(b) The act of communication to the public by satellite occurs solely in the Member State where, under the control and responsibility of the broadcasting organization, the programme-carrying signals are introduced into an uninterrupted chain of communication leading to the satellite and down towards the earth.
(c) If the programme-carrying signals are encrypted, then there is communication to the public by satellite on condition that the means for decrypting the broadcast are provided to the public by the broadcasting organization or with its consent.
(d) Where an act of communication to the public by satellite occurs in a non-Community State which does not provide the level of protection provided for under Chapter II,
(I) if the programme-carrying signals are transmitted to the satellite from an uplink station situated in a Member State, that act of communication to the public by satellite shall be deemed to have occurred in that Member State and the rights provided for under Chapter II shall be exercisable against the person operating the uplink station; or
(II) if there is no use of an uplink station situated in a Member State but a broadcasting organization established in a Member State has commissioned the act of communication to the public by satellite, that act shall be deemed to have occurred in the Member State in which the broadcasting organization has its principal establishment in the Community and the rights provided for under Chapter II shall be exercisable against the broadcasting organization.

3. For the purposes of this Directive, 'cable retransmission' means the simultaneous, unaltered and unabridged retransmission by a cable or microwave system for reception by the public of an initial transmission from another Member State, by wire or over the air, including that by satellite, of television or radio programmes intended for reception by the public.

4. For the purposes of this Directive 'collecting society' means any organization which manages or administers copyright or rights related to copyright as its sole purpose or as one of its main purposes.
5. For the purposes of this Directive, the principal director of a cinematographic or audiovisual work shall be considered as its author or one of its authors. Member States may provide for others to be considered as its co-authors.

CHAPTER II: BROADCASTING OF PROGRAMMES BY SATELLITE

Article 2 - Broadcasting right

Member States shall provide an exclusive right for the author to authorize the communication to the public by satellite of copyright works, subject to the provisions set out in this chapter.

Article 3 - Acquisition of broadcasting rights

1. Member States shall ensure that the authorization referred to in Article 2 may be acquired only be agreement.
2. A Member State may provide that a collective agreement between a collecting society and a broadcasting organization concerning a given category of works may be extended to rightholders of the same category who are not represented by the collecting society, provided that:
- the communication to the public by satellite simulcasts a terrestrial broadcast by the same broadcaster, and
- the unrepresented rightholder shall, at any time, have the possibility of excluding the extension of the collective agreement to his works and of exercising his rights either individually or collectively.
3. Paragraph 2 shall not apply to cinematographic works, including works created by a process analogous to cinematography.
4. Where the law of a Member State provides for the extension of a collective agreement in accordance with the provisions of paragraph 2, that Member States shall inform the Commission which broadcasting organizations are entitled to avail themselves of that law. The Commission shall publish this information in the Official Journal of the European Communities (C series).

Article 4 - Rights of performers, phonogram producers and broadcasting organizations

1. For the purposes of communication to the public by satellite, the rights of performers, phonogram producers and broadcasting organizations shall be protected in accordance with the provisions of Articles 6, 7, 8 and 10 of Directive 92/100/EEC.
2. For the purposes of paragraph 1, 'broadcasting by wireless means' in Directive 92/100/EEC shall be understood as including communication to the public by satellite.
3. With regard to the exercise of the rights referred to in paragraph 1, Articles 2 (7) and 12 of Directive 92/100/EEC shall apply.

Article 5 - Relation between copyright and related rights

Protection of copyright-related rights under this Directive shall leave intact and shall in no way affect the protection of copyright.

Article 6 - Minimum protection

1. Member States may provide for more far-reaching protection for holders of rights related to copyright than that required by Article 8 of Directive 92/100/EEC.

2. In applying paragraph 1 Member States shall observe the definitions contained in Article 1 (1) and (2).

Article 7 - Transitional provisions

1. With regard to the application in time of the rights referred to in Article 4 (1) of this Directive, Article 13 (1), (2), (6) and (7) of Directive 92/100/EEC shall apply. Article 13 (4) and (5) of Directive 92/100/EEC shall apply mutatis mutandis.
2. Agreements concerning the exploitation of works and other protected subject matter which are in force on the date mentioned in Article 14 (1) shall be subject to the provisions of Articles 1 (2), 2 and 3 as from 1 January 2000 if they expire after that date.
3. When an international co-production agreement concluded before the date mentioned in Article 14 (1) between a co-producer from a Member State and one or more co-producers from other Member States or third countries expressly provides for a system of division of exploitation rights between the co-producers by geographical areas for all means of communication to the public, without distinguishing the arrangement applicable to communication to the public by satellite from the provisions applicable to the other means of communication, and where communication to the public by satellite of the co-production would prejudice the exclusivity, in particular the language exclusivity, of one of the co-producers or his assignees in a given territory, the authorization by one of the co-producers or his assignees for a communication to the public by satellite shall require the prior consent of the holder of that exclusivity, whether co-producer or assignee.

CHAPTER III: CABLE RETRANSMISSION

Article 8 - Cable retransmission right

1. Member States shall ensure that when programmes from other Member States are retransmitted by cable in their territory the applicable copyright and related rights are observed and that such retransmission takes place on the basis of individual or collective contractual agreements between copyright owners, holders of related rights and cable operators.
2. Notwithstanding paragraph 1, Member States may retain until 31 December 1997 such statutory licence systems which are in operation or expressly provided for by national law on 31 July 1991.

Article 9 - Exercise of the cable retransmission right

1. Member States shall ensure that the right of copyright owners and holders or related rights to grant or refuse authorization to a cable operator for a cable retransmission may be exercised only through a collecting society.
2. Where a rightholder has not transferred the management of his rights to a collecting society, the collecting society which manages rights of the same category shall be deemed to be mandated to manage his rights. Where more than one collecting society manages rights of that category, the rightholder shall be free to choose which of those collecting societies is deemed to be mandated to manage his rights. A rightholder referred to in this paragraph shall have the same rights and obligations resulting from the agreement between the cable operator and the collecting society which is deemed to be mandated to manage his rights as the rightholders who have mandated that collecting society and he shall be able to claim those rights within a period, to be fixed by the Member State concerned, which shall not be shorter than three years from the date of the cable retransmission which includes his work or other protected subject matter.

3. A Member State may provide that, when a rightholder authorizes the initial transmission within its territory of a work or other protected subject matter, he shall be deemed to have agreed not to exercise his cable retransmission rights on an individual basis but to exercise them in accordance with the provisions of this Directive.

Article 10 - Exercise of the cable retransmission right by broadcasting organizations

Member States shall ensure that Article 9 does not apply to the rights exercised by a broadcasting organization in respect of its own transmission, irrespective of whether the rights concerned are its own or have been transferred to it by other copyright owners and/or holders of related rights.

Article 11 - Mediators

1. Where no agreement is concluded regarding authorization of the cable retransmission of a broadcast, Member States shall ensure that either party may call upon the assistance of one or more mediators.
2. The task of the mediators shall be to provide assistance with negotiation. They may also submit proposals to the parties.
3. It shall be assumed that all the parties accept a proposal as referred to in paragraph 2 if none of them expresses its opposition within a period of three months. Notice of the proposal and of any opposition thereto shall be served on the parties concerned in accordance with the applicable rules concerning the service of legal documents.
4. The mediators shall be so selected that their independence and impartiality are beyond reasonable doubt.

Article 12 - Prevention of the abuse of negotiating positions

1. Member States shall ensure by means of civil or administrative law, as appropriate, that the parties enter and conduct negotiations regarding authorization for cable retransmission in good faith and do not prevent or hinder negotiation without valid justification.
2. A Member State which, on the date mentioned in Article 14 (1), has a body with jurisdiction in its territory over cases where the right to retransmit a programme by cable to the public in that Member State has been unreasonably refused or offered on unreasonable terms by a broadcasting organization may retain that body.
3. Paragraph 2 shall apply for a transitional period of eight years from the date mentioned in Article 14 (1).

CHAPTER IV: GENERAL PROVISIONS

Article 13 - Collective administration of rights

This Directive shall be without prejudice to the regulation of the activities of collecting societies by the Member States.

Article 14 - Final provisions

1. Member States shall bring into force the laws, regulations and administrative provisions necessary to comply with this Directive before 1 January 1995. They shall immediately inform the Commission thereof.
   When Member States adopt these measures, the latter shall contain a reference to this Directive or shall be accompanied by such reference at the time of their official publication. The methods of making such a reference shall be laid down by the Member States.
2. Member States shall communicate to the Commission the provisions of national law which they adopt in the field covered by this Directive.

3. Not later than 1 January 2000, the Commission shall submit to the European Parliament, the Council and the Economic and Social Committee a report on the application of this Directive and, if necessary, make further proposals to adapt it to developments in the audio and audiovisual sector.

Article 15 - Addressees

This Directive is addressed to the Member States.

COUNCIL DIRECTIVE 93/98/EEC
OF 29 OCTOBER 1993
HARMONIZING THE TERM OF PROTECTION OF COPYRIGHT AND CERTAIN RELATED RIGHTS

(Official Journal L 290, 24/11/1993, p. 0009 – 0013)

THE COUNCIL OF THE EUROPEAN COMMUNITIES,

Having regard to the Treaty establishing the European Economic Community, and in particular Articles 57 (2), 66 and 100a thereof,
Having regard to the proposal from the Commission[1],
In cooperation with the European Parliament[2],
Having regard to the opinion of the Economic and Social Committee[3],

(1) Whereas the Berne Convention for the protection of literary and artistic works and the International Convention for the protection of performers, producers of phonograms and broadcasting organizations (Rome Convention) lay down only minimum terms of protection of the rights they refer to, leaving the Contracting States free to grant longer terms; whereas certain Member States have exercised this entitlement; whereas in addition certain Member States have not become party to the Rome Convention;

(2) Whereas there are consequently differences between the national laws governing the terms of protection of copyright and related rights, which are liable to impede the free movement of goods and freedom to provide services, and to distort competition in the common market; whereas therefore with a view to the smooth operation of the internal market, the laws of the Member States should be harmonized so as to make terms of protection identical throughout the Community;

(3) Whereas harmonization must cover not only the terms of protection as such, but also certain implementing arrangements such as the date from which each term of protection is calculated;

(4) Whereas the provisions of this Directive do not affect the application by the Member States of the provisions of Article 14a (2) (b), (c) and (d) and (3) of the Berne Convention;

(5) Whereas the minimum term of protection laid down by the Berne Convention, namely the life of the author and 50 years after his death, was intended to provide protection for the author and the first two generations of his descendants; whereas the average lifespan in the Community has grown longer, to the point where this term is no longer sufficient to cover two generations;

(6) Whereas certain Member States have granted a term longer than 50 years after the death of the author in order to offset the effects of the world wars on the exploitation of authors' works;

(7) Whereas for the protection of related rights certain Member States have introduced a term of 50 years after lawful publication or lawful communication to the public;

(8) Whereas under the Community position adopted for the Uruguay Round negotiations under the General Agreement on Tariffs and Trade (GATT) the term of protection for producers of phonograms should be 50 years after first publication;

(9) Whereas due regard for established rights is one of the general principles of law protected by the Community legal order; whereas, therefore, a harmonization of the terms of protection of copyright and related rights cannot have the effect of reducing the protection currently

---

[1] OJ No C 92, 11. 4. 1992, p. 6 and OJ No C 27, 30. 1. 1993, p. 7.
[2] OJ No C 337, 21. 12. 1992, p. 205 and Decision of 27 October 1993 (not yet published in the Official Journal).
[3] OJ No C 287, 4. 11. 1992, p. 53.

enjoyed by rightholders in the Community; whereas in order to keep the effects of transitional measures to a minimum and to allow the internal market to operate in practice, the harmonization of the term of protection should take place on a long term basis;
(10) Whereas in its communication of 17 January 1991 'Follow-up to the Green Paper - Working programme of the Commission in the field of copyright and neighbouring rights' the Commission stresses the need to harmonize copyright and neighbouring rights at a high level of protection since these rights are fundamental to intellectual creation and stresses that their protection ensures the maintenance and development of creativity in the interest of authors, cultural industries, consumers and society as a whole;
(11) Whereas in order to establish a high level of protection which at the same time meets the requirements of the internal market and the need to establish a legal environment conducive to the harmonious development of literary and artistic creation in the Community, the term of protection for copyright should be harmonized at 70 years after the death of the author or 70 years after the work is lawfully made available to the public, and for related rights at 50 years after the event which sets the term running;
(12) Whereas collections are protected according to Article 2 (5) of the Berne Convention when, by reason of the selection and arrangement of their content, they constitute intellectual creations; whereas those works are protected as such, without prejudice to the copyright in each of the works forming part of such collections, whereas in consequence specific terms of protection may apply to works included in collections;
(13) Whereas in all cases where one or more physical persons are identified as authors the term of protection should be calculated after their death; whereas the question of authorship in the whole or a part of a work is a question of fact which the national courts may have to decide;
(14) Whereas terms of protection should be calculated from the first day of January of the year following the relevant event, as they are in the Berne and Rome Conventions;
(15) Whereas Article 1 of Council Directive 91/250/EEC of 14 May 1991 on the legal protection of computer programs[4] provides that Member States are to protect computer programs, by copyright, as literary works within the meaning of the Berne Convention; whereas this Directive harmonizes the term of protection of literary works in the Community; whereas Article 8 of Directive 91/250/EEC, which merely makes provisional arrangements governing the term of protection of computer programs, should accordingly be repealed;
(16) Whereas Articles 11 and 12 of Council Directive 92/100/EEC of 19 November 1992 on rental right and lending right and on certain rights related to copyright in the field of intellectual property[5] make provision for minimum terms of protection only, subject to any further harmonization; whereas this Directive provides such further harmonization; whereas these Articles should accordingly be repealed;
(17) Whereas the protection of photographs in the Member States is the subject of varying regimes; whereas in order to achieve a sufficient harmonization of the term of protection of photographic works, in particular of those which, due to their artistic or professional character, are of importance within the internal market, it is necessary to define the level of originality required in this Directive; whereas a photographic work within the meaning of the Berne Convention is to be considered original if it is the author's own intellectual creation reflecting his personality, no other criteria such as merit or purpose being taken into account; whereas the protection of other photographs should be left to national law;
(18) Whereas, in order to avoid differences in the term of protection as regards related rights it is necessary to provide the same starting point for the calculation of the term throughout the Community; whereas the performance, fixation, transmission, lawful publication, and lawful communication to the public, that is to say the means of making a subject of a related right

---

[4] OJ No L 122, 17. 5. 1991, p. 42.
[5] OJ No L 346, 27. 11. 1992, p. 61.

perceptible in all appropriate ways to persons in general, should be taken into account for the calculation of the term of protection regardless of the country where this performance, fixation, transmission, lawful publication, or lawful communication to the public takes place;
(19) Whereas the rights of broadcasting organizations in their broadcasts, whether these broadcasts are transmitted by wire or over the air, including by cable or satellite, should not be perpetual; whereas it is therefore necessary to have the term of protection running from the first transmission of a particular broadcast only; whereas this provision is understood to avoid a new term running in cases where a broadcast is identical to a previous one;
(20) Whereas the Member States should remain free to maintain or introduce other rights related to copyright in particular in relation to the protection of critical and scientific publications; whereas, in order to ensure transparency at Community level, it is however necessary for Member States which introduce new related rights to notify the Commission;
(21) Whereas it is useful to make clear that the harmonization brought about by this Directive does not apply to moral rights;
(22) Whereas, for works whose country of origin within the meaning of the Berne Convention is a third country and whose author is not a Community national, comparison of terms of protection should be applied, provided that the term accorded in the Community does not exceed the term laid down in this Directive;
(23) Whereas where a rightholder who is not a Community national qualifies for protection under an international agreement the term of protection of related rights should be the same as that laid down in this Directive, except that it should not exceed that fixed in the country of which the rightholder is a national;
(24) Whereas comparison of terms should not result in Member States being brought into conflict with their international obligations;
(25) Whereas, for the smooth functioning of the internal market this Directive should be applied as from 1 July 1995;
(26) Whereas Member States should remain free to adopt provisions on the interpretation, adaptation and further execution of contracts on the exploitation of protected works and other subject matter which were concluded before the extension of the term of protection resulting from this Directive;
(27) Whereas respect of acquired rights and legitimate expectations is part of the Community legal order; whereas Member States may provide in particular that in certain circumstances the copyright and related rights which are revived pursuant to this Directive may not give rise to payments by persons who undertook in good faith the exploitation of the works at the time when such works lay within the public domain,

HAS ADOPTED THIS DIRECTIVE:

Article 1 - Duration of authors' rights

1. The rights of an author of a literary or artistic work within the meaning of Article 2 of the Berne Convention shall run for the life of the author and for 70 years after his death, irrespective of the date when the work is lawfully made available to the public.
2. In the case of a work of joint authorship the term referred to in paragraph 1 shall be calculated from the death of the last surviving author.
3. In the case of anonymous or pseudonymous works, the term of protection shall run for seventy years after the work is lawfully made available to the public. However, when the pseudonym adopted by the author leaves no doubt as to his identity, or if the author discloses his identity during the period referred to in the first sentence, the term of protection applicable shall be that laid down in paragraph 1.

4. Where a Member State provides for particular provisions on copyright in respect of collective works or for a legal person to be designated as the rightholder, the term of protection shall be calculated according to the provisions of paragraph 3, except if the natural persons who have created the work as such are identified as such in the versions of the work which are made available to the public. This paragraph is without prejudice to the rights of identified authors whose identifiable contributions are included in such works, to which contributions paragraph 1 or 2 shall apply.
5. Where a work is published in volumes, parts, instalments, issues or episodes and the term of protection runs from the time when the work was lawfully made available to the public, the term of protection shall run for each such item separately.
6. In the case of works for which the term of protection is not calculated from the death of the author or authors and which have not been lawfully made available to the public within seventy years from their creation, the protection shall terminate.

Article 2 - Cinematographic or audiovisual works

1. The principal director of a cinematographic or audiovisual work shall be considered as its author or one of its authors. Member States shall be free to designate other co-authors.
2. The term of protection of cinematographic or audiovisual works shall expire 70 years after the death of the last of the following persons to survive, whether or not these persons are designated as co-authors: the principal director, the author of the screenplay, the author of the dialogue and the composer of music specifically created for use in the cinematographic or audiovisual work.

Article 3 - Duration of related rights

1. The rights of performers shall expire 50 years after the date of the performance. However, if a fixation of the performance is lawfully published or lawfully communicated to the public within this period, the rights shall expire 50 years from the date of the first such publication or the first such communication to the public, whichever is the earlier.
2. The rights of producers of phonograms shall expire 50 years after the fixation is made. However, if the phonogram is lawfully published or lawfully communicated to the public during this period, the rights shall expire 50 years from the date of the first such publication or the first such communication to the public, whichever is the earlier.
3. The rights of producers of the first fixation of a film shall expire 50 years after the fixation is made. However, if the film is lawfully published or lawfully communicated to the public during this period, the rights shall expire 50 years from the date of the first such publication or the first such communication to the public, whichever is the earlier. The term 'film' shall designate a cinematographic or audiovisual work or moving images, whether or not accompanied by sound.
4. The rights of broadcasting organizations shall expire 50 years after the first transmission of a broadcast, whether this broadcast is transmitted by wire or over the air, including by cable or satellite.

Article 4 - Protection of previously unpublished works

Any person who, after the expiry of copyright protection, for the first time lawfully publishes or lawfully communicates to the public a previously unpublished work, shall benefit from a protection equivalent to the economic rights of the author. The term of protection of such rights shall be 25 years from the time when the work was first lawfully published or lawfully communicated to the public.

Article 5 - Critical and scientific publications

Member States may protect critical and scientific publications of works which have come into the public domain. The maximum term of protection of such rights shall be 30 years from the time when the publication was first lawfully published.

Article 6 - Protection of photographs

Photographs which are original in the sense that they are the author's own intellectual creation shall be protected in accordance with Article 1. No other criteria shall be applied to determine their eligibility for protection. Member States may provide for the protection of other photographs.

Article 7 - Protection vis-à-vis third countries

1. Where the country of origin of a work, within the meaning of the Berne Convention, is a third country, and the author of the work is not a Community national, the term of protection granted by the Member States shall expire on the date of expiry of the protection granted in the country of origin of the work, but may not exceed the term laid down in Article 1.
2. The terms of protection laid down in Article 3 shall also apply in the case of rightholders who are not Community nationals, provided Member States grant them protection. However, without prejudice to the international obligations of the Member States, the term of protection granted by Member States shall expire no later than the date of expiry of the protection granted in the country of which the rightholder is a national and may not exceed the term laid down in Article 3.
3. Member States which, at the date of adoption of this Directive, in particular pursuant to their international obligations, granted a longer term of protection than that which would result from the provisions, referred to in paragraphs 1 and 2 may maintain this protection until the conclusion of international agreements on the term of protection by copyright or related rights.

Article 8 - Calculation of terms

The terms laid down in this Directive are calculated from the first day of January of the year following the event which gives rise to them.

Article 9 - Moral rights

This Directive shall be without prejudice to the provisions of the Member States regulating moral rights.

Article 10 - Application in time

1. Where a term of protection, which is longer than the corresponding term provided for by this Directive, is already running in a Member State on the date referred to in Article 13 (1), this Directive shall not have the effect of shortening that term of protection in that Member State.
2. The terms of protection provided for in this Directive shall apply to all works and subject matter which are protected in at least one Member State, on the date referred to in Article 13 (1), pursuant to national provisions on copyright or related rights or which meet the criteria for protection under Directive 92/100/EEC.
3. This Directive shall be without prejudice to any acts of exploitation performed before the date referred to in Article 13 (1). Member States shall adopt the necessary provisions to protect in particular acquired rights of third parties.
4. Member States need not apply the provisions of Article 2 (1) to cinematographic or audiovisual works created before 1 July 1994.

5. Member States may determine the date as from which Article 2 (1) shall apply, provided that date is no later than 1 July 1997.

Article 11 - Technical adaptation

1. Article 8 of Directive 91/250/EEC is hereby repealed.
2. Articles 11 and 12 of Directive 92/100/EEC are hereby repealed.

Article 12 - Notification procedure

Member States shall immediately notify the Commission of any governmental plan to grant new related rights, including the basic reasons for their introduction and the term of protection envisaged.

Article 13 - General provisions

1. Member States shall bring into force the laws, regulations and administrative provisions necessary to comply with Articles 1 to 11 of this Directive before 1 July 1995. When Member States adopt these provisions, they shall contain a reference to this Directive or shall be accompanied by such reference at the time of their official publication. The methods of making such a reference shall be laid down by the Member States. Member States shall communicate to the Commission the texts of the provisions of national law which they adopt in the field governed by this Directive.
2. Member States shall apply Article 12 from the date of notification of this Directive.

Article 14 - Adressees

This Directive is addressed to the Member States.

COMMISSION REGULATION (EC) NO 240/96
OF 31 JANUARY 1996
ON THE APPLICATION OF ARTICLE 85 (3) OF THE TREATY TO CERTAIN CATEGORIES OF TECHNOLOGY TRANSFER AGREEMENTS

(Official Journal L 031, 09/02/1996, p. 0002 - 0013)

THE COMMISSION OF THE EUROPEAN COMMUNITIES,

Having regard to the Treaty establishing the European Community,
Having regard to Council Regulation No 19/65/EEC of 2 March 1965 on the application of Article 85 (3) of the Treaty to certain categories of agreements and concerted practices[1] as last amended by the Act of Accession of Austria, Finland and Sweden, and in particular Article 1 thereof,
Having published a draft of this Regulation[2],
After consulting the Advisory Committee on Restrictive Practices and Dominant Positions,

Whereas:
(1) Regulation No 19/65/EEC empowers the Commission to apply Article 85 (3) of the Treaty by regulation to certain categories of agreements and concerted practices falling within the scope of Article 85 (1) which include restrictions imposed in relation to the acquisition or use of industrial property rights - in particular of patents, utility models, designs or trademarks - or to the rights arising out of contracts for assignment of, or the right to use, a method of manufacture of knowledge relating to use or to the application of industrial processes.
(2) The Commission has made use of this power by adopting Regulation (EEC) No 2349/84 of 23 July 1984 on the application of Article 85 (3) of the Treaty to certain categories of patent licensing agreements[3], as last amended by Regulation (EC) No 2131/95[4], and Regulation (EEC) No 556/89 of 30 November 1988 on the application of Article 85 (3) of the Treaty to certain categories of know-how licensing agreements[5], as last amended by the Act of Accession of Austria, Finland and Sweden.
(3) These two block exemptions ought to be combined into a single regulation covering technology transfer agreements, and the rules governing patent licensing agreements and agreements for the licensing of know-how ought to be harmonized and simplified as far as possible, in order to encourage the dissemination of technical knowledge in the Community and to promote the manufacture of technically more sophisticated products. In those circumstances Regulation (EEC) No 556/89 should be repealed.
(4) This Regulation should apply to the licensing of Member States' own patents, Community patents[6] and European patents[7] ('pure' patent licensing agreements). It should also apply to agreements for the licensing of non-patented technical information such as descriptions of manufacturing processes, recipes, formulae, designs or drawings, commonly termed 'know-how' ('pure' know-how licensing agreements), and to combined patent and know-how licensing agreements ('mixed' agreements), which are playing an increasingly important role

---

[1] OJ No 36, 6. 3. 1965, p. 533/65.
[2] OJ No C 178, 30. 6. 1994, p. 3.
[3] OJ No L 219, 16. 8. 1984, p. 15.
[4] OJ No L 214, 8. 9. 1995, p. 6.
[5] OJ No L 61, 4. 3. 1989, p. 1.
[6] Convention for the European patent for the common market (Community Patent Convention) of 15 December 1975, OJ No L 17, 26. 1. 1976, p. 1.
[7] Convention on the grant of European patents (European Patent Convention) of 5 October 1973.

in the transfer of technology. For the purposes of this Regulation, a number of terms are defined in Article 10.

(5)　Patent or know-how licensing agreements are agreements whereby one undertaking which holds a patent or know-how ('the licensor') permits another undertaking ('the licensee') to exploit the patent thereby licensed, or communicates the know-how to it, in particular for purposes of manufacture, use or putting on the market. In the light of experience acquired so far, it is possible to define a category of licensing agreements covering all or part of the common market which are capable of falling within the scope of Article 85 (1) but which can normally be regarded as satisfying the conditions laid down in Article 85 (3), where patents are necessary for the achievement of the objects of the licensed technology by a mixed agreement or where know-how - whether it is ancillary to patents or independent of them - is secret, substantial and identified in any appropriate form. These criteria are intended only to ensure that the licensing of the know-how or the grant of the patent licence justifies a block exemption of obligations restricting competition. This is without prejudice to the right of the parties to include in the contract provisions regarding other obligations, such as the obligation to pay royalties, even if the block exemption no longer applies.

(6)　It is appropriate to extend the scope of this Regulation to pure or mixed agreements containing the licensing of intellectual property rights other than patents (in particular, trademarks, design rights and copyright, especially software protection), when such additional licensing contributes to the achievement of the objects of the licensed technology and contains only ancillary provisions.

(7)　Where such pure or mixed licensing agreements contain not only obligations relating to territories within the common market but also obligations relating to non-member countries, the presence of the latter does not prevent this Regulation from applying to the obligations relating to territories within the common market. Where licensing agreements for non-member countries or for territories which extend beyond the frontiers of the Community have effects within the common market which may fall within the scope of Article 85 (1), such agreements should be covered by this Regulation to the same extent as would agreements for territories within the common market.

(8)　The objective being to facilitate the dissemination of technology and the improvement of manufacturing processes, this Regulation should apply only where the licensee himself manufactures the licensed products or has them manufactured for his account, or where the licensed product is a service, provides the service himself or has the service provided for his account, irrespective of whether or not the licensee is also entitled to use confidential information provided by the licensor for the promotion and sale of the licensed product. The scope of this Regulation should therefore exclude agreements solely for the purpose of sale. Also to be excluded from the scope of this Regulation are agreements relating to marketing know-how communicated in the context of franchising arrangements and certain licensing agreements entered into in connection with arrangements such as joint ventures or patent pools and other arrangements in which a licence is granted in exchange for other licences not related to improvements to or new applications of the licensed technology. Such agreements pose different problems which cannot at present be dealt with in a single regulation (Article 5).

(9)　Given the similarity between sale and exclusive licensing, and the danger that the requirements of this Regulation might be evaded by presenting as assignments what are in fact exclusive licenses restrictive of competition, this Regulation should apply to agreements concerning the assignment and acquisition of patents or know-how where the risk associated with exploitation remains with the assignor. It should also apply to licensing agreements in which the licensor is not the holder of the patent or know-how but is authorized by the holder to grant the licence (as in the case of sub-licences) and to licensing agreements in which the parties' rights or obligations are assumed by connected undertakings (Article 6).

(10) Exclusive licensing agreements, i.e. agreements in which the licensor undertakes not to exploit the licensed technology in the licensed territory himself or to grant further licences there, may not be in themselves incompatible with Article 85 (1) where they are concerned with the introduction and protection of a new technology in the licensed territory, by reason of the scale of the research which has been undertaken, of the increase in the level of competition, in particular inter-brand competition, and of the competitiveness of the undertakings concerned resulting from the dissemination of innovation within the Community. In so far as agreements of this kind fall, in other circumstances, within the scope of Article 85 (1), it is appropriate to include them in Article 1 in order that they may also benefit from the exemption.

(11) The exemption of export bans on the licensor and on the licensees does not prejudice any developments in the case law of the Court of Justice in relation to such agreements, notably with respect to Articles 30 to 36 and Article 85 (1). This is also the case, in particular, regarding the prohibition on the licensee from selling the licensed product in territories granted to other licensees (passive competition).

(12) The obligations listed in Article 1 generally contribute to improving the production of goods and to promoting technical progress. They make the holders of patents or know-how more willing to grant licences and licensees more inclined to undertake the investment required to manufacture, use and put on the market a new product or to use a new process. Such obligations may be permitted under this Regulation in respect of territories where the licensed product is protected by patents as long as these remain in force.

(13) Since the point at which the know-how ceases to be secret can be difficult to determine, it is appropriate, in respect of territories where the licensed technology comprises know-how only, to limit such obligations to a fixed number of years. Moreover, in order to provide sufficient periods of protection, it is appropriate to take as the starting-point for such periods the date on which the product is first put on the market in the Community by a licensee.

(14) Exemption under Article 85 (3) of longer periods of territorial protection for know-how agreements, in particular in order to protect expensive and risky investment or where the parties were not competitors at the date of the grant of the licence, can be granted only by individual decision. On the other hand, parties are free to extend the term of their agreements in order to exploit any subsequent improvement and to provide for the payment of additional royalties. However, in such cases, further periods of territorial protection may be allowed only starting from the date of licensing of the secret improvements in the Community, and by individual decision. Where the research for improvements results in innovations which are distinct from the licensed technology the parties may conclude a new agreement benefitting from an exemption under this Regulation.

(15) Provision should also be made for exemption of an obligation on the licensee not to put the product on the market in the territories of other licensees, the permitted period for such an obligation (this obligation would ban not just active competition but passive competition too) should, however, be limited to a few years from the date on which the licensed product is first put on the market in the Community by a licensee, irrespective of whether the licensed technology comprises know-how, patents or both in the territories concerned.

(16) The exemption of territorial protection should apply for the whole duration of the periods thus permitted, as long as the patents remain in force or the know-how remains secret and substantial. The parties to a mixed patent and know-how licensing agreement must be able to take advantage in a particular territory of the period of protection conferred by a patent or by the know-how, whichever is the longer.

(17) The obligations listed in Article 1 also generally fulfil the other conditions for the application of Article 85 (3). Consumers will, as a rule, be allowed a fair share of the benefit resulting from the improvement in the supply of goods on the market. To safeguard this effect, however, it is right to exclude from the application of Article 1 cases where the parties agree to

refuse to meet demand from users or resellers within their respective territories who would resell for export, or to take other steps to impede parallel imports. The obligations referred to above thus only impose restrictions which are indispensable to the attainment of their objectives.

(18) It is desirable to list in this Regulation a number of obligations that are commonly found in licensing agreements but are normally not restrictive of competition, and to provide that in the event that because of the particular economic or legal circumstances they should fall within Article 85 (1), they too will be covered by the exemption. This list, in Article 2, is not exhaustive.

(19) This Regulation must also specify what restrictions or provisions may not be included in licensing agreements if these are to benefit from the block exemption. The restrictions listed in Article 3 may fall under the prohibition of Article 85 (1), but in their case there can be no general presumption that, although they relate to the transfer of technology, they will lead to the positive effects required by Article 85 (3), as would be necessary for the granting of a block exemption. Such restrictions can be declared exempt only by an individual decision, taking account of the market position of the undertakings concerned and the degree of concentration on the relevant market.

(20) The obligations on the licensee to cease using the licensed technology after the termination of the agreement (Article 2 (1) (3)) and to make improvements available to the licensor (Article 2 (1) (4)) do not generally restrict competition. The post-term use ban may be regarded as a normal feature of licensing, as otherwise the licensor would be forced to transfer his know-how or patents in perpetuity. Undertakings by the licensee to grant back to the licensor a licence for improvements to the licensed know-how and/or patents are generally not restrictive of competition if the licensee is entitled by the contract to share in future experience and inventions made by the licensor. On the other hand, a restrictive effect on competition arises where the agreement obliges the licensee to assign to the licensor rights to improvements of the originally licensed technology that he himself has brought about (Article 3 (6)).

(21) The list of clauses which do not prevent exemption also includes an obligation on the licensee to keep paying royalties until the end of the agreement independently of whether or not the licensed know-how has entered into the public domain through the action of third parties or of the licensee himself (Article 2 (1) (7)). Moreover, the parties must be free, in order to facilitate payment, to spread the royalty payments for the use of the licensed technology over a period extending beyond the duration of the licensed patents, in particular by setting lower royalty rates. As a rule, parties do not need to be protected against the foreseeable financial consequences of an agreement freely entered into, and they should therefore be free to choose the appropriate means of financing the technology transfer and sharing between them the risks of such use. However, the setting of rates of royalty so as to achieve one of the restrictions listed in Article 3 renders the agreement ineligible for the block exemption.

(22) An obligation on the licensee to restrict his exploitation of the licensed technology to one or more technical fields of application ('fields of use') or to one or more product markets is not caught by Article 85 (1) either, since the licensor is entitled to transfer the technology only for a limited purpose (Article 2 (1) (8)).

(23) Clauses whereby the parties allocate customers within the same technological field of use or the same product market, either by an actual prohibition on supplying certain classes of customer or through an obligation with an equivalent effect, would also render the agreement ineligible for the block exemption where the parties are competitors for the contract products (Article 3 (4)). Such restrictions between undertakings which are not competitors remain subject to the opposition procedure. Article 3 does not apply to cases where the patent or know-how licence is granted in order to provide a single customer with a second source of

supply. In such a case, a prohibition on the second licensee from supplying persons other than the customer concerned is an essential condition for the grant of a second licence, since the purpose of the transaction is not to create an independent supplier in the market. The same applies to limitations on the quantities the licensee may supply to the customer concerned (Article 2 (1) (13)).

(24) Besides the clauses already mentioned, the list of restrictions which render the block exemption inapplicable also includes restrictions regarding the selling prices of the licensed product or the quantities to be manufactured or sold, since they seriously limit the extent to which the licensee can exploit the licensed technology and since quantity restrictions particularly may have the same effect as export bans (Article 3 (1) and (5)). This does not apply where a licence is granted for use of the technology in specific production facilities and where both a specific technology is communicated for the setting-up, operation and maintenance of these facilities and the licensee is allowed to increase the capacity of the facilities or to set up further facilities for its own use on normal commercial terms. On the other hand, the licensee may lawfully be prevented from using the transferred technology to set up facilities for third parties, since the purpose of the agreement is not to permit the licensee to give other producers access to the licensor's technology while it remains secret or protected by patent (Article 2 (1) (12)).

(25) Agreements which are not automatically covered by the exemption because they contain provisions that are not expressly exempted by this Regulation and not expressly excluded from exemption, including those lsited in Article 4 (2), may, in certain circumstances, nonetheless be presumed to be eligible for application of the block exemption. It will be possible for the Commission rapidly to establish whether this is the case on the basis of the information undertakings are obliged to provide under Commission Regulation (EC) No 3385/94[8]. The Commission may waive the requirement to supply specific information required in form A/B but which it does not deem necessary. The Commission will generally be content with communication of the text of the agreement and with an estimate, based on directly available data, of the market structure and of the licensee's market share. Such agreements should therefore be deemed to be covered by the exemption provided for in this Regulation where they are notified to the Commission and the Commission does not oppose the application of the exemption within a specified period of time.

(26) Where agreements exempted under this Regulation nevertheless have effects incompatible with Article 85 (3), the Commission may withdraw the block exemption, in particular where the licensed products are not faced with real competition in the licensed territory (Article 7). This could also be the case where the licensee has a strong position on the market. In assessing the competition the Commission will pay special attention to cases where the licensee has more than 40 % of the whole market for the licensed products and of all the products or services which customers consider interchangeable or substitutable on account of their characteristics, prices and intended use.

(27) Agreements which come within the terms of Articles 1 and 2 and which have neither the object nor the effect of restricting competition in any other way need no longer be notified. Nevertheless, undertakings will still have the right to apply in individual cases for negative clearance or for exemption under Article 85 (3) in accordance with Council Regulation No 17[9], as last amended by the Act of Accession of Austria, Finland and Sweden. They can in particular notify agreements obliging the licensor not to grant other licences in the territory, where the licensee's market share exceeds or is likely to exceed 40 %.

HAS ADOPTED THIS REGULATION:

---

[8] OJ No L 377, 31. 12. 1994, p. 28.
[9] OJ No 13, 21. 2. 1962, p. 204/62.

Article 1

1. Pursuant to Article 85 (3) of the Treaty and subject to the conditions set out below, it is hereby declared that Article 85 (1) of the Treaty shall not apply to pure patent licensing or know-how licensing agreements and to mixed patent and know-how licensing agreements, including those agreements containing ancillary provisions relating to intellectual property rights other than patents, to which only two undertakings are party and which include one or more of the following obligations:
    (1) an obligation on the licensor not to license other undertakings to exploit the licensed technology in the licensed territory;
    (2) an obligation on the licensor not to exploit the licensed technology in the licensed territory himself;
    (3) an obligation on the licensee not to exploit the licensed technology in the territory of the licensor within the common market;
    (4) an obligation on the licensee not to manufacture or use the licensed product, or use the licensed process, in territories within the common market which are licensed to other licensees;
    (5) an obligation on the licensee not to pursue an active policy of putting the licensed product on the market in the territories within the common market which are licensed to other licensees, and in particular not to engage in advertising specifically aimed at those territories or to establish any branch or maintain an distribution depot there;
    (6) an obligation on the licensee not to put the licensed product on the market in the territories licensed to other licensees within the common market in response to unsolicited orders;
    (7) an obligation on the licensee to use only the licensor's trademark or get up to distinguish the licensed product during the term of the agreement, provided that the licensee is not prevented from identifying himself as the manufacturer of the licensed products;
    (8) an obligation on the licensee to limit his production of the licensed product to the quantities he requires in manufacturing his own products and to sell the licensed product only as an integral part of or a replacement part for his own products or otherwise in connection with the sale of his own products, provided that such quantities are freely determined by the licensee.
2. Where the agreement is a pure patent licensing agreement, the exemption of the obligations referred to in paragraph 1 is granted only to the extent that and for as long as the licensed product is protected by parallel patents, in the territories respectively of the licensee (points (1), (2), (7) and (8)), the licensor (point (3)) and other licensees (points (4) and (5). The exemption of the obligation referred to in point (6) of paragraph 1 is granted for a period not exceeding five years from the date when the licensed product is first put on the market within the common market by one of the licensees, to the extent that and for as long as, in these territories, this product is protected by parallel patents.
3. Where the agreement is a pure know-how licensing agreement, the period for which the exemption of the obligations referred to in points (1) to (5) of paragraph 1 is granted may not exceed ten years from the date when the licensed product is first put on the market within the common market by one of the licensees.

    The exemption of the obligation referred to in point (6) of paragraph 1 is granted for a period not exceeding five years from the date when the licensed product is first put on the market within the common market by one of the licensees.

    The obligations referred to in points (7) and (8) of paragraph 1 are exempted during the lifetime of the agreement for as long as the know-how remains secret and substantial.

    However, the exemption in paragraph 1 shall apply only where the parties have identified in any appropriate form the initial know-how and any subsequent improvements to it which become available to one party and are communicated to the other party pursuant to the terms of the agreement and to the purpose thereof, and only for as long as the know-how remains secret and substantial.

4. Where the agreement is a mixed patent and know-how licensing agreement, the exemption of the obligations referred to in points (1) to (5) of paragraph 1 shall apply in Member States in which the licensed technology is protected by necessary patents for as long as the licensed product is protected in those Member States by such patents if the duration of such protection exceeds the periods specified in paragraph 3.

The duration of the exemption provided in point (6) of paragraph 1 may not exceed the five-year period provided for in paragraphs 2 and 3.

However, such agreements qualify for the exemption referred to in paragraph 1 only for as long as the patents remain in force or to the extent that the know-how is identified and for as long as it remains secret and substantial whichever period is the longer.

5. The exemption provided for in paragraph 1 shall also apply where in a particular agreement the parties undertake obligations of the types referred to in that paragraph but with a more limited scope than is permitted by that paragraph.

Article 2

1. Article 1 shall apply notwithstanding the presence in particular of any of the following clauses, which are generally not restrictive of competition:
   (1) an obligation on the licensee not to divulge the know-how communicated by the licensor; the licensee may be held to this obligation after the agreement has expired;
   (2) an obligation on the licensee not to grant sublicences or assign the licence;
   (3) an obligation on the licensee not to exploit the licensed know-how or patents after termination of the agreement in so far and as long as the know-how is still secret or the patents are still in force;
   (4) an obligation on the licensee to grant to the licensor a licence in respect of his own improvements to or his new applications of the licensed technology, provided:
   - that, in the case of severable improvements, such a licence is not exclusive, so that the licensee is free to use his own improvements or to license them to third parties, in so far as that does not involve disclosure of the know-how communicated by the licensor that is still secret,
   - and that the licensor undertakes to grant an exclusive or non-exclusive licence of his own improvements to the licensee;
   (5) an obligation on the licensee to observe minimum quality specifications, including technical specifications, for the licensed product or to procure goods or services from the licensor or from an undertaking designated by the licensor, in so far as these quality specifications, products or services are necessary for:
      (a) a technically proper exploitation of the licensed technology; or
      (b) ensuring that the product of the licensee conforms to the minimum quality specifications that are applicable to the licensor and other licensees;
      and to allow the licensor to carry out related checks;
   (6) obligations:
      (a) to inform the licensor of misappropriation of the know-how or of infringements of the licensed patents; or
      (b) to take or to assist the licensor in taking legal action against such misappropriation or infringements;
   (7) an obligation on the licensee to continue paying the royalties:
      (a) until the end of the agreement in the amounts, for the periods and according to the methods freely determined by the parties, in the event of the know-how becoming publicly known other than by action of the licensor, without prejudice

to the payment of any additional damages in the event of the know-how becoming publicly known by the action of the licensee in breach of the agreement;
- (b) over a period going beyond the duration of the licensed patents, in order to facilitate payment;
(8) an obligation on the licensee to restrict his exploitation of the licensed technology to one or more technical fields of application covered by the licensed technology or to one or more product markets;
(9) an obligation on the licensee to pay a minimum royalty or to produce a minimum quantity of the licensed product or to carry out a minimum number of operations exploiting the licensed technology;
(10) an obligation on the licensor to grant the licensee any more favourable terms that the licensor may grant to another undertaking after the agreement is entered into;
(11) an obligation on the licensee to mark the licensed product with an indication of the licensor's name or of the licensed patent;
(12) an obligation on the licensee not to use the licensor's technology to construct facilities for third parties; this is without prejudice to the right of the licensee to increase the capacity of his facilities or to set up additional facilities for his own use on normal commercial terms, including the payment of additional royalties;
(13) an obligation on the licensee to supply only a limited quantity of the licensed product to a particular customer, where the licence was granted so that the customer might have a second source of supply inside the licensed territory; this provision shall also apply where the customer is the licensee, and the licence which was granted in order to provide a second source of supply provides that the customer is himself to manufacture the licensed products or to have them manufactured by a subcontractor;
(14) a reservation by the licensor of the right to exercise the rights conferred by a patent to oppose the exploitation of the technology by the licensee outside the licensed territory;
(15) a reservation by the licensor of the right to terminate the agreement if the licensee contests the secret or substantial nature of the licensed know-how or challenges the validity of licensed patents within the common market belonging to the licensor or undertakings connected with him;
(16) a reservation by the licensor of the right to terminate the licence agreement of a patent if the licensee raises the claim that such a patent is not necessary;
(17) an obligation on the licensee to use his best endeavours to manufacture and market the licensed product;
(18) a reservation by the licensor of the right to terminate the exclusivity granted to the licensee and to stop licensing improvements to him when the licensee enters into competition within the common market with the licensor, with undertakings connected with the licensor or with other undertakings in respect of research and development, production, use or distribution of competing products, and to require the licensee to prove that the licensed know-how is not being used for the production of products and the provision of services other than those licensed.
2. In the event that, because of particular circumstances, the clauses referred to in paragraph 1 fall within the scope of Article 85 (1), they shall also be exempted even if they are not accompanied by any of the obligations exempted by Article 1.
3. The exemption in paragraph 2 shall also apply where an agreement contains clauses of the types referred to in paragraph 1 but with a more limited scope than is permitted by that paragraph.

Article 3

Article 1 and Article 2 (2) shall not apply where:

(1) one party is restricted in the determination of prices, components of prices or discounts for the licensed products;
(2) one party is restricted from competing within the common market with the other party, with undertakings connected with the other party or with other undertakings in respect of research and development, production, use or distribution of competing products without prejudice to the provisions of Article 2 (1) (17) and (18);
(3) one or both of the parties are required without any objectively justified reason:
   (a) to refuse to meet orders from users or resellers in their respective territories who would market products in other territories within the common market;
   (b) to make it difficult for users or resellers to obtain the products from other resellers within the common market, and in particular to exercise intellectual property rights or take measures so as to prevent users or resellers from obtaining outside, or from putting on the market in the licensed territory products which have been lawfully put on the market within the common market by the licensor or with his consent;
   or do so as a result of a concerted practice between them;
(4) the parties were already competing manufacturers before the grant of the licence and one of them is restricted, within the same technical field of use or within the same product market, as to the customers he may serve, in particular by being prohibited from supplying certain classes of user, employing certain forms of distribution or, with the aim of sharing customers, using certain types of packaging for the products, save as provided in Article 1 (1) (7) and Article 2 (1) (13);
(5) the quantity of the licensed products one party may manufacture or sell or the number of operations exploiting the licensed technology he may carry out are subject to limitations, save as provided in Article (1) (8) and Article 2 (1) (13);
(6) the licensee is obliged to assign in whole or in part to the licensor rights to improvements to or new applications of the licensed technology;
(7) the licensor is required, albeit in separate agreements or through automatic prolongation of the initial duration of the agreement by the inclusion of any new improvements, for a period exceeding that referred to in Article 1 (2) and (3) not to license other undertakings to exploit the licensed technology in the licensed territory, or a party is required for a period exceeding that referred to in Article 1 (2) and (3) or Article 1 (4) not to exploit the licensed technology in the territory of the other party or of other licensees.

Article 4

1. The exemption provided for in Articles 1 and 2 shall also apply to agreements containing obligations restrictive of competition which are not covered by those Articles and do not fall within the scope of Article 3, on condition that the agreements in question are notified to the Commission in accordance with the provisions of Articles 1, 2 and 3 of Regulation (EC) No 3385/94 and that the Commission does not oppose such exemption within a period of four months.
2. Paragraph 1 shall apply, in particular, where:
   (a) the licensee is obliged at the time the agreement is entered into to accept quality specifications or further licences or to procure goods or services which are not necessary for a technically satisfactory exploitation of the licensed technology or for ensuring that the production of the licensee conforms to the quality standards that are respected by the licensor and other licensees;
   (b) the licensee is prohibited from contesting the secrecy or the substantiality of the licensed know-how or from challenging the validity of patents licensed within the common market belonging to the licensor or undertakings connected with him.

3. The period of four months referred to in paragraph 1 shall run from the date on which the notification takes effect in accordance with Article 4 of Regulation (EC) No 3385/94.
4. The benefit of paragraphs 1 and 2 may be claimed for agreements notified before the entry into force of this Regulation by submitting a communication to the Commission referring expressly to this Article and to the notification. Paragraph 3 shall apply mutatis mutandis.
5. The Commission may oppose the exemption within a period of four months. It shall oppose exemption if it receives a request to do so from a Member State within two months of the transmission to the Member State of the notification referred to in paragraph 1 or of the communication referred to in paragraph 4. This request must be justified on the basis of considerations relating to the competition rules of the Treaty.
6. The Commission may withdraw the opposition to the exemption at any time. However, where the opposition was raised at the request of a Member State and this request is maintained, it may be withdrawn only after consultation of the Advisory Committee on Restrictive Practices and Dominant Positions.
7. If the opposition is withdrawn because the undertakings concerned have shown that the conditions of Article 85 (3) are satisfied, the exemption shall apply from the date of notification.
8. If the opposition is withdrawn because the undertakings concerned have amended the agreement so that the conditions of Article 85 (3) are satisfied, the exemption shall apply from the date on which the amendments take effect.
9. If the Commission opposes exemption and the opposition is not withdrawn, the effects of the notification shall be governed by the provisions of Regulation No 17.

Article 5

1. This Regulation shall not apply to:
    (1) agreements between members of a patent or know-how pool which relate to the pooled technologies;
    (2) licensing agreements between competing undertakings which hold interests in a joint venture, or between one of them and the joint venture, if the licensing agreements relate to the activities of the joint venture;
    (3) agreements under which one party grants the other a patent and/or know-how licence and in exchange the other party, albeit in separate agreements or through connected undertakings, grants the first party a patent, trademark or know-how licence or exclusive sales rights, where the parties are competitors in relation to the products covered by those agreements;
    (4) licensing agreements containing provisions relating to intellectual property rights other than patents which are not ancillary;
    (5) agreements entered into solely for the purpose of sale.
2. This Regulation shall nevertheless apply:
    (1) to agreements to which paragraph 1 (2) applies, under which a parent undertaking grants the joint venture a patent or know-how licence, provided that the licensed products and the other goods and services of the participating undertakings which are considered by users to be interchangeable or substitutable in view of their characteristics, price and intended use represent:
        - in case of a licence limited to production, not more than 20 %, and
        - in case of a licence covering production and distribution, not more than 10 %;
        of the market for the licensed products and all interchangeable or substitutable goods and services;
    (2) to agreements to which paragraph 1 (1) applies and to reciprocal licences within the meaning of paragraph 1 (3), provided the parties are not subject to any territorial restriction within the common market with regard to the manufacture, use or putting

on the market of the licensed products or to the use of the licensed or pooled technologies.
3. This Regulation shall continue to apply where, for two consecutive financial years, the market shares in paragraph 2 (1) are not exceeded by more than one-tenth; where that limit is exceeded, this Regulation shall continue to apply for a period of six months from the end of the year in which the limit was exceeded.

Article 6

This Regulation shall also apply to:
- (1) agreements where the licensor is not the holder of the know-how or the patentee, but is authorized by the holder or the patentee to grant a licence;
- (2) assignments of know-how, patents or both where the risk associated with exploitation remains with the assignor, in particular where the sum payable in consideration of the assignment is dependent on the turnover obtained by the assignee in respect of products made using the know-how or the patents, the quantity of such products manufactured or the number of operations carried out employing the know-how or the patents;
- (3) licensing agreements in which the rights or obligations of the licensor or the licensee are assumed by undertakings connected with them.

Article 7

The Commission may withdraw the benefit of this Regulation, pursuant to Article 7 of Regulation No 19/65/EEC, where it finds in a particular case that an agreement exempted by this Regulation nevertheless has certain effects which are incompatible with the conditions laid down in Article 85 (3) of the Treaty, and in particular where:
- (1) the effect of the agreement is to prevent the licensed products from being exposed to effective competition in the licensed territory from identical goods or services or from goods or services considered by users as interchangeable or substitutable in view of their characteristics, price and intended use, which may in particular occur where the licensee's market share exceeds 40 %;
- (2) without prejudice to Article 1 (1) (6), the licensee refuses, without any objectively justified reason, to meet unsolicited orders from users or resellers in the territory of other licensees;
- (3) the parties:
  - (a) without any objectively justified reason, refuse to meet orders from users or resellers in their respective territories who would market the products in other territories within the common market; or
  - (b) make it difficult for users or resellers to obtain the products from other resellers within the common market, and in particular where they exercise intellectual property rights or take measures so as to prevent resellers or users from obtaining outside, or from putting on the market in the licensed territory products which have been lawfully put on the market within the common market by the licensor or with his consent;
- (4) the parties were competing manufacturers at the date of the grant of the licence and obligations on the licensee to produce a minimum quantity or to use his best endeavours as referred to in Article 2 (1), (9) and (17) respectively have the effect of preventing the licensee from using competing technologies.

Article 8

1. For purposes of this Regulation:

(a) patent applications;
(b) utility models;
(c) applications for registration of utility models;
(d) topographies of semiconductor products;
(e) certificates d'utilité and certificates d'addition under French law;
(f) applications for certificates d'utilité and certificates d'addition under French law;
(g) supplementary protection certificates for medicinal products or other products for which such supplementary protection certificates may be obtained;
(h) plant breeder's certificates,

shall be deemed to be patents.

2. This Regulation shall also apply to agreements relating to the exploitation of an invention if an application within the meaning of paragraph 1 is made in respect of the invention for a licensed territory after the date when the agreements were entered into but within the time-limits set by the national law or the international convention to be applied.

3. This Regulation shall furthermore apply to pure patent or know-how licensing agreements or to mixed agreements whose initial duration is automatically prolonged by the inclusion of any new improvements, whether patented or not, communicated by the licensor, provided that the licensee has the right to refuse such improvements or each party has the right to terminate the agreement at the expiry of the initial term of an agreement and at least every three years thereafter.

Article 9

1. Information acquired pursuant to Article 4 shall be used only for the purposes of this Regulation.

2. The Commission and the authorities of the Member States, their officials and other servants shall not disclose information acquired by them pursuant to this Regulation of the kind covered by the obligation of professional secrecy.

3. The provisions of paragraphs 1 and 2 shall not prevent publication of general information or surveys which do not contain information relating to particular undertakings or associations of undertakings.

Article 10

For purposes of this Regulation:

(1) 'know-how' means a body of technical information that is secret, substantial and identified in any appropriate form;

(2) 'secret' means that the know-how package as a body or in the precise configuration and assembly of its components is not generally known or easily accessible, so that part of its value consists in the lead which the licensee gains when it is communicated to him; it is not limited to the narrow sense that each individual component of the know-how should be totally unknown or unobtainable outside the licensor's business;

(3) 'substantial' means that the know-how includes information which must be useful, i.e. can reasonably be expected at the date of conclusion of the agreement to be capable of improving the competitive position of the licensee, for example by helping him to enter a new market or giving him an advantage in competition with other manufacturers or providers of services who do not have access to the licensed secret know-how or other comparable secret know-how;

(4) 'identified' means that the know-how is described or recorded in such a manner as to make it possible to verify that it satisfies the criteria of secrecy and substantiality and to ensure that the licensee is not unduly restricted in his exploitation of his own technology, to be identified the know-how can either be set out in the licence agreement or in a separate document or recorded in any other appropriate form at the

latest when the know-how is transferred or shortly thereafter, provided that the separate document or other record can be made available if the need arises;

(5) 'necessary patents' are patents where a licence under the patent is necessary for the putting into effect of the licensed technology in so far as, in the absence of such a licence, the realization of the licensed technology would not be possible or would by possible only to a lesser extent or in more difficult or costly conditions. Such patents must therefore be of technical, legal or economic interest to the licensee;

(6) 'licensing agreement' means pure patent licensing agreements and pure know-how licensing agreements as well as mixed patent and know-how licensing agreements;

(7) 'licensed technology' means the initial manufacturing know-how or the necessary product and process patents, or both, existing at the time the first licensing agreement is concluded, and improvements subsequently made to the know-how or patents, irrespective of whether and to what extent they are exploited by the parties or by other licensees;

(8) 'the licensed products' are goods or services the production or provision of which requires the use of the licensed technology;

(9) 'the licensee's market share' means the proportion which the licensed products and other goods or services provided by the licensee, which are considered by users to be interchangeable or substitutable for the licensed products in view of their characteristics, price and intended use, represent the entire market for the licensed products and all other interchangeable or substitutable goods and services in the common market or a substantial part of it;

(10) 'exploitation' refers to any use of the licensed technology in particular in the production, active or passive sales in a territory even if not coupled with manufacture in that territory, or leasing of the licensed products;

(11) 'the licensed territory' is the territory covering all or at least part of the common market where the licensee is entitled to exploit the licensed technology;

(12) 'territory of the licensor' means territories in which the licensor has not granted any licences for patents and/or know-how covered by the licensing agreement;

(13) 'parallel patents' means patents which, in spite of the divergences which remain in the absence of any unification of national rules concerning industrial property, protect the same invention in various Member States;

(14) 'connected undertakings' means:
   (a) undertakings in which a party to the agreement, directly or indirectly:
      - owns more than half the capital or business assets, or
      - has the power to exercise more than half the voting rights, or
      - has the power to appoint more than half the members of the supervisory board, board of directors or bodies legally representing the undertaking, or
      - has the right to manage the affairs of the undertaking;
   (b) undertakings which, directly or indirectly, have in or over a party to the agreement the rights or powers listed in (a);
   (c) undertakings in which an undertaking referred to in (b), directly or indirectly, has the rights or powers listed in (a);
   (d) undertakings in which the parties to the agreement or undertakings connected with them jointly have the rights or powers listed in (a): such jointly controlled undertakings are considered to be connected with each of the parties to the agreement;

(15) 'ancillary provisions' are provisions relating to the exploitation of intellectual property rights other than patents, which contain no obligations restrictive of competition other than those also attached to the licensed know-how or patents and exempted under this Regulation;

(16) 'obligation' means both contractual obligation and a concerted practice;
(17) 'competing manufacturers' or manufacturers of 'competing products' means manufacturers who sell products which, in view of their characteristics, price and intended use, are considered by users to be interchangeable or substitutable for the licensed products.

Article 11

1. Regulation (EEC) No 556/89 is hereby repealed with effect from 1 April 1996.
2. Regulation (EEC) No 2349/84 shall continue to apply until 31 March 1996.
3. The prohibition in Article 85 (1) of the Treaty shall not apply to agreements in force on 31 March 1996 which fulfil the exemption requirements laid down by Regulation (EEC) No 2349/84 or (EEC) No 556/89.

Article 12

1. The Commission shall undertake regular assessments of the application of this Regulation, and in particular of the opposition procedure provided for in Article 4.
2. The Commission shall draw up a report on the operation of this Regulation before the end of the fourth year following its entry into force and shall, on that basis, assess whether any adaptation of the Regulation is desirable.

Article 13

This Regulation shall enter into force on 1 April 1996.
It shall apply until 31 March 2006.
Article 11 (2) of this Regulation shall, however, enter into force on 1 January 1996.
This Regulation shall be binding in its entirety and directly applicable in all Member States.

DIRECTIVE 96/9/EC OF THE EUROPEAN PARLIAMENT AND OF THE COUNCIL OF 11 MARCH 1996 ON THE LEGAL PROTECTION OF DATABASES

(Official Journal L 077, 27/03/1996, p.0020)

THE EUROPEAN PARLIAMENT AND THE COUNCIL OF THE EUROPEAN UNION,

Having regard to the Treaty establishing the European Community, and in particular Article 57 (2), 66 and 100a thereof,
Having regard to the proposal from the Commission,[1]
Having regard to the opinion of the Economic and Social Committee,[2]

Acting in accordance with the procedure laid down in Article 189b of the Treaty,[3]

(1) Whereas databases are at present not sufficiently protected in all Member States by existing legislation; whereas such protection, where it exists, has different attributes;

(2) Whereas such differences in the legal protection of databases offered by the legislation of the Member States have direct negative effects on the functioning of the internal market as regards databases and in particular on the freedom of natural and legal persons to provide on-line database goods and services on the basis of harmonized legal arrangements throughout the Community; whereas such differences could well become more pronounced as Member States introduce new legislation in this field, which is now taking on an increasingly international dimension;

(3) Whereas existing differences distorting the functioning of the internal market need to be removed and new ones prevented from arising, while differences not adversely affecting the functioning of the internal market or the development of an information market within the Community need not be removed or prevented from arising;

(4) Whereas copyright protection for databases exists in varying forms in the Member States according to legislation or case-law, and whereas, if differences in legislation in the scope and conditions of protection remain between the Member States, such unharmonized intellectual property rights can have the effect of preventing the free movement of goods or services within the Community;

(5) Whereas copyright remains an appropriate form of exclusive right for authors who have created databases;

(6) Whereas, nevertheless, in the absence of a harmonized system of unfair-competition legislation or of case-law, other measures are required in addition to prevent the unauthorized extraction and/or re-utilization of the contents of a database;

(7) Whereas the making of databases requires the investment of considerable human, technical and financial resources while such databases can be copied or accessed at a fraction of the cost needed to design them independently;

(8) Whereas the unauthorized extraction and/or re-utilization of the contents of a database constitute acts which can have serious economic and technical consequences;

---

[1] OJ No C 156, 23. 6. 1992, p. 4 and OJ No C 308, 15. 11. 1993, p. 1.

[2] OJ No C 19, 25. 1. 1993, p. 3.

[3] Opinion of the European Parliament of 23 June 1993 (OJ No C 194, 19. 7. 1993, p. 144), Common Position of the Council of 10 July 1995 (OJ No C 288, 30. 10. 1995, p. 14), Decision of the European Parliament of 14 December 1995 (OJ No C 17, 22 1. 1996) and Council Decision of 26 February 1996.

(9) Whereas databases are a vital tool in the development of an information market within the Community; whereas this tool will also be of use in many other fields;
(10) Whereas the exponential growth, in the Community and worldwide, in the amount of information generated and processed annually in all sectors of commerce and industry calls for investment in all the Member States in advanced information processing systems;
(11) Whereas there is at present a very great imbalance in the level of investment in the database sector both as between the Member States and between the Community and the world's largest database-producing third countries;
(12) Whereas such an investment in modern information storage and processing systems will not take place within the Community unless a stable and uniform legal protection regime is introduced for the protection of the rights of makers of databases;
(13) Whereas this Directive protects collections, sometimes called 'compilations', of works, data or other materials which are arranged, stored and accessed by means which include electronic, electromagnetic or electro-optical processes or analogous processes;
(14) Whereas protection under this Directive should be extended to cover non-electronic databases;
(15) Whereas the criteria used to determine whether a database should be protected by copyright should be defined to the fact that the selection or the arrangement of the contents of the database is the author's own intellectual creation; whereas such protection should cover the structure of the database;
(16) Whereas no criterion other than originality in the sense of the author's intellectual creation should be applied to determine the eligibility of the database for copyright protection, and in particular no aesthetic or qualitative criteria should be applied;
(17) Whereas the term 'database' should be understood to include literary, artistic, musical or other collections of works or collections of other material such as texts, sound, images, numbers, facts, and data; whereas it should cover collections of independent works, data or other materials which are systematically or methodically arranged and can be individually accessed; whereas this means that a recording or an audiovisual, cinematographic, literary or musical work as such does not fall within the scope of this Directive;
(18) Whereas this Directive is without prejudice to the freedom of authors to decide whether, or in what manner, they will allow their works to be included in a database, in particular whether or not the authorization given is exclusive; whereas the protection of databases by the sui generis right is without prejudice to existing rights over their contents, and whereas in particular where an author or the holder of a related right permits some of his works or subject matter to be included in a database pursuant to a non-exclusive agreement, a third party may make use of those works or subject matter subject to the required consent of the author or of the holder of the related right without the sui generis right of the maker of the database being invoked to prevent him doing so, on condition that those works or subject matter are neither extracted from the database nor re-utilized on the basis thereof;
(19) Whereas, as a rule, the compilation of several recordings of musical performances on a CD does not come within the scope of this Directive, both because, as a compilation, it does not meet the conditions for copyright protection and because it does not represent a substantial enough investment to be eligible under the sui generis right;
(20) Whereas protection under this Directive may also apply to the materials necessary for the operation or consultation of certain databases such as thesaurus and indexation systems;
(21) Whereas the protection provided for in this Directive relates to databases in which works, data or other materials have been arranged systematically or methodically; whereas it is not necessary for those materials to have been physically stored in an organized manner;
(22) Whereas electronic databases within the meaning of this Directive may also include devices such as CD-ROM and CD-i;

(23) Whereas the term 'database' should not be taken to extend to computer programs used in the making or operation of a database, which are protected by Council Directive 91/250/EEC of 14 May 1991 on the legal protection of computer programs[4];
(24) Whereas the rental and lending of databases in the field of copyright and related rights are governed exclusively by Council Directive 92/100/EEC of 19 November 1992 on rental right and lending right and on certain rights related to copyright in the field of intellectual property[5];
(25) Whereas the term of copyright is already governed by Council Directive 93/98/EEC of 29 October 1993 harmonizing the term of protection of copyright and certain related rights[6];
(26) Whereas works protected by copyright and subject matter protected by related rights, which are incorporated into a database, remain nevertheless protected by the respective exclusive rights and may not be incorporated into, or extracted from, the database without the permission of the rightholder or his successors in title;
(27) Whereas copyright in such works and related rights in subject matter thus incorporated into a database are in no way affected by the existence of a separate right in the selection or arrangement of these works and subject matter in a database;
(28) Whereas the moral rights of the natural person who created the database belong to the author and should be exercised according to the legislation of the Member States and the provisions of the Berne Convention for the Protection of Literary and Artistic Works; whereas such moral rights remain outside the scope of this Directive;
(29) Whereas the arrangements applicable to databases created by employees are left to the discretion of the Member States; whereas, therefore nothing in this Directive prevents Member States from stipulating in their legislation that where a database is created by an employee in the execution of his duties or following the instructions given by his employer, the employer exclusively shall be entitled to exercise all economic rights in the database so created, unless otherwise provided by contract;
(30) Whereas the author's exclusive rights should include the right to determine the way in which his work is exploited and by whom, and in particular to control the distribution of his work to unauthorized persons;
(31) Whereas the copyright protection of databases includes making databases available by means other than the distribution of copies;
(32) Whereas Member States are required to ensure that their national provisions are at least materially equivalent in the case of such acts subject to restrictions as are provided for by this Directive;
(33) Whereas the question of exhaustion of the right of distribution does not arise in the case of on-line databases, which come within the field of provision of services; whereas this also applies with regard to a material copy of such a database made by the user of such a service with the consent of the rightholder; whereas, unlike CD-ROM or CD-i, where the intellectual property is incorporated in a material medium, namely an item of goods, every on-line service is in fact an act which will have to be subject to authorization where the copyright so provides;
(34) Whereas, nevertheless, once the rightholder has chosen to make available a copy of the database to a user, whether by an on-line service or by other means of distribution, that lawful user must be able to access and use the database for the purposes and in the way set out in the agreement with the rightholder, even if such access and use necessitate performance of otherwise restricted acts;
(35) Whereas a list should be drawn up of exceptions to restricted acts, taking into account the fact that copyright as covered by this Directive applies only to the selection or arrangements of the contents of a database; whereas Member States should be given the option of providing for such exceptions in certain cases; whereas, however, this option should be exercised in

---

[4] OJ No L 122, 17. 5. 1991, p. 42. Directive as last amended by Directive 93/98/EEC (OJ No L
[5] OJ No L 346, 27. 11. 1992, p. 61.
[6] OJ No L 290, 24. 11. 1993, p. 9.

accordance with the Berne Convention and to the extent that the exceptions relate to the structure of the database; whereas a distinction should be drawn between exceptions for private use and exceptions for reproduction for private purposes, which concerns provisions under national legislation of some Member States on levies on blank media or recording equipment;

(36) Whereas the term 'scientific research' within the meaning of this Directive covers both the natural sciences and the human sciences;

(37) Whereas Article 10 (1) of the Berne Convention is not affected by this Directive;

(38) Whereas the increasing use of digital recording technology exposes the database maker to the risk that the contents of his database may be copied and rearranged electronically, without his authorization, to produce a database of identical content which, however, does not infringe any copyright in the arrangement of his database;

(39) Whereas, in addition to aiming to protect the copyright in the original selection or arrangement of the contents of a database, this Directive seeks to safeguard the position of makers of databases against misappropriation of the results of the financial and professional investment made in obtaining and collection the contents by protecting the whole or substantial parts of a database against certain acts by a user or competitor;

(40) Whereas the object of this sui generis right is to ensure protection of any investment in obtaining, verifying or presenting the contents of a database for the limited duration of the right; whereas such investment may consist in the deployment of financial resources and/or the expending of time, effort and energy;

(41) Whereas the objective of the sui generis right is to give the maker of a database the option of preventing the unauthorized extraction and/or re-utilization of all or a substantial part of the contents of that database; whereas the maker of a database is the person who takes the initiative and the risk of investing; whereas this excludes subcontractors in particular from the definition of maker;

(42) Whereas the special right to prevent unauthorized extraction and/or re-utilization relates to acts by the user which go beyond his legitimate rights and thereby harm the investment; whereas the right to prohibit extraction and/or re-utilization of all or a substantial part of the contents relates not only to the manufacture of a parasitical competing product but also to any user who, through his acts, causes significant detriment, evaluated qualitatively or quantitatively, to the investment;

(43) Whereas, in the case of on-line transmission, the right to prohibit re-utilization is not exhausted either as regards the database or as regards a material copy of the database or of part thereof made by the addressee of the transmission with the consent of the rightholder;

(44) Whereas, when on-screen display of the contents of a database necessitates the permanent or temporary transfer of all or a substantial part of such contents to another medium, that act should be subject to authorization by the rightholder;

(45) Whereas the right to prevent unauthorized extraction and/or re-utilization does not in any way constitute an extension of copyright protection to mere facts or data;

(46) Whereas the existence of a right to prevent the unauthorized extraction and/or re-utilization of the whole or a substantial part of works, data or materials from a database should not give rise to the creation of a new right in the works, data or materials themselves;

(47) Whereas, in the interests of competition between suppliers of information products and services, protection by the sui generis right must not be afforded in such a way as to facilitate abuses of a dominant position, in particular as regards the creation and distribution of new products and services which have an intellectual, documentary, technical, economic or commercial added value; whereas, therefore, the provisions of this Directive are without prejudice to the application of Community or national competition rules;

(48) Whereas the objective of this Directive, which is to afford an appropriate and uniform level of protection of databases as a means to secure the remuneration of the maker of the database,

is different from the aim of Directive 95/46/EC of the European Parliament and of the Council of 24 October 1995 on the protection of individuals with regard to the processing of personal data and on the free movement of such data[7], which is to guarantee free circulation of personal data on the basis of harmonized rules designed to protect fundamental rights, notably the right to privacy which is recognized in Article 8 of the European Convention for the Protection of Human Rights and Fundamental Freedoms; whereas the provisions of this Directive are without prejudice to data protection legislation;

(49) Whereas, notwithstanding the right to prevent extraction and/or re-utilization of all or a substantial part of a database, it should be laid down that the maker of a database or rightholder may not prevent a lawful user of the database from extracting and re-utilizing insubstantial parts; whereas, however, that user may not unreasonably prejudice either the legitimate interests of the holder of the sui generis right or the holder of copyright or a related right in respect of the works or subject matter contained in the database;

(50) Whereas the Member States should be given the option of providing for exceptions to the right to prevent the unauthorized extraction and/or re-utilization of a substantial part of the contents of a database in the case of extraction for private purposes, for the purposes of illustration for teaching or scientific research, or where extraction and/or re-utilization are/is carried out in the interests of public security or for the purposes of an administrative or judicial procedure; whereas such operations must not prejudice the exclusive rights of the maker to exploit the database and their purpose must not be commercial;

(51) Whereas the Member States, where they avail themselves of the option to permit a lawful user of a database to extract a substantial part of the contents for the purposes of illustration for teaching or scientific research, may limit that permission to certain categories of teaching or scientific research institution;

(52) Whereas those Member States which have specific rules providing for a right comparable to the sui generis right provided for in this Directive should be permitted to retain, as far as the new right is concerned, the exceptions traditionally specified by such rules;

(53) Whereas the burden of proof regarding the date of completion of the making of a database lies with the maker of the database;

(54) Whereas the burden of proof that the criteria exist for concluding that a substantial modification of the contents of a database is to be regarded as a substantial new investment lies with the maker of the database resulting from such investment;

(55) Whereas a substantial new investment involving a new term of protection may include a substantial verification of the contents of the database;

(56) Whereas the right to prevent unauthorized extraction and/or re-utilization in respect of a database should apply to databases whose makers are nationals or habitual residents of third countries or to those produced by legal persons not established in a Member State, within the meaning of the Treaty, only if such third countries offer comparable protection to databases produced by nationals of a Member State or persons who have their habitual residence in the territory of the Community;

(57) Whereas, in addition to remedies provided under the legislation of the Member States for infringements of copyright or other rights, Member States should provide for appropriate remedies against unauthorized extraction and/or re-utilization of the contents of a database;

(58) Whereas, in addition to the protection given under this Directive to the structure of the database by copyright, and to its contents against unauthorized extraction and/or re-utilization under the sui generis right, other legal provisions in the Member States relevant to the supply of database goods and services continue to apply;

---

[7] OJ No L 281, 23. 11. 1995, p. 31.

(59) Whereas this Directive is without prejudice to the application to databases composed of audiovisual works of any rules recognized by a Member State's legislation concerning the broadcasting of audiovisual programmes;

(60) Whereas some Member States currently protect under copyright arrangements databases which do not meet the criteria for eligibility for copyright protection laid down in this Directive; whereas, even if the databases concerned are eligible for protection under the right laid down in this Directive to prevent unauthorized extraction and/or re-utilization of their contents, the term of protection under that right is considerably shorter than that which they enjoy under the national arrangements currently in force; whereas harmonization of the criteria for determining whether a database is to be protected by copyright may not have the effect of reducing the term of protection currently enjoyed by the rightholders concerned; whereas a derogation should be laid down to that effect; whereas the effects of such derogation must be confined to the territories of the Member States concerned,

HAVE ADOPTED THIS DIRECTIVE:

CHAPTER I: SCOPE

Article 1 - Scope

1. This Directive concerns the legal protection of databases in any form.
2. For the purposes of this Directive, 'database' shall mean a collection of independent works, data or other materials arranged in a systematic or methodical way and individually accessible by electronic or other means.
3. Protection under this Directive shall not apply to computer programs used in the making or operation of databases accessible by electronic means.

Article 2 - Limitations on the scope

This Directive shall apply without prejudice to Community provisions relating to:
(a) the legal protection of computer programs;
(b) rental right, lending right and certain rights related to copyright in the field of intellectual property;
(c) the term of protection of copyright and certain related rights.

CHAPTER II: COPYRIGHT

Article 3 - Object of protection

1. In accordance with this Directive, databases which, by reason of the selection or arrangement of their contents, constitute the author's own intellectual creation shall be protected as such by copyright. No other criteria shall be applied to determine their eligibility for that protection.
2. The copyright protection of databases provided for by this Directive shall not extend to their contents and shall be without prejudice to any rights subsisting in those contents themselves.

Article 4 - Database authorship

1. The author of a database shall be the natural person or group of natural persons who created the base or, where the legislation of the Member States so permits, the legal person designated as the rightholder by that legislation.

2. Where collective works are recognized by the legislation of a Member State, the economic rights shall be owned by the person holding the copyright.
3. In respect of a database created by a group of natural persons jointly, the exclusive rights shall be owned jointly.

Article 5 - Restricted acts

In respect of the expression of the database which is protectable by copyright, the author of a database shall have the exclusive right to carry out or to authorize:
(a) temporary or permanent reproduction by any means and in any form, in whole or in part;
(b) translation, adaptation, arrangement and any other alteration;
(c) any form of distribution to the public of the database or of copies thereof. The first sale in the Community of a copy of the database by the rightholder or with his consent shall exhaust the right to control resale of that copy within the Community;
(d) any communication, display or performance to the public;
(e) any reproduction, distribution, communication, display or performance to the public of the results of the acts referred to in (b).

Article 6 - Exceptions to restricted acts

1. The performance by the lawful user of a database or of a copy thereof of any of the acts listed in Article 5 which is necessary for the purposes of access to the contents of the databases and normal use of the contents by the lawful user shall not require the authorization of the author of the database. Where the lawful user is authorized to use only part of the database, this provision shall apply only to that part.
2. Member States shall have the option of providing for limitations on the rights set out in Article 5 in the following cases:
(a) in the case of reproduction for private purposes of a non-electronic database;
(b) where there is use for the sole purpose of illustration for teaching or scientific research, as long as the source is indicated and to the extent justified by the non-commercial purpose to be achieved;
(c) where there is use for the purposes of public security or for the purposes of an administrative or judicial procedure;
(d) where other exceptions to copyright which are traditionally authorized under national law are involved, without prejudice to points (a), (b) and (c).
3. In accordance with the Berne Convention for the protection of Literary and Artistic Works, this Article may not be interpreted in such a way as to allow its application to be used in a manner which unreasonably prejudices the rightholder's legitimate interests or conflicts with normal exploitation of the database.

CHAPTER III: SUI GENERIS RIGHT

Article 7 - Object of protection

1. Member States shall provide for a right for the maker of a database which shows that there has been qualitatively and/or quantitatively a substantial investment in either the obtaining, verification or presentation of the contents to prevent extraction and/or re-utilization of the whole or of a substantial part, evaluated qualitatively and/or quantitatively, of the contents of that database.
2. For the purposes of this Chapter:
(a) 'extraction' shall mean the permanent or temporary transfer of all or a substantial part of the contents of a database to another medium by any means or in any form;

(b) 're-utilization' shall mean any form of making available to the public all or a substantial part of the contents of a database by the distribution of copies, by renting, by on-line or other forms of transmission. The first sale of a copy of a database within the Community by the rightholder or with his consent shall exhaust the right to control resale of that copy within the Community;

Public lending is not an act of extraction or re-utilization.

3. The right referred to in paragraph 1 may be transferred, assigned or granted under contractual licence.
4. The right provided for in paragraph 1 shall apply irrespective of the eligibility of that database for protection by copyright or by other rights. Moreover, it shall apply irrespective of eligibility of the contents of that database for protection by copyright or by other rights. Protection of databases under the right provided for in paragraph 1 shall be without prejudice to rights existing in respect of their contents.
5. The repeated and systematic extraction and/or re-utilization of insubstantial parts of the contents of the database implying acts which conflict with a normal exploitation of that database or which unreasonably prejudice the legitimate interests of the maker of the database shall not be permitted.

Article 8 - Rights and obligations of lawful users

1. The maker of a database which is made available to the public in whatever manner may not prevent a lawful user of the database from extracting and/or re-utilizing insubstantial parts of its contents, evaluated qualitatively and/or quantitatively, for any purposes whatsoever. Where the lawful user is authorized to extract and/or re-utilize only part of the database, this paragraph shall apply only to that part.
2. A lawful user of a database which is made available to the public in whatever manner may not perform acts which conflict with normal exploitation of the database or unreasonably prejudice the legitimate interests of the maker of the database.
3. A lawful user of a database which is made available to the public in any manner may not cause prejudice to the holder of a copyright or related right in respect of the works or subject matter contained in the database.

Article 9 - Exceptions to the sui generis right

Member States may stipulate that lawful users of a database which is made available to the public in whatever manner may, without the authorization of its maker, extract or re-utilize a substantial part of its contents:

(a) in the case of extraction for private purposes of the contents of a non-electronic database;
(b) in the case of extraction for the purposes of illustration for teaching or scientific research, as long as the source is indicated and to the extent justified by the non-commercial purpose to be achieved;
(c) in the case of extraction and/or re-utilization for the purposes of public security or an administrative or judicial procedure.

Article 10 - Term of protection

1. The right provided for in Article 7 shall run from the date of completion of the making of the database. It shall expire fifteen years from the first of January of the year following the date of completion.
2. In the case of a database which is made available to the public in whatever manner before expiry of the period provided for in paragraph 1, the term of protection by that right shall expire fifteen years from the first of January of the year following the date when the database was first made available to the public.

3. Any substantial change, evaluated qualitatively or quantitatively, to the contents of a database, including any substantial change resulting from the accumulation of successive additions, deletions or alterations, which would result in the database being considered to be a substantial new investment, evaluated qualitatively or quantitatively, shall qualify the database resulting from that investment for its own term of protection.

Article 11 - Beneficiaries of protection under the sui generis right

1. The right provided for in Article 7 shall apply to database whose makers or rightholders are nationals of a Member State or who have their habitual residence in the territory of the Community.
2. Paragraph 1 shall also apply to companies and firms formed in accordance with the law of a Member State and having their registered office, central administration or principal place of business within the Community; however, where such a company or firm has only its registered office in the territory of the Community, its operations must be genuinely linked on an ongoing basis with the economy of a Member State.
3. Agreements extending the right provided for in Article 7 to databases made in third countries and falling outside the provisions of paragraphs 1 and 2 shall be concluded by the Council acting on a proposal from the Commission. The term of any protection extended to databases by virtue of that procedure shall not exceed that available pursuant to Article 10.

CHAPTER IV: COMMON PROVISIONS

Article 12 - Remedies

Member States shall provide appropriate remedies in respect of infringements of the rights provided for in this Directive.

Article 13 - Continued application of other legal provisions

This Directive shall be without prejudice to provisions concerning in particular copyright, rights related to copyright or any other rights or obligations subsisting in the data, works or other materials incorporated into a database, patent rights, trade marks, design rights, the protection of national treasures, laws on restrictive practices and unfair competition, trade secrets, security, confidentiality, data protection and privacy, access to public documents, and the law of contract.

Article 14 - Application over time

1. Protection pursuant to this Directive as regards copyright shall also be available in respect of databases created prior to the date referred to Article 16 (1) which on that date fulfil the requirements laid down in this Directive as regards copyright protection of databases.
2. Notwithstanding paragraph 1, where a database protected under copyright arrangements in a Member State on the date of publication of this Directive does not fulfil the eligibility criteria for copyright protection laid down in Article 3 (1), this Directive shall not result in any curtailing in that Member State of the remaining term of protection afforded under those arrangements.
3. Protection pursuant to the provisions of this Directive as regards the right provided for in Article 7 shall also be available in respect of databases the making of which was completed not more than fifteen years prior to the date referred to in Article 16 (1) and which on that date fulfil the requirements laid down in Article 7.
4. The protection provided for in paragraphs 1 and 3 shall be without prejudice to any acts concluded and rights acquired before the date referred to in those paragraphs.

5. In the case of a database the making of which was completed not more than fifteen years prior to the date referred to in Article 16 (1), the term of protection by the right provided for in Article 7 shall expire fifteen years from the first of January following that date.

Article 15 - Binding nature of certain provisions

Any contractual provision contrary to Articles 6 (1) and 8 shall be null and void.

Article 16 - Final provisions

1. Member States shall bring into force the laws, regulations and administrative provisions necessary to comply with this Directive before 1 January 1998. When Member States adopt these provisions, they shall contain a reference to this Directive or shall be accompanied by such reference on the occasion of their official publication. The methods of making such reference shall be laid down by Member States.
2. Member States shall communicate to the Commission the text of the provisions of domestic law which they adopt in the field governed by this Directive.
3. Not later than at the end of the third year after the date referred to in paragraph 1, and every three years thereafter, the Commission shall submit to the European Parliament, the Council and the Economic and Social Committee a report on the application of this Directive, in which, inter alia, on the basis of specific information supplied by the Member States, it shall examine in particular the application of the sui generis right, including Articles 8 and 9, and shall verify especially whether the application of this right has led to abuse of a dominant position or other interference with free competition which would justify appropriate measures being taken, including the establishment of non-voluntary licensing arrangements. Where necessary, it shall submit proposals for adjustment of this Directive in line with developments in the area of databases.

Article 17 - Addressees

This Directive is addressed to the Member States.

DIRECTIVE 2001/29/EC OF THE EUROPEAN PARLIAMENT AND OF THE COUNCIL OF 22 MAY 2001 ON THE HARMONISATION OF CERTAIN ASPECTS OF COPYRIGHT AND RELATED RIGHTS IN THE INFORMATION SOCIETY

(Official Journal L 167, 22/06/2001, p. 0010)
(with Corrigendum, Official Journal L 006, 10/01/2001, p. 0070 - 0070)

THE EUROPEAN PARLIAMENT AND THE COUNCIL OF THE EUROPEAN UNION,

Having regard to the Treaty establishing the European Community, and in particular Articles 47(2), 55 and 95 thereof,
Having regard to the proposal from the Commission[1],
Having regard to the Opinion of the Economic and Social Committee[2],

Acting in accordance with the procedure laid down in Article 251 of the Treaty[3],

Whereas:

(1) The Treaty provides for the establishment of an internal market and the institution of a system ensuring that competition in the internal market is not distorted. Harmonisation of the laws of the Member States on copyright and related rights contributes to the achievement of these objectives.

(2) The European Council, meeting at Corfu on 24 and 25 June 1994, stressed the need to create a general and flexible legal framework at Community level in order to foster the development of the information society in Europe. This requires, inter alia, the existence of an internal market for new products and services. Important Community legislation to ensure such a regulatory framework is already in place or its adoption is well under way. Copyright and related rights play an important role in this context as they protect and stimulate the development and marketing of new products and services and the creation and exploitation of their creative content.

(3) The proposed harmonisation will help to implement the four freedoms of the internal market and relates to compliance with the fundamental principles of law and especially of property, including intellectual property, and freedom of expression and the public interest.

(4) A harmonised legal framework on copyright and related rights, through increased legal certainty and while providing for a high level of protection of intellectual property, will foster substantial investment in creativity and innovation, including network infrastructure, and lead in turn to growth and increased competitiveness of European industry, both in the area of content provision and information technology and more generally across a wide range of industrial and cultural sectors. This will safeguard employment and encourage new job creation.

(5) Technological development has multiplied and diversified the vectors for creation, production and exploitation. While no new concepts for the protection of intellectual property are needed, the current law on copyright and related rights should be adapted and supplemented to respond adequately to economic realities such as new forms of exploitation.

---

[1] OJ C 108, 7.4.1998, p. 6 and OJ C 180, 25.6.1999, p. 6.
[2] OJ C 407, 28.12.1998, p. 30.
[3] Opinion of the European Parliament of 10 February 1999 (OJ C 150, 28.5.1999, p. 171), Council Common Position of 28 September 2000 (OJ C 344, 1.12.2000, p. 1) and Decision of the European Parliament of 14 February 2001 (not yet published in the Official Journal). Council Decision of 9 April 2001.

(6) Without harmonisation at Community level, legislative activities at national level which have already been initiated in a number of Member States in order to respond to the technological challenges might result in significant differences in protection and thereby in restrictions on the free movement of services and products incorporating, or based on, intellectual property, leading to a refragmentation of the internal market and legislative inconsistency. The impact of such legislative differences and uncertainties will become more significant with the further development of the information society, which has already greatly increased transborder exploitation of intellectual property. This development will and should further increase. Significant legal differences and uncertainties in protection may hinder economies of scale for new products and services containing copyright and related rights.

(7) The Community legal framework for the protection of copyright and related rights must, therefore, also be adapted and supplemented as far as is necessary for the smooth functioning of the internal market. To that end, those national provisions on copyright and related rights which vary considerably from one Member State to another or which cause legal uncertainties hindering the smooth functioning of the internal market and the proper development of the information society in Europe should be adjusted, and inconsistent national responses to the technological developments should be avoided, whilst differences not adversely affecting the functioning of the internal market need not be removed or prevented.

(8) The various social, societal and cultural implications of the information society require that account be taken of the specific features of the content of products and services.

(9) Any harmonisation of copyright and related rights must take as a basis a high level of protection, since such rights are crucial to intellectual creation. Their protection helps to ensure the maintenance and development of creativity in the interests of authors, performers, producers, consumers, culture, industry and the public at large. Intellectual property has therefore been recognised as an integral part of property.

(10) If authors or performers are to continue their creative and artistic work, they have to receive an appropriate reward for the use of their work, as must producers in order to be able to finance this work. The investment required to produce products such as phonograms, films or multimedia products, and services such as "on-demand" services, is considerable. Adequate legal protection of intellectual property rights is necessary in order to guarantee the availability of such a reward and provide the opportunity for satisfactory returns on this investment.

(11) A rigorous, effective system for the protection of copyright and related rights is one of the main ways of ensuring that European cultural creativity and production receive the necessary resources and of safeguarding the independence and dignity of artistic creators and performers.

(12) Adequate protection of copyright works and subject-matter of related rights is also of great importance from a cultural standpoint. Article 151 of the Treaty requires the Community to take cultural aspects into account in its action.

(13) A common search for, and consistent application at European level of, technical measures to protect works and other subject-matter and to provide the necessary information on rights are essential insofar as the ultimate aim of these measures is to give effect to the principles and guarantees laid down in law.

(14) This Directive should seek to promote learning and culture by protecting works and other subject-matter while permitting exceptions or limitations in the public interest for the purpose of education and teaching.

(15) The Diplomatic Conference held under the auspices of the World Intellectual Property Organisation (WIPO) in December 1996 led to the adoption of two new Treaties, the "WIPO Copyright Treaty" and the "WIPO Performances and Phonograms Treaty", dealing respectively with the protection of authors and the protection of performers and phonogram producers. Those Treaties update the international protection for copyright and related rights significantly, not least with regard to the so-called "digital agenda", and improve the means to fight piracy world-wide. The Community and a majority of Member States have already

signed the Treaties and the process of making arrangements for the ratification of the Treaties by the Community and the Member States is under way. This Directive also serves to implement a number of the new international obligations.

(16) Liability for activities in the network environment concerns not only copyright and related rights but also other areas, such as defamation, misleading advertising, or infringement of trademarks, and is addressed horizontally in Directive 2000/31/EC of the European Parliament and of the Council of 8 June 2000 on certain legal aspects of information society services, in particular electronic commerce, in the internal market ("Directive on electronic commerce")[4], which clarifies and harmonises various legal issues relating to information society services including electronic commerce. This Directive should be implemented within a timescale similar to that for the implementation of the Directive on electronic commerce, since that Directive provides a harmonised framework of principles and provisions relevant inter alia to important parts of this Directive. This Directive is without prejudice to provisions relating to liability in that Directive.

(17) It is necessary, especially in the light of the requirements arising out of the digital environment, to ensure that collecting societies achieve a higher level of rationalisation and transparency with regard to compliance with competition rules.

(18) This Directive is without prejudice to the arrangements in the Member States concerning the management of rights such as extended collective licences.

(19) The moral rights of rightholders should be exercised according to the legislation of the Member States and the provisions of the Berne Convention for the Protection of Literary and Artistic Works, of the WIPO Copyright Treaty and of the WIPO Performances and Phonograms Treaty. Such moral rights remain outside the scope of this Directive.

(20) This Directive is based on principles and rules already laid down in the Directives currently in force in this area, in particular Directives 91/250/EEC[5], 92/100/EEC[6], 93/83/EEC[7], 93/98/EEC[8] and 96/9/EC[9], and it develops those principles and rules and places them in the context of the information society. The provisions of this Directive should be without prejudice to the provisions of those Directives, unless otherwise provided in this Directive.

(21) This Directive should define the scope of the acts covered by the reproduction right with regard to the different beneficiaries. This should be done in conformity with the acquis communautaire. A broad definition of these acts is needed to ensure legal certainty within the internal market.

(22) The objective of proper support for the dissemination of culture must not be achieved by sacrificing strict protection of rights or by tolerating illegal forms of distribution of counterfeited or pirated works.

(23) This Directive should harmonise further the author's right of communication to the public. This right should be understood in a broad sense covering all communication to the public not present at the place where the communication originates. This right should cover any such transmission or retransmission of a work to the public by wire or wireless means, including broadcasting. This right should not cover any other acts.

---

[4] OJ L 178, 17.7.2000, p. 1.

[5] Council Directive 91/250/EEC of 14 May 1991 on the legal protection of computer programs (OJ L 122, 17.5.1991, p. 42). Directive as amended by Directive 93/98/EEC.

[6] Council Directive 92/100/EEC of 19 November 1992 on rental right and lending right and on certain rights related to copyright in the field of intellectual property (OJ L 346, 27.11.1992, p. 61). Directive as amended by Directive 93/98/EEC.

[7] Council Directive 93/83/EEC of 27 September 1993 on the coordination of certain rules concerning copyright and rights related to copyright applicable to satellite broadcasting and cable retransmission (OJ L 248, 6.10.1993, p. 15).

[8] Council Directive 93/98/EEC of 29 October 1993 harmonising the term of protection of copyright and certain related rights (OJ L 290, 24.11.1993, p. 9).

[9] Directive 96/9/EC of the European Parliament and of the Council of 11 March 1996 on the legal protection of databases (OJ L 77, 27.3.1996, p. 20).

(24) The right to make available to the public subject-matter referred to in Article 3(2) should be understood as covering all acts of making available such subject-matter to members of the public not present at the place where the act of making available originates, and as not covering any other acts.

(25) The legal uncertainty regarding the nature and the level of protection of acts of on-demand transmission of copyright works and subject-matter protected by related rights over networks should be overcome by providing for harmonised protection at Community level. It should be made clear that all rightholders recognised by this Directive should have an exclusive right to make available to the public copyright works or any other subject-matter by way of interactive on-demand transmissions. Such interactive on-demand transmissions are characterised by the fact that members of the public may access them from a place and at a time individually chosen by them.

(26) With regard to the making available in on-demand services by broadcasters of their radio or television productions incorporating music from commercial phonograms as an integral part thereof, collective licensing arrangements are to be encouraged in order to facilitate the clearance of the rights concerned.

(27) The mere provision of physical facilities for enabling or making a communication does not in itself amount to communication within the meaning of this Directive.

(28) Copyright protection under this Directive includes the exclusive right to control distribution of the work incorporated in a tangible article. The first sale in the Community of the original of a work or copies thereof by the rightholder or with his consent exhausts the right to control resale of that object in the Community. This right should not be exhausted in respect of the original or of copies thereof sold by the rightholder or with his consent outside the Community. Rental and lending rights for authors have been established in Directive 92/100/EEC. The distribution right provided for in this Directive is without prejudice to the provisions relating to the rental and lending rights contained in Chapter I of that Directive.

(29) The question of exhaustion does not arise in the case of services and on-line services in particular. This also applies with regard to a material copy of a work or other subject-matter made by a user of such a service with the consent of the rightholder. Therefore, the same applies to rental and lending of the original and copies of works or other subject-matter which are services by nature. Unlike CD-ROM or CD-I, where the intellectual property is incorporated in a material medium, namely an item of goods, every on-line service is in fact an act which should be subject to authorisation where the copyright or related right so provides.

(30) The rights referred to in this Directive may be transferred, assigned or subject to the granting of contractual licences, without prejudice to the relevant national legislation on copyright and related rights.

(31) A fair balance of rights and interests between the different categories of rightholders, as well as between the different categories of rightholders and users of protected subject-matter must be safeguarded. The existing exceptions and limitations to the rights as set out by the Member States have to be reassessed in the light of the new electronic environment. Existing differences in the exceptions and limitations to certain restricted acts have direct negative effects on the functioning of the internal market of copyright and related rights. Such differences could well become more pronounced in view of the further development of transborder exploitation of works and cross-border activities. In order to ensure the proper functioning of the internal market, such exceptions and limitations should be defined more harmoniously. The degree of their harmonisation should be based on their impact on the smooth functioning of the internal market.

(32) This Directive provides for an exhaustive enumeration of exceptions and limitations to the reproduction right and the right of communication to the public. Some exceptions or limitations only apply to the reproduction right, where appropriate. This list takes due account of the different legal traditions in Member States, while, at the same time, aiming to ensure a

functioning internal market. Member States should arrive at a coherent application of these exceptions and limitations, which will be assessed when reviewing implementing legislation in the future.

(33) The exclusive right of reproduction should be subject to an exception to allow certain acts of temporary reproduction, which are transient or incidental reproductions, forming an integral and essential part of a technological process carried out for the sole purpose of enabling either efficient transmission in a network between third parties by an intermediary, or a lawful use of a work or other subject-matter to be made. The acts of reproduction concerned should have no separate economic value on their own. To the extent that they meet these conditions, this exception should include acts which enable browsing as well as acts of caching to take place, including those which enable transmission systems to function efficiently, provided that the intermediary does not modify the information and does not interfere with the lawful use of technology, widely recognised and used by industry, to obtain data on the use of the information. A use should be considered lawful where it is authorised by the rightholder or not restricted by law.

(34) Member States should be given the option of providing for certain exceptions or limitations for cases such as educational and scientific purposes, for the benefit of public institutions such as libraries and archives, for purposes of news reporting, for quotations, for use by people with disabilities, for public security uses and for uses in administrative and judicial proceedings.

(35) In certain cases of exceptions or limitations, rightholders should receive fair compensation to compensate them adequately for the use made of their protected works or other subject-matter. When determining the form, detailed arrangements and possible level of such fair compensation, account should be taken of the particular circumstances of each case. When evaluating these circumstances, a valuable criterion would be the possible harm to the rightholders resulting from the act in question. In cases where rightholders have already received payment in some other form, for instance as part of a licence fee, no specific or separate payment may be due. The level of fair compensation should take full account of the degree of use of technological protection measures referred to in this Directive. In certain situations where the prejudice to the rightholder would be minimal, no obligation for payment may arise.

(36) The Member States may provide for fair compensation for rightholders also when applying the optional provisions on exceptions or limitations which do not require such compensation.

(37) Existing national schemes on reprography, where they exist, do not create major barriers to the internal market. Member States should be allowed to provide for an exception or limitation in respect of reprography.

(38) Member States should be allowed to provide for an exception or limitation to the reproduction right for certain types of reproduction of audio, visual and audio-visual material for private use, accompanied by fair compensation. This may include the introduction or continuation of remuneration schemes to compensate for the prejudice to rightholders. Although differences between those remuneration schemes affect the functioning of the internal market, those differences, with respect to analogue private reproduction, should not have a significant impact on the development of the information society. Digital private copying is likely to be more widespread and have a greater economic impact. Due account should therefore be taken of the differences between digital and analogue private copying and a distinction should be made in certain respects between them.

(39) When applying the exception or limitation on private copying, Member States should take due account of technological and economic developments, in particular with respect to digital private copying and remuneration schemes, when effective technological protection measures are available. Such exceptions or limitations should not inhibit the use of technological measures or their enforcement against circumvention.

(40) Member States may provide for an exception or limitation for the benefit of certain non-profit making establishments, such as publicly accessible libraries and equivalent institutions, as well as archives. However, this should be limited to certain special cases covered by the reproduction right. Such an exception or limitation should not cover uses made in the context of on-line delivery of protected works or other subject-matter. This Directive should be without prejudice to the Member States' option to derogate from the exclusive public lending right in accordance with Article 5 of Directive 92/100/EEC. Therefore, specific contracts or licences should be promoted which, without creating imbalances, favour such establishments and the disseminative purposes they serve.

(41) When applying the exception or limitation in respect of ephemeral recordings made by broadcasting organisations it is understood that a broadcaster's own facilities include those of a person acting on behalf of and under the responsibility of the broadcasting organisation.

(42) When applying the exception or limitation for non-commercial educational and scientific research purposes, including distance learning, the non-commercial nature of the activity in question should be determined by that activity as such. The organisational structure and the means of funding of the establishment concerned are not the decisive factors in this respect.

(43) It is in any case important for the Member States to adopt all necessary measures to facilitate access to works by persons suffering from a disability which constitutes an obstacle to the use of the works themselves, and to pay particular attention to accessible formats.

(44) When applying the exceptions and limitations provided for in this Directive, they should be exercised in accordance with international obligations. Such exceptions and limitations may not be applied in a way which prejudices the legitimate interests of the rightholder or which conflicts with the normal exploitation of his work or other subject-matter. The provision of such exceptions or limitations by Member States should, in particular, duly reflect the increased economic impact that such exceptions or limitations may have in the context of the new electronic environment. Therefore, the scope of certain exceptions or limitations may have to be even more limited when it comes to certain new uses of copyright works and other subject-matter.

(45) The exceptions and limitations referred to in Article 5(2), (3) and (4) should not, however, prevent the definition of contractual relations designed to ensure fair compensation for the rightholders insofar as permitted by national law.

(46) Recourse to mediation could help users and rightholders to settle disputes. The Commission, in cooperation with the Member States within the Contact Committee, should undertake a study to consider new legal ways of settling disputes concerning copyright and related rights.

(47) Technological development will allow rightholders to make use of technological measures designed to prevent or restrict acts not authorised by the rightholders of any copyright, rights related to copyright or the sui generis right in databases. The danger, however, exists that illegal activities might be carried out in order to enable or facilitate the circumvention of the technical protection provided by these measures. In order to avoid fragmented legal approaches that could potentially hinder the functioning of the internal market, there is a need to provide for harmonised legal protection against circumvention of effective technological measures and against provision of devices and products or services to this effect.

(48) Such legal protection should be provided in respect of technological measures that effectively restrict acts not authorised by the rightholders of any copyright, rights related to copyright or the sui generis right in databases without, however, preventing the normal operation of electronic equipment and its technological development. Such legal protection implies no obligation to design devices, products, components or services to correspond to technological measures, so long as such device, product, component or service does not otherwise fall under the prohibition of Article 6. Such legal protection should respect proportionality and should not prohibit those devices or activities which have a commercially

significant purpose or use other than to circumvent the technical protection. In particular, this protection should not hinder research into cryptography.
(49) The legal protection of technological measures is without prejudice to the application of any national provisions which may prohibit the private possession of devices, products or components for the circumvention of technological measures.
(50) Such a harmonised legal protection does not affect the specific provisions on protection provided for by Directive 91/250/EEC. In particular, it should not apply to the protection of technological measures used in connection with computer programs, which is exclusively addressed in that Directive. It should neither inhibit nor prevent the development or use of any means of circumventing a technological measure that is necessary to enable acts to be undertaken in accordance with the terms of Article 5(3) or Article 6 of Directive 91/250/EEC. Articles 5 and 6 of that Directive exclusively determine exceptions to the exclusive rights applicable to computer programs.
(51) The legal protection of technological measures applies without prejudice to public policy, as reflected in Article 5, or public security. Member States should promote voluntary measures taken by rightholders, including the conclusion and implementation of agreements between rightholders and other parties concerned, to accommodate achieving the objectives of certain exceptions or limitations provided for in national law in accordance with this Directive. In the absence of such voluntary measures or agreements within a reasonable period of time, Member States should take appropriate measures to ensure that rightholders provide beneficiaries of such exceptions or limitations with appropriate means of benefiting from them, by modifying an implemented technological measure or by other means. However, in order to prevent abuse of such measures taken by rightholders, including within the framework of agreements, or taken by a Member State, any technological measures applied in implementation of such measures should enjoy legal protection.
(52) When implementing an exception or limitation for private copying in accordance with Article 5(2)(b), Member States should likewise promote the use of voluntary measures to accommodate achieving the objectives of such exception or limitation. If, within a reasonable period of time, no such voluntary measures to make reproduction for private use possible have been taken, Member States may take measures to enable beneficiaries of the exception or limitation concerned to benefit from it. Voluntary measures taken by rightholders, including agreements between rightholders and other parties concerned, as well as measures taken by Member States, do not prevent rightholders from using technological measures which are consistent with the exceptions or limitations on private copying in national law in accordance with Article 5(2)(b), taking account of the condition of fair compensation under that provision and the possible differentiation between various conditions of use in accordance with Article 5(5), such as controlling the number of reproductions. In order to prevent abuse of such measures, any technological measures applied in their implementation should enjoy legal protection.
(53) The protection of technological measures should ensure a secure environment for the provision of interactive on-demand services, in such a way that members of the public may access works or other subject-matter from a place and at a time individually chosen by them. Where such services are governed by contractual arrangements, the first and second subparagraphs of Article 6(4) do not apply. Non-interactive forms of online use should remain subject to those provisions.
(54) Important progress has been made in the international standardisation of technical systems of identification of works and protected subject-matter in digital format. In an increasingly networked environment, differences between technological measures could lead to an incompatibility of systems within the Community. Compatibility and interoperability of the different systems should be encouraged. It would be highly desirable to encourage the development of global systems.

Copyright in the Information Society Directive (2001/29/EC)

(55) Technological development will facilitate the distribution of works, notably on networks, and this will entail the need for rightholders to identify better the work or other subject-matter, the author or any other rightholder, and to provide information about the terms and conditions of use of the work or other subject-matter in order to render easier the management of rights attached to them. Rightholders should be encouraged to use markings indicating, in addition to the information referred to above, inter alia their authorisation when putting works or other subject-matter on networks.

(56) There is, however, the danger that illegal activities might be carried out in order to remove or alter the electronic copyright-management information attached to it, or otherwise to distribute, import for distribution, broadcast, communicate to the public or make available to the public works or other protected subject-matter from which such information has been removed without authority. In order to avoid fragmented legal approaches that could potentially hinder the functioning of the internal market, there is a need to provide for harmonised legal protection against any of these activities.

(57) Any such rights-management information systems referred to above may, depending on their design, at the same time process personal data about the consumption patterns of protected subject-matter by individuals and allow for tracing of on-line behaviour. These technical means, in their technical functions, should incorporate privacy safeguards in accordance with Directive 95/46/EC of the European Parliament and of the Council of 24 October 1995 on the protection of individuals with regard to the processing of personal data and the free movement of such data[10].

(58) Member States should provide for effective sanctions and remedies for infringements of rights and obligations as set out in this Directive. They should take all the measures necessary to ensure that those sanctions and remedies are applied. The sanctions thus provided for should be effective, proportionate and dissuasive and should include the possibility of seeking damages and/or injunctive relief and, where appropriate, of applying for seizure of infringing material.

(59) In the digital environment, in particular, the services of intermediaries may increasingly be used by third parties for infringing activities. In many cases such intermediaries are best placed to bring such infringing activities to an end. Therefore, without prejudice to any other sanctions and remedies available, rightholders should have the possibility of applying for an injunction against an intermediary who carries a third party's infringement of a protected work or other subject-matter in a network. This possibility should be available even where the acts carried out by the intermediary are exempted under Article 5. The conditions and modalities relating to such injunctions should be left to the national law of the Member States.

(60) The protection provided under this Directive should be without prejudice to national or Community legal provisions in other areas, such as industrial property, data protection, conditional access, access to public documents, and the rule of media exploitation chronology, which may affect the protection of copyright or related rights.

(61) In order to comply with the WIPO Performances and Phonograms Treaty, Directives 92/100/EEC and 93/98/EEC should be amended,

HAVE ADOPTED THIS DIRECTIVE:

CHAPTER I: OBJECTIVE AND SCOPE

Article 1 - Scope

1. This Directive concerns the legal protection of copyright and related rights in the framework of the internal market, with particular emphasis on the information society.

---

[10] OJ L 281, 23.11.1995, p. 31.

2. Except in the cases referred to in Article 11, this Directive shall leave intact and shall in no way affect existing Community provisions relating to:
(a) the legal protection of computer programs;
(b) rental right, lending right and certain rights related to copyright in the field of intellectual property;
(c) copyright and related rights applicable to broadcasting of programmes by satellite and cable retransmission;
(d) the term of protection of copyright and certain related rights;
(e) the legal protection of databases.

CHAPTER II: RIGHTS AND EXCEPTIONS

Article 2 - Reproduction right

Member States shall provide for the exclusive right to authorise or prohibit direct or indirect, temporary or permanent reproduction by any means and in any form, in whole or in part:
(a) for authors, of their works;
(b) for performers, of fixations of their performances;
(c) for phonogram producers, of their phonograms;
(d) for the producers of the first fixations of films, in respect of the original and copies of their films;
(e) for broadcasting organisations, of fixations of their broadcasts, whether those broadcasts are transmitted by wire or over the air, including by cable or satellite.

Article 3 - Right of communication to the public of works and right of making available to the public other subject-matter

1. Member States shall provide authors with the exclusive right to authorise or prohibit any communication to the public of their works, by wire or wireless means, including the making available to the public of their works in such a way that members of the public may access them from a place and at a time individually chosen by them.
2. Member States shall provide for the exclusive right to authorise or prohibit the making available to the public, by wire or wireless means, in such a way that members of the public may access them from a place and at a time individually chosen by them:
(a) for performers, of fixations of their performances;
(b) for phonogram producers, of their phonograms;
(c) for the producers of the first fixations of films, of the original and copies of their films;
(d) for broadcasting organisations, of fixations of their broadcasts, whether these broadcasts are transmitted by wire or over the air, including by cable or satellite.
3. The rights referred to in paragraphs 1 and 2 shall not be exhausted by any act of communication to the public or making available to the public as set out in this Article.

Article 4 - Distribution right

1. Member States shall provide for authors, in respect of the original of their works or of copies thereof, the exclusive right to authorise or prohibit any form of distribution to the public by sale or otherwise.
2. The distribution right shall not be exhausted within the Community in respect of the original or copies of the work, except where the first sale or other transfer of ownership in the Community of that object is made by the rightholder or with his consent.

Article 5 - Exceptions and limitations

1. Temporary acts of reproduction referred to in Article 2, which are transient or incidental, which are an integral and essential part of a technological process and the sole purpose of which is to enable:[11]
(a) a transmission in a network between third parties by an intermediary or
(b) a lawful use of a work or other subject-matter to be made, and which have no independent economic significance, shall be exempted from the reproduction right provided for in Article 2.
2. Member States may provide for exceptions or limitations to the reproduction right provided for in Article 2 in the following cases:
(a) in respect of reproductions on paper or any similar medium, effected by the use of any kind of photographic technique or by some other process having similar effects, with the exception of sheet music, provided that the rightholders receive fair compensation;
(b) in respect of reproductions on any medium made by a natural person for private use and for ends that are neither directly nor indirectly commercial, on condition that the rightholders receive fair compensation which takes account of the application or non-application of technological measures referred to in Article 6 to the work or subject-matter concerned;
(c) in respect of specific acts of reproduction made by publicly accessible libraries, educational establishments or museums, or by archives, which are not for direct or indirect economic or commercial advantage;
(d) in respect of ephemeral recordings of works made by broadcasting organisations by means of their own facilities and for their own broadcasts; the preservation of these recordings in official archives may, on the ground of their exceptional documentary character, be permitted;
(e) in respect of reproductions of broadcasts made by social institutions pursuing non-commercial purposes, such as hospitals or prisons, on condition that the rightholders receive fair compensation.
3. Member States may provide for exceptions or limitations to the rights provided for in Articles 2 and 3 in the following cases:
(a) use for the sole purpose of illustration for teaching or scientific research, as long as the source, including the author's name, is indicated, unless this turns out to be impossible, and to the extent justified by the non-commercial purpose to be achieved;
(b) uses, for the benefit of people with a disability, which are directly related to the disability and of a non-commercial nature, to the extent required by the specific disability;
(c) reproduction by the press, communication to the public or making available of published articles on current economic, political or religious topics or of broadcast works or other subject-matter of the same character, in cases where such use is not expressly reserved, and as long as the source, including the author's name, is indicated, or use of works or other subject-matter in connection with the reporting of current events, to the extent justified by the informatory purpose and as long as the source, including the author's name, is indicated, unless this turns out to be impossible;
(d) quotations for purposes such as criticism or review, provided that they relate to a work or other subject-matter which has already been lawfully made available to the public, that, unless this turns out to be impossible, the source, including the author's name, is indicated, and that their use is in accordance with fair practice, and to the extent required by the specific purpose;

---

[11] Corrigendum to Directive 2001/29/EC of the European Parliament and of the Council of 22 May 2001 on the harmonisation of certain aspects of copyright and related rights in the information society (OJ L 167 of 22.6.2001), Official Journal L 006 , 10/01/2001 P. 0070 – 0070.

(e) use for the purposes of public security or to ensure the proper performance or reporting of administrative, parliamentary or judicial proceedings;
(f) use of political speeches as well as extracts of public lectures or similar works or subject-matter to the extent justified by the informatory purpose and provided that, the source, including the author's name, is indicated, except where this turns out to be impossible;
(g) use during religious celebrations or official celebrations organised by a public authority;
(h) use of works, such as works of architecture or sculpture, made to be located permanently in public places;
(i) incidental inclusion of a work or other subject-matter in other material;
(j) use for the purpose of advertising the public exhibition or sale of artistic works, to the extent necessary to promote the event, excluding any other commercial use;
(k) use for the purpose of caricature, parody or pastiche;
(l) use in connection with the demonstration or repair of equipment;
(m) use of an artistic work in the form of a building or a drawing or plan of a building for the purposes of reconstructing the building;
(n) use by communication or making available, for the purpose of research or private study, to individual members of the public by dedicated terminals on the premises of establishments referred to in paragraph 2(c) of works and other subject-matter not subject to purchase or licensing terms which are contained in their collections;
(o) use in certain other cases of minor importance where exceptions or limitations already exist under national law, provided that they only concern analogue uses and do not affect the free circulation of goods and services within the Community, without prejudice to the other exceptions and limitations contained in this Article.
4. Where the Member States may provide for an exception or limitation to the right of reproduction pursuant to paragraphs 2 and 3, they may provide similarly for an exception or limitation to the right of distribution as referred to in Article 4 to the extent justified by the purpose of the authorised act of reproduction.
5. The exceptions and limitations provided for in paragraphs 1, 2, 3 and 4 shall only be applied in certain special cases which do not conflict with a normal exploitation of the work or other subject-matter and do not unreasonably prejudice the legitimate interests of the rightholder.

CHAPTER III: PROTECTION OF TECHNOLOGICAL MEASURES AND RIGHTS-MANAGEMENT INFORMATION

Article 6 - Obligations as to technological measures

1. Member States shall provide adequate legal protection against the circumvention of any effective technological measures, which the person concerned carries out in the knowledge, or with reasonable grounds to know, that he or she is pursuing that objective.
2. Member States shall provide adequate legal protection against the manufacture, import, distribution, sale, rental, advertisement for sale or rental, or possession for commercial purposes of devices, products or components or the provision of services which:
(a) are promoted, advertised or marketed for the purpose of circumvention of, or
(b) have only a limited commercially significant purpose or use other than to circumvent, or
(c) are primarily designed, produced, adapted or performed for the purpose of enabling or facilitating the circumvention of, any effective technological measures.
3. For the purposes of this Directive, the expression "technological measures" means any technology, device or component that, in the normal course of its operation, is designed to prevent or restrict acts, in respect of works or other subject-matter, which are not authorised by the rightholder of any copyright or any right related to copyright as provided for by law or the sui generis right provided for in Chapter III of Directive 96/9/EC. Technological measures shall be deemed "effective" where the use of a protected work or other subject-

matter is controlled by the rightholders through application of an access control or protection process, such as encryption, scrambling or other transformation of the work or other subject-matter or a copy control mechanism, which achieves the protection objective.

4. Notwithstanding the legal protection provided for in paragraph 1, in the absence of voluntary measures taken by rightholders, including agreements between rightholders and other parties concerned, Member States shall take appropriate measures to ensure that rightholders make available to the beneficiary of an exception or limitation provided for in national law in accordance with Article 5(2)(a), (2)(c), (2)(d), (2)(e), (3)(a), (3)(b) or (3)(e) the means of benefiting from that exception or limitation, to the extent necessary to benefit from that exception or limitation and where that beneficiary has legal access to the protected work or subject-matter concerned.

A Member State may also take such measures in respect of a beneficiary of an exception or limitation provided for in accordance with Article 5(2)(b), unless reproduction for private use has already been made possible by rightholders to the extent necessary to benefit from the exception or limitation concerned and in accordance with the provisions of Article 5(2)(b) and (5), without preventing rightholders from adopting adequate measures regarding the number of reproductions in accordance with these provisions.

The technological measures applied voluntarily by rightholders, including those applied in implementation of voluntary agreements, and technological measures applied in implementation of the measures taken by Member States, shall enjoy the legal protection provided for in paragraph 1.

The provisions of the first and second subparagraphs shall not apply to works or other subject-matter made available to the public on agreed contractual terms in such a way that members of the public may access them from a place and at a time individually chosen by them.

When this Article is applied in the context of Directives 92/100/EEC and 96/9/EC, this paragraph shall apply mutatis mutandis.

Article 7 - Obligations concerning rights-management information

1. Member States shall provide for adequate legal protection against any person knowingly performing without authority any of the following acts:
(a) the removal or alteration of any electronic rights-management information;
(b) the distribution, importation for distribution, broadcasting, communication or making available to the public of works or other subject-matter protected under this Directive or under Chapter III of Directive 96/9/EC from which electronic rights-management information has been removed or altered without authority,

if such person knows, or has reasonable grounds to know, that by so doing he is inducing, enabling, facilitating or concealing an infringement of any copyright or any rights related to copyright as provided by law, or of the sui generis right provided for in Chapter III of Directive 96/9/EC.

2. For the purposes of this Directive, the expression "rights-management information" means any information provided by rightholders which identifies the work or other subject-matter referred to in this Directive or covered by the sui generis right provided for in Chapter III of Directive 96/9/EC, the author or any other rightholder, or information about the terms and conditions of use of the work or other subject-matter, and any numbers or codes that represent such information.

The first subparagraph shall apply when any of these items of information is associated with a copy of, or appears in connection with the communication to the public of, a work or other subject-matter referred to in this Directive or covered by the sui generis right provided for in Chapter III of Directive 96/9/EC.

CHAPTER IV: COMMON PROVISIONS

Article 8 - Sanctions and remedies

1. Member States shall provide appropriate sanctions and remedies in respect of infringements of the rights and obligations set out in this Directive and shall take all the measures necessary to ensure that those sanctions and remedies are applied. The sanctions thus provided for shall be effective, proportionate and dissuasive.
2. Each Member State shall take the measures necessary to ensure that rightholders whose interests are affected by an infringing activity carried out on its territory can bring an action for damages and/or apply for an injunction and, where appropriate, for the seizure of infringing material as well as of devices, products or components referred to in Article 6(2).
3. Member States shall ensure that rightholders are in a position to apply for an injunction against intermediaries whose services are used by a third party to infringe a copyright or related right.

Article 9 - Continued application of other legal provisions

This Directive shall be without prejudice to provisions concerning in particular patent rights, trade marks, design rights, utility models, topographies of semi-conductor products, type faces, conditional access, access to cable of broadcasting services, protection of national treasures, legal deposit requirements, laws on restrictive practices and unfair competition, trade secrets, security, confidentiality, data protection and privacy, access to public documents, the law of contract.

Article 10 - Application over time

1. The provisions of this Directive shall apply in respect of all works and other subject-matter referred to in this Directive which are, on 22 December 2002, protected by the Member States' legislation in the field of copyright and related rights, or which meet the criteria for protection under the provisions of this Directive or the provisions referred to in Article 1(2).
2. This Directive shall apply without prejudice to any acts concluded and rights acquired before 22 December 2002.

Article 11 - Technical adaptations

1. Directive 92/100/EEC is hereby amended as follows:
(a) Article 7 shall be deleted;
(b) Article 10(3) shall be replaced by the following:
"3. The limitations shall only be applied in certain special cases which do not conflict with a normal exploitation of the subject-matter and do not unreasonably prejudice the legitimate interests of the rightholder.".
2. Article 3(2) of Directive 93/98/EEC shall be replaced by the following:
"2. The rights of producers of phonograms shall expire 50 years after the fixation is made.
However, if the phonogram has been lawfully published within this period, the said rights shall expire 50 years from the date of the first lawful publication. If no lawful publication has taken place within the period mentioned in the first sentence, and if the phonogram has been lawfully communicated to the public within this period, the said rights shall expire 50 years from the date of the first lawful communication to the public.
However, where through the expiry of the term of protection granted pursuant to this paragraph in its version before amendment by Directive 2001/29/EC of the European Parliament and of the Council of 22 May 2001 on the harmonisation of certain aspects of copyright and related rights in the information society[12] the rights of producers of

---

[12] OJ L 167, 22.6.2001, p. 10.

phonograms are no longer protected on 22 December 2002, this paragraph shall not have the effect of protecting those rights anew. "

Article 12 - Final provisions

1. Not later than 22 December 2004 and every three years thereafter, the Commission shall submit to the European Parliament, the Council and the Economic and Social Committee a report on the application of this Directive, in which, inter alia, on the basis of specific information supplied by the Member States, it shall examine in particular the application of Articles 5, 6 and 8 in the light of the development of the digital market. In the case of Article 6, it shall examine in particular whether that Article confers a sufficient level of protection and whether acts which are permitted by law are being adversely affected by the use of effective technological measures. Where necessary, in particular to ensure the functioning of the internal market pursuant to Article 14 of the Treaty, it shall submit proposals for amendments to this Directive.
2. Protection of rights related to copyright under this Directive shall leave intact and shall in no way affect the protection of copyright.
3. A contact committee is hereby established. It shall be composed of representatives of the competent authorities of the Member States. It shall be chaired by a representative of the Commission and shall meet either on the initiative of the chairman or at the request of the delegation of a Member State.
4. The tasks of the committee shall be as follows:
(a) to examine the impact of the Directive on the functioning of the internal market, and to highlight any difficulties,
(b) to organise consultations on all questions deriving from the application of this Directive;
(c) to facilitate the exchange of information on relevant developments in legislation and case-law, as well as relevant economic, social, cultural and technological developments;
(d) to act as a forum for the assessment of the digital market in works and other items, including private copying and the use of technological measures.

Article 13 - Implementation

1. Member States shall bring into force the laws, regulations and administrative provisions necessary to comply with this Directive before 22 December 2002. They shall forthwith inform the Commission thereof.
When Member States adopt these measures, they shall contain a reference to this Directive or shall be accompanied by such reference on the occasion of their official publication. The methods of making such reference shall be laid down by Member States.
2. Member States shall communicate to the Commission the text of the provisions of domestic law which they adopt in the field governed by this Directive.

Article 14 - Entry into force

This Directive shall enter into force on the day of its publication in the Official Journal of the European Communities.

Article 15 - Addressees

This Directive is addressed to the Member States.

COUNCIL REGULATION (EC) NO 6/2002
OF 12 DECEMBER 2001
ON COMMUNITY DESIGNS

(Official Journal L 003, 05/01/2002, p. 0001 - 0024)

THE COUNCIL OF THE EUROPEAN UNION,

Having regard to the Treaty establishing the European Community, and in particular Article 308 thereof,
Having regard to the proposal from the Commission[1],
Having regard to the opinion of the European Parliament[2],
Having regard to the opinion of the Economic and Social Committee[3],

Whereas:
(1) A unified system for obtaining a Community design to which uniform protection is given with uniform effect throughout the entire territory of the Community would further the objectives of the Community as laid down in the Treaty.
(2) Only the Benelux countries have introduced a uniform design protection law. In all the other Member States the protection of designs is a matter for the relevant national law and is confined to the territory of the Member State concerned. Identical designs may be therefore protected differently in different Member States and for the benefit of different owners. This inevitably leads to conflicts in the course of trade between Member States.
(3) The substantial differences between Member States' design laws prevent and distort Community-wide competition. In comparison with domestic trade in, and competition between, products incorporating a design, trade and competition within the Community are prevented and distorted by the large number of applications, offices, procedures, laws, nationally circumscribed exclusive rights and the combined administrative expense with correspondingly high costs and fees for the applicant. Directive 98/71/EC of the European Parliament and of the Council of 13 October 1998 on the legal protection of designs[4] contributes to remedying this situation.
(4) The effect of design protection being limited to the territory of the individual Member States whether or not their laws are approximated, leads to a possible division of the internal market with respect to products incorporating a design which is the subject of national rights held by different individuals, and hence constitutes an obstacle to the free movement of goods.
(5) This calls for the creation of a Community design which is directly applicable in each Member State, because only in this way will it be possible to obtain, through one application made to the Office for Harmonisation in the Internal Market (Trade Marks and Design) in accordance with a single procedure under one law, one design right for one area encompassing all Member States.
(6) Since the objectives of the proposed action, namely, the protection of one design right for one area encompassing all the Member States, cannot be sufficiently achieved by the Member States by reason of the scale and the effects of the creation of a Community design and a Community design authority and can therefore, and can therefore be better achieved at Community level, the Community may adopt measures, in accordance with the principle of subsidiarity as set out in Article 5 of the Treaty. In accordance with the principle of

---

[1] OJ C 29, 31.1.1994, p. 20 and OJ C 248, 29.8.2000, p. 3.
[2] OJ C 67, 1.3.2001, p. 318.
[3] OJ C 110, 2.5.1995 and OJ C 75, 15.3.2000, p. 35.
[4] OJ L 289, 28.10.1998, p. 28.

proportionality, as set out in that Article, this Regulation does not go beyond what is necessary in order to achieve those objectives.
(7) Enhanced protection for industrial design not only promotes the contribution of individual designers to the sum of Community excellence in the field, but also encourages innovation and development of new products and investment in their production.
(8) Consequently a more accessible design-protection system adapted to the needs of the internal market is essential for Community industries.
(9) The substantive provisions of this Regulation on design law should be aligned with the respective provisions in Directive 98/71/EC.
(10) Technological innovation should not be hampered by granting design protection to features dictated solely by a technical function. It is understood that this does not entail that a design must have an aesthetic quality. Likewise, the interoperability of products of different makes should not be hindered by extending protection to the design of mechanical fittings. Consequently, those features of a design which are excluded from protection for those reasons should not be taken into consideration for the purpose of assessing whether other features of the design fulfil the requirements for protection.
(11) The mechanical fittings of modular products may nevertheless constitute an important element of the innovative characteristics of modular products and present a major marketing asset, and therefore should be eligible for protection.
(12) Protection should not be extended to those component parts which are not visible during normal use of a product, nor to those features of such part which are not visible when the part is mounted, or which would not, in themselves, fulfil the requirements as to novelty and individual character. Therefore, those features of design which are excluded from protection for these reasons should not be taken into consideration for the purpose of assessing whether other features of the design fulfil the requirements for protection.
(13) Full-scale approximation of the laws of the Member States on the use of protected designs for the purpose of permitting the repair of a complex product so as to restore its original appearance, where the design is applied to or incorporated in a product which constitutes a component part of a complex product upon whose appearance the protected design is dependent, could not be achieved through Directive 98/71/EC. Within the framework of the conciliation procedure on the said Directive, the Commission undertook to review the consequences of the provisions of that Directive three years after the deadline for transposition of the Directive in particular for the industrial sectors which are most affected. Under these circumstances, it is appropriate not to confer any protection as a Community design for a design which is applied to or incorporated in a product which constitutes a component part of a complex product upon whose appearance the design is dependent and which is used for the purpose of the repair of a complex product so as to restore its original appearance, until the Council has decided its policy on this issue on the basis of a Commission proposal.
(14) The assessment as to whether a design has individual character should be based on whether the overall impression produced on an informed user viewing the design clearly differs from that produced on him by the existing design corpus, taking into consideration the nature of the product to which the design is applied or in which it is incorporated, and in particular the industrial sector to which it belongs and the degree of freedom of the designer in developing the design.
(15) A Community design should, as far as possible, serve the needs of all sectors of industry in the Community.
(16) Some of those sectors produce large numbers of designs for products frequently having a short market life where protection without the burden of registration formalities is an advantage and the duration of protection is of lesser significance. On the other hand, there are sectors of industry which value the advantages of registration for the greater legal certainty it

provides and which require the possibility of a longer term of protection corresponding to the foreseeable market life of their products.
(17) This calls for two forms of protection, one being a short-term unregistered design and the other being a longer term registered design.
(18) A registered Community design requires the creation and maintenance of a register in which will be registered all those applications which comply with formal conditions and which have been accorded a date of filing. This registration system should in principle not be based upon substantive examination as to compliance with requirements for protection prior to registration, thereby keeping to a minimum the registration and other procedural burdens on applicants.
(19) A Community design should not be upheld unless the design is new and unless it also possesses an individual character in comparison with other designs.
(20) It is also necessary to allow the designer or his successor in title to test the products embodying the design in the market place before deciding whether the protection resulting from a registered Community design is desirable. To this end it is necessary to provide that disclosures of the design by the designer or his successor in title, or abusive disclosures during a period of 12 months prior to the date of the filing of the application for a registered Community design should not be prejudicial in assessing the novelty or the individual character of the design in question.
(21) The exclusive nature of the right conferred by the registered Community design is consistent with its greater legal certainty. It is appropriate that the unregistered Community design should, however, constitute a right only to prevent copying. Protection could not therefore extend to design products which are the result of a design arrived at independently by a second designer. This right should also extend to trade in products embodying infringing designs.
(22) The enforcement of these rights is to be left to national laws. It is necessary therefore to provide for some basic uniform sanctions in all Member States. These should make it possible, irrespective of the jurisdiction under which enforcement is sought, to stop the infringing acts.
(23) Any third person who can establish that he has in good faith commenced use even for commercial purposes within the Community, or has made serious and effective preparations to that end, of a design included within the scope of protection of a registered Community design, which has not been copied from the latter, may be entitled to a limited exploitation of that design.
(24) It is a fundamental objective of this Regulation that the procedure for obtaining a registered Community design should present the minimum cost and difficulty to applicants, so as to make it readily available to small and medium-sized enterprises as well as to individual designers.
(25) Those sectors of industry producing large numbers of possibly short-lived designs over short periods of time of which only some may be eventually commercialised will find advantage in the unregistered Community design. Furthermore, there is also a need for these sectors to have easier recourse to the registered Community design. Therefore, the option of combining a number of designs in one multiple application would satisfy that need. However, the designs contained in a multiple application may be dealt with independently of each other for the purposes of enforcement of rights, licensing, rights in rem, levy of execution, insolvency proceedings, surrender, renewal, assignment, deferred publication or declaration of invalidity.
(26) The normal publication following registration of a Community design could in some cases destroy or jeopardise the success of a commercial operation involving the design. The facility of a deferment of publication for a reasonable period affords a solution in such cases.
(27) A procedure for hearing actions concerning validity of a registered Community design in a single place would bring savings in costs and time compared with procedures involving different national courts.

(28) It is therefore necessary to provide safeguards including a right of appeal to a Board of Appeal, and ultimately to the Court of Justice. Such a procedure would assist the development of uniform interpretation of the requirements governing the validity of Community designs.
(29) It is essential that the rights conferred by a Community design can be enforced in an efficient manner throughout the territory of the Community.
(30) The litigation system should avoid as far as possible "forum shopping". It is therefore necessary to establish clear rules of international jurisdiction.
(31) This Regulation does not preclude the application to designs protected by Community designs of the industrial property laws or other relevant laws of the Member States, such as those relating to design protection acquired by registration or those relating to unregistered designs, trade marks, patents and utility models, unfair competition or civil liability.
(32) In the absence of the complete harmonisation of copyright law, it is important to establish the principle of cumulation of protection under the Community design and under copyright law, whilst leaving Member States free to establish the extent of copyright protection and the conditions under which such protection is conferred.
(33) The measures necessary for the implementation of this Regulation should be adopted in accordance with Council Decision 1999/468/EC of 28 June 1999 laying down the procedures for the exercise of implementing powers conferred on the Commission[5],

HAS ADOPTED THIS REGULATION:

TITLE I - GENERAL PROVISIONS

Article 1 - Community design

1. A design which complies with the conditions contained in this Regulation is hereinafter referred to as a "Community design".
2. A design shall be protected:
(a) by an "unregistered Community design", if made available to the public in the manner provided for in this Regulation;
(b) by a "registered Community design", if registered in the manner provided for in this Regulation.
3. A Community design shall have a unitary character. It shall have equal effect throughout the Community. It shall not be registered, transferred or surrendered or be the subject of a decision declaring it invalid, nor shall its use be prohibited, save in respect of the whole Community. This principle and its implications shall apply unless otherwise provided in this Regulation.

Article 2 - Office

The Office for Harmonisation in the Internal Market (Trade Marks and Designs), hereinafter referred to as "the Office", instituted by Council Regulation (EC) No 40/94 of 20 December 1993 on the Community trade mark[6], hereinafter referred to as the "Regulation on the Community trade mark", shall carry out the tasks entrusted to it by this Regulation.

TITLE II - THE LAW RELATING TO DESIGNS

---

[5] OJ L 184, 17.7.1999, p. 23.
[6] OJ L 11, 14.1.1994, p. 1. Regulation as last amended by Regulation (EC) No 3288/94 (OJ L 349, 31.12.1994, p. 83).

SECTION 1: REQUIREMENTS FOR PROTECTION

Article 3 - Definitions

For the purposes of this Regulation:
(a) "design" means the appearance of the whole or a part of a product resulting from the features of, in particular, the lines, contours, colours, shape, texture and/or materials of the product itself and/or its ornamentation;
(b) "product" means any industrial or handicraft item, including inter alia parts intended to be assembled into a complex product, packaging, get-up, graphic symbols and typographic typefaces, but excluding computer programs;
(c) "complex product" means a product which is composed of multiple components which can be replaced permitting disassembly and re-assembly of the product.

Article 4 - Requirements for protection

1. A design shall be protected by a Community design to the extent that it is new and has individual character.
2. A design applied to or incorporated in a product which constitutes a component part of a complex product shall only be considered to be new and to have individual character:
(a) if the component part, once it has been incorporated into the complex product, remains visible during normal use of the latter; and
(b) to the extent that those visible features of the component part fulfil in themselves the requirements as to novelty and individual character.
3. "Normal use" within the meaning of paragraph (2)(a) shall mean use by the end user, excluding maintenance, servicing or repair work.

Article 5 - Novelty

1. A design shall be considered to be new if no identical design has been made available to the public:
(a) in the case of an unregistered Community design, before the date on which the design for which protection is claimed has first been made available to the public;
(b) in the case of a registered Community design, before the date of filing of the application for registration of the design for which protection is claimed, or, if priority is claimed, the date of priority.
2. Designs shall be deemed to be identical if their features differ only in immaterial details.

Article 6 - Individual character

1. A design shall be considered to have individual character if the overall impression it produces on the informed user differs from the overall impression produced on such a user by any design which has been made available to the public:
(a) in the case of an unregistered Community design, before the date on which the design for which protection is claimed has first been made available to the public;
(b) in the case of a registered Community design, before the date of filing the application for registration or, if a priority is claimed, the date of priority.
2. In assessing individual character, the degree of freedom of the designer in developing the design shall be taken into consideration.

Article 7 - Disclosure

1. For the purpose of applying Articles 5 and 6, a design shall be deemed to have been made available to the public if it has been published following registration or otherwise, or exhibited, used in trade or otherwise disclosed, before the date referred to in Articles 5(1)(a)

and 6(1)(a) or in Articles 5(1)(b) and 6(1)(b), as the case may be, except where these events could not reasonably have become known in the normal course of business to the circles specialised in the sector concerned, operating within the Community. The design shall not, however, be deemed to have been made available to the public for the sole reason that it has been disclosed to a third person under explicit or implicit conditions of confidentiality.

2. A disclosure shall not be taken into consideration for the purpose of applying Articles 5 and 6 and if a design for which protection is claimed under a registered Community design has been made available to the public:
(a) by the designer, his successor in title, or a third person as a result of information provided or action taken by the designer or his successor in title; and
(b) during the 12-month period preceding the date of filing of the application or, if a priority is claimed, the date of priority.
3. Paragraph 2 shall also apply if the design has been made available to the public as a consequence of an abuse in relation to the designer or his successor in title.

Article 8 - Designs dictated by their technical function and designs of interconnections

1. A Community design shall not subsist in features of appearance of a product which are solely dictated by its technical function.
2. A Community design shall not subsist in features of appearance of a product which must necessarily be reproduced in their exact form and dimensions in order to permit the product in which the design is incorporated or to which it is applied to be mechanically connected to or placed in, around or against another product so that either product may perform its function.
3. Notwithstanding paragraph 2, a Community design shall under the conditions set out in Articles 5 and 6 subsist in a design serving the purpose of allowing the multiple assembly or connection of mutually interchangeable products within a modular system.

Article 9 - Designs contrary to public policy or morality

A Community design shall not subsist in a design which is contrary to public policy or to accepted principles of morality.

SECTION 2: SCOPE AND TERM OF PROTECTION

Article 10 - Scope of protection

1. The scope of the protection conferred by a Community design shall include any design which does not produce on the informed user a different overall impression.
2. In assessing the scope of protection, the degree of freedom of the designer in developing his design shall be taken into consideration.

Article 11 Commencement and term of protection of the unregistered Community design

1. A design which meets the requirements under Section 1 shall be protected by an unregistered Community design for a period of three years as from the date on which the design was first made available to the public within the Community.
2. For the purpose of paragraph 1, a design shall be deemed to have been made available to the public within the Community if it has been published, exhibited, used in trade or otherwise disclosed in such a way that, in the normal course of business, these events could reasonably have become known to the circles specialised in the sector concerned, operating within the Community. The design shall not, however, be deemed to have been made available to the

public for the sole reason that it has been disclosed to a third person under explicit or implicit conditions of confidentiality.

Article 12 - Commencement and term of protection of the registered Community design

Upon registration by the Office, a design which meets the requirements under Section 1 shall be protected by a registered Community design for a period of five years as from the date of the filing of the application. The right holder may have the term of protection renewed for one or more periods of five years each, up to a total term of 25 years from the date of filing.

Article 13 - Renewal

1. Registration of the registered Community design shall be renewed at the request of the right holder or of any person expressly authorised by him, provided that the renewal fee has been paid.
2. The Office shall inform the right holder of the registered Community design and any person having a right entered in the register of Community designs, referred to in Article 72, hereafter referred to as the "register" in respect of the registered Community design, of the expiry of the registration in good time before the said expiry. Failure to give such information shall not involve the responsibility of the Office.
3. The request for renewal shall be submitted and the renewal fee paid within a period of six months ending on the last day of the month in which protection ends. Failing this, the request may be submitted and the fee paid within a further period of six months from the day referred to in the first sentence, provided that an additional fee is paid within this further period.
4. Renewal shall take effect from the day following the date on which the existing registration expires. The renewal shall be entered in the register.

SECTION 3: RIGHT TO THE COMMUNITY DESIGN

Article 14 - Right to the Community design

1. The right to the Community design shall vest in the designer or his successor in title.
2. If two or more persons have jointly developed a design, the right to the Community design shall vest in them jointly.
3. However, where a design is developed by an employee in the execution of his duties or following the instructions given by his employer, the right to the Community design shall vest in the employer, unless otherwise agreed or specified under national law.

Article 15 - Claims relating to the entitlement to a Community design

1. If an unregistered Community design is disclosed or claimed by, or a registered Community design has been applied for or registered in the name of, a person who is not entitled to it under Article 14, the person entitled to it under that provision may, without prejudice to any other remedy which may be open to him, claim to become recognised as the legitimate holder of the Community design.
2. Where a person is jointly entitled to a Community design, that person may, in accordance with paragraph 1, claim to become recognised as joint holder.
3. Legal proceedings under paragraphs 1 or 2 shall be barred three years after the date of publication of a registered Community design or the date of disclosure of an unregistered Community design. This provision shall not apply if the person who is not entitled to the Community design was acting in bad faith at the time when such design was applied for or disclosed or was assigned to him.

4. In the case of a registered Community design, the following shall be entered in the register:
(a) the mention that legal proceedings under paragraph 1 have been instituted;
(b) the final decision or any other termination of the proceedings;
(c) any change in the ownership of the registered Community design resulting from the final decision.

Article 16 - Effects of a judgement on entitlement to a registered Community design

1. Where there is a complete change of ownership of a registered Community design as a result of legal proceedings under Article 15(1), licences and other rights shall lapse upon the entering in the register of the person entitled.
2. If, before the institution of the legal proceedings under Article 15(1) has been registered, the holder of the registered Community design or a licensee has exploited the design within the Community or made serious and effective preparations to do so, he may continue such exploitation provided that he requests within the period prescribed by the implementing regulation a non-exclusive licence from the new holder whose name is entered in the register. The licence shall be granted for a reasonable period and upon reasonable terms.
3. Paragraph 2 shall not apply if the holder of the registered Community design or the licensee was acting in bad faith at the time when he began to exploit the design or to make preparations to do so.

Article 17 - Presumption in favour of the registered holder of the design

The person in whose name the registered Community design is registered or, prior to registration, the person in whose name the application is filed, shall be deemed to be the person entitled in any proceedings before the Office as well as in any other proceedings.

Article 18 - Right of the designer to be cited

The designer shall have the right, in the same way as the applicant for or the holder of a registered Community design, to be cited as such before the Office and in the register. If the design is the result of teamwork, the citation of the team may replace the citation of the individual designers.

SECTION 4: EFFECTS OF THE COMMUNITY DESIGN

Article 19 - Rights conferred by the Community design

1. A registered Community design shall confer on its holder the exclusive right to use it and to prevent any third party not having his consent from using it. The aforementioned use shall cover, in particular, the making, offering, putting on the market, importing, exporting or using of a product in which the design is incorporated or to which it is applied, or stocking such a product for those purposes.
2. An unregistered Community design shall, however, confer on its holder the right to prevent the acts referred to in paragraph 1 only if the contested use results from copying the protected design.
   The contested use shall not be deemed to result from copying the protected design if it results from an independent work of creation by a designer who may be reasonably thought not to be familiar with the design made available to the public by the holder.
3. Paragraph 2 shall also apply to a registered Community design subject to deferment of publication as long as the relevant entries in the register and the file have not been made available to the public in accordance with Article 50(4).

Article 20 - Limitation of the rights conferred by a Community design

1. The rights conferred by a Community design shall not be exercised in respect of:
   (a) acts done privately and for non-commercial purposes;
   (b) acts done for experimental purposes;
   (c) acts of reproduction for the purpose of making citations or of teaching, provided that such acts are compatible with fair trade practice and do not unduly prejudice the normal exploitation of the design, and that mention is made of the source.
2. In addition, the rights conferred by a Community design shall not be exercised in respect of:
   (a) the equipment on ships and aircraft registered in a third country when these temporarily enter the territory of the Community;
   (b) the importation in the Community of spare parts and accessories for the purpose of repairing such craft;
   (c) the execution of repairs on such craft.

Article 21 - Exhaustion of rights

The rights conferred by a Community design shall not extend to acts relating to a product in which a design included within the scope of protection of the Community design is incorporated or to which it is applied, when the product has been put on the market in the Community by the holder of the Community design or with his consent.

Article 22 - Rights of prior use in respect of a registered Community design

1. A right of prior use shall exist for any third person who can establish that before the date of filing of the application, or, if a priority is claimed, before the date of priority, he has in good faith commenced use within the Community, or has made serious and effective preparations to that end, of a design included within the scope of protection of a registered Community design, which has not been copied from the latter.
2. The right of prior use shall entitle the third person to exploit the design for the purposes for which its use had been effected, or for which serious and effective preparations had been made, before the filing or priority date of the registered Community design.
3. The right of prior use shall not extend to granting a licence to another person to exploit the design.
4. The right of prior use cannot be transferred except, where the third person is a business, along with that part of the business in the course of which the act was done or the preparations were made.

Article 23 - Government use

Any provision in the law of a Member State allowing use of national designs by or for the government may be applied to Community designs, but only to the extent that the use is necessary for essential defence or security needs.

SECTION 5: INVALIDITY

Article 24 - Declaration of invalidity

1. A registered Community design shall be declared invalid on application to the Office in accordance with the procedure in Titles VI and VII or by a Community design court on the basis of a counterclaim in infringement proceedings.
2. A Community design may be declared invalid even after the Community design has lapsed or has been surrendered.

3. An unregistered Community design shall be declared invalid by a Community design court on application to such a court or on the basis of a counterclaim in infringement proceedings.

Article 25 - Grounds for invalidity

1. A Community design may be declared invalid only in the following cases:
(a) if the design does not correspond to the definition under Article 3(a);
(b) if it does not fulfil the requirements of Articles 4 to 9;
(c) if, by virtue of a court decision, the right holder is not entitled to the Community design under Article 14;
(d) if the Community design is in conflict with a prior design which has been made available to the public after the date of filing of the application or, if a priority is claimed, the date of priority of the Community design, and which is protected from a date prior to the said date by a registered Community design or an application for such a design, or by a registered design right of a Member State, or by an application for such a right;
(e) if a distinctive sign is used in a subsequent design, and Community law or the law of the Member State governing that sign confers on the right holder of the sign the right to prohibit such use;
(f) if the design constitutes an unauthorised use of a work protected under the copyright law of a Member State;
(g) if the design constitutes an improper use of any of the items listed in Article 6ter of the "Paris Convention" for the Protection of Industrial Property hereafter referred to as the "Paris Convention", or of badges, emblems and escutcheons other than those covered by the said Article 6ter and which are of particular public interest in a Member State.
2. The ground provided for in paragraph (1)(c) may be invoked solely by the person who is entitled to the Community design under Article 14.
3. The grounds provided for in paragraph (1)(d), (e) and (f) may be invoked solely by the applicant for or holder of the earlier right.
4. The ground provided for in paragraph (1)(g) may be invoked solely by the person or entity concerned by the use.
5. Paragraphs 3 and 4 shall be without prejudice to the freedom of Member States to provide that the grounds provided for in paragraphs 1(d) and (g) may also be invoked by the appropriate authority of the Member State in question on its own initiative.
6. A registered Community design which has been declared invalid pursuant to paragraph (1)(b), (e), (f) or (g) may be maintained in an amended form, if in that form it complies with the requirements for protection and the identity of the design is retained. "Maintenance" in an amended form may include registration accompanied by a partial disclaimer by the holder of the registered Community design or entry in the register of a court decision or a decision by the Office declaring the partial invalidity of the registered Community design.

Article 26 - Consequences of invalidity

1. A Community design shall be deemed not to have had, as from the outset, the effects specified in this Regulation, to the extent that it has been declared invalid.
2. Subject to the national provisions relating either to claims for compensation for damage caused by negligence or lack of good faith on the part of the holder of the Community design, or to unjust enrichment, the retroactive effect of invalidity of the Community design shall not affect:
(a) any decision on infringement which has acquired the authority of a final decision and been enforced prior to the invalidity decision;
(b) any contract concluded prior to the invalidity decision, in so far as it has been performed before the decision; however, repayment, to an extent justified by the circumstances, of sums paid under the relevant contract may be claimed on grounds of equity.

TITLE III - COMMUNITY DESIGNS AS OBJECTS OF PROPERTY

Article 27 - Dealing with Community designs as national design rights

1. Unless Articles 28, 29, 30, 31 and 32 provide otherwise, a Community design as an object of property shall be dealt with in its entirety, and for the whole area of the Community, as a national design right of the Member State in which:
(a) the holder has his seat or his domicile on the relevant date; or
(b) where point (a) does not apply, the holder has an establishment on the relevant date.
2. In the case of a registered Community design, paragraph 1 shall apply according to the entries in the register.
3. In the case of joint holders, if two or more of them fulfil the condition under paragraph 1, the Member State referred to in that paragraph shall be determined:
(a) in the case of an unregistered Community design, by reference to the relevant joint holder designated by them by common agreement;
(b) in the case of a registered Community design, by reference to the first of the relevant joint holders in the order in which they are mentioned in the register.
4. Where paragraphs 1, 2 and 3 do not apply, the Member State referred to in paragraph 1 shall be the Member State in which the seat of the Office is situated.

Article 28 - Transfer of the registered Community design

The transfer of a registered Community design shall be subject to the following provisions:
(a) at the request of one of the parties, a transfer shall be entered in the register and published;
(b) until such time as the transfer has been entered in the register, the successor in title may not invoke the rights arising from the registration of the Community design;
(c) where there are time limits to be observed in dealings with the Office, the successor in title may make the corresponding statements to the Office once the request for registration of the transfer has been received by the Office;
(d) all documents which by virtue of Article 66 require notification to the holder of the registered Community design shall be addressed by the Office to the person registered as holder or his representative, if one has been appointed.

Article 29 - Rights in rem on a registered Community design

1. A registered Community design may be given as security or be the subject of rights in rem.
2. On request of one of the parties, the rights mentioned in paragraph 1 shall be entered in the register and published.

Article 30 - Levy of execution

1. A registered Community design may be levied in execution.
2. As regards the procedure for levy of execution in respect of a registered Community design, the courts and authorities of the Member State determined in accordance with Article 27 shall have exclusive jurisdiction.
3. On request of one of the parties, levy of execution shall be entered in the register and published.

Article 31 - Insolvency proceedings

1. The only insolvency proceedings in which a Community design may be involved shall be those opened in the Member State within the territory of which the centre of a debtor's main interests is situated.
2. In the case of joint proprietorship of a Community design, paragraph 1 shall apply to the share of the joint proprietor.
3. Where a Community design is involved in insolvency proceedings, on request of the competent national authority an entry to this effect shall be made in the register and published in the Community Designs Bulletin referred to in Article 73(1).

Article 32 - Licensing

1. A Community design may be licensed for the whole or part of the Community. A licence may be exclusive or non-exclusive.
2. Without prejudice to any legal proceedings based on the law of contract, the holder may invoke the rights conferred by the Community design against a licensee who contravenes any provision in his licensing contract with regard to its duration, the form in which the design may be used, the range of products for which the licence is granted and the quality of products manufactured by the licensee.
3. Without prejudice to the provisions of the licensing contract, the licensee may bring proceedings for infringement of a Community design only if the right holder consents thereto. However, the holder of an exclusive licence may bring such proceedings if the right holder in the Community design, having been given notice to do so, does not himself bring infringement proceedings within an appropriate period.
4. A licensee shall, for the purpose of obtaining compensation for damage suffered by him, be entitled to intervene in an infringement action brought by the right holder in a Community design.
5. In the case of a registered Community design, the grant or transfer of a licence in respect of such right shall, at the request of one of the parties, be entered in the register and published.

Article 33 - Effects vis-à-vis third parties

1. The effects vis-à-vis third parties of the legal acts referred to in Articles 28, 29, 30 and 32 shall be governed by the law of the Member State determined in accordance with Article 27.
2. However, as regards registered Community designs, legal acts referred to in Articles 28, 29 and 32 shall only have effect vis-à-vis third parties in all the Member States after entry in the register. Nevertheless, such an act, before it is so entered, shall have effect vis-à-vis third parties who have acquired rights in the registered Community design after the date of that act but who knew of the act at the date on which the rights were acquired.
3. Paragraph 2 shall not apply to a person who acquires the registered Community design or a right concerning the registered Community design by way of transfer of the whole of the undertaking or by any other universal succession.
4. Until such time as common rules for the Member States in the field of insolvency enter into force, the effects vis-à-vis third parties of insolvency proceedings shall be governed by the law of the Member State in which such proceedings are first brought under the national law or the regulations applicable in this field.

Article 34 - The application for a registered Community design as an object of property

1. An application for a registered Community design as an object of property shall be dealt with in its entirety, and for the whole area of the Community, as a national design right of the Member State determined in accordance with Article 27.

2. Articles 28, 29, 30, 31, 32 and 33 shall apply mutatis mutandis to applications for registered Community designs. Where the effect of one of these provisions is conditional upon an entry in the register, that formality shall be performed upon registration of the resulting registered Community design.

TITLE IV - APPLICATION FOR A REGISTERED COMMUNITY DESIGN

SECTION 1: FILING OF APPLICATIONS AND THE CONDITIONS WHICH GOVERN THEM

Article 35 - Filing and forwarding of applications

1. An application for a registered Community design shall be filed, at the option of the applicant:
(a) at the Office; or
(b) at the central industrial property office of a Member State; or
(c) in the Benelux countries, at the Benelux Design Office.
2. Where the application is filed at the central industrial property office of a Member State or at the Benelux Design Office, that office shall take all steps to forward the application to the Office within two weeks after filing. It may charge the applicant a fee which shall not exceed the administrative costs of receiving and forwarding the application.
3. As soon as the Office has received an application which has been forwarded by a central industrial property office of a Member State or by the Benelux Design Office, it shall inform the applicant accordingly, indicating the date of its receipt at the Office.
4. No less than 10 years after the entry into force of this Regulation, the Commission shall draw up a report on the operation of the system of filing applications for registered Community designs, accompanied by any proposals for revision that it may deem appropriate.

Article 36 - Conditions with which applications must comply

1. An application for a registered Community design shall contain:
(a) a request for registration;
(b) information identifying the applicant;
(c) a representation of the design suitable for reproduction. However, if the object of the application is a two-dimensional design and the application contains a request for deferment of publication in accordance with Article 50, the representation of the design may be replaced by a specimen.
2. The application shall further contain an indication of the products in which the design is intended to be incorporated or to which it is intended to be applied.
3. In addition, the application may contain:
(a) a description explaining the representation or the specimen;
(b) a request for deferment of publication of the registration in accordance with Article 50;
(c) information identifying the representative if the applicant has appointed one;
(d) the classification of the products in which the design is intended to be incorporated or to which it is intended to be applied according to class;
(e) the citation of the designer or of the team of designers or a statement under the applicant's responsibility that the designer or the team of designers has waived the right to be cited.
4. The application shall be subject to the payment of the registration fee and the publication fee. Where a request for deferment under paragraph 3(b) is filed, the publication fee shall be replaced by the fee for deferment of publication.

5. The application shall comply with the conditions laid down in the implementing regulation.
6. The information contained in the elements mentioned in paragraph 2 and in paragraph 3(a) and (d) shall not affect the scope of protection of the design as such.

Article 37 - Multiple applications

1. Several designs may be combined in one multiple application for registered Community designs. Except in cases of ornamentation, this possibility is subject to the condition that the products in which the designs are intended to be incorporated or to which they are intended to be applied all belong to the same class of the International Classification for Industrial Designs.
2. Besides the fees referred to in Article 36(4), the multiple application shall be subject to payment of an additional registration fee and an additional publication fee. Where the multiple application contains a request for deferment of publication, the additional publication fee shall be replaced by the additional fee for deferment of publication. The additional fees shall correspond to a percentage of the basic fees for each additional design.
3. The multiple application shall comply with the conditions of presentation laid down in the implementing regulation.
4. Each of the designs contained in a multiple application or registration may be dealt with separately from the others for the purpose of applying this Regulation. It may in particular, separately from the others, be enforced, licensed, be the subject of a right in rem, a levy of execution or insolvency proceedings, be surrendered, renewed or assigned, be the subject of deferred publication or be declared invalid. A multiple application or registration may be divided into separate applications or registrations only under the conditions set out in the implementing regulation.

Article 38 - Date of filing

1. The date of filing of an application for a registered Community design shall be the date on which documents containing the information specified in Article 36(1) are filed with the Office by the applicant, or, if the application has been filed with the central industrial property office of a Member State or with the Benelux Design Office, with that office.
2. By derogation from paragraph 1, the date of filing of an application filed with the central industrial property office of a Member State or with the Benelux Design Office and reaching the Office more than two months after the date on which documents containing the information specified in Article 36(1) have been filed shall be the date of receipt of such documents by the Office.

Article 39 - Equivalence of Community filing with national filing

An application for a registered Community design which has been accorded a date of filing shall, in the Member States, be equivalent to a regular national filing, including where appropriate the priority claimed for the said application.

Article 40 - Classification

For the purpose of this Regulation, use shall be made of the Annex to the Agreement establishing an International Classification for Industrial Designs, signed at Locarno on 8 October 1968.

SECTION 2: PRIORITY

Article 41 - Right of priority

1. A person who has duly filed an application for a design right or for a utility model in or for any State party to the Paris Convention for the Protection of Industrial Property, or to the Agreement establishing the World Trade Organisation, or his successors in title, shall enjoy, for the purpose of filing an application for a registered Community design in respect of the same design or utility model, a right of priority of six months from the date of filing of the first application.
2. Every filing that is equivalent to a regular national filing under the national law of the State where it was made or under bilateral or multilateral agreements shall be recognised as giving rise to a right of priority.
3. "Regular national filing" means any filing that is sufficient to establish the date on which the application was filed, whatever may be the outcome of the application.
4. A subsequent application for a design which was the subject of a previous first application, and which is filed in or in respect of the same State, shall be considered as the first application for the purpose of determining priority, provided that, at the date of the filing of the subsequent application, the previous application has been withdrawn, abandoned or refused without being open to public inspection and without leaving any rights outstanding, and has not served as a basis for claiming priority. The previous application may not thereafter serve as a basis for claiming a right of priority.
5. If the first filing has been made in a State which is not a party to the Paris Convention, or to the Agreement establishing the World Trade Organisation, paragraphs 1 to 4 shall apply only in so far as that State, according to published findings, grants, on the basis of a filing made at the Office and subject to conditions equivalent to those laid down in this Regulation, a right of priority having equivalent effect.

Article 42 - Claiming priority

An applicant for a registered Community design desiring to take advantage of the priority of a previous application shall file a declaration of priority and a copy of the previous application. If the language of the latter is not one of the languages of the Office, the Office may require a translation of the previous application in one of those languages.

Article 43 - Effect of priority right

The effect of the right of priority shall be that the date of priority shall count as the date of the filing of the application for a registered Community design for the purpose of Articles 5, 6, 7, 22, 25(1)(d) and 50(1).

Article 44 - Exhibition priority

1. If an applicant for a registered Community design has disclosed products in which the design is incorporated, or to which it is applied, at an official or officially recognised international exhibition falling within the terms of the Convention on International Exhibitions signed in Paris on 22 November 1928 and last revised on 30 November 1972, he may, if he files the application within a period of six months from the date of the first disclosure of such products, claim a right of priority from that date within the meaning of Article 43.
2. An applicant who wishes to claim priority pursuant to paragraph 1, under the conditions laid down in the implementing regulation, must file evidence that he has disclosed at an exhibition the products in or to which the design is incorporated or applied.

3. An exhibition priority granted in a Member State or in a third country does not extend the period of priority laid down in Article 41.

TITLE V - REGISTRATION PROCEDURE

Article 45 - Examination as to formal requirements for filing

1. The Office shall examine whether the application complies with the requirements laid down in Article 36(1) for the accordance of a date of filing.
2. The Office shall examine whether:
(a) the application complies with the other requirements laid down in Article 36(2), (3), (4) and (5) and, in the case of a multiple application, Article 37(1) and (2);
(b) the application meets the formal requirements laid down in the implementing regulation for the implementation of Articles 36 and 37;
(c) the requirements of Article 77(2) are satisfied;
(d) the requirements concerning the claim to priority are satisfied, if a priority is claimed.
3. The conditions for the examination as to the formal requirements for filing shall be laid down in the implementing regulation.

Article 46 - Remediable deficiencies

1. Where, in carrying out the examination under Article 45, the Office notes that there are deficiencies which may be corrected, the Office shall request the applicant to remedy them within the prescribed period.
2. If the deficiencies concern the requirements referred to in Article 36(1) and the applicant complies with the Office's request within the prescribed period, the Office shall accord as the date of filing the date on which the deficiencies are remedied. If the deficiencies are not remedied within the prescribed period, the application shall not be dealt with as an application for a registered Community design.
3. If the deficiencies concern the requirements, including the payment of fees, as referred to in Article 45(2)(a), (b) and (c) and the applicant complies with the Office's request within the prescribed period, the Office shall accord as the date of filing the date on which the application was originally filed. If the deficiencies or the default in payment are not remedied within the prescribed period, the Office shall refuse the application.
4. If the deficiencies concern the requirements referred to in Article 45(2)(d), failure to remedy them within the prescribed period shall result in the loss of the right of priority for the application.

Article 47 - Grounds for non-registrability

1. If the Office, in carrying out the examination pursuant to Article 45, notices that the design for which protection is sought:
(a) does not correspond to the definition under Article 3(a); or
(b) is contrary to public policy or to accepted principles of morality, it shall refuse the application.
2. The application shall not be refused before the applicant has been allowed the opportunity of withdrawing or amending the application or of submitting his observations.

Article 48 - Registration

If the requirements that an application for a registered Community design must satisfy have been fulfilled and to the extent that the application has not been refused by virtue of Article 47, the

Office shall register the application in the Community design Register as a registered Community design. The registration shall bear the date of filing of the application referred to in Article 38.

Article 49 - Publication

Upon registration, the Office shall publish the registered Community design in the Community Designs Bulletin as mentioned in Article 73(1). The contents of the publication shall be set out in the implementing regulation.

Article 50 - Deferment of publication

1. The applicant for a registered Community design may request, when filing the application, that the publication of the registered Community design be deferred for a period of 30 months from the date of filing the application or, if a priority is claimed, from the date of priority.
2. Upon such request, where the conditions set out in Article 48 are satisfied, the registered Community design shall be registered, but neither the representation of the design nor any file relating to the application shall, subject to Article 74(2), be open to public inspection.
3. The Office shall publish in the Community Designs Bulletin a mention of the deferment of the publication of the registered Community design. The mention shall be accompanied by information identifying the right holder in the registered Community design, the date of filing the application and any other particulars prescribed by the implementing regulation.
4. At the expiry of the period of deferment, or at any earlier date on request by the right holder, the Office shall open to public inspection all the entries in the register and the file relating to the application and shall publish the registered Community design in the Community Designs Bulletin, provided that, within the time limit laid down in the implementing regulation:
(a) the publication fee and, in the event of a multiple application, the additional publication fee are paid;
(b) where use has been made of the option pursuant to Article 36(1)(c), the right holder has filed with the Office a representation of the design.
If the right holder fails to comply with these requirements, the registered Community design shall be deemed from the outset not to have had the effects specified in this Regulation.
5. In the case of multiple applications, paragraph 4 need only be applied to some of the designs included therein.
6. The institution of legal proceedings on the basis of a registered Community design during the period of deferment of publication shall be subject to the condition that the information contained in the register and in the file relating to the application has been communicated to the person against whom the action is brought.

TITLE VI - SURRENDER AND INVALIDITY OF THE REGISTERED COMMUNITY DESIGN

Article 51 - Surrender

1. The surrender of a registered Community design shall be declared to the Office in writing by the right holder. It shall not have effect until it has been entered in the register.
2. If a Community design which is subject to deferment of publication is surrendered it shall be deemed from the outset not to have had the effects specified in this Regulation.
3. A registered Community design may be partially surrendered provided that its amended form complies with the requirements for protection and the identity of the design is retained.

4. Surrender shall be registered only with the agreement of the proprietor of a right entered in the register. If a licence has been registered, surrender shall be entered in the register only if the right holder in the registered Community design proves that he has informed the licensee of his intention to surrender. This entry shall be made on expiry of the period prescribed by the implementing regulation.
5. If an action pursuant to Article 14 relating to the entitlement to a registered Community design has been brought before a Community design court, the Office shall not enter the surrender in the register without the agreement of the claimant.

Article 52 - Application for a declaration of invalidity

1. Subject to Article 25(2), (3), (4) and (5), any natural or legal person, as well as a public authority empowered to do so, may submit to the Office an application for a declaration of invalidity of a registered Community design.
2. The application shall be filed in a written reasoned statement. It shall not be deemed to have been filed until the fee for an application for a declaration of invalidity has been paid.
3. An application for a declaration of invalidity shall not be admissible if an application relating to the same subject matter and cause of action, and involving the same parties, has been adjudicated on by a Community design court and has acquired the authority of a final decision.

Article 53 - Examination of the application

1. If the Office finds that the application for a declaration of invalidity is admissible, the Office shall examine whether the grounds for invalidity referred to in Article 25 prejudice the maintenance of the registered Community design.
2. In the examination of the application, which shall be conducted in accordance with the implementing regulation, the Office shall invite the parties, as often as necessary, to file observations, within a period to be fixed by the Office, on communications from the other parties or issued by itself.
3. The decision declaring the registered Community design invalid shall be entered in the register upon becoming final.

Article 54 - Participation in the proceedings of the alleged infringer

1. In the event of an application for a declaration of invalidity of a registered Community design being filed, and as long as no final decision has been taken by the Office, any third party who proves that proceedings for infringement of the same design have been instituted against him may be joined as a party in the invalidity proceedings on request submitted within three months of the date on which the infringement proceedings were instituted.
The same shall apply in respect of any third party who proves both that the right holder of the Community design has requested that he cease an alleged infringement of the design and that he has instituted proceedings for a court ruling that he is not infringing the Community design.
2. The request to be joined as a party shall be filed in a written reasoned statement. It shall not be deemed to have been filed until the invalidity fee, referred to in Article 52(2), has been paid. Thereafter the request shall, subject to any exceptions laid down in the implementing regulation, be treated as an application for a declaration of invalidity.

TITLE VII - APPEALS

Article 55 - Decisions subject to appeal

1. An appeal shall lie from decisions of the examiners, the Administration of Trade Marks and Designs and Legal Division and Invalidity Divisions. It shall have suspensive effect.
2. A decision which does not terminate proceedings as regards one of the parties can only be appealed together with the final decision, unless the decision allows separate appeal.

Article 56 - Persons entitled to appeal and to be parties to appeal proceedings

Any party to proceedings adversely affected by a decision may appeal. Any other parties to the proceedings shall be parties to the appeal proceedings as of right.

Article 57 - Time limit and form of appeal

Notice of appeal must be filed in writing at the Office within two months after the date of notification of the decision appealed from. The notice shall be deemed to have been filed only when the fee for appeal has been paid. Within four months after the date of notification of the decision, a written statement setting out the grounds of appeal must be filed.

Article 58 - Interlocutory revision

1. If the department whose decision is contested considers the appeal to be admissible and well founded, it shall rectify its decision. This shall not apply where the appellant is opposed by another party to the proceedings.
2. If the decision is not rectified within one month after receipt of the statement of grounds, the appeal shall be remitted to the Board of Appeal without delay and without comment as to its merits.

Article 59 - Examination of appeals

1. If the appeal is admissible, the Board of Appeal shall examine whether the appeal is to be allowed.
2. In the examination of the appeal, the Board of Appeal shall invite the parties, as often as necessary, to file observations, within a period to be fixed by the Board of Appeal, on communications from the other parties or issued by itself.

Article 60 - Decisions in respect of appeals

1. Following the examination as to the merits of the appeal, the Board of Appeal shall decide on the appeal. The Board of Appeal may either exercise any power within the competence of the department which was responsible for the decision appealed against or remit the case to that department for further prosecution.
2. If the Board of Appeal remits the case for further prosecution to the department whose decision was appealed, that department shall be bound by the ratio decidendi of the Board of Appeal, in so far as the facts are the same.
3. The decisions of the Boards of Appeal shall take effect only from the date of expiry of the period referred to in Article 61(5) or, if an action has been brought before the Court of Justice within that period, from the date of rejection of such action.

Article 61 - Actions before the Court of Justice

1. Actions may be brought before the Court of Justice against decisions of the Boards of Appeal on appeals.

2. The action may be brought on grounds of lack of competence, infringement of an essential procedural requirement, infringement of the Treaty, of this Regulation or of any rule of law relating to their application or misuse of power.
3. The Court of Justice has jurisdiction to annul or to alter the contested decision.
4. The action shall be open to any party to proceedings before the Board of Appeal adversely affected by its decision.
5. The action shall be brought before the Court of Justice within two months of the date of notification of the decision of the Board of Appeal.
6. The Office shall be required to take the necessary measures to comply with the judgment of the Court of Justice.

TITLE VIII - PROCEDURE BEFORE THE OFFICE

SECTION 1: GENERAL PROVISIONS

Article 62 - Statement of reasons on which decisions are based

Decisions of the Office shall state the reasons on which they are based. They shall be based only on reasons or evidence on which the parties concerned have had an opportunity to present their comments.

Article 63 - Examination of the facts by the Office of its own motion

1. In proceedings before it the Office shall examine the facts of its own motion. However, in proceedings relating to a declaration of invalidity, the Office shall be restricted in this examination to the facts, evidence and arguments provided by the parties and the relief sought.
2. The Office may disregard facts or evidence which are not submitted in due time by the parties concerned.

Article 64 - Oral proceedings

1. If the Office considers that oral proceedings would be expedient, they shall be held either at the instance of the Office or at the request of any party to the proceedings.
2. Oral proceedings, including delivery of the decision, shall be public, unless the department before which the proceedings are taking place decides otherwise in cases where admission of the public could have serious and unjustified disadvantages, in particular for a party to the proceedings.

Article 65 - Taking of evidence

1. In any proceedings before the Office the means of giving or obtaining evidence shall include the following:
(a) hearing the parties;
(b) requests for information;
(c) the production of documents and items of evidence;
(d) hearing witnesses;
(e) opinions by experts;
(f) statements in writing, sworn or affirmed or having a similar effect under the law of the State in which the statement is drawn up.
2. The relevant department of the Office may commission one of its members to examine the evidence adduced.

3. If the Office considers it necessary for a party, witness or expert to give evidence orally, it shall issue a summons to the person concerned to appear before it.
4. The parties shall be informed of the hearing of a witness or expert before the Office. They shall have the right to be present and to put questions to the witness or expert.

Article 66 - Notification

The Office shall, as a matter of course, notify those concerned of decisions and summonses and of any notice or other communication from which a time limit is reckoned, or of which those concerned must be notified under other provisions of this Regulation or of the implementing regulation, or of which notification has been ordered by the President of the Office.

Article 67 - Restitutio in integrum

1. The applicant for or holder of a registered Community design or any other party to proceedings before the Office who, in spite of all due care required by the circumstances having been taken, was unable to observe a time limit vis-à-vis the Office shall, upon application, have his rights re-established if the non-observance in question has the direct consequence, by virtue of the provisions of this Regulation, of causing the loss of any rights or means of redress.
2. The application must be filed in writing within two months of the removal of the cause of non-compliance with the time limit. The omitted act must be completed within this period. The application shall only be admissible within the year immediately following the expiry of the unobserved time limit. In the case of non-submission of the request for renewal of registration or of non-payment of a renewal fee, the further period of six months provided for in the second sentence of Article 13(3) shall be deducted from the period of one year.
3. The application must state the grounds on which it is based and must set out the facts on which it relies. It shall not be deemed to be filed until the fee for the re-establishment of rights has been paid.
4. The department competent to decide on the omitted act shall decide upon the application.
5. The provisions of this Article shall not be applicable to the time limits referred to in paragraph 2 and Article 41(1).
6. Where the applicant for or holder of a registered Community design has his rights re-established, he may not invoke his rights vis-à-vis a third party who, in good faith, in the course of the period between the loss of rights in the application for or registration of the registered Community design and publication of the mention of re-establishment of those rights, has put on the market products in which a design included within the scope of protection of the registered Community design is incorporated or to which it is applied.
7. A third party who may avail himself of the provisions of paragraph 6 may bring third party proceedings against the decision re-establishing the rights of the applicant for or holder of the registered Community design within a period of two months as from the date of publication of the mention of re-establishment of those rights.
8. Nothing in this Article shall limit the right of a Member State to grant restitutio in integrum in respect of time limits provided for in this Regulation and to be complied with vis-à-vis the authorities of such State.

Article 68 - Reference to general principles

In the absence of procedural provisions in this Regulation, the implementing regulation, the fees regulation or the rules of procedure of the Boards of Appeal, the Office shall take into account the principles of procedural law generally recognised in the Member States.

Article 69 - Termination of financial obligations

1. Rights of the Office to the payment of fees shall be barred four years from the end of the calendar year in which the fee fell due.
2. Rights against the Office for the refunding of fees or sums of money paid in excess of a fee shall be barred after four years from the end of the calendar year in which the right arose.
3. The periods laid down in paragraphs 1 and 2 shall be interrupted, in the case covered by paragraph 1, by a request for payment of the fee and, in the case covered by paragraph 2, by a reasoned claim in writing. On interruption it shall begin again immediately and shall end at the latest six years after the end of the year in which it originally began, unless in the meantime judicial proceedings to enforce the right have begun. In this case the period shall end at the earliest one year after the judgment has acquired the authority of a final decision.

SECTION 2: COSTS

Article 70 - Apportionment of costs

1. The losing party in proceedings for a declaration of invalidity of a registered Community design or appeal proceedings shall bear the fees incurred by the other party as well as all costs incurred by him essential to the proceedings, including travel and subsistence and the remuneration of an agent, adviser or advocate, within the limits of scales set for each category of costs under the conditions laid down in the implementing regulation.
2. However, where each party succeeds on some and fails on other heads, or if reasons of equity so dictate, the Invalidity Division or Board of Appeal shall decide a different apportionment of costs.
3. A party who terminates the proceedings by surrendering the registered Community design or by not renewing its registration or by withdrawing the application for a declaration of invalidity or the appeal, shall bear the fees and the costs incurred by the other party as stipulated in paragraphs 1 and 2.
4. Where a case does not proceed to judgment, the costs shall be at the discretion of the Invalidity Division or Board of Appeal.
5. Where the parties conclude before the Invalidity Division or Board of Appeal a settlement of costs differing from that provided for in paragraphs 1, 2, 3 and 4, the body concerned shall take note of that agreement.
6. On request, the registry of the Invalidity Division or Board of Appeal shall fix the amount of the costs to be paid pursuant to the preceding paragraphs. The amount so determined may be reviewed by a decision of the Invalidity Division or Board of Appeal on a request filed within the period prescribed by the implementing regulation.

Article 71 - Enforcement of decisions fixing the amount of costs

1. Any final decision of the Office fixing the amount of costs shall be enforceable.
2. Enforcement shall be governed by the rules of civil procedure in force in the State in the territory of which it is carried out. The order for its enforcement shall be appended to the decision, without any other formality than verification of the authenticity of the decision, by the national authority which the government of each Member State shall designate for this purpose and shall make known to the Office and to the Court of Justice.
3. When these formalities have been completed on application by the party concerned, the latter may proceed to enforcement in accordance with the national law, by bringing the matter directly before the competent authority.

4. Enforcement may be suspended only by a decision of the Court of Justice. However, the courts of the Member State concerned shall have jurisdiction over complaints that enforcement is being carried out in an irregular manner.

SECTION 3: INFORMING THE PUBLIC AND THE OFFICIAL AUTHORITIES OF THE MEMBER STATES

Article 72 - Register of Community designs

The Office shall keep a register to be known as the register of Community designs, which shall contain those particulars of which the registration is provided for by this Regulation or by the implementing regulation. The register shall be open to public inspection, except to the extent that Article 50(2) provides otherwise.

Article 73 - Periodical publications

1. This Office shall periodically publish a Community Designs Bulletin containing entries open to public inspection in the register as well as other particulars the publication of which is prescribed by this Regulation or by the implementing regulation.
2. Notices and information of a general character issued by the President of the Office, as well as any other information relevant to this Regulation or its implementation, shall be published in the Official Journal of the Office.

Article 74 - Inspection of files

1. The files relating to applications for registered Community designs which have not yet been published or the files relating to registered Community designs which are subject to deferment of publication in accordance with Article 50 or which, being subject to such deferment, have been surrendered before or on the expiry of that period, shall not be made available for inspection without the consent of the applicant for or the right holder in the registered Community design.
2. Any person who can establish a legitimate interest may inspect a file without the consent of the applicant for or holder of the registered Community design prior to the publication or after the surrender of the latter in the case provided for in paragraph 1.
   This shall in particular apply if the interested person proves that the applicant for or the holder of the registered Community design has taken steps with a view to invoking against him the right under the registered Community design.
3. Subsequent to the publication of the registered Community design, the file may be inspected on request.
4. However, where a file is inspected pursuant to paragraph 2 or 3, certain documents in the file may be withheld from inspection in accordance with the provisions of the implementing regulation.

Article 75 - Administrative cooperation

Unless otherwise provided in this Regulation or in national laws, the Office and the courts or authorities of the Member States shall on request give assistance to each other by communicating information or opening files for inspection.

Where the Office opens files to inspection by courts, public prosecutors' offices or central industrial property offices, the inspection shall not be subject to the restrictions laid down in Article 74.

Article 76 - Exchange of publications

1. The Office and the central industrial property offices of the Member States shall despatch to each other on request and for their own use one or more copies of their respective publications free of charge.
2. The Office may conclude agreements relating to the exchange or supply of publications.

SECTION 4: REPRESENTATION

Article 77 - General principles of representation

1. Subject to paragraph 2, no person shall be compelled to be represented before the Office.
2. Without prejudice to the second subparagraph of paragraph 3, natural or legal persons not having either their domicile or their principal place of business or a real and effective industrial or commercial establishment in the Community must be represented before the Office in accordance with Article 78(1) in all proceedings before the Office established by this Regulation, other than in filing an application for a registered Community design; the implementing regulation may permit other exceptions.
3. Natural or legal persons having their domicile or principal place of business or a real and effective industrial or commercial establishment in the Community may be represented before the Office by one of their employees, who must file with it a signed authorisation for inclusion in the files, the details of which are set out in the implementing regulation.
An employee of a legal person to which this paragraph applies may also represent other legal persons which have economic connections with the first legal person, even if those other legal persons have neither their domicile nor their principal place of business nor a real and effective industrial or commercial establishment within the Community.

Article 78 - Professional representation

1. Representation of natural or legal persons in proceedings before the Office under this Regulation may only be undertaken by:
(a) any legal practitioner qualified in one of the Member States and having his place of business within the Community, to the extent that he is entitled, within the said State, to act as a representative in industrial property matters; or
(b) any professional representatives whose name has been entered on the list of professional representatives referred to in Article 89(1)(b) of the Regulation on the Community trade mark; or
(c) persons whose names are entered on the special list of professional representatives for design matters referred to in paragraph 4.
2. The persons referred to in paragraph 1(c) shall only be entitled to represent third persons in proceedings on design matters before the Office.
3. The implementing regulation shall provide whether and under what conditions representatives must file with the Office a signed authorisation for insertion on the files.
4. Any natural person may be entered on the special list of professional representatives in design matters, if he fulfils the following conditions:
(a) he must be a national of one of the Member States;
(b) he must have his place of business or employment in the Community;
(c) he must be entitled to represent natural or legal persons in design matters before the central industrial property office of a Member State or before the Benelux Design Office. Where, in that State, the entitlement to represent in design matters is not conditional upon the requirement of special professional qualifications, persons applying to be entered on the list must have habitually acted in design matters before the central industrial property office of

the said State for at least five years. However, persons whose professional qualification to represent natural or legal persons in design matters before the central industrial property office of one of the Member States is officially recognised in accordance with the regulations laid by such State shall not be subject to the condition of having exercised the profession.

5. Entry on the list referred to in paragraph 4 shall be effected upon request, accompanied by a certificate furnished by the central industrial property office of the Member State concerned, which must indicate that the conditions laid down in the said paragraph are fulfilled.
6. The President of the Office may grant exemption from:
(a) the requirement of paragraph 4(a) in special circumstances;
(b) the requirement of paragraph 4(c), second sentence, if the applicant furnishes proof that he has acquired the requisite qualification in another way.
7. The conditions under which a person may be removed from the list shall be laid down in the implementing regulation.

TITLE IX - JURISDICTION AND PROCEDURE IN LEGAL ACTIONS RELATING TO COMMUNITY DESIGNS

SECTION 1: JURISDICTION AND ENFORCEMENT

Article 79 - Application of the Convention on Jurisdiction and Enforcement

1. Unless otherwise specified in this Regulation, the Convention on Jurisdiction and the Enforcement of Judgements in Civil and Commercial Matters, signed in Brussels on 27 September 1968[7], hereinafter referred to as the "Convention on Jurisdiction and Enforcement", shall apply to proceedings relating to Community designs and applications for registered Community designs, as well as to proceedings relating to actions on the basis of Community designs and national designs enjoying simultaneous protection.
2. The provisions of the Convention on Jurisdiction and Enforcement which are rendered applicable by the paragraph 1 shall have effect in respect of any Member State solely in the text which is in force in respect of that State at any given time.
3. In the event of proceedings in respect of the actions and claims referred to in Article 85:
(a) Articles 2, 4, 5(1), (3), (4) and (5), 16(4) and 24 of the Convention on Jurisdiction and Enforcement shall not apply;
(b) Articles 17 and 18 of that Convention shall apply subject to the limitations in Article 82(4) of this Regulation;
(c) the provisions of Title II of that Convention which are applicable to persons domiciled in a Member State shall also be applicable to persons who do not have a domicile in any Member State but have an establishment therein.
4. The provisions of the Convention on Jurisdiction and Enforcement shall not have effect in respect of any Member State for which that Convention has not yet entered into force. Until such entry into force, proceedings referred to in paragraph 1 shall be governed in such a Member State by any bilateral or multilateral convention governing its relationship with another Member State concerned, or, if no such convention exists, by its domestic law on jurisdiction, recognition and enforcement of decisions.

---

[7] OJ L 299, 31.12.1972, p. 32. Convention as amended by the Conventions on the Accession to that Convention of the States acceding to the European Communities.

SECTION 2: DISPUTES CONCERNING THE INFRINGEMENT AND VALIDITY OF COMMUNITY DESIGNS

Article 80 - Community design courts

1. The Member States shall designate in their territories as limited a number as possible of national courts and tribunals of first and second instance (Community design courts) which shall perform the functions assigned to them by this Regulation.
2. Each Member State shall communicate to the Commission not later than 6 March 2005 a list of Community design courts, indicating their names and their territorial jurisdiction.
3. Any change made after communication of the list referred to in paragraph 2 in the number, names or territorial jurisdiction of the Community design courts shall be notified without delay by the Member State concerned to the Commission.
4. The information referred to in paragraphs 2 and 3 shall be notified by the Commission to the Member States and published in the Official Journal of the European Communities.
5. As long as a Member State has not communicated the list as stipulated in paragraph 2, jurisdiction for any proceedings resulting from an action covered by Article 81 for which the courts of that State have jurisdiction pursuant to Article 82 shall lie with that court of the State in question which would have jurisdiction ratione loci and ratione materiae in the case of proceedings relating to a national design right of that State.

Article 81 - Jurisdiction over infringement and validity

The Community design courts shall have exclusive jurisdiction:
(a) for infringement actions and - if they are permitted under national law - actions in respect of threatened infringement of Community designs;
(b) for actions for declaration of non-infringement of Community designs, if they are permitted under national law;
(c) for actions for a declaration of invalidity of an unregistered Community design;
(d) for counterclaims for a declaration of invalidity of a Community design raised in connection with actions under (a).

Article 82 - International jurisdiction

1. Subject to the provisions of this Regulation and to any provisions of the Convention on Jurisdiction and Enforcement applicable by virtue of Article 79, proceedings in respect of the actions and claims referred to in Article 81 shall be brought in the courts of the Member State in which the defendant is domiciled or, if he is not domiciled in any of the Member States, in any Member State in which he has an establishment.
2. If the defendant is neither domiciled nor has an establishment in any of the Member States, such proceedings shall be brought in the courts of the Member State in which the plaintiff is domiciled or, if he is not domiciled in any of the Member States, in any Member State in which he has an establishment.
3. If neither the defendant nor the plaintiff is so domiciled or has such an establishment, such proceedings shall be brought in the courts of the Member State where the Office has its seat.
4. Notwithstanding paragraphs 1, 2 and 3:
(a) Article 17 of the Convention on Jurisdiction and Enforcement shall apply if the parties agree that a different Community design court shall have jurisdiction;
(b) Article 18 of that Convention shall apply if the defendant enters an appearance before a different Community design court.
5. Proceedings in respect of the actions and claims referred to in Article 81(a) and (d) may also be brought in the courts of the Member State in which the act of infringement has been committed or threatened.

Article 83 - Extent of jurisdiction on infringement

1. A Community design court whose jurisdiction is based on Article 82(1), (2) (3) or (4) shall have jurisdiction in respect of acts of infringement committed or threatened within the territory of any of the Member States.
2. A Community design court whose jurisdiction is based on Article 82(5) shall have jurisdiction only in respect of acts of infringement committed or threatened within the territory of the Member State in which that court is situated.

Article 84 - Action or counterclaim for a declaration of invalidity of a Community design

1. An action or a counterclaim for a declaration of invalidity of a Community design may only be based on the grounds for invalidity mentioned in Article 25.
2. In the cases referred to in Article 25(2), (3), (4) and (5) the action or the counterclaim may be brought solely by the person entitled under those provisions.
3. If the counterclaim is brought in a legal action to which the right holder of the Community design is not already a party, he shall be informed thereof and may be joined as a party to the action in accordance with the conditions set out in the law of the Member State where the court is situated.
4. The validity of a Community design may not be put in issue in an action for a declaration of non-infringement.

Article 85 - Presumption of validity - defence as to the merits

1. In proceedings in respect of an infringement action or an action for threatened infringement of a registered Community design, the Community design court shall treat the Community design as valid. Validity may be challenged only with a counterclaim for a declaration of invalidity. However, a plea relating to the invalidity of a Community design, submitted otherwise than by way of counterclaim, shall be admissible in so far as the defendant claims that the Community design could be declared invalid on account of an earlier national design right, within the meaning of Article 25(1)(d), belonging to him.
2. In proceedings in respect of an infringement action or an action for threatened infringement of an unregistered Community design, the Community design court shall treat the Community design as valid if the right holder produces proof that the conditions laid down in Article 11 have been met and indicates what constitutes the individual character of his Community design. However, the defendant may contest its validity by way of a plea or with a counterclaim for a declaration of invalidity.

Article 86 - Judgements of invalidity

1. Where in a proceeding before a Community design court the Community design has been put in issue by way of a counterclaim for a declaration of invalidity:
(a) if any of the grounds mentioned in Article 25 are found to prejudice the maintenance of the Community design, the court shall declare the Community design invalid;
(b) if none of the grounds mentioned in Article 25 is found to prejudice the maintenance of the Community design, the court shall reject the counterclaim.
2. The Community design court with which a counterclaim for a declaration of invalidity of a registered Community design has been filed shall inform the Office of the date on which the counterclaim was filed. The latter shall record this fact in the register.
3. The Community design court hearing a counterclaim for a declaration of invalidity of a registered Community design may, on application by the right holder of the registered Community design and after hearing the other parties, stay the proceedings and request the defendant to submit an application for a declaration of invalidity to the Office within a time limit which the court shall determine. If the application is not made within the time limit, the

proceedings shall continue; the counterclaim shall be deemed withdrawn. Article 91(3) shall apply.
4. Where a Community design court has given a judgment which has become final on a counterclaim for a declaration of invalidity of a registered Community design, a copy of the judgment shall be sent to the Office. Any party may request information about such transmission. The Office shall mention the judgment in the register in accordance with the provisions of the implementing regulation.
5. No counterclaim for a declaration of invalidity of a registered Community design may be made if an application relating to the same subject matter and cause of action, and involving the same parties, has already been determined by the Office in a decision which has become final.

Article 87 - Effects of the judgement on invalidity

When it has become final, a judgment of a Community design court declaring a Community design invalid shall have in all the Member States the effects specified in Article 26.

Article 88 - Applicable law

1. The Community design courts shall apply the provisions of this Regulation.
2. On all matters not covered by this Regulation, a Community design court shall apply its national law, including its private international law.
3. Unless otherwise provided in this Regulation, a Community design court shall apply the rules of procedure governing the same type of action relating to a national design right in the Member State where it is situated.

Article 89 - Sanctions in actions for infringement

1. Where in an action for infringement or for threatened infringement a Community design court finds that the defendant has infringed or threatened to infringe a Community design, it shall, unless there are special reasons for not doing so, order the following measures:
(a) an order prohibiting the defendant from proceeding with the acts which have infringed or would infringe the Community design;
(b) an order to seize the infringing products;
(c) an order to seize materials and implements predominantly used in order to manufacture the infringing goods, if their owner knew the effect for which such use was intended or if such effect would have been obvious in the circumstances;
(d) any order imposing other sanctions appropriate under the circumstances which are provided by the law of the Member State in which the acts of infringement or threatened infringement are committed, including its private international law.
2. The Community design court shall take such measures in accordance with its national law as are aimed at ensuring that the orders referred to in paragraph 1 are complied with.

Article 90 - Provisional measures, including protective measures

1. Application may be made to the courts of a Member State, including Community design courts, for such provisional measures, including protective measures, in respect of a Community design as may be available under the law of that State in respect of national design rights even if, under this Regulation, a Community design court of another Member State has jurisdiction as to the substance of the matter.
2. In proceedings relating to provisional measures, including protective measures, a plea otherwise than by way of counterclaim relating to the invalidity of a Community design submitted by the defendant shall be admissible. Article 85(2) shall, however, apply mutatis mutandis.

3. A Community design court whose jurisdiction is based on Article 82(1), (2), (3) or (4) shall have jurisdiction to grant provisional measures, including protective measures, which, subject to any necessary procedure for recognition and enforcement pursuant to Title III of the Convention on Jurisdiction and Enforcement, are applicable in the territory of any Member State. No other court shall have such jurisdiction.

Article 91 - Specific rules on related actions

1. A Community design court hearing an action referred to in Article 81, other than an action for a declaration of non-infringement, shall, unless there are special grounds for continuing the hearing, of its own motion after hearing the parties, or at the request of one of the parties and after hearing the other parties, stay the proceedings where the validity of the Community design is already in issue before another Community design court on account of a counterclaim or, in the case of a registered Community design, where an application for a declaration of invalidity has already been filed at the Office.
2. The Office, when hearing an application for a declaration of invalidity of a registered Community design, shall, unless there are special grounds for continuing the hearing, of its own motion after hearing the parties, or at the request of one of the parties and after hearing the other parties, stay the proceedings where the validity of the registered Community design is already in issue on account of a counterclaim before a Community design court. However, if one of the parties to the proceedings before the Community design court so requests, the court may, after hearing the other parties to these proceedings, stay the proceedings. The Office shall in this instance continue the proceedings pending before it.
3. Where the Community design court stays the proceedings it may order provisional measures, including protective measures, for the duration of the stay.

Article 92 - Jurisdiction of Community design courts of second instance - further appeal

1. An appeal to the Community design courts of second instance shall lie from judgments of the Community design courts of first instance in respect of proceedings arising from the actions and claims referred to in Article 81.
2. The conditions under which an appeal may be lodged with a Community design court of second instance shall be determined by the national law of the Member State in which that court is located.
3. The national rules concerning further appeal shall be applicable in respect of judgments of Community design courts of second instance.

SECTION 3: OTHER DISPUTES CONCERNING COMMUNITY DESIGNS

Article 93 - Supplementary provisions on the jurisdiction of national courts other than Community design courts

1. Within the Member State whose courts have jurisdiction under Article 79(1) or (4), those courts shall have jurisdiction for actions relating to Community designs other than those referred to in Article 81 which would have jurisdiction ratione loci and ratione materiae in the case of actions relating to a national design right in that State.
2. Actions relating to a Community design, other than those referred to in Article 81, for which no court has jurisdiction pursuant to Article 79(1) and (4) and paragraph 1 of this Article may be heard before the courts of the Member State in which the Office has its seat.

Article 94 - Obligation of the national court

A national court which is dealing with an action relating to a Community design other than the actions referred to in Article 81 shall treat the design as valid. Articles 85(2) and 90(2) shall, however, apply mutatis mutandis.

TITLE X - EFFECTS ON THE LAWS OF THE MEMBER STATES

Article 95 - Parallel actions on the basis of Community designs and national design rights

1. Where actions for infringement or for threatened infringement involving the same cause of action and between the same parties are brought before the courts of different Member States, one seized on the basis of a Community design and the other seized on the basis of a national design right providing simultaneous protection, the court other than the court first seized shall of its own motion decline jurisdiction in favour of that court. The court which would be required to decline jurisdiction may stay its proceedings if the jurisdiction of the other court is contested.
2. The Community design court hearing an action for infringement or threatened infringement on the basis of a Community design shall reject the action if a final judgment on the merits has been given on the same cause of action and between the same parties on the basis of a design right providing simultaneous protection.
3. The court hearing an action for infringement or for threatened infringement on the basis of a national design right shall reject the action if a final judgment on the merits has been given on the same cause of action and between the same parties on the basis of a Community design providing simultaneous protection.
4. Paragraphs 1, 2 and 3 shall not apply in respect of provisional measures, including protective measures.

Article 96 - Relationship to other forms of protection under national law

1. The provisions of this Regulation shall be without prejudice to any provisions of Community law or of the law of the Member States concerned relating to unregistered designs, trade marks or other distinctive signs, patents and utility models, typefaces, civil liability and unfair competition.
2. A design protected by a Community design shall also be eligible for protection under the law of copyright of Member States as from the date on which the design was created or fixed in any form. The extent to which, and the conditions under which, such a protection is conferred, including the level of originality required, shall be determined by each Member State.

TITLE XI - SUPPLEMENTARY PROVISIONS CONCERNING THE OFFICE

SECTION 1: GENERAL PROVISIONS

Article 97 - General provision

Unless otherwise provided in this Title, Title XII of the Regulation on the Community trade mark shall apply to the Office with regard to its tasks under this Regulation.

Article 98 - Language of proceedings

1. The application for a registered Community design shall be filed in one of the official languages of the Community.

2. The applicant must indicate a second language which shall be a language of the Office the use of which he accepts as a possible language of proceedings before the Office.
If the application was filed in a language which is not one of the languages of the Office, the Office shall arrange to have the application translated into the language indicated by the applicant.
3. Where the applicant for a registered Community design is the sole party to proceedings before the Office, the language of proceedings shall be the language used for filing the application. If the application was made in a language other then the languages of the Office, the Office may send written communications to the applicant in the second language indicated by the applicant in his application.
4. In the case of invalidity proceedings, the language of proceedings shall be the language used for filing the application for a registered Community design if this is one of the languages of the Office. If the application was made in a language other than the languages of the Office, the language of proceedings shall be the second language indicated in the application.
The application for a declaration of invalidity shall be filed in the language of proceedings.
Where the language of proceedings is not the language used for filing the application for a registered Community design, the right holder of the Community design may file observations in the language of filing. The Office shall arrange to have those observations translated into the language of proceedings.
The implementing regulation may provide that the translation expenses to be borne by the Office may not, subject to a derogation granted by the Office where justified by the complexity of the case, exceed an amount to be fixed for each category of proceedings on the basis of the average size of statements of case received by the Office. Expenditure in excess of this amount may be allocated to the losing party in accordance with Article 70.
5. Parties to invalidity proceedings may agree that a different official language of the Community is to be the language of the proceedings.

Article 99 - Publication and register

1. All information the publication of which is prescribed by this Regulation or the implementing regulation shall be published in all the official languages of the Community.
2. All entries in the Register of Community designs shall be made in all the official languages of the Community.
3. In cases of doubt, the text in the language of the Office in which the application for a registered Community design was filed shall be authentic. If the application was filed in an official language of the Community other than one of the languages of the Office, the text in the second language indicated by the applicant shall be authentic.

Article 100 - Supplementary powers of the President

In addition to the functions and powers conferred on the President of the Office by Article 119 of the Regulation on the Community trade mark, the President may place before the Commission any proposal to amend this Regulation, the implementing regulation, the fees regulation and any other rule to the extent that they apply to registered Community designs, after consulting the Administrative Board and, in the case of the fees regulation, the Budget Committee.

Article 101 - Supplementary powers of the Administrative Board

In addition to the powers conferred on it by Article 121 et seq of the Regulation on the Community trade mark or by other provisions of this Regulation, the Administrative Board;
(a) shall set the date for the first filing of applications for registered Community designs pursuant to Article 111(2);

(b) shall be consulted before adoption of the guidelines for examination as to formal requirements, examination as to grounds for refusal of registration and invalidity proceedings in the Office and in the other cases provided for in this Regulation.

SECTION 2: PROCEDURES

Article 102 - Competence

For taking decisions in connection with the procedures laid down in this Regulation the following shall be competent:
(a) examiners;
(b) the Administration of Trade Marks and Designs and Legal Division;
(c) Invalidity Divisions;
(d) Boards of Appeal.

Article 103 - Examiners

An examiner shall be responsible for taking decisions on behalf of the Office in relation to an application for a registered Community design.

Article 104 - The Administration of Trade Marks and Designs and Legal Division

1. The Administration of Trade Marks and Legal Division provided for by Article 128 of the Regulation on the Community trade mark shall become the Administration of Trade Marks and Designs and Legal Division.
2. In addition to the powers conferred upon it by the Regulation on the Community trade mark, it shall be responsible for taking those decisions required by this Regulation which do not fall within the competence of an examiner or an Invalidity Division. It shall in particular be responsible for decisions in respect of entries in the register.

Article 105 - Invalidity Divisions

1. An Invalidity Division shall be responsible for taking decisions in relation to applications for declarations of invalidity of registered Community designs.
2. An Invalidity Division shall consist of three members. At least one of the members must be legally qualified.

Article 106 - Boards of Appeal

In addition to the powers conferred upon it by Article 131 of the Regulation on the Community trade mark, the Boards of Appeal instituted by that Regulation shall be responsible for deciding on appeals from decisions of the examiners, the Invalidity Divisions and from the decisions of the Administration of Trade Marks and Designs and Legal Division as regards their decisions concerning Community designs.

TITLE XII - FINAL PROVISIONS

Article 107 - Implementing regulation

1. The rules implementing this Regulation shall be adopted in an implementing regulation.
2. In addition to the fees already provided for in this Regulation, fees shall be charged, in accordance with the detailed rules of application laid down in the implementing regulation and in a fees regulation, in the cases listed below:

(a) late payment of the registration fee;
(b) late payment of the publication fee;
(c) late payment of the fee for deferment of publication;
(d) late payment of additional fees for multiple applications;
(e) issue of a copy of the certificate of registration;
(f) registration of the transfer of a registered Community design;
(g) registration of a licence or another right in respect of a registered Community design;
(h) cancellation of the registration of a licence or another right;
(i) issue of an extract from the register;
(j) inspection of the files;
(k) issue of copies of file documents;
(l) communication of information in a file;
(m) review of the determination of the procedural costs to be refunded;
(n) issue of certified copies of the application.
3. The implementing regulation and the fees regulation shall be adopted and amended in accordance with the procedure laid down in Article 109(2).

Article 108 - Rules of procedure of the Boards of Appeal

The rules of procedure of the Boards of Appeal shall apply to appeals heard by those Boards under this Regulation, without prejudice to any necessary adjustment or additional provision, adopted in accordance with the procedure laid down in Article 109(2).

Article 109 - Committee

1. The Commission shall be assisted by a Committee.
2. Where reference is made to this paragraph, Articles 5 and 7 of Decision 1999/468/EC shall apply.

    The period laid down in Article 5(6) of Decision 1999/468/EC shall be set at three months.
3. The Committee shall adopt its rules of procedure

Article 110 - Transitional provision

1. Until such time as amendments to this Regulation enter into force on a proposal from the Commission on this subject, protection as a Community design shall not exist for a design which constitutes a component part of a complex product used within the meaning of Article 19(1) for the purpose of the repair of that complex product so as to restore its original appearance.
2. The proposal from the Commission referred to in paragraph 1 shall be submitted together with, and take into consideration, any changes which the Commission shall propose on the same subject pursuant to Article 18 of Directive 98/71/EC.

Article 111 - Entry into force

1. This Regulation shall enter into force on the 60th day following its publication in the Official Journal of the European Communities.
2. Applications for registered Community designs may be filed at the Office from the date fixed by the Administrative Board on the recommendation of the President of the Office.
3. Applications for registered Community designs filed within three months before the date referred to in paragraph 2 shall be deemed to have been filed on that date.

This Regulation shall be binding in its entirety and directly applicable in all Member States.
Done at Brussels, 12 December 2001.

3. Electronic Payments

COMMISSION RECOMMENDATION 97/489/EC
OF 30 JULY 1997
CONCERNING TRANSACTIONS BY ELECTRONIC PAYMENT INSTRUMENTS AND IN PARTICULAR THE RELATIONSHIP BETWEEN ISSUER AND HOLDER

(Official Journal L 208, 02/08/1997, p. 0052 – 0058)

THE COMMISSION OF THE EUROPEAN COMMUNITIES,

Having regard to the Treaty establishing the European Community and in particular Article 155, second indent, thereof,

(1) Whereas one of the main objectives of the Community is to ensure the full functioning of the internal market of which payment systems are essential parts; whereas transactions made by electronic payment instruments account for an increasing proportion of the volume and the value of domestic and cross-border payments; whereas, given the current context of rapid innovation and technological progress, this trend is expected to accelerate notably as a consequence of the wide array of innovative businesses, markets and trading communities engendered by electronic commerce;

(2) Whereas it is important for individuals and businesses to be able to use electronic payment instruments throughout the Community; whereas this recommendation seeks to follow up progress made towards the completion of the internal market, notably in the light of the liberalization of capital movements, and will also contribute to the implementation of economic and monetary union;

(3) Wereas this recommendation covers transactions effected by electronic payment instruments; whereas, for the purposes of this recommendation, these include instruments allowing for (remote) access to a customer's account, notably payment cards and phone- and home-banking applications; whereas transactions by means of a payment card shall cover electronic and non-electronic payment by means of a payment card, including processes for which a signature is required and a voucher is produced; whereas, for the purposes of this recommendation, means of payment instruments also include reloadable electronic money instruments in the form of stored-value cards and electronic tokens stored on network computer memory; whereas reloadable electronic money instruments, because of their features, in particular the possible link to the holder's account, are those for which the need for customer protection is strongest; whereas, as far as electronic money instruments are concerned, coverage under this recommendation is therefore limited to instruments of the reloadable type;

(4) Whereas this recommendation is intended to contribute to the advent of the information society and, in particular, electronic commerce by promoting customer confidence in and retailer acceptance of these instruments; whereas, to this end, the Commission will also consider the possibility of modernizing and updating its recommendation 87/598/EEC[1], with a view to establishing a clear framework for the relationship between acquirers and acceptors in respect of electronic payment instruments; whereas, in line with those objectives, this

---
[1] OJ No L 365, 24. 12. 1987, p. 72.

recommendation sets out minimum information requirements which should be contained in the terms and conditions applied to transactions made by electronic payment instruments, as well as the minimum obligations and liabilities of the parties concerned; whereas such terms and conditions should be set out in writing, including where appropriate by electronic means, and maintain a fair balance between the interests of the parties concerned; whereas, in compliance with Council Directive 93/13/EEC of 5 April 1993 on unfair terms in consumer contracts[2], such terms and conditions should in particular be in an understandable and comprehensible form;

(5) Whereas, with a view to ensuring transparency, this recommendation sets out the minimum requirements needed to ensure an adequate level of customer information upon conclusion of a contract as well as subsequent to transactions effected by means of a payment instrument, including information on charges, exchange rates and interest rates; whereas, for the purpose of informing the holder of the manner of calculation of the interest rate, reference is to be made to Council Directive 87/102/EEC of 22 December 1986 for the approximation of the laws, regulations and administrative provisions of the Member States concerning consumer credit[3], as amended by Directive 90/88/EEC[4];

(6) Whereas this recommendation sets out minimum requirements concerning the obligations and liabilities of the parties concerned; whereas information to a holder should include a clear statement of the extent of the customer's obligation as holder of an electronic payment instrument enabling him/her to make payments in favour in third persons, as well as to perform certain financial transactions for himself/herself;

(7) Whereas, to improve customer's access to redress, this recommendation calls on Member States to ensure that there are adequate and effective means for the settlement of disputes between a holder and an issuer; whereas the Commission published on 14 February 1996 a plan of action on consumer access to justice and the settlement of consumer disputes in the internal market; whereas that plan of action includes specific initiatives to promote out-of-court procedures; whereas objective criteria (Annex II) are suggested to ensure the reliability of those procedures and provision is made for the use of standardized claims forms (Annex III);

(8) Whereas this recommendation seeks to ensure a high level of consumer protection in the field of electronic payment instruments;

(9) Whereas it is essential that transactions effected by means of electronic payment instruments should be the subject of records in order that transactions can be traced and errors can be rectified; whereas the burden of proof to show that a transaction was accurately recorded and entered into the accounts and was not affected by technical breakdown or other deficiency should lie upon the issuer;

(10) Whereas, without prejudice to any rights of a holder under national law, payment instructions given by a holder in respect of transactions effected by means of an electronic payment instrument should be irrevocable, except if the amount was not determined when the order was given;

(11) Whereas rules need to be specified concerning the issuer's liability for non-execution or for defective execution of a holder's payment instructions and for transactions which have not been authorized by him/her, subject always to the holder's own obligations in the case of lost or stolen electronic payment instruments;

(12) Whereas the Commission will monitor the implementation of this Recommendation and, if it finds the implementation unsatisfactory, it intends to propose the appropriate binding legislation covering the issues dealt with in this recommendation,

---

[2] OJ No L 95, 21. 4. 1993, p. 29.

[3] OJ No L 42, 12. 2. 1987, p. 48.

[4] OJ No L 61, 10. 3. 1990, p. 14.

Commission Recommendation on Transactions by Electronic Payment Instruments (97/489/EC)

HEREBY RECOMMENDS:

SECTION I: SCOPE AND DEFINITIONS

Article 1 - Scope

1. This Recommendation applies to the following transactions:
(a) transfers of funds, other than those ordered and executed by financial institutions, effected by means of an electronic payment instrument;
(b) cash withdrawals by means of an electronic payment instrument and the loading (and unloading) of an electronic money instrument, at devices such as cash dispensing machines and automated teller machines and at the premises of the issuer or an institution who is under contract to accept the payment instrument.
2. By way of derogation from paragraph 1, Article 4 (1), the second and third indents of Article 5 (b), Article 6, Article 7 (2) (c), (d) and the first indent of (e), Article 8 (1), (2) and (3) and Article 9 (2) do not apply to transactions effected by means of an electronic money instrument. However, where the electronic money instrument is used to load (and unload) value through remote access to the holder's account, this Recommendation is applicable in its entirety.
3. This recommendation does not apply to:
(a) payments by cheques;
(b) the guarantee function of certain cards in relation to payments by cheques.

Article 2 - Definitions

For the purpose of this recommendation, the following definitions apply:
(a) 'electronic payment instrument' means an instrument enabling its holder to effect transactions of the kind specified in Article 1 (1). This covers both remote access payment instruments and electronic money instruments;
(b) 'remote access payment instrument' means an instrument enabling a holder to access funds held on his/her account at an institution, whereby payment is allowed to be made to a payee and usually requiring a personal identification code and/or any other similar proof of identity. This includes in particular payment cards (whether credit, debit, deferred debit or charge cards) and phone- and home-banking applications;
(c) 'electronic money instrument' means a reloadable payment instrument other than a remote access payment instrument, whether a stored-value card or a computer memory, on which value units are stored electronically, enabling its holder to effect transactions of the kind specified in Article 1 (1);
(d) 'financial institution' means an institution as defined in Article 4 (1) of Council Regulation (EC) No 3604/93[5];
(e) 'issuer' means a person who, in the course of his business, makes available to another person a payment instrument pursuant to a contract concluded with him/her;
(f) 'holder' means a person who, pursuant to a contract concluded between him/her and an issuer, holds a payment instrument.

---
[5] OJ No L 332, 31. 12. 1993, p. 4.

SECTION II: TRANSPARENCY OF CONDITIONS FOR TRANSACTIONS

Article 3 - Minimum information contained in the terms and conditions governing the issuing and use of an electronic payment instrument

1. Upon signature of the contract or in any event in good time prior to delivering an electronic payment instrument, the issuer communicates to the holder the contractual terms and conditions (hereinafter referred to as 'the terms') governing the issue and use of that electronic payment instrument. The terms indicate the law applicable to the contract.
2. The terms are set out in writing, including where appropriate by electronic means, in easily understandable words and in a readily comprehensive form, and are available at least in the official language or languages of the Member State in which the electronic payment instrument is offered.
3. The terms include at least:
(a) a description of the electronic payment instrument, including where appropriate the technical requirements with respect to the holder's communication equipment authorized for use, and the way in which it can be used, including the financial limits applied, if any;
(b) a description of the holder's and issuer's respective obligations and liabilities; they include a description of the reasonable steps that the holder must take to keep safe the electronic payment instrument and the means (such as a personal identification number or other code) which enable it to be used;
(c) where applicable, the normal period within which the holder's account will be debited or credited, including the value date, or, where the holder has no account with the issuer, the normal period within which he/she will be invoiced;
(d) the types of any charges payable by the holder. In particular, this includes where applicable details of the following charges:
- the amount of any initial and annual fees,
- any commission fees and charges payable by the holder to the issuer for particular types of transactions,
- any interest rate, including the manner of its calculation, which may be applied;
(e) the period of time during which a given transaction can be contested by the holder and an indication of the redress and complaints procedures available to the holder and the method of gaining access to them.
4. If the electronic payment instrument is usable for transactions abroad (outside the country of issuing/affiliation), the following information is also communicated to the holder:
(a) an indication of the amount of any fees and charges levied for foreign currency transactions, including where appropriate the rates;
(b) the reference exchange rate used for converting foreign currency transactions, including the relevant date for determining such a rate.

Article 4 - Information subsequent to a transaction

1. The issuer supplies the holder with information relating to the transactions effected by means of an electronic payment instrument. This information, set out in writing, including where appropriate by electronic means, and in a readily comprehensible form, includes at least:
(a) a reference enabling the holder to identify the transaction, including, where appropriate, the information relating to the acceptor at/with which the transaction took place;
(b) the amount of the transaction debited to the holder in billing currency and, where applicable, the amount in foreign currency;
(c) the amount of any fees and charges applied for particular types of transactions.

The issuer also provides the holder with the exchange rate used for converting foreign currency transactions.

2. The issuer of an electronic money instrument provides the holder with the possibility of verifying the last five transactions executed with the instrument and the outstanding value stored thereon.

SECTION III: OBLIGATIONS AND LIABILITIES OF THE PARTIES TO A CONTRACT

Article 5 - Obligations of the holder

The holder:
(a) uses the electronic payment instrument in accordance with the terms governing the issuing and use of a payment instrument; in particular, the holder takes all reasonable steps to keep safe the electronic payment instrument and the means (such as a personal identification number or other code) which enable it to be used;
(b) notifies the issuer (or the entity specified by the latter) without delay after becoming aware of:
- the loss or theft of the electronic payment instrument or of the means which enable it to be used,
- the recording on his/her account of any unauthorized transaction,
- any error or other irregularity in the maintaining of that account by the issuer;
(c) does not record his personal identification number or other code in any easily recognizable form, in particular on the electronic payment instrument or on any item which he/she keeps or carries with the electronic payment instrument;
(d) does not countermand an order which he/she has given by means of his/her electronic payment instrument, except if the amount was not determined when the order was given.

Article 6 - Liabilities of the holder

1. Up to the time of notification, the holder bears the loss sustained in consequence of the loss or theft of the electronic payment instrument up to a limit, which may not exceed ECU 150, except where he/she acted with extreme negligence, in contravention of relevant provisions under Article 5 (a), (b) or (c), or fraudulently, in which case such a limit does not apply.
2. As soon as the holder has notified the issuer (or the entity specified by the latter) as required by Article 5 (b), except where he/she acted fraudulently, he/she is not thereafter liable for the loss arising in consequence of the loss or theft of his/her electronic payment instrument.
3. By derogation from paragraphs 1 and 2, the holder is not liable if the payment instrument has been used, without physical presentation or electronic identification (of the instrument itself). The use of a confidential code or any other similar proof of identity is not, by itself, sufficient to entail the holder's liability.

Article 7 - Obligations of the issuer

1. The issuer may alter the terms, provided that sufficient notice of the change is given individually to the holder to enable him/her to withdraw if he/she so chooses. A period of not less than one month is specified after which time the holder is deemed to have accepted the terms if he/she has not withdrawn.
   However, any significant change to the actual interest rate is not subject to the provisions of the first subparagraph and comes into effect upon the date specified in the publication of such a change. In this event, and without prejudice to the right of the holder to withdraw from the contract, the issuer informs the holder individually thereof as soon as possible.
2. The issuer:

(a) does not disclose the holder's personal identification number or other code, except to the holder;
(b) does not dispatch an unsolicited electronic payment instrument, except where it is a replacement for an electronic payment instrument already held by the holder;
(c) keeps for a sufficient period of time, internal records to enable the transactions referred to in Article 1 (1) to be traced and errors to be rectified;
(d) ensures that appropriate means are available to enable the holder to make the notification required under Article 5 (b). Where notification is made by telephone, the issuer (or the entity specified by the latter) provides the holder with the means of proof that he/she has made such a notification;
(e) proves, in any dispute with the holder concerning a transaction referred to in Article 1 (1), and without prejudice to any proof to the contrary that may be produced by the holder, that the transaction:
- was accurately recorded and entered into accounts,
- was not affected by technical breakdown or other deficiency.

Article 8 - Liabilities of the issuer

1. The issuer is liable, subject to Article 5, Article 6 and Article 7 (2) (a) and (e):
(a) for the non-execution or defective execution of the holder's transactions referred to in Article 1 (1), even if a transaction is initiated at devices/terminals or through equipment which are not under the issuer's direct or exclusive control, provided that the transaction is not initiated at devices/terminals or through equipment unauthorized for use by the issuer;
(b) for transactions not authorized by the holder, as well as for any error or irregularity attributable to the issuer in the maintaining of the holder's account.
2. Without prejudice to paragraph 3, the amount of the liability indicated in paragraph 1 consists of:
(a) the amount of the unexecuted or defectively executed transaction and, if any, interest thereon;
(b) the sum required to restore the holder to the position he/she was in before the unauthorized transaction took place.
3. Any further financial consequences, and, in particular, those concerning the extent of the damage for which compensation is to be paid, are borne by the issuer in accordance with the law applicable to the contract concluded between the issuer and the holder.
4. The issuer is liable to the holder of an electronic money instrument for the lost amount of value stored on the instrument and for the defective execution of the holder's transactions, where the loss or defective execution is attributable to a malfunction of the instrument, of the device/terminal or any other equipment authorized for use, provided that the malfunction was not caused by the holder knowingly or in breach of Article 3 (3) (a).

SECTION IV: NOTIFICATION, SETTLEMENT OF DISPUTES AND FINAL PROVISION

Article 9 - Notification

1. The issuer (or the entity specified by him) provides means whereby a holder may at any time of day or night notify the loss or theft of his/her electronic payment instrument.
2. The issuer (or the entity specified by him), upon receipt of notification, is under the obligation, even if the holder acted with extreme negligence or fraudulently, to take all reasonable action open to him to stop any further use of the electronic payment instrument.

Article 10 - Settlement of disputes

Member States are invited to ensure that there are adequate and effective means for the settlement of disputes between a holder and an issuer.

Article 11 - Final provision

Member States are invited to take the measures necessary to ensure that the issuers of electronic payment instruments conduct their activities in accordance with Articles 1 to 9 by not later than 31 December 1998.

DIRECTIVE 2000/12/EC OF THE EUROPEAN PARLIAMENT AND OF THE COUNCIL OF 20 MARCH 2000 RELATING TO THE TAKING UP AND PURSUIT OF THE BUSINESS OF CREDIT INSTITUTIONS

(Official Journal L 126, 26/05/2000, p. 0001 – 0059)
(Amended by Directive 2000/28/EC, OJ L 275, 27/10/2000, p. 0037 – 0038)

THE EUROPEAN PARLIAMENT AND THE COUNCIL OF THE EUROPEAN UNION,

Having regard to the Treaty establishing the European Community, and in particular the first and third sentences of Article 47(2) thereof,
Having regard to the proposal from the Commission,
Having regard to the opinion of the Economic and Social Committee[1],

Acting in accordance with the procedure laid down in Article 251 of the Treaty[2],

Whereas:

(1) Council Directive 73/183/EEC of 28 June 1973 on the abolition of restrictions on freedom of establishment and freedom to provide services in respect of self-employed activities of banks and other financial institutions[3], first Council Directive (77/780/EEC) of 12 December 1977 on the coordination of laws, regulations and administrative provisions relating to the taking up and pursuit of the business of credit institutions[4], Council Directive 89/299/EEC of 17 April 1989 on the own funds of credit institutions[5], second Council Directive 89/646/EEC of 15 December 1989 on the coordination of laws, regulations and administrative provisions relating to the taking up and pursuit of the business of credit institutions[6], Council Directive 89/647/EEC of 18 December 1989 on a solvency ratio for credit institutions[7], Council Directive 92/30/EEC of 6 April 1992 on the supervision of credit institutions on a consolidated basis[8], and Council Directive 92/121/EEC of 21 December 1992 on the monitoring and control of large exposures of credit institutions[9] have been frequently and substantially amended. For reasons of clarity and rationality, the said Directives therefore, should be codified and combined in a single text.

(2) Pursuant to the Treaty, any discriminatory treatment with regard to establishment and to the provision of services, based either on nationality or on the fact that an undertaking is not established in the Member State where the services are provided, is prohibited.

(3) In order to make it easier to take up and pursue the business of credit institutions, it is necessary to eliminate the most obstructive differences between the laws of the Member States as regards the rules to which these institutions are subject.

---

[1] OJ C 157, 25.5.1998, p. 13.
[2] Opinion of the European Parliament of 18 January 2000 (not yet published in the Official Journal) and Council Decision of 13 March 2000 (not yet published in the Official Journal).
[3] OJ L 194, 16.7.1973, p. 1.
[4] OJ L 322, 17.12.1977, p. 30. Directive as last amended by Directive 98/33/EC (OJ L 204, 21.7.1998, p. 29).
[5] OJ L 124, 5.5.1989, p. 16. Directive as last amended by Directive 92/30/EEC (OJ L 110, 28.4.1992, p. 52).
[6] OJ L 386, 30.12.1989, p. 1. Directive as last amended by Directive 95/26/EC (OJ L 168, 18.7.1995, p. 7).
[7] OJ L 386, 30.12.1989, p. 14. Directive as last amended by Directive 98/33/EC.
[8] OJ L 110, 28.4.1992, p. 52.
[9] OJ L 29, 5.2.1993, p. 1. Directive as amended by the 1994 Act of Accession.

(4) This Directive constitutes the essential instrument for the achievement of the internal market, a course determined by the Single European Act and set out in timetable form in the Commission's White Paper, from the point of view of both the freedom of establishment and the freedom to provide financial services, in the field of credit institutions.

(5) Measures to coordinate credit institutions must, both in order to protect savings and to create equal conditions of competition between these institutions, apply to all of them. Due regard must be had, where applicable, to the objective differences in their statutes and their proper aims as laid down by national laws.

(6) The scope of those measures should therefore be as broad as possible, covering all institutions whose business is to receive repayable funds from the public, whether in the form of deposits or in other forms such as the continuing issue of bonds and other comparable securities and to grant credits for their own account. Exceptions must be provided for in the case of certain credit institutions to which this Directive cannot apply. The provisions of this Directive shall not prejudice the application of national laws which provide for special supplementary authorisations permitting credit institutions to carry on specific activities or undertake specific kinds of operations.

(7) The approach which has been adopted is to achieve only the essential harmonisation necessary and sufficient to secure the mutual recognition of authorisation and of prudential supervision systems, making possible the granting of a single licence recognised throughout the Community and the application of the principle of home Member State prudential supervision. Therefore, the requirement that a programme of operations must be produced should be seen merely as a factor enabling the competent authorities to decide on the basis of more precise information using objective criteria. A measure of flexibility may none the less be possible as regards the requirements on the legal form of credit institutions of the protection of banking names.

(8) Equivalent financial requirement for credit institutions are necessary to ensure similar safeguards for savers and fair conditions of competition between comparable groups of credit institutions. Pending further coordination, appropriate structural ratios should be formulated that will make it possible within the framework of cooperation between national authorities to observe, in accordance with standard methods, the position of comparable types of credit institutions. This procedure should help to bring about the gradual approximation of the systems of coefficients established and applied by the Member States. It is necessary, however to make a distinction between coefficients intended to ensure the sound management of credit institutions and those established for the purposes of economic and monetary policy.

(9) The principles of mutual recognition and home Member State supervision require that Member States' competent authorities should not grant or should withdraw authorisation where factors such as content of the activities programmes, the geographical distribution or the activities actually carried on indicate clearly that a credit institution has opted for the legal system of one Member State for the purpose of evading the stricter standards in force in another Member State within whose territory it carries on or intends to carry on the greater part of its activities. A credit institution which is a legal person must be authorised in the Member State in which it has its registered office. A credit institution which is not a legal person must have its head office in the Member State in which it has been authorised. In addition, Member States must require that a credit institution's head office always be situated in its home Member State and that it actually operates there.

(10) The competent authorities should not authorise or continue the authorisation of a credit institution where they are liable to be prevented from effectively exercising their supervisory functions by the close links between that institution and other natural or legal persons. Credit institutions already authorised must also satisfy the competent authorities in that respect. The definition of "close links" in this Directive lays down minimum criteria. That does not prevent Member States from applying it to situations other than those envisaged by the definition. The

sole fact of having acquired a significant proportion of a company's capital does not constitute participation, within the meaning of "close links", if that holding has been acquired solely as a temporary investment which does not make it possible to exercise influence over the structure or financial policy of the institution.

(11) The reference to the supervisory authorities' effective exercise of their supervisory functions covers supervision on a consolidated basis which must be exercised over a credit institution where the provisions of Community law so provide. In such cases, the authorities applied to for authorisation must be able to identify the authorities competent to exercise supervision on a consolidated basis over that credit institution.

(12) The home Member State may also establish rules stricter than those laid down in Article 5(1), first subparagraph and (2), and Articles 7, 16, 30, 51 and 65 for institutions authorised by its competent authorities.

(13) The abolition of the authorisation requirement with respect to the branches of Community credit institutions necessitates the abolition of endowment capital.

(14) By virtue of mutual recognition, the approach chosen permits credit institutions authorised in their home Member States to carry on, throughout the Community, any or all of the activities listed in Annex I by establishing branches or by providing services. The carrying-on of activities not listed in the said Annex enjoys the right of establishment and the freedom to provide services under the general provisions of the Treaty.

(15) It is appropriate, however to extend mutual recognition to the activities listed in Annex I when they are carried on by financial institutions which are subsidiaries of credit institutions, provided that such subsidiaries are covered by the consolidated supervision of their parent undertakings and meet certain strict conditions.

(16) The host Member State may, in connection with the exercise of the right of establishment and the freedom to provide services, require compliance with specific provisions of its own national laws or regulations on the part of institutions not authorised as credit institutions in their home Member States and with regard to activities not listed in Annex I provided that, on the one hand, such provisions are compatible with Community law and are intended to protect the general good and that, on the other hand, such institutions or such activities are not subject to equivalent rules under this legislation or regulations of their home Member States.

(17) The Member States must ensure that there are no obstacles to carrying on activities receiving mutual recognition in the same manner as in the home Member State, as long as the latter do not conflict with legal provisions protecting the general good in the host Member State.

(18) There is a necessary link between the objective of this Directive and the liberalisation of capital movements being brought about by other Community legislation. In any case the measures regarding the liberalisation of banking services must be in harmony with the measures liberalising capital movements.

(19) The rules governing branches of credit institutions having their head office outside the Community should be analogous in all Member States. It is important at the present time to provide that such rules may not be more favourable than those for branches of institutions from another Member State. It should be specified that the Community may conclude agreements with third countries providing for the application of rules which accord such branches the same treatment throughout its territory, account being taken of the principle of reciprocity. The branches of credit institutions authorised in third countries do not enjoy the freedom to provide services under the second paragraph of Article 49 of the Treaty or the freedom of establishment in Member States other than those in which they are established. However, requests for the authorisation of subsidiaries or of the acquisition of holdings made by undertakings governed by the laws of third countries are subject to a procedure intended to ensure that Community credit institutions receive reciprocal treatment in the third countries in question.

(20) The authorisations granted to credit institutions by the competent national authorities pursuant to this Directive have Community-wide, and no longer merely nationwide, application. Existing reciprocity clauses have therefore no effect. A flexible procedure is therefore needed to make it possible to assess reciprocity on a Community basis. The aim of this procedure is not to close the Community's financial markets but rather, as the Community intends to keep its financial markets open to the rest of the world, to improve the liberalisation of the global financial markets in other third countries. To that end, this Directive provides for procedures for negotiating with third countries and, as a last resort, for the possibility of taking measures involving the suspension of new applications for authorisation or the restriction of new authorisations.

(21) It is desirable that agreement should be reached, on the basis of reciprocity, between the Community and third countries with a view to allowing the practical exercise of consolidated supervision over the largest possible geographical area.

(22) Responsibility for supervising the financial soundness of a credit institution, and in particular its solvency, rests with the competent authorities of its home Member State. The host Member State's competent authorities retain responsibility for the supervision of liquidity and monetary policy. The supervision of market risk must be the subject of close cooperation between the competent authorities of the home and host Member States.

(23) The smooth operation of the internal banking market requires not only legal rules but also close and regular cooperation between the competent authorities of the Member States. For the consideration of problems concerning individual credit institutions the "groupe de contact" (contact group) set up between the banking supervisory authorities remains the most appropriate forum. That group is a suitable body for the mutual exchange of information provided for in Article 28.

(24) That mutual information procedure does not in any case replace the bilateral collaboration established by Article 28. The competent host Member State authorities can, without prejudice to their powers of proper control, continue either, in an emergency, on their own initiative or following the initiative of the competent home Member State authorities, to verify that the activities of a credit institution established within their territories comply with the relevant laws and with the principles of sound administrative and accounting procedures and adequate internal control.

(25) It is appropriate to allow the exchange of information between the competent authorities and authorities or bodies which, by virtue of their function, help to strengthen the stability of the financial system. In order to preserve the confidential nature of the information forwarded, the list of addressees must remain within strict limits.

(26) Certain behaviour, such as fraud and insider offences, is liable to affect the stability, including the integrity, of the financial system, even when involving institutions other than credit institutions.

(27) It is necessary to specify the conditions under which such exchanges of information are authorised.

(28) Where it is stipulated that information may be disclosed only with the express agreement of the competent authorities, these may, where appropriate, make their agreement subject to compliance with strict conditions.

(29) Exchanges of information between, on the one hand, the competent authorities and, on the other, central banks and other bodies with a similar function in their capacity as monetary authorities and, where appropriate, other public authorities responsible for supervising payment systems should also be authorised.

(30) For the purpose of strengthening the prudential supervision of credit institutions and protection of clients of credit institutions, it should be stipulated that an auditor must have a duty to report promptly to the competent authorities, wherever, as provided for by this Directive, he becomes aware, while carrying out his tasks, of certain facts which are liable to

have a serious effect on the financial situation or the administrative and accounting organisation of a credit institution. Having regard to the aim in view, it is desirable for the Member State to provide that such a duty should apply in all circumstances where such facts are discovered by an auditor during the performance of his tasks in an undertaking which has close links with a credit institution. The duty of auditors to communicate, where appropriate, to the competent authorities certain facts and decisions concerning a credit institution which they discover during the performance of their tasks in a non-financial undertaking does not in itself change the nature of their tasks in that undertaking nor the manner in which they must perform those tasks in that undertaking.

(31) Common basic standards for the own funds of credit institutions are a key factor in the creation of an internal banking market since own funds serve to ensure the continuity of credit institutions and to protect savings. Such harmonisation strengthens the supervision of credit institutions and contributes to further coordination in the banking sector.

(32) Such standards must apply to all credit institutions authorised in the Community.

(33) The own funds of a credit institutions can serve to absorb losses which are not matched by a sufficient volume of profits. The own funds also serve as an important yardstick for the competent authorities, in particular for the assessment of the solvency of credit institutions and for other prudential purposes.

(34) Credit institutions, in an internal banking market, engage in direct competition with each other, and the definitions and standards pertaining to own funds must therefore be equivalent. To that end, the criteria for determining the composition of own funds must not be left solely to Member States. The adoption of common basic standards will be in the best interests of the Community in that it will prevent distortions of competition and will strengthen the Community banking system.

(35) The definition of own funds laid down in this Directive provides for a maximum of items and qualifying amounts, leaving it to the discretion of each Member State to use all or some of such items or to adopt lower ceilings for the qualifying amounts.

(36) This Directive specifies the qualifying criteria for certain own funds items, and the Member States remain free to apply more stringent provisions.

(37) At the initial stage common basic standards are defined in broad terms in order to encompass all the items making up own funds in the different Member States.

(38) According to the nature of the items making up own funds, this Directive distinguishes between on the one hand, items constituting original own funds and, on the other, those constituting additional own funds.

(39) To reflect the fact that items constituting additional own funds are not of the same nature as those constituting original own funds, the amount of the former included in own funds must not exceed the original own funds. Moreover, the amount of certain items of additional own funds included must not exceed one half of the original own funds.

(40) In order to avoid distortions of competition, public credit institutions must not include in their own funds guarantees granted them by the Member States or local authorities.

(41) Whenever in the course of supervision it is necessary to determine the amount of the consolidated own funds of a group of credit institutions, the calculation shall be effected in accordance with this Directive.

(42) The precise accounting technique to be used for the calculation of own funds, the solvency ratio, and for the assessment of the concentration of exposures must take account of the provisions of Council Directive 86/635/EEC of 8 December 1986 on the annual accounts and consolidated accounts of banks and other financial institutions[10], which incorporates certain

---

[10] OJ L 372, 31.12.1986, p. 1.

(43) adaptations of the provisions of Council Directive 83/349/EEC of 13 June 1983 based on Article 44(2)(g) of the Treaty on consolidated accounts[11].
(43) The provisions on own funds form part of the wider international effort to bring about approximation of the rules in force in major countries regarding the adequacy of own funds.
(44) The Commission will draw up a report and periodically examine, with the aim of tightening them, the provisions on own funds and thus achieving greater convergence on a common definition of own funds. Such convergence will allow the alignment of Community credit institutions' own funds.
(45) The provisions on solvency ratios are the outcome of work carried out by the Banking Advisory Committee which is responsible for making suggestions to the Commission with a view to coordinating the coefficients applicable in the Member States.
(46) The establishment of an appropriate solvency ratio plays a central role in the supervision of credit institutions.
(47) A ratio which weights assets and off-balance-sheet items according to the degree of credit risk is a particularly useful measure of solvency.
(48) The development of common standards for own funds in relation to assets and off-balance-sheet items exposed to credit risk is, accordingly, an essential aspect of the harmonisation necessary for the achievement of the mutual recognition of supervision techniques and thus the completion of the internal banking market.
(49) In that respect, the provisions on a solvency ratio must be considered in conjunction with other specific instruments also harmonising the fundamental techniques of the supervision of credit institutions.
(50) In an internal banking market, institutions are required to enter into direct competition with one another and the common solvency standards in the form of a minimum ratio prevent distortions of competition and strengthen the Community banking system.
(51) This Directive provides for different weightings to be given to guarantees issued by different financial institutions. The Commission accordingly undertakes to examine whether this Directive taken as a whole significantly distorts competition between credit institutions and insurance undertakings and, in the light of that examination, to consider whether any remedial measures are justified.
(52) Annex III lays down the treatment of off-balance-sheet items in the context of the calculation of credit institutions' capital requirements. With a view to the smooth functioning of the internal market and in particular with a view to ensuring a level playing field Member States are obliged to strive for uniform assessment of contractual netting agreements by their competent authorities. Annex III takes account of the work of an international forum of banking supervisors on the supervisory recognition of bilateral netting, in particular the possibility of calculating the own-funds requirements for certain transactions on the basis of a net rather than a gross amount provided that there are legally binding agreements which ensure that the credit risk is confined to the net amount. For internationally active credit institutions and groups of credit institutions in a wide range of third countries, which compete with Community credit institutions, the rules adopted on the wider international level will result in a refined supervisory treatment of over-the-counter (OTC) derivative instruments. This refinement results in a more appropriate compulsory capital cover taking into account the risk-reducing effects of supervisorily recognised contractual netting agreements on potential future credit risks. The clearing of OTC derivative instruments provided by clearing houses acting as a central counterparty plays an important role in certain Member States. It is appropriate to recognise the benefits from such a clearing in terms of a reduction of credit risk and related systemic risk in the prudential treatment of credit risk. It is necessary for the current and potential future exposures arising from cleared OTC derivatives contracts to be fully

---

[11] OJ L 193, 18.7.1983, p. 1. Directive as last amended by Directive 90/605/EEC (OJ L 317, 16.11.1990, p. 60).

collateralised and for the risk of a build-up of the clearing house's exposures beyond the market value of posted collateral to be eliminated in order for cleared OTC derivatives to be granted for a transitional period the same prudential treatment as exchange-traded derivatives. The competent authorities must be satisfied as to the level of the initial margins and variation margins required and the quality of and the level of protection provided by the posted collateral. For credit institutions incorporated in the Member States, Annex III creates a similar possibility for the recognition of bilateral netting by the competent authorities and thereby offers them equal conditions of competition. The rules are both well balanced and appropriate for the further reinforcement of the application of prudential supervisory measures to credit institutions. The competent authorities in the Member States should ensure that the calculation of add-ons is based on effective rather than apparent national amounts.

(53) The minimum ratio provided for in this Directive reinforces the capital of credit institutions in the Community. A level of 8 % has been adopted following a statistical survey of capital requirements in force at the beginning of 1988.

(54) The essential rules for monitoring large exposures of credit institutions should be harmonised. Member States should still be able to adopt provisions more stringent than those provided for by this Directive.

(55) The monitoring and control of a credit institution's exposures is an integral part of its supervision. Excessive concentration of exposures to a single client or group of connected clients may result in an unacceptable risk of loss. Such a situation may be considered prejudicial to the solvency of a credit institution.

(56) In an internal banking market, credit institutions are engaged in direct competition with one another and monitoring requirements throughout the Community should therefore be equivalent. To that end, the criteria applied to determining the concentration of exposures must be the subject of legally binding rules at Community level and cannot be left entirely to the discretion of the Member States. The adoption of common rules will therefore best serve the Community's interests, since it will prevent differences in the conditions of competition, while strengthening the Community's banking system.

(57) The provisions on a solvency ratio for credit institutions include a list of credit risks which may be incurred by credit institutions. That list should therefore be used also for the definition of exposures for the purposes of limits to large exposures. It is not, however, appropriate to refer on principle to the weightings or degrees of risk laid down in the said provisions. Those weightings and degrees of risk were devised for the purpose of establishing a general solvency requirement to cover the credit risk of credit institutions. In the context of the regulation of large exposures, the aim is to limit the maximum loss that a credit institution may incur through any single client or group of connected clients. It is therefore appropriate to adopt a prudent approach in which, as a general rule, account is taken of the nominal value of exposures, but no weightings or degrees of risk are applied.

(58) When a credit institution incurs an exposure to its own parent undertaking or to other subsidiaries of its parent undertaking, particular prudence is necessary. The management of exposures incurred by credit institutions must be carried out in a fully autonomous manner, in accordance with the principles of sound banking management, without regard to any considerations other than those principles. The provision of this Directive require that where the influence exercised by persons directly or indirectly holding a qualifying participation in a credit institution is likely to operate to the detriment of the sound and prudent management of that institution, the competent authorities shall take appropriate measures to put an end to that situation. In the field of large exposures, specific standards should also be laid down for exposures incurred by a credit institution to its own group, and in such cases more stringent restrictions are justified than for other exposures. More stringent restrictions need not, however be applied where the parent undertaking is a financial holding company or a credit institution or where the other subsidiaries are either credit or financial institutions or

undertakings offering ancillary banking services, provided that all such undertakings are covered by the supervision of the credit institution on a consolidated basis. In such cases the consolidated monitoring of the group of undertakings allows for an adequate level of supervision, and does not require the imposition of more stringent limits on exposure. Under this approach banking groups will also be encouraged to organise their structures in such a way as to allow consolidated monitoring, which is desirable because a more comprehensive level of monitoring is possible.

(59) In order to be effective, supervision on a consolidated basis must be applied to all banking groups, including those the parent undertakings of which are not credit institutions. The competent authorities must hold the necessary legal instruments to be able to exercise such supervision.

(60) In the case of groups with diversified activities the parent undertakings of which control at least one credit institution subsidiary, the competent authorities must be able to assess the financial situation of a credit institution in such a group. Pending subsequent coordination, the Member States may lay down appropriate methods of consolidation for the achievement of the objective of this Directive. The competent authorities must at least have the means of obtaining from all undertakings within a group the information necessary for the performance of their function. Cooperation between the authorities responsible for the supervision of different financial sectors must be established in the case of groups of undertakings carrying on a range of financial activities.

(61) The Member States can, furthermore, refuse or withdraw banking authorisation in the case of certain group structures considered inappropriate for carrying on banking activities, in particular because such structures could not be supervised effectively. In this respect the competent authorities have the powers mentioned in the first subparagraph of Article 7(1), Article 7(2), point (c) of Article 14(1), and Article 16 of this Directive, in order to ensure the sound and prudent management of credit institutions.

(62) The Member States can equally apply appropriate supervision techniques to groups with structures not covered by this Directive. If such structures become common, this Directive should be extended to cover them.

(63) Supervision on a consolidated basis must take in all activities defined in Annex I. All undertakings principally engaged in such activities must therefore be included in supervision on a consolidated basis. As a result, the definition of financial institutions must be widened in order to cover such activities.

(64) Directive 86/635/EEC, together with Directive 83/349/EEC, established the rules of consolidation applicable to consolidated accounts published by credit institutions. It is therefore possible to define more precisely the methods to be used in prudential supervision exercised on a consolidated basis.

(65) Supervision of credit institutions on a consolidated basis must be aimed at, in particular, protecting the interests of the depositors of the said institutions and ensuring the stability of the financial system.

(66) The examination of problems connected with matters covered by this Directive as well as by other Directive on the business of credit institutions requires cooperation between the competent authorities and the Commission within a banking advisory committee, particularly when conducted with a view to closer coordination. The Banking Advisory Committee of the competent authorities of the Member States does not rule out other forms of cooperation between authorities which supervise the taking up and pursuit of the business of credit institutions and, in particular, cooperation within the "groupe de contact" (contact group) set up between the banking supervisory authorities.

(67) Technical modifications to the detailed rules laid down in this Directive may from time to time be necessary to take account of new developments in the banking sector. The Commission shall accordingly make such modifications as are necessary, after consulting the

Banking Advisory Committee, within the limits of the implementing powers conferred on the Commission by the Treaty. The measures necessary for the implementation of this Directive should be adopted in accordance with Council Decision 1999/468/EC of 28 June 1999 laying down the procedures for the exercise of implementing powers conferred on the Commission[12].

(68) Article 36(1) of this Directive permits joint and several commitments of borrowers in the case of credit institutions organised as cooperative societies or funds to be treated as own funds items under Article 34(2)(7). The Danish Government has expressed a strong interest in having its few mortgage credit institutions organised as cooperative societies or funds converted into public limited liability companies. In order to facilitate the conversion or to make it possible, a temporary derogation allowing them to include part of their joint and several commitments as own funds is required. This temporary derogation should not adversely affect competition between credit institutions.

(69) The application of a 20 % weighting to credit institutions' holdings of mortgage bonds may unsettle a national financial market on which such instruments play a preponderant role. In this case, provisional measures are taken to apply a 10 % risk weighting. The market for securitisation is undergoing rapid development. It is therefore desirable that the Commission should examine with the Member States the prudential treatment of asset-backed securities and put forward, before 22 June 1999, proposals aimed at adapting existing legislation in order to define an appropriate prudential treatment for asset-backed securities. The competent authorities may authorise a 50 % weighting to assets secured by mortgages on offices or on multipurpose commercial premises until 31 December 2006. The property to which the mortgage relates must be subject to rigorous assessment criteria and regular revaluation to take account of the developments in the commercial property market. The property must be either occupied or let by the owner. Loans for property development are excluded from this 50 % weighting.

(70) In order to ensure harmonious application of the provisions on large exposures, Member States should be allowed to provide for the two-stage application of the new limits. For smaller credit institutions, a longer transitional period may be warranted inasmuch as too rapid an application of the 25 % rule could reduce their lending activity too abruptly.

(71) Moreover, the harmonisation of the conditions relating to the reorganisation and winding-up of credit institutions is also proceeding.

(72) The arrangements necessary for the supervision of liquidity risks will also have to be harmonised.

(73) This Directive must no affect to obligations of the Member States concerning the deadlines for transposition set out in Annex V, Part B,

HAVE ADOPTED THIS DIRECTIVE:

TITLE I: DEFINITIONS AND SCOPE

Article 1 - Definitions

For the purpose of this Directive:
1. "credit institution" shall mean an undertaking whose business is to receive deposits or other repayable funds from the public and to grant credits for its own account.
   For the purposes of applying the supervision on a consolidated basis, shall be considered as a credit institution, a credit institution according to the first paragraph and any private or

---

[12] OJ L 184, 17.7.1999, p. 23.

public undertaking which corresponds to the definition in the first paragraph and which has been authorised in a third country.

For the purposes of applying the supervision and control of large exposures, shall be considered as a credit institution, a credit institution according to the first paragraph, including branches of a credit institution in third countries and any private or public undertaking, including its branches, which corresponds to the definition in the first paragraph and which has been authorised in a third country;

2. "authorisation" shall mean an instrument issued in any form by the authorities by which the right to carry on the business of a credit institution is granted;
3. "branch" shall mean a place of business which forms a legally dependent part of a credit institution and which carries out directly all or some of the transactions inherent in the business of credit institutions; any number of places of business set up in the same Member State by a credit institution with headquarters in another Member State shall be regarded as a single branch;
4. "competent authorities" shall mean the national authorities which are empowered by law or regulation to supervise credit institutions;
5. "financial institution" shall mean an undertaking other than a credit institution, the principal activity of which is to acquire holdings or to carry on one or more of the activities listed in points 2 to 12 of Annex I;
6. "home Member State" shall mean the Member State in which a credit institution has been authorised in accordance with Articles 4 to 11;
7. "host Member State" shall mean the Member State in which a credit institution has a branch or in which it provides services;
8. "control" shall mean the relationship between a parent undertaking and a subsidiary, as defined in Article 1 of Directive 83/349/EEC, or a similar relationship between any natural or legal person and an undertaking;
9. "participation" for the purposes of supervision on a consolidated basis shall mean the ownership, direct or indirect, of 20 % or more of the voting rights or capital of an undertaking;
10. "qualifiying holding" shall mean a direct or indirect holding in an undertaking which represents 10 % or more of the capital or of the voting rights or which makes it possible to exercise a significant influence over the management of the undertaking in which a holding subsists.
11. "initial capital" shall mean capital as defined in Article 34(2)(1) and (2);
12. "parent undertaking" shall mean a parent undertaking as defined in Articles 1 and 2 of Directive 83/349/EEC.

    It shall, for the purposes of supervision on a consolidated basis and control of large exposures, mean a parent undertaking within the meaning of Article 1(1) of Directive 83/349/EEC and any undertaking which, in the opinion of the competent authorities, effectively exercises a dominant influence over another undertaking;
13. "subsidiary" shall mean a subsidiary undertaking as defined in Articles 1 and 2 of Directive 83/349/EEC.

    It shall, for the purposes of supervision on a consolidated basis and control of large exposures, mean a subsidiary undertaking within the meaning of Article 1(1) of Directive 83/349/EEC and any undertaking over which, in the opinion of the competent authorities, a parent undertaking effectively exercises a dominant influence.

    All subsidiaries of subsidiary undertakings shall also be considered subsidiaries of the undertaking that is their original parent;
14. "Zone A" shall comprise all the Member States and all other countries which are full members of the Organisation for Economic Cooperation and Development (OECD) and those countries which have concluded special lending arrangements with the International

Monetary Fund (IMF) associated with the Fund's general arrangements to borrow (GAB). Any country which reschedules its external sovereign debt is, however, precluded from Zone A for a period of five years;

15. "Zone B" shall comprise all countries not in Zone A;
16. "Zone A credit institutions" shall mean all credit institutions authorised in the Member States, in accordance with Article 4, including their branches in third countries, and all private and public undertakings covered by the definitions in point 1, first subparagraph and authorised in other Zone A countries, including their branches;
17. "Zone B credit institutions" shall mean all private and public undertakings authorised outside Zone A covered by the definition in point 1, first subparagraph, including their branches within the Community;
18. "non-bank sector" shall mean all borrowers other than credit institutions as defined in points 16 and 17, central governments and central banks, regional governments and local authorities, the European Communities, the European Investment Bank (EIB) and multilateral development banks as defined in point 19;
19. "multilateral development banks" shall mean the International Bank for Reconstruction and Development, the International Finance Corporation, the Inter-American Development Bank, the Asian Development Bank, the African Development Bank, the Council of Europe Resettlement Fund, the Nordic Investment Bank, the Caribbean Development Bank, the European Bank for Reconstruction and Development, the European Investment Fund and the Inter-American Investment Corporation;
20. "'full-risk', 'medium-risk', 'medium/low-risk' and 'low-risk' off-balance-sheet items" shall mean the items described in Article 43(2) and listed in Annex II;
21. "financial holding company" shall mean a financial institution, the subsidiary undertakings of which are either exclusively or mainly credit institutions or financial institutions, one at least of such subsidiaries being a credit institution;
22. "mixed-activity holding company" shall mean a parent undertaking, other than a financial holding company or a credit institution the subsidiaries of which include at least one credit institution;
23. "ancillary banking services undertaking" shall mean an undertaking the principal activity of which consists in owning or managing property, managing data-processing services, or any other similar activity which is ancillary to the principal activity of one or more credit institutions;
24. "exposures" for the purpose of applying Articles 48, 49 and 50 shall mean the assets and off-balance-sheet items referred to in Article 43 and in Annexes II and IV thereto, without application of the weightings or degrees of risk there provided for; the risks referred to in Annex IV must be calculated in accordance with one of the methods set out in Annex III, without application of the weightings for counterparty risk; all elements entirely covered by own funds may, with the agreement of the competent authorities, be excluded from the definition of exposures provided that such own funds are not included in the calculation of the solvency ratio or of other monitoring ratios provided for in this Directive and in other Community acts; exposures shall not include:
- in the case of foreign exchange transactions, exposures incurred in the ordinary course of settlement during the 48 hours following payment, or
- in the case of transactions for the purchase or sale of securities, exposures incurred in the ordinary course of settlement during the five working days following payment or delivery of the securities, whichever is the earlier;
25. "group of connected clients" shall mean:
- two or more natural or legal persons who, unless it is shown otherwise, constitute a single risk because one of them, directly or indirectly, has control over the other or others or

- two or more natural or legal persons between whom there is no relationship of control as defined in the first indent but who are to be regarded as constituting a single risk because they are so interconnected that, if one of them were to experience financial problems, the other or all of the others would be likely to encounter repayment difficulties;
26. "close links" shall mean a situation in which two or more natural or legal persons are linked by:
(a) participation, which shall mean the ownership, direct or by way of control, of 20 % or more of the voting rights or capital of an undertaking, or
(b) control, which shall mean the relationship between a parent undertaking and asubsidiary, in all the cases referred to in Article 1(1) and (2) of Directive 83/349/EEC, or a similar relationship between any natural or legal person and an undertaking; any subsidiary undertaking of a subsidiary undertaking shall also be considered a subsidiary of the parent undertaking which is at the head of those undertakings.

A situation in which two or more natural or legal persons are permanently linked to one and the same person by a control relationship shall also be regarded as constituting a close link between such persons.
27. "recognised exchanges" shall mean exchanges recognised by the competent authorities which:

(i) function regularly,

(ii) have rules, issued or approved by the appropriate authorities of the home country of the exchange, which define the conditions for the operation of the exchange, the conditions of access to the exchange as well as the conditions that must be satisfied by a contract before it can effectively be dealt on the exchange,

(iii) have a clearing mechanism that provides for contracts listed in Annex IV to be subject to daily margin requirements providing an appropriate protection in the opinion of the competent authorities.

Article 2 - Scope

1. This Directive concerns the taking up and pursuit of the business of credit institutions. This Directive shall apply to all credit institutions.
2. Articles 25 and 52 to 56 shall also apply to financial holding companies and mixed-activity holding companies which have their head offices in the Community.

The institutions permanently excluded by paragraph 3, with the exception, however, of the Member States' central banks, shall be treated as financial institutions for the purposes of Articles 25 and 52 to 56.
3. This Directive shall not apply to:
- the central banks of Member States,
- post office giro institutions,
- in Belgium, the "Institut de Réescompte et de Garantie/Herdiscontering- en Waarborginstituut",
- in Denmark, the "Dansk Eksportfinansieringsfond", the "Danmarks Skibskreditfond", and "Dansk Landbrugs Realkreditfond",
- in Germany, the "Kreditanstalt für Wiederaufbau", undertakings which are recognised under the "Wohnungsgemeinnützigkeitsgesetz" as bodies of State housing policy and are not mainly engaged in banking transactions, and undertakings recognised under that law as non-profit housing undertakings,
- in Greece, the Elliniki Trapeza Viomichanikis Anaptyxeos, the Tamio Parakatathikon kai Danion, and the Tachidromiko Tamieftirio,
- in Spain, the "Instituto de Crédito Oficial",
- in France, the "Caisse des dépôts et consignations",
- in Ireland, credit unions and the friendly societies,

- in Italy, the "Cassa depositi e prestiti",
- in the Netherlands, the "Netherlandse Investeringsbank voor Ontwikkelingslanden NV", the "NV Noordelijke Ontwikkelingsmaatschappij", the "NV Industriebank Limburgs Instituut voor Ontwikkeling en Financiering" and the "Overijsselse Ontwikkelingsmaatschappij NV",
- in Austria, undertakings recognised as housing associations in the public interest and the "Österreichische Kontrollbank AG",
- in Portugal, "Caixas Económicas" existing on 1 January 1986 with the exception of those incorporated as limited companies and of the "Caixa Económica Montepio Geral",
- in Finland, the "Teollisen yhteistyön rahasto Oy/Fonden för industriellt samarbete AB", and the "Kera Oy/Kera Ab",
- in Sweden, the "Svenska Skeppshypotekskassan",
- in the United Kingdom, the National Savings Bank, the Commonwealth Development Finance Company Ltd, the Agricultural Mortgage Corporation Ltd, the Scottish Agricultural Securities Corporation Ltd, the Crown Agents for overseas governments and administrations, credit unions and municipal banks.

4. The Council, acting on a proposal from the Commission, which, for this purpose, shall consult the Committee referred to in Article 57 (hereinafter referred to as the "Banking Advisory Committee") shall decide on any amendments to the list in paragraph 3.

5. Credit institutions situated in the same Member State and permanently affiliated, on 15 December 1977, to a central body which supervises them and which is established in that same Member State, may be exempted from the requirements of Articles 6(1), 8 and 59 if, no later than 15 December 1979, national law provides that:

- the commitments of the central body and affiliated institutions are joint and several liabilities or the commitments of its affiliated institutions are entirely guaranteed by the central body,
- the solvency and liquidity of the central body and of all the affiliated institutions are monitored as a whole on the basis of consolidated accounts,
- the management of the central body is empowered to issue instructions to the management of the affiliated institutions.

Credit institutions operating locally which are affiliated, subsequent to 15 December 1977, to a central body within the meaning of the first subparagraph, may benefit from the conditions laid down therein if they constitute normal additions to the network belonging to that central body.

In the case of credit institutions other than those which are set up in areas newly reclaimed from the sea or have resulted from scission or mergers of existing institutions dependent or answerable to the central body, the Council, acting on a proposal from the Commission, which shall for this purpose, consult the Banking Advisory Committee, may lay down additional rules for the application of the second subparagraph including the repeal of exemptions provided for in the first subparagraph, where it is of the opinion that the affiliation of new institutions benefiting from the arrangements laid down in the second subparagraph might have an adverse effect on competition. The Council shall decide by a qualified majority.

6. A credit institution which, as defined in the first subparagraph of paragraph 5, is affiliated to a central body in the same Member State may also be exempted from the provisions of Article 5, and also Articles 40 to 51, and 65 provided that, without prejudice to the application of those provisions to the central body, the whole as constituted by the central body together with its affiliated institutions is subject to the abovementioned provisions a consolidated basis.

In case of exemption, Articles 13, 18, 19, 20(1) to (6), 21 and 22 shall apply to the whole as constituted by the central body together with its affiliated institutions.

Banking Directive (2000/12/EC)

Article 3 - Prohibition for undertakings other than credit institutions from carrying on the business of taking deposits or other repayable funds from the public

The Member States shall prohibit persons or undertakings that are not credit institutions from carrying on the business of taking deposits or other repayable funds from the public. This prohibition shall not apply to the taking of deposits or other funds repayable by a Member State or by a Member State's regional or local authorities or by public international bodies of which one or more Member States are members or to cases expressly covered by national or Community legislation, provided that those activities are subject to regulations and controls intended to protect depositors and investors and applicable to those cases.

TITLE II: REQUIREMENTS FOR ACCESS TO THE TAKING UP AND PURSUIT OF THE BUSINESS OF CREDIT INSTITUTIONS

Article 4 - Authorisation

Member States shall require credit institutions to obtain authorisation before commencing their activities. They shall lay down the requirements for such authorisation subject to Articles 5 to 9, and notify them to both the Commission and the Banking Advisory Committee.

Article 5 - Initial capital

1. Without prejudice to other general conditions laid down by national law, the competent authorities shall not grant authorisation when the credit institution does not possess separate own funds or in cases where initial capital is less than EUR 5 million.
   Member States may decide that credit institutions which do not fulfil the requirement of separate own funds and which were in existence on 15 December 1979 may continue to carry on their business. They may exempt such credit institutions from complying with the requirement contained in the first subparagraph of Article 6(1).
2. The Member States shall, however, have the option of granting authorisation to particular categories of credit institutions the initial capital of which is less than that prescribed in paragraph 1. In such cases:
(a) the initial capital shall not be less than EUR 1 million,
(b) the Member States concerned must notify the Commission of their reasons for making use of the option provided for in this paragraph,
(c) when the list referred to in Article 11 is published, the name of each credit institution that does not have the minimum capital prescribed in paragraph 1 shall be annotated to that effect.
3. A credit institution's own funds may not fall below the amount of initial capital required by paragraphs 1 and 2 at the time of its authorisation.
4. The Member States may decide that credit institutions already in existence on 1 January 1993, the own funds of which do not attain the levels prescribed for initial capital in paragraphs 1 and 2, may continue to carry on their activities. In that event, their own funds may not fall below the highest level reached with effect from 22 December 1989.
5. If control of a credit institution falling within the category referred to in paragraph 4 is taken by a natural or legal person other than the person who controlled the institution previously, the own funds of that institution must attain at least the level prescribed for initial capital in paragraphs 1 and 2.
6. In certain specific circumstances and with the consent of the competent authorities, where there is a merger of two or more credit institutions falling within the category referred to in paragraph 4, the own funds of the institution resulting from the merger may not fall below

the total own funds of the merged institutions at the time of the merger, as long as the appropriate levels pursuant to paragraphs 1 and 2 have not been attained.
7. If, in the cases referred to in paragraphs 3, 4 and 6, the own funds should be reduced, the competent authorities may, where the circumstances justify it, allow an institution a limited period in which to rectify its situation or cease its activities.

Article 6 - Management body and place of the head office of credit institutions

1. The competent authorities shall grant an authorisation to the credit institution only when there are at least two persons who effectively direct the business of the credit institution. Moreover, the authorities concerned shall not grant authorisation if these persons are not of sufficiently good repute or lack sufficient experience to perform such duties.
2. Each Member State shall require that:
- any credit institution which is a legal person and which, under its national law, has a registered office have its head office in the same Member State as its registered office,
- any other credit institution have its head office in the Member State which issued its authorisation and in which it actually carries on its business.

Article 7 - Shareholders and members

1. The competent authorities shall not grant authorisation for the taking-up of the business of credit institutions before they have been informed of the identities of the shareholders or members, whether direct or indirect, natural or legal persons, that have qualifying holdings, and of the amounts of those holdings.
For the purpose of the definition of qualifying holding in the context of this Article, the voting rights referred to in Article 7 of Council Directive 88/627/EEC[13] shall be taken into consideration.
2. The competent authorities shall refuse authorisation if, taking into account the need to ensure the sound and prudent management of a credit institution, they are not satisfied as to the suitability of the abovementioned shareholders or members.
3. Where close links exist between the credit institution and other natural or legal persons, the competent authorities shall grant authorisation only if those links do not prevent the effective exercise of their supervisory functions.
The competent authorities shall also refuse authorisation if the laws, regulations or administrative provisions of a non-member country governing one or more natural or legal persons with which the credit institution has close links, or difficulties involved in their enforcement, prevent the effective exercise of their supervisory functions.
The competent authorities shall require credit institutions to provide them with the information they require to monitor compliance with the conditions referred to in this paragraph on a continuous basis.

Article 8 - Programme of operations and structural organisation

Member States shall require applications for authorisation to be accompanied by a programme of operations setting out, inter alia, the types of business envisaged and the structural organisation of the institution.

Article 9 - Economic needs

Member States may not require the application for authorisation to be examined in terms of the economic needs of the market.

---

[13] Council Directive 88/627/EEC of 12 December 1988 on the information to be published when a major holding in a listed company is acquired or disposed of (OJ L 348, 17.12.1988, p. 62).

Article 10 - Authorisation refusal

Reasons shall be given whenever an authorisation is refused and the applicant shall be notified thereof within six months of receipt of the application or, should the latter be incomplete, within six months of the applicant's sending the information required for the decision. A decision shall, in any case, be taken within 12 months of the receipt of the application.

Article 11 - Notification of the authorisation to the Commission

Every authorisation shall be notified to the Commission. Each credit institution shall be entered in a list which the Commission shall publish in the Official Journal of the European Communities and shall keep up to date.

Article 12 - Prior consultation with the competent authorities of other Member States

There must be prior consultation with the competent authorities of the other Member State involved on the authorisation of a credit institution which is:
- a subsidiary of a credit institution authorised in another Member State, or
- a subsidiary of the parent undertaking of a credit institution authorised in another Member State, or
- controlled by the same persons, whether natural or legal, as control a credit institution authorised in another Member State.

Article 13 - Branches of credit institutions authorised in another Member State

Host Member States may not require authorisation or endowment capital for branches of credit institutions authorised in other Member States. The establishment and supervision of such branches shall be effected as prescribed in Articles 17, 20(l) to (6) and Articles 22 and 26.

Article 14 - Withdrawal of authorisation

1. The competent authorities may withdraw the authorisation issued to a credit institution only where such an institution:
(a) does not make use of the authorisation within 12 months, expressly renounces the authorisation or has ceased to engage in business for more than six months, if the Member State concerned has made no provision for the authorisation to lapse in such cases;
(b) has obtained the authorisation through false statements or any other irregular means;
(c) no longer fulfils the conditions under which authorisation was granted;
(d) no longer possesses sufficient own funds or can no longer be relied on to fulfil its obligations towards its creditors, and in particular no longer provides security for the assets entrusted to it;
(e) falls within one of the other cases where national law provides for withdrawal of authorisation.
2. Reasons must be given for any withdrawal of authorisation and those concerned informed thereof; such withdrawal shall be notified to the Commission.

Article 15 - Name

For the purpose of exercising their activities, credit institutions may, notwithstanding any provisions concerning the use of the words "bank", "savings bank" or other banking names which may exist in the host Member State, use throughout the territory of the Community the same name as they use in the Member State in which their head office is situated. In the event of there being any danger of confusion, the host Member State may, for the purposes of clarification, require that the name be accompanied by certain explanatory particulars.

Article 16 - Qualifiying holding in a credit institution

1. The Member States shall require any natural or legal person who proposes to hold, directly or indirectly a qualifying holding in a credit institution first to inform the competent authorities, telling them of the size of the intended holding. Such a person must likewise inform the competent authorities if he proposes to increase his qualifying holding so that the proportion of the voting rights or of the capital held by him would reach or exceed 20 %, 33 % or 50 % or so that the credit institution would become his subsidiary.

   Without prejudice to the provisions of paragraph 2, the competent authorities shall have a maximum of three months from the date of the notification provided for in the first subparagraph to oppose such a plan if, in view of the need to ensure sound and prudent management of the credit institution, they are not satisfied as to the suitability of the person referred to in the first subparagraph. If they do not oppose the plan referred to in the first subparagraph, they may fix a maximum period for its implementation.

2. If the acquirer of the holdings referred to in paragraph 1 is a credit institution authorised in another Member State or the parent undertaking of a credit institution authorised in another Member State or a natural or legal person controlling a credit institution authorised in another Member State and if, as a result of that acquisition, the institution, in which the acquirer proposes to hold a holding would become a subsidiary or subject to the control of the acquirer, the assessment of the acquisition must be the subject of the prior consultation referred to in Article 12.

3. The Member States shall require any natural or legal person who proposes to dispose, directly or indirectly, of a qualifying holding in a credit institution first to inform the competent authorities, telling them of the size of his intended holding. Such a person must likewise inform the competent authorities if he proposes to reduce his qualifying holding so that the proportion of the voting rights or of the capital held by him would fall below 20 %, 33 % or 50 % or so that the credit institution would cease to be his subsidiary.

4. On becoming aware of them, credit institutions shall inform the competent authorities of any acquisitions or disposals of holdings in their capital that cause holdings to exceed or fall below one of the thresholds referred to in paragraphs 1 and 3.

   They shall also, at least once a year, inform them of the names of shareholders and members possessing qualifying holdings and the sizes of such holdings as shown, for example, by the information received at the annual general meetings of shareholders and members or as a result of compliance with the regulations relating to companies listed on stock exchanges.

5. The Member States shall require that, where the influence exercised by the persons referred to in paragraph 1 is likely to operate to the detriment of the prudent and sound management of the institution, the competent authorities shall take appropriate measures to put an end to that situation. Such measures may consist for example in injunctions, sanctions against directors and managers, or the suspension of the exercise of the voting rights attaching to the shares held by the shareholders or members in question.

   Similar measures shall apply to natural or legal persons failing to comply with the obligation to provide prior information, as laid down in paragraph 1. If a holding is acquired despite the opposition of the competent authorities, the Member States shall, regardless of any other sanctions to be adopted, provide either for exercise of the corresponding voting rights to be suspended, or for the nullity of votes cast or for the possibility of their annulment.

6. For the purposes of the definition of qualifying holding and other levels of holding set out in this Article, the voting rights referred to in Article 7 of Directive 88/627/EEC shall be taken into consideration.

Article 17 - Procedures and internal control mechanisms

Home Member State competent authorities shall require that every credit institution have sound administrative and accounting procedures and adequate internal control mechanisms.

TITLE III: PROVISIONS CONCERNING THE FREEDOM OF ESTABLISHMENT AND THE FREEDOM TO PROVIDE SERVICES

Article 18 - Credit institutions

The Member States shall provide that the activities listed in Annex I may be carried on within their territories, in accordance with Articles 20(1) to (6), 21(1) and (2), and 22, either by the establishment of a branch or by way of the provision of services, by any credit institution authorised and supervised by the competent authorities of another Member State, provided that such activities are covered by the authorisation.

Article 19 - Financial institutions

The Member States shall also provide that the activities listed in Annex I may be carried on within their territories, in accordance with Articles 20(1) to (6), 21(1) and (2), and 22, either by the establishment of a branch or by way of the provision of services, by any financial institution from another Member State, whether a subsidiary of a credit institution or the jointly-owned subsidiary of two or more credit institutions, the memorandum and articles of association of which permit the carrying on of those activities and which fulfils each of the following conditions:
- the parent undertaking or undertakings must be authorised as credit institutions in the Member State by the law of which the subsidiary is governed,
- the activities in question must actually be carried on within the territory of the same Member State,
- the parent undertaking or undertakings must hold 90 % or more of the voting rights attaching to shares in the capital of the subsidiary,
- the parent undertaking or undertakings must satisfy the competent authorities regarding the prudent management of the subsidiary and must have declared, with the consent of the relevant home Member State competent authorities, that they jointly and severally guarantee the commitments entered into by the subsidiary,
- the subsidiary must be effectively included, for the activities in question in particular, in the consolidated supervision of the parent undertaking, or of each of the parent undertakings, in accordance with Articles 52 to 56, in particular for the calculation of the solvency ratio, for the control of large exposures and for purposes of the limitation of holdings provided for in Article 51.

Compliance with these conditions must be verified by the competent authorities of the home Member State and the latter must supply the subsidiary with a certificate of compliance which must form part of the notification referred to in Articles 20(1) to (6), and 21(1) and (2).

The competent authorities of the home Member State shall ensure the supervision of the subsidiary in accordance with Articles 5(3), 16, 17, 26, 28, 29, 30, and 32.

The provisions mentioned in this Article shall apply mutatis mutandis to subsidiaries, subject to the necessary modifications. In particular, the words "credit institution" should be read as "financial institution fulfilling the conditions laid down in Article 19" and the word "authorisation" as "memorandum and articles of association".

The second subparagraph of Article 20(3) shall read:"The home Member State competent authorities shall also communicate the amount of own funds of the subsidiary financial institution and the consolidated solvency ratio of the credit institution which is its parent undertaking".

If a financial institution eligible under this Article should cease to fulfil any of the conditions imposed, the home Member State shall notify the competent authorities of the host Member State and the activities carried on by that institution in the host Member State become subject to the legislation of the host Member State.

Article 20 - Exercise of the right of establishment

1. A credit institution wishing to establish a branch within the territory of another Member State shall notify the competent authorities of its Member State.
2. The Member State shall require every credit institution wishing to establish a branch in another Member State to provide the following information when effecting the notification referred to in paragraph 1:
(a) the Member State within the territory of which it plans to establish a branch;
(b) a programme of operations setting out, inter alia, the types of business envisaged and the structural organisation of the branch;
(c) the address in the host Member State from which documents may be obtained;
(d) the names of those responsible for the management of the branch.
3. Unless the competent authorities of the home Member State have reason to doubt the adequacy of the administrative structure or the financial situation of the credit institution, taking into account the activities envisaged, they shall within three months of receipt of the information referred to in paragraph 2 communicate that information to the competent authorities of the host Member State and shall inform the institution accordingly.

   The home Member State competent authorities shall also communicate the amount of own funds and the solvency ratio of the credit institution.

   Where the competent authorities of the home Member State refuse to communicate the information referred to in paragraph 2 to the competent authorities of the host Member State, they shall give reasons for their refusal to the institution concerned within three months of receipt of all the information. That refusal or failure to reply shall be subject to a right to apply to the courts in the home Member State.
4. Before the branch of a credit institution commences its activities the competent authorities of the host Member State shall, within two months of receiving the information mentioned in paragraph 3, prepare for the supervision of the credit institution in accordance with Article 22 and if necessary indicate the conditions under which, in the interest of the general good, those activities must be carried on in the host Member State.
5. On receipt of a communication from the competent authorities of the host Member State, or in the event of the expiry of the period provided for in paragraph 4 without receipt of any communication from the latter, the branch may be established and commence its activities.
6. In the event of a change in any of the particulars communicated pursuant to paragraph 2(b), (c) or (d), a credit institution shall give written notice of the change in question to the competent authorities of the home and host Member States at least one month before making the change so as to enable the competent authorities of the home Member State to take a decision pursuant to paragraph 3 and the competent authorities of the host Member State to take a decision on the change pursuant to paragraph 4.
7. Branches which have commenced their activities, in accordance with the provisions in force in their host Member States, before 1 January 1993, shall be presumed to have been subject to the procedure laid down in paragraphs 1 to 5. They shall be governed, from the abovementioned date, by paragraph 6, and by Articles 18, 19, 22 and 29.

Article 21 - Exercise of the freedom to provide services

1. Any credit institution wishing to exercise the freedom to provide services by carrying on its activities within the territory of another Member State for the first time shall notify the competent authorities of the home Member State, of the activities on the list in Annex I which it intends to carry on.
2. The competent authorities of the home Member State shall, within one month of receipt of the notification mentioned in paragraph 1, send that notification to the competent authorities of the host Member State.

3. This Article shall not affect rights acquired by credit institutions providing services before 1 January 1993.

Article 22 - Power of the competent authorities of the host Member State

1. Host Member States may, for statistical purposes, require that all credit institutions having branches within their territories shall report periodically on their activities in those host Member States to the competent authorities of those host Member States.

   In discharging the responsibilities imposed on them in Article 27, host Member States may require that branches of credit institutions from other Member States provide the same information as they require from national credit institutions for that purpose.

2. Where the competent authorities of a host Member State ascertain than an institution having a branch or providing services within its territory is not complying with the legal provisions adopted in that State pursuant to the provisions of this Directive involving powers of the host Member State's competent authorities, those authorities shall require the institution concerned to put an end to that irregular situation.

3. If the institution concerned fails to take the necessary steps, the competent authorities of the host Member State shall inform the competent authorities of the home Member State accordingly. The competent authorities of the home Member State shall, at the earliest opportunity, take all appropriate measures to ensure that the institution concerned puts an end to that irregular situation. The nature of those measures shall be communicated to the competent authorities of the host Member State.

4. If, despite the measures taken by the home Member State or because such measures prove inadequate or are not available in the Member State in question, the institution persists in violating the legal rules referred to in paragraph 2 in force in the host Member State, the latter State may, after informing the competent authorities of the home Member State, take appropriate measures to prevent or to punish further irregularities and, in so far as is necessary, to prevent that institution from initiating further transactions within its territory. The Member States shall ensure that within their territories it is possible to serve the legal documents necessary for these measures on credit institutions.

5. The provisions of paragraph 1 to 4 shall not affect the power of host Member States to take appropriate measures to prevent or to punish irregularities committed within their territories which are contrary to the legal rules they have adopted in the interest of the general good. This shall include the possibility of preventing offending institutions from initiating any further transactions within their territories.

6. Any measure adopted pursuant to paragraph 3, 4 and 5 involving penalties or restrictions on the exercise of the freedom to provide services must be properly justified and communicated to the institution concerned. Every such measure shall be subject to a right of appeal to the courts in the Member State the authorities of which adopted it.

7. Before following the procedure provided for in paragraph 2, 3 and 4, the competent authorities of the host Member State may, in emergencies, take any precautionary measures necessary to protect the interests of depositors, investors and others to whom services are provided. The Commission and the competent authorities of the other Member States concerned must be informed of such measures at the earliest opportunity.

   The Commission may, after consulting the competent authorities of the Member States concerned, decide that the Member State in question must amend or abolish those measures.

8. Host Member States may exercise the powers conferred on them under this Directive by taking appropriate measures to prevent or to punish irregularities committed within their territories. This shall include the possibility of preventing institutions from initiating further transactions within their territories.

9. In the event of the withdrawal of authorisation the competent authorities of the host Member State shall be informed and shall take appropriate measures to prevent the institution

concerned from initiating further transactions within its territory and to safeguard the interests of depositors. Every two years the Commission shall submit a report on such cases to the Banking Advisory Committee.
10. The Member States shall inform the Commission of the number and type of cases in which there has been a refusal pursuant to Article 20(1) to (6) or in which measures have been taken in accordance with paragraph 4 of this Article. Every two years the Commission shall submit a report on such cases to the Banking Advisory Committee.
11. Nothing in this Article shall prevent credit institutions with head offices in other Member States from advertising their services through all available means of communication in the host Member State, subject to any rules governing the form and the content of such advertising adopted in the interest of the general good.

TITLE IV: RELATIONS WITH THIRD COUNTRIES

Article 23 - Notification of the subsidiaries of third countries' undertakings and conditions of access to the markets of these countries

1. The competent authorities of the Member States shall inform the Commission:
(a) of any authorisation of a direct or indirect subsidiary one or more parent undertakings of which are governed by the laws of a third country. The Commission shall inform the Banking Advisory Committee accordingly;
(b) whenever such a parent undertaking acquires a holding in a Community credit institution such that the latter would become its subsidiary. The Commission shall inform the Banking Advisory Committee accordingly.
When authorisation is granted to the direct or indirect subsidiary of one or more parent undertakings governed by the law of third countries, the structure of the group shall be specified in the notification which the competent authorities shall address to the Commission in accordance with Article 11.
2. The Member States shall inform the Commission of any general difficulties encountered by their credit institutions in establishing themselves or carrying on banking activities in a third country.
3. The Commission shall periodically draw up a report examining the treatment accorded to Community credit institutions in third countries, in the terms referred to in paragraphs 4 and 5, as regards establishment and the carrying-on of banking activities, and the acquisition of holdings in third-country credit institutions. The Commission shall submit those reports to the Council, together with any appropriate proposals.
4. Whenever it appears to the Commission, either on the basis of the reports referred to in paragraph 3 or on the basis of other information, that a third country is not granting Community credit institutions effective market access comparable to that granted by the Community to credit institutions from that third country, the Commission may submit proposals to the Council for the appropriate mandate for negotiation with a view to obtaining comparable competitive opportunities for Community credit institutions. The Council shall decide by a qualified majority.
5. Whenever it appears to the Commission, either on the basis of the reports referred to in paragraph 3 or on the basis of other information that Community credit institutions in a third country do not receive national treatment offering the same competitive opportunities as are available to domestic credit institutions and the conditions of effective market access are not fulfilled, the Commission may initiate negotiations in order to remedy the situation.
In the circumstances described in the first subparagraph, it may also be decided at any time, and in addition to initiating negotiations, in accordance with the procedure laid down in Article 60(2), that the competent authorities of the Member States must limit or suspend

their decisions regarding requests pending at the moment of the decision or future requests for authorisations and the acquisition of holdings by direct or indirect parent undertakings governed by the laws of the third country in question. The duration of the measures referred to may not exceed three months.

Before the end of that three-month period, and in the light of the results of the negotiations, the Council may, acting on a proposal from the Commission, decide by a qualified majority whether the measures shall be continued.

Such limitations or suspension may not apply to the setting up of subsidiaries by credit institutions or their subsidiaries duly authorised in the Community, or to the acquisition of holdings in Community credit institutions by such institutions or subsidiaries.

6. Whenever it appears to the Commission that one of the situations described in paragraphs 4 and 5 obtains, the Member States shall inform it at its request:
(a) of any request for the authorisation of a direct or indirect subsidiary one or more parent undertakings of which are governed by the laws of the third country in question;
(b) whenever they are informed in accordance with Article 16 that such an undertaking proposes to acquire a holding in a Community credit institution such that the latter would become its subsidiary.

This obligation to provide information shall lapse whenever an agreement is reached with the third country referred to in paragraph 4 or 5 or when the measures referred to in the second and third subparagraphs of paragraph 5 cease to apply.

7. Measures taken pursuant to this Article comply with the Community's obligations under any international agreements, bilateral or multilateral, governing the taking-up and pursuit of the business of credit institutions.

Article 24 - Branches of credit institutions having their head offices outside the Community

1. Member States shall not apply to branches of credit institutions having their head office outside the Community, when commencing or carrying on their business, provisions which result in more favourable treatment than that accorded to branches of credit institutions having their head office in the Community.
2. The competent authorities shall notify the Commission and the Banking Advisory Committee of all authorisations for branches granted to credit institutions having their head office outside the Community.
3. Without prejudice to paragraph 1, the Community may, through agreements concluded in accordance with the Treaty with one or more third countries, agree to apply provisions which, on the basis of the principle of reciprocity, accord to branches of a credit institution having its head office outside the Community identical treatment throughout the territory of the Community.

Article 25 - Cooperation with third countries' competent authorities regarding supervision on a consolidated basis

1. The Commission may submit proposals to the Council, either at the request of a Member State or on its own initiative, for the negotiation of agreements with one or more third countries regarding the means of exercising supervision on a consolidated basis over:
- credit institutions the parent undertakings of which have their head offices situated in a third country, and
- credit institutions situated in third countries the parent undertakings of which, whether credit institutions or financial holding companies, have their head offices in the Community.
2. The agreements referred to in paragraph 1 shall in particular seek to ensure both:
- that the competent authorities of the Member States are able to obtain the information necessary for the supervision, on the basis of their consolidated financial situations, of credit institutions or financial holding companies situated in the Community and which have as

subsidiaries credit institutions or financial institutions situated outside the Community, or holding participation in such institutions,
- that the competent authorities of third countries are able to obtain the information necessary for the supervision of parent undertakings the head offices of which are situated within their territories and which have as subsidiaries credit institutions or financial institutions situated in one or more Member States or holding participation in such institutions.
3. The Commission and the Banking Advisory Committee shall examine the outcome of the negotiations referred to in paragraph 1 and the resulting situation.

TITLE V: PRINCIPLES AND TECHNICAL INSTRUMENTS FOR PRUDENTIAL SUPERVISION

CHAPTER 1: PRINCIPLES OF PRUDENTIAL SUPERVISION

Article 26 - Competence of control of the home Member State

1. The prudential supervision of a credit institution, including that of the activities it carries on accordance with Articles 18 and 19, shall be the responsibility of the competent authorities of the home Member State, without prejudice to those provisions of this Directive which give responsibility to the authorities of the host Member State.
2. Paragraph 1 shall not prevent supervision on a consolidated basis pursuant to this Directive.

Article 27 - Competence of the host Member State

Host Member States shall retain responsibility in cooperation with the competent authorities of the home Member State for the supervision of the liquidity of the branches of credit institutions pending further coordination. Without prejudice to the measures necessary for the reinforcement of the European Monetary System, host Member States shall retain complete responsibility for the measures resulting from the implementation of their monetary policies. Such measures may not provide for discriminatory or restrictive treatment based on the fact that a credit institution is authorised in another Member State.

Article 28 - Collaboration concerning supervision

The competent authorities of the Member States concerned shall collaborate closely in order to supervise the activities of credit institutions operating, in particular by having established branches there, in one or more Member States other than that in which their head offices are situated. They shall supply one another with all information concerning the management and ownership of such credit institutions that is likely to facilitate their supervision and the examination of the conditions for their authorisation, and all information likely to facilitate the monitoring of such institutions, in particular with regard to liquidity, solvency, deposit guarantees, the limiting of large exposures, administrative and accounting procedures and internal control mechanisms.

Article 29 - On-the-spot verification of branches established in another Member State

1. Host Member States shall provide that, where a credit institution authorised in another Member State carries on its activities through a branch, the competent authorities of the home Member State may, after having first informed the competent authorities of the host Member State, carry out themselves or through the intermediary of persons they appoint for that purpose on-the-spot verification of the information referred to in Article 28.
2. The competent authorities of the home Member State may also, for purposes of the verification of branches, have recourse to one of the other procedures laid down in Article 56(7).

3. This Article shall not affect the right of the competent authorities of the host Member State to carry out, in the discharge of their responsibilities under this Directive, on-the-spot verifications of branches established within their territory.

Article 30 - Exchange of information and professional secrecy

1. The Member States shall provide that all persons working or who have worked for the competent authorities, as well as auditors or experts acting on behalf of the competent authorities, shall be bound by the obligation of professional secrecy. This means that no confidential information which they may receive in the course of their duties may be divulged to any person or authority whatsoever, except in summary or collective form, such that individual institutions cannot be identified, without prejudice to cases covered by criminal law.
Nevertheless, where a credit institution has been declared bankrupt or is being compulsorily wound up, confidential information which does not concern third parties involved in attempts to rescue that credit institution may be divulged in civil or commercial proceedings.
2. Paragraph 1 shall not prevent the competent authorities of the various Member States from exchanging information in accordance with this Directive and with other Directives applicable to credit institutions. That information shall be subject to the conditions of professional secrecy indicated in paragraph 1.
3. Member States may conclude cooperation agreements, providing for exchanges of information, with the competent authorities of third countries or with authorities or bodies of third countries as defined in paragraphs 5 and 6 only if the information disclosed is subject to guarantees of professional secrecy at least equivalent to those referred to in this Article. Such exchange of information must be for the purpose of performing the supervisory task of the authorities or bodies mentioned.
Where the information originates in another Member State, it may not be disclosed without the express agreement of the competent authorities which have disclosed it and, where appropriate, solely for the purposes for which those authorities gave their agreement.
4. Competent authorities receiving confidential information under paragraphs 1 or 2 may use it only in the course of their duties:
- to check that the conditions governing the taking-up of the business of credit institutions are met and to facilitate monitoring, on a non-consolidated or consolidated basis, of the conduct of such business, especially with regard to the monitoring of liquidity, solvency, large exposures, and administrative and accounting procedures and internal control mechanisms, or
- to impose sanctions, or
- in an administrative appeal against a decision of the competent authority, or
- in court proceedings initiated pursuant to Article 33 or to special provisions provided for in this in other Directives adopted in the field of credit institutions.
5. Paragraphs 1 and 4 shall not preclude the exchange of information within a Member State, where there are two or more competent authorities in the same Member State, or between Member States, between competent authorities and:
- authorities entrusted with the public duty of supervising other financial organisations and insurance companies and the authorities responsible for the supervision of financial markets,
- bodies involved in the liquidation and bankruptcy of credit institutions and in other similar procedures,
- persons responsible for carrying out statutory audits of the accounts of credit institutions and other financial institutions,
in the discharge of their supervisory functions, and the disclosure to bodies which administer deposit-guarantee schemes of information necessary to the exercise of their functions. The

Banking Directive (2000/12/EC)

information received shall be subject to the conditions of professional secrecy indicated in paragraph 1.

6. Notwithstanding paragraphs 1 to 4, Member States may authorise exchanges of information between, the competent authorities and:
- the authorities responsible for overseeing the bodies, involved in the liquidation and bankruptcy of credit institutions and other similar procedures, or
- the authorities responsible for overseeing persons charged with carrying out statutory audits of the accounts of insurance undertakings, credit institutions, investment firms and other financial institutions.

Member States which have recourse to the provisions of the first subparagraph shall require at least that the following conditions are met:
- the information shall be for the purpose of performing the supervisory task referred to in the first subparagraph,
- information received in this context shall be subject to the conditions of professional secrecy imposed in paragraph 1,
- where the information originates in another Member State, it may not be disclosed without the express agreement of the competent authorities which have disclosed it and, where appropriate, solely for the purposes for which those authorities gave their agreement.

Member States shall communicate to the Commission and to the other Member States the name of the authorities which may receive information pursuant to this paragraph.

7. Notwithstanding paragraphs 1 to 4, Member States may, with the aim of strengthening the stability, including integrity, of the financial system, authorise the exchange of information between the competent authorities and the authorities or bodies responsible under law for the detection and investigation of breaches of company law.

Member States which have recourse to the provision in the first subparagraph shall require at least that the following conditions are met:
- the information shall be for the purpose of performing the task referred to in the first subparagraph,
- information received in this context shall be subject to the conditions of professional secrecy imposed in paragraph 1,
- where the information originates in another Member State, it may not be disclosed without the express agreement of the competent authorities which have disclosed it and, where appropriate, solely for the purposes for which those authorities gave their agreement.

Where, in a Member State, the authorities or bodies referred to in the first subparagraph perform their task of detection or investigation with the aid, in view of their specific competence, of persons appointed for that purpose and not employed in the public sector, the possibility of exchanging information provided for in the first subparagraph may be extended to such persons under the conditions stipulated in the second subparagraph.

In order to implement the third indent of the second subparagraph, the authorities or bodies referred to in the first subparagraph shall communicate to the competent authorities which have disclosed the information, the names and precise responsibilities of the persons to whom it is to be sent.

Member States shall communicate to the Commission and to the other Member States the names of the authorities or bodies which may receive information pursuant to this paragraph.

Before 31 December 2000, the Commission shall draw up a report on the application of the provisions of this paragraph.

8. This Article shall not prevent a competent authority from transmitting:
- to central banks and other bodies with a similar function in their capacity as monetary authorities,
- where appropriate to other public authorities responsible for overseeing payment systems,

information intended for the performance of their task, nor shall it prevent such authorities or bodies from communicating to the competent authorities such information as they may need for the purposes of paragraph 4. Information received in this context shall be subject to the conditions of professional secrecy imposed in this Article.

9. In addition, notwithstanding the provisions referred to in paragraphs 1 and 4, the Member States may, by virtue of provisions laid down by law, authorise the disclosure of certain information to other departments of their central government administrations responsible for legislation on the supervision of credit institutions financial institutions, investment services and insurance companies and to inspectors acting on behalf of those departments.

However, such disclosures may be made only where necessary for reasons of prudential control.

However, the Member States shall provide that information received under paragraphs 2 and 5 and that obtained by means of the on-the-spot verification referred to in Article 29(1) and (2) may never be disclosed in the cases referred to in this paragraph except with the express consent of the competent authorities which disclosed the information or of the competent authorities of the Member State in which on-the-spot verification was carried out.

10. This Article shall not prevent the competent authorities from communicating the information referred to in paragraphs 1 to 4 to a clearing house or other similar body recognised under national law for the provision of clearing or settlement services for one of their Member States' markets if they consider that it is necessary to communicate the information in order to ensure the proper functioning of those bodies in relation to defaults or potential defaults by market participants. The information received in this context shall be subject to the conditions of professional secrecy imposed in paragraph 1. The Member States shall, however, ensure that information received under paragraph 2 may not be disclosed in the circumstances referred to in this paragraph without the express consent of the competent authorities which disclosed it.

Article 31 - Duty of persons responsible for the legal control of annual and consolidated accounts

1. Member States shall provide at least that:
(a) any person authorised within the meaning of Council Directive 84/253/EEC[14], performing in a credit institution the task described in Article 51 of Council Directive 78/660/EEC[15], or Article 37 of Council Directive 83/349/EEC, or Article 31 of Directive 85/611/EEC[16], or any other statutory task, shall have a duty to report promptly to the competent authorities any fact or decision concerning that institution of which he has become aware while carrying out that task which is liable to:
- constitute a material breach of the laws, regulations or administrative provisions which lay down the conditions governing authorisation or which specifically govern pursuit of the activities of credit institutions, or
- affect the continuous functioning of the credit institution, or
- lead to refusal to certify the accounts or to the expression of reservations;
(b) that person shall likewise have a duty to report any fact and decisions of which he becomes aware in the course of carrying out a task as described in (a) in an undertaking having close

---

[14] Eighth Council Directive (84/253/EEC) of 10 April 1984 based on Article 44(2)(g) of the Treaty on the approval of persons responsible for carrying out the statutory audits of accounting documents (OJ L 126, 12.5.1984, p. 20).

[15] Fourth Council Directive (78/660/EEC) of 25 July 1978 based on Article 44(2)(g) of the Treaty on the annual accounts of certain types of companies (OJ L 222, 14.8.1978, p. 11). Directive as last amended by Directive 1999/60/EC (OJ L 62, 26.6.1999, p. 65).

[16] Council Directive 85/611/EEC of 20 December 1985 on the coordination of laws, regulations and administrative provisions relating to undertakings for collective investment in transferable securities (UCITS) (OJ L 375, 31.12.1985, p. 3). Directive as last amended by Directive 95/26/EC (OJ L 168, 18.7.1995, p. 7).

links resulting from a control relationship with the credit institution within which he is carrying out the abovementioned task.
2. The disclosure in good faith to the competent authorities, by persons authorised within the meaning of Directive 84/253/EEC, of any fact or decision referred to in paragraph 1 shall not constitute a breach of any restriction on disclosure of information imposed by contract or by any legislative, regulatory or administrative provision and shall not involve such persons in liability of any kind.

Article 32 - Power of sanction of the competent authorities

Without prejudice to the procedures for the withdrawal of authorisations and the provisions of criminal law, the Member States shall provide that their respective competent authorities may, as against credit institutions or those who effectively control the business of credit institutions which breach laws, regulations or administrative provisions concerning the supervision or pursuit of their activities, adopt or impose in respect of them penalties or measures aimed specifically at ending observed breaches or the causes of such breaches.

Article 33 -Right to apply to the courts

Member States shall ensure that decisions taken in respect of a credit institution in pursuance of laws, regulations and administrative provisions adopted in accordance with this Directive may be subject to the right to apply to the courts. The same shall apply where no decision is taken within six months of its submission in respect of an application for authorisation which contains all the information required under the provisions in force.

CHAPTER 2: TECHNICAL INSTRUMENTS OF PRUDENTIAL SUPERVISION

SECTION 1: OWN FUNDS

Article 34 - General principles

1. Wherever a Member State lays down by law, regulation or administrative action a provision in implementation of Community legislation concerning the prudential supervision of an operative credit institution which uses the term or refers to the concept of own funds, it shall bring this term or concept into line with the definition given in paragraphs 2, 3 and 4 and Articles 35 to 38.
2. Subject to the limits imposed in Article 38, the unconsolidated own funds of credit institutions shall consist of the following items:
(1) capital within the meaning of Article 22 of Directive 86/635/EEC, in so far as it has been paid up, plus share premium accounts but excluding cumulative preferential shares;
(2) reserves within the meaning of Article 23 of Directive 86/635/EEC and profits and losses brought forward as a result of the application of the final profit or loss. The Member States may permit inclusion of interim profits before a formal decision has been taken only if these profits have been verified by persons responsible for the auditing of the accounts and if it is proved to the satisfaction of the competent authorities that the amount thereof has been evaluated in accordance with the principles set out in Directive 86/635/EEC and is net of any foreseeable charge or dividend;
(3) funds for general banking risks within the meaning of Article 38 of Directive 86/635/EEC;
(4) revaluation reserves within the meaning of Article 33 of Directive 78/660/EEC;
(5) value adjustments within the meaning of Article 37(2) of Directive 86/635/EEC;
(6) other items within the meaning of Article 35;

(7) the commitments of the members of credit institutions set up as cooperative societies and the joint and several commitments of the borrowers of certain institutions organised as funds, as referred to in Article 36(1);
(8) fixed-term cumulative preferential shares and subordinated loan capital as referred to in Article 36(3).

The following items shall be deducted in accordance with Article 38:

(9) own shares at book value held by a credit institution;
(10) intangible assets within the meaning of Article 4(9) ("Assets") of Directive 86/635/EEC;
(11) material losses of the current financial year;
(12) holdings in other credit and financial institutions amounting to more than 10 % of their capital, subordinated claims and the instruments referred to in Article 35 which a credit institution holds in respect of credit and financial institutions in which it has holdings exceeding 10 % of the capital in each case.
Where shares in another credit or financial institution are held temporarily for the purposes of a financial assistance operation designed to reorganise and save that institution, the competent authority may waive this provision;
(13) holdings in other credit and financial institutions of up to 10 % of their capital, the subordinated claims and the instruments referred to in Article 35 which a credit institution holds in respect of credit and financial institutions other than those referred to in point (12) in respect of the amount of the total of such holdings, subordinated claims and instruments which exceed 10 % of that credit institution's own funds calculated before the deduction of items in point (12) and in this point.

Pending subsequent coordination of the provisions on consolidation, Member States may provide that, for the calculation of unconsolidated own funds, parent companies subject to supervision on a consolidated basis need not deduct their holdings in other credit institutions or financial institutions which are included in the consolidation. This provision shall apply to all the prudential rules harmonised by Community acts.

3. The concept of own funds as defined in points (1) to (8) of paragraph 2 embodies a maximum number of items and amounts. The use of those items and the fixing of lower ceilings, and the deduction of items other than those listed in points (9) to (13) of paragraph 2 shall be left to the discretion of the Member States. Member States shall nevertheless be obliged to consider increased convergence with a view to a common definition of own funds.
To that end, the Commission shall, by 1 January 1996 at the latest, submit a report to the European Parliament and to the Council on the application of this Article and Articles 35 to 39, accompanied, where appropriate, by such proposals for amendment as it shall deem necessary. Not later than 1 January 1998, the European Parliament and the Council shall, acting in accordance with the procedure laid down in Article 251 of the Treaty and after consultation of the Economic and Social Committee, examine the definition of own funds with a view to the uniform application of the common definition.

4. The items listed in points (1) to (5) of paragraph 2 must be available to a credit institution for unrestricted and immediate use to cover risks or losses as soon as these occur. The amount must be net of any foreseeable tax charge at the moment of its calculation or be suitably adjusted in so far as such tax charges reduce the amount up to which these items may be applied to cover risks or losses.

Article 35 - Other items

1. The concept of own funds used by a Member State may include other items provided that, whatever their legal or accounting designations might be, they have the following characteristics:
(a) they are freely available to the credit institution to cover normal banking risks where revenue or capital losses have not yet been identified;
(b) their existence is disclosed in internal accounting records;
(c) their amount is determined by the management of the credit institution, verified by independent auditors, made known to the competent authorities and placed under the supervision of the latter.
2. Securities of indeterminate duration and other instruments that fulfil the following conditions may also be accepted as other items:
(a) they may not be reimbursed on the bearer's initiative or without the prior agreement of the competent authority;
(b) the debt agreement must provide for the credit institution to have the option of deferring the payment of interest on the debt;
(c) the lender's claims on the credit institution must be wholly subordinated to those of all non-subordinated creditors;
(d) the documents governing the issue of the securities must provide for debt and unpaid interest to be such as to absorb losses, whilst leaving the credit institution in a position to continue trading;
(e) only fully paid-up amounts shall be taken into account.

To these may be added cumulative preferential shares other than those referred to in point 8 of Article 34(2).

Article 36 - Other provisions concerning own funds

1. The commitments of the members of credit institutions set up as cooperative societies referred to in point 7 of Article 34(2), shall comprise those societies' uncalled capital; together with the legal commitments of the members of those cooperative societies to make additional non-refundable payments should the credit institution incur a loss, in which case it must be possible to demand those payments without delay.

   The joint and several commitments of borrowers in the case of credit institutions organised as funds shall be treated in the same way as the preceding items.

   All such items may be included in own funds in so far as they are counted as the own funds of institutions of this category under national law.
2. Member States shall not include in the own funds of public credit institutions guarantees which they or their local authorities extend to such entities.
3. Member States or the competent authorities may include fixed-term cumulative preferential shares referred to in point (8) of Article 34(2) and subordinated loan capital referred to in that provision in own funds, if binding agreements exist under which, in the event of the bankruptcy or liquidation of the credit institution, they rank after the claims of all other creditors and are not to be repaid until all other debts outstanding at the time have been settled.

Subordinated loan capital must also fulfil the following criteria:
(a) only fully paid-up funds may be taken into account;
(b) the loans involved must have an original maturity of at least five years, after which they may be repaid; if the maturity of the debt is not fixed, they shall be repayable only subject to five years' notice unless the loans are no longer considered as own funds or unless the prior consent of the competent authorities is specifically required for early repayment. The competent authorities may grant permission for the early repayment of such loans provided

the request is made at the initiative of the issuer and the solvency of the credit institution in question is not affected;
(c) the extent to which they may rank as own funds must be gradually reduced during at least the last five years before the repayment date;
(d) the loan agreement must not include any clause providing that in specified circumstances, other than the winding-up of the credit institution, the debt will become repayable before the agreed repayment date.

Article 37 - Calculation of own funds on a consolidated basis

1. Where the calculation is to be made on a consolidated basis, the consolidated amounts relating to the items listed under Article 34(2) shall be used in accordance with the rules laid down in Articles 52 to 56. Moreover, the following may, when they are credit ("negative") items, be regarded as consolidated reserves for the calculation of own funds:
- any minority interests within the meaning of Article 21 of Directive 83/349/EEC, where the global integration method is used,
- the first consolidation difference within the meaning of Articles 19, 30 and 31 of Directive 83/349/EEC,
- the translation differences included in consolidated reserves in accordance with Article 39(6) of Directive 86/635/EEC,
- any difference resulting from the inclusion of certain participating interests in accordance with the method prescribed in Article 33 of Directive 83/349/EEC.
2. Where the above are debit ("positive") items, they must be deducted in the calculation of consolidated own funds.

Article 38 - Deductions and limits

1. The items referred to in points (4) to (8) of Article 34(2), shall be subject to the following limits:
(a) the total of the items in points (4) to (8) may not exceed a maximum of 100 % of the items in points (1) plus (2) and (3) minus (9), (10) and (11);
(b) the total of the items in points (7) and (8) may not exceed a maximum of 50 % of the items in points (1) plus (2) and (3) minus (9), (10) and (11);
(c) the total of the items in points (12) and (13) shall be deducted from the total of the items.
2. The competent authorities may authorise credit institutions to exceed the limit laid down in paragraph 1 in temporary and exceptional circumstances.

Article 39 - Provision of proof to the competent authorities

Compliance with the conditions laid down in Article 34(2), (3) and (4) and Articles 35 to 38 must be proved to the satisfaction of the competent authorities.

SECTION 2: SOLVENCY RATIO

Article 40 - General principles

1. The solvency ratio expresses own funds, as defined in Article 41, as a proportion of total assets and off-balance-sheet items, risk-adjusted in accordance with Article 42.
2. The solvency ratios of credit institutions which are neither parent undertakings as defined in Article 1 of Directive 83/349/EEC, nor subsidiaries of such undertakings shall be calculated on an individual basis.
3. The solvency ratios of credit institutions which are parent undertakings shall be calculated on a consolidated basis in accordance with the methods laid down in this Directive and in Directive 86/635/EEC.

4. The competent authorities responsible for authorising and supervising a parent undertaking which is a credit institution may also require the calculation of a subconsolidated or unconsolidated ratio in respect of that parent undertaking and of any of its subsidiaries which are subject to authorisation and supervision by them. Where such monitoring of the satisfactory allocation of capital within a banking group is not carried out, other measures must be taken to attain that end.
5. Without prejudice to credit institutions' compliance with the requirements of paragraphs 2, 3 and 4, and of Article 52(8) and (9), the competent authorities shall ensure that ratios are calculated not less than twice each year, either by credit institutions themselves, which shall communicate the results and any component data required to the competent authorities, or by the competent authorities, using data supplied by the credit institutions.
6. The valuation of assets and off-balance-sheet items shall be effected in accordance with Directive 86/635/EEC.

Article 41 - The numerator: own funds

Own funds as defined in this Directive shall form the numerator of the solvency ratio.

Article 42 - The denominator: risk-adjusted assets and off-balance-sheet items

1. Degrees of credit risk, expressed as percentage weightings, shall be assigned to asset items in accordance with Articles 43 and 44, and exceptionally Articles 45, 62 and 63. The balance-sheet value of each asset shall then be multiplied by the relevant weighting to produce a risk-adjusted value.
2. In the case of the off-balance-sheet items listed in Annex II, a two-stage calculation as prescribed in Article 43(2) shall be used.
3. In the case of the off-balance-sheet items referred to in Article 43(3), the potential costs of replacing contracts in the event of counterparty default shall be calculated by means of one of the two methods set out in Annex III. Those costs shall be multiplied by the relevant counterparty weightings in Article 43(1), except the 100 % weightings as provided for there shall be replaced by 50 % weightings to produce risk-adjusted values.
4. The total of the risk-adjusted values of the assets and off-balance-sheet items mentioned in paragraphs 2 and 3 shall be the denominator of the solvency ratio.

Article 43 - Risk weightings

1. The following weightings shall be applied to the various categories of asset items, although the competent authorities may fix higher weightings as they see fit:
(a) Zero weighting
(1) cash in hand and equivalent items;
(2) asset items constituting claims on Zone A central governments and central banks;
(3) asset items constituting claims on the European Communities;
(4) asset items constituting claims carrying the explicit guarantees of Zone A central governments and central banks or of the European Communities;
(5) asset items constituting claims on Zone B central governments and central banks denominated and funded in the national currencies of the borrowers;
(6) asset items constituting claims carrying the explicit guarantees of Zone B central governments and central banks denominated and funded in the national currency common to the guarantor and the borrower;
(7) asset items secured to the satisfaction of the competent authorities, by collateral in the form of Zone A central government or central bank securities or securities issued by the European Communities or by cash deposits placed with the lending institution or by certificates of deposit or similar instruments issued by and lodged with the latter;

(b) 20 % weighting
(1) asset items constituting claims on the EIB;
(2) asset items constituting claims on multilateral development banks;
(3) asset items constituting claims carrying the explicit guarantee of the EIB;
(4) asset items constituting claims carrying the explicit guarantees of multilateral development banks;
(5) asset items constituting claims on Zone A regional governments or local authorities, subject to Article 44;
(6) asset items constituting claims carrying the explicit guarantees of Zone A regional governments or local authorities, subject to Article 44;
(7) asset items constituting claims on Zone A credit institutions but not constituting such institutions' own funds;
(8) asset items constituting claims with a maturity of one year or less, on Zone B credit institutions, other than securities issued by such institutions which are recognised as components of their own funds;
(9) asset items carrying the explicit guarantees of Zone A credit institutions;
(10) asset items constituting claims with a maturity of one year or less carrying the explicit guarantees of Zone B credit institutions;
(11) asset items secured, to the satisfaction of the competent authorities, by collateral in the form of securities issued by the EIB or by multilateral development banks;
(12) cash items in the process of collection;

(c) 50 % weighting
(1) loans fully and completely secured, to the satisfaction of the competent authorities, by mortgages on residential property which is or will be occupied or let by the borrower, and loans fully and completely secured, to the satisfaction of the competent authorities, by shares in Finnish residential housing companies, operating in accordance with the Finnish Housing Company Act of 1991 or subsequent equivalent legislation, in respect of residential property which is or will be occupied or let by the borrower;
"mortgage-backed securities" which may be treated as loans referred to in the first subparagraph or in Article 62(1), if the competent authorities consider, having regard to the legal framework in force in each Member State, that they are equivalent in the light of the credit risk. Without prejudice to the types of securities which may be included in and are capable of fulfilling the conditions in this point 1, "mortgage-backed securities" may include instruments within the meaning of Section B(1)(a) and (b) of the Annex to Council Directive 93/22/EEC[17]. The competent authorities must in particular be satisfied that:
  (i) such securities are fully and directly backed by a pool of mortgages which are of the same nature as those defined in the first subparagraph or in Article 62(1) and are fully performing when the mortgage-backed securities are created;
  (ii) an acceptable high-priority charge on the underlying mortgage-asset items is held either directly by investors in mortgage-backed securities or on their behalf by a trustee or mandated representative in the same proportion to the securities which they hold;
(2) prepayments and accrued income: these assets shall be subject to the weighting corresponding to the counterparty where a credit institution is able to determine it in accordance with Directive 86/635/EEC. Otherwise, where it is unable to determine the counterparty, it shall apply a flat-rate weighting of 50 %;

---

[17] Council Directive 93/22/EEC of 10 May 1993 on investment services in the securities field (OJ L 141, 11.6.1993, p. 27). Directive as last amended by Directive 97/9/EC (OJ L 84, 26.3.1997, p. 22).

(d) 100 % weighting
(1) asset items constituting claims on Zone B central governments and central banks except where denominated and funded in the national currency of the borrower;
(2) asset items constituting claims on Zone B regional governments or local authorities;
(3) asset items constituting claims with a maturity of more than one year on Zone B credit institutions;
(4) asset items constituting claims on the Zone A and Zone B non-bank sectors;
(5) tangible "Assets" within the meaning of Article 4(10) of Directive 86/635/EEC;
(6) holdings of shares, participation and other components of the own funds of other credit institutions which are not deducted from the own funds of the lending institutions;
(7) all other assets except where deducted from own funds.

2. The following treatment shall apply to off-balance-sheet items other than those covered in paragraph 3. They shall first be grouped according to the risk groupings set out in Annex II. The full value of the full-risk items shall be taken into account, 50 % of the value of the medium-risk items and 20 % of the medium/low-risk items, while the value of low-risk items shall be set at zero. The second stage shall be to multiply the off-balance-sheet values, adjusted as described above, by the weightings attributable to the relevant counterparties in accordance with the treatment of asset items prescribed in paragraph 1 and Article 44. In the case of asset sale and repurchase agreements and outright forward purchases, the weightings shall be those attaching to the assets in question and not to the counterparties to the transactions. The portion of unpaid capital subscribed to the European Investment Fund may be weighted at 20 %.

3. The methods set out in Annex III shall be applied to the off-balance-sheet items listed in Annex IV except for:
- contracts traded on recognised exchanges,
- foreign-exchange contracts (except contracts concerning gold) with an original maturity of 14 calendar days or less.

Until 31 December 2006, the competent authorities of Member States may exempt from the application of the methods set out in Annex III over-the-counter (OTC) contracts cleared by a clearing house where the latter acts as the legal counterparty and all participants fully collateralise on a daily basis the exposure they present to the clearing house, thereby providing a protection covering both the current exposure and the potential future exposure. The competent authorities must be satisfied that the posted collateral gives the same level of protection as collateral which complies with paragraph 1(a)(7) and that the risk of a build-up of the clearing house's exposures beyond the market value of posted collateral is eliminated. Member States shall inform the Commission of the use they make of this option.

4. Where off-balance-sheet items carry explicit guarantees, they shall be weighted as if they had been incurred on behalf of the guarantor rather than the counterparty. Where the potential exposure arising from off-balance-sheet transactions is fully and completely secured, to the satisfaction of the competent authorities, by any of the asset items recognised as collateral in paragraph 1(a)(7) and (b)(11), weightings of 0 % or 20 % shall apply depending on the collateral in question.

The Member States may apply a 50 % weighting to off-balance-sheet items which are sureties or guarantees having the character of credit substitutes and which are fully guaranteed, to the satisfaction of the competent authorities, by mortgages meeting the conditions set out in paragraph 1(c)(1), subject to the guarantor having a direct right to such collateral.

5. Where asset and off-balance-sheet items are given a lower weighting because of the existence of explicit guarantees or collateral acceptable to the competent authorities, the lower weighting shall apply only to that part which is guaranteed or which is fully covered by the collateral.

Article 44 - Weighting of claims for regional governments or local authorities of the Member States

1. Notwithstanding the requirements of Article 43(1)(b), the Member States may fix a weighting of 0 % for their own regional governments and local authorities if there is no difference in risk between claims on the latter and claims on their central governments because of the revenue-raising powers of the regional governments and local authorities and the existence of specific institutional arrangements the effect of which is to reduce the chances of default by the latter. A zero-weighting fixed in accordance with these criteria shall apply to claims on and off-balance-sheet items incurred on behalf of the regional governments and local authorities in question and claims on others and off-balance-sheet items incurred on behalf of others and guaranteed by those regional governments and local authorities or secured, to the satisfaction of the competent authorities concerned, by collateral in the form of securities issued by those regional governments or local authorities.
2. The Member States shall notify the Commission if they believe a zero-weighting to be justified according to the criteria laid down in paragraph 1. The Commission shall circulate that information. Other Member States may offer the credit institutions under the supervision of their competent authorities the possibility of applying a zero-weighting where they undertake business with the regional governments or local authorities in question or where they hold claims guaranteed by the latter, including collateral in the form of securities.

Article 45 - Other weighting

1. Without prejudice to Article 44(1) the Member States may apply a weighting of 20 % to asset items which are secured, to the satisfaction of the competent authorities concerned, by collateral in the form of securities issued by Zone A regional governments or local authorities, by deposits placed with Zone A credit institutions other than the lending institution, or by certificates of deposit or similar instruments issued by such credit institutions.
2. The Member States may apply a weighting of 10 % to claims on institutions specialising in the inter-bank and public-debt markets in their home Member States and subject to close supervision by the competent authorities where those asset items are fully and completely secured, to the satisfaction of the competent authorities of the home Member States, by a combination of asset items mentioned in Article 43(1)(a) and (b) recognised by the latter as constituting adequate collateral.
3. The Member States shall notify the Commission of any provisions adopted pursuant to paragraphs 1 and 2 and of the grounds for such provisions. The Commission shall forward that information to the Member States. The Commission shall periodically examine the implications of those provisions in order to ensure that they do not result in any distortions of competition.

Article 46 - Administrative bodies and non-commercial undertakings

For the purposes of Article 43 (1)(b), the competent authorities may include within the concept of regional governments and local authorities non-commercial administrative bodies responsible to regional governments or local authorities or authorities which, in the view of the competent authorities, exercise the same responsibilities as regional and local authorities.

The competent authorities may also include within the concept of regional governments and local authorities, churches and religious communities constituted in the form of a legal person under public law, in so far as they raise taxes in accordance with legislation conferring on them the right to do so. However, in this case the option set out in Article 44 shall not apply.

Article 47 - Solvency ratio level

1. Credit institutions shall be required permanently to maintain the ratio defined in Article 40 at a level of at least 8 %.
2. Notwithstanding paragraph 1, the competent authorities may prescribe higher minimum ratios as they consider appropriate.
3. If the ratio falls below 8 % the competent authorities shall ensure that the credit institution in question takes appropriate measures to restore the ratio to the agreed minimum as quickly as possible.

SECTION 3: LARGE EXPOSURES

Article 48 - Reporting of large exposures

1. A credit institution's exposure to a client or group of connected clients shall be considered a large exposure where its value is equal to or exceeds 10 % of its own funds.
2. A credit institution shall report every large exposure within the meaning of paragraph 1 to the competent authorities. Member States shall provide that reporting is to be carried out, at their discretion, in accordance with one of the following two methods:
- reporting of all large exposures at least once a year, combined with reporting during the year of all new large exposures and any increases in existing large exposures of at least 20 % with respect to the previous communication,
- reporting of all large exposures at least four times a year.
3. Exposures exempted under Article 49(7)(a), (b), (c), (d), (f), (g) and (h) need not, however, be reported as laid down in paragraph 2. The reporting frequency laid down in the second indent to paragraph 2 may be reduced to twice a year for the exposures referred to in Article 49(7)(e) and (i), and also in paragraphs 8, 9 and 10.
4. The competent authorities shall require that every credit institution have sound administrative and accounting procedures and adequate internal control mechanisms for the purpose of identifying and recording all large exposures and subsequent changes to them, as defined and required by this Directive, and for that of monitoring those exposures in the light of each credit institution's own exposure policies.

Where a credit institution invokes paragraph 3, it shall keep a record of the grounds advanced for at least one year after the event giving rise to the dispensation, so that the competent authorities may establish whether it is justified.

Article 49 - Limits on large exposures

1. A credit institution may not incur an exposure to a client or group of connected clients the value of which exceed 25 % of its own funds.
2. Where that client or group of connected clients is the parent undertaking or subsidiary of the credit institution and/or one or more subsidiaries of that parent undertaking, the percentage laid down in paragraph 1 shall be reduced to 20 %. Member States may, however, exempt the exposures incurred to such clients from the 20 % limit if they provide for specific monitoring of such exposures by other measures or procedures. They shall inform the Commission and the Banking Advisory Committee of the content of such measures or procedures.

3. A credit institution may not incur large exposures which in total exceed 800 % of its own funds.
4. Member States may impose limits more stringent than those laid down in paragraphs 1, 2 and 3.
5. A credit institution shall at all times comply with the limits laid down in paragraphs 1, 2 and 3 in respect of its exposures. If in an exceptional case exposures exceed those limits, that fact must be reported without delay to the competent authorities which may, where the circumstances warrant it, allow the credit institution a limited period of time in which to comply with the limits.
6. Member States may fully or partially exempt from the application of paragraphs 1, 2 and 3 exposures incurred by a credit institution to its parent undertaking, to other subsidiaries of that parent undertaking or to its own subsidiaries, in so far as those undertakings are covered by the supervision on a consolidated basis to which the credit institution itself is subject, in accordance with this Directive or with equivalent standards in force in a third country.
7. Member States may fully or partially exempt the following exposures from the application of paragraphs 1, 2 and 3:
(a) asset items constituting claims on Zone A central governments or central banks;
(b) asset items constituting claims on the European Communities;
(c) asset items constituting claims carrying the explicit guarantees of Zone A central governments or central banks or of the European Communities;
(d) other exposures attributable to, or guaranteed by, Zone A central governments or central banks or the European Communities;
(e) asset items constituting claims on and other exposures to Zone B central governments or central banks which are denominated and, where applicable, funded in the national currencies of the borrowers;
(f) asset items and other exposures secured, to the satisfaction of the competent authorities, by collateral in the form of Zone A central government or central bank securities, or securities issued by the European Communities or by Member State regional or local authorities for which Article 44 lays down a zero weighting for solvency purposes;
(g) asset items and other exposures secured, to the satisfaction of the competent authorities, by collateral in the form of cash deposits placed with the lending institution or with a credit institution which is the parent undertaking or a subsidiary of the lending institution;
(h) asset items and other exposures secured, to the satisfaction of the competent authorities, by collateral in the form of certificates of deposit issued by the lending institution or by a credit institution which is the parent undertaking or a subsidiary of the lending institution and lodged with either of them;
(i) asset items constituting claims on and other exposures to credit institutions, with a maturity of one year or less, but not constituting such institutions' own funds;
(j) asset items constituting claims on and other exposures to those institutions which are not credit institutions but which fulfil the conditions referred to in Article 45(2), with a maturity of one year or less, and secured in accordance with the same paragraph;
(k) bills of trade and other similar bills, with a maturity of one year or less, bearing the signatures of other credit institutions;
(l) debt securities as defined in Article 22(4) of Directive 85/611/EEC;
(m) pending subsequent coordination, holdings in the insurance companies referred to in Article 51(3) up to 40 % of the own funds of the credit institution acquiring such a holding;
(n) asset items constituting claims on regional or central credit institutions with which the lending institution is associated in a network in accordance with legal or statutory provisions and which are responsible, under those provisions, for cash-clearing operations within the network;

(o) exposures secured, to the satisfaction of the competent authorities, by collateral in the form of securities other than those referred to in (f) provided that those securities are not issued by the credit institution itself, its parent company or one of their subsidiaries, or by the client or group of connected clients in question. The securities used as collateral must be valued at market price, have a value that exceeds the exposures guaranteed and be either traded on a stock exchange or effectively negotiable and regularly quoted on a market operated under the auspices of recognised professional operators and allowing, to the satisfaction of the competent authorities of the Member State of origin of the credit institution, for the establishment of an objective price such that the excess value of the securities may be verified at any time. The excess value required shall be 100 % it shall, however, be 150 % in the case of shares and 50 % in the case of debt securities issued by credit institutions, Member State regional or local authorities other than those referred to in Article 44, and in the case of debt securities issued by the EIB and multilateral development banks. Securities used as collateral may not constitute credit institutions' own funds;

(p) loans secured, to the satisfaction of the competent authorities, by mortgages on residential property or by shares in Finnish residential housing companies, operating in accordance with the Finnish Housing Company Act of 1991 or subsequent equivalent legislation and leasing transactions under which the lessor retains full ownership of the residential property leased for as long as the lessee has not exercised his option to purchase, in all cases up to 50 % of the value of the residential property concerned. The value of the property shall be calculated, to the satisfaction of the competent authorities, on the basis of strict valuation standards laid down by law, regulation or administrative provisions. Valuation shall be carried out at least once a year. For the purposes of this point residential property shall mean a residence to be occupied or let by the borrower;

(q) 50 % of the medium/low-risk off-balance-sheet items referred to in Annex II;

(r) subject to the competent authorities' agreement, guarantees other than loan guarantees which have a legal or regulatory basis and are given for their members by mutual guarantee schemes possessing the status of credit institutions, subject to a weighting of 20 % of their amount.

Member States shall inform the Commission of the use they make of this option in order to ensure that it does not result in distortions of competition;

(s) the low-risk off-balance-sheet items referred to in Annex II, to the extent that an agreement has been concluded with the client or group of connected clients under which the exposure may be incurred only if it has been ascertained that it will not cause the limits applicable under paragraphs 1, 2 and 3 to be exceeded.

8. For the purposes of paragraphs 1, 2 and 3, Member States may apply a weighting of 20 % to asset items constituting claims on Member State regional and local authorities and to other exposures to or guaranteed by such authorities; subject to the conditions laid down in Article 44, however, Member States may reduce that rate to 0 %.

9. For the purposes of paragraphs 1, 2 and 3, Member States may apply a weighting of 20 % to asset items constituting claims on and other exposures to credit institutions with a maturity of more than one but not more than three years and a weighting of 50 % to asset items constituting claims on credit institutions with a maturity of more than three years, provided that the latter are represented by debt instruments that were issued by a credit institution and that those debt instruments are, in the opinion of the competent authorities, effectively negotiable on a market made up of professional operators and are subject to daily quotation on that market, or the issue of which was authorised by the competent authorities of the Member State of origin of the issuing credit institutions. In no case may any of these items constitute own funds.

10. By way of derogation from paragraphs 7(i) and 9, Member States may apply a weighting of 20 % to asset items constituting claims on and other exposures to credit institutions, regardless of their maturity.
11. Where an exposure to a client is guaranteed by a third party, or by collateral in the form of securities issued by a third party under the conditions laid down in paragraph 7(o), Member States may:
- treat the exposure as having been incurred to the third party rather than to the client, if the exposure is directly and unconditionally guaranteed by that third party, to the satisfaction of the competent authorities,
- treat the exposure as having been incurred to the third party rather than to the client, if the exposure defined in paragraph 7(o) is guaranteed by collateral under the conditions there laid down.
12. By 1 January 1999 at the latest, the Council shall, on the basis of a report from the Commission, examine the treatment of interbank exposures provided for in paragraphs 7(i), 9 and 10. The Council shall decide on any changes to be made on a proposal from the Commission.

Article 50 - Supervision on a consolidated or unconsolidated basis of large exposures

1. If the credit institution is neither a parent undertaking nor a subsidiary, compliance with the obligations imposed in Articles 48 and 49 or in any other Community provision applicable to this area shall be monitored on an unconsolidated basis.
2. In the other cases, compliance with the obligations imposed in Articles 48 and 49 or in any other Community provision applicable to this area shall be monitored on a consolidated basis in accordance with Articles 52 to 56.
3. Member States may waive monitoring on an individual or subconsolidated basis of compliance with the obligations imposed in Articles 48 and 49 or in any other Community provision applicable to this area by a credit institution which, as a parent undertaking, is subject to monitoring on a consolidated basis and by any subsidiary of such a credit institution which is subject to their authoritisation and supervision and is covered by monitoring on a consolidated basis.

   Member States also waive such monitoring where the parent undertaking is a financial holding company established in the same Member State as the credit institution, provided that company is subject to the same monitoring as credit institutions.

   In the cases referred to in the first and second subparagraphs measures must be taken to ensure the satisfactory allocation of risks within the group.

SECTION 4: QUALIFYING HOLDINGS OUTSIDE THE FINANCIAL SECTOR

Article 51 - Limits to non-financial qualifying holdings

1. No credit institution may have a qualifying holding the amount of which exceeds 15 % of its own funds in an undertaking which is neither a credit institution, nor a financial institution, nor an undertaking carrying on an activity referred to in the second subparagraph of Article 43(2)(f) of Directive 86/635/EEC.
2. The total amount of a credit institution's qualifying holdings in undertakings other than credit institutions, financial institutions or undertakings carrying on activities referred to in the second subparagraph of Article 43(2)(f) of Directive 86/635/EEC may not exceed 60 % of its own funds.

3. The Member States need not apply the limits laid down in paragraphs 1 and 2 to holdings in insurance companies as defined in Directive 73/239/EEC[18], and Directive 79/267/EEC[19].
4. Shares held temporarily during a financial reconstruction or rescue operation or during the normal course of underwriting or in an institution's own name on behalf of others shall not be counted as qualifying holdings for the purpose of calculating the limits laid down in paragraphs 1 and 2. Shares which are not financial fixed assets as defined in Article 35(2) of Directive 86/635/EEC shall not be included.
5. The limits laid down in paragraphs 1 and 2 may be exceeded only in exceptional circumstances. In such cases, however, the competent authorities shall require a credit institution either to increase its own funds or to take other equivalent measures.
6. The Member States may provide that the competent authorities shall not apply the limits laid down in paragraphs 1 and 2 if they provide that 100 % of the amounts by which a credit institution's qualifying holdings exceed those limits must be covered by own funds and that the latter shall not be included in the calculation of the solvency ratio. If both the limits laid down in paragraphs 1 and 2 are exceeded, the amount to be covered by own funds shall be the greater of the excess amounts.

CHAPTER 3: SUPERVISION ON A CONSOLIDATED BASIS

Article 52 - Supervision on a consolidated basis of credit institutions

1. Every credit institution which has a credit institution or a financial institution as a subsidiary or which holds a participation in such institutions shall be subject, to the extent and in the manner prescribed in Article 54, to supervision on the basis of its consolidated financial situation. Such supervision shall be exercised at least in the areas referred to in paragraphs 5 and 6.
2. Every credit institution the parent undertaking of which is a financial holding company shall be subject, to the extent and in the manner prescribed in Article 54, to supervision on the basis of the consolidated financial situation of that financial holding company. Such supervision shall be exercised at least in the areas referred to in paragraphs 5 and 6. The consolidation of the financial situation of the financial holding company shall not in any way imply that the competent authorities are required to play a supervisory role in relation to the financial holding company standing alone.
3. The Member States or the competent authorities responsible for exercising supervision on a consolidated basis pursuant to Article 53 may decide in the cases listed below that a credit institution, financial institution or auxiliary banking services undertaking which is a subsidiary or in which a participation is held need not be included in the consolidation:
- if the undertaking that should be included is situated in a third country where there are legal impediments to the transfer of the necessary information,
- if, in the opinion of the competent authorities, the undertaking that should be included is of negligible interest only with respect to the objectives of monitoring credit institutions and in all cases if the balance-sheet total of the undertaking that should be included is less than the smaller of the following two amounts: EUR 10 million or 1 % of the balance-sheet total of the parent undertaking or the undertaking that holds the participation. If several undertakings meet the above criteria, they must nevertheless be included in the consolidation where

---

[18] First Council Directive 73/239/EEC of 24 July 1973 on the coordination of laws, regulations and administrative provisions relating to the taking-up and pursuit of the business of direct insurance other than life assurance (OJ L 228, 16.8.1973, p. 3). Directive as last amended by Directive 95/26/EC.

[19] First Council Directive 79/267/EEC of 5 March 1979 on the coordination of laws, regulations and administrative provisions relating to the taking-up and pursuit of the business of direct life assurance (OJ L 63, 13.3.1979, p. 1). Directive as last amended by Directive 95/26/EC.

- collectively they are of non-negligible interest with respect to the aforementioned objectives, or
- if, in the opinion of the competent authorities responsible for exercising supervision on a consolidated basis, the consolidation of the financial situation of the undertaking that should be included would be inappropriate or misleading as far as the objectives of the supervision of credit institutions are concerned.
4. When the competent authorities of a Member State do not include a credit institution subsidiary in supervision on a consolidated basis under one of the cases provided for in the second and third indents of paragraph 3, the competent authorities of the Member State in which that credit institution subsidiary is situated may ask the parent undertaking for information which may facilitate their supervision of that credit institution.
5. Supervision of solvency, and of the adequacy of own funds to cover market risks and control of large exposures shall be exercised on a consolidated basis in accordance with this Article and Articles 53 to 56. Member States shall adopt any measures necessary, where appropriate, to include financial holding companies in consolidated supervision, in accordance with paragraph 2.

    Compliance with the limits set in Article 51(1) and (2) shall be supervised and controlled on the basis of the consolidated or subconsolidated financial situation of the credit institution.
6. The competent authorities shall ensure that, in all the undertakings included in the scope of the supervision on a consolidated basis that is exercised over a credit institution in implementation of paragraphs 1 and 2, there are adequate internal control mechanisms for the production of any data and information which would be relevant for the purposes of supervision on a consolidated basis.
7. Without prejudice to specific provisions contained in other directives, Member States may waive application, on an individual or subconsolidated basis, of the rules laid down in paragraph 5 to a credit institution that, as a parent undertaking, is subject to supervision on a consolidated basis, and to any subsidiary of such a credit institution which is subject to their authorisation and supervision and is included in the supervision on a consolidated basis of the credit institution which is the parent company. The same exemption option shall be allowed where the parent undertaking is a financial holding company which has its head office in the same Member State as the credit institution, provided that it is subject to the same supervision as that exercised over credit institutions, and in particular the standards laid down in paragraph 5.

    In both cases set out in the first subparagraph, steps must be taken to ensure that capital is distributed adequately within the banking group.

    If the competent authorities apply those rules individually to such credit institutions, they may, for the purpose of calculating own funds, make use of the provision in the last subparagraph of Article 3(2).
8. Where a credit institution the parent of which is a credit institution has been authorised and is situated in another Member State, the competent authorities which granted that authorisation shall apply the rules laid down in paragraph 5 to that institution on an individual or, when appropriate, a subconsolidated basis.
9. Notwithstanding the requirements of paragraph 8, the competent authorities responsible for authorising the subsidiary of a parent undertaking which is a credit institution may, by bilateral agreement, delegate their responsibility for supervision to the competent authorities which authorised and supervise the parent undertaking so that they assume responsibility for supervising the subsidiary in accordance with this Directive. The Commission must be kept informed of the existence and content of such agreements. It shall forward such information to the competent authorities of the other Member States and to the Banking Advisory Committee.

10. Member States shall provide that their competent authorities responsible for exercising supervision on a consolidated basis may ask the subsidiaries of a credit institution or a financial holding company which are not included within the scope of supervision on a consolidated basis for the information referred to in Article 55. In such a case, the procedures for transmitting and verifying the information laid down in that Article shall apply.

Article 53 - Competent authorities responsible for exercising supervision on a consolidated basis

1. Where a parent undertaking is a credit institution, supervision on a consolidated basis shall be exercised by the competent authorities that authorised it under Article 4.
2. Where the parent of a credit institution is a financial holding company, supervision on a consolidated basis shall be exercised by the competent authorities which authorised that credit institution under Article 4.

   However, where credit institutions authorised in two or more Member States have as their parent the same financial holding company, supervision on a consolidated basis shall be exercised by the competent authorities of the credit institution authorised in the Member State in which the financial holding company was set up.

   If no credit institution subsidiary has been authorised in the Member State in which the financial holding company was set up, the competent authorities of the Member States concerned (including those of the Member State in which the financial holding company was set up) shall seek to reach agreement as to who amongst them will exercise supervision on a consolidated basis. In the absence of such agreement, supervision on a consolidated basis shall be exercised by the competent authorities that authorised the credit institution with the greatest balance-sheet total; if that figure is the same, supervision on a consolidated basis shall be exercised by the competent authorities which first gave the authorisation referred to in Article 4.
3. The competent authorities concerned may by common agreement waive the rules laid down in the first and second subparagraph of paragraph 2.
4. The agreements referred to in the third subparagraph of paragraph 2 and in paragraph 3 shall provide for procedures for cooperation and for the transmission of information such that the objectives of supervision on a consolidated basis can be attained.
5. Where Member States have more than one competent authority for the prudential supervision of credit institutions and financial institutions, Member States shall take the requisite measures to organise coordination between such authorities.

Article 54 - Form and extent of consolidation

1. The competent authorities responsible for exercising supervision on a consolidated basis must, for the purposes of supervision, require full consolidation of all the credit institutions and financial institutions which are subsidiaries of a parent undertaking.

   However, proportional consolidation may be prescribed where, in the opinion of the competent authorities, the liability of a parent undertaking holding a share of the capital is limited to that share of the capital because of the liability of the other shareholders or members whose solvency is satisfactory. The liability of the other shareholders and members must be clearly established, if necessary by means of formal signed commitments.
2. The competent authorities responsible for carrying out supervision on a consolidated basis must, in order to do so, require the proportional consolidation of participations in credit institutions and financial institutions managed by an undertaking included in the consolidation together with one or more undertakings not included in the consolidation, where those undertakings' liability is limited to the share of the capital they hold.

3. In the case of participations or capital ties other than those referred to in paragraphs 1 and 2, the competent authorities shall determine whether and how consolidation is to be carried out. In particular, they may permit or require use of the equity method. That method shall not, however, constitute inclusion of the undertakings concerned in supervision on a consolidated basis.
4. Without prejudice to paragraphs 1, 2 and 3, the competent authorities shall determine whether and how consolidation is to be carried out in the following cases:
-   where, in the opinion of the competent authorities, a credit institution exercises a significant influence over one or more credit institutions or financial institutions, but without holding a participation or other capital ties in these institutions,
-   where two or more credit institutions or financial institutions are placed under single management other than pursuant to a contract or clauses of their memoranda or articles of association,
-   where two or more credit institutions or financial institutions have administrative, management or supervisory bodies with the same persons constituting a majority.

In particular, the competent authorities may permit, or require use of, the method provided for in Article 12 of Directive 83/349/EEC. That method shall not, however, constitute inclusion of the undertakings concerned in consolidated supervision.

5. Where consolidated supervision is required pursuant to Article 52(1) and (2), ancillary banking services undertakings shall be included in consolidations in the cases, and in accordance with the methods laid down in paragraphs 1 to 4 of this Article.

Article 55 - Information to be supplied by mixed-activity holding companies and their subsidiaries

1. Pending further coordination of consolidation methods, Member States shall provide that, where the parent undertaking of one or more credit institutions is a mixed-activity holding company, the competent authorities responsible for the authorisation and supervision of those credit institutions shall, by approaching the mixed-activity holding company and its subsidiaries either directly or via credit institution subsidiaries, require them to supply any information which would be relevant for the purpose of supervising the credit institution subsidiaries.
2. Member States shall provide that their competent authorities may carry out, or have carried out by external inspectors, on-the-spot inspections to verify information received from mixed-activity holding companies and their subsidiaries. If the mixed-activity holding company or one of its subsidiaries is an insurance undertaking, the procedure laid down in Article 56(4) may also be used. If a mixed-activity holding company or one of its subsidiaries is situated in a Member State other than that in which the credit institution subsidiary is situated, on-the-spot verification of information shall be carried out in accordance with the procedure laid down in Article 56(7).

Article 56 - Measures to facilitate supervision on a consolidated basis

1. Member States shall take the necessary steps to ensure that there are no legal impediments preventing the undertakings included within the scope of supervision on a consolidated basis, mixed-activity holding companies and their subsidiaries, or subsidiaries of the kind covered in Article 52(10), from exchanging amongst themselves any information which would be relevant for the purposes of supervision in accordance with Articles 52 to 55 and this Article.
2. Where a parent undertaking and any of its subsidiaries that are credit institutions are situated in different Member States, the competent authorities of each Member State shall

communicate to each other all relevant information which may allow or aid the exercise of supervision on a consolidated basis.

Where the competent authorities of the Member State in which a parent undertaking is situated do not themselves exercise supervision on a consolidated basis pursuant to Article 53, they may be invited by the competent authorities responsible for exercising such supervision to ask the parent undertaking for any information which would be relevant for the purposes of supervision on a consolidated basis and to transmit it to these authorities.

3. Member States shall authorise the exchange between their competent authorities of the information referred to in paragraph 2, on the understanding that, in the case of financial holding companies, financial institutions or ancillary banking services undertakings, the collection or possession of information shall not in any way imply that the competent authorities are required to play a supervisory role in relation to those institutions or undertakings standing alone.

Similarly, Member States shall authorise their competent authorities to exchange the information referred to in Article 55 on the understanding that the collection or possession of information does not in any way imply that the competent authorities play a supervisory role in relation to the mixed-activity holding company and those of its subsidiaries which are not credit institutions, or to subsidiaries of the kind covered in Article 52(10).

4. Where a credit institution, financial holding company or a mixed-activity holding company controls one or more subsidiaries which are insurance companies or other undertakings providing investment services which are subject to authorisation, the competent authorities and the authorities entrusted with the public task of supervising insurance undertakings or those other undertakings providing investment services shall cooperate closely. Without prejudice to their respective responsibilities, those authorities shall provide one another with any information likely to simplify their task and to allow supervision of the activity and overall financial situation of the undertakings they supervise.

5. Information received, in the framework of supervision on a consolidated basis, and in particular any exchange of information between competent authorities which is provided for in this Directive, shall be subject to the obligation of professional secrecy defined in Article 30.

6. The competent authorities responsible for supervision on a consolidated basis shall establish lists of the financial holding companies referred to in Article 52(2). Those lists shall be communicated to the competent authorities of the other Member States and to the Commission.

7. Where, in applying this Directive, the competent authorities of one Member State wish in specific cases to verify the information concerning a credit institution, a financial holding company, a financial institution, an ancillary banking services undertaking, a mixed-activity holding company, a subsidiary of the kind covered in Article 55 or a subsidiary of the kind covered in Article 52(10), situated in another Member State, they must ask the competent authorities of that other Member State to have that verification carried out. The authorities which receive such a request must, within the framework of their competence, act upon it either by carrying out the verification themselves, by allowing the authorities who made the request to carry it out, or by allowing an auditor or expert to carry it out.

8. Without prejudice to their provisions of criminal law, Member States shall ensure that penalties or measures aimed at ending observed breaches or the causes of such breaches may be imposed on financial holding companies and mixed-activity holding companies, or their effective managers, that infringe laws, regulation or administrative provisions enacted to implement Articles 52 to 55 and this Article. In certain cases, such measures may require the intervention of the courts. The competent authorities shall cooperate closely to ensure that the abovementioned penalties or measures produce the desired results, especially when the

central administration or main establishment of a financial holding company or of a mixed-activity holding company is not located at its head office.

TITLE VI: BANKING ADVISORY COMMITTEE

Article 57 - Composition and tasks of the Banking Advisory Committee

1. A Banking Advisory Committee of the competent authorities of the Member States shall be set up alongside the Commission.
2. The tasks of the Banking Advisory Committee shall be to assist the Commission in ensuring the proper implementation of this Directive. Further it shall carry out the other tasks prescribed by this Directive and shall assist the Commission in the preparation of new proposals to the Council concerning further coordination in the sphere of credit institutions.
3. The Banking Advisory Committee shall not concern itself with concrete problems relating to individual credit institutions.
4. The Banking Advisory Committee shall be composed of not more than three representatives from each Member State and from the Commission. These representatives may be accompanied by advisers from time to time and subject to the prior agreement of the Committee. The Committee may also invite qualified persons and experts to participate in its meetings. The secretariat shall be provided by the Commission.
5. The Banking Advisory Committee shall adopt its rules of procedure and elect a chairman from among the representatives of Member States. It shall meet at regular intervals and whenever the situation demands. The Commission may ask the Committee to hold an emergency meeting if it considers that the situation so requires.
6. The Banking Advisory Committee's discussions and the outcome thereof shall be confidential except when the Committee decides otherwise.

Article 58 - Examination of the requirements for authorisation

The Banking Advisory Committee shall examine the content given by the competent authorities to requirements listed in Articles 5(1) and 6(1), any other requirements which the Member States apply and the information which must be included in the programme of operations, and shall, where appropriate, make suggestions to the Commission with a view to a more detailed coordination.

Article 59 - Observation ratios

1. Pending subsequent coordination, the competent authorities shall, for the purposes of observation and, if necessary, in addition to such coefficients as may be applied by them, establish ratios between the various assets and/or liabilities of credit institutions with a view to monitoring their solvency and liquidity and the other measures which may serve to ensure that savings are protected.

    To this end, the Banking Advisory Committee shall decide on the content of the various factors of the observation ratios referred to in the first subparagraph and lay down the method to be applied in calculating them.

    Where appropriate, the Banking Advisory Committee shall be guided by technical consultations between the supervisory authorities of the categories of institutions concerned.
2. The observation ratios established in pursuance of paragraph 1 shall be calculated at least every six months.
3. The Banking Advisory Committee shall examine the results of analyses carried out by the supervisory authorities referred to in the third subparagraph of paragraph 1 on the basis of the calculations referred to in paragraph 2.

4. The Banking Advisory Committee may make suggestions to the Commission with a view to coordinating the coefficients applicable in the Member States.

TITLE VII: POWERS OF EXECUTION

Article 60 - Technical adaptations

1. Without prejudice, regarding own funds, to the report referred to in the second subparagraph of Article 34(3), the technical adaptations in the following areas shall be adopted in accordance with the procedure laid down in paragraph 2:
   - clarification of the definitions in order to take account in the application of this Directive of developments on financial markets,
   - clarification of the definitions to ensure uniform application of this Directive in the Community,
   - the alignment of terminology on and the framing of definitions in accordance with subsequent acts on credit institutions and related matters,
   - the definition of "Zone A" in Article 1(14),
   - the definition of "multilateral development banks" in Article 1(19),
   - alteration of the amount of initial capital prescribed in Article 5 to take account of developments in the economic and monetary field,
   - expansion of the content of the list referred to in Articles 18 and 19 and set out in Annex I or adaptation of the terminology used in that list to take account of developments on financial markets,
   - the areas in which the competent authorities must exchange information as listed in Article 28,
   - amendment of the definitions of the assets listed in Article 43 in order to take account of developments on financial markets,
   - the list and classification of off-balance-sheet items in Annexes II and IV and their treatment in the calculation of the ratio as described in Articles 42, 43 and 44 and Annex III,
   - a temporary reduction in the minimum ratio prescribed in Article 47 or the weighting prescribed in Article 43 in order to take account of specific circumstances,
   - clarification of exemptions provided for in Article 49(5) to (10).
2. The Commission shall be assisted by a committee.
   Where reference is made to this paragraph, Articles 5 and 7 of Decision 1999/468/EC shall apply, having regard to the provisions of Article 8 thereof.
   The period laid down in Article 5(6) of Decision 1999/468/EC shall be set at three months.
   The Committee shall adopt its rules of procedure.

TITLE VIII: TRANSITIONAL AND FINAL PROVISIONS

CHAPTER 1: TRANSITIONAL PROVISIONS

Article 61 - Transitional provisions regarding Article 36

Denmark may allow its mortgage credit institutions organised as cooperative societies or funds before 1 January 1990 and converted into public limited liability companies to continue to include joint and several commitments of members, or of borrowers as referred to in Article 36(1) claims on whom are treated in the same way as such joint and several commitments, in their own funds, subject to the following limits:

(a) the basis for calculation of the part of joint and several commitments of borrowers shall be the total of the items referred to in Article 34(2)(1) and (2), minus those referred to in Article 34(2)(9), (10) and (11);
(b) the basis for calculation on 1 January 1991 or, if converted at a later date, on the date on conversion, shall be the maximum basis for calculation. The basis for calculation may never exceed the maximum basis for calculation;
(c) the maximum basis for calculation shall, from 1 January 1997, be reduced by half of the proceeds from any issue of new capital, as defined in Article 34(2)(1), made after that date; and
(d) the maximum amount of joint and several commitments of borrowers to be included as own funds must never exceed:
50 % in 1991 and 1992,
45 % in 1993 and 1994,
40 % in 1995 and 1996,
35 % in 1997,
30 % in 1998,
20 % in 1999,
10 % in 2000, and
0 % after 1 January 2001, of the basis for calculation.

Article 62 - Transitional provisions regarding Article 43

1. Until 31 December 2006, the competent authorities of the Member States may authorise their credit institutions to apply a 50 % risk weighting to loans fully and completely secured to their satisfaction by mortgages on offices or on multi-purpose commercial premises situated within the territory of those Member States that allow the 50 % risk weighting, subject to the following conditions:
(i) the 50 % risk weighting applies to the part of the loan that does not exceed a limit calculated according to either (a) or (b):
(a) 50 % of the market value of the property in question.

The market value of the property must be calculated by two independent valuers making independent assessments at the time the loan is made. The loan must be based on the lower of the two valuations.

The property shall be revalued at least once a year by one valuer. For loans not exceeding EUR 1 million and 5 % of the own funds of the credit institution, the property shall be revalued at least every three years by one valuer;
(b) 50 % of the market value of the property or 60 % of the mortgage lending value, whichever is lower, in those Member States that have laid down rigorous criteria for the assessment of the mortgage lending value in statutory or regulatory provisions.

The mortgage lending value shall means the value of the property as determined by a valuer making a prudent assessment of the future marketability of the property by taking into account long-term sustainable aspects of the property, the normal and local market conditions, the current use and alternative appropriate uses of the property. Speculative elements shall not be taken into account in the assessment of the mortgage lending value. The mortgage lending value shall be documented n a transparent and clear manner.

At least every three years or if the market falls by more than 10 % the mortgage lending value and in particular the underlying assumptions concerning the development of the relevant market, shall be reassessed.

In both (a) and (b) "market value" shall mean the price at which the property could be sold under private contract between a willing seller and an arm's-length buyer on the date of valuation, it being assumed that the property is publicly exposed to the market, that market conditions permit orderly disposal and that a normal period, having regard to the nature of the property, is available for the negotiation of the sale;

(ii) the 100 % risk weighting applies to the part of the loan that exceeds the limits set out in (i);
(iii) the property must be either used or let by the owner.

The first subparagraph shall not prevent the competent authorities of a Member State, which applies a higher risk weighting in its territory, from allowing, under the conditions defined above, the 50 % risk weighting to apply for this type of lending in the territories of those Member States that allow the 50 % risk weighting.

The competent authorities of the Member States may allow their credit institutions to apply a 50 % risk weighting to the loans outstanding on 21 July 2000 provided that the conditions listed in this paragraph are fulfilled. In this case the property shall be valued according to the assessment criteria laid down above not later than 21 July 2003.

For loans granted before 31 December 2006, the 50 % risk weighting remains applicable until their maturity, if the credit institution is bound to observe the contractual terms.

Until 31 December 2006, the competent authorities of the Member State may also authorise their credit institutions to apply a 50 % risk weighting to the part of the loans fully and completely secured to their satisfaction by shares in Finnish housing companies operating in accordance with the Finnish Housing Company Act of 1991 or subsequent equivalent legislation, provided that the conditions laid down in this paragraph are fulfilled.

Member States shall inform the Commission of the use they make of this paragraph.

2. Member States may apply a 50 % risk weighting to property leasing transactions concluded before 31 December 2006 and concerning assets for business use situated in the country of the head office and governed by statutory provisions whereby the lessor retains full ownership of the rented asset until the tenant exercises his option to purchase. Member States shall inform the Commission of the use they make of this paragraph.

3. Article 43(3) shall not affect the competent authorities' recognition of bilateral contracts for novation concluded concerning:
- Belgium, before 23 April 1996,
- Denmark, before 1 June 1996,
- Germany, before 30 October 1996,
- Greece, before 27 March 1997,
- Spain, before 7 January 1997,
- France, before 30 May 1996,
- Ireland, before 27 June 1996,
- Italy, before 30 July 1996,
- Luxembourg, before 29 May 1996,
- the Netherlands, before 1 July 1996,
- Austria, before 30 December 1996,
- Portugal, before 15 January 1997,
- Finland, before 21 August 1996,
- Sweden, before 1 June 1996, and
- United Kingdom, before 30 April 1996.

Article 63 - Transitional provisions regarding Article 47

1. A credit institution, the minimum ratio of which has not reached the 8 % prescribed in Article 47(1), by 1 January 1991, must gradually approach that level by successive stages. It may not allow the ratio to fall below the level reached before that objective has been

attained. Any fluctuation should be temporary and the competent authorities should be apprised of the reasons for it.
2. For not more than five years after 1 January 1993, the Member States may fix a weighting of 10 % for the bonds defined in Article 22(4) of Directive 85/611/EEC and maintain if for credit institutions when and if they consider it necessary, to avoid grave disturbances in the operation of their markets. Such exceptions shall be reported to the Commission.
3. For not more than seven years after 1 January 1993, Article 47(1) shall not apply to the Agricultural Bank of Greece. However, the latter must approach the level prescribed in Article 47(1) by successive stages according to the method described in paragraph 1 of this Article.

Article 64 - Transitional provisions regarding Article 49

1. If, on 5 February 1993, a credit institution had already incurred an exposure or exposures exceeding either the large exposure limit or the aggregate large exposure limit laid down in Article 49, the competent authorities shall require the credit institution concerned to take steps to have that exposure or those exposures brought within the limits laid down in Article 49.
2. The process of having such an exposure or exposures brought within authorised limits shall be devised, adopted, implemented and completed within the period which the competent authorities consider consistent with the principle of sound administration and fair competition. The competent authorities shall inform the Commission and the Banking Advisory Committee of the schedule for the general process adopted.
3. A credit institution may not take any measure which would cause the exposures referred to in paragraph 1 to exceed their level on 5 February 1993
4. The period applicable under paragraph 2 shall expire no later than 31 December 2001. Exposures with a longer maturity, for which the lending institution is bound to observe the contractual terms, may be continued until their maturity.
5. Until 31 December 1998, Member States may increase the limit laid down in Article 49(1) to 40 % and the limit laid down in Article 49(2) to 30 %. In such cases and subject to paragraphs 1 to 4, the time limit for bringing the exposures existing at the end of this period within the limit laid down in Article 49 shall expire on 31 December 2001.
6. In the case of credit institutions the own funds of which do not exceed EUR 7 million and only in the case of such institutions, Member States may extend the time limits laid down in paragraph 5 by five years. Member States that avail themselves of the option provided for in this paragraph shall take steps to prevent distortions of competition and shall inform the Commission and the Banking Advisory Committee thereof.
7. In the cases referred to in paragraphs 5 and 6, an exposure may be considered a large exposure if its value is equal to or exceeds 15 % of own funds.
8. Until 31 December 2001 Member States may substitute a frequency of at least twice a year for the frequency of notification of large exposures referred to in the second indent of Article 48(2).
9. Member States may fully or partially exempt from the application of Article 49(1), (2) and (3) exposures incurred by a credit institution consisting of mortgage loans as defined in Article 62(1) concluded before 1 January 2002 as well as property leasing transactions as defined in Article 62(2) concluded before 1 January 2002, in both cases up to 50 % of the value of the property concerned.
The same treatment applies to loans secured, to the satisfaction of the competent authorities, by shares in Finnish residential housing companies, operating in accordance with the Finnish Housing Company Act of 1991 or subsequent equivalent legislation which are similar to the mortgage loans referred to in the first subparagraph.

Article 65 - Transitional provisions regarding Article 51

Credit institutions which, on 1 January 1993, exceeded the limits laid down in Articles 51(1) and (2) shall have until 1 January 2003 to comply with them.

CHAPTER 2: FINAL PROVISIONS

Article 66 - Commission information

Member States shall communicate to the Commission the texts of the main laws, regulations and administrative provisions which they adopt in the field covered by this Directive.

Article 67 - Repealed Directives

1. Directives 73/183/EEC, 77/780/EEC, 89/299/EEC, 89/646/EEC, 89/647/EEC, 92/30/EEC and 92/121/EEC, as amended by the Directives set out in Annex V, Part A, are hereby repealed without prejudice to the obligations of the Member States concerning the deadlines for transposition of the said Directives listed in Annex V, Part B.
2. References to the repealed Directives shall be construed as references to this Directive and should be read in accordance with the correlation table in Annex VI.

Article 68 - Implementation

This Directive shall enter into force on the 20th day following its publication in the Official Journal of the European Communities.

Article 69 - Addressees

This Directive is addressed to the Member States.

ANNEX I: LIST OF ACTIVITIES SUBJECT TO MUTUAL RECOGNITION

1. Acceptance of deposits and other repayable funds
2. Lending[20]
3. Financial leasing
4. Money transmission services
5. Issuing and administering means of payment (e.g. credit cards, travellers' cheques and bankers' drafts)
6. Guarantees and commitments
7. Trading for own account or for account of customers in:
(a) money market instruments (cheques, bills, certificates of deposit, etc.)
(b) foreign exchange;
(c) financial futures and options;
(d) exchange and interest-rate instruments;
(e) transferable securities
8. Participation in securities issues and the provision of services related to such issues
9. Advice to undertakings on capital structure, industrial strategy and related questions and advice as well as services relating to mergers and the purchase of undertakings

---

[20] Including, inter alia:
- consumer credit,
- mortgage credit,
- factoring, with or without recourse,
- financing of commercial transactions (including forfeiting).

10. Money broking
11. Portfolio management and advice
12. Safekeeping and administration of securities
13. Credit reference services
14. Safe custody services

ANNEX II - CLASSIFICATION OF OFF-BALANCE-SHEET ITEMS

[…]

ANNEX III: THE TREATMENT OF OFF-BALANCE-SHEET ITEMS

[…]

ANNEX IV: TYPES OF OFF-BALANCE-SHEET ITEMS

[…]

ANNEX V

PART A
REPEALED DIRECTIVES TOGETHER WITH THEIR SUCCESSIVE AMENDMENTS
(referred to in Article 67)

Council Directive 73/183/EEC
Council Directive 77/780/EEC
    Council Directive 85/345/EEC
    Council Directive 86/137/EEC
    Council Directive 86/524/EEC
    Council Directive 89/646/EEC
    Directive 95/26/EC of the European Parliament and of the Council,
        only Article 1, first indent, Article 2(1), first indent and (2), first indent, Article 3(2), Article 4(2), (3) and (4), as regards references to Directive 77/780/EEC, and (6), and Article 5, first indent
    Council Directive 96/13/EC
    Directive 98/33/EC of the European Parliament and of the Council
Council Directive 89/299/EEC
    Council Directive 91/633/EEC
    Council Directive 92/16/EEC
    Council Directive 92/30/EEC
Council Directive 89/646/EEC
    Council Directive 92/30/EEC
    Directive 95/26/EC of the European Parliament and of the Council
        only Article 1, first indent
Council Directive 89/647/EEC
    Commission Directive 91/31/EEC
    Council Directive 92/30/EEC
    Commission Directive 94/7/EC
    Commission Directive 95/15/EC

Commission Directive 95/67/EC
Directive 96/10/EC of the European Parliament and of the Council
Directive 98/32/EC of the European Parliament and of the Council
Directive 98/33/EC of the European Parliament and of the Council (Article 2)
Council Directive 92/30/EEC
Council Directive 92/121/EEC

PART B
DEADLINES FOR IMPLEMENTATION
(referred to in Article 67)

[…]

DIRECTIVE 2000/28/EC OF THE EUROPEAN PARLIAMENT AND OF THE COUNCIL OF 18 SEPTEMBER 2000 AMENDING DIRECTIVE 2000/12/EC RELATING TO THE TAKING UP AND PURSUIT OF THE BUSINESS OF CREDIT INSTITUTIONS

(Official Journal L 275, 27/10/2000, p. 0037 – 0038)

THE EUROPEAN PARLIAMENT AND THE COUNCIL OF THE EUROPEAN UNION,

Having regard to the Treaty establishing the European Community, and in particular the first and third sentences of Article 47(2) thereof,
Having regard to the proposal from the Commission[1],
Having regard to the opinion of the Economic and Social Committee[2],
Having regard to the opinion of the European Central Bank[3],

Acting in accordance with the procedure laid down in Article 251 of the Treaty[4],

Whereas:
(1) In accordance with the objectives of the Treaty, it is desirable to promote harmonious development of the activities of credit institutions throughout the Community, in particular as regards the issuance of electronic money.
(2) Certain institutions limit their activity primarily to the issuance of electronic money. To avoid any distortion of competition between electronic money issuers, even as regards application of monetary policy measures, it is advisable that these institutions, subject to suitable specific provisions taking into account their special characteristics, be brought within the scope of Directive 2000/12/EC[5].
(3) It is advisable, consequently, to extend to these institutions the definition of credit institutions provided for in Article 1 of Directive 2000/12/EC.
(4) Directive 2000/46/EC of the European Parliament and of the Council of 18 September 2000 on the taking up, pursuit and prudential supervision of the business of electronic money institutions[6] defines electronic money institutions.
(5) It is necessary for electronic money to be redeemable to ensure bearer confidence,

HAVE ADOPTED THIS DIRECTIVE:

Article 1

Directive 2000/12/EC is hereby amended as follows:
1. Article 1, point 1, first subparagraph shall be replaced by the following text:
"1. 'Credit institution' shall mean:
(a) an undertaking whose business is to receive deposits or other repayable funds from the public and to grant credits for its own account; or

---

[1] OJ C 317, 15.10.1998, p. 12.
[2] OJ C 101, 12.4.1999, p. 64.
[3] OJ C 189, 6.7.1999, p. 7.
[4] Opinion of the European Parliament of 15 April 1999 (OJ C 219, 30.7.1999, p. 421), confirmed on 27 October 1999, Council Common Position of 29 November 1999 (OJ C 26, 28.1.2000, p. 12) and Decision of the European Parliament of 11 April 2000 (not yet published in the Official Journal).
[5] Directive 2000/12/EC of the European Parliament and of the Council of 20 March 2000 relating to the taking up and pursuit of the business of credit institutions (OJ L 126, 26.5.2000, p. 1).
[6] See page 39 of this Official Journal.

(b) an electronic money institution within the meaning of Directive 2000/46/EC of the European Parliament and of the Council of 18 September 2000 on the taking up, pursuit and prudential supervision of the business of electronic money institutions[7]."

2. The following Article shall be added to Title V:
"Article 33a
Article 3 of Directive 2000/46/EC shall apply to credit institutions."

Article 2

1. Member States shall bring into force the laws, regulations and administrative provisions necessary to comply with this Directive not later than 27 April 2002. They shall immediately inform the Commission thereof.

   When Member States adopt these measures, they shall contain a reference to this Directive or shall be accompanied by such reference on the occasion of their official publication. The methods of making such a reference shall be laid down by the Member States.

2. Member States shall communicate to the Commission the text of the main provisions of national law which they adopt in the field covered by this Directive.

Article 3

This Directive shall enter into force on the day of its publication in the Official Journal of the European Communities.

Article 4

This Directive is addressed to the Member States.

---

[7] OJ L 275, 27.10.2000, p. 39.

DIRECTIVE 2000/46/EC OF THE EUROPEAN PARLIAMENT AND OF THE COUNCIL OF 18 SEPTEMBER 2000 ON THE TAKING UP, PURSUIT OF AND PRUDENTIAL SUPERVISION OF THE BUSINESS OF ELECTRONIC MONEY INSTITUTIONS

(Official Journal L 275, 27/10/2000, p. 0039)

THE EUROPEAN PARLIAMENT AND THE COUNCIL OF THE EUROPEAN UNION,

Having regard to the Treaty establishing the European Community, and in particular the first and third sentences of Article 47(2) thereof,
Having regard to the proposal from the Commission[1],
Having regard to the opinion of the Economic and Social Committee[2],
Having regard to the opinion of the European Central Bank[3],

Acting in accordance with the procedure laid down in Article 251 of the Treaty[4],

Whereas:
(1) Credit institutions within the meaning of Article 1, point 1, first subparagraph (b) of Directive 2000/12/EC[5] are limited in the scope of their activities.
(2) It is necessary to take account of the specific characteristics of these institutions and to provide the appropriate measures necessary to co-ordinate and harmonise Member States' laws, regulations and administrative provisions relating to the taking up, pursuit and prudential supervision of the business of electronic money institutions.
(3) For the purposes of this Directive, electronic money can be considered an electronic surrogate for coins and banknotes, which is stored o a electronic device such as a chip card or computer memory and which is generally intended for the purpose of effecting electronic payments of limited amounts.
(4) The approach adopted is appropriate to achieve only the essential harmonisation necessary and sufficient to secure the mutual recognition of authorisation and prudential supervision of electronic money institutions, making possible the granting of a single licence recognised throughout the Community and designed to ensure bearer confidence and the application of the principle of home Member State prudential supervision .
(5) Within the wider context of the rapidly evolving electronic commerce it is desirable to provide a regulatory framework that assists electronic money in delivering its full potential benefits and that avoids hampering technological innovation in particular. Therefore, this Directive introduces a technology-neutral legal framework that harmonises the prudential supervision of electronic money institutions to the extent necessary for ensuring their sound and prudent operation and their financial integrity in particular.
(6) Credit institutions, by virtue of point 5 of A ex I to Directive 2000/12/EC, are already allowed to issue and administer means of payment including electronic money and to carry on such activities Community-wide subject to mutual recognition and to the comprehensive

---

[1] OJ C 317, 15.10.1998, p. 7.
[2] OJ C 101, 12.4.1999, p. 64.
[3] OJ C 189, 6.7.1999, p. 7.
[4] Opinion of the European Parliament of 15 April 1999 (OJ C 219, 30.7.1999, p. 415), confirmed on 27 October 1999, Council Common Position of 29 November 1999 (OJ C 26, 28.1.2000, p. 1) and Decision of the European Parliament of 11 April 2000 (not yet published in the Official Journal). Decision of the Council of 16 June 2000.
[5] Directive 2000/12/EC of the European Parliament and of the Council of 20 March 2000 relating to the taking up and pursuit of the business of credit institutions (OJ L 126, 26.5.2000, p. 1). Directive as last amended by Directive 2000/28/EC (see page 37 of this Official Journal).

prudential supervisory system applying to them in accordance with the European banking Directives.

(7) The introduction of a separate prudential supervisory regime for electronic money institutions, which, although calibrated o the prudential supervisory regime applying to other credit institutions and Directive 2000/12/EC except Title V, Chapters 2 a d 3 thereof in particular, differs from that regime, is justified and desirable because the issuance of electronic money does not constitute in itself, in view of its specific character as an electronic surrogate for coins and banknotes, a deposit-taking activity pursuant to Article 3 of Directive 2000/12/EC, if the received funds are immediately exchanged for electronic money.

(8) The receipt of funds from the public in exchange for electronic money, which results in a credit balance left on account with the issuing institution, constitutes the receipt of deposits or other repayable funds for the purpose of Directive 2000/12/EC.

(9) It is necessary for electronic money to be redeemable to ensure bearer confidence. Redeemability does not imply, in itself, that the funds received in exchange for electronic money shall be regarded as deposits or other repayable funds for the purpose of Directive 2000/12/EC.

(10) Redeemability should always be understood to be at par value.

(11) In order to respond to the specific risks associated with the issuance of electronic money this prudential supervisory regime must be more targeted and, accordingly, less cumbersome than the prudential supervisory regime applying to credit institutions, notably as regards reduced initial capital requirements and the non-application of Directive 93/6/EEC[6] and Title V, Chapter 2, Sections II and III of Directive 2000/12/EC.

(12) However, it is necessary to preserve a level playing field between electronic money institutions and other credit institutions issuing electronic money and, thus, to ensure fair competition among a wider range of institutions to the benefit of bearers. This is achieved since the above mentioned less cumbersome features of the prudential supervisory regime applying to electronic money institutions are balanced by provisions that are more stringent than those applying to other credit institutions, notably as regards restrictions on the business activities which electronic money institutions may carry on and, particularly, prudent limitations of their investments aimed at ensuring that their financial liabilities related to outstanding electronic money are backed at all times by sufficiently liquid low risk assets.

(13) Pending the harmonisation of prudential supervision of outsourced activities for credit institutions it is appropriate that electronic money institutions have sound and prudent management and control procedures. With a view to the possibility of operational and other ancillary functions related to the issuance of electronic money being performed by undertakings which are not subject to prudential supervision it is essential that electronic money institutions have in place internal structures which should respond to the financial and non-financial risks to which they are exposed.

(14) The issuance of electronic money may affect the stability of the financial system and the smooth operation of payments systems. Close co-operation in assessing the integrity of electronic money schemes is called for.

(15) It is appropriate to afford compete t authorities the possibility of waiving some or all of the requirements imposed by this Directive for electronic money institutions which operate only within the territories of the respective Member States.

(16) Adoption of this Directive constitutes the most appropriate means of achieving the desired objectives. This Directive is limited to the minimum necessary to achieve these objectives and does not go beyond what is necessary for this purpose.

(17) Provision should be made for the review of this Directive in the light of experience of developments in the market and the protection of bearers of electronic money.

---

[6] Council Directive 93/6/EEC of 15 March 1993 on the capital adequacy of investment firms and credit institutions (OJ L 141, 11.6.1993, p. 1). Directive as last amended by Directive 98/33/EC (OJ L 204, 21.7.1998, p. 29).

(18) The Banking Advisory Committee has been consulted on the adoption of this Directive,

HAVE ADOPTED THIS DIRECTIVE:

Article 1 - Scope, definitions and restriction of activities

1. This Directive shall apply to electronic money institutions.
2. It shall not apply to the institutions referred to in Article 2(3) of Directive 2000/12/EC.
3. For the purposes of this Directive:
(a) 'electronic money institution' shall mean an undertaking or any other legal person, other than a credit institution as defined in Article 1, point 1, first subparagraph (a) of Directive 2000/12/EC which issues means of payment in the form of electronic money;
(b) 'electronic money' shall mean monetary value as represented by a claim on the issuer which is:
(i) stored on an electronic device;
(ii) issued on receipt of funds of an amount not less in value than the monetary value issued;
(iii) accepted as means of payment by undertakings other than the issuer.
4. Member States shall prohibit persons or undertakings that are not credit institutions, as defined in Article 1, point 1, first subparagraph of Directive 2000/12/EC, from carrying on the business of issuing electronic money.
5. The business activities of electronic money institutions other than the issuing of electronic money shall be restricted to:
(a) the provision of closely related financial and non-financial services such as the administering of electronic money by the performance of operational and other ancillary functions related to its issuance, and the issuing and administering of other means of payment but excluding the granting of a y form of credit; and
(b) the storing of data on the electronic device on behalf of other undertakings or public institutions.

Electronic money institutions shall not have any holdings in other undertakings except where these undertakings perform operational or other ancillary functions related to electronic money issued or distributed by the institution concerned.

Article 2 - Application of Banking Directives

1. Save where otherwise expressly provided for, only references to credit institutions in Directive 91/308/EEC (1) and Directive 2000/12/EC except Title V, Chapter 2 thereof shall apply to electronic money institutions.
2. Articles 5, 11, 13, 19, 20(7), 51 a d 59 of Directive 2000/12/EC shall not apply. The mutual recognition arrangements provided for in Directive 2000/12/EC shall not apply to electronic money institutions' business activities other than the issuance of electronic money.
3. The receipt of funds within the meaning of Article 1(3)(b)(ii) does not constitute a deposit or other repayable funds according to Article 3 of Directive 2000/12/EC, if the funds received are immediately exchanged for electronic money.

Article 3 - Redeemability

1. A bearer of electronic money may, during the period of validity, ask the issuer to redeem it at par value in coins and banknotes or by a transfer to an account free of charges other than those strictly necessary to carry out that operation.
2. The contract between the issuer and the bearer shall clearly state the conditions of redemption.

3. The contract may stipulate a minimum threshold for redemption. The threshold may not exceed EUR 10.

Article 4 - Initial capital and ongoing own funds requirements

1. Electronic money institutions shall have an initial capital, as defined in Article 34(2), subparagraphs (1) and (2) of Directive 2000/12/EC, of not less than EUR 1 million. Notwithstanding paragraphs 2 and 3, their own funds, as defined in Directive 2000/12/EC, shall not fall below that amount.
2. Electronic money institutions shall have at all times own funds which are equal to or above 2 % of the higher of the current amount or the average of the preceding six months' total amount of their financial liabilities related to outstanding electronic money.
3. Where an electronic money institution has not completed a six months' period of business, including the day it starts up, it shall have own funds which are equal to or above 2 % of the higher of the current amount or the six months' target total amount of its financial liabilities related to outstanding electronic money. The six months' target total amount of the institution's financial liabilities related to outstanding electronic money shall be evidenced by its business plan subject to any adjustment to that plan having been required by the competent authorities.

Article 5 - Limitations of investments

1. Electronic money institutions shall have investments of an amount of no less than their financial liabilities related to outstanding electronic money in the following assets only:
(a) asset items which according to Article 43(1)(a) (1), (2), (3) and (4) and Article 44(1) of Directive 2000/12/EC attract a zero credit risk weighting and which are sufficiently liquid;
(b) sight deposits held with Zone A credit institutions as defined in Directive 2000/12/EC; and
(c) debt instruments which are:
(i) sufficiently liquid;
(ii) not covered by paragraph 1(a);
(iii) recognised by competent authorities as qualifying items within the meaning of Article 2(12) of Directive 93/6/EEC; and
(iv) issued by undertakings other than undertakings which have a qualifying holding, as defined in Article 1 of Directive 2000/12/EC, in the electronic money institution concerned or which must be included in those undertakings' consolidated accounts.
2. Investments referred to in paragraph 1(b) a d (c) may not exceed 20 times the own funds of the electronic money institution concerned and shall be subject to limitations which are at least as stringent as those applying to credit institutions in accordance with Title V, Chapter 2, Section III of Directive 2000/12/EC.
3. For the purpose of hedging market risks arising from the issuance of electronic money and from the investments referred to in paragraph 1, electronic money institutions may use sufficiently liquid interest-rate and foreign-exchange-related off balance-sheet items in the form of exchange-traded (i.e. not OTC) derivative instruments where they are subject to daily margin requirements or foreign exchange contracts with an original maturity of 14 calendar days or less. The use of derivative instruments according to the first sentence is permissible only if the full elimination of market risks is intended and, to the extent possible, achieved.
4. Member States shall impose appropriate limitations on the market risks electronic money institutions may incur from the investments referred to in paragraph 1.
5. For the purpose of applying paragraph 1, assets shall be valued at the lower of cost or market value.
6. If the value of the assets referred to in paragraph 1 falls below the amount of financial liabilities related to outstanding electronic money, the competent authorities shall ensure that

the electronic money institution in question takes appropriate measures to remedy that situation promptly. To this end, and for a temporary period only, the competent authorities may allow the institution's financial liabilities related to outstanding electronic money to be backed by assets other than those referred to in paragraph 1 up to am amount not exceeding the lower of 5 % of these liabilities or the institution's total amount of own funds.

Article 6 - Verification of specific requirements by the competent authorities

The competent authorities shall ensure that the calculations justifying compliance with Articles 4 and 5 are made, not less than twice each year, either by electronic money institutions themselves, which shall communicate them, and any component data required, to the competent authorities, or by competent authorities, using data supplied by the electronic money institutions.

Article 7 - Sound and prudent operation

Electronic money institutions shall have sound and prudent management, administrative and accounting procedures and adequate internal control mechanisms. These should respond to the financial and non-financial risks to which the institution is exposed including technical and procedural risks as well as risks connected to its cooperation with any undertaking performing operational or other ancillary functions related to its business activities.

Article 8 - Waive

1. Member States may allow their competent authorities to waive the application of some or all of the provisions of this Directive and the application of Directive 2000/12/EC to electronic money institutions in cases where either:
(a) the total business activities of the type referred to in Article 1(3)(a) of this Directive of the institution generate a total amount of financial liabilities related to outstanding electronic money that normally does not exceed EUR 5 million and ever exceeds EUR 6 million ; or
(b) the electronic money issued by the institution is accepted as a means of payment only by any subsidiaries of the institution which perform operational or other ancillary functions related to electronic money issued or distributed by the institution , any parent undertaking of the institution or any other subsidiaries of that parent undertaking; or
(c) electronic money issued by the institution is accepted as payment only by a limited umber of undertakings, which can be clearly distinguished by:
(i) their location in the same premises or other limited local area; or
(ii) their close financial or business relationship with the issuing institution , such as a common marketing or distribution scheme.

The underlying contractual arrangements must provide that the electronic storage device at the disposal of bearers for the purpose of making payments is subject to a maximum storage amount of not more than EUR 150.

2. An electronic money institution for which a waiver has bee granted under paragraph 1 shall not benefit from the mutual recognition arrangements provided for in Directive 2000/12/EC.
3. Member States shall require that all electronic money institutions to which the application of this Directive and Directive 2000/12/EC has been waived report periodically on their activities including the total amount of financial liabilities related to electronic money.

Article 9 - Grandfathering

Electronic money institutions subject to this Directive which have commenced their activity in accordance with the provisions in force in the Member State in which they have their head office before the date of entry into force of the provisions adopted in implementation of this Directive or the date referred to in Article 10(1), whichever date is earlier, shall be presumed to be authorised. The Member States shall oblige such electronic money institutions to submit all relevant information to the competent authorities in order to allow them to assess within six months from the date of entry into force of the provisions adopted in implementation of this Directive, whether the institutions comply with the requirements pursuant to this Directive, which measures need to be taken in order to ensure compliance, or whether a withdrawal of authorisation is appropriate. If compliance is not ensured within six months from the date referred to in Article 10(1), the electronic money institution shall not benefit from mutual recognition after that time.

Article 10 - Implementation

1. Member States shall bring into force the laws, regulations and administrative provisions necessary to comply with this Directive not later than 27 April 2002. They shall immediately inform the Commission thereof.
When Member States adopt these measures, they shall contain a reference to this Directive or shall be accompanied by such reference on the occasion of their official publication. The methods of making such a reference shall be laid down by the Member States.
2. Member States shall communicate to the Commission the text of the main provisions of national law, which they adopt in the field covered by this Directive.

Article 11 - Review

Not later than 27 April 2005 the Commission shall present a report to the European Parliament and the Council on the application of this Directive, in particular on:
- the measures to protect the bearers of electronic money, including the possible need to introduce a guarantee scheme,
- capital requirements,
- waivers, and
- the possible need to prohibit interest being paid on funds received in exchange for electronic money,

accompanied where appropriate by a proposal for its revision.

Article 12 - Entry into force

This Directive shall enter into force on the day of its publication in the *Official Journal of the European Communities*.

Article 13 – Addressees

This Directive is addressed to the Member States.

4. E-Contracting

UNCITRAL MODEL LAW ON ELECTRONIC COMMERCE

UNITED NATIONS COMMISSION ON INTERNATIONAL TRADE LAW (UNCITRAL)

51/162 Model Law on Electronic Commerce adopted by the United Nations Commission on International Trade Law, 16 December 1996
with additional article 5 bis as adopted in 1998

(Source: http://www.uncitral.org/en-index.htm)

Part One. Electronic Commerce in General

CHAPTER I: GENERAL PROVISIONS

Article 1 - Sphere of application[*]

This Law[**] applies to any kind of information in the form of a data message used in the context[***] of commercial[****] activities.

Article 2 - Definitions

For the purposes of this Law:

(a) "Data message" means information generated, sent, received or stored by electronic, optical or similar means including, but not limited to, electronic data interchange (EDI), electronic mail, telegram, telex or telecopy;

(b) "Electronic data interchange (EDI)" means the electronic transfer from computer to computer of information using an agreed standard to structure the information;

(c) "Originator" of a data message means a person by whom, or on whose behalf, the data message purports to have been sent or generated prior to storage, if any, but it does not include a person acting as an intermediary with respect to that data message;

(d) "Addressee" of a data message means a person who is intended by the originator to receive the data message, but does not include a person acting as an intermediary with respect to that data message;

---

[*] The Commission suggests the following text for States that might wish to limit the applicability of this Law to international data messages:
"This Law applies to a data message as defined in paragraph (1) of article 2 where the data message relates to international commerce."

[**] This Law does not override any rule of law intended for the protection of consumers.

[***] The Commission suggests the following text for States that might wish to extend the applicability of this Law: "This Law applies to any kind of information in the form of a data message, except in the following situations: [...]."

[****] The term "commercial" should be given a wide interpretation so as to cover matters arising from all relationships of a commercial nature, whether contractual or not. Relationships of a commercial nature include, but are not limited to, the following transactions: any trade transaction for the supply or exchange of goods or services; distribution agreement; commercial representation or agency; factoring; leasing; construction of works; consulting; engineering; licensing; investment; financing; banking; insurance; exploitation agreement or concession; joint venture and other forms of industrial or business cooperation; carriage of goods or passengers by air, sea, rail or road.

(e) "Intermediary", with respect to a particular data message, means a person who, on behalf of another person, sends, receives or stores that data message or provides other services with respect to that data message;
(f) "Information system" means a system for generating, sending, receiving, storing or otherwise processing data messages.

Article 3 - Interpretation

(1) In the interpretation of this Law, regard is to be had to its international origin and to the need to promote uniformity in its application and the observance of good faith.
(2) Questions concerning matters governed by this Law which are not expressly settled in it are to be settled in conformity with the general principles on which this Law is based.

Article 4 - Variation by agreement

(1) As between parties involved in generating, sending, receiving, storing or otherwise processing data messages, and except as otherwise provided, the provisions of chapter III may be varied by agreement.
(2) Paragraph (1) does not affect any right that may exist to modify by agreement any rule of law referred to in chapter II.

CHAPTER II: APPLiCATION OF LEGAL REQUIREMENTS TO DATA MESSAGES

Article 5 - Legal recognition of data messages

Information shall not be denied legal effect, validity or enforce- ability solely on the grounds that it is in the form of a data message.

Article 5 bis - Incorporation by reference (as adopted by the Commission at its thirty-first session, in June 1998)

Information shall not be denied legal effect, validity or enforceability solely on the grounds that it is not contained in the data message purporting to give rise to such legal effect, but is merely referred to in that data message.

Article 6 - Writing

(1) Where the law requires information to be in writing, that requirement is met by a data message if the information contained therein is accessible so as to be usable for subsequent reference.
(2) Paragraph (1) applies whether the requirement therein is in the form of an obligation or whether the law simply provides consequences for the information not being in writing.
(3) The provisions of this article do not apply to the following: [...].

Article 7 - Signature

(1) Where the law requires a signature of a person, that requirement is met in relation to a data message if:
(a) a method is used to identify that person and to indicate that person's approval of the information contained in the data message; and
(b) that method is as reliable as was appropriate for the purpose for which the data message was generated or communicated, in the light of all the circumstances, including any relevant agreement.

(2) Paragraph (1) applies whether the requirement therein is in the form of an obligation or whether the law simply provides consequences for the absence of a signature.
(3) The provisions of this article do not apply to the following: [...].

Article 8 - Original

(1) Where the law requires information to be presented or retained in its original form, that requirement is met by a data message if:
(a) there exists a reliable assurance as to the integrity of the information from the time when it was first generated in its final form, as a data message or otherwise; and
(b) where it is required that information be presented, that information is capable of being displayed to the person to whom it is to be presented.
(2) Paragraph (1) applies whether the requirement therein is in the form of an obligation or whether the law simply provides consequences for the information not being presented or retained in its original form.
(3) For the purposes of subparagraph (a) of paragraph (1):
(a) the criteria for assessing integrity shall be whether the information has remained complete and unaltered, apart from the addition of any endorsement and any change which arises in the normal course of communication, storage and display; and
(b) the standard of reliability required shall be assessed in the light of the purpose for which the information was generated and in the light of all the relevant circumstances.
(4) The provisions of this article do not apply to the following: [...].

Article 9 - Admissibility and evidential weight of data messages

(1) In any legal proceedings, nothing in the application of the rules of evidence shall apply so as to deny the admissibility of a data message in evidence:
(a) on the sole ground that it is a data message; or,
(b) if it is the best evidence that the person adducing it could reasonably be expected to obtain, on the grounds that it is not in its original form.
(2) Information in the form of a data message shall be given due evidential weight. In assessing the evidential weight of a data message, regard shall be had to the reliability of the manner in which the data message was generated, stored or communicated, to the reliability of the manner in which the integrity of the information was maintained, to the manner in which its originator was identified, and to any other relevant factor.

Article 10 - Retention of data messages

(1) Where the law requires that certain documents, records or information be retained, that requirement is met by retaining data messages, provided that the following conditions are satisfied:
(a) the information contained therein is accessible so as to be usable for subsequent reference; and
(b) the data message is retained in the format in which it was generated, sent or received, or in a format which can be demonstrated to represent accurately the information generated, sent or received; and
(c) such information, if any, is retained as enables the identification of the origin and destination of a data message and the date and time when it was sent or received.
(2) An obligation to retain documents, records or information in accordance with paragraph (1) does not extend to any information the sole purpose of which is to enable the message to be sent or received.

(3) A person may satisfy the requirement referred to in paragraph (1) by using the services of any other person, provided that the conditions set forth in subparagraphs (a), (b) and (c) of paragraph (1) are met.

CHAPTER III: COMMUNICATION OF DATA MESSAGES

Article 11 - Formation and validity of contracts

(1) In the context of contract formation, unless otherwise agreed by the parties, an offer and the acceptance of an offer may be expressed by means of data messages. Where a data message is used in the formation of a contract, that contract shall not be denied validity or enforceability on the sole ground that a data message was used for that purpose.
(2) The provisions of this article do not apply to the following: [...].

Article 12 - Recognition by parties of data messages

(1) As between the originator and the addressee of a data message, a declaration of will or other statement shall not be denied legal effect, validity or enforceability solely on the grounds that it is in the form of a data message.
(2) The provisions of this article do not apply to the following: [...].

Article 13 - Attribution of data messages

(1) A data message is that of the originator if it was sent by the originator itself.
(2) As between the originator and the addressee, a data message is deemed to be that of the originator if it was sent:
(a) by a person who had the authority to act on behalf of the originator in respect of that data message; or
(b) by an information system programmed by, or on behalf of, the originator to operate automatically.
(3) As between the originator and the addressee, an addressee is entitled to regard a data message as being that of the originator, and to act on that assumption, if:
(a) in order to ascertain whether the data message was that of the originator, the addressee properly applied a procedure previously agreed to by the originator for that purpose; or
(b) the data message as received by the addressee resulted from the actions of a person whose relationship with the originator or with any agent of the originator enabled that person to gain access to a method used by the originator to identify data messages as its own.
(4) Paragraph (3) does not apply:
(a) as of the time when the addressee has both received notice from the originator that the data message is not that of the originator, and had reasonable time to act accordingly; or
(b) in a case within paragraph (3)(b), at any time when the addressee knew or should have known, had it exercised reasonable care or used any agreed procedure, that the data message was not that of the originator.
(5) Where a data message is that of the originator or is deemed to be that of the originator, or the addressee is entitled to act on that assumption, then, as between the originator and the addressee, the addressee is entitled to regard the data message as received as being what the originator intended to send, and to act on that assumption. The addressee is not so entitled when it knew or should have known, had it exercised reasonable care or used any agreed procedure, that the transmission resulted in any error in the data message as received.
(6) The addressee is entitled to regard each data message received as a separate data message and to act on that assumption, except to the extent that it duplicates another data message

and the addressee knew or should have known, had it exercised reasonable care or used any agreed procedure, that the data message was a duplicate.

Article 14 - Acknowledgement of receipt

(1) Paragraphs (2) to (4) of this article apply where, on or before sending a data message, or by means of that data message, the originator has requested or has agreed with the addressee that receipt of the data message be acknowledged.

(2) Where the originator has not agreed with the addressee that the acknowledgement be given in a particular form or by a particular method, an acknowledgement may be given by

(a) any communication by the addressee, automated or otherwise, or
(b) any conduct of the addressee,

sufficient to indicate to the originator that the data message has been received.

(3) Where the originator has stated that the data message is conditional on receipt of the acknowledgement, the data message is treated as though it has never been sent, until the acknowledgement is received.

(4) Where the originator has not stated that the data message is conditional on receipt of the acknowledgement, and the acknowledgement has not been received by the originator within the time specified or agreed or, if no time has been specified or agreed, within a reasonable time, the originator:

(a) may give notice to the addressee stating that no acknowledgement has been received and specifying a reasonable time by which the acknowledgement must be received; and
(b) if the acknowledgement is not received within the time specified in subparagraph (a), may, upon notice to the addressee, treat the data message as though it had never been sent, or exercise any other rights it may have.

(5) Where the originator receives the addressee's acknowledgement of receipt, it is presumed that the related data message was received by the addressee. That presumption does not imply that the data message corresponds to the message received.

(6) Where the received acknowledgement states that the related data message met technical requirements, either agreed upon or set forth in applicable standards, it is presumed that those requirements have been met.

(7) Except in so far as it relates to the sending or receipt of the data message, this article is not intended to deal with the legal consequences that may flow either from that data message or from the acknowledgement of its receipt.

Article 15 - Time and place of dispatch and receipt of data messages

(1) Unless otherwise agreed between the originator and the addressee, the dispatch of a data message occurs when it enters an information system outside the control of the originator or of the person who sent the data message on behalf of the originator.

(2) Unless otherwise agreed between the originator and the addressee, the time of receipt of a data message is determined as follows:

(a) if the addressee has designated an information system for the purpose of receiving data messages, receipt occurs:
(i) at the time when the data message enters the designated information system; or
(ii) if the data message is sent to an information system of the addressee that is not the designated information system, at the time when the data message is retrieved by the addressee;
(b) if the addressee has not designated an information system, receipt occurs when the data message enters an information system of the addressee.

(3) Paragraph (2) applies notwithstanding that the place where the information system is located may be different from the place where the data message is deemed to be received under paragraph (4).

(4) Unless otherwise agreed between the originator and the addressee, a data message is deemed to be dispatched at the place where the originator has its place of business, and is deemed to be received at the place where the addressee has its place of business. For the purposes of this paragraph:
(i) if the originator or the addressee has more than one place of business, the place of business is that which has the closest relationship to the underlying transaction or, where there is no underlying transaction, the principal place of business;
(ii) if the originator or the addressee does not have a place of business, reference is to be made to its habitual residence.
(5) The provisions of this article do not apply to the following: [...].

Part Two. Electronic Commerce in Specific Areas

CHAPTER I: CARRIAGE OF GOODS

Article 16 - Actions related to contracts of carriage of goods

Without derogating from the provisions of part one of this Law, this chapter applies to any action in connection with, or in pursuance of, a contract of carriage of goods, including but not limited to:
(a)
(i) furnishing the marks, number, quantity or weight of goods;
(ii) stating or declaring the nature or value of goods;
(iii) issuing a receipt for goods;
(iv) confirming that goods have been loaded;
(b)
(i) notifying a person of terms and conditions of the contract;
(ii) giving instructions to a carrier;
(c)
(i) claiming delivery of goods;
(ii) authorizing release of goods;
(iii) giving notice of loss of, or damage to, goods;
(d) giving any other notice or statement in connection with the performance of the contract;
(e) undertaking to deliver goods to a named person or a person authorized to claim delivery;
(f) granting, acquiring, renouncing, surrendering, transferring or negotiating rights in goods;
(g) acquiring or transferring rights and obligations under the contract.

Article 17 - Transport documents

(1) Subject to paragraph (3), where the law requires that any action referred to in article 16 be carried out in writing or by using a paper document, that requirement is met if the action is carried out by using one or more data messages.
(2) Paragraph (1) applies whether the requirement therein is in the form of an obligation or whether the law simply provides consequences for failing either to carry out the action in writing or to use a paper document.
(3) If a right is to be granted to, or an obligation is to be acquired by, one person and no other person, and if the law requires that, in order to effect this, the right or obligation must be conveyed to that person by the transfer, or use of, a paper document, that requirement is met if the right or obligation is conveyed by using one or more data messages, provided that a reliable method is used to render such data message or messages unique.

(4) For the purposes of paragraph (3), the standard of reliability required shall be assessed in the light of the purpose for which the right or obligation was conveyed and in the light of all the circumstances, including any relevant agreement.

(5) Where one or more data messages are used to effect any action in subparagraphs (f) and (g) of article 16, no paper document used to effect any such action is valid unless the use of data messages has been terminated and replaced by the use of paper documents. A paper document issued in these circumstances shall contain a statement of such termination. The replacement of data messages by paper documents shall not affect the rights or obligations of the parties involved.

(6) If a rule of law is compulsorily applicable to a contract of carriage of goods which is in, or is evidenced by, a paper document, that rule shall not be inapplicable to such a contract of carriage of goods which is evidenced by one or more data messages by reason of the fact that the contract is evidenced by such data message or messages instead of by a paper document.

(7) The provisions of this article do not apply to the following: [...].

UNCITRAL MODEL LAW ON ELECTRONIC SIGNATURES

(Excerpt from the report of the United Nations Commission on International Trade Law on the work of its thirty-fourth session, held at Vienna, from 25 June to 13 July 2001. The text of the UNCITRAL Model Law on Electronic Signatures was adopted on 5 July 2001)

(Source: http://www.uncitral.org/)

Annex II

UNCITRAL Model Law on Electronic Signatures (2001)

Article 1 - Sphere of application

This Law applies where electronic signatures are used in the context* of commercial** activities. It does not override any rule of law intended for the protection of consumers.

Article 2 - Definitions

For the purposes of this Law:
(a) "Electronic signature" means data in electronic form in, affixed to or logically associated with, a data message, which may be used to identify the signatory in relation to the data message and to indicate the signatory's approval of the information contained in the data message;
(b) "Certificate" means a data message or other record confirming the link between a signatory and signature creation data;
(c) "Data message" means information generated, sent, received or stored by electronic, optical or similar means including, but not limited to, electronic data interchange (EDI), electronic mail, telegram, telex or telecopy;
(d) "Signatory" means a person that holds signature creation data and acts either on its own behalf or on behalf of the person it represents;
(e) "Certification service provider" means a person that issues certificates and may provide other services related to electronic signatures;
(f) "Relying party" means a person that may act on the basis of a certificate or an electronic signature.

Article 3 - Equal treatment of signature technologies

Nothing in this Law, except article 5, shall be applied so as to exclude, restrict or deprive of legal effect any method of creating an electronic signature that satisfies the requirements referred to in article 6, paragraph 1, or otherwise meets the requirements of applicable law.

---

* The Commission suggests the following text for States that might wish to extend the applicability of this Law:
"This Law applies where electronic signatures are used, except in the following situations: [...].".

** The term "commercial" should be given a wide interpretation so as to cover matters arising from all relationships of a commercial nature, whether contractual or not. Relationships of a commercial nature include, but are not limited to, the following transactions: any trade transaction for the supply or exchange of goods or services; distribution agreement; commercial representation or agency; factoring; leasing; construction of works; consulting; engineering; licensing; investment; financing; banking; insurance; exploitation agreement or concession; joint venture and other forms of industrial or business cooperation; carriage of goods or passengers by air, sea, rail or road.

Article 4 - Interpretation

1. In the interpretation of this Law, regard is to be had to its international origin and to the need to promote uniformity in its application and the observance of good faith.
2. Questions concerning matters governed by this Law which are not expressly settled in it are to be settled in conformity with the general principles on which this Law is based.

Article 5 - Variation by agreement

The provisions of this Law may be derogated from or their effect may be varied by agreement, unless that agreement would not be valid or effective under applicable law.

Article 6 - Compliance with a requirement for a signature

1. Where the law requires a signature of a person, that requirement is met in relation to a data message if an electronic signature is used that is as reliable as was appropriate for the purpose for which the data message was generated or communicated, in the light of all the circumstances, including any relevant agreement.
2. Paragraph 1 applies whether the requirement referred to therein is in the form of an obligation or whether the law simply provides consequences for the absence of a signature.
3. An electronic signature is considered to be reliable for the purpose of satisfying the requirement referred to in paragraph 1 if:
 (a) The signature creation data are, within the context in which they are used, linked to the signatory and to no other person;
 (b) The signature creation data were, at the time of signing, under the control of the signatory and of no other person;
 (c) Any alteration to the electronic signature, made after the time of signing, is detectable; and
 (d) Where a purpose of the legal requirement for a signature is to provide assurance as to the integrity of the information to which it relates, any alteration made to that information after the time of signing is detectable.
4. Paragraph 3 does not limit the ability of any person:
 (a) To establish in any other way, for the purpose of satisfying the requirement referred to in paragraph 1, the reliability of an electronic signature; or
 (b) To adduce evidence of the non-reliability of an electronic signature.
5. The provisions of this article do not apply to the following: [...].

Article 7 - Satisfaction of article 6

1. [*Any person, organ or authority, whether public or private, specified by the enacting State as competent*] may determine which electronic signatures satisfy the provisions of article 6 of this Law.
2. Any determination made under paragraph 1 shall be consistent with recognized international standards.
3. Nothing in this article affects the operation of the rules of private international law.

Article 8 - Conduct of the signatory

1. Where signature creation data can be used to create a signature that has legal effect, each signatory shall:
 (a) Exercise reasonable care to avoid unauthorized use of its signature creation data;
 (b) Without undue delay, utilize means made available by the certification service provider pursuant to article 9 of this Law, or otherwise use reasonable efforts, to notify any person that may reasonably be expected by the signatory to rely on or to provide services in support of the electronic signature if:
  (i) The signatory knows that the signature creation data have been compromised; or

(ii) The circumstances known to the signatory give rise to a substantial risk that the signature creation data may have been compromised;
(c) Where a certificate is used to support the electronic signature, exercise reasonable care to ensure the accuracy and completeness of all material representations made by the signatory that are relevant to the certificate throughout its life cycle or that are to be included in the certificate.
2. A signatory shall bear the legal consequences of its failure to satisfy the requirements of paragraph 1.

Article 9 - Conduct of the certification service provider

1. Where a certification service provider provides services to support an electronic signature that may be used for legal effect as a signature, that certification service provider shall:
(a) Act in accordance with representations made by it with respect to its policies and practices;
(b) Exercise reasonable care to ensure the accuracy and completeness of all material representations made by it that are relevant to the certificate throughout its life cycle or that are included in the certificate;
(c) Provide reasonably accessible means that enable a relying party to ascertain from the certificate:
   (i) The identity of the certification service provider;
   (ii) That the signatory that is identified in the certificate had control of the signature creation data at the time when the certificate was issued;
   (iii) That signature creation data were valid at or before the time when the certificate was issued;
(d) Provide reasonably accessible means that enable a relying party to ascertain, where relevant, from the certificate or otherwise:
   (i) The method used to identify the signatory;
   (ii) Any limitation on the purpose or value for which the signature creation data or the certificate may be used;
   (iii) That the signature creation data are valid and have not been compromised;
   (iv) Any limitation on the scope or extent of liability stipulated by the certification service provider;
   (v) Whether means exist for the signatory to give notice pursuant to article 8, paragraph 1 (b), of this Law;
   (vi) Whether a timely revocation service is offered;
(e) Where services under subparagraph (d) (v) are offered, provide a means for a signatory to give notice pursuant to article 8, paragraph 1 (b), of this Law and, where services under subparagraph (d) (vi) are offered, ensure the availability of a timely revocation service;
(f) Utilize trustworthy systems, procedures and human resources in performing its services.
2. A certification service provider shall bear the legal consequences of its failure to satisfy the requirements of paragraph 1.

Article 10 - Trustworthiness

For the purposes of article 9, paragraph 1 (f), of this Law in determining whether, or to what extent, any systems, procedures and human resources utilized by a certification service provider are trustworthy, regard may be had to the following factors:
   (a) Financial and human resources, including existence of assets;
   (b) Quality of hardware and software systems;
   (c) Procedures for processing of certificates and applications for certificates and retention of records;
   (d) Availability of information to signatories identified in certificates and to potential relying parties;

(e) Regularity and extent of audit by an independent body;
(f) The existence of a declaration by the State, an accreditation body or the certification service provider regarding compliance with or existence of the foregoing; or
(g) Any other relevant factor.

Article 11 - Conduct of the relying party

A relying party shall bear the legal consequences of its failure:
(a) To take reasonable steps to verify the reliability of an electronic signature; or
(b) Where an electronic signature is supported by a certificate, to take reasonable steps:
  (i) To verify the validity, suspension or revocation of the certificate; and
  (ii) To observe any limitation with respect to the certificate.

Article 12 - Recognition of foreign certificates and electronic signatures

1. In determining whether, or to what extent, a certificate or an electronic signature is legally effective, no regard shall be had:
(a) To the geographic location where the certificate is issued or the electronic signature created or used; or
(b) To the geographic location of the place of business of the issuer or signatory.
2. A certificate issued outside [*the enacting State*] shall have the same legal effect in [*the enacting State*] as a certificate issued in [*the enacting State*] if it offers a substantially equivalent level of reliability.
3. An electronic signature created or used outside [*the enacting State*] shall have the same legal effect in [*the enacting State*] as an electronic signature created or used in [*the enacting State*] if it offers a substantially equivalent level of reliability.
4. In determining whether a certificate or an electronic signature offers a substantially equivalent level of reliability for the purposes of paragraph 2 or 3, regard shall be had to recognized international standards and to any other relevant factors.

Where, notwithstanding paragraphs 2, 3 and 4, parties agree, as between themselves, to the use of certain types of electronic signatures or certificates, that agreement shall be recognized as sufficient for the purposes of cross-border recognition, unless that agreement would not be valid or effective under applicable law.

INTERNATIONAL LEAGUE FOR COMPETITION LAW - CODE OF CONDUCT IN REGARD TO FAIR COMPETITION IN ELECTRONIC COMMERCE

(Source: http://www.uni-muenster.de/Jura.itm/hoeren/materialien/lidc.htm)

(1) Whereas in general there are no differences in the application of national competition law in electronic commerce compared to the traditional marketing of goods and services;

(2) Whereas the general principles are similar from a worldwide perspective, at least in the developed countries;

(3) Whereas there are minor differences between the national competition laws as to electronic commerce, for instance considering unsolicited electronic mail messages or electronic goods or services;

(4) Whereas there is a chance to harmonize the regulations on online marketing, at least within Europe and other industrialized nations;

(5) Whereas greater problems arise in the context of conflict of laws as possible criteria for applying national law to internet cases is yet not harmonized;

(6) Whereas the effect of the country of origin rule (introduced within the EU as a part of the EU Directive on Certain Legal Aspects of Electronic Commerce) on private international law remains unclear;

(7) Whereas at least outside the scope of the Brussels and Lugano Convention the execution of court decisions within a transborder Internet context is very often complicated, sometimes even impossible;

(8) Whereas informal and voluntary ways of enforcing common principles of online marketing should be explored, such as codes of conduct and alternative dispute resolution procedures;

THE LEAGUE HEREBY ADOPTS THE FOLLOWING RESOLUTION:

I. The LIDC recognises that a Code of Conduct summarizing the common structure of regulations concerning online marketing would be helpful for online providers and users.

II. The LIDC agrees upon the attached "Code of Conduct in regard to Fair Competition in Electronic Commerce".

III. The LIDC proposes that the Code of Conduct will be sent to the concerned international and national organizations (such as World Trade Organization, WIPO, ICC) for further integration in the discussion on internet regulation.

SECTION 1: SCOPE

[Application] This regulatory framework applies to commercial communication taking place on the Internet. It is aimed solely at fair competition in the context of electronic commerce and is to be regarded as a voluntary, self-restrictive addition to existing legal requirements.

The code as a whole should be clearly focused on issues relating to fair competition. By concentrating on a limited scope and taking certain issues out of consideration (i.e. data protection), the code can serve as an effective instrument for this particular segment of electronic commerce.

SECTION 2: TERMS AND DEFINITIONS

Introductory note to this section: In order to prevent that regulations are misinterpreted - unintentionally or on purpose —, it is important to agree on a set of terms and definitions that is as precise and easy to handle as possible.

In this Code,

Cookie means an electronic file which is stored by an Internet provider on the computer of the user in order to store certain data of the user and/or his computer and make them available to the provider.

Customer means a person buying goods or services over the Internet.

Deep linking means the use of hyperlinks to make references to particular parts of a website without going to the homepage.

Frame means a special part of a homepage where general information is displayed apart and independently of other contents of the website.

Hyperlink means any technical tool which permits the linking of one homepage to another.

Inline linking means the use of frame technology in a way that conceals the true origin of the information displayed within the frame.

Intermediary service means the person who is carrying out the process of accumulating consumers on the Internet, thereby serving as a intermediary between merchant and consumer group.

Internet auction means the sale of goods through bidding that is carried out over the Internet.

Merchant means a person selling goods or services over the Internet.

Metadata means data which is used as part of the HTML code to identify the content of a website.

Person means a human being as well as a legal entity and a any other third party.

Power shopping describes an accumulation of consumers that is gathered through over the Internet in order to buy goods or services at a reduced price that is granted by the providers of goods or services merchant to buyers that order large quantities of the product or service in question.

Resource means content, i. e. any material accessible via the Internet, regardless of the specific transmission protocol.

This is to extend the Code's scope beyond the main way of communication via the WWW (HTTP protocol) and to ensure that protocols such as FTP, SMTP, POP etc. are included. It should be clear that most regulations apply to Internet content and cannot be avoided by simply using a technically different communication channel. The advantage of such broad definition is that it covers a large variety of material distributed via the Internet (i. e. audio files, software, graphics) and need not be changed if technology extends existing standards or advances beyond the WWW.

Technological terms related to the communication on the Internet itself, not its content, are to be understood by the standards definitions of the WWW consortium.

This is to assure that regulations concerning technical issues cannot be misinterpreted. By using technical terms in compliance with the internationally accepted standards, their meaning will be capable of being understood beyond the scope of this Code of Conduct. The use of such terms also avoids the need to define each technological term specifically. Such information is available at http://www.w3.org/.

User means the person requesting resources via the Internet.

SECTION 3: REGULATIONS

I. General Provisions as regards Commercial Communication

[General requirements on resources] Resources provided on the Internet should not be false or misleading. They should be clear, comprehensible and valid. It should be possible to identify the person responsible for the resource. Identification information should include the name and legal form of the person, full name of the authorised representative, full postal and eMail address as well as digital or non-digital registration numbers or certificates suitable or used in off-line contexts for identification purposes, i. e. Trade register numbers, VAT numbers etc, digital certificates etc.

The last part does not specify what kind of registration number would be appropriate with regard to the fact that specific means of registration and identification may differ from country to country.

[Accessibility] Resources should be designed in a way that allows the user to access identification information directly, regardless of which hierarchic level of the information system resources are requested. The user should not need more than two steps to obtain the identification information. Online advertisers should not covertly disable the back button of the customer's browser or appliance or otherwise interfere with a visitor's ability to exit a site.

[Presentation] Identification information should be presented accurately, should be readily accessible online and be (in addition) provided in a printable version. The design of identification information should not be easily overridden by the users' software settings.

The last part assumes that the possibility of presenting information in one specific way on the Internet is limited by technology.

[Transparency] Commercial communication has to be clearly and unambiguously identifiable as such, as soon as it is received by the recipient. In a context where it is difficult to distinguish between editorial content and advertising, the advertising should be labelled as such.

[Limited and transparent collection of data] It is not suitable to collect more information on the user than is voluntarily and knowingly given by the user.

If user information is supposed to be processed or used for other purposes than the single electronic commerce transaction, the user must be notified and must be given the opportunity to object.

This is to ensure that user information is not exploited unless the user is aware of it and has stated his or her consent prior to further processing. This regulation is intended to avoid unauthorised and convert collection of user information through online observation of eMail or IP addresses, the users' hard- or software or data related to the connection.

[Embedding sanctions in contract] Host provider and other persons in an intermediary position between merchants and consumers should ensure that, within the context of contracts which they enter into, they provide for effective sanctions that can be enforced against persons who break this Code of Conduct.

[Complaint procedures] Host provider and other persons in a mediary position between merchants and consumers should provide for sufficient complaint procedures. They should reserve themselves the right to take a resource from the Internet that is the subject of a substantial complaint until the dispute is settled.

II. Provisions regarding specific Means of Communication

1. Commercial Electronic Mail Messages

Introductory note: The League discovered that there are different opinions on the legality of unsolicited electronic mail messages. Some states seem to prefer opt-in solutions; others adhere to opt-out principles. The League decided to take the opt-out model as a minimum standard for the code irrespective of further discussions.

[Directories] No person should initiate the transmission, conspire with another to initiate the transmission or assist the transmission of a commercial electronic mail message if the addressee is listed in "robinson" directories stating that the addressee objects to receiving commercial electronic mail messages except for his or her explicit request.

[Do not contact policy] Online businesses that engage in unsolicited email marketing should identify their postings as an advertisement in the subject of their message. In addition, they have to post and adhere to a "Do not contact" policy that at a minimum enables those customers who do not wish to be contacted online to "opt out" online from future solicitations. This policy should be available both on the website and in any email other than those relating to a particular order. The technical facilities for "opting out" should be easy to handle and react in a short time.

[False or misleading subject lines] No person should initiate the transmission, conspire with another to initiate the transmission or assist the transmission of a commercial electronic mail message if the sender knows or has reason to know that the message contains false or misleading information in the subject line.

[Concealed origin or transmission pass] No person should initiate the transmission, conspire with another to initiate the transmission or assist the transmission of a commercial electronic mail message if the sender knows or has reason to know that his message misrepresents or obscures any information in identifying the point of origin or the transmission pass of a commercial electronic mail message.

2. Frames and Hyperlinks

[Notification, objection] A person whose web pages or other resources accessible via the Internet are pointed to by frame or hyperlink technique should be notified upon publication of the frame or the hyperlink unless the link points to informative or educational content. No person should continue pointing towards other person's resources if there is knowledge or a substantial reason to know that the other person objects that frames or hyperlinks point towards its resources.

A notification upon publication should only be pursued if it is possible to fulfil this requirement with reasonable effort. Nevertheless, if there is clear objection or substantial reason to assume objection, it must be ensured that the person does not continue using frames or hyperlinks.

[Inline linking] If frames are used to display information of a third party, the true origin of the information should be clearly and unmistakenly visible. It is not sufficient that merely the third party's URL appears in the URL column. Use of third party's information should be indicated directly by the link pointing towards the information itself or directly in relation to that link. Neither the link itself nor the frame design should suggest otherwise.

[Deep linking] It is not suitable to exploit the third party's work, contacts, references or its effort in collecting, processing or presenting the information by misrepresenting it as one's own.

[Correctness] If hyperlinks are used, this should not be done in a misleading or hostile context. A hyperlink should always show an objective relation to the content to which it is directed. In particular online advertisers should not mislead online customers by creating the false impression of sponsorship, endorsement, popularity, trustworthiness, product quality or business size through the misuse of hyperlinks, other technology, or another's intellectual property.

3. Metadata

[Correctness] Metadata should be correct and give a reasonable summary of the document they are part of. No person should set metadata that is suitable for generating confusion or that is likely to conceal the documents' true content.

[Intended use] Metadata should not be misused with the intention of obtaining an inappropriate ranking in search engine results.

[Competitors] Metadata should not give the impression that information of competitors or third parties is used with their permission if this is not the case.

4. Cookies

[Optionality] The user should be informed as to the intended purpose of a cookie. Cookies cannot be used unless there is a prior express consent of the person concerned. There should be no disadvantage in access, use or functionality of the system if cookies are not accepted.

[Expiration] Cookies should always have a reasonable expiration date .

5. Power shopping

Power shopping/community shopping is a useful instrument if the customer knows the price at the moment it is ordered. If customers act on a merchant's decision to grant reduced prices if a product is ordered in large capacities, it is not up to the merchant to change that decision or to exclude power shopping by customers. Since both parties may benefit from power shopping — the merchant may sell, in total, more products than without the benefit of power shopping while the customer is able to buy at a reduced price — it seems to be more a matter of business decisions than a question of self-regulation.

Nevertheless, persons who provide the intermediary services should respect a merchant's decision not to engage in power shopping. The question is whether if the responsibility on this matter should rest with the intermediary service (so that the intermediary service would be requested to be aware of the merchants' power shopping policies) or with the merchants (so that the merchants would have to be aware of power shopping activities and come to a decision whether power shopping is welcome or not).

[Principle] Intermediary services should only engage in power shopping with merchants who offer goods or services at a reduced bulk price.

[Merchants] Intermediary services should make clear on which terms a merchant is chosen as a power shopping partner. The criteria should be objective, related to the purpose, transparent and accessible. It should also be transparent in which way merchant and intermediary services are related, i. e. by contract.

[Customers] Intermediary services should provide for transparent terms on which customers are eligible to take part in power shopping. The criteria should be objective, related to the purpose, transparent and accessible. Persons related to merchants that are power shopping partners of the intermediary service should be excluded from power shopping with the merchant they are related to.

[Registry] Intermediary services should register their customers prior to power shopping.

6. Internet Auctions

[Principle] Persons hosting auctions on the Internet should provide for a comprehensible description of the auction process and notify the user of the auctions' character.

[Customers] Auction services should provide for transparent terms on which persons are eligible to take part in the auction. The criteria should be objective, related to the purpose, transparent and accessible.

[Registry] Auction services should register their customers prior to the auction.

SECTION 4 : ENFORCEMENT

Introductory note to this section: This Code is meant to help organizations or any other concerned body to build up their own system of regulating online marketing. In particular, it might be used as a sample for drafting voluntary codes of conduct (perhaps in combination with a quality label system). Therefore, enforcement depends on the possible sanctions within the organization concerned.

[Measures] Breach of this Code can be enforced inter alia by

1. Publication of the act leading to the breach, including the person responsible, in journals or websites, also including the site of the offender.

2. Notification of the offender and a request to stop the offensive behavior.

3. Taking the questionable material off the Internet.

4. Requesting the offender to pay a substantial fine without prejudice to damages.

[Complaint procedure] Everyone should have the possibility to submit complaints to the concerned body, which provides a sufficient administrative process in which the complaint can be settled in a simple and quick way.

[Dispute resolution procedure] Online merchants should use at least one mechanism that provides customers with either a guarantee of satisfaction or a fair method for resolving differences with regard to a transaction. If an online merchant offers third party dispute resolution, it should use a trusted third party that offers impartial, accessible, and timely dispute resolution procedures that are free to customers or at a charge to customers that is not disproportionate to the value of goods or services involved in the dispute. Online merchants should provide customers with easy-to-find and understandable contact information for such third parties, including a link to any third party sites used for such means.

Transparency Directive (98/34/EC)

DIRECTIVE 98/34/EC OF THE EUROPEAN PARLIAMENT AND OF THE COUNCIL
OF 22 JUNE 1998
LAYING DOWN A PROCEDURE FOR THE PROVISION OF INFORMATION IN THE FIELD OF TECHNICAL STANDARDS AND REGULATIONS

(Official Journal L 204, 21/07/1998, p. 0037)

THE EUROPEAN PARLIAMENT AND THE COUNCIL OF THE EUROPEAN UNION,

Having regard to the Treaty establishing the European Community, and in particular Articles 100a, 213 and 43 thereof,
Having regard to the proposal from the Commission[1],
Having regard to the opinion of the Economic and Social Committee[2],

Acting in accordance with the procedure laid down in Article 189b of the Treaty[3],

(1) Whereas Council Directive 83/189/EEC of 28 March 1983 laying down a procedure for the provision of information in the field of technical standards and regulations[4] has been variously and substantially amended; whereas for reasons of clarity and rationality the said Directive should be consolidated;

(2) Whereas the internal market comprises an area without internal frontiers in which the free movement of goods, persons, services and capital is ensured; whereas, therefore, the prohibition of quantitative restrictions on the movement of goods and of measures having an equivalent effect is one of the basic principles of the Community;

(3) Whereas in order to promote the smooth functioning of the internal market, as much transparency as possible should be ensured as regards national initiatives for the establishment of technical standards or regulations;

(4) Whereas barriers to trade resulting from technical regulations relating to products may be allowed only where they are necessary in order to meet essential requirements and have an objective in the public interest of which they constitute the main guarantee;

(5) Whereas it is essential for the Commission to have the necessary information at its disposal before the adoption of technical provisions; whereas, consequently, the Member States which are required to facilitate the achievement of its task pursuant to Article 5 of the Treaty must notify it of their projects in the field of technical regulations;

(6) Whereas all the Member States must also be informed of the technical regulations contemplated by any one Member State;

(7) Whereas the aim of the internal market is to create an environment that is conducive to the competitiveness of undertakings; whereas increased provision of information is one way of helping undertakings to make more of the advantages inherent in this market; whereas it is therefore necessary to enable economic operators to give their assessment of the impact of the national technical regulations proposed by other Member States, by providing for the regular

---

[1] OJ C 78, 12.3.1997, p. 4.
[2] OJ C 133, 28.4.1997, p. 5.
[3] Opinion of the European Parliament of 17 September 1997 (OJ C 304, 6.10.1997, p. 79), Council Common Position of 23 February 1998 (OJ C 110, 8.4.1998, p. 1) and Decision of the European Parliament of 30 April 1998 (OJ C 152, 18.5.1998). Decision of the Council of 28 May 1998.
[4] OJ L 109, 26.4.1983, p. 8. Directive as last amended by Commission Decision 96/139/EC (OJ L 32, 10.2.1996, p. 31).

(8) Whereas it is appropriate, in the interests of legal certainty, that Member States publicly announce that a national technical regulation has been adopted in accordance with the formalities laid down in this Directive;

(9) Whereas, as far as technical regulations for products are concerned, the measures designed to ensure the proper functioning or the continued development of the market include greater transparency of national intentions and a broadening of the criteria and conditions for assessing the potential effect of the proposed regulations on the market;

(10) Whereas it is therefore necessary to assess all the requirements laid down in respect of a product and to take account of developments in national practices for the regulation of products;

(11) Whereas requirements, other than technical specifications, referring to the life cycle of a product after it has been placed on the market are liable to affect the free movement of that product or to create obstacles to the proper functioning of the internal market;

(12) Whereas it is necessary to clarify the concept of a de facto technical regulation; whereas, in particular, the provisions by which the public authority refers to technical specifications or other requirements, or encourages the observance thereof, and the provisions referring to products with which the public authority is associated, in the public interest, have the effect of conferring on such requirements or specifications a more binding value than they would otherwise have by virtue of their private origin;

(13) Whereas the Commission and the Member States must also be allowed sufficient time in which to propose amendments to a contemplated measure, in order to remove or reduce any barriers which it might create to the free movement of goods;

(14) Whereas the Member State concerned must take account of these amendments when formulating the definitive text of the measure envisaged;

(15) Whereas it is inherent in the internal market that, in particular where the principle of mutual recognition cannot be implemented by the Member States, the Commission adopts or proposes the adoption of binding Community acts; whereas a specific temporary standstill period has been established in order to prevent the introduction of national measures from compromising the adoption of binding Community acts by the Council or the Commission in the same field;

(16) Whereas the Member State in question must, pursuant to the general obligations laid down in Article 5 of the Treaty, defer implementation of the contemplated measure for a period sufficient to allow either a joint examination of the proposed amendments or the preparation of a proposal for a binding act of the Council or the adoption of a binding act of the Commission; whereas the time limits laid down in the Agreement of the representatives of the Governments of the Member States meeting within the Council of 28 May 1969 providing for standstill and notification to the Commission[5], as amended by the Agreement of 5 March 1973[6], have proved inadequate in the cases concerned and should accordingly be extended;

(17) Whereas the procedure concerning the standstill arrangement and notification of the Commission contained in the abovementioned agreement of 28 May 1969 remains applicable to products subject to that procedure which are not covered by this Directive;

(18) Whereas, with a view to facilitating the adoption of Community measures by the Council, Member States should refrain from adopting technical regulations once the Council has adopted a common position on a Commission proposal concerning that sector;

(19) Whereas, in practice, national technical standards may have the same effects on the free movement of goods as technical regulations;

---

[5] OJ C 76, 17.6.1969, p. 9.
[6] OJ C 9, 15.3.1973, p. 3.

(20) Whereas it would therefore appear necessary to inform the Commission of draft standards under similar conditions to those which apply to technical regulations; whereas, pursuant to Article 213 of the Treaty, the Commission may, within the limits and under the conditions laid down by the Council in accordance with the provisions of the Treaty, collect any information and carry out any checks required for the performance of the tasks entrusted to it;

(21) Whereas it is also necessary for the Member States and the standards institutions to be informed of standards contemplated by standards institutions in the other Member States;

(22) Whereas systematic notification is actually necessary only in the case of new subjects for standardisation and in so far as the treatment of these subjects at national level may give rise to differences in national standards which are liable to disturb the functioning of the market as a result; whereas any subsequent notification or communication relating to the progress of national activities must depend on the interest in such activities expressed by those to whom this new subject has already been communicated;

(23) Whereas the Commission must nevertheless be able to request the communication of all or part of the national standardisation programmes so that it can review the development of standardisation activity in particular economic sectors;

(24) Whereas the European standardisation system must be organised by and for the parties concerned, on a basis of coherence, transparency, openness, consensus, independence of special interests, efficiency and decision-making based on national representation;

(25) Whereas the functioning of standardisation in the Community must be based on fundamental rights for the national standardisation bodies, such as the possibility of obtaining draft standards, being informed of the action taken in response to comments submitted, being associated with national standardisation activities or requesting the preparation of European standards in place of national standards; whereas it is for the Member States to take the appropriate measures in their power to ensure that their standardisation bodies observe these rights;

(26) Whereas the provisions concerning the standstill arrangements applicable to national standardisation bodies when a European standard is in preparation must be brought into line with the relevant provisions adopted by the standardisation bodies within the framework of the European standardisation bodies;

(27) Whereas it is necessary to set up a Standing Committee, the members of which will be appointed by the Member States with the task of helping the Commission to examine draft national standards and cooperating in its efforts to lessen any adverse effects thereof on the free movement of goods;

(28) Whereas the Standing Committee should be consulted on the draft standardisation requests referred to in this Directive;

(29) Whereas this Directive must not affect the obligations of the Member States concerning the deadlines for transposition of the Directives set out in Annex III, Part B,

HAVE ADOPTED THIS DIRECTIVE:

Article 1

For the purposes of this Directive, the following meanings shall apply:
1. 'product', any industrially manufactured product and any agricultural product, including fish products;
2. 'technical specification', a specification contained in a document which lays down the characteristics required of a product such as levels of quality, performance, safety or dimensions, including the requirements applicable to the product as regards the name under which the product is sold, terminology, symbols, testing and test methods, packaging, marking or labelling and conformity assessment procedures.

The term 'technical specification' also covers production methods and processes used in respect of agricultural products as referred to Article 38(1) of the Treaty, products intended for human and animal consumption, and medicinal products as defined in Article 1 of Directive 65/65/EEC[7], as well as production methods and processes relating to other products, where these have an effect on their characteristics;

3. 'other requirements', a requirement, other than a technical specification, imposed on a product for the purpose of protecting, in particular, consumers or the environment, and which affects its life cycle after it has been placed on the market, such as conditions of use, recycling, reuse or disposal, where such conditions can significantly influence the composition or nature of the product or its marketing;

4. 'standard', a technical specification approved by a recognised standardisation body for repeated or continuous application, with which compliance is not compulsory and which is one of the following:

- international standard: a standard adopted by an international standardisation organisation and made available to the public,
- European standard: a standard adopted by a European standardisation body and made available to the public,
- national standard: a standard adopted by a national standardisation body and made available to the public;

5. 'standards programme', a work programme of a recognised standardisation body listing the subjects on which standardisation work is being carried out;

6. 'draft standard', document containing the text of the technical specifications concerning a given subject, which is being considered for adoption in accordance with the national standards procedure, as that document stands after the preparatory work and as circulated for public comment or scrutiny;

7. 'European standardisation body', a body referred to in Annex I;

8. 'national standardisation body', a body referred to in Annex II;

9. 'technical regulation', technical specifications and other requirements, including the relevant administrative provisions, the observance of which is compulsory, de jure or de facto, in the case of marketing or use in a Member State or a major part thereof, as well as laws, regulations or administrative provisions of Member States, except those provided for in Article 10, prohibiting the manufacture, importation, marketing or use of a product. De facto technical regulations include:

- laws, regulations or administrative provisions of a Member State which refer either to technical specifications or other requirements or to professional codes or codes of practice which in turn refer to technical specifications or other requirements and compliance with which confers a presumption of conformity with the obligations imposed by the aforementioned laws, regulations or administrative provisions,
- voluntary agreements to which a public authority is a contracting party and which provide, in the public interest, for compliance with technical specifications or other requirements, excluding public procurement tender specifications,
- technical specifications or other requirements which are linked to fiscal or financial measures affecting the consumption of products by encouraging compliance with such technical specifications or other requirements; technical specifications or other requirements linked to national social-security systems are not included.

This comprises technical regulations imposed by the authorities designated by the Member States and appearing on a list to be drawn up by the Commission before 1 July 1995, in the framework of the Committee referred to in Article 5.

---

[7] Council Directive 65/65/EEC of 26 January 1965 on the approximation of provisions laid down by law, regulation or administrative action relating to medicinal products (OJ 22, 9.2.1965, p. 369/65), Directive as last amended by Directive 93/39/EEC (OJ L 214, 24.8.1993, p. 22).

The same procedure shall be used for amending this list;
10. 'draft technical regulation', the text of a technical specification or other requirement, including administrative provisions formulated with the aim of enacting it or of ultimately having it enacted as a technical regulation, the text being at a stage of preparation at which substantial amendments can still be made.

This Directive shall not apply to those measures Member States consider necessary under the Treaty for the protection of persons, in particular workers, when products are used, provided that such measures do not affect the products.

Article 2

1. The Commission and the standardisation bodies referred to in Annexes I and II shall be informed of the new subjects for which the national bodies referred to in Annex II have decided, by including them in their standards programme, to prepare or amend a standard, unless it is an identical or equivalent transposition of an international or European standard.
2. The information referred to in paragraph 1 shall indicate, in particular, whether the standard concerned:
- will transpose an international standard without being the equivalent,
- will be a new national standard, or
- will amend a national standard.

After consulting the Committee referred to in Article 5, the Commission may draw up rules for the consolidated presentation of this information and a plan and criteria governing the presentation of this information in order to facilitate its evaluation.

3. The Commission may ask for all or part of the standards programmes to be communicated to it.
   It shall make this information available to the Member States in a form which allows the different programmes to be assessed and compared.
4. Where appropriate, the Commission shall amend Annex II on the basis of communications from the Member States.
5. The Council shall decide, on the basis of a proposal from the Commission, on any amendment to Annex I.

Article 3

The standardisation bodies referred to in Annexes I and II, and the Commission, shall be sent all draft standards on request; they shall be kept informed by the body concerned of the action taken on any comments they have made relating to drafts.

Article 4

1. Member States shall take all necessary steps to ensure that their standardisation bodies:
- communicate information in accordance with Articles 2 and 3,
- publish the draft standards in such a way that comments may also be obtained from parties established in other Member States,
- grant the other bodies referred to in Annex II the right to be involved passively or actively (by sending an observer) in the planned activities,
- do not object to a subject for standardisation in their work programme being discussed at European level in accordance with the rules laid down by the European standardisation bodies and undertake no action which may prejudice a decision in this regard.
2. Member States shall refrain in particular from any act of recognition, approval or use by reference to a national standard adopted in breach of Articles 2 and 3 and of paragraph 1 of this Article.

Article 5

A Standing Committee shall be set up consisting of representatives appointed by the Member States who may call on the assistance of experts or advisers; its chairman shall be a representative of the Commission.
The Committee shall draw up its own rules of procedure.

Article 6

1. The Committee shall meet at least twice a year with the representatives of the standards institutions referred to in Annexes I and II.
2. The Commission shall submit to the Committee a report on the implementation and application of the procedures set out in this Directive, and shall present proposals aimed at eliminating existing or foreseeable barriers to trade.
3. The Committee shall express its opinion on the communications and proposals referred to in paragraph 2 and may in this connection propose, in particular, that the Commission:
   - request the European standards institutions to draw up a European standard within a given time limit,
   - ensure where necessary, in order to avoid the risk of barriers to trade, that initially the Member States concerned decide amongst themselves on appropriate measures,
   - take all appropriate measures,
   - identify the areas where harmonisation appears necessary, and, should the case arise, undertake appropriate harmonisation in a given sector.
4. The Committee must be consulted by the Commission:
   (a) before any amendment is made to the lists in Annexes I and II (Article 2(1));
   (b) when drawing up the rules for the consolidated presentation of information and the plan and criteria for the presentation of standards programmes (Article 2(2));
   (c) when deciding on the actual system whereby the exchange of information provided for in this Directive is to be effected and on any change to it;
   (d) when reviewing the operation of the system set up by this Directive;
   (e) on the requests to the standards institutions referred to in the first indent of paragraph 3.
5. The Committee may be consulted by the Commission on any preliminary draft technical regulation received by the latter.
6. Any question regarding the implementation of this Directive may be submitted to the Committee at the request of its chairman or of a Member State.
7. The proceedings of the Committee and the information to be submitted to it shall be confidential.
   However, the Committee and the national authorities may, provided that the necessary precautions are taken, consult, for an expert opinion, natural or legal persons, including persons in the private sector.

Article 7

1. Member States shall take all appropriate measures to ensure that, during the preparation of a European standard referred to in the first indent of Article 6(3) or after its approval, their standardisation bodies do not take any action which could prejudice the harmonisation intended and, in particular, that they do not publish in the field in question a new or revised national standard which is not completely in line with an existing European standard.
2. Paragraph 1 shall not apply to the work of standards institutions undertaken at the request of the public authorities to draw up technical specifications or a standard for specific products for the purpose of enacting a technical regulation for such products. Member States shall communicate all requests of the kind referred to in the preceding

subparagraph to the Commission as draft technical regulations, in accordance with Article 8(1), and shall state the grounds for their enactment.

Article 8

1. Subject to Article 10, Member States shall immediately communicate to the Commission any draft technical regulation, except where it merely transposes the full text of an international or European standard, in which case information regarding the relevant standard shall suffice; they shall also let the Commission have a statement of the grounds which make the enactment of such a technical regulation necessary, where these have not already been made clear in the draft.

   Where appropriate, and unless it has already been sent with a prior communication, Member States shall simultaneously communicate the text of the basic legislative or regulatory provisions principally and directly concerned, should knowledge of such text be necessary to assess the implications of the draft technical regulation.

   Member States shall communicate the draft again under the above conditions if they make changes to the draft that have the effect of significantly altering its scope, shortening the timetable originally envisaged for implementation, adding specifications or requirements, or making the latter more restrictive.

   Where, in particular, the draft seeks to limit the marketing or use of a chemical substance, preparation or product on grounds of public health or of the protection of consumers or the environment, Member States shall also forward either a summary or the references of all relevant data relating to the substance, preparation or product concerned and to known and available substitutes, where such information may be available, and communicate the anticipated effects of the measure on public health and the protection of the consumer and the environment, together with an analysis of the risk carried out as appropriate in accordance with the general principles for the risk evaluation of chemical substances as referred to in Article 10(4) of Regulation (EEC) No 793/93[8] in the case of an existing substance or in Article 3(2) of Directive 67/548/EEC[9], in the case of a new substance.

   The Commission shall immediately notify the other Member States of the draft and all documents which have been forwarded to it; it may also refer this draft, for an opinion, to the Committee referred to in Article 5 and, where appropriate, to the committee responsible for the field in question.

   With respect to the technical specifications or other requirements referred to in the second subparagraph of Article 1(9), third indent, the detailed comments or opinions of the Commission or the Member States may concern only the aspect which may hinder trade and not the fiscal or financial aspect of the measure.

2. The Commission and the Member States may make comments to the Member State which has forwarded a draft technical regulation; that Member State shall take such comments into account as far as possible in the subsequent preparation of the technical regulation.

3. Member States shall communicate the definitive text of a technical regulation to the Commission without delay.

4. Information supplied under this Article shall not be confidential except at the express request of the notifying Member State. Any such request shall be supported by reasons. In cases of this kind, if necessary precautions are taken, the Committee referred to in Article 5 and the national authorities may seek expert advice from physical or legal persons in the private sector.

---

[8] Council Regulation (EEC) No 793/93 of 23 March 1993 on the evaluation and control of the risks of existing substances (OJ L 84, 5.4.1993, p. 1).

[9] Council Directive 67/548/EEC of 27 June 1967 on the approximation of the laws, regulations and administrative provisions relating to the classification, packaging and labelling of dangerous substances (OJ L 196, 16.8.1967, p. 1). Directive, as amended by Directive 92/32/EEC, (OJ L 154, 5.6.1992, p. 1).

5. When draft technical regulations form part of measures which are required to be communicated to the Commission at the draft stage under another Community act, Member States may make a communication within the meaning of paragraph 1 under that other act, provided that they formally indicate that the said communication also constitutes a communication for the purposes of this Directive.

The absence of a reaction from the Commission under this Directive to a draft technical regulation shall not prejudice any decision which might be taken under other Community acts.

Article 9

1. Member States shall postpone the adoption of a draft technical regulation for three months from the date of receipt by the Commission of the communication referred to in Article 8(1).
2. Member States shall postpone:
- for four months the adoption of a draft technical regulation in the form of a voluntary agreement within the meaning of Article 1(9), second indent,
- without prejudice to paragraphs 3, 4 and 5, for six months the adoption of any other draft technical regulation, from the date of receipt by the Commission of the communication referred to in Article 8(1) if the Commission or another Member State delivers a detailed opinion, within three months of that date, to the effect that the measure envisaged may create obstacles to the free movement of goods within the internal market.

The Member State concerned shall report to the Commission on the action it proposes to take on such detailed opinions. The Commission shall comment on this reaction.

3. Member States shall postpone the adoption of a draft technical regulation for 12 months from the date of receipt by the Commission of the communication referred to in Article 8(1) if, within the three months following that date, the Commission announces its intention to propose or adopt a directive, regulation or decision on the matter in accordance with Article 189 of the Treaty.
4. Member States shall postpone the adoption of a draft technical regulation for 12 months from the date of receipt by the Commission of the communication referred to in Article 8(1) if, within the three months following that date, the Commission announces its finding that the draft technical regulation concerns a matter which is covered by a proposal for a directive, regulation or decision presented to the Council in accordance with Article 189 of the Treaty.
5. If the Council adopts a common position during the standstill period referred to in paragraphs 3 and 4, that period shall, subject to paragraph 6, be extended to 18 months.
6. The obligations referred to in paragraphs 3, 4 and 5 shall lapse:
- when the Commission informs the Member States that it no longer intends to propose or adopt a binding Community act,
- when the Commission informs the Member States of the withdrawal of its draft or proposal,
- when the Commission or the Council has adopted a binding Community act.
7. Paragraphs 1 to 5 shall not apply in those cases where, for urgent reasons, occasioned by serious and unforeseeable circumstances relating to the protection of public health or safety, the protection of animals or the preservation of plants, a Member State is obliged to prepare technical regulations in a very short space of time in order to enact and introduce them immediately without any consultations being possible. The Member State shall give, in the communication referred to in Article 8, the reasons which warrant the urgency of the measures taken. The Commission shall give its views on the communication as soon as possible. It shall take appropriate action in cases where improper use is made of this procedure. The European Parliament shall be kept informed by the Commission.

Article 10

1. Articles 8 and 9 shall not apply to those laws, regulations and administrative provisions of the Member States or voluntary agreements by means of which Member States:
   - comply with binding Community acts which result in the adoption of technical specifications,
   - fulfil the obligations arising out of international agreements which result in the adoption of common technical specifications in the Community,
   - make use of safeguard clauses provided for in binding Community acts,
   - apply Article 8(1) of Directive 92/59/EEC[10],
   - restrict themselves to implementing a judgment of the Court of Justice of the European Communities,
   - restrict themselves to amending a technical regulation within the meaning of Article 1(9) of this Directive, in accordance with a Commission request, with a view to removing an obstacle to trade.
2. Article 9 shall not apply to the laws, regulations and administrative provisions of the Member States prohibiting manufacture insofar as they do not impede the free movement of products.
3. Article 9(3) to (6) shall not apply to the voluntary agreements referred to in Article 1(9), second indent.
4. Article 9 shall not apply to the technical specifications or other requirements referred to in Article 1(9), third indent.

Article 11

The Commission shall report every two years to the European Parliament, the Council and the Economic and Social Committee on the results of the application of this Directive. Lists of standardisation work entrusted to the European standardisation organisations pursuant to this Directive, as well as statistics on the notifications received, shall be published on an annual basis in the Official Journal of the European Communities.

Article 12

When Member States adopt a technical regulation, it shall contain a reference to this Directive or shall be accompanied by such reference on the occasion of its official publication. The methods of making such reference shall be laid down by Member States.

Article 13

1. The Directives and Decisions listed in Annex III, Part A are hereby repealed without prejudice to the obligations of the Member States concerning the deadlines for transposition of the said Directives, set out in Annex III, Part B.
2. References to the repealed directives and decisions shall be construed as references to this Directive and shall be read in accordance with the correlation table set out in Annex IV.

Article 14

This Directive shall enter into force on the 20th day following that of its publication in the Official Journal of the European Communities.

---

[10] Council Directive 92/59/EEC of 29 June 1992 on general product safety (OJ L 228, 11.8.1992, p. 24).

Article 15

This Directive is addressed to the Member States.

ANNEX I

EUROPEAN STANDARDISATION BODIES

CEN - European Committee for Standardisation
Cenelec - European Committee for Electrotechnical Standardisation
ETSI- European Telecommunications Standards Institute

ANNEX II

NATIONAL STANDARDISATION BODIES

[...]

ANNEX III

PART A - Repealed Directives and Decisions (referred to by Article 13)

Directive 83/189/EEC and its following amendments
Council Directive 88/182/EEC
Commission Decision 90/230/EEC
Commission Decision 92/400/EEC
Directive 94/10/EC of the European Parliament and Council
Commission Decision 96/139/EC

PART B - List of deadlines for transposition into national law
(referred to in Article 13)

Directive	Deadline for transposition
83/189/EEC (OJ L 109, 26.4.1983, p. 8)	31.3.1984
88/182/EEC (OJ L 81, 26.3.1988, p. 75)	1.1.1989
94/10/EC (OJ L 100, 19.4.1994, p. 30)	1.7.1995

ANNEX IV

CORRELATION TABLE

Directive 83/189/EEC	This Directive
Article 1	Article 1
Article 2	Article 2
Article 3	Article 3
Article 4	Article 4
Article 5	Article 5
Article 6	Article 6
Article 7	Article 7
Article 8	Article 8

Transparency Directive (98/34/EC)

Article 9	Article 9
Article 10	Article 10
Article 11	Article 11
Article 12	Article 12
—	Article 13
—	Article 14
—	Article 15
Annex I	Annex I
Annex II	Annex II
—	Annex III
—	Annex IV

DIRECTIVE 98/48/EC OF THE EUROPEAN PARLIAMENT AND OF THE COUNCIL OF 20 JULY 1998 AMENDING DIRECTIVE 98/34/EC LAYING DOWN A PROCEDURE FOR THE PROVISION OF INFORMATION IN THE FIELD OF TECHNICAL STANDARDS AND REGULATIONS

(Official Journal L 217, 05/08/1998, p. 0018)

THE EUROPEAN PARLIAMENT AND THE COUNCIL OF THE EUROPEAN UNION,

Having regard to the Treaty establishing the European Community, and in particular Articles 100a and 213 thereof,
Having regard to the proposal from the Commission[1],
Having regard to the opinion of the Economic and Social Committee[2],
Acting in accordance with the procedure laid down in Article 189b of the Treaty[3],

(1) Whereas, in order to promote the smooth functioning of the internal market, as much transparency as possible should be ensured as regards the future national rules and regulations applying to Information Society services, by amending Directive 98/34/EC[4];

(2) Whereas a wide variety of services within the meaning of Articles 59 and 60 of the Treaty will benefit by the opportunities afforded by the Information Society of being provided at a distance, electronically and at the individual request of a recipient of services;

(3) Whereas the area without internal frontiers comprising the internal market enables providers of such services to develop their cross-border activities with a view to increasing their competitiveness, and thus affords citizens new opportunities to transmit and receive information regardless of frontiers, and consumers new forms of access to goods and services;

(4) Whereas the extension of the scope of Directive 98/34/EC should not prevent Member States from taking account of the different social, societal and cultural implications inherent in the advent of the Information Society; whereas, in particular, the use of the procedural rules laid down in that Directive for Information Society services should not affect cultural policy measures, particularly in the audiovisual field, which Member States might adopt in accordance with Community law, taking account of their linguistic diversity, their specific national and regional characteristics and their cultural heritage; whereas the development of the Information Society should ensure, in any event, proper access of European citizens to the European cultural heritage supplied in a digital environment;

(5) Whereas Directive 98/34/EC is not intended to apply to national rules relating to fundamental rights, such as constitutional provisions concerning freedom of expression and, more particularly, freedom of the press; whereas it is not intended to apply to the general criminal law either; whereas, furthermore, it does not apply to agreements governed by private law between credit institutions, in particular, to agreements on the execution of payments between credit institutions;

---

[1] OJ C 307, 16. 10. 1996, p. 11, and OJ C 65, 28. 2. 1998, p. 12.

[2] OJ C 158, 26. 5. 1997, p. 1.

[3] Opinion of the European Parliament of 16 May 1997 (OJ C 167, 2. 6. 1997, p. 238), Council Common Position of 26 January 1998 (OJ C 62, 26. 2. 1998, p. 48) and Decision of the European Parliament of 14 May 1998 (OJ C 167, 1. 6. 1998). Council Decision of 29 June 1998.

[4] OJ L 204, 21. 7. 1998, p. 37.

(6) Whereas the European Council has stressed the need to create a clear and stable legal framework at Community level in order to foster the development of the Information Society; whereas Community law and the rules governing the internal market in particular, including both the principles enshrined in the Treaty and secondary legislation, already constitute a basic legal framework for the development of such services;

(7) Whereas it should be possible to adapt the existing national rules and regulations applicable to services available at the present so as to take account of new Information Society services, either with a view to ensuring that the general interest is better protected or, on the other hand, with a view to simplifying such rules and regulations where their application is disproportionate to the objectives they pursue;

(8) Whereas, without coordination at Community level, this foreseeable regulatory activity at national level might give rise to restrictions on the free movement of services and the freedom of establishment, leading in turn to a refragmentation of the internal market, over-regulation and regulatory inconsistencies;

(9) Whereas, in order to ensure real and effective protection of the general-interest objectives involved in the development of the Information Society, there is a need for a coordinated approach at Community level when questions relating to activities with such highly transnational connotations as those of the new services are dealt with;

(10) Whereas, in the case of telecommunications services, there is already harmonisation at Community level or, in some cases, arrangements for mutual recognition, and whereas the existing Community legislation provides for adaptations to take account of technological developments and the supply of new services and, as a result, the majority of national regulations concerning telecommunications services will not be subject to notification under this Directive since they will come under the exemptions set out in Article 10(1) or Article 1 point 5 of Directive 98/34/EC; whereas, nevertheless, certain national provisions specifically aimed at matters which are not subject to Community legislation may affect the free movement of Information Society services and to that extent they must be notified;

(11) Whereas, for the other still little known fields of the Information Society, it would, however, be premature to coordinate national rules and regulations by means of extensive or exhaustive harmonisation at Community level of the substantive law, given that enough is not yet known about the form the new services will take or their nature, that there is as yet at national level no specific regulatory activity in this field, and that the need for, and content of, such harmonisation in the light of the internal market cannot be defined at this stage;

(12) Whereas it is therefore necessary to preserve the smooth functioning of the internal market and to avert the risks of refragmentation by providing for a procedure for the provision of information, the holding of consultations, and administrative cooperation in respect of new draft rules and regulations; whereas such a procedure will help, inter alia, to ensure that the Treaty, in particular Articles 52 and 59 thereof, is effectively applied and, where necessary, to detect any need to protect the general interest at Community level; whereas, moreover, the improved application of the Treaty made possible by such an information procedure will have the effect of reducing the need for Community rules to what is strictly necessary and proportional in the light of the internal market and the protection of general-interest objectives; whereas, lastly, such a procedure will enable businesses to exploit the advantages of the internal market more effectively;

(13) Whereas Directive 98/34/EC pursues the same objectives and whereas this procedure is effective, being the most comprehensive one for attaining these objectives; whereas the experience that has been gained in implementing that Directive and the procedures provided for therein can be applied to draft rules on Information Society services; whereas the procedure it lays down is now well established among national authorities;

(14) Whereas, moreover, in accordance with Article 7a of the Treaty, the internal market comprises an area without internal frontiers in which the free movement of goods, persons, services and capital is ensured and whereas Directive 98/34/EC provides only for an administrative cooperation procedure and not for any harmonisation of substantive rules;

(15) Whereas, therefore, amendment of Directive 98/34/EC with a view to applying it to draft rules and regulations on Information Society services is the approach best suited, with regard to the legal framework of the said services, to meeting effectively the need for transparency in the internal market;

(16) Whereas notification should be provided for notably in the case of rules which are likely to evolve in future; whereas services which are provided at a distance, electronically, and at the individual request of a recipient of services (Information Society services) are likely, in view of their diversity and their future growth, to necessitate and generate the largest number of new rules and regulations; whereas provision must accordingly be made for the notification of draft rules and regulations relating to such services;

(17) Whereas specific rules on the taking-up and pursuit of service activities which are capable of being carried on in the manner described above should thus be communicated even where they are included in rules and regulations with a more general purpose; whereas, however, general regulations which do not contain any provision specifically aimed at such services need not be notified;

(18) Whereas 'rules on the taking-up and pursuit of service activities' means rules laying down requirements concerning Information Society services, such as those relating to service providers, services and recipients of services and to economic activities capable of being provided electronically, at a distance and at the individual request of the recipient of the services; whereas, for example, rules on the establishment of service providers, in particular those on authorisation or licensing arrangements, are accordingly covered; whereas a provision specifically aimed at Information Society services must be considered as being such a rule even if part of a more general regulation; whereas, on the other hand, measures of direct and individual concern to certain specific recipients (such as, for example, telecommunications licences) would not be covered;

(19) Whereas, under Article 60 of the Treaty as interpreted by the case-law of the Court of Justice, 'services' means those normally provided for remuneration; whereas that characteristic is absent in the case of activities which a State carries out without economic consideration in the context of its duties in particular in the social, cultural, educational and judicial fields; whereas national provisions concerning such activities are not covered by the definition given in Article 60 of the Treaty and therefore do not fall within the scope of this Directive;

(20) Whereas this Directive is without prejudice to the scope of Council Directive 89/552/EEC of 3 October 1989 on the coordination of certain provisions laid down by law, regulation or administrative action in Member States concerning the pursuit of television broadcasting activities[5], as amended by Directive 97/36/EC of the European Parliament and of the Council[6], or any future amendments;

(21) Whereas, in any event, this Directive does not cover draft national provisions aimed at transposing the content of Community directives in force or awaiting adoption inasmuch as they are already subject to specific examination; whereas it accordingly covers neither national rules and regulations transposing Directive 89/552/EEC, as amended by Directive 97/36/EC, or any future amendments, nor national rules and regulations transposing, or adopted subsequently within the context of, Directive 97/13/EC of the European Parliament and of the

---

[5] OJ L 298, 17. 10. 1989, p. 23.
[6] OJ L 202, 30. 7. 1997, p. 1.

Council of 10 April 1997 on a common framework for general authorisations and individual licences for telecommunications services[7];

(22) Whereas, moreover, provision should be made for exceptional cases in which national rules and regulations concerning Information Society services might be adopted immediately and whereas it is also important to allow this possibility solely for urgent reasons linked to serious and unforeseeable circumstances, such as circumstances of which there was no previous knowledge and the origin of which is not attributable to any action on the part of the authorities of the Member State concerned, so as not to jeopardize the objective of prior consultation and administrative cooperation inherent in this Directive;

(23) Whereas it is appropriate for a Member State to postpone for twelve months - or possibly eighteen months in the case of a common position of the Council - the adoption of a draft rule on services only where the draft rule relates to a matter which falls within the scope of a proposal for a directive, regulation or decision which the Commission has already submitted to the Council; whereas this standstill obligation may be imposed by the Commission on the relevant Member State only if the draft national rule contains provisions which are not substantively consistent with the proposal submitted by the Commission;

(24) Whereas definition of the framework for the provision of information and the holding of consultations at Community level as established by this Directive is a precondition for consistent and effective participation by the Community in work involving matters relating to the regulatory aspects of Information Society services in the international context;

(25) Whereas it is appropriate that, in the context of the functioning of Directive 98/34/EC, the Committee provided for in Article 5 thereof should meet specifically to examine questions relating to Information Society services;

(26) Whereas, by the same token, it should be noted that whenever a national measure is required also to be notified at the draft stage under another Community act, the Member State concerned may make a single communication under that other act, by indicating that that communication constitutes a communication also for the purpose of this Directive;

(27) Whereas the Commission will at regular intervals investigate developments in the market for new services in the field of the Information Society, especially in the framework of the convergence between telecommunications, information technology and media and, where necessary, take initiatives in order to adapt rules promptly in order to encourage the European development of new services,

HAVE ADOPTED THIS DIRECTIVE:

Article 1

Directive 98/34/EC is amended as follows:
1. the title shall be replaced by the following:
"Directive of the European Parliament and of the Council laying down a procedure for the provision of information in the field of technical standards and regulations and of rules on Information Society services";
2. Article 1 is amended as follows:
(a) the following new point shall be inserted:
"2. "service", any Information Society service, that is to say, any service normally provided for remuneration, at a distance, by electronic means and at the individual request of a recipient of services.
For the purposes of this definition:

---

[7] OJ L 117, 7. 5. 1997, p. 15.

Directive amending Transparency Directive (98/48/EC)

- "at a distance" means that the service is provided without the parties being simultaneously present,
- "by electronic means" means that the service is sent initially and received at its destination by means of electronic equipment for the processing (including digital compression) and storage of data, and entirely transmitted, conveyed and received by wire, by radio, by optical means or by other electromagnetic means,
- "at the individual request of a recipient of services" means that the service is provided through the transmission of data on individual request.

An indicative list of services not covered by this definition is set out in Annex V.
This Directive shall not apply to:
- radio broadcasting services,
- television broadcasting services covered by point (a) of Article 1 of Directive 89/552/EEC[*];

(b) points 2 and 3 shall become points 3 and 4 respectively;
(c) the following new point shall be inserted:

"5. "rule on services", requirement of a general nature relating to the taking-up and pursuit of service activities within the meaning of point 2, in particular provisions concerning the service provider, the services and the recipient of services, excluding any rules which are not specifically aimed at the services defined in that point.

This Directive shall not apply to rules relating to matters which are covered by Community legislation in the field of telecommunications services, as defined by Directive 90/387/EEC[*].

This Directive shall not apply to rules relating to matters which are covered by Community legislation in the field of financial services, as listed non-exhaustively in Annex VI to this Directive.

With the exception of Article 8(3), this Directive shall not apply to rules enacted by or for regulated markets within the meaning of Directive 93/22/EEC or by or for other markets or bodies carrying out clearing or settlement functions for those markets.

For the purposes of this definition:
- a rule shall be considered to be specifically aimed at Information Society services where, having regard to its statement of reasons and its operative part, the specific aim and object of all or some of its individual provisions is to regulate such services in an explicit and targeted manner,
- a rule shall not be considered to be specifically aimed at Information Society services if it affects such services only in an implicit or incidental manner.

(d) points 4 to 8 shall become points 6 to 10;
(e) point 9 shall be renumbered 11 and shall read as follows:

"11. "technical regulation", technical specifications and other requirements or rules on services, including the relevant administrative provisions, the observance of which is compulsory, de jure or de facto, in the case of marketing, provision of a service, establishment of a service operator or use in a Member State or a major part thereof, as well as laws, regulations or administrative provisions of Member States, except those provided for in Article 10, prohibiting the manufacture, importation, marketing or use of a product or prohibiting the provision or use of a service, or establishment as a service provider.

De facto technical regulations include:
- laws, regulations or administrative provisions of a Member State which refer either to technical specifications or to other requirements or to rules on services, or to professional

---

[*] OJ L 298, 17.10.1989, p. 23. Directive as last amended by Directive 97/36/EC (OJ L 202, 30.7.1997, p. 1).

[*] OJ L 192, 24.7.1990, p. 1. Directive as amended by Directive 97/51/EC (OJ L 295, 29.10.1997 p. 23).

- codes or codes of practice which in turn refer to technical specifications or to other requirements or to rules on services, compliance with which confers a presumption of conformity with the obligations imposed by the aforementioned laws, regulations or administrative provisions,
- voluntary agreements to which a public authority is a contracting party and which provide, in the general interest, for compliance with technical specifications or other requirements or rules on services, excluding public procurement tender specifications,
- technical specifications or other requirements or rules on services which are linked to fiscal or financial measures affecting the consumption of products or services by encouraging compliance with such technical specifications or other requirements or rules on services; technical specifications or other requirements or rules on services linked to national social security systems are not included.

This comprises technical regulations imposed by the authorities designated by the Member States and appearing on a list to be drawn up by the Commission before 5 August 1999*), in the framework of the Committee referred to in Article 5.

The same procedure shall be used for amending this list; '

(f) point 10 shall be renumbered 12 and the first subparagraph shall read as follows:

"11. "draft technical regulation", the text of a technical specification or other requirement or of a rule on services, including administrative provisions, formulated with the aim of enacting it or of ultimately having it enacted as a technical regulation, the text being at a stage of preparation at which substantial amendments can still be made; "

3. Article 6 shall be amended as follows:

(a) the following subparagraph shall be added to paragraph 1:

"The Committee shall meet in a specific composition to examine questions concerning Information Society services. ";

(b) the following paragraph shall be added:

"8. With respect to rules on services, the Commission and the Committee may consult natural or legal persons from industry or academia, and where possible representative bodies, capable of delivering an expert opinion on the social and societal aims and consequences of any draft rule on services, and take notice of their advice whenever requested to do so.";

4. The sixth subparagraph of Article 8(1) shall be replaced by the following:

"With respect to the technical specifications or other requirements or rules on services referred to in the third indent of the second subparagraph of point 11 of Article 1, the comments or detailed opinions of the Commission or Member States may concern only aspects which may hinder trade or, in respect of rules on services, the free movement of services or the freedom of establishment of service operators and not the fiscal or financial aspects of the measure. ";

5. Article 9 shall be amended as follows:

(a) Paragraphs 2 and 3 shall be replaced by the following:

"2. Member States shall postpone:

- for four months the adoption of a draft technical regulation in the form of a voluntary agreement within the meaning of the second indent of the second subparagraph of point 11 of Article 1,
- without prejudice to paragraphs 3, 4 and 5, for six months the adoption of any other draft technical regulation (except for draft rules on services),from the date of receipt by the Commission of the communication referred to in Article 8(1) if the Commission or another Member State delivers a detailed opinion, within three months of that date, to the effect that the measure envisaged may create obstacles to the free movement of goods within the internal market;

without prejudice to paragraphs 4 and 5, for four months the adoption of any draft rule on services, from the date of receipt by the Commission of the communication referred to in Article 8(1) if the Commission or another Member State delivers a detailed opinion, within three months of that date, to the effect that the measure envisaged may create obstacles to the free movement of services or to the freedom of establishment of service operators within the internal market. With regard to draft rules on services, detailed opinions from the Commission or Member States may not affect any cultural policy measures, in particular in the audiovisual sphere, which Member States might adopt in accordance with Community law, taking account of their linguistic diversity, their specific national and regional characteristics and their cultural heritage. The Member State concerned shall report to the Commission on the action it proposes to take on such detailed opinions. The Commission shall comment on this reaction. With respect to rules on services, the Member State concerned shall indicate, where appropriate, the reasons why the detailed opinions cannot be taken into account.

3. With the exclusion of draft rules relating to services, Member States shall postpone the adoption of a draft technical regulation for twelve months from the date of receipt by the Commission of the communication referred to in Article 8(1) if, within three months of that date, the Commission announces its intention of proposing or adopting a directive, regulation or decision on the matter in accordance with Article 189 of the Treaty. ";

(b) Paragraph 7 shall be replaced by the following:

"7. Paragraphs 1 to 5 shall not apply in cases where:

- for urgent reasons, occasioned by serious and unforeseeable circumstances relating to the protection of public health or safety, the protection of animals or the preservation of plants, and for rules on services, also for public policy, notably the protection of minors, a Member State is obliged to prepare technical regulations in a very short space of time in order to enact and introduce them immediately without any consultations being possible or

- for urgent reasons occasioned by serious circumstances relating to the protection of the security and the integrity of the financial system, notably the protection of depositors, investors and insured persons, a Member State is obliged to enact and implement rules on financial services immediately.

In the communication referred to in Article 8, the Member State shall give reasons for the urgency of the measures taken. The Commission shall give its views on the communication as soon as possible. It shall take appropriate action in cases where improper use is made of this procedure. The European Parliament shall be kept informed by the Commission. ";

6. Article 10 shall be amended as follows:

(a) the first and second indents of paragraph 1 shall be replaced by the following:

"- comply with binding Community acts which result in the adoption of technical specifications or rules on services,

- fulfil the obligations arising out of international agreements which result in the adoption of common technical specifications or rules on services in the Community; "

(b) the sixth indent of paragraph 1 shall be replaced by the following:

"- restrict themselves to amending a technical regulation within the meaning of point 11 of Article 1, in accordance with a Commission request, with a view to removing an obstacle to trade or, in the case of rules on services, to the free movement of services or the freedom of establishment of service operators. ";

(c) paragraphs 3 and 4 shall be replaced by the following:

"3. Paragraphs 3 to 6 of Article 9 shall not apply to the voluntary agreements referred to in the second indent of the second subparagraph of point 11 of Article 1.

4. Article 9 shall not apply to the technical specifications or other requirements or the rules on services referred to in the third indent of the second subparagraph of point 11 of Article 1. ";

7. Annexes V and VI, which appear in the Annex to this Directive, shall be added.

Article 2

1. Member States shall bring into force the regulations and administrative provisions necessary in order to comply with this Directive by 5 August 1999. They shall forthwith inform the Commission thereof.
   When Member States adopt these measures, they shall contain a reference to this Directive or shall be accompanied by such reference on the occasion of their official publication. The methods of making such reference shall be laid down by Member States.
2. Member States shall communicate the main provisions of national law which they adopt in the field covered by this Directive to the Commission.

Article 3

Not later than two years from the date referred to in the first subparagraph of Article 2(1), the Commission shall submit to the European Parliament and the Council an evaluation of the application of Directive 98/34/EC in particular in the light of technological and market developments for the services referred to in point 2 of Article 1. Not later than three years from the date referred to in the first subparagraph of Article 2(1), the Commission shall, if necessary, make proposals to the European Parliament and to the Council for a revision of the said Directive. To this end, the Commission shall take into account any observations that might be communicated to it by Member States.

Article 4

This Directive shall enter into force on the day of its publication in the Official Journal of the European Communities.

Article 5

This Directive is addressed to the Member States.

ANNEX

ANNEX V

Indicative list of services not covered by the second subparagraph of point 2 of Article 1

1. Services not provided "at a distance"
   Services provided in the physical presence of the provider and the recipient, even if they involve the use of electronic devices
   (a) medical examinations or treatment at a doctor's surgery using electronic equipment where the patient is physically present;
   (b) consultation of an electronic catalogue in a shop with the customer on site;
   (c) plane ticket reservation at a travel agency in the physical presence of the customer by means of a network of computers;
   (d) electronic games made available in a video-arcade where the customer is physically present.
2. Services not provided "by electronic means"
   - Services having material content even though provided via electronic devices:
   (a) automatic cash or ticket dispensing machines (banknotes, rail tickets);

(b) access to road networks, car parks, etc., charging for use, even if there are electronic devices at the entrance/exit controlling access and/or ensuring correct payment is made,
- Off-line services: distribution of CD roms or software on diskettes,
- Services which are not provided via electronic processing/inventory systems:
(a) voice telephony services;
(b) telefax/telex services;
(c) services provided via voice telephony or fax;
(d) telephone/telefax consultation of a doctor;
(e) telephone/telefax consultation of a lawyer;
(f) telephone/telefax direct marketing.
3. Services not supplied "at the individual request of a recipient of services"
Services provided by transmitting data without individual demand for simultaneous reception by an unlimited number of individual receivers (point to multipoint transmission):
(a) television broadcasting services (including near-video on-demand services), covered by point (a) of Article 1 of Directive 89/552/EEC;
(b) radio broadcasting services;
(c) (televised) teletext.

ANNEX VI

Indicative list of the financial services covered by the third subparagraph of point 5 of Article 1
- Investment services
- Insurance and reinsurance operations
- Banking services
- Operations relating to pension funds
- Services relating to dealings in futures or options

Such services include in particular:
(a) investment services referred to in the Annex to Directive 93/22/EEC[1]; services of collective investment undertakings,
(b) services covered by the activities subject to mutual recognition referred to in the Annex to Directive 89/646/EEC[2],
(c) operations covered by the insurance and reinsurance activities referred to in:
- Article 1 of Directive 73/239/EEC[3],
- the Annex to Directive 79/267/EEC[4],
- Directive 64/225/EEC[5],
- Directives 92/49/EEC[6] and 92/96/EEC[7].

---

[1] OJ L 141, 11. 6. 1993, p. 27.

[2] OJ L 386, 30. 12. 1989, p. 1. Directive as amended by Directive 92/30/EEC (OJ L 110, 28. 4. 1992, p. 52).

[3] OJ L 228, 16.8.1973, p. 3. Directive as last amended by Directive 92/49/EEC (OJ L 228, 11.8.1992, p.1).

[4] OJ L 63, 13. 3. 1979, p. 1. Directive as last amended by Directive 90/619/EEC (OJ L 330, 29. 11. 1990, p. 50).

[5] OJ 56, 4. 4. 1964, p. 878/64. Directive as amended by the 1973 Act of Accession.

[6] OJ L 228, 11. 8. 1992, p. 1.

Directive amending Transparency Directive (98/48/EC)

---

[7] OJ L 360, 9. 12. 1992, p. 1.

DIRECTIVE 1999/93/EC OF THE EUROPEAN PARLIAMENT AND OF THE COUNCIL OF 13 DECEMBER 1999 ON A COMMUNITY FRAMEWORK FOR ELECTRONIC SIGNATURES

(Official Journal L 013, 19/01/2000, p. 0012)

THE EUROPEAN PARLIAMENT AND THE COUNCIL OF THE EUROPEAN UNION,

Having regard to the Treaty establishing the European Community, and in particular Articles 47(2), 55 and 95 thereof,
Having regard to the proposal from the Commission,[1]
Having regard to the opinion of the Economic and Social Committee,[2]
Having regard to the opinion of the Committee of the Regions,[3]

Acting in accordance with the procedure laid down in Article 251 of the Treaty,[4]

Whereas:
(1) On 16 April 1997 the Commission presented to the European Parliament, the Council, the Economic and Social Committee and the Committee of the Regions a Communication on a European Initiative in Electronic Commerce;
(2) On 8 October 1997 the Commission presented to the European Parliament, the Council, the Economic and Social Committee and the Committee of the Regions a Communication on ensuring security and trust in electronic communication - towards a European framework for digital signatures and encryption;
(3) On 1 December 1997 the Council invited the Commission to submit as soon as possible a proposal for a Directive of the European Parliament and of the Council on digital signatures;
(4) Electronic communication and commerce necessitate " electronic signatures" and related services allowing data authentication; divergent rules with respect to legal recognition of electronic signatures and the accreditation of certification-service providers in the Member States may create a significant barrier to the use of electronic communications and electronic commerce; on the other hand, a clear Community framework regarding the conditions applying to electronic signatures will strengthen confidence in, and general acceptance of, the new technologies; legislation in the Member States should not hinder the free movement of goods and services in the internal market;
(5) The interoperability of electronic-signature products should be promoted; in accordance with Article 14 of the Treaty, the internal market comprises an area without internal frontiers in which the free movement of goods is ensured; essential requirements specific to electronic-signature products must be met in order to ensure free movement within the internal market and to build trust in electronic signatures, without prejudice to Council Regulation (EC) No 3381/94 of 19 December 1994 setting up a Community regime for the control of exports of dual-use goods[5] and Council Decision 94/942/CFSP of 19 December 1994 on the joint action adopted by the Council concerning the control of exports of dual-use goods[6];

---

[1] OJ C 325, 23.10.1998, p. 5.

[2] OJ C 40, 15.2.1999, p. 29.

[3] OJ C 93, 6.4.1999, p. 33.

[4] Opinion of the European Parliament of 13 January 1999 (OJ C 104, 14.4.1999, p. 49), Council Common Position of 28 June 1999 (OJ C 243, 27.8.1999, p. 33) and Decision of the European Parliament of 27 October 1999 (not yet published in the Official Journal). Council Decision of 30 November 1999.

[5] OJ L 367, 31.12.1994, p. 1. Regulation as amended by Regulation (EC) No 837/95 (OJ L 90, 21.4.1995, p. 1).

[6] OJ L 367, 31.12.1994, p. 8. Decision as last amended by Decision 99/193/CFSP (OJ L 73, 19.3.1999, p. 1).

(6) This Directive does not harmonise the provision of services with respect to the confidentiality of information where they are covered by national provisions concerned with public policy or public security;

(7) The internal market ensures the free movement of persons, as a result of which citizens and residents of the European Union increasingly need to deal with authorities in Member States other than the one in which they reside; the availability of electronic communication could be of great service in this respect;

(8) Rapid technological development and the global character of the Internet necessitate an approach which is open to various technologies and services capable of authenticating data electronically;

(9) Electronic signatures will be used in a large variety of circumstances and applications, resulting in a wide range of new services and products related to or using electronic signatures; the definition of such products and services should not be limited to the issuance and management of certificates, but should also encompass any other service and product using, or ancillary to, electronic signatures, such as registration services, time-stamping services, directory services, computing services or consultancy services related to electronic signatures;

(10) The internal market enables certification-service-providers to develop their cross-border activities with a view to increasing their competitiveness, and thus to offer consumers and businesses new opportunities to exchange information and trade electronically in a secure way, regardless of frontiers; in order to stimulate the Community-wide provision of certification services over open networks, certification-service-providers should be free to provide their services without prior authorisation; prior authorisation means not only any permission whereby the certification-service-provider concerned has to obtain a decision by national authorities before being allowed to provide its certification services, but also any other measures having the same effect;

(11) Voluntary accreditation schemes aiming at an enhanced level of service-provision may offer certification-service-providers the appropriate framework for developing further their services towards the levels of trust, security and quality demanded by the evolving market; such schemes should encourage the development of best practice among certification-service-providers; certification-service-providers should be left free to adhere to and benefit from such accreditation schemes;

(12) Certification services can be offered either by a public entity or a legal or natural person, when it is established in accordance with the national law; whereas Member States should not prohibit certification-service-providers from operating outside voluntary accreditation schemes; it should be ensured that such accreditation schemes do not reduce competition for certification services;

(13) Member States may decide how they ensure the supervision of compliance with the provisions laid down in this Directive; this Directive does not preclude the establishment of private-sector-based supervision systems; this Directive does not oblige certification-service-providers to apply to be supervised under any applicable accreditation scheme;

(14) It is important to strike a balance between consumer and business needs;

(15) Annex III covers requirements for secure signature-creation devices to ensure the functionality of advanced electronic signatures; it does not cover the entire system environment in which such devices operate; the functioning of the internal market requires the Commission and the Member States to act swiftly to enable the bodies charged with the conformity assessment of secure signature devices with Annex III to be designated; in order to meet market needs conformity assessment must be timely and efficient;

(16) This Directive contributes to the use and legal recognition of electronic signatures within the Community; a regulatory framework is not needed for electronic signatures exclusively used within systems, which are based on voluntary agreements under private law between a specified number of participants; the freedom of parties to agree among themselves the terms

and conditions under which they accept electronically signed data should be respected to the extent allowed by national law; the legal effectiveness of electronic signatures used in such systems and their admissibility as evidence in legal proceedings should be recognised;
(17) This Directive does not seek to harmonise national rules concerning contract law, particularly the formation and performance of contracts, or other formalities of a non-contractual nature concerning signatures; for this reason the provisions concerning the legal effect of electronic signatures should be without prejudice to requirements regarding form laid down in national law with regard to the conclusion of contracts or the rules determining where a contract is concluded;
(18) The storage and copying of signature-creation data could cause a threat to the legal validity of electronic signatures;
(19) Electronic signatures will be used in the public sector within national and Community administrations and in communications between such administrations and with citizens and economic operators, for example in the public procurement, taxation, social security, health and justice systems;
(20) Harmonised criteria relating to the legal effects of electronic signatures will preserve a coherent legal framework across the Community; national law lays down different requirements for the legal validity of hand-written signatures; whereas certificates can be used to confirm the identity of a person signing electronically; advanced electronic signatures based on qualified certificates aim at a higher level of security; advanced electronic signatures which are based on a qualified certificate and which are created by a secure-signature-creation device can be regarded as legally equivalent to hand-written signatures only if the requirements for hand-written signatures are fulfilled;
(21) In order to contribute to the general acceptance of electronic authentication methods it has to be ensured that electronic signatures can be used as evidence in legal proceedings in all Member States; the legal recognition of electronic signatures should be based upon objective criteria and not be linked to authorisation of the certification-service-provider involved; national law governs the legal spheres in which electronic documents and electronic signatures may be used; this Directive is without prejudice to the power of a national court to make a ruling regarding conformity with the requirements of this Directive and does not affect national rules regarding the unfettered judicial consideration of evidence;
(22) Certification-service-providers providing certification-services to the public are subject to national rules regarding liability;
(23) The development of international electronic commerce requires cross-border arrangements involving third countries; in order to ensure interoperability at a global level, agreements on multilateral rules with third countries on mutual recognition of certification services could be beneficial;
(24) In order to increase user confidence in electronic communication and electronic commerce, certification-service-providers must observe data protection legislation and individual privacy;
(25) Provisions on the use of pseudonyms in certificates should not prevent Member States from requiring identification of persons pursuant to Community or national law;
(26) The measures necessary for the implementation of this Directive are to be adopted in accordance with Council Decision 1999/468/EC of 28 June 1999 laying down the procedures for the exercise of implementing powers conferred on the Commission[7];
(27) Two years after its implementation the Commission will carry out a review of this Directive so as, inter alia, to ensure that the advance of technology or changes in the legal environment have not created barriers to achieving the aims stated in this Directive; it should examine the implications of associated technical areas and submit a report to the European Parliament and the Council on this subject;

---

[7] OJ L 184, 17.7.1999, p. 23.

(28) In accordance with the principles of subsidiarity and proportionality as set out in Article 5 of the Treaty, the objective of creating a harmonised legal framework for the provision of electronic signatures and related services cannot be sufficiently achieved by the Member States and can therefore be better achieved by the Community; this Directive does not go beyond what is necessary to achieve that objective,

HAVE ADOPTED THIS DIRECTIVE:

Article 1 - Scope

The purpose of this Directive is to facilitate the use of electronic signatures and to contribute to their legal recognition. It establishes a legal framework for electronic signatures and certain certification-services in order to ensure the proper functioning of the internal market.

It does not cover aspects related to the conclusion and validity of contracts or other legal obligations where there are requirements as regards form prescribed by national or Community law nor does it affect rules and limits, contained in national or Community law, governing the use of documents.

Article 2 - Definitions

For the purpose of this Directive:

1. "electronic signature" means data in electronic form which are attached to or logically associated with other electronic data and which serve as a method of authentication;
2. "advanced electronic signature" means an electronic signature which meets the following requirements:
(a) it is uniquely linked to the signatory;
(b) it is capable of identifying the signatory;
(c) it is created using means that the signatory can maintain under his sole control; and
(d) it is linked to the data to which it relates in such a manner that any subsequent change of the data is detectable;
3. "signatory" means a person who holds a signature-creation device and acts either on his own behalf or on behalf of the natural or legal person or entity he represents;
4. "signature-creation data" means unique data, such as codes or private cryptographic keys, which are used by the signatory to create an electronic signature;
5. "signature-creation device" means configured software or hardware used to implement the signature-creation data;
6. "secure-signature-creation device" means a signature-creation device which meets the requirements laid down in Annex III;
7. "signature-verification-data" means data, such as codes or public cryptographic keys, which are used for the purpose of verifying an electronic signature;
8. "signature-verification device" means configured software or hardware used to implement the signature-verification-data;
9. "certificate" means an electronic attestation which links signature-verification data to a person and confirms the identity of that person;
10. "qualified certificate" means a certificate which meets the requirements laid down in Annex I and is provided by a certification-service-provider who fulfils the requirements laid down in Annex II;
11. "certification-service-provider" means an entity or a legal or natural person who issues certificates or provides other services related to electronic signatures;
12. "electronic-signature product" means hardware or software, or relevant components thereof, which are intended to be used by a certification-service-provider for the provision of electronic-signature services or are intended to be used for the creation or verification of electronic signatures;

13. "voluntary accreditation" means any permission, setting out rights and obligations specific to the provision of certification services, to be granted upon request by the certification-service-provider concerned, by the public or private body charged with the elaboration of, and supervision of compliance with, such rights and obligations, where the certification-service-provider is not entitled to exercise the rights stemming from the permission until it has received the decision by the body.

Article 3 - Market access

1. Member States shall not make the provision of certification services subject to prior authorisation.
2. Without prejudice to the provisions of paragraph 1, Member States may introduce or maintain voluntary accreditation schemes aiming at enhanced levels of certification-service provision. All conditions related to such schemes must be objective, transparent, proportionate and non-discriminatory. Member States may not limit the number of accredited certification-service-providers for reasons which fall within the scope of this Directive.
3. Each Member State shall ensure the establishment of an appropriate system that allows for supervision of certification-service-providers which are established on its territory and issue qualified certificates to the public.
4. The conformity of secure signature-creation-devices with the requirements laid down in Annex III shall be determined by appropriate public or private bodies designated by Member States. The Commission shall, pursuant to the procedure laid down in Article 9, establish criteria for Member States to determine whether a body should be designated.

   A determination of conformity with the requirements laid down in Annex III made by the bodies referred to in the first subparagraph shall be recognised by all Member States.
5. The Commission may, in accordance with the procedure laid down in Article 9, establish and publish reference numbers of generally recognised standards for electronic-signature products in the Official Journal of the European Communities. Member States shall presume that there is compliance with the requirements laid down in Annex II, point (f), and Annex III when an electronic signature product meets those standards.
6. Member States and the Commission shall work together to promote the development and use of signature-verification devices in the light of the recommendations for secure signature-verification laid down in Annex IV and in the interests of the consumer.
7. Member States may make the use of electronic signatures in the public sector subject to possible additional requirements. Such requirements shall be objective, transparent, proportionate and non-discriminatory and shall relate only to the specific characteristics of the application concerned. Such requirements may not constitute an obstacle to cross-border services for citizens.

Article 4 - Internal market principles

1. Each Member State shall apply the national provisions which it adopts pursuant to this Directive to certification-service-providers established on its territory and to the services which they provide. Member States may not restrict the provision of certification-services originating in another Member State in the fields covered by this Directive.
2. Member States shall ensure that electronic-signature products which comply with this Directive are permitted to circulate freely in the internal market.

Article 5 - Legal effects of electronic signatures

1. Member States shall ensure that advanced electronic signatures which are based on a qualified certificate and which are created by a secure-signature-creation device:

(a) satisfy the legal requirements of a signature in relation to data in electronic form in the same manner as a handwritten signature satisfies those requirements in relation to paper-based data; and
(b) are admissible as evidence in legal proceedings.
2. Member States shall ensure that an electronic signature is not denied legal effectiveness and admissibility as evidence in legal proceedings solely on the grounds that it is:
- in electronic form, or
- not based upon a qualified certificate, or
- not based upon a qualified certificate issued by an accredited certification-service-provider, or
- not created by a secure signature-creation device.

Article 6 - Liability

1. As a minimum, Member States shall ensure that by issuing a certificate as a qualified certificate to the public or by guaranteeing such a certificate to the public a certification-service-provider is liable for damage caused to any entity or legal or natural person who reasonably relies on that certificate:
(a) as regards the accuracy at the time of issuance of all information contained in the qualified certificate and as regards the fact that the certificate contains all the details prescribed for a qualified certificate;
(b) for assurance that at the time of the issuance of the certificate, the signatory identified in the qualified certificate held the signature-creation data corresponding to the signature-verification data given or identified in the certificate;
(c) for assurance that the signature-creation data and the signature-verification data can be used in a complementary manner in cases where the certification-service-provider generates them both;
unless the certification-service-provider proves that he has not acted negligently.
2. As a minimum Member States shall ensure that a certification-service-provider who has issued a certificate as a qualified certificate to the public is liable for damage caused to any entity or legal or natural person who reasonably relies on the certificate for failure to register revocation of the certificate unless the certification-service-provider proves that he has not acted negligently.
3. Member States shall ensure that a certification-service-provider may indicate in a qualified certificate limitations on the use of that certificate. provided that the limitations are recognisable to third parties. The certification-service-provider shall not be liable for damage arising from use of a qualified certificate which exceeds the limitations placed on it.
4. Member States shall ensure that a certification-service-provider may indicate in the qualified certificate a limit on the value of transactions for which the certificate can be used, provided that the limit is recognisable to third parties.
The certification-service-provider shall not be liable for damage resulting from this maximum limit being exceeded.
5. The provisions of paragraphs 1 to 4 shall be without prejudice to Council Directive 93/13/EEC of 5 April 1993 on unfair terms in consumer contracts.[8]

Article 7 - International aspects

1. Member States shall ensure that certificates which are issued as qualified certificates to the public by a certification-service-provider established in a third country are recognised as legally equivalent to certificates issued by a certification-service-provider established within the Community if:

---
[8] OJ L 95, 21.4.1993, p. 29.

(a) the certification-service-provider fulfils the requirements laid down in this Directive and has been accredited under a voluntary accreditation scheme established in a Member State; or
(b) a certification-service-provider established within the Community which fulfils the requirements laid down in this Directive guarantees the certificate; or
(c) the certificate or the certification-service-provider is recognised under a bilateral or multilateral agreement between the Community and third countries or international organisations.
2. In order to facilitate cross-border certification services with third countries and legal recognition of advanced electronic signatures originating in third countries, the Commission shall make proposals, where appropriate, to achieve the effective implementation of standards and international agreements applicable to certification services. In particular, and where necessary, it shall submit proposals to the Council for appropriate mandates for the negotiation of bilateral and multilateral agreements with third countries and international organisations. The Council shall decide by qualified majority.
3. Whenever the Commission is informed of any difficulties encountered by Community undertakings with respect to market access in third countries, it may, if necessary, submit proposals to the Council for an appropriate mandate for the negotiation of comparable rights for Community undertakings in these third countries. The Council shall decide by qualified majority.

Measures taken pursuant to this paragraph shall be without prejudice to the obligations of the Community and of the Member States under relevant international agreements.

Article 8 - Data protection

1. Member States shall ensure that certification-service-providers and national bodies responsible for accreditation or supervision comply with the requirements laid down in Directive 95/46/EC of the European Parliament and of the Council of 24 October 1995 on the protection of individuals with regard to the processing of personal data and on the free movement of such data.[9]
2. Member States shall ensure that a certification-service-provider which issues certificates to the public may collect personal data only directly from the data subject, or after the explicit consent of the data subject, and only insofar as it is necessary for the purposes of issuing and maintaining the certificate. The data may not be collected or processed for any other purposes without the explicit consent of the data subject.
3. Without prejudice to the legal effect given to pseudonyms under national law, Member States shall not prevent certification service providers from indicating in the certificate a pseudonym instead of the signatory's name.

Article 9 - Committee

1. The Commission shall be assisted by an "Electronic-Signature Committee", hereinafter referred to as "the committee".
2. Where reference is made to this paragraph, Articles 4 and 7 of Decision 1999/468/EC shall apply, having regard to the provisions of Article 8 thereof.
The period laid down in Article 4(3) of Decision 1999/468/EC shall be set at three months.
3. The Committee shall adopt its own rules of procedure.

---

[9] OJ L 281, 23.11.1995, p. 31.

Article 10 - Tasks of the committee

The committee shall clarify the requirements laid down in the Annexes of this Directive, the criteria referred to in Article 3(4) and the generally recognised standards for electronic signature products established and published pursuant to Article 3(5), in accordance with the procedure laid down in Article 9(2).

Article 11 - Notification

1. Member States shall notify to the Commission and the other Member States the following:
(a) information on national voluntary accreditation schemes, including any additional requirements pursuant to Article 3(7);
(b) the names and addresses of the national bodies responsible for accreditation and supervision as well as of the bodies referred to in Article 3(4);
(c) the names and addresses of all accredited national certification service providers.
2. Any information supplied under paragraph 1 and changes in respect of that information shall be notified by the Member States as soon as possible.

Article 12 - Review

1. The Commission shall review the operation of this Directive and report thereon to the European Parliament and to the Council by 19 July 2003 at the latest.
2. The review shall inter alia assess whether the scope of this Directive should be modified, taking account of technological, market and legal developments. The report shall in particular include an assessment, on the basis of experience gained, of aspects of harmonisation. The report shall be accompanied, where appropriate, by legislative proposals.

Article 13 - Implementation

1. Member States shall bring into force the laws, regulations and administrative provisions necessary to comply with this Directive before 19 July 2001. They shall forthwith inform the Commission thereof.
When Member States adopt these measures, they shall contain a reference to this Directive or shall be accompanied by such a reference on the occasion of their official publication. The methods of making such reference shall be laid down by the Member States.
2. Member States shall communicate to the Commission the text of the main provisions of domestic law which they adopt in the field governed by this Directive.

Article 14 - Entry into force

This Directive shall enter into force on the day of its publication in the Official Journal of the European Communities

Article 15 - Addressees

This Directive is addressed to the Member States.

ANNEX I - Requirements for qualified certificates

Qualified certificates must contain:
(a) an indication that the certificate is issued as a qualified certificate;
(b) the identification of the certification-service-provider and the State in which it is established;
(c) the name of the signatory or a pseudonym, which shall be identified as such;

(d) provision for a specific attribute of the signatory to be included if relevant, depending on the purpose for which the certificate is intended;
(e) signature-verification data which correspond to signature-creation data under the control of the signatory;
(f) an indication of the beginning and end of the period of validity of the certificate;
(g) the identity code of the certificate;
(h) the advanced electronic signature of the certification-service-provider issuing it;
(i) limitations on the scope of use of the certificate, if applicable; and
(j) limits on the value of transactions for which the certificate can be used, if applicable.

ANNEX II - Requirements for certification-service-providers issuing qualified certificates

Certification-service-providers must:

(a) demonstrate the reliability necessary for providing certification services;
(b) ensure the operation of a prompt and secure directory and a secure and immediate revocation service;
(c) ensure that the date and time when a certificate is issued or revoked can be determined precisely;
(d) verify, by appropriate means in accordance with national law, the identity and, if applicable, any specific attributes of the person to which a qualified certificate is issued;
(e) employ personnel who possess the expert knowledge, experience, and qualifications necessary for the services provided, in particular competence at managerial level, expertise in electronic signature technology and familiarity with proper security procedures; they must also apply administrative and management procedures which are adequate and correspond to recognised standards;
(f) use trustworthy systems and products which are protected against modification and ensure the technical and cryptographic security of the process supported by them;
(g) take measures against forgery of certificates, and, in cases where the certification-service-provider generates signature-creation data, guarantee confidentiality during the process of generating such data;
(h) maintain sufficient financial resources to operate in conformity with the requirements laid down in the Directive, in particular to bear the risk of liability for damages, for example, by obtaining appropriate insurance;
(i) record all relevant information concerning a qualified certificate for an appropriate period of time, in particular for the purpose of providing evidence of certification for the purposes of legal proceedings. Such recording may be done electronically;
(j) not store or copy signature-creation data of the person to whom the certification-service-provider provided key management services;
(k) before entering into a contractual relationship with a person seeking a certificate to support his electronic signature inform that person by a durable means of communication of the precise terms and conditions regarding the use of the certificate, including any limitations on its use, the existence of a voluntary accreditation scheme and procedures for complaints and dispute settlement. Such information, which may be transmitted electronically, must be in writing and in readily understandable language. Relevant parts of this information must also be made available on request to third-parties relying on the certificate;
(l) use trustworthy systems to store certificates in a verifiable form so that:
- only authorised persons can make entries and changes,
- information can be checked for authenticity,
- certificates are publicly available for retrieval in only those cases for which the certificate-holder's consent has been obtained, and

- any technical changes compromising these security requirements are apparent to the operator.

ANNEX III - Requirements for secure signature-creation devices

1. Secure signature-creation devices must, by appropriate technical and procedural means, ensure at the least that:
(a) the signature-creation-data used for signature generation can practically occur only once, and that their secrecy is reasonably assured;
(b) the signature-creation-data used for signature generation cannot, with reasonable assurance, be derived and the signature is protected against forgery using currently available technology;
(c) the signature-creation-data used for signature generation can be reliably protected by the legitimate signatory against the use of others.
2. Secure signature-creation devices must not alter the data to be signed or prevent such data from being presented to the signatory prior to the signature process.

ANNEX IV - Recommendations for secure signature verification

During the signature-verification process it should be ensured with reasonable certainty that:
(i) the data used for verifying the signature correspond to the data displayed to the verifier;
(ii) the signature is reliably verified and the result of that verification is correctly displayed;
(iii) the verifier can, as necessary, reliably establish the contents of the signed data;
(iv) the authenticity and validity of the certificate required at the time of signature verification are reliably verified;
(v) the result of verification and the signatory's identity are correctly displayed;
(vi) the use of a pseudonym is clearly indicated; and
(vii) any security-relevant changes can be detected.

DIRECTIVE 2000/31/EC OF THE EUROPEAN PARLIAMENT AND OF THE COUNCIL OF 8 JUNE 2000 ON CERTAIN LEGAL ASPECTS OF INFORMATION SOCIETY SERVICES, IN PARTICULAR ELECTRONIC COMMERCE, IN THE INTERNAL MARKET

(Official Journal L 178, 17/07/2000, p. 0001)

THE EUROPEAN PARLIAMENT AND THE COUNCIL OF THE EUROPEAN UNION,

Having regard to the Treaty establishing the European Community, and in particular Articles 47(2), 55 and 95 thereof,
Having regard to the proposal from the Commission[1],
Having regard to the opinion of the Economic and Social Committee[2],

Acting in accordance with the procedure laid down in Article 251 of the Treaty[3],

Whereas:
(1) The European Union is seeking to forge ever closer links between the States and peoples of Europe, to ensure economic and social progress; in accordance with Article 14(2) of the Treaty, the internal market comprises an area without internal frontiers in which the free movements of goods, services and the freedom of establishment are ensured; the development of information society services within the area without internal frontiers is vital to eliminating the barriers which divide the European peoples.
(2) The development of electronic commerce within the information society offers significant employment opportunities in the Community, particularly in small and medium-sized enterprises, and will stimulate economic growth and investment in innovation by European companies, and can also enhance the competitiveness of European industry, provided that everyone has access to the Internet.
(3) Community law and the characteristics of the Community legal order are a vital asset to enable European citizens and operators to take full advantage, without consideration of borders, of the opportunities afforded by electronic commerce; this Directive therefore has the purpose of ensuring a high level of Community legal integration in order to establish a real area without internal borders for information society services.
(4) It is important to ensure that electronic commerce could fully benefit from the internal market and therefore that, as with Council Directive 89/552/EEC of 3 October 1989 on the coordination of certain provisions laid down by law, regulation or administrative action in Member States concerning the pursuit of television broadcasting activities[4], a high level of Community integration is achieved.
(5) The development of information society services within the Community is hampered by a number of legal obstacles to the proper functioning of the internal market which make less attractive the exercise of the freedom of establishment and the freedom to provide services;

---

[1] OJ C 30, 5.2.1999, p. 4.

[2] OJ C 169, 16.6.1999, p. 36.

[3] Opinion of the European Parliament of 6 May 1999 (OJ C 279, 1.10.1999, p. 389), Council common position of 28 February 2000 (OJ C 128, 8.5.2000, p. 32) and Decision of the European Parliament of 4 May 2000 (not yet published in the Official Journal).

[4] OJ L 298, 17.10.1989, p. 23. Directive as amended by Directive 97/36/EC of the European Parliament and of the Council (OJ L 202, 30.7.1997, p. 60).

these obstacles arise from divergences in legislation and from the legal uncertainty as to which national rules apply to such services; in the absence of coordination and adjustment of legislation in the relevant areas, obstacles might be justified in the light of the case-law of the Court of Justice of the European Communities; legal uncertainty exists with regard to the extent to which Member States may control services originating from another Member State.

(6) In the light of Community objectives, of Articles 43 and 49 of the Treaty and of secondary Community law, these obstacles should be eliminated by coordinating certain national laws and by clarifying certain legal concepts at Community level to the extent necessary for the proper functioning of the internal market; by dealing only with certain specific matters which give rise to problems for the internal market, this Directive is fully consistent with the need to respect the principle of subsidiarity as set out in Article 5 of the Treaty.

(7) In order to ensure legal certainty and consumer confidence, this Directive must lay down a clear and general framework to cover certain legal aspects of electronic commerce in the internal market.

(8) The objective of this Directive is to create a legal framework to ensure the free movement of information society services between Member States and not to harmonise the field of criminal law as such.

(9) The free movement of information society services can in many cases be a specific reflection in Community law of a more general principle, namely freedom of expression as enshrined in Article 10(1) of the Convention for the Protection of Human Rights and Fundamental Freedoms, which has been ratified by all the Member States; for this reason, directives covering the supply of information society services must ensure that this activity may be engaged in freely in the light of that Article, subject only to the restrictions laid down in paragraph 2 of that Article and in Article 46(1) of the Treaty; this Directive is not intended to affect national fundamental rules and principles relating to freedom of expression.

(10) In accordance with the principle of proportionality, the measures provided for in this Directive are strictly limited to the minimum needed to achieve the objective of the proper functioning of the internal market; where action at Community level is necessary, and in order to guarantee an area which is truly without internal frontiers as far as electronic commerce is concerned, the Directive must ensure a high level of protection of objectives of general interest, in particular the protection of minors and human dignity, consumer protection and the protection of public health; according to Article 152 of the Treaty, the protection of public health is an essential component of other Community policies.

(11) This Directive is without prejudice to the level of protection for, in particular, public health and consumer interests, as established by Community acts; amongst others, Council Directive 93/13/EEC of 5 April 1993 on unfair terms in consumer contracts[5] and Directive 97/7/EC of the European Parliament and of the Council of 20 May 1997 on the protection of consumers in respect of distance contracts[6] form a vital element for protecting consumers in contractual matters; those Directives also apply in their entirety to information society services; that same Community acquis, which is fully applicable to information society services, also embraces in particular Council Directive 84/450/EEC of 10 September 1984 concerning misleading and comparative advertising[7], Council Directive 87/102/EEC of 22 December 1986 for the approximation of the laws, regulations and administrative provisions of the Member States concerning consumer credit[8], Council Directive 93/22/EEC of 10 May 1993 on investment

---

[5] OJ L 95, 21.4.1993, p. 29.

[6] OJ L 144, 4.6.1999, p. 19.

[7] OJ L 250, 19.9.1984, p. 17. Directive as amended by Directive 97/55/EC of the European Parliament and of the Council (OJ L 290, 23.10.1997, p. 18).

[8] OJ L 42, 12.2.1987, p. 48. Directive as last amended by Directive 98/7/EC of the European Parliament and of the Council (OJ L 101, 1.4.1998, p. 17).

services in the securities field[9], Council Directive 90/314/EEC of 13 June 1990 on package travel, package holidays and package tours[10], Directive 98/6/EC of the European Parliament and of the Council of 16 February 1998 on consumer production in the indication of prices of products offered to consumers[11], Council Directive 92/59/EEC of 29 June 1992 on general product safety[12], Directive 94/47/EC of the European Parliament and of the Council of 26 October 1994 on the protection of purchasers in respect of certain aspects on contracts relating to the purchase of the right to use immovable properties on a timeshare basis[13], Directive 98/27/EC of the European Parliament and of the Council of 19 May 1998 on injunctions for the protection of consumers' interests[14], Council Directive 85/374/EEC of 25 July 1985 on the approximation of the laws, regulations and administrative provisions concerning liability for defective products[15], Directive 1999/44/EC of the European Parliament and of the Council of 25 May 1999 on certain aspects of the sale of consumer goods and associated guarantees[16], the future Directive of the European Parliament and of the Council concerning the distance marketing of consumer financial services and Council Directive 92/28/EEC of 31 March 1992 on the advertising of medicinal products[17]; this Directive should be without prejudice to Directive 98/43/EC of the European Parliament and of the Council of 6 July 1998 on the approximation of the laws, regulations and administrative provisions of the Member States relating to the advertising and sponsorship of tobacco products[18] adopted within the framework of the internal market, or to directives on the protection of public health; this Directive complements information requirements established by the abovementioned Directives and in particular Directive 97/7/EC.

(12) It is necessary to exclude certain activities from the scope of this Directive, on the grounds that the freedom to provide services in these fields cannot, at this stage, be guaranteed under the Treaty or existing secondary legislation; excluding these activities does not preclude any instruments which might prove necessary for the proper functioning of the internal market; taxation, particularly value added tax imposed on a large number of the services covered by this Directive, must be excluded form the scope of this Directive.

(13) This Directive does not aim to establish rules on fiscal obligations nor does it pre-empt the drawing up of Community instruments concerning fiscal aspects of electronic commerce.

(14) The protection of individuals with regard to the processing of personal data is solely governed by Directive 95/46/EC of the European Parliament and of the Council of 24 October 1995 on the protection of individuals with regard to the processing of personal data and on the free movement of such data[19] and Directive 97/66/EC of the European Parliament and of the Council of 15 December 1997 concerning the processing of personal data and the protection of privacy in the telecommunications sector[20] which are fully applicable to information society services; these Directives already establish a Community legal framework in the field of personal data and therefore it is not necessary to cover this issue in this Directive in order to ensure the smooth functioning of the internal market, in particular the free movement of personal data between Member States; the implementation and application of this Directive

---

[9] OJ L 141, 11.6.1993, p. 27. Directive as last amended by Directive 97/9/EC of the European Parliament and of the Council (OJ L 84, 26.3.1997, p. 22).
[10] OJ L 158, 23.6.1990, p. 59.
[11] OJ L 80, 18.3.1998, p. 27.
[12] OJ L 228, 11.8.1992, p. 24.
[13] OJ L 280, 29.10.1994, p. 83.
[14] OJ L 166, 11.6.1998, p. 51. Directive as amended by Directive 1999/44/EC (OJ L 171, 7.7.1999, p. 12).
[15] OJ L 210, 7.8.1985, p. 29. Directive as amended by Directive 1999/34/EC (OJ L 141, 4.6.1999, p. 20).
[16] OJ L 171, 7.7.1999, p. 12.
[17] OJ L 113, 30.4.1992, p. 13.
[18] OJ L 213, 30.7.1998, p. 9.
[19] OJ L 281, 23.11.1995, p. 31.
[20] OJ L 24, 30.1.1998, p. 1.

should be made in full compliance with the principles relating to the protection of personal data, in particular as regards unsolicited commercial communication and the liability of intermediaries; this Directive cannot prevent the anonymous use of open networks such as the Internet.

(15) The confidentiality of communications is guaranteed by Article 5 Directive 97/66/EC; in accordance with that Directive, Member States must prohibit any kind of interception or surveillance of such communications by others than the senders and receivers, except when legally authorised.

(16) The exclusion of gambling activities from the scope of application of this Directive covers only games of chance, lotteries and betting transactions, which involve wagering a stake with monetary value; this does not cover promotional competitions or games where the purpose is to encourage the sale of goods or services and where payments, if they arise, serve only to acquire the promoted goods or services.

(17) The definition of information society services already exists in Community law in Directive 98/34/EC of the European Parliament and of the Council of 22 June 1998 laying down a procedure for the provision of information in the field of technical standards and regulations and of rules on information society services[21] and in Directive 98/84/EC of the European Parliament and of the Council of 20 November 1998 on the legal protection of services based on, or consisting of, conditional access[22]; this definition covers any service normally provided for remuneration, at a distance, by means of electronic equipment for the processing (including digital compression) and storage of data, and at the individual request of a recipient of a service; those services referred to in the indicative list in Annex V to Directive 98/34/EC which do not imply data processing and storage are not covered by this definition.

(18) Information society services span a wide range of economic activities which take place on-line; these activities can, in particular, consist of selling goods on-line; activities such as the delivery of goods as such or the provision of services off-line are not covered; information society services are not solely restricted to services giving rise to on-line contracting but also, in so far as they represent an economic activity, extend to services which are not remunerated by those who receive them, such as those offering on-line information or commercial communications, or those providing tools allowing for search, access and retrieval of data; information society services also include services consisting of the transmission of information via a communication network, in providing access to a communication network or in hosting information provided by a recipient of the service; television broadcasting within the meaning of Directive EEC/89/552 and radio broadcasting are not information society services because they are not provided at individual request; by contrast, services which are transmitted point to point, such as video-on-demand or the provision of commercial communications by electronic mail are information society services; the use of electronic mail or equivalent individual communications for instance by natural persons acting outside their trade, business or profession including their use for the conclusion of contracts between such persons is not an information society service; the contractual relationship between an employee and his employer is not an information society service; activities which by their very nature cannot be carried out at a distance and by electronic means, such as the statutory auditing of company accounts or medical advice requiring the physical examination of a patient are not information society services.

(19) The place at which a service provider is established should be determined in conformity with the case-law of the Court of Justice according to which the concept of establishment involves the actual pursuit of an economic activity through a fixed establishment for an indefinite period; this requirement is also fulfilled where a company is constituted for a given

---

[21] OJ L 204, 21.7.1998, p. 37. Directive as amended by Directive 98/48/EC (OJ L 217, 5.8.1998, p. 18).
[22] OJ L 320, 28.11.1998, p. 54.

period; the place of establishment of a company providing services via an Internet website is not the place at which the technology supporting its website is located or the place at which its website is accessible but the place where it pursues its economic activity; in cases where a provider has several places of establishment it is important to determine from which place of establishment the service concerned is provided; in cases where it is difficult to determine from which of several places of establishment a given service is provided, this is the place where the provider has the centre of his activities relating to this particular service.
(20) The definition of "recipient of a service" covers all types of usage of information society services, both by persons who provide information on open networks such as the Internet and by persons who seek information on the Internet for private or professional reasons.
(21) The scope of the coordinated field is without prejudice to future Community harmonisation relating to information society services and to future legislation adopted at national level in accordance with Community law; the coordinated field covers only requirements relating to on-line activities such as on-line information, on-line advertising, on-line shopping, on-line contracting and does not concern Member States' legal requirements relating to goods such as safety standards, labelling obligations, or liability for goods, or Member States' requirements relating to the delivery or the transport of goods, including the distribution of medicinal products; the coordinated field does not cover the exercise of rights of pre-emption by public authorities concerning certain goods such as works of art.
(22) Information society services should be supervised at the source of the activity, in order to ensure an effective protection of public interest objectives; to that end, it is necessary to ensure that the competent authority provides such protection not only for the citizens of its own country but for all Community citizens; in order to improve mutual trust between Member States, it is essential to state clearly this responsibility on the part of the Member State where the services originate; moreover, in order to effectively guarantee freedom to provide services and legal certainty for suppliers and recipients of services, such information society services should in principle be subject to the law of the Member State in which the service provider is established.
(23) This Directive neither aims to establish additional rules on private international law relating to conflicts of law nor does it deal with the jurisdiction of Courts; provisions of the applicable law designated by rules of private international law must not restrict the freedom to provide information society services as established in this Directive.
(24) In the context of this Directive, notwithstanding the rule on the control at source of information society services, it is legitimate under the conditions established in this Directive for Member States to take measures to restrict the free movement of information society services.
(25) National courts, including civil courts, dealing with private law disputes can take measures to derogate from the freedom to provide information society services in conformity with conditions established in this Directive.
(26) Member States, in conformity with conditions established in this Directive, may apply their national rules on criminal law and criminal proceedings with a view to taking all investigative and other measures necessary for the detection and prosecution of criminal offences, without there being a need to notify such measures to the Commission.
(27) This Directive, together with the future Directive of the European Parliament and of the Council concerning the distance marketing of consumer financial services, contributes to the creating of a legal framework for the on-line provision of financial services; this Directive does not pre-empt future initiatives in the area of financial services in particular with regard to the harmonisation of rules of conduct in this field; the possibility for Member States, established in this Directive, under certain circumstances of restricting the freedom to provide information society services in order to protect consumers also covers measures in the area of financial services in particular measures aiming at protecting investors.

(28) The Member States' obligation not to subject access to the activity of an information society service provider to prior authorisation does not concern postal services covered by Directive 97/67/EC of the European Parliament and of the Council of 15 December 1997 on common rules for the development of the internal market of Community postal services and the improvement of quality of service[23] consisting of the physical delivery of a printed electronic mail message and does not affect voluntary accreditation systems, in particular for providers of electronic signature certification service.

(29) Commercial communications are essential for the financing of information society services and for developing a wide variety of new, charge-free services; in the interests of consumer protection and fair trading, commercial communications, including discounts, promotional offers and promotional competitions or games, must meet a number of transparency requirements; these requirements are without prejudice to Directive 97/7/EC; this Directive should not affect existing Directives on commercial communications, in particular Directive 98/43/EC.

(30) The sending of unsolicited commercial communications by electronic mail may be undesirable for consumers and information society service providers and may disrupt the smooth functioning of interactive networks; the question of consent by recipient of certain forms of unsolicited commercial communications is not addressed by this Directive, but has already been addressed, in particular, by Directive 97/7/EC and by Directive 97/66/EC; in Member States which authorise unsolicited commercial communications by electronic mail, the setting up of appropriate industry filtering initiatives should be encouraged and facilitated; in addition it is necessary that in any event unsolicited commercial communities are clearly identifiable as such in order to improve transparency and to facilitate the functioning of such industry initiatives; unsolicited commercial communications by electronic mail should not result in additional communication costs for the recipient.

(31) Member States which allow the sending of unsolicited commercial communications by electronic mail without prior consent of the recipient by service providers established in their territory have to ensure that the service providers consult regularly and respect the opt-out registers in which natural persons not wishing to receive such commercial communications can register themselves.

(32) In order to remove barriers to the development of cross-border services within the Community which members of the regulated professions might offer on the Internet, it is necessary that compliance be guaranteed at Community level with professional rules aiming, in particular, to protect consumers or public health; codes of conduct at Community level would be the best means of determining the rules on professional ethics applicable to commercial communication; the drawing-up or, where appropriate, the adaptation of such rules should be encouraged without prejudice to the autonomy of professional bodies and associations.

(33) This Directive complements Community law and national law relating to regulated professions maintaining a coherent set of applicable rules in this field.

(34) Each Member State is to amend its legislation containing requirements, and in particular requirements as to form, which are likely to curb the use of contracts by electronic means; the examination of the legislation requiring such adjustment should be systematic and should cover all the necessary stages and acts of the contractual process, including the filing of the contract; the result of this amendment should be to make contracts concluded electronically workable; the legal effect of electronic signatures is dealt with by Directive 1999/93/EC of the European Parliament and of the Council of 13 December 1999 on a Community framework for

---

[23] OJ L 15, 21.1.1998, p. 14.

electronic signatures[24]; the acknowledgement of receipt by a service provider may take the form of the on-line provision of the service paid for.
(35) This Directive does not affect Member States' possibility of maintaining or establishing general or specific legal requirements for contracts which can be fulfilled by electronic means, in particular requirements concerning secure electronic signatures.
(36) Member States may maintain restrictions for the use of electronic contracts with regard to contracts requiring by law the involvement of courts, public authorities, or professions exercising public authority; this possibility also covers contracts which require the involvement of courts, public authorities, or professions exercising public authority in order to have an effect with regard to third parties as well as contracts requiring by law certification or attestation by a notary.
(37) Member States' obligation to remove obstacles to the use of electronic contracts concerns only obstacles resulting from legal requirements and not practical obstacles resulting from the impossibility of using electronic means in certain cases.
(38) Member States' obligation to remove obstacles to the use of electronic contracts is to be implemented in conformity with legal requirements for contracts enshrined in Community law.
(39) The exceptions to the provisions concerning the contracts concluded exclusively by electronic mail or by equivalent individual communications provided for by this Directive, in relation to information to be provided and the placing of orders, should not enable, as a result, the by-passing of those provisions by providers of information society services.
(40) Both existing and emerging disparities in Member States' legislation and case-law concerning liability of service providers acting as intermediaries prevent the smooth functioning of the internal market, in particular by impairing the development of cross-border services and producing distortions of competition; service providers have a duty to act, under certain circumstances, with a view to preventing or stopping illegal activities; this Directive should constitute the appropriate basis for the development of rapid and reliable procedures for removing and disabling access to illegal information; such mechanisms could be developed on the basis of voluntary agreements between all parties concerned and should be encouraged by Member States; it is in the interest of all parties involved in the provision of information society services to adopt and implement such procedures; the provisions of this Directive relating to liability should not preclude the development and effective operation, by the different interested parties, of technical systems of protection and identification and of technical surveillance instruments made possible by digital technology within the limits laid down by Directives 95/46/EC and 97/66/EC.
(41) This Directive strikes a balance between the different interests at stake and establishes principles upon which industry agreements and standards can be based.
(42) The exemptions from liability established in this Directive cover only cases where the activity of the information society service provider is limited to the technical process of operating and giving access to a communication network over which information made available by third parties is transmitted or temporarily stored, for the sole purpose of making the transmission more efficient; this activity is of a mere technical, automatic and passive nature, which implies that the information society service provider has neither knowledge of nor control over the information which is transmitted or stored.
(43) A service provider can benefit from the exemptions for "mere conduit" and for "caching" when he is in no way involved with the information transmitted; this requires among other things that he does not modify the information that he transmits; this requirement does not cover manipulations of a technical nature which take place in the course of the transmission as they do not alter the integrity of the information contained in the transmission.

---

[24] OJ L 13, 19.1.2000, p. 12.

(44) A service provider who deliberately collaborates with one of the recipients of his service in order to undertake illegal acts goes beyond the activities of "mere conduit" or "caching" and as a result cannot benefit from the liability exemptions established for these activities.
(45) The limitations of the liability of intermediary service providers established in this Directive do not affect the possibility of injunctions of different kinds; such injunctions can in particular consist of orders by courts or administrative authorities requiring the termination or prevention of any infringement, including the removal of illegal information or the disabling of access to it.
(46) In order to benefit from a limitation of liability, the provider of an information society service, consisting of the storage of information, upon obtaining actual knowledge or awareness of illegal activities has to act expeditiously to remove or to disable access to the information concerned; the removal or disabling of access has to be undertaken in the observance of the principle of freedom of expression and of procedures established for this purpose at national level; this Directive does not affect Member States' possibility of establishing specific requirements which must be fulfilled expeditiously prior to the removal or disabling of information.
(47) Member States are prevented from imposing a monitoring obligation on service providers only with respect to obligations of a general nature; this does not concern monitoring obligations in a specific case and, in particular, does not affect orders by national authorities in accordance with national legislation.
(48) This Directive does not affect the possibility for Member States of requiring service providers, who host information provided by recipients of their service, to apply duties of care, which can reasonably be expected from them and which are specified by national law, in order to detect and prevent certain types of illegal activities.
(49) Member States and the Commission are to encourage the drawing-up of codes of conduct; this is not to impair the voluntary nature of such codes and the possibility for interested parties of deciding freely whether to adhere to such codes.
(50) It is important that the proposed directive on the harmonisation of certain aspects of copyright and related rights in the information society and this Directive come into force within a similar time scale with a view to establishing a clear framework of rules relevant to the issue of liability of intermediaries for copyright and relating rights infringements at Community level.
(51) Each Member State should be required, where necessary, to amend any legislation which is liable to hamper the use of schemes for the out-of-court settlement of disputes through electronic channels; the result of this amendment must be to make the functioning of such schemes genuinely and effectively possible in law and in practice, even across borders.
(52) The effective exercise of the freedoms of the internal market makes it necessary to guarantee victims effective access to means of settling disputes; damage which may arise in connection with information society services is characterised both by its rapidity and by its geographical extent; in view of this specific character and the need to ensure that national authorities do not endanger the mutual confidence which they should have in one another, this Directive requests Member States to ensure that appropriate court actions are available; Member States should examine the need to provide access to judicial procedures by appropriate electronic means.
(53) Directive 98/27/EC, which is applicable to information society services, provides a mechanism relating to actions for an injunction aimed at the protection of the collective interests of consumers; this mechanism will contribute to the free movement of information society services by ensuring a high level of consumer protection.
(54) The sanctions provided for under this Directive are without prejudice to any other sanction or remedy provided under national law; Member States are not obliged to provide criminal sanctions for infringement of national provisions adopted pursuant to this Directive.

(55) This Directive does not affect the law applicable to contractual obligations relating to consumer contracts; accordingly, this Directive cannot have the result of depriving the consumer of the protection afforded to him by the mandatory rules relating to contractual obligations of the law of the Member State in which he has his habitual residence.
(56) As regards the derogation contained in this Directive regarding contractual obligations concerning contracts concluded by consumers, those obligations should be interpreted as including information on the essential elements of the content of the contract, including consumer rights, which have a determining influence on the decision to contract.
(57) The Court of Justice has consistently held that a Member State retains the right to take measures against a service provider that is established in another Member State but directs all or most of his activity to the territory of the first Member State if the choice of establishment was made with a view to evading the legislation that would have applied to the provider had he been established on the territory of the first Member State.
(58) This Directive should not apply to services supplied by service providers established in a third country; in view of the global dimension of electronic commerce, it is, however, appropriate to ensure that the Community rules are consistent with international rules; this Directive is without prejudice to the results of discussions within international organisations (amongst others WTO, OECD, Uncitral) on legal issues.
(59) Despite the global nature of electronic communications, coordination of national regulatory measures at European Union level is necessary in order to avoid fragmentation of the internal market, and for the establishment of an appropriate European regulatory framework; such coordination should also contribute to the establishment of a common and strong negotiating position in international forums.
(60) In order to allow the unhampered development of electronic commerce, the legal framework must be clear and simple, predictable and consistent with the rules applicable at international level so that it does not adversely affect the competitiveness of European industry or impede innovation in that sector.
(61) If the market is actually to operate by electronic means in the context of globalisation, the European Union and the major non-European areas need to consult each other with a view to making laws and procedures compatible.
(62) Cooperation with third countries should be strengthened in the area of electronic commerce, in particular with applicant countries, the developing countries and the European Union's other trading partners.
(63) The adoption of this Directive will not prevent the Member States from taking into account the various social, societal and cultural implications which are inherent in the advent of the information society; in particular it should not hinder measures which Member States might adopt in conformity with Community law to achieve social, cultural and democratic goals taking into account their linguistic diversity, national and regional specificities as well as their cultural heritage, and to ensure and maintain public access to the widest possible range of information society services; in any case, the development of the information society is to ensure that Community citizens can have access to the cultural European heritage provided in the digital environment.
(64) Electronic communication offers the Member States an excellent means of providing public services in the cultural, educational and linguistic fields.
(65) The Council, in its resolution of 19 January 1999 on the consumer dimension of the information society[25], stressed that the protection of consumers deserved special attention in this field; the Commission will examine the degree to which existing consumer protection rules provide insufficient protection in the context of the information society and will identify, where necessary, the deficiencies of this legislation and those issues which could require

---

[25] OJ C 23, 28.1.1999, p. 1.

additional measures; if need be, the Commission should make specific additional proposals to resolve such deficiencies that will thereby have been identified,

HAVE ADOPTED THIS DIRECTIVE:

CHAPTER I: GENERAL PROVISIONS

Article 1 - Objective and scope

1. This Directive seeks to contribute to the proper functioning of the internal market by ensuring the free movement of information society services between the Member States.
2. This Directive approximates, to the extent necessary for the achievement of the objective set out in paragraph 1, certain national provisions on information society services relating to the internal market, the establishment of service providers, commercial communications, electronic contracts, the liability of intermediaries, codes of conduct, out-of-court dispute settlements, court actions and cooperation between Member States.
3. This Directive complements Community law applicable to information society services without prejudice to the level of protection for, in particular, public health and consumer interests, as established by Community acts and national legislation implementing them in so far as this does not restrict the freedom to provide information society services.
4. This Directive does not establish additional rules on private international law nor does it deal with the jurisdiction of Courts.
5. This Directive shall not apply to:
(a) the field of taxation;
(b) questions relating to information society services covered by Directives 95/46/EC and 97/66/EC;
(c) questions relating to agreements or practices governed by cartel law;
(d) the following activities of information society services:
- the activities of notaries or equivalent professions to the extent that they involve a direct and specific connection with the exercise of public authority,
- the representation of a client and defence of his interests before the courts,
- gambling activities which involve wagering a stake with monetary value in games of chance, including lotteries and betting transactions.
6. This Directive does not affect measures taken at Community or national level, in the respect of Community law, in order to promote cultural and linguistic diversity and to ensure the defence of pluralism.

Article 2 - Definitions

For the purpose of this Directive, the following terms shall bear the following meanings:
(a) "information society services": services within the meaning of Article 1(2) of Directive 98/34/EC as amended by Directive 98/48/EC;
(b) "service provider": any natural or legal person providing an information society service;
(c) "established service provider": a service provider who effectively pursues an economic activity using a fixed establishment for an indefinite period. The presence and use of the technical means and technologies required to provide the service do not, in themselves, constitute an establishment of the provider;
(d) "recipient of the service": any natural or legal person who, for professional ends or otherwise, uses an information society service, in particular for the purposes of seeking information or making it accessible;
(e) "consumer": any natural person who is acting for purposes which are outside his or her trade, business or profession;

(f) "commercial communication": any form of communication designed to promote, directly or indirectly, the goods, services or image of a company, organisation or person pursuing a commercial, industrial or craft activity or exercising a regulated profession. The following do not in themselves constitute commercial communications:
- information allowing direct access to the activity of the company, organisation or person, in particular a domain name or an electronic-mail address,
- communications relating to the goods, services or image of the company, organisation or person compiled in an independent manner, particularly when this is without financial consideration;
(g) "regulated profession": any profession within the meaning of either Article 1(d) of Council Directive 89/48/EEC of 21 December 1988 on a general system for the recognition of higher-education diplomas awarded on completion of professional education and training of at least three-years' duration[26] or of Article 1(f) of Council Directive 92/51/EEC of 18 June 1992 on a second general system for the recognition of professional education and training to supplement Directive 89/48/EEC[27];
(h) "coordinated field": requirements laid down in Member States' legal systems applicable to information society service providers or information society services, regardless of whether they are of a general nature or specifically designed for them.
(i) The coordinated field concerns requirements with which the service provider has to comply in respect of:
- the taking up of the activity of an information society service, such as requirements concerning qualifications, authorisation or notification,
- the pursuit of the activity of an information society service, such as requirements concerning the behaviour of the service provider, requirements regarding the quality or content of the service including those applicable to advertising and contracts, or requirements concerning the liability of the service provider;
(j) The coordinated field does not cover requirements such as:
- requirements applicable to goods as such,
- requirements applicable to the delivery of goods,
- requirements applicable to services not provided by electronic means.

Article 3 - Internal market

1. Each Member State shall ensure that the information society services provided by a service provider established on its territory comply with the national provisions applicable in the Member State in question which fall within the coordinated field.
2. Member States may not, for reasons falling within the coordinated field, restrict the freedom to provide information society services from another Member State.
3. Paragraphs 1 and 2 shall not apply to the fields referred to in the Annex.
4. Member States may take measures to derogate from paragraph 2 in respect of a given information society service if the following conditions are fulfilled:
(a) the measures shall be:
(I) necessary for one of the following reasons:
- public policy, in particular the prevention, investigation, detection and prosecution of criminal offences, including the protection of minors and the fight against any incitement to hatred on grounds of race, sex, religion or nationality, and violations of human dignity concerning individual persons,
- the protection of public health,
- public security, including the safeguarding of national security and defence,

---

[26] OJ L 19, 24.1.1989, p. 16.
[27] OJ L 209, 24.7.1992, p. 25. Directive as last amended by Commission Directive 97/38/EC (OJ L 184, 12.7.1997, p. 31).

- the protection of consumers, including investors;
(II) taken against a given information society service which prejudices the objectives referred to in point (i) or which presents a serious and grave risk of prejudice to those objectives;
(III) proportionate to those objectives;
(b) before taking the measures in question and without prejudice to court proceedings, including preliminary proceedings and acts carried out in the framework of a criminal investigation, the Member State has:
- asked the Member State referred to in paragraph 1 to take measures and the latter did not take such measures, or they were inadequate,
- notified the Commission and the Member State referred to in paragraph 1 of its intention to take such measures.
5. Member States may, in the case of urgency, derogate from the conditions stipulated in paragraph 4(b). Where this is the case, the measures shall be notified in the shortest possible time to the Commission and to the Member State referred to in paragraph 1, indicating the reasons for which the Member State considers that there is urgency.
6. Without prejudice to the Member State's possibility of proceeding with the measures in question, the Commission shall examine the compatibility of the notified measures with Community law in the shortest possible time; where it comes to the conclusion that the measure is incompatible with Community law, the Commission shall ask the Member State in question to refrain from taking any proposed measures or urgently to put an end to the measures in question.

CHAPTER II: PRINCIPLES

SECTION 1: ESTABLISHMENT AND INFORMATION REQUIREMENTS

Article 4 - Principle excluding prior authorisation

1. Member States shall ensure that the taking up and pursuit of the activity of an information society service provider may not be made subject to prior authorisation or any other requirement having equivalent effect.
2. Paragraph 1 shall be without prejudice to authorisation schemes which are not specifically and exclusively targeted at information society services, or which are covered by Directive 97/13/EC of the European Parliament and of the Council of 10 April 1997 on a common framework for general authorisations and individual licences in the field of telecommunications services[28].

Article 5 - General information to be provided

1. In addition to other information requirements established by Community law, Member States shall ensure that the service provider shall render easily, directly and permanently accessible to the recipients of the service and competent authorities, at least the following information:
(a) the name of the service provider;
(b) the geographic address at which the service provider is established;
(c) the details of the service provider, including his electronic mail address, which allow him to be contacted rapidly and communicated with in a direct and effective manner;
(d) where the service provider is registered in a trade or similar public register, the trade register in which the service provider is entered and his registration number, or equivalent means of identification in that register;

---

[28] OJ L 117, 7.5.1997, p. 15.

(e) where the activity is subject to an authorisation scheme, the particulars of the relevant supervisory authority;
(f) as concerns the regulated professions:
- any professional body or similar institution with which the service provider is registered,
- the professional title and the Member State where it has been granted,
- a reference to the applicable professional rules in the Member State of establishment and the means to access them;
(g) where the service provider undertakes an activity that is subject to VAT, the identification number referred to in Article 22(1) of the sixth Council Directive 77/388/EEC of 17 May 1977 on the harmonisation of the laws of the Member States relating to turnover taxes - Common system of value added tax: uniform basis of assessment[29].
2. In addition to other information requirements established by Community law, Member States shall at least ensure that, where information society services refer to prices, these are to be indicated clearly and unambiguously and, in particular, must indicate whether they are inclusive of tax and delivery costs.

SECTION 2: COMMERCIAL COMMUNICATIONS

Article 6 - Information to be provided

In addition to other information requirements established by Community law, Member States shall ensure that commercial communications which are part of, or constitute, an information society service comply at least with the following conditions:
(a) the commercial communication shall be clearly identifiable as such;
(b) the natural or legal person on whose behalf the commercial communication is made shall be clearly identifiable;
(c) promotional offers, such as discounts, premiums and gifts, where permitted in the Member State where the service provider is established, shall be clearly identifiable as such, and the conditions which are to be met to qualify for them shall be easily accessible and be presented clearly and unambiguously;
(d) promotional competitions or games, where permitted in the Member State where the service provider is established, shall be clearly identifiable as such, and the conditions for participation shall be easily accessible and be presented clearly and unambiguously.

Article 7 - Unsolicited commercial communication

1. In addition to other requirements established by Community law, Member States which permit unsolicited commercial communication by electronic mail shall ensure that such commercial communication by a service provider established in their territory shall be identifiable clearly and unambiguously as such as soon as it is received by the recipient.
2. Without prejudice to Directive 97/7/EC and Directive 97/66/EC, Member States shall take measures to ensure that service providers undertaking unsolicited commercial communications by electronic mail consult regularly and respect the opt-out registers in which natural persons not wishing to receive such commercial communications can register themselves.

Article 8 - Regulated professions

1. Member States shall ensure that the use of commercial communications which are part of, or constitute, an information society service provided by a member of a regulated profession is

---

[29] OJ L 145, 13.6.1977, p. 1. Directive as last amended by Directive 1999/85/EC (OJ L 277, 28.10.1999, p. 34).

permitted subject to compliance with the professional rules regarding, in particular, the independence, dignity and honour of the profession, professional secrecy and fairness towards clients and other members of the profession.
2. Without prejudice to the autonomy of professional bodies and associations, Member States and the Commission shall encourage professional associations and bodies to establish codes of conduct at Community level in order to determine the types of information that can be given for the purposes of commercial communication in conformity with the rules referred to in paragraph 1
3. When drawing up proposals for Community initiatives which may become necessary to ensure the proper functioning of the Internal Market with regard to the information referred to in paragraph 2, the Commission shall take due account of codes of conduct applicable at Community level and shall act in close cooperation with the relevant professional associations and bodies.
4. This Directive shall apply in addition to Community Directives concerning access to, and the exercise of, activities of the regulated professions.

SECTION 3: CONTRACTS CONCLUDED BY ELECTRONIC MEANS

Article 9 - Treatment of contracts

1. Member States shall ensure that their legal system allows contracts to be concluded by electronic means. Member States shall in particular ensure that the legal requirements applicable to the contractual process neither create obstacles for the use of electronic contracts nor result in such contracts being deprived of legal effectiveness and validity on account of their having been made by electronic means.
2. Member States may lay down that paragraph 1 shall not apply to all or certain contracts falling into one of the following categories:
(a) contracts that create or transfer rights in real estate, except for rental rights;
(b) contracts requiring by law the involvement of courts, public authorities or professions exercising public authority;
(c) contracts of suretyship granted and on collateral securities furnished by persons acting for purposes outside their trade, business or profession;
(d) contracts governed by family law or by the law of succession.
3. Member States shall indicate to the Commission the categories referred to in paragraph 2 to which they do not apply paragraph 1. Member States shall submit to the Commission every five years a report on the application of paragraph 2 explaining the reasons why they consider it necessary to maintain the category referred to in paragraph 2(b) to which they do not apply paragraph 1.

Article 10 - Information to be provided

1. In addition to other information requirements established by Community law, Member States shall ensure, except when otherwise agreed by parties who are not consumers, that at least the following information is given by the service provider clearly, comprehensibly and unambiguously and prior to the order being placed by the recipient of the service:
(a) the different technical steps to follow to conclude the contract;
(b) whether or not the concluded contract will be filed by the service provider and whether it will be accessible;
(c) the technical means for identifying and correcting input errors prior to the placing of the order;
(d) the languages offered for the conclusion of the contract.

2. Member States shall ensure that, except when otherwise agreed by parties who are not consumers, the service provider indicates any relevant codes of conduct to which he subscribes and information on how those codes can be consulted electronically.
3. Contract terms and general conditions provided to the recipient must be made available in a way that allows him to store and reproduce them.
4. Paragraphs 1 and 2 shall not apply to contracts concluded exclusively by exchange of electronic mail or by equivalent individual communications.

Article 11 - Placing of the order

1. Member States shall ensure, except when otherwise agreed by parties who are not consumers, that in cases where the recipient of the service places his order through technological means, the following principles apply:
- the service provider has to acknowledge the receipt of the recipient's order without undue delay and by electronic means,
- the order and the acknowledgement of receipt are deemed to be received when the parties to whom they are addressed are able to access them.
2. Member States shall ensure that, except when otherwise agreed by parties who are not consumers, the service provider makes available to the recipient of the service appropriate, effective and accessible technical means allowing him to identify and correct input errors, prior to the placing of the order.
3. Paragraph 1, first indent, and paragraph 2 shall not apply to contracts concluded exclusively by exchange of electronic mail or by equivalent individual communications.

SECTION 4: LIABILITY OF INTERMEDIARY SERVICE PROVIDERS

Article 12 - "Mere conduit"

1. Where an information society service is provided that consists of the transmission in a communication network of information provided by a recipient of the service, or the provision of access to a communication network, Member States shall ensure that the service provider is not liable for the information transmitted, on condition that the provider:
(a) does not initiate the transmission;
(b) does not select the receiver of the transmission; and
(c) does not select or modify the information contained in the transmission.
2. The acts of transmission and of provision of access referred to in paragraph 1 include the automatic, intermediate and transient storage of the information transmitted in so far as this takes place for the sole purpose of carrying out the transmission in the communication network, and provided that the information is not stored for any period longer than is reasonably necessary for the transmission.
3. This Article shall not affect the possibility for a court or administrative authority, in accordance with Member States' legal systems, of requiring the service provider to terminate or prevent an infringement.

Article 13 - "Caching"

1. Where an information society service is provided that consists of the transmission in a communication network of information provided by a recipient of the service, Member States shall ensure that the service provider is not liable for the automatic, intermediate and temporary storage of that information, performed for the sole purpose of making more efficient the information's onward transmission to other recipients of the service upon their request, on condition that:

(a) the provider does not modify the information;
(b) the provider complies with conditions on access to the information;
(c) the provider complies with rules regarding the updating of the information, specified in a manner widely recognised and used by industry;
(d) the provider does not interfere with the lawful use of technology, widely recognised and used by industry, to obtain data on the use of the information; and
(e) the provider acts expeditiously to remove or to disable access to the information it has stored upon obtaining actual knowledge of the fact that the information at the initial source of the transmission has been removed from the network, or access to it has been disabled, or that a court or an administrative authority has ordered such removal or disablement.
2. This Article shall not affect the possibility for a court or administrative authority, in accordance with Member States' legal systems, of requiring the service provider to terminate or prevent an infringement.

Article 14 - Hosting

1. Where an information society service is provided that consists of the storage of information provided by a recipient of the service, Member States shall ensure that the service provider is not liable for the information stored at the request of a recipient of the service, on condition that:
(a) the provider does not have actual knowledge of illegal activity or information and, as regards claims for damages, is not aware of facts or circumstances from which the illegal activity or information is apparent; or
(b) the provider, upon obtaining such knowledge or awareness, acts expeditiously to remove or to disable access to the information.
2. Paragraph 1 shall not apply when the recipient of the service is acting under the authority or the control of the provider.
3. This Article shall not affect the possibility for a court or administrative authority, in accordance with Member States' legal systems, of requiring the service provider to terminate or prevent an infringement, nor does it affect the possibility for Member States of establishing procedures governing the removal or disabling of access to information.

Article 15 - No general obligation to monitor

1. Member States shall not impose a general obligation on providers, when providing the services covered by Articles 12, 13 and 14, to monitor the information which they transmit or store, nor a general obligation actively to seek facts or circumstances indicating illegal activity.
2. Member States may establish obligations for information society service providers promptly to inform the competent public authorities of alleged illegal activities undertaken or information provided by recipients of their service or obligations to communicate to the competent authorities, at their request, information enabling the identification of recipients of their service with whom they have storage agreements.

CHAPTER III: IMPLEMENTATION

Article 16 - Codes of conduct

1. Member States and the Commission shall encourage:
(a) the drawing up of codes of conduct at Community level, by trade, professional and consumer associations or organisations, designed to contribute to the proper implementation of Articles 5 to 15;

(b) the voluntary transmission of draft codes of conduct at national or Community level to the Commission;
(c) the accessibility of these codes of conduct in the Community languages by electronic means;
(d) the communication to the Member States and the Commission, by trade, professional and consumer associations or organisations, of their assessment of the application of their codes of conduct and their impact upon practices, habits or customs relating to electronic commerce;
(e) the drawing up of codes of conduct regarding the protection of minors and human dignity.
2. Member States and the Commission shall encourage the involvement of associations or organisations representing consumers in the drafting and implementation of codes of conduct affecting their interests and drawn up in accordance with paragraph 1(a). Where appropriate, to take account of their specific needs, associations representing the visually impaired and disabled should be consulted.

Article 17 - Out-of-court dispute settlement

1. Member States shall ensure that, in the event of disagreement between an information society service provider and the recipient of the service, their legislation does not hamper the use of out-of-court schemes, available under national law, for dispute settlement, including appropriate electronic means.
2. Member States shall encourage bodies responsible for the out-of-court settlement of, in particular, consumer disputes to operate in a way which provides adequate procedural guarantees for the parties concerned.
3. Member States shall encourage bodies responsible for out-of-court dispute settlement to inform the Commission of the significant decisions they take regarding information society services and to transmit any other information on the practices, usages or customs relating to electronic commerce.

Article 18 - Court actions

1. Member States shall ensure that court actions available under national law concerning information society services' activities allow for the rapid adoption of measures, including interim measures, designed to terminate any alleged infringement and to prevent any further impairment of the interests involved.
2. The Annex to Directive 98/27/EC shall be supplemented as follows:
"11. Directive 2000/31/EC of the European Parliament and of the Council of 8 June 2000 on certain legal aspects on information society services, in particular electronic commerce, in the internal market (Directive on electronic commerce) (OJ L 178, 17.7.2000, p. 1)."

Article 19 - Cooperation

1. Member States shall have adequate means of supervision and investigation necessary to implement this Directive effectively and shall ensure that service providers supply them with the requisite information.
2. Member States shall cooperate with other Member States; they shall, to that end, appoint one or several contact points, whose details they shall communicate to the other Member States and to the Commission.
3. Member States shall, as quickly as possible, and in conformity with national law, provide the assistance and information requested by other Member States or by the Commission, including by appropriate electronic means.
4. Member States shall establish contact points which shall be accessible at least by electronic means and from which recipients and service providers may:

(a) obtain general information on contractual rights and obligations as well as on the complaint and redress mechanisms available in the event of disputes, including practical aspects involved in the use of such mechanisms;
(b) obtain the details of authorities, associations or organisations from which they may obtain further information or practical assistance.
5. Member States shall encourage the communication to the Commission of any significant administrative or judicial decisions taken in their territory regarding disputes relating to information society services and practices, usages and customs relating to electronic commerce. The Commission shall communicate these decisions to the other Member States.

Article 20 - Sanctions

Member States shall determine the sanctions applicable to infringements of national provisions adopted pursuant to this Directive and shall take all measures necessary to ensure that they are enforced. The sanctions they provide for shall be effective, proportionate and dissuasive.

CHAPTER IV: FINAL PROVISIONS

Article 21 - Re-examination

1. Before 17 July 2003, and thereafter every two years, the Commission shall submit to the European Parliament, the Council and the Economic and Social Committee a report on the application of this Directive, accompanied, where necessary, by proposals for adapting it to legal, technical and economic developments in the field of information society services, in particular with respect to crime prevention, the protection of minors, consumer protection and to the proper functioning of the internal market.
2. In examining the need for an adaptation of this Directive, the report shall in particular analyse the need for proposals concerning the liability of providers of hyperlinks and location tool services, "notice and take down" procedures and the attribution of liability following the taking down of content. The report shall also analyse the need for additional conditions for the exemption from liability, provided for in Articles 12 and 13, in the light of technical developments, and the possibility of applying the internal market principles to unsolicited commercial communications by electronic mail.

Article 22 - Transposition

1. Member States shall bring into force the laws, regulations and administrative provisions necessary to comply with this Directive before 17 January 2002. They shall forthwith inform the Commission thereof.
2. When Member States adopt the measures referred to in paragraph 1, these shall contain a reference to this Directive or shall be accompanied by such reference at the time of their official publication. The methods of making such reference shall be laid down by Member States.

Article 23 - Entry into force

This Directive shall enter into force on the day of its publication in the Official Journal of the European Communities.

Article 24 - Addressees

This Directive is addressed to the Member States.

ANNEX - DEROGATIONS FROM ARTICLE 3

As provided for in Article 3(3), Article 3(1) and (2) do not apply to:
- copyright, neighbouring rights, rights referred to in Directive 87/54/EEC[1] and Directive 96/9/EC[2] as well as industrial property rights,
- the emission of electronic money by institutions in respect of which Member States have applied one of the derogations provided for in Article 8(1) of Directive 2000/46/EC[3],
- Article 44(2) of Directive 85/611/EEC[4],
- Article 30 and Title IV of Directive 92/49/EEC[5], Title IV of Directive 92/96/EEC[6], Articles 7 and 8 of Directive 88/357/EEC[7] and Article 4 of Directive 90/619/EEC[8],
- the freedom of the parties to choose the law applicable to their contract,
- contractual obligations concerning consumer contacts,
- formal validity of contracts creating or transferring rights in real estate where such contracts are subject to mandatory formal requirements of the law of the Member State where the real estate is situated,
- the permissibility of unsolicited commercial communications by electronic mail.

---

[1] OJ L 24, 27.1.1987, p. 36.
[2] OJ L 77, 27.3.1996, p. 20.
[3] Not yet published in the Official Journal.
[4] OJ L 375, 31.12.1985, p. 3. Directive as last amended by Directive 95/26/EC (OJ L 168, 18.7.1995, p. 7).
[5] OJ L 228, 11.8.1992, p. 1. Directive as last amended by Directive 95/26/EC.
[6] OJ L 360, 9.12.1992, p. 2. Directive as last amended by Directive 95/26/EC.
[7] OJ L 172, 4.7.1988, p. 1. Directive as last amended by Directive 92/49/EC.
[8] OJ L 330, 29.11.1990, p. 50. Directive as last amended by Directive 92/96/EC.

5. Consumer Protection

DIRECTIVE 97/7/EC OF THE EUROPEAN PARLIAMENT AND OF THE COUNCIL
OF 20 MAY 1997
ON THE PROTECTION OF CONSUMERS IN RESPECT OF DISTANCE CONTRACTS

(Official Journal L 144, 04/06/1997, p. 0019)

THE EUROPEAN PARLIAMENT AND THE COUNCIL OF THE EUROPEAN UNION,

Having regard to the Treaty establishing the European Community, and in particular Article 100a thereof,
Having regard to the proposal from the Commission,[1]
Having regard to the opinion of the Economic and Social Committee,[2]

Acting in accordance with the procedure laid down in Article 189b of the Treaty,[3] in the light of the joint text approved by the Conciliation Committee on 27 November 1996,

(1) Whereas, in connection with the attainment of the aims of the internal market, measures must be taken for the gradual consolidation of that market;
(2) Whereas the free movement of goods and services affects not only the business sector but also private individuals; whereas it means that consumers should be able to have access to the goods and services of another Member State on the same terms as the population of that State;
(3) Whereas, for consumers, cross-border distance selling could be one of the main tangible results of the completion of the internal market, as noted, inter alia, in the communication from the Commission to the Council entitled 'Towards a single market in distribution'; whereas it is essential to the smooth operation of the internal market for consumers to be able to have dealings with a business outside their country, even if it has a subsidiary in the consumer's country of residence;
(4) Whereas the introduction of new technologies is increasing the number of ways for consumers to obtain information about offers anywhere in the Community and to place orders; whereas some Member States have already taken different or diverging measures to protect consumers in respect of distance selling, which has had a detrimental effect on competition between businesses in the internal market; whereas it is therefore necessary to introduce at Community level a minimum set of common rules in this area;
(5) Whereas paragraphs 18 and 19 of the Annex to the Council resolution of 14 April 1975 on a preliminary programme of the European Economic Community for a consumer protection and information policy[4] point to the need to protect the purchasers of goods or services from demands for payment for unsolicited goods and from high-pressure selling methods;

---

[1] OJ No C 156, 23. 6. 1992, p. 14 and OJ No C 308, 15. 11. 1993, p. 18.
[2] OJ No C 19, 25. 1. 1993, p. 111.
[3] Opinion of the European Parliament of 26 May 1993 (OJ No C 176, 28. 6. 1993, p. 95), Council common position of 29 June 1995 (OJ No C 288, 30. 10. 1995, p. 1) and Decision of the European Parliament of 13 December 1995 (OJ No C 17, 22. 1. 1996, p. 51). Decision of the European Parliament of 16 January 1997 and Council Decision of 20 January 1997.
[4] OJ No C 92, 25. 4. 1975, p. 1.

(6) Whereas paragraph 33 of the communication from the Commission to the Council entitled 'A new impetus for consumer protection policy', which was approved by the Council resolution of 23 June 1986,[5] states that the Commission will submit proposals regarding the use of new information technologies enabling consumers to place orders with suppliers from their homes;

(7) Whereas the Council resolution of 9 November 1989 on future priorities for relaunching consumer protection policy[6] calls upon the Commission to give priority to the areas referred to in the Annex to that resolution; whereas that Annex refers to new technologies involving teleshopping; whereas the Commission has responded to that resolution by adopting a three-year action plan for consumer protection policy in the European Economic Community (1990-1992); whereas that plan provides for the adoption of a Directive;

(8) Whereas the languages used for distance contracts are a matter for the Member States;

(9) Whereas contracts negotiated at a distance involve the use of one or more means of distance communication; whereas the various means of communication are used as part of an organized distance sales or service-provision scheme not involving the simultaneous presence of the supplier and the consumer; whereas the constant development of those means of communication does not allow an exhaustive list to be compiled but does require principles to be defined which are valid even for those which are not as yet in widespread use;

(10) Whereas the same transaction comprising successive operations or a series of separate operations over a period of time may give rise to different legal descriptions depending on the law of the Member States; whereas the provisions of this Directive cannot be applied differently according to the law of the Member States, subject to their recourse to Article 14; whereas, to that end, there is therefore reason to consider that there must at least be compliance with the provisions of this Directive at the time of the first of a series of successive operations or the first of a series of separate operations over a period of time which may be considered as forming a whole, whether that operation or series of operations are the subject of a single contract or successive, separate contracts;

(11) Whereas the use of means of distance communication must not lead to a reduction in the information provided to the consumer; whereas the information that is required to be sent to the consumer should therefore be determined, whatever the means of communication used; whereas the information supplied must also comply with the other relevant Community rules, in particular those in Council Directive 84/450/EEC of 10 September 1984 relating to the approximation of the laws, regulations and administrative provisions of the Member States concerning misleading advertising[7]; whereas, if exceptions are made to the obligation to provide information, it is up to the consumer, on a discretionary basis, to request certain basic information such as the identity of the supplier, the main characteristics of the goods or services and their price;

(12) Whereas in the case of communication by telephone it is appropriate that the consumer receive enough information at the beginning of the conversation to decide whether or not to continue;

(13) Whereas information disseminated by certain electronic technologies is often ephemeral in nature insofar as it is not received on a permanent medium; whereas the consumer must therefore receive written notice in good time of the information necessary for proper performance of the contract;

(14) Whereas the consumer is not able actually to see the product or ascertain the nature of the service provided before concluding the contract; whereas provision should be made, unless otherwise specified in this Directive, for a right of withdrawal from the contract; whereas, if this right is to be more than formal, the costs, if any, borne by the consumer when exercising

---

[5] OJ No C 167, 5. 7. 1986, p. 1.
[6] OJ No C 294, 22. 11. 1989, p. 1.
[7] OJ No L 250, 19. 9. 1984, p. 17.

the right of withdrawal must be limited to the direct costs for returning the goods; whereas this right of withdrawal shall be without prejudice to the consumer's rights under national laws, with particular regard to the receipt of damaged products and services or of products and services not corresponding to the description given in the offer of such products or services; whereas it is for the Member States to determine the other conditions and arrangements following exercise of the right of withdrawal;

(15) Whereas it is also necessary to prescribe a time limit for performance of the contract if this is not specified at the time of ordering;

(16) Whereas the promotional technique involving the dispatch of a product or the provision of a service to the consumer in return for payment without a prior request from, or the explicit agreement of, the consumer cannot be permitted, unless a substitute product or service is involved;

(17) Whereas the principles set out in Articles 8 and 10 of the European Convention for the Protection of Human Rights and Fundamental Freedoms of 4 November 1950 apply; whereas the consumer's right to privacy, particularly as regards freedom from certain particularly intrusive means of communication, should be recognized; whereas specific limits on the use of such means should therefore be stipulated; whereas Member States should take appropriate measures to protect effectively those consumers, who do not wish to be contacted through certain means of communication, against such contacts, without prejudice to the particular safeguards available to the consumer under Community legislation concerning the protection of personal data and privacy;

(18) Whereas it is important for the minimum binding rules contained in this Directive to be supplemented where appropriate by voluntary arrangements among the traders concerned, in line with Commission recommendation 92/295/EEC of 7 April 1992 on codes of practice for the protection of consumers in respect of contracts negotiated at a distance[8];

(19) Whereas in the interest of optimum consumer protection it is important for consumers to be satisfactorily informed of the provisions of this Directive and of codes of practice that may exist in this field;

(20) Whereas non-compliance with this Directive may harm not only consumers but also competitors; whereas provisions may therefore be laid down enabling public bodies or their representatives, or consumer organizations which, under national legislation, have a legitimate interest in consumer protection, or professional organizations which have a legitimate interest in taking action, to monitor the application thereof;

(21) Whereas it is important, with a view to consumer protection, to address the question of cross-border complaints as soon as this is feasible; whereas the Commission published on 14 February 1996 a plan of action on consumer access to justice and the settlement of consumer disputes in the internal market; whereas that plan of action includes specific initiatives to promote out-of-court procedures; whereas objective criteria (Annex II) are suggested to ensure the reliability of those procedures and provision is made for the use of standardized claims forms (Annex III);

(22) Whereas in the use of new technologies the consumer is not in control of the means of communication used; whereas it is therefore necessary to provide that the burden of proof may be on the supplier;

(23) Whereas there is a risk that, in certain cases, the consumer may be deprived of protection under this Directive through the designation of the law of a non-member country as the law applicable to the contract; whereas provisions should therefore be included in this Directive to avert that risk;

(24) Whereas a Member State may ban, in the general interest, the marketing on its territory of certain goods and services through distance contracts; whereas that ban must comply with

---

[8] OJ No L 156, 10. 6. 1992, p. 21.

Community rules; whereas there is already provision for such bans, notably with regard to medicinal products, under Council Directive 89/552/EEC of 3 October 1989 on the coordination of certain provisions laid down by law, regulation or administrative action in Member States concerning the pursuit of television broadcasting activities[9] and Council Directive 92/28/EEC of 31 March 1992 on the advertising of medicinal products for human use,[10]

HAVE ADOPTED THIS DIRECTIVE:

Article 1 - Object

The object of this Directive is to approximate the laws, regulations and administrative provisions of the Member States concerning distance contracts between consumers and suppliers.

Article 2 - Definitions

For the purposes of this Directive:
(1) 'distance contract' means any contract concerning goods or services concluded between a supplier and a consumer under an organized distance sales or service-provision scheme run by the supplier, who, for the purpose of the contract, makes exclusive use of one or more means of distance communication up to and including the moment at which the contract is concluded;
(2) 'consumer' means any natural person who, in contracts covered by this Directive, is acting for purposes which are outside his trade, business or profession;
(3) 'supplier' means any natural or legal person who, in contracts covered by this Directive, is acting in his commercial or professional capacity;
(4) 'means of distance communication' means any means which, without the simultaneous physical presence of the supplier and the consumer, may be used for the conclusion of a contract between those parties. An indicative list of the means covered by this Directive is contained in Annex I;
(5) 'operator of a means of communication' means any public or private natural or legal person whose trade, business or profession involves making one or more means of distance communication available to suppliers.

Article 3 - Exemptions

1. This Directive shall not apply to contracts:
- relating to financial services, a non-exhaustive list of which is given in Annex II,
- concluded by means of automatic vending machines or automated commercial premises,
- concluded with telecommunications operators through the use of public payphones,
- concluded for the construction and sale of immovable property or relating to other immovable property rights, except for rental,
- concluded at an auction.
2. Articles 4, 5, 6 and 7 (1) shall not apply:
- to contracts for the supply of foodstuffs, beverages or other goods intended for everyday consumption supplied to the home of the consumer, to his residence or to his workplace by regular roundsmen,
- to contracts for the provision of accommodation, transport, catering or leisure services, where the supplier undertakes, when the contract is concluded, to provide these services on a specific date or within a specific period; exceptionally, in the case of outdoor leisure events, the supplier can reserve the right not to apply Article 7 (2) in specific circumstances.

---

[9] OJ No L 298, 17. 10. 1989, p. 23.
[10] OJ No L 113, 30. 4. 1992, p. 13.

Article 4 - Prior information

1. In good time prior to the conclusion of any distance contract, the consumer shall be provided with the following information:
   (a) the identity of the supplier and, in the case of contracts requiring payment in advance, his address;
   (b) the main characteristics of the goods or services;
   (c) the price of the goods or services including all taxes;
   (d) delivery costs, where appropriate;
   (e) the arrangements for payment, delivery or performance;
   (f) the existence of a right of withdrawal, except in the cases referred to in Article 6 (3);
   (g) the cost of using the means of distance communication, where it is calculated other than at the basic rate;
   (h) the period for which the offer or the price remains valid;
   (i) where appropriate, the minimum duration of the contract in the case of contracts for the supply of products or services to be performed permanently or recurrently.
2. The information referred to in paragraph 1, the commercial purpose of which must be made clear, shall be provided in a clear and comprehensible manner in any way appropriate to the means of distance communication used, with due regard, in particular, to the principles of good faith in commercial transactions, and the principles governing the protection of those who are unable, pursuant to the legislation of the Member States, to give their consent, such as minors.
3. Moreover, in the case of telephone communications, the identity of the supplier and the commercial purpose of the call shall be made explicitly clear at the beginning of any conversation with the consumer.

Article 5 - Written confirmation of information

1. The consumer must receive written confirmation or confirmation in another durable medium available and accessible to him of the information referred to in Article 4 (1) (a) to (f), in good time during the performance of the contract, and at the latest at the time of delivery where goods not for delivery to third parties are concerned, unless the information has already been given to the consumer prior to conclusion of the contract in writing or on another durable medium available and accessible to him. In any event the following must be provided:
   - written information on the conditions and procedures for exercising the right of withdrawal, within the meaning of Article 6, including the cases referred to in the first indent of Article 6 (3),
   - the geographical address of the place of business of the supplier to which the consumer may address any complaints, - information on after-sales services and guarantees which exist,
   - the conclusion for cancelling the contract, where it is of unspecified duration or a duration exceeding one year.
2. Paragraph 1 shall not apply to services which are performed through the use of a means of distance communication, where they are supplied on only one occasion and are invoiced by the operator of the means of distance communication. Nevertheless, the consumer must in all cases be able to obtain the geographical address of the place of business of the supplier to which he may address any complaints.

Article 6 - Right of withdrawal

1. For any distance contract the consumer shall have a period of at least seven working days in which to withdraw from the contract without penalty and without giving any reason. The only charge that may be made to the consumer because of the exercise of his right of

withdrawal is the direct cost of returning the goods. The period for exercise of this right shall begin:
- in the case of goods, from the day of receipt by the consumer where the obligations laid down in Article 5 have been fulfilled,
- in the case of services, from the day of conclusion of the contract or from the day on which the obligations laid down in Article 5 were fulfilled if they are fulfilled after conclusion of the contract, provided that this period does not exceed the three-month period referred to in the following subparagraph.

If the supplier has failed to fulfil the obligations laid down in Article 5, the period shall be three months. The period shall begin:
- in the case of goods, from the day of receipt by the consumer,
- in the case of services, from the day of conclusion of the contract.

If the information referred to in Article 5 is supplied within this three-month period, the seven working day period referred to in the first subparagraph shall begin as from that moment.

2. Where the right of withdrawal has been exercised by the consumer pursuant to this Article, the supplier shall be obliged to reimburse the sums paid by the consumer free of charge. The only charge that may be made to the consumer because of the exercise of his right of withdrawal is the direct cost of returning the goods. Such reimbursement must be carried out as soon as possible and in any case within 30 days.

3. Unless the parties have agreed otherwise, the consumer may not exercise the right of withdrawal provided for in paragraph 1 in respect of contracts:
- for the provision of services if performance has begun, with the consumer's agreement, before the end of the seven working day period referred to in paragraph 1,
- for the supply of goods or services the price of which is dependent on fluctuations in the financial market which cannot be controlled by the supplier,
- for the supply of goods made to the consumer's specifications or clearly personalized or which, by reason of their nature, cannot be returned or are liable to deteriorate or expire rapidly,
- for the supply of audio or video recordings or computer software which were unsealed by the consumer,
- for the supply of newspapers, periodicals and magazines,- for gaming and lottery services.

4. The Member States shall make provision in their legislation to ensure that:
- if the price of goods or services is fully or partly covered by credit granted by the supplier, or
- if that price is fully or partly covered by credit granted to the consumer by a third party on the basis of an agreement between the third party and the supplier, the credit agreement shall be cancelled, without any penalty, if the consumer exercises his right to withdraw from the contract in accordance with paragraph 1.

Member States shall determine the detailed rules for cancellation of the credit agreement.

Article 7 - Performance

1. Unless the parties have agreed otherwise, the supplier must execute the order within a maximum of 30 days from the day following that on which the consumer forwarded his order to the supplier.
2. Where a supplier fails to perform his side of the contract on the grounds that the goods or services ordered are unavailable, the consumer must be informed of this situation and must be able to obtain a refund of any sums he has paid as soon as possible and in any case within 30 days.
3. Nevertheless, Member States may lay down that the supplier may provide the consumer with goods or services of equivalent quality and price provided that this possibility was provided for prior to the conclusion of the contract or in the contract. The consumer shall be

informed of this possibility in a clear and comprehensible manner. The cost of returning the goods following exercise of the right of withdrawal shall, in this case, be borne by the supplier, and the consumer must be informed of this. In such cases the supply of goods or services may not be deemed to constitute inertia selling within the meaning of Article 9.

Article 8 - Payment by card

Member States shall ensure that appropriate measures exist to allow a consumer:
- to request cancellation of a payment where fraudulent use has been made of his payment card in connection with distance contracts covered by this Directive,
- in the event of fraudulent use, to be recredited with the sums paid or have them returned.

Article 9 - Inertia selling

Member States shall take the measures necessary to:
- prohibit the supply of goods or services to a consumer without their being ordered by the consumer beforehand, where such supply involves a demand for payment,
- exempt the consumer from the provision of any consideration in cases of unsolicited supply, the absence of a response not constituting consent.

Article 10 - Restrictions on the use of certain means of distance communication

1. Use by a supplier of the following means requires the prior consent of the consumer:
- automated calling system without human intervention (automatic calling machine),
- facsimile machine (fax).
2. Member States shall ensure that means of distance communication, other than those referred to in paragraph 1, which allow individual communications may be used only where there is no clear objection from the consumer.

Article 11 - Judicial or administrative redress

1. Member States shall ensure that adequate and effective means exist to ensure compliance with this Directive in the interests of consumers.
2. The means referred to in paragraph 1 shall include provisions whereby one or more of the following bodies, as determined by national law, may take action under national law before the courts or before the competent administrative bodies to ensure that the national provisions for the implementation of this Directive are applied:
(a) public bodies or their representatives;
(b) consumer organizations having a legitimate interest in protecting consumers;
(c) professional organizations having a legitimate interest in acting.
3.
(a) Member States may stipulate that the burden of proof concerning the existence of prior information, written confirmation, compliance with time-limits or consumer consent can be placed on the supplier.
(b) Member States shall take the measures needed to ensure that suppliers and operators of means of communication, where they are able to do so, cease practices which do not comply with measures adopted pursuant to this Directive.
4. Member States may provide for voluntary supervision by self-regulatory bodies of compliance with the provisions of this Directive and recourse to such bodies for the settlement of disputes to be added to the means which Member States must provided to ensure compliance with the provisions of this Directive.

Article 12 - Binding nature

1. The consumer may not waive the rights conferred on him by the transposition of this Directive into national law.
2. Member States shall take the measures needed to ensure that the consumer does not lose the protection granted by this Directive by virtue of the choice of the law of a non-member country as the law applicable to the contract if the latter has close connection with the territory of one or more Member States.

Article 13 - Community rules

1. The provisions of this Directive shall apply insofar as there are no particular provisions in rules of Community law governing certain types of distance contracts in their entirety.
2. Where specific Community rules contain provisions governing only certain aspects of the supply of goods or provision of services, those provisions, rather than the provisions of this Directive, shall apply to these specific aspects of the distance contracts.

Article 14 - Minimal clause

Member States may introduce or maintain, in the area covered by this Directive, more stringent provisions compatible with the Treaty, to ensure a higher level of consumer protection. Such provisions shall, where appropriate, include a ban, in the general interest, on the marketing of certain goods or services, particularly medicinal products, within their territory by means of distance contracts, with due regard for the Treaty.

Article 15 - Implementation

1. Member States shall bring into force the laws, regulations and administrative provisions necessary to comply with this Directive no later than three years after it enters into force. They shall forthwith inform the Commission thereof.
2. When Member States adopt the measures referred to in paragraph 1, these shall contain a reference to this Directive or shall be accompanied by such reference on the occasion of their official publication. The procedure for such reference shall be laid down by Member States.
3. Member States shall communicate to the Commission the text of the provisions of national law which they adopt in the field governed by this Directive.
4. No later than four years after the entry into force of this Directive the Commission shall submit a report to the European Parliament and the Council on the implementation of this Directive, accompanied if appropriate by a proposal for the revision thereof.

Article 16 - Consumer information

Member States shall take appropriate measures to inform the consumer of the national law transposing this Directive and shall encourage, where appropriate, professional organizations to inform consumers of their codes of practice.

Article 17 - Complaints systems

The Commission shall study the feasibility of establishing effective means to deal with consumers' complaints in respect of distance selling. Within two years after the entry into force of this Directive the Commission shall submit a report to the European Parliament and the Council on the results of the studies, accompanied if appropriate by proposals.

Article 18 - Entry into force

This Directive shall enter into force on the day of its publication in the Official Journal of the European Communities.

Article 19 - Addressees

This Directive is addressed to the Member States.

ANNEX I

Means of communication covered by Article 2 (4):

- Unaddressed printed matter
- Addressed printed matter
- Standard letter
- Press advertising with order form
- Catalogue
- Telephone with human intervention
- Telephone without human intervention (automatic calling machine, audiotext)
- Radio
- Videophone (telephone with screen)
- Videotex (microcomputer and television screen) with keyboard or touch screen
- Electronic mail
- Facsimile machine (fax)
- Television (teleshopping).

ANNEX II

Financial services within the meaning of Article 3 (1):

- Investment services
- Insurance and reinsurance operations
- Banking services
- Operations relating to dealings in futures or options.

Such services include in particular:

- investment services referred to in the Annex to Directive 93/22/EEC[11]; services of collective investment undertakings,
- services covered by the activities subject to mutual recognition referred to in the Annex to Directive 89/646/EEC[12];
- operations covered by the insurance and reinsurance activities referred to in:
- Article 1 of Directive 73/239/EEC[13],
- the Annex to Directive 79/267/EEC[14],

---

[11] OJ No L 141, 11. 6. 1993, p. 27.
[12] OJ No L 386, 30. 12. 1989, p. 1. Directive as amended by Directive 92/30/EEC (OJ No L 110, 28. 4. 1992, p. 52).
[13] OJ No L 228, 16. 8. 1973, p. 3. Directive as last amended by Directive 92/49/EEC (OJ No L 228, 11. 8. 1992, p. 1).

- Directive 64/225/EEC[15],
- Directives 92/49/EEC[16] and 92/96/EEC[17].

---

[14] OJ No L 63, 13. 3. 1979, p. 1. Directive as last amended by Directive 90/619/EEC (OJ No L 330, 29. 11. 1990, p. 50).
[15] OJ No 56, 4. 4. 1964, p. 878/64. Directive as amended by the 1973 Act of Accession.
[16] OJ No L 228, 11. 8. 1992, p. 1.
[17] OJ No L 360, 9. 12. 1992, p. 1.

DIRECTIVE 2002/65/EC OF THE EUROPEAN PARLIAMENT AND OF THE COUNCIL OF 23 SEPTEMBER 2002 CONCERNING THE DISTANCE MARKETING OF CONSUMER FINANCIAL SERVICES AND AMENDING COUNCIL DIRECTIVE 90/619/EEC AND DIRECTIVES 97/7/EC AND 98/27/EC

(Official Journal L 271, 09/10/2002, p. 0016 – 0024)

THE EUROPEAN PARLIAMENT AND THE COUNCIL OF THE EUROPEAN UNION,

Having regard to the Treaty establishing the European Community, and in particular Article 47(2), Article 55 and Article 95 thereof,
Having regard to the proposal from the Commission[1],
Having regard to the opinion of the Economic and Social Committee[2],

Acting in accordance with the procedure laid down in Article 251 of the Treaty[3],

Whereas:
(1) It is important, in the context of achieving the aims of the single market, to adopt measures designed to consolidate progressively this market and those measures must contribute to attaining a high level of consumer protection, in accordance with Articles 95 and 153 of the Treaty.
(2) Both for consumers and suppliers of financial services, the distance marketing of financial services will constitute one of the main tangible results of the completion of the internal market.
(3) Within the framework of the internal market, it is in the interest of consumers to have access without discrimination to the widest possible range of financial services available in the Community so that they can choose those that are best suited to their needs. In order to safeguard freedom of choice, which is an essential consumer right, a high degree of consumer protection is required in order to enhance consumer confidence in distance selling.
(4) It is essential to the smooth operation of the internal market for consumers to be able to negotiate and conclude contracts with a supplier established in other Member States, regardless of whether the supplier is also established in the Member State in which the consumer resides.
(5) Because of their intangible nature, financial services are particularly suited to distance selling and the establishment of a legal framework governing the distance marketing of financial services should increase consumer confidence in the use of new techniques for the distance marketing of financial services, such as electronic commerce.
(6) This Directive should be applied in conformity with the Treaty and with secondary law, including Directive 2000/31/EC[4] on electronic commerce, the latter being applicable solely to the transactions which it covers.

---

[1] OJ C 385, 11.12.1998, p. 10 and OJ C 177 E, 27.6.2000, p. 21.
[2] OJ C 169, 16.6.1999, p. 43.
[3] Opinion of the European Parliament of 5 May 1999 (OJ C 279, 1.10.1999, p. 207), Council Common Position of 19 December 2001 (OJ C 58 E, 5.3.2002, p. 32) and Decision of the European Parliament of 14 May 2002 (not yet published in the Official Journal). Council Decision of 26 June 2002 (not yet published in the Official Journal).
[4] OJ L 178, 17.7.2000, p. 1.

(7) This Directive aims to achieve the objectives set forth above without prejudice to Community or national law governing freedom to provide services or, where applicable, host Member State control and/or authorisation or supervision systems in the Member States where this is compatible with Community legislation.

(8) Moreover, this Directive, and in particular its provisions relating to information about any contractual clause on law applicable to the contract and/or on the competent court does not affect the applicability to the distance marketing of consumer financial services of Council Regulation (EC) No 44/2001 of 22 December 2000 on jurisdiction and the recognition and enforcement of judgements in civil and commercial matters[5] or of the 1980 Rome Convention on the law applicable to contractual obligations.

(9) The achievement of the objectives of the Financial Services Action Plan requires a higher level of consumer protection in certain areas. This implies a greater convergence, in particular, in non harmonised collective investment funds, rules of conduct applicable to investment services and consumer credits. Pending the achievement of the above convergence, a high level of consumer protection should be maintained.

(10) Directive 97/7/EC of the European Parliament and of the Council of 20 May 1997 on the protection of consumers in respect of distance contracts[6], lays down the main rules applicable to distance contracts for goods or services concluded between a supplier and a consumer. However, that Directive does not cover financial services.

(11) In the context of the analysis conducted by the Commission with a view to ascertaining the need for specific measures in the field of financial services, the Commission invited all the interested parties to transmit their comments, notably in connection with the preparation of its Green Paper entitled "Financial Services - Meeting Consumers' Expectations". The consultations in this context showed that there is a need to strengthen consumer protection in this area. The Commission therefore decided to present a specific proposal concerning the distance marketing of financial services.

(12) The adoption by the Member States of conflicting or different consumer protection rules governing the distance marketing of consumer financial services could impede the functioning of the internal market and competition between firms in the market. It is therefore necessary to enact common rules at Community level in this area, consistent with no reduction in overall consumer protection in the Member States.

(13) A high level of consumer protection should be guaranteed by this Directive, with a view to ensuring the free movement of financial services. Member States should not be able to adopt provisions other than those laid down in this Directive in the fields it harmonises, unless otherwise specifically indicated in it.

(14) This Directive covers all financial services liable to be provided at a distance. However, certain financial services are governed by specific provisions of Community legislation which continue to apply to those financial services. However, principles governing the distance marketing of such services should be laid down.

(15) Contracts negotiated at a distance involve the use of means of distance communication which are used as part of a distance sales or service-provision scheme not involving the simultaneous presence of the supplier and the consumer. The constant development of those means of communication requires principles to be defined that are valid even for those means which are not yet in widespread use. Therefore, distance contracts are those the offer, negotiation and conclusion of which are carried out at a distance.

(16) A single contract involving successive operations or separate operations of the same nature performed over time may be subject to different legal treatment in the different Member States, but it is important that this Directive be applied in the same way in all the Member

---

[5] OJ L 12, 16.1.2001, p. 1.

[6] OJ L 144, 4.6.1997, p. 19.

States. To that end, it is appropriate that this Directive should be considered to apply to the first of a series of successive operations or separate operations of the same nature performed over time which may be considered as forming a whole, irrespective of whether that operation or series of operations is the subject of a single contract or several successive contracts.
(17) An "initial service agreement" may be considered to be for example the opening of a bank account, acquiring a credit card, concluding a portfolio management contract, and "operations" may be considered to be for example the deposit or withdrawal of funds to or from the bank account, payment by credit card, transactions made within the framework of a portfolio management contract. Adding new elements to an initial service agreement, such as a possibility to use an electronic payment instrument together with one's existing bank account, does not constitute an "operation" but an additional contract to which this Directive applies. The subscription to new units of the same collective investment fund is considered to be one of "successive operations of the same nature".
(18) By covering a service-provision scheme organised by the financial services provider, this Directive aims to exclude from its scope services provided on a strictly occasional basis and outside a commercial structure dedicated to the conclusion of distance contracts.
(19) The supplier is the person providing services at a distance. This Directive should however also apply when one of the marketing stages involves an intermediary. Having regard to the nature and degree of that involvement, the pertinent provisions of this Directive should apply to such an intermediary, irrespective of his or her legal status.
(20) Durable mediums include in particular floppy discs, CD-ROMs, DVDs and the hard drive of the consumer's computer on which the electronic mail is stored, but they do not include Internet websites unless they fulfil the criteria contained in the definition of a durable medium.
(21) The use of means of distance communications should not lead to an unwarranted restriction on the information provided to the client. In the interests of transparency this Directive lays down the requirements needed to ensure that an appropriate level of information is provided to the consumer both before and after conclusion of the contract. The consumer should receive, before conclusion of the contract, the prior information needed so as to properly appraise the financial service offered to him and hence make a well-informed choice. The supplier should specify how long his offer applies as it stands.
(22) Information items listed in this Directive cover information of a general nature applicable to all kinds of financial services. Other information requirements concerning a given financial service, such as the coverage of an insurance policy, are not solely specified in this Directive. This kind of information should be provided in accordance, where applicable, with relevant Community legislation or national legislation in conformity with Community law.
(23) With a view to optimum protection of the consumer, it is important that the consumer is adequately informed of the provisions of this Directive and of any codes of conduct existing in this area and that he has a right of withdrawal.
(24) When the right of withdrawal does not apply because the consumer has expressly requested the performance of a contract, the supplier should inform the consumer of this fact.
(25) Consumers should be protected against unsolicited services. Consumers should be exempt from any obligation in the case of unsolicited services, the absence of a reply not being construed as signifying consent on their part. However, this rule should be without prejudice to the tacit renewal of contracts validly concluded between the parties whenever the law of the Member States permits such tacit renewal.
(26) Member States should take appropriate measures to protect effectively consumers who do not wish to be contacted through certain means of communication or at certain times. This Directive should be without prejudice to the particular safeguards available to consumers under Community legislation concerning the protection of personal data and privacy.

(27) With a view to protecting consumers, there is a need for suitable and effective complaint and redress procedures in the Member States with a view to settling potential disputes between suppliers and consumers, by using, where appropriate, existing procedures.
(28) Member States should encourage public or private bodies established with a view to settling disputes out of court to cooperate in resolving cross-border disputes. Such cooperation could in particular entail allowing consumers to submit to extra-judicial bodies in the Member State of their residence complaints concerning suppliers established in other Member States. The establishment of FIN-NET offers increased assistance to consumers when using cross-border services.
(29) This Directive is without prejudice to extension by Member States, in accordance with Community law, of the protection provided by this Directive to non-profit organisations and persons making use of financial services in order to become entrepreneurs.
(30) This Directive should also cover cases where the national legislation includes the concept of a consumer making a binding contractual statement.
(31) The provisions in this Directive on the supplier's choice of language should be without prejudice to provisions of national legislation, adopted in conformity with Community law governing the choice of language.
(32) The Community and the Member States have entered into commitments in the context of the General Agreement on Trade in Services (GATS) concerning the possibility for consumers to purchase banking and investment services abroad. The GATS entitles Member States to adopt measures for prudential reasons, including measures to protect investors, depositors, policy-holders and persons to whom a financial service is owed by the supplier of the financial service. Such measures should not impose restrictions going beyond what is required to ensure the protection of consumers.
(33) In view of the adoption of this Directive, the scope of Directive 97/7/EC and Directive 98/27/EC of the European Parliament and of the Council of 19 May 1998 on injunctions for the protection of consumers' interests[7] and the scope of the cancellation period in Council Directive 90/619/EEC of 8 November 1990 on the coordination of laws, regulations and administrative provisions relating to direct life assurance, laying down provisions to facilitate the effective exercise of freedom to provide services[8] should be adapted.
(34) Since the objectives of this Directive, namely the establishment of common rules on the distance marketing of consumer financial services cannot be sufficiently achieved by the Member States and can therefore be better achieved at Community level, the Community may adopt measures, in accordance with the principles of subsidiarity as set out in Article 5 of the Treaty. In accordance with the principle of proportionality, as set out in that Article, this Directive does not go beyond what is necessary to achieve that objective,

HAVE ADOPTED THIS DIRECTIVE:

Article 1 - Object and scope

1. The object of this Directive is to approximate the laws, regulations and administrative provisions of the Member States concerning the distance marketing of consumer financial services.
2. In the case of contracts for financial services comprising an initial service agreement followed by successive operations or a series of separate operations of the same nature performed over time, the provisions of this Directive shall apply only to the initial agreement.

---

[7] OJ L 166, 11.6.1998, p. 51. Directive as last amended by Directive 2000/31/EC (OJ L 178, 17.7.2001, p. 1).

[8] OJ L 330, 29.11.1990, p. 50. Directive as last amended by Directive 92/96/EEC (OJ L 360, 9.12.1992, p. 1).

In case there is no initial service agreement but the successive operations or the separate operations of the same nature performed over time are performed between the same contractual parties, Articles 3 and 4 apply only when the first operation is performed. Where, however, no operation of the same nature is performed for more than one year, the next operation will be deemed to be the first in a new series of operations and, accordingly, Articles 3 and 4 shall apply.

Article 2 - Definitions

For the purposes of this Directive:
(a) "distance contract" means any contract concerning financial services concluded between a supplier and a consumer under an organised distance sales or service-provision scheme run by the supplier, who, for the purpose of that contract, makes exclusive use of one or more means of distance communication up to and including the time at which the contract is concluded;
(b) "financial service" means any service of a banking, credit, insurance, personal pension, investment or payment nature;
(c) "supplier" means any natural or legal person, public or private, who, acting in his commercial or professional capacity, is the contractual provider of services subject to distance contracts;
(d) "consumer" means any natural person who, in distance contracts covered by this Directive, is acting for purposes which are outside his trade, business or profession;
(e) "means of distance communication" refers to any means which, without the simultaneous physical presence of the supplier and the consumer, may be used for the distance marketing of a service between those parties;
(f) "durable medium" means any instrument which enables the consumer to store information addressed personally to him in a way accessible for future reference for a period of time adequate for the purposes of the information and which allows the unchanged reproduction of the information stored;
(g) "operator or supplier of a means of distance communication" means any public or private, natural or legal person whose trade, business or profession involves making one or more means of distance communication available to suppliers.

Article 3 - Information to the consumer prior to the conclusion of the distance contract

1. In good time before the consumer is bound by any distance contract or offer, he shall be provided with the following information concerning:
(1) the supplier
    (a) the identity and the main business of the supplier, the geographical address at which the supplier is established and any other geographical address relevant for the customer's relations with the supplier;
    (b) the identity of the representative of the supplier established in the consumer's Member State of residence and the geographical address relevant for the customer's relations with the representative, if such a representative exists;
    (c) when the consumer's dealings are with any professional other than the supplier, the identity of this professional, the capacity in which he is acting vis-à-vis the consumer, and the geographical address relevant for the customer's relations with this professional;
    (d) where the supplier is registered in a trade or similar public register, the trade register in which the supplier is entered and his registration number or an equivalent means of identification in that register;
    (e) where the supplier's activity is subject to an authorisation scheme, the particulars of the relevant supervisory authority;

(2) the financial service
   (a) a description of the main characteristics of the financial service;
   (b) the total price to be paid by the consumer to the supplier for the financial service, including all related fees, charges and expenses, and all taxes paid via the supplier or, when an exact price cannot be indicated, the basis for the calculation of the price enabling the consumer to verify it;
   (c) where relevant notice indicating that the financial service is related to instruments involving special risks related to their specific features or the operations to be executed or whose price depends on fluctuations in the financial markets outside the supplier's control and that historical performances are no indicators for future performances;
   (d) notice of the possibility that other taxes and/or costs may exist that are not paid via the supplier or imposed by him;
   (e) any limitations of the period for which the information provided is valid;
   (f) the arrangements for payment and for performance;
   (g) any specific additional cost for the consumer of using the means of distance communication, if such additional cost is charged;
(3) the distance contract
   (a) the existence or absence of a right of withdrawal in accordance with Article 6 and, where the right of withdrawal exists, its duration and the conditions for exercising it, including information on the amount which the consumer may be required to pay on the basis of Article 7(1), as well as the consequences of non-exercise of that right;
   (b) the minimum duration of the distance contract in the case of financial services to be performed permanently or recurrently;
   (c) information on any rights the parties may have to terminate the contract early or unilaterally by virtue of the terms of the distance contract, including any penalties imposed by the contract in such cases;
   (d) practical instructions for exercising the right of withdrawal indicating, inter alia, the address to which the notification of a withdrawal should be sent;
   (e) the Member State or States whose laws are taken by the supplier as a basis for the establishment of relations with the consumer prior to the conclusion of the distance contract;
   (f) any contractual clause on law applicable to the distance contract and/or on competent court;
   (g) in which language, or languages, the contractual terms and conditions, and the prior information referred to in this Article are supplied, and furthermore in which language, or languages, the supplier, with the agreement of the consumer, undertakes to communicate during the duration of this distance contract;
(4) redress
   (a) whether or not there is an out-of-court complaint and redress mechanism for the consumer that is party to the distance contract and, if so, the methods for having access to it;
   (b) the existence of guarantee funds or other compensation arrangements, not covered by Directive 94/19/EC of the European Parliament and of the Council of 30 May 1994 on deposit guarantee schemes[9] and Directive 97/9/EC of the European Parliament and of the Council of 3 March 1997 on investor compensation schemes[10].
2. The information referred to in paragraph 1, the commercial purpose of which must be made clear, shall be provided in a clear and comprehensible manner in any way appropriate to the

---

[9] OJ L 135, 31.5.1994, p. 5.
[10] OJ L 84, 26.3.1997, p. 22.

means of distance communication used, with due regard, in particular, to the principles of good faith in commercial transactions, and the principles governing the protection of those who are unable, pursuant to the legislation of the Member States, to give their consent, such as minors.

3. In the case of voice telephony communications
(a) the identity of the supplier and the commercial purpose of the call initiated by the supplier shall be made explicitly clear at the beginning of any conversation with the consumer;
(b) subject to the explicit consent of the consumer only the following information needs to be given:
- the identity of the person in contact with the consumer and his link with the supplier,
- a description of the main characteristics of the financial service,
- the total price to be paid by the consumer to the supplier for the financial service including all taxes paid via the supplier or, when an exact price cannot be indicated, the basis for the calculation of the price enabling the consumer to verify it,
- notice of the possibility that other taxes and/or costs may exist that are not paid via the supplier or imposed by him,
- the existence or absence of a right of withdrawal in accordance with Article 6 and, where the right of withdrawal exists, its duration and the conditions for exercising it, including information on the amount which the consumer may be required to pay on the basis of Article 7(1).

The supplier shall inform the consumer that other information is available on request and of what nature this information is. In any case the supplier shall provide the full information when he fulfils his obligations under Article 5.

4. Information on contractual obligations, to be communicated to the consumer during the pre-contractual phase, shall be in conformity with the contractual obligations which would result from the law presumed to be applicable to the distance contract if the latter were concluded.

Article 4 - Additional information requirements

1. Where there are provisions in the Community legislation governing financial services which contain prior information requirements additional to those listed in Article 3(1), these requirements shall continue to apply.
2. Pending further harmonisation, Member States may maintain or introduce more stringent provisions on prior information requirements when the provisions are in conformity with Community law.
3. Member States shall communicate to the Commission national provisions on prior information requirements under paragraphs 1 and 2 of this Article when these requirements are additional to those listed in Article 3(1). The Commission shall take account of the communicated national provisions when drawing up the report referred to in Article 20(2).
4. The Commission shall, with a view to creating a high level of transparency by all appropriate means, ensure that information, on the national provisions communicated to it, is made available to consumers and suppliers.

Article 5 - Communication of the contractual terms and conditions and of the prior information

1. The supplier shall communicate to the consumer all the contractual terms and conditions and the information referred to in Article 3(1) and Article 4 on paper or on another durable medium available and accessible to the consumer in good time before the consumer is bound by any distance contract or offer.
2. The supplier shall fulfil his obligation under paragraph 1 immediately after the conclusion of the contract, if the contract has been concluded at the consumer's request using a means of

distance communication which does not enable providing the contractual terms and conditions and the information in conformity with paragraph 1.
3. At any time during the contractual relationship the consumer is entitled, at his request, to receive the contractual terms and conditions on paper. In addition, the consumer is entitled to change the means of distance communication used, unless this is incompatible with the contract concluded or the nature of the financial service provided.

Article 6 - Right of withdrawal

1. The Member States shall ensure that the consumer shall have a period of 14 calendar days to withdraw from the contract without penalty and without giving any reason. However, this period shall be extended to 30 calendar days in distance contracts relating to life insurance covered by Directive 90/619/EEC and personal pension operations.
The period for withdrawal shall begin:
- either from the day of the conclusion of the distance contract, except in respect of the said life assurance, where the time limit will begin from the time when the consumer is informed that the distance contract has been concluded, or
- from the day on which the consumer receives the contractual terms and conditions and the information in accordance with Article 5(1) or (2), if that is later than the date referred to in the first indent.

Member States, in addition to the right of withdrawal, may provide that the enforceability of contracts relating to investment services is suspended for the same period provided for in this paragraph.
2. The right of withdrawal shall not apply to:
(a) financial services whose price depends on fluctuations in the financial market outside the suppliers control, which may occur during the withdrawal period, such as services related to:
- foreign exchange,
- money market instruments,
- transferable securities,
- units in collective investment undertakings,
- financial-futures contracts, including equivalent cash-settled instruments,
- forward interest-rate agreements (FRAs),
- interest-rate, currency and equity swaps,
- options to acquire or dispose of any instruments referred to in this point including equivalent cash-settled instruments. This category includes in particular options on currency and on interest rates;
(b) travel and baggage insurance policies or similar short-term insurance policies of less than one month's duration;
(c) contracts whose performance has been fully completed by both parties at the consumer's express request before the consumer exercises his right of withdrawal.
3. Member States may provide that the right of withdrawal shall not apply to:
(a) any credit intended primarily for the purpose of acquiring or retaining property rights in land or in an existing or projected building, or for the purpose of renovating or improving a building, or
(b) any credit secured either by mortgage on immovable property or by a right related to immovable property, or
(c) declarations by consumers using the services of an official, provided that the official confirms that the consumer is guaranteed the rights under Article 5(1).

This paragraph shall be without prejudice to the right to a reflection time to the benefit of the consumers that are resident in those Member States where it exists, at the time of the adoption of this Directive.

4. Member States making use of the possibility set out in paragraph 3 shall communicate it to the Commission.
5. The Commission shall make available the information communicated by Member States to the European Parliament and the Council and shall ensure that it is also available to consumers and suppliers who request it.
6. If the consumer exercises his right of withdrawal he shall, before the expiry of the relevant deadline, notify this following the practical instructions given to him in accordance with Article 3(1)(3)(d) by means which can be proved in accordance with national law. The deadline shall be deemed to have been observed if the notification, if it is on paper or on another durable medium available and accessible to the recipient, is dispatched before the deadline expires.
7. This Article does not apply to credit agreements cancelled under the conditions of Article 6(4) of Directive 97/7/EC or Article 7 of Directive 94/47/EC of the European Parliament and of the Council of 26 October 1994 on the protection of purchasers in respect of certain aspects of contracts relating to the purchase of the right to use immovable properties on a timeshare basis[11].

If to a distance contract of a given financial service another distance contract has been attached concerning services provided by the supplier or by a third party on the basis of an agreement between the third party and the supplier, this additional distance contract shall be cancelled, without any penalty, if the consumer exercises his right of withdrawal as provided for in Article 6(1).
8. The provisions of this Article are without prejudice to the Member States' laws and regulations governing the cancellation or termination or non-enforceability of a distance contract or the right of a consumer to fulfil his contractual obligations before the time fixed in the distance contract. This applies irrespective of the conditions for and the legal effects of the winding-up of the contract.

Article 7 - Payment of the service provided before withdrawal

1. When the consumer exercises his right of withdrawal under Article 6(1) he may only be required to pay, without any undue delay, for the service actually provided by the supplier in accordance with the contract. The performance of the contract may only begin after the consumer has given his approval. The amount payable shall not:
    - exceed an amount which is in proportion to the extent of the service already provided in comparison with the full coverage of the contract,
    - in any case be such that it could be construed as a penalty.
2. Member States may provide that the consumer cannot be required to pay any amount when withdrawing from an insurance contract.
3. The supplier may not require the consumer to pay any amount on the basis of paragraph 1 unless he can prove that the consumer was duly informed about the amount payable, in conformity with Article 3(1)(3)(a). However, in no case may he require such payment if he has commenced the performance of the contract before the expiry of the withdrawal period provided for in Article 6(1) without the consumer's prior request.
4. The supplier shall, without any undue delay and no later than within 30 calendar days, return to the consumer any sums he has received from him in accordance with the distance contract, except for the amount referred to in paragraph 1. This period shall begin from the day on which the supplier receives the notification of withdrawal.
5. The consumer shall return to the supplier any sums and/or property he has received from the supplier without any undue delay and no later than within 30 calendar days. This period shall begin from the day on which the consumer dispatches the notification of withdrawal.

---

[11] OJ L 280, 29.10.1994, p. 83.

Article 8 - Payment by card

Member States shall ensure that appropriate measures exist to allow a consumer:
- to request cancellation of a payment where fraudulent use has been made of his payment card in connection with distance contracts,
- in the event of such fraudulent use, to be re-credited with the sum paid or have them returned.

Article 9 - Unsolicited services

Without prejudice to Member States provisions on the tacit renewal of distance contracts, when such rules permit tacit renewal, Member States shall take the necessary measures to:
- prohibit the supply of financial services to a consumer without a prior request on his part, when this supply includes a request for immediate or deferred payment,
- exempt the consumer from any obligation in the event of unsolicited supplies, the absence of a reply not constituting consent.

Article 10 - Unsolicited communications

1. The use by a supplier of the following distance communication techniques shall require the consumer's prior consent:
(a) automated calling systems without human intervention (automatic calling machines);
(b) fax machines.
2. Member States shall ensure that means of distance communication other than those referred to in paragraph 1, when they allow individual communications:
(a) shall not be authorised unless the consent of the consumers concerned has been obtained, or
(b) may only be used if the consumer has not expressed his manifest objection.
3. The measures referred to in paragraphs 1 and 2 shall not entail costs for consumers.

Article 11 - Sanctions

Member States shall provide for appropriate sanctions in the event of the supplier's failure to comply with national provisions adopted pursuant to this Directive.

They may provide for this purpose in particular that the consumer may cancel the contract at any time, free of charge and without penalty.

These sanctions must be effective, proportional and dissuasive.

Article 12 - Imperative nature of this Directive's provisions

1. Consumers may not waive the rights conferred on them by this Directive.
2. Member States shall take the measures needed to ensure that the consumer does not lose the protection granted by this Directive by virtue of the choice of the law of a non-member country as the law applicable to the contract, if this contract has a close link with the territory of one or more Member States.

Article 13 - Judicial and administrative redress

1. Member States shall ensure that adequate and effective means exist to ensure compliance with this Directive in the interests of consumers.
2. The means referred to in paragraph 1 shall include provisions whereby one or more of the following bodies, as determined by national law, may take action in accordance with national law before the courts or competent administrative bodies to ensure that the national provisions for the implementation of this Directive are applied:
(a) public bodies or their representatives;
(b) consumer organisations having a legitimate interest in protecting consumers;

(c) professional organisations having a legitimate interest in acting.
3. Member States shall take the measures necessary to ensure that operators and suppliers of means of distance communication put an end to practices that have been declared to be contrary to this Directive, on the basis of a judicial decision, an administrative decision or a decision issued by a supervisory authority notified to them, where those operators or suppliers are in a position to do so.

Article 14 - Out-of-court redress

1. Member States shall promote the setting up or development of adequate and effective out-of-court complaints and redress procedures for the settlement of consumer disputes concerning financial services provided at distance.
2. Member States shall, in particular, encourage the bodies responsible for out-of-court settlement of disputes to cooperate in the resolution of cross-border disputes concerning financial services provided at distance.

Article 15 - Burden of proof

Without prejudice to Article 7(3), Member States may stipulate that the burden of proof in respect of the supplier's obligations to inform the consumer and the consumer's consent to conclusion of the contract and, where appropriate, its performance, can be placed on the supplier.

Any contractual term or condition providing that the burden of proof of the respect by the supplier of all or part of the obligations incumbent on him pursuant to this Directive should lie with the consumer shall be an unfair term within the meaning of Council Directive 93/13/EEC of 5 April 1993 on unfair terms in consumer contracts[12].

Article 16 - Transitional measures

Member States may impose national rules which are in conformity with this Directive on suppliers established in a Member State which has not yet transposed this Directive and whose law has no obligations corresponding to those provided for in this Directive.

Article 17 - Directive 90/619/EC

In Article 15(1) of Directive 90/619/EEC the first subparagraph shall be replaced by the following: "1. Each Member State shall prescribe that a policyholder who concludes an individual life-assurance contract shall have a period of 30 calendar days, from the time when he was informed that the contract had been concluded, within which to cancel the contract."

Article 18 - Directive 97/7/EC

Directive 97/7/EC is hereby amended as follows:
1. the first indent of Article 3(1) shall be replaced by the following: "- relating to any financial service to which Directive 2002/65/EC of the European Parliament and of the Council of 23 September 2002 concerning the distance marketing of consumer financial services and amending Council Directive 90/619/EEC and Directives 97/7/EC and 98/27/EC[13] applies,";
2. Annex II shall be deleted.

Article 19 - Directive 98/27/EC

The following point shall be added to the Annex of Directive 98/27/EC: "11. Directive 2002/65/EC of the European Parliament and of the Council of 23 September 2002 concerning the

---

[12] OJ L 95, 21.4.1993, p. 29.
[13] OJ L 271, 9.10.2002, p. 16.

distance marketing of consumer financial services and amending Council Directive 90/619/EEC and Directives 97/7/EC and 98/27/EC[14]."

Article 20 - Review

1. Following the implementation of this Directive, the Commission shall examine the functioning of the internal market in financial services in respect of the marketing of those services. It should seek to analyse and detail the difficulties that are, or might be faced by both consumers and suppliers, in particular arising from differences between national provisions regarding information and right of withdrawal.
2. Not later than 9 April 2006 the Commission shall report to the European Parliament and the Council on the problems facing both consumers and suppliers seeking to buy and sell financial services, and shall submit, where appropriate, proposals to amend and/or further harmonise the information and right of withdrawal provisions in Community legislation concerning financial services and/or those covered in Article 3.

Article 21 - Transposition

1. Member States shall bring into force the laws, regulations and administrative provisions necessary to comply with this Directive not later than 9 October 2004. They shall forthwith inform the Commission thereof.
   When Member States adopt these measures, they shall contain a reference to this Directive or shall be accompanied by such a reference on the occasion of their official publication. The methods of making such reference shall be laid down by Member States.
2. Member States shall communicate to the Commission the text of the main provisions of national law which they adopt in the field governed by this Directive together with a table showing how the provisions of this Directive correspond to the national provisions adopted.

Article 22 - Entry into force

This Directive shall enter into force on the day of its publication in the Official Journal of the European Communities.

Article 23 - Addressees

This Directive is addressed to the Member States.

---

[14] OJ L 271, 9.10.2002, p. 16.

RECOMMENDATION OF THE OECD COUNCIL CONCERNING GUIDELINES FOR CONSUMER PROTECTION IN THE CONTEXT OF ELECTRONIC COMMERCE

Consumer laws, policies and practices limit fraudulent, misleading and unfair commercial conduct. Such protections are indispensable in building consumer confidence and establishing a more balanced relationship between businesses and consumers in commercial transactions.

The inherently international nature of the digital networks and computer technologies that comprise the electronic marketplace requires a global approach to consumer protection as part of a transparent and predictable legal and self-regulatory framework for electronic commerce. The global network environment challenges the abilities of each country or jurisdiction to adequately address issues related to consumer protection in the context of electronic commerce. Disparate national policies may impede the growth of electronic commerce, and as such, these consumer protection issues may be addressed most effectively through international consultation and co-operation. OECD Member governments have recognised that internationally co-ordinated approaches may be needed to exchange information and establish a general understanding about how to address these issues.

Governments are challenged to help facilitate social development and economic growth based on emerging network technologies, and to provide their citizens with effective and transparent consumer protection for electronic commerce. A variety of consumer protection laws exist that govern business practices. Many OECD Member countries have begun to review existing consumer protection laws and practices to determine whether or not changes need to be made to accommodate the unique aspects of electronic commerce. Member countries are also examining ways in which self-regulatory efforts can assist in providing effective and fair protection for consumers in that context. Reaching these objectives requires insight and input from throughout civil society, and all of these initiatives should be undertaken as part of a global co-operative effort among governments, business, consumers and their representatives.

In April of 1998, the OECD Committee on Consumer Policy began to develop a set of general guidelines to protect consumers participating in electronic commerce without erecting barriers to trade. These guidelines represent a recommendation to governments, businesses, consumers, and their representatives as to the core characteristics of effective consumer protection for electronic commerce. However, nothing contained herein should restrict any party from exceeding these guidelines nor preclude Member countries from retaining or adopting more stringent provisions to protect consumers online. In particular, the purpose of the guidelines is to provide both a framework and a set of principles to assist:

    i) Governments in reviewing, formulating and implementing consumer and law enforcement policies, practices, and regulations if necessary for effective consumer protection in the context of electronic commerce;

    ii) Business associations, consumer groups and self-regulatory bodies, by providing guidance as to the core characteristics of effective consumer protection that should be considered in reviewing, formulating, and implementing self-regulatory schemes in the context of electronic commerce; and

    iii) Individual businesses and consumers engaged in electronic commerce, by providing clear guidance as to the core characteristics of information disclosure and fair business practices that businesses should provide and consumers should expect in the context of electronic commerce.

In light of the above, the Council,

    Having regard to Article 5 b) of the Convention on the Organisation for Economic Co-operation and Development of 14th December 1960;

Having regard to the Ministerial Declaration on Consumer Protection in the Context of Electronic Commerce of 8-9 October 1998 [C(98)177 (Annex 2)];

Having regard to the Recommendation of the Council concerning Guidelines Governing the Protection of Privacy and Transborder Flows of Personal Data of 23 September 1980 [C(80)58(Final)], and the Ministerial Declaration on the Protection of Privacy on Global Networks of 8-9 October 1998 [C(98)177 (Annex 1)];

Having regard to the Ministerial Declaration on Authentication for Electronic Commerce of 8-9 October 1998 [(C98)177 (Annex 3)];

Having regard to the Recommendation of the Council concerning Guidelines for the Security of Information Systems of 26-27 November 1992 [C(92)188/FINAL)], and the OECD Recommendation concerning Guidelines on Cryptography Policy of 27 March 1997 [C(97)62/FINAL] ;

Recognising that electronic commerce may offer consumers new and substantial benefits, including convenience, access to a wide range of goods and services, and the ability to gather and compare information about such goods and services;

Recognising that certain special characteristics of electronic commerce, such as the ease and speed with which businesses and consumers can communicate about goods and services and engage in cross-border transactions, may create commercial situations which are unfamiliar to consumers and which may put their interests at risk, it is increasingly important for consumers and businesses to be informed and aware of their rights and obligations in the electronic marketplace;

Recognising that rules regarding applicable law and jurisdiction in the consumer context could have implications for a broad range of issues in electronic commerce, just as rules regarding applicable law and jurisdiction in other contexts could have implications for consumer protection;

Recognising that consumer confidence in electronic commerce is enhanced by the continued development of transparent and effective consumer protection mechanisms that limit the presence of fraudulent, misleading or unfair commercial conduct online;

Considering that electronic commerce should be open and accessible to all consumers; and

Considering that governments, businesses, consumers and their representatives should devote special attention to the development of effective cross-border redress systems.

RECOMMENDS THAT MEMBER COUNTRIES:

Take the necessary steps to implement the relevant sections of the Guidelines contained in the Annex attached to this Recommendation;

Widely disseminate the Guidelines to all relevant governmental departments and agencies, to business sectors involved in electronic commerce, to consumer representatives, to the media, to educational institutions, and to other relevant public interest groups;

Encourage businesses, consumers, and their representatives to take an active role in promoting the implementation of the Guidelines at the international, national, and local levels;

Encourage governments, businesses, consumers and their representatives to participate in and consider the recommendations of ongoing examinations of rules regarding applicable law and jurisdiction;

Invite non-member countries to take account of the terms of this Recommendation in reviewing their consumer policies, initiatives and regulations;

Consult, co-operate, and facilitate information sharing among themselves and non-member countries, businesses, consumers, and their representatives, at both national and international levels, in providing effective consumer protection in the context of electronic commerce in accordance with the Guidelines;

Implement the Guidelines in a manner that encourages the development of new business models and technology applications that benefit consumers; and encourage consumers to take advantage of all tools available to strengthen their position as buyers; and

INSTRUCTS the Committee on Consumer Policy to exchange information on progress and experiences with respect to the implementation of this Recommendation, review that information and report to the Council in 2002, or sooner, and, as appropriate, thereafter.

ANNEX

GUIDELINES

PART ONE - SCOPE

These Guidelines apply only to business-to-consumer electronic commerce and not to businessto-business transactions.

PART TWO - GENERAL PRINCIPLES

I. TRANSPARENT AND EFFECTIVE PROTECTION

Consumers who participate in electronic commerce should be afforded transparent and effective consumer protection that is not less than the level of protection afforded in other forms of commerce.

Governments, businesses, consumers, and their representatives should work together to achieve such protection and determine what changes may be necessary to address the special circumstances of electronic commerce.

II. FAIR BUSINESS, ADVERTISING AND MARKETING PRACTICES

Businesses engaged in electronic commerce should pay due regard to the interests of consumersand act in accordance with fair business, advertising and marketing practices.

- Businesses should not make any representation, or omission, or engage in any practice that is likely to be deceptive, misleading, fraudulent or unfair.
- Businesses selling, promoting or marketing goods or services to consumers should not engage in practices that are likely to cause unreasonable risk of harm to consumers.
- Whenever businesses make information available about themselves or the goods or services they provide, they should present such information in a clear, conspicuous, accurate and easily accessible manner.
- Businesses should comply with any representations they make regarding policies or practices relating to their transactions with consumers.
- Businesses should take into account the global nature of electronic commerce and, wherever possible, should consider the various regulatory characteristics of the markets they target.
- Businesses should not exploit the special characteristics of electronic commerce to hide their true identity or location, or to avoid compliance with consumer protection standards and/or enforcement mechanisms.
- Businesses should not use unfair contract terms.
- Advertising and marketing should be clearly identifiable as such.
- Advertising and marketing should identify the business on whose behalf the marketing or advertising is being conducted where failure to do so would be deceptive.
- Businesses should be able to substantiate any express or implied representations as long as the representations are maintained, and for a reasonable time thereafter.
- Businesses should develop and implement effective and easy-to-use procedures that allow consumers to choose whether or not they wish to receive unsolicited commercial e-mail messages.
- Where consumers have indicated that they do not want to receive unsolicited commercial e-mail messages, such choice should be respected.

- In a number of countries, unsolicited commercial e-mail is subject to specific legal or selfregulatory requirements.
- Businesses should take special care in advertising or marketing that is targeted to children, the elderly, the seriously ill, and others who may not have the capacity to fully understand the information with which they are presented.

III. ONLINE DISCLOSURES

A. INFORMATION ABOUT THE BUSINESS

Businesses engaged in electronic commerce with consumers should provide accurate, clear and easily accessible information about themselves sufficient to allow, at a minimum:

i) Identification of the business - including the legal name of the business and the name under which the business trades; the principal geographic address for the business; email address or other electronic means of contact, or telephone number; and, where applicable, an address for registration purposes and any relevant government registration or license numbers;
ii) Prompt, easy and effective consumer communication with the business;
iii) Appropriate and effective resolution of disputes;
iv) Service of legal process; and
v) Location of the business and its principals by law enforcement and regulatory officials

Where a business publicises its membership in any relevant self-regulatory scheme, business association, dispute resolution organisation or other certification body, the business should provide consumers with appropriate contact details and an easy method of verifying that membership and of accessing the relevant codes and practices of the certification body.

B. INFORMATION ABOUT THE GOODS OR SERVICES

Businesses engaged in electronic commerce with consumers should provide accurate and easily accessible information describing the goods or services offered; sufficient to enable consumers to make an informed decision about whether to enter into the transaction and in a manner that makes it possible for consumers to maintain an adequate record of such information.

C. INFORMATION ABOUT THE TRANSACTION

Businesses engaged in electronic commerce should provide sufficient information about the terms, conditions and costs associated with a transaction to enable consumers to make an informed decision about whether to enter into the transaction.

- Such information should be clear, accurate, easily accessible, and provided in manner that gives consumers an adequate opportunity for review before entering into the transaction.
- Where more than one language is available to conduct a transaction, businesses should make available in those same languages all information necessary for consumers to make an informed decision about the transaction.
- Businesses should provide consumers with a clear and full text of the relevant terms and conditions of the transaction in a manner that makes it possible for consumers to access and maintain an adequate record of such information.
- Where applicable and appropriate given the transaction, such information should include the following:
    i) an itemisation of total costs collected and/or imposed by the business;
    ii) notice of the existence of other routinely applicable costs to the consumer that are not collected and/or imposed by the business;
    iii) terms of delivery or performance;
    iv) terms, conditions, and methods of payment;

v)   restrictions, limitations or conditions of purchase, such as parental/guardian approval requirements, geographic or time restrictions;
vi) instructions for proper use including safety and health care warnings;
vii) information relating to available after-sales service
viii) details of and conditions related to withdrawal, termination, return, exchange, cancellation and/or refund policy information; and
ix) available warranties and guarantees.

All information that refers to costs should indicate the applicable currency.

IV. CONFIRMATION PROCESS

To avoid ambiguity concerning the consumer's intent to make a purchase, the consumer should be able, before concluding the purchase, to identify precisely the goods or services he or she wishes to purchase; identify and correct any errors or modify the order; express an informed and deliberate consent to the purchase; and retain a complete and accurate record of the transaction

The consumer should be able to cancel the transaction before concluding the purchase.

V. PAYMENT

Consumers should be provided with easy-to-use, secure payment mechanisms and information on the level of security such mechanisms afford.

Limitations of liability for unauthorised or fraudulent use of payment systems, and chargeback mechanisms offer powerful tools to enhance consumer confidence and their development and use should be encouraged in the context of electronic commerce.

VI. DISPUTE RESOLUTION AND REDRESS

A. APPLICABLE LAW AND JURISDICTION

Business-to-consumer cross-border transactions, whether carried out electronically or otherwise, are subject to the existing framework on applicable law and jurisdiction.

Electronic commerce poses challenges to this existing framework. Therefore, consideration should be given to whether the existing framework for applicable law and jurisdiction should be modified, or applied differently, to ensure effective and transparent consumer protection in the context of the continued growth of electronic commerce.

In considering whether to modify the existing framework, governments should seek to ensure that the framework provides fairness to consumers and business, facilitates electronic commerce, results in consumers having a level of protection not less than that afforded in other forms of commerce, and provides consumers with meaningful access to fair and timely dispute resolution and redress without undue cost or burden.

B. ALTERNATIVE DISPUTE RESOLUTION AND REDRESS

Consumers should be provided meaningful access to fair and timely alternative dispute resolution and redress without undue cost or burden.

Businesses, consumer representatives and governments should work together to continue to use and develop fair, effective and transparent self-regulatory and other policies and procedures, including alternative dispute resolution mechanisms, to address consumer complaints and to resolve consumer disputes arising from business-to-consumer electronic commerce, with special attention to cross-border transactions.

i)   Businesses and consumer representatives should continue to establish fair, effective and transparent internal mechanisms to address and respond to consumer complaints and difficulties in a fair and timely manner and without undue cost or burden to the consumer. Consumers should be encouraged to take advantage of such mechanisms.

ii) Businesses and consumer representatives should continue to establish co-operative selfregulatory programs to address consumer complaints and to assist consumers in resolving disputes arising from business-to-consumer electronic commerce.
iii) Businesses, consumer representatives and governments should work together to continue to provide consumers with the option of alternative dispute resolution mechanisms that provide effective resolution of the dispute in a fair and timely manner and without undue cost or burden to the consumer.
iv) In implementing the above, businesses, consumer representatives and governments should employ information technologies innovatively and use them to enhance consumer awareness and freedom of choice.

In addition, further study is required to meet the objectives of Section VI at an international level.

VII. PRIVACY

Business-to-consumer electronic commerce should be conducted in accordance with the recognised privacy principles set out in the OECD Guidelines Governing the Protection of Privacy and Transborder Flow of Personal Data (1980), and taking into account the OECD Ministerial Declaration on the Protection of Privacy on Global Networks (1998), to provide appropriate and effective protection for consumers.

VIII. EDUCATION AND AWARENESS

Governments, business and consumer representatives should work together to educate consumers about electronic commerce, to foster informed decision-making by consumers participating in electronic commerce, and to increase business and consumer awareness of the consumer protection framework that applies to their online activities.

Governments, business, the media, educational institutions and consumer representatives should make use of all effective means to educate consumers and businesses, including innovative techniques made possible by global networks.

Governments, consumer representatives and businesses should work together to provide information to consumers and businesses globally about relevant consumer protection laws and remedies in an easily accessible and understandable form.

PART THREE - IMPLEMENTATION

To achieve the purpose of this Recommendation, Member countries should at the national and international level, and in co-operation with businesses, consumers and their representatives:

a) review and, if necessary, promote self-regulatory practices and/or adopt and adapt laws and practices to make such laws and practices applicable to electronic commerce, having in mind the principles of technology and media neutrality;
b) encourage continued private sector leadership that includes the participation of consumer representatives in the development of effective self-regulatory mechanisms that contain specific, substantive rules for dispute resolution and compliance mechanisms;
c) encourage continued private sector leadership in the development of technology as a tool to protect and empower consumers;
d) promote the existence, purpose and contents of the Guidelines as widely as possible and encourage their use; and
e) facilitate consumers' ability to both access consumer education information and advice and to file complaints related to electronic commerce.

PART FOUR - GLOBAL CO-OPERATION

In order to provide effective consumer protection in the context of global electronic commerce Member countries should:

Facilitate communication, co-operation, and, where appropriate the development and enforcement of joint initiatives at the international level among businesses, consumer representatives and governments.

Through their judicial, regulatory, and law enforcement authorities co-operate at the international level, as appropriate, through information exchange, co-ordination, communication, and joint action to combat cross-border fraudulent, misleading and unfair commercial conduct.

Make use of existing international networks and enter into bilateral and/or multilateral agreements or other arrangements as necessary and appropriate, to accomplish such co-operation.

Work toward building consensus, both at the national and international levels, on core consumer protections to further the goals of enhancing consumer confidence, ensuring predictability for businesses, and protecting consumers.

Co-operate and work toward developing agreements or other arrangements for the mutual recognition and enforcement of judgments resulting from disputes between consumers and businesses, and judgments resulting from law enforcement actions taken to combat fraudulent, misleading or unfair commercial conduct.

6. Data Protection

DIRECTIVE 95/46/EC OF THE EUROPEAN PARLIAMENT AND OF THE COUNCIL OF 24 OCTOBER 1995 ON THE PROTECTION OF INDIVIDUALS WITH REGARD TO THE PROCESSING OF PERSONAL DATA AND ON THE FREE MOVEMENT OF SUCH DATA

(Official Journal L 281, 23/11/1995, p. 0031)

THE EUROPEAN PARLIAMENT AND THE COUNCIL OF THE EUROPEAN UNION,

Having regard to the Treaty establishing the European Community, and in particular Article 100a thereof,
Having regard to the proposal from the Commission[1],
Having regard to the opinion of the Economic and Social Committee[2],

Acting in accordance with the procedure referred to in Article 189b of the Treaty[3],

(1) Whereas the objectives of the Community, as laid down in the Treaty, as amended by the Treaty on European Union, include creating an ever closer union among the peoples of Europe, fostering closer relations between the States belonging to the Community, ensuring economic and social progress by common action to eliminate the barriers which divide Europe, encouraging the constant improvement of the living conditions of its peoples, preserving and strengthening peace and liberty and promoting democracy on the basis of the fundamental rights recognized in the constitution and laws of the Member States and in the European Convention for the Protection of Human Rights and Fundamental Freedoms;

(2) Whereas data-processing systems are designed to serve man; whereas they must, whatever the nationality or residence of natural persons, respect their fundamental rights and freedoms, notably the right to privacy, and contribute to economic and social progress, trade expansion and the well-being of individuals;

(3) Whereas the establishment and functioning of an internal market in which, in accordance with Article 7a of the Treaty, the free movement of goods, persons, services and capital is ensured require not only that personal data should be able to flow freely from one Member State to another, but also that the fundamental rights of individuals should be safeguarded;

(4) Whereas increasingly frequent recourse is being had in the Community to the processing of personal data in the various spheres of economic and social activity; whereas the progress made in information technology is making the processing and exchange of such data considerably easier;

(5) Whereas the economic and social integration resulting from the establishment and functioning of the internal market within the meaning of Article 7a of the Treaty will necessarily lead to a substantial increase in cross-border flows of personal data between all

---

[1] OJ No C 277, 5. 11. 1990, p. 3 and OJ No C 311, 27. 11. 1992, p. 30.
[2] OJ No C 159, 17. 6. 1991, p. 38.
[3] Opinion of the European Parliament of 11 March 1992 (OJ No C 94, 13. 4. 1992, p. 198), confirmed on 2 December 1993 (OJ No C 342, 20. 12. 1993, p. 30); Council common position of 20 February 1995 (OJ No C 93, 13. 4. 1995, p. 1) and Decision of the European Parliament of 15 June 1995 (OJ No C 166, 3. 7. 1995).

those involved in a private or public capacity in economic and social activity in the Member States; whereas the exchange of personal data between undertakings in different Member States is set to increase; whereas the national authorities in the various Member States are being called upon by virtue of Community law to collaborate and exchange personal data so as to be able to perform their duties or carry out tasks on behalf of an authority in another Member State within the context of the area without internal frontiers as constituted by the internal market;

(6) Whereas, furthermore, the increase in scientific and technical cooperation and the coordinated introduction of new telecommunications networks in the Community necessitate and facilitate cross-border flows of personal data;

(7) Whereas the difference in levels of protection of the rights and freedoms of individuals, notably the right to privacy, with regard to the processing of personal data afforded in the Member States may prevent the transmission of such data from the territory of one Member State to that of another Member State; whereas this difference may therefore constitute an obstacle to the pursuit of a number of economic activities at Community level, distort competition and impede authorities in the discharge of their responsibilities under Community law; whereas this difference in levels of protection is due to the existence of a wide variety of national laws, regulations and administrative provisions;

(8) Whereas, in order to remove the obstacles to flows of personal data, the level of protection of the rights and freedoms of individuals with regard to the processing of such data must be equivalent in all Member States; whereas this objective is vital to the internal market but cannot be achieved by the Member States alone, especially in view of the scale of the divergences which currently exist between the relevant laws in the Member States and the need to coordinate the laws of the Member States so as to ensure that the cross-border flow of personal data is regulated in a consistent manner that is in keeping with the objective of the internal market as provided for in Article 7a of the Treaty; whereas Community action to approximate those laws is therefore needed;

(9) Whereas, given the equivalent protection resulting from the approximation of national laws, the Member States will no longer be able to inhibit the free movement between them of personal data on grounds relating to protection of the rights and freedoms of individuals, and in particular the right to privacy; whereas Member States will be left a margin for manoeuvre, which may, in the context of implementation of the Directive, also be exercised by the business and social partners; whereas Member States will therefore be able to specify in their national law the general conditions governing the lawfulness of data processing; whereas in doing so the Member States shall strive to improve the protection currently provided by their legislation; whereas, within the limits of this margin for manoeuvre and in accordance with Community law, disparities could arise in the implementation of the Directive, and this could have an effect on the movement of data within a Member State as well as within the Community;

(10) Whereas the object of the national laws on the processing of personal data is to protect fundamental rights and freedoms, notably the right to privacy, which is recognized both in Article 8 of the European Convention for the Protection of Human Rights and Fundamental Freedoms and in the general principles of Community law; whereas, for that reason, the approximation of those laws must not result in any lessening of the protection they afford but must, on the contrary, seek to ensure a high level of protection in the Community;

(11) Whereas the principles of the protection of the rights and freedoms of individuals, notably the right to privacy, which are contained in this Directive, give substance to and amplify those contained in the Council of Europe Convention of 28 January 1981 for the Protection of Individuals with regard to Automatic Processing of Personal Data;

(12) Whereas the protection principles must apply to all processing of personal data by any person whose activities are governed by Community law; whereas there should be excluded

the processing of data carried out by a natural person in the exercise of activities which are exclusively personal or domestic, such as correspondence and the holding of records of addresses;
(13) Whereas the activities referred to in Titles V and VI of the Treaty on European Union regarding public safety, defence, State security or the activities of the State in the area of criminal laws fall outside the scope of Community law, without prejudice to the obligations incumbent upon Member States under Article 56 (2), Article 57 or Article 100a of the Treaty establishing the European Community; whereas the processing of personal data that is necessary to safeguard the economic well-being of the State does not fall within the scope of this Directive where such processing relates to State security matters;
(14) Whereas, given the importance of the developments under way, in the framework of the information society, of the techniques used to capture, transmit, manipulate, record, store or communicate sound and image data relating to natural persons, this Directive should be applicable to processing involving such data;
(15) Whereas the processing of such data is covered by this Directive only if it is automated or if the data processed are contained or are intended to be contained in a filing system structured according to specific criteria relating to individuals, so as to permit easy access to the personal data in question;
(16) Whereas the processing of sound and image data, such as in cases of video surveillance, does not come within the scope of this Directive if it is carried out for the purposes of public security, defence, national security or in the course of State activities relating to the area of criminal law or of other activities which do not come within the scope of Community law;
(17) Whereas, as far as the processing of sound and image data carried out for purposes of journalism or the purposes of literary or artistic expression is concerned, in particular in the audiovisual field, the principles of the Directive are to apply in a restricted manner according to the provisions laid down in Article 9;
(18) Whereas, in order to ensure that individuals are not deprived of the protection to which they are entitled under this Directive, any processing of personal data in the Community must be carried out in accordance with the law of one of the Member States; whereas, in this connection, processing carried out under the responsibility of a controller who is established in a Member State should be governed by the law of that State;
(19) Whereas establishment on the territory of a Member State implies the effective and real exercise of activity through stable arrangements; whereas the legal form of such an establishment, whether simply branch or a subsidiary with a legal personality, is not the determining factor in this respect; whereas, when a single controller is established on the territory of several Member States, particularly by means of subsidiaries, he must ensure, in order to avoid any circumvention of national rules, that each of the establishments fulfils the obligations imposed by the national law applicable to its activities;
(20) Whereas the fact that the processing of data is carried out by a person established in a third country must not stand in the way of the protection of individuals provided for in this Directive; whereas in these cases, the processing should be governed by the law of the Member State in which the means used are located, and there should be guarantees to ensure that the rights and obligations provided for in this Directive are respected in practice;
(21) Whereas this Directive is without prejudice to the rules of territoriality applicable in criminal matters;
(22) Whereas Member States shall more precisely define in the laws they enact or when bringing into force the measures taken under this Directive the general circumstances in which processing is lawful; whereas in particular Article 5, in conjunction with Articles 7 and 8, allows Member States, independently of general rules, to provide for special processing conditions for specific sectors and for the various categories of data covered by Article 8;

(23) Whereas Member States are empowered to ensure the implementation of the protection of individuals both by means of a general law on the protection of individuals as regards the processing of personal data and by sectorial laws such as those relating, for example, to statistical institutes;
(24) Whereas the legislation concerning the protection of legal persons with regard to the processing data which concerns them is not affected by this Directive;
(25) Whereas the principles of protection must be reflected, on the one hand, in the obligations imposed on persons, public authorities, enterprises, agencies or other bodies responsible for processing, in particular regarding data quality, technical security, notification to the supervisory authority, and the circumstances under which processing can be carried out, and, on the other hand, in the right conferred on individuals, the data on whom are the subject of processing, to be informed that processing is taking place, to consult the data, to request corrections and even to object to processing in certain circumstances;
(26) Whereas the principles of protection must apply to any information concerning an identified or identifiable person; whereas, to determine whether a person is identifiable, account should be taken of all the means likely reasonably to be used either by the controller or by any other person to identify the said person; whereas the principles of protection shall not apply to data rendered anonymous in such a way that the data subject is no longer identifiable; whereas codes of conduct within the meaning of Article 27 may be a useful instrument for providing guidance as to the ways in which data may be rendered anonymous and retained in a form in which identification of the data subject is no longer possible;
(27) Whereas the protection of individuals must apply as much to automatic processing of data as to manual processing; whereas the scope of this protection must not in effect depend on the techniques used, otherwise this would create a serious risk of circumvention; whereas, nonetheless, as regards manual processing, this Directive covers only filing systems, not unstructured files; whereas, in particular, the content of a filing system must be structured according to specific criteria relating to individuals allowing easy access to the personal data; whereas, in line with the definition in Article 2 (c), the different criteria for determining the constituents of a structured set of personal data, and the different criteria governing access to such a set, may be laid down by each Member State; whereas files or sets of files as well as their cover pages, which are not structured according to specific criteria, shall under no circumstances fall within the scope of this Directive;
(28) Whereas any processing of personal data must be lawful and fair to the individuals concerned; whereas, in particular, the data must be adequate, relevant and not excessive in relation to the purposes for which they are processed; whereas such purposes must be explicit and legitimate and must be determined at the time of collection of the data; whereas the purposes of processing further to collection shall not be incompatible with the purposes as they were originally specified;
(29) Whereas the further processing of personal data for historical, statistical or scientific purposes is not generally to be considered incompatible with the purposes for which the data have previously been collected provided that Member States furnish suitable safeguards; whereas these safeguards must in particular rule out the use of the data in support of measures or decisions regarding any particular individual;
(30) Whereas, in order to be lawful, the processing of personal data must in addition be carried out with the consent of the data subject or be necessary for the conclusion or performance of a contract binding on the data subject, or as a legal requirement, or for the performance of a task carried out in the public interest or in the exercise of official authority, or in the legitimate interests of a natural or legal person, provided that the interests or the rights and freedoms of the data subject are not overriding; whereas, in particular, in order to maintain a balance between the interests involved while guaranteeing effective competition, Member States may determine the circumstances in which personal data may be used or disclosed to a third party

in the context of the legitimate ordinary business activities of companies and other bodies; whereas Member States may similarly specify the conditions under which personal data may be disclosed to a third party for the purposes of marketing whether carried out commercially or by a charitable organization or by any other association or foundation, of a political nature for example, subject to the provisions allowing a data subject to object to the processing of data regarding him, at no cost and without having to state his reasons;

(31) Whereas the processing of personal data must equally be regarded as lawful where it is carried out in order to protect an interest which is essential for the data subject's life;

(32) Whereas it is for national legislation to determine whether the controller performing a task carried out in the public interest or in the exercise of official authority should be a public administration or another natural or legal person governed by public law, or by private law such as a professional association;

(33) Whereas data which are capable by their nature of infringing fundamental freedoms or privacy should not be processed unless the data subject gives his explicit consent; whereas, however, derogations from this prohibition must be explicitly provided for in respect of specific needs, in particular where the processing of these data is carried out for certain health-related purposes by persons subject to a legal obligation of professional secrecy or in the course of legitimate activities by certain associations or foundations the purpose of which is to permit the exercise of fundamental freedoms;

(34) Whereas Member States must also be authorized, when justified by grounds of important public interest, to derogate from the prohibition on processing sensitive categories of data where important reasons of public interest so justify in areas such as public health and social protection - especially in order to ensure the quality and cost-effectiveness of the procedures used for settling claims for benefits and services in the health insurance system - scientific research and government statistics; whereas it is incumbent on them, however, to provide specific and suitable safeguards so as to protect the fundamental rights and the privacy of individuals;

(35) Whereas, moreover, the processing of personal data by official authorities for achieving aims, laid down in constitutional law or international public law, of officially recognized religious associations is carried out on important grounds of public interest;

(36) Whereas where, in the course of electoral activities, the operation of the democratic system requires in certain Member States that political parties compile data on people's political opinion, the processing of such data may be permitted for reasons of important public interest, provided that appropriate safeguards are established;

(37) Whereas the processing of personal data for purposes of journalism or for purposes of literary of artistic expression, in particular in the audiovisual field, should qualify for exemption from the requirements of certain provisions of this Directive in so far as this is necessary to reconcile the fundamental rights of individuals with freedom of information and notably the right to receive and impart information, as guaranteed in particular in Article 10 of the European Convention for the Protection of Human Rights and Fundamental Freedoms; whereas Member States should therefore lay down exemptions and derogations necessary for the purpose of balance between fundamental rights as regards general measures on the legitimacy of data processing, measures on the transfer of data to third countries and the power of the supervisory authority; whereas this should not, however, lead Member States to lay down exemptions from the measures to ensure security of processing; whereas at least the supervisory authority responsible for this sector should also be provided with certain ex-post powers, e.g. to publish a regular report or to refer matters to the judicial authorities;

(38) Whereas, if the processing of data is to be fair, the data subject must be in a position to learn of the existence of a processing operation and, where data are collected from him, must be given accurate and full information, bearing in mind the circumstances of the collection;

(39) Whereas certain processing operations involve data which the controller has not collected directly from the data subject; whereas, furthermore, data can be legitimately disclosed to a third party, even if the disclosure was not anticipated at the time the data were collected from the data subject; whereas, in all these cases, the data subject should be informed when the data are recorded or at the latest when the data are first disclosed to a third party;

(40) Whereas, however, it is not necessary to impose this obligation of the data subject already has the information; whereas, moreover, there will be no such obligation if the recording or disclosure are expressly provided for by law or if the provision of information to the data subject proves impossible or would involve disproportionate efforts, which could be the case where processing is for historical, statistical or scientific purposes; whereas, in this regard, the number of data subjects, the age of the data, and any compensatory measures adopted may be taken into consideration;

(41) Whereas any person must be able to exercise the right of access to data relating to him which are being processed, in order to verify in particular the accuracy of the data and the lawfulness of the processing; whereas, for the same reasons, every data subject must also have the right to know the logic involved in the automatic processing of data concerning him, at least in the case of the automated decisions referred to in Article 15 (1); whereas this right must not adversely affect trade secrets or intellectual property and in particular the copyright protecting the software; whereas these considerations must not, however, result in the data subject being refused all information;

(42) Whereas Member States may, in the interest of the data subject or so as to protect the rights and freedoms of others, restrict rights of access and information; whereas they may, for example, specify that access to medical data may be obtained only through a health professional;

(43) Whereas restrictions on the rights of access and information and on certain obligations of the controller may similarly be imposed by Member States in so far as they are necessary to safeguard, for example, national security, defence, public safety, or important economic or financial interests of a Member State or the Union, as well as criminal investigations and prosecutions and action in respect of breaches of ethics in the regulated professions; whereas the list of exceptions and limitations should include the tasks of monitoring, inspection or regulation necessary in the three last-mentioned areas concerning public security, economic or financial interests and crime prevention; whereas the listing of tasks in these three areas does not affect the legitimacy of exceptions or restrictions for reasons of State security or defence;

(44) Whereas Member States may also be led, by virtue of the provisions of Community law, to derogate from the provisions of this Directive concerning the right of access, the obligation to inform individuals, and the quality of data, in order to secure certain of the purposes referred to above;

(45) Whereas, in cases where data might lawfully be processed on grounds of public interest, official authority or the legitimate interests of a natural or legal person, any data subject should nevertheless be entitled, on legitimate and compelling grounds relating to his particular situation, to object to the processing of any data relating to himself; whereas Member States may nevertheless lay down national provisions to the contrary;

(46) Whereas the protection of the rights and freedoms of data subjects with regard to the processing of personal data requires that appropriate technical and organizational measures be taken, both at the time of the design of the processing system and at the time of the processing itself, particularly in order to maintain security and thereby to prevent any unauthorized processing; whereas it is incumbent on the Member States to ensure that controllers comply with these measures; whereas these measures must ensure an appropriate level of security, taking into account the state of the art and the costs of their implementation in relation to the risks inherent in the processing and the nature of the data to be protected;

(47) Whereas where a message containing personal data is transmitted by means of a telecommunications or electronic mail service, the sole purpose of which is the transmission of such messages, the controller in respect of the personal data contained in the message will normally be considered to be the person from whom the message originates, rather than the person offering the transmission services; whereas, nevertheless, those offering such services will normally be considered controllers in respect of the processing of the additional personal data necessary for the operation of the service;

(48) Whereas the procedures for notifying the supervisory authority are designed to ensure disclosure of the purposes and main features of any processing operation for the purpose of verification that the operation is in accordance with the national measures taken under this Directive;

(49) Whereas, in order to avoid unsuitable administrative formalities, exemptions from the obligation to notify and simplification of the notification required may be provided for by Member States in cases where processing is unlikely adversely to affect the rights and freedoms of data subjects, provided that it is in accordance with a measure taken by a Member State specifying its limits; whereas exemption or simplification may similarly be provided for by Member States where a person appointed by the controller ensures that the processing carried out is not likely adversely to affect the rights and freedoms of data subjects; whereas such a data protection official, whether or not an employee of the controller, must be in a position to exercise his functions in complete independence;

(50) Whereas exemption or simplification could be provided for in cases of processing operations whose sole purpose is the keeping of a register intended, according to national law, to provide information to the public and open to consultation by the public or by any person demonstrating a legitimate interest;

(51) Whereas, nevertheless, simplification or exemption from the obligation to notify shall not release the controller from any of the other obligations resulting from this Directive;

(52) Whereas, in this context, ex post facto verification by the competent authorities must in general be considered a sufficient measure;

(53) Whereas, however, certain processing operation are likely to pose specific risks to the rights and freedoms of data subjects by virtue of their nature, their scope or their purposes, such as that of excluding individuals from a right, benefit or a contract, or by virtue of the specific use of new technologies; whereas it is for Member States, if they so wish, to specify such risks in their legislation;

(54) Whereas with regard to all the processing undertaken in society, the amount posing such specific risks should be very limited; whereas Member States must provide that the supervisory authority, or the data protection official in cooperation with the authority, check such processing prior to it being carried out; whereas following this prior check, the supervisory authority may, according to its national law, give an opinion or an authorization regarding the processing; whereas such checking may equally take place in the course of the preparation either of a measure of the national parliament or of a measure based on such a legislative measure, which defines the nature of the processing and lays down appropriate safeguards;

(55) Whereas, if the controller fails to respect the rights of data subjects, national legislation must provide for a judicial remedy; whereas any damage which a person may suffer as a result of unlawful processing must be compensated for by the controller, who may be exempted from liability if he proves that he is not responsible for the damage, in particular in cases where he establishes fault on the part of the data subject or in case of force majeure; whereas sanctions must be imposed on any person, whether governed by private of public law, who fails to comply with the national measures taken under this Directive;

(56) Whereas cross-border flows of personal data are necessary to the expansion of international trade; whereas the protection of individuals guaranteed in the Community by this

Directive does not stand in the way of transfers of personal data to third countries which ensure an adequate level of protection; whereas the adequacy of the level of protection afforded by a third country must be assessed in the light of all the circumstances surrounding the transfer operation or set of transfer operations;

(57) Whereas, on the other hand, the transfer of personal data to a third country which does not ensure an adequate level of protection must be prohibited;

(58) Whereas provisions should be made for exemptions from this prohibition in certain circumstances where the data subject has given his consent, where the transfer is necessary in relation to a contract or a legal claim, where protection of an important public interest so requires, for example in cases of international transfers of data between tax or customs administrations or between services competent for social security matters, or where the transfer is made from a register established by law and intended for consultation by the public or persons having a legitimate interest; whereas in this case such a transfer should not involve the entirety of the data or entire categories of the data contained in the register and, when the register is intended for consultation by persons having a legitimate interest, the transfer should be made only at the request of those persons or if they are to be the recipients;

(59) Whereas particular measures may be taken to compensate for the lack of protection in a third country in cases where the controller offers appropriate safeguards; whereas, moreover, provision must be made for procedures for negotiations between the Community and such third countries;

(60) Whereas, in any event, transfers to third countries may be effected only in full compliance with the provisions adopted by the Member States pursuant to this Directive, and in particular Article 8 thereof;

(61) Whereas Member States and the Commission, in their respective spheres of competence, must encourage the trade associations and other representative organizations concerned to draw up codes of conduct so as to facilitate the application of this Directive, taking account of the specific characteristics of the processing carried out in certain sectors, and respecting the national provisions adopted for its implementation;

(62) Whereas the establishment in Member States of supervisory authorities, exercising their functions with complete independence, is an essential component of the protection of individuals with regard to the processing of personal data;

(63) Whereas such authorities must have the necessary means to perform their duties, including powers of investigation and intervention, particularly in cases of complaints from individuals, and powers to engage in legal proceedings; whereas such authorities must help to ensure transparency of processing in the Member States within whose jurisdiction they fall;

(64) Whereas the authorities in the different Member States will need to assist one another in performing their duties so as to ensure that the rules of protection are properly respected throughout the European Union;

(65) Whereas, at Community level, a Working Party on the Protection of Individuals with regard to the Processing of Personal Data must be set up and be completely independent in the performance of its functions; whereas, having regard to its specific nature, it must advise the Commission and, in particular, contribute to the uniform application of the national rules adopted pursuant to this Directive;

(66) Whereas, with regard to the transfer of data to third countries, the application of this Directive calls for the conferment of powers of implementation on the Commission and the establishment of a procedure as laid down in Council Decision 87/373/EEC[4];

(67) Whereas an agreement on a modus vivendi between the European Parliament, the Council and the Commission concerning the implementing measures for acts adopted in accordance

---

[4] OJ No L 197, 18. 7. 1987, p. 33.

with the procedure laid down in Article 189b of the EC Treaty was reached on 20 December 1994;
(68) Whereas the principles set out in this Directive regarding the protection of the rights and freedoms of individuals, notably their right to privacy, with regard to the processing of personal data may be supplemented or clarified, in particular as far as certain sectors are concerned, by specific rules based on those principles;
(69) Whereas Member States should be allowed a period of not more than three years from the entry into force of the national measures transposing this Directive in which to apply such new national rules progressively to all processing operations already under way; whereas, in order to facilitate their cost-effective implementation, a further period expiring 12 years after the date on which this Directive is adopted will be allowed to Member States to ensure the conformity of existing manual filing systems with certain of the Directive's provisions; whereas, where data contained in such filing systems are manually processed during this extended transition period, those systems must be brought into conformity with these provisions at the time of such processing;
(70) Whereas it is not necessary for the data subject to give his consent again so as to allow the controller to continue to process, after the national provisions taken pursuant to this Directive enter into force, any sensitive data necessary for the performance of a contract concluded on the basis of free and informed consent before the entry into force of these provisions;
(71) Whereas this Directive does not stand in the way of a Member State's regulating marketing activities aimed at consumers residing in territory in so far as such regulation does not concern the protection of individuals with regard to the processing of personal data;
(72) Whereas this Directive allows the principle of public access to official documents to be taken into account when implementing the principles set out in this Directive,

HAVE ADOPTED THIS DIRECTIVE:

CHAPTER I: GENERAL PROVISIONS

Article 1 - Object of the Directive

1. In accordance with this Directive, Member States shall protect the fundamental rights and freedoms of natural persons, and in particular their right to privacy with respect to the processing of personal data.
2. Member States shall neither restrict nor prohibit the free flow of personal data between Member States for reasons connected with the protection afforded under paragraph 1.

Article 2 - Definitions

For the purposes of this Directive:
(a) 'personal data' shall mean any information relating to an identified or identifiable natural person ('data subject'); an identifiable person is one who can be identified, directly or indirectly, in particular by reference to an identification number or to one or more factors specific to his physical, physiological, mental, economic, cultural or social identity;
(b) 'processing of personal data' ('processing') shall mean any operation or set of operations which is performed upon personal data, whether or not by automatic means, such as collection, recording, organization, storage, adaptation or alteration, retrieval, consultation, use, disclosure by transmission, dissemination or otherwise making available, alignment or combination, blocking, erasure or destruction;
(c) 'personal data filing system' ('filing system') shall mean any structured set of personal data which are accessible according to specific criteria, whether centralized, decentralized or dispersed on a functional or geographical basis;

(d) 'controller' shall mean the natural or legal person, public authority, agency or any other body which alone or jointly with others determines the purposes and means of the processing of personal data; where the purposes and means of processing are determined by national or Community laws or regulations, the controller or the specific criteria for his nomination may be designated by national or Community law;
(e) 'processor' shall mean a natural or legal person, public authority, agency or any other body which processes personal data on behalf of the controller;
(f) 'third party' shall mean any natural or legal person, public authority, agency or any other body other than the data subject, the controller, the processor and the persons who, under the direct authority of the controller or the processor, are authorized to process the data;
(g) 'recipient' shall mean a natural or legal person, public authority, agency or any other body to whom data are disclosed, whether a third party or not; however, authorities which may receive data in the framework of a particular inquiry shall not be regarded as recipients;
(h) 'the data subject's consent' shall mean any freely given specific and informed indication of his wishes by which the data subject signifies his agreement to personal data relating to him being processed.

Article 3 - Scope

1. This Directive shall apply to the processing of personal data wholly or partly by automatic means, and to the processing otherwise than by automatic means of personal data which form part of a filing system or are intended to form part of a filing system.
2. This Directive shall not apply to the processing of personal data:
- in the course of an activity which falls outside the scope of Community law, such as those provided for by Titles V and VI of the Treaty on European Union and in any case to processing operations concerning public security, defence, State security (including the economic well-being of the State when the processing operation relates to State security matters) and the activities of the State in areas of criminal law,
- by a natural person in the course of a purely personal or household activity.

Article 4 - National law applicable

1. Each Member State shall apply the national provisions it adopts pursuant to this Directive to the processing of personal data where:
(a) the processing is carried out in the context of the activities of an establishment of the controller on the territory of the Member State; when the same controller is established on the territory of several Member States, he must take the necessary measures to ensure that each of these establishments complies with the obligations laid down by the national law applicable;
(b) the controller is not established on the Member State's territory, but in a place where its national law applies by virtue of international public law;
(c) the controller is not established on Community territory and, for purposes of processing personal data makes use of equipment, automated or otherwise, situated on the territory of the said Member State, unless such equipment is used only for purposes of transit through the territory of the Community.
2. In the circumstances referred to in paragraph 1 (c), the controller must designate a representative established in the territory of that Member State, without prejudice to legal actions which could be initiated against the controller himself.

CHAPTER II: GENERAL RULE ON THE LAWFULNESS OF THE PROCESSING OF PERSONAL DATA

Article 5

Member States shall, within the limits of the provisions of this Chapter, determine more precisely the conditions under which the processing of personal data is lawful.

SECTION I: PRINCIPLES RELATING TO DATA QUALITY

Article 6

1. Member States shall provide that personal data must be:
   (a) processed fairly and lawfully;
   (b) collected for specified, explicit and legitimate purposes and not further processed in a way incompatible with those purposes. Further processing of data for historical, statistical or scientific purposes shall not be considered as incompatible provided that Member States provide appropriate safeguards;
   (c) adequate, relevant and not excessive in relation to the purposes for which they are collected and/or further processed;
   (d) accurate and, where necessary, kept up to date; every reasonable step must be taken to ensure that data which are inaccurate or incomplete, having regard to the purposes for which they were collected or for which they are further processed, are erased or rectified;
   (e) kept in a form which permits identification of data subjects for no longer than is necessary for the purposes for which the data were collected or for which they are further processed. Member States shall lay down appropriate safeguards for personal data stored for longer periods for historical, statistical or scientific use.
2. It shall be for the controller to ensure that paragraph 1 is complied with.

SECTION II: CRITERIA FOR MAKING DATA PROCESSING LEGITIMATE

Article 7

Member States shall provide that personal data may be processed only if:
(a) the data subject has unambiguously given his consent; or
(b) processing is necessary for the performance of a contract to which the data subject is party or in order to take steps at the request of the data subject prior to entering into a contract; or
(c) processing is necessary for compliance with a legal obligation to which the controller is subject; or
(d) processing is necessary in order to protect the vital interests of the data subject; or
(e) processing is necessary for the performance of a task carried out in the public interest or in the exercise of official authority vested in the controller or in a third party to whom the data are disclosed; or
(f) processing is necessary for the purposes of the legitimate interests pursued by the controller or by the third party or parties to whom the data are disclosed, except where such interests are overridden by the interests for fundamental rights and freedoms of the data subject which require protection under Article 1 (1).

SECTION III: SPECIAL CATEGORIES OF PROCESSING

Article 8 - The processing of special categories of data

1. Member States shall prohibit the processing of personal data revealing racial or ethnic origin, political opinions, religious or philosophical beliefs, trade-union membership, and the processing of data concerning health or sex life.
2. Paragraph 1 shall not apply where:
(a) the data subject has given his explicit consent to the processing of those data, except where the laws of the Member State provide that the prohibition referred to in paragraph 1 may not be lifted by the data subject's giving his consent; or
(b) processing is necessary for the purposes of carrying out the obligations and specific rights of the controller in the field of employment law in so far as it is authorized by national law providing for adequate safeguards; or
(c) processing is necessary to protect the vital interests of the data subject or of another person where the data subject is physically or legally incapable of giving his consent; or
(d) processing is carried out in the course of its legitimate activities with appropriate guarantees by a foundation, association or any other non-profit-seeking body with a political, philosophical, religious or trade-union aim and on condition that the processing relates solely to the members of the body or to persons who have regular contact with it in connection with its purposes and that the data are not disclosed to a third party without the consent of the data subjects; or
(e) the processing relates to data which are manifestly made public by the data subject or is necessary for the establishment, exercise or defence of legal claims.
3. Paragraph 1 shall not apply where processing of the data is required for the purposes of preventive medicine, medical diagnosis, the provision of care or treatment or the management of health-care services, and where those data are processed by a health professional subject under national law or rules established by national competent bodies to the obligation of professional secrecy or by another person also subject to an equivalent obligation of secrecy.
4. Subject to the provision of suitable safeguards, Member States may, for reasons of substantial public interest, lay down exemptions in addition to those laid down in paragraph 2 either by national law or by decision of the supervisory authority.
5. Processing of data relating to offences, criminal convictions or security measures may be carried out only under the control of official authority, or if suitable specific safeguards are provided under national law, subject to derogations which may be granted by the Member State under national provisions providing suitable specific safeguards. However, a complete register of criminal convictions may be kept only under the control of official authority. Member States may provide that data relating to administrative sanctions or judgements in civil cases shall also be processed under the control of official authority.
6. Derogations from paragraph 1 provided for in paragraphs 4 and 5 shall be notified to the Commission.
7. Member States shall determine the conditions under which a national identification number or any other identifier of general application may be processed.

Article 9 - Processing of personal data and freedom of expression

Member States shall provide for exemptions or derogations from the provisions of this Chapter, Chapter IV and Chapter VI for the processing of personal data carried out solely for journalistic purposes or the purpose of artistic or literary expression only if they are necessary to reconcile the right to privacy with the rules governing freedom of expression.

SECTION IV: INFORMATION TO BE GIVEN TO THE DATA SUBJECT

Article 10 - Information in cases of collection of data from the data subject

Member States shall provide that the controller or his representative must provide a data subject from whom data relating to himself are collected with at least the following information, except where he already has it:
(a) the identity of the controller and of his representative, if any;
(b) the purposes of the processing for which the data are intended;
(c) any further information such as
- the recipients or categories of recipients of the data,
- whether replies to the questions are obligatory or voluntary, as well as the possible consequences of failure to reply,
- the existence of the right of access to and the right to rectify the data concerning him in so far as such further information is necessary, having regard to the specific circumstances in which the data are collected, to guarantee fair processing in respect of the data subject.

Article 11 - Information where the data have not been obtained from the data subject

1. Where the data have not been obtained from the data subject, Member States shall provide that the controller or his representative must at the time of undertaking the recording of personal data or if a disclosure to a third party is envisaged, no later than the time when the data are first disclosed provide the data subject with at least the following information, except where he already has it:
(a) the identity of the controller and of his representative, if any;
(b) the purposes of the processing;
(c) any further information such as
- the categories of data concerned,
- the recipients or categories of recipients,
- the existence of the right of access to and the right to rectify the data concerning him in so far as such further information is necessary, having regard to the specific circumstances in which the data are processed, to guarantee fair processing in respect of the data subject.
2. Paragraph 1 shall not apply where, in particular for processing for statistical purposes or for the purposes of historical or scientific research, the provision of such information proves impossible or would involve a disproportionate effort or if recording or disclosure is expressly laid down by law. In these cases Member States shall provide appropriate safeguards.

SECTION V: THE DATA SUBJECT'S RIGHT OF ACCESS TO DATA

Article 12 - Right of access

Member States shall guarantee every data subject the right to obtain from the controller:
(a) without constraint at reasonable intervals and without excessive delay or expense:
- confirmation as to whether or not data relating to him are being processed and information at least as to the purposes of the processing, the categories of data concerned, and the recipients or categories of recipients to whom the data are disclosed,
- communication to him in an intelligible form of the data undergoing processing and of any available information as to their source,
- knowledge of the logic involved in any automatic processing of data concerning him at least in the case of the automated decisions referred to in Article 15 (1);

(b) as appropriate the rectification, erasure or blocking of data the processing of which does not comply with the provisions of this Directive, in particular because of the incomplete or inaccurate nature of the data;
(c) notification to third parties to whom the data have been disclosed of any rectification, erasure or blocking carried out in compliance with (b), unless this proves impossible or involves a disproportionate effort.

SECTION VI: EXEMPTIONS AND RESTRICTIONS

Article 13 - Exemptions and restrictions

1. Member States may adopt legislative measures to restrict the scope of the obligations and rights provided for in Articles 6 (1), 10, 11 (1), 12 and 21 when such a restriction constitutes a necessary measures to safeguard:
(a) national security;
(b) defence;
(c) public security;
(d) the prevention, investigation, detection and prosecution of criminal offences, or of breaches of ethics for regulated professions;
(e) an important economic or financial interest of a Member State or of the European Union, including monetary, budgetary and taxation matters;
(f) a monitoring, inspection or regulatory function connected, even occasionally, with the exercise of official authority in cases referred to in (c), (d) and (e);
(g) the protection of the data subject or of the rights and freedoms of others.
2. Subject to adequate legal safeguards, in particular that the data are not used for taking measures or decisions regarding any particular individual, Member States may, where there is clearly no risk of breaching the privacy of the data subject, restrict by a legislative measure the rights provided for in Article 12 when data are processed solely for purposes of scientific research or are kept in personal form for a period which does not exceed the period necessary for the sole purpose of creating statistics.

SECTION VII: THE DATA SUBJECT'S RIGHT TO OBJECT

Article 14 - The data subject's right to object

Member States shall grant the data subject the right:
(a) at least in the cases referred to in Article 7 (e) and (f), to object at any time on compelling legitimate grounds relating to his particular situation to the processing of data relating to him, save where otherwise provided by national legislation. Where there is a justified objection, the processing instigated by the controller may no longer involve those data;
(b) to object, on request and free of charge, to the processing of personal data relating to him which the controller anticipates being processed for the purposes of direct marketing, or to be informed before personal data are disclosed for the first time to third parties or used on their behalf for the purposes of direct marketing, and to be expressly offered the right to object free of charge to such disclosures or uses. Member States shall take the necessary measures to ensure that data subjects are aware of the existence of the right referred to in the first subparagraph of (b).

Article 15 - Automated individual decisions

1. Member States shall grant the right to every person not to be subject to a decision which produces legal effects concerning him or significantly affects him and which is based solely on automated processing of data intended to evaluate certain personal aspects relating to him, such as his performance at work, creditworthiness, reliability, conduct, etc.
2. Subject to the other Articles of this Directive, Member States shall provide that a person may be subjected to a decision of the kind referred to in paragraph 1 if that decision:
(a) is taken in the course of the entering into or performance of a contract, provided the request for the entering into or the performance of the contract, lodged by the data subject, has been satisfied or that there are suitable measures to safeguard his legitimate interests, such as arrangements allowing him to put his point of view; or
(b) is authorized by a law which also lays down measures to safeguard the data subject's legitimate interests.

SECTION VIII: CONFIDENTIALITY AND SECURITY OF PROCESSING

Article 16 - Confidentiality of processing

Any person acting under the authority of the controller or of the processor, including the processor himself, who has access to personal data must not process them except on instructions from the controller, unless he is required to do so by law.

Article 17 - Security of processing

1. Member States shall provide that the controller must implement appropriate technical and organizational measures to protect personal data against accidental or unlawful destruction or accidental loss, alteration, unauthorized disclosure or access, in particular where the processing involves the transmission of data over a network, and against all other unlawful forms of processing. Having regard to the state of the art and the cost of their implementation, such measures shall ensure a level of security appropriate to the risks represented by the processing and the nature of the data to be protected.
2. The Member States shall provide that the controller must, where processing is carried out on his behalf, choose a processor providing sufficient guarantees in respect of the technical security measures and organizational measures governing the processing to be carried out, and must ensure compliance with those measures.
3. The carrying out of processing by way of a processor must be governed by a contract or legal act binding the processor to the controller and stipulating in particular that:
- the processor shall act only on instructions from the controller,
- the obligations set out in paragraph 1, as defined by the law of the Member State in which the processor is established, shall also be incumbent on the processor.
4. For the purposes of keeping proof, the parts of the contract or the legal act relating to data protection and the requirements relating to the measures referred to in paragraph 1 shall be in writing or in another equivalent form.

SECTION IX: NOTIFICATION

Article 18 - Obligation to notify the supervisory authority

1. Member States shall provide that the controller or his representative, if any, must notify the supervisory authority referred to in Article 28 before carrying out any wholly or partly

automatic processing operation or set of such operations intended to serve a single purpose or several related purposes.
2. Member States may provide for the simplification of or exemption from notification only in the following cases and under the following conditions:
- where, for categories of processing operations which are unlikely, taking account of the data to be processed, to affect adversely the rights and freedoms of data subjects, they specify the purposes of the processing, the data or categories of data undergoing processing, the category or categories of data subject, the recipients or categories of recipient to whom the data are to be disclosed and the length of time the data are to be stored, and/or
- where the controller, in compliance with the national law which governs him, appoints a personal data protection official, responsible in particular:
- for ensuring in an independent manner the internal application of the national provisions taken pursuant to this Directive
- for keeping the register of processing operations carried out by the controller, containing the items of information referred to in Article 21 (2), thereby ensuring that the rights and freedoms of the data subjects are unlikely to be adversely affected by the processing operations.
3. Member States may provide that paragraph 1 does not apply to processing whose sole purpose is the keeping of a register which according to laws or regulations is intended to provide information to the public and which is open to consultation either by the public in general or by any person demonstrating a legitimate interest.
4. Member States may provide for an exemption from the obligation to notify or a simplification of the notification in the case of processing operations referred to in Article 8 (2) (d).
5. Member States may stipulate that certain or all non-automatic processing operations involving personal data shall be notified, or provide for these processing operations to be subject to simplified notification.

Article 19 - Contents of notification

1. Member States shall specify the information to be given in the notification. It shall include at least:
(a) the name and address of the controller and of his representative, if any;
(b) the purpose or purposes of the processing;
(c) a description of the category or categories of data subject and of the data or categories of data relating to them;
(d) the recipients or categories of recipient to whom the data might be disclosed;
(e) proposed transfers of data to third countries;
(f) a general description allowing a preliminary assessment to be made of the appropriateness of the measures taken pursuant to Article 17 to ensure security of processing.
2. Member States shall specify the procedures under which any change affecting the information referred to in paragraph 1 must be notified to the supervisory authority.

Article 20 - Prior checking

1. Member States shall determine the processing operations likely to present specific risks to the rights and freedoms of data subjects and shall check that these processing operations are examined prior to the start thereof.
2. Such prior checks shall be carried out by the supervisory authority following receipt of a notification from the controller or by the data protection official, who, in cases of doubt, must consult the supervisory authority.

3. Member States may also carry out such checks in the context of preparation either of a measure of the national parliament or of a measure based on such a legislative measure, which define the nature of the processing and lay down appropriate safeguards.

Article 21 - Publicizing of processing operations

1. Member States shall take measures to ensure that processing operations are publicized.
2. Member States shall provide that a register of processing operations notified in accordance with Article 18 shall be kept by the supervisory authority. The register shall contain at least the information listed in Article 19 (1) (a) to (e).The register may be inspected by any person.
3. Member States shall provide, in relation to processing operations not subject to notification, that controllers or another body appointed by the Member States make available at least the information referred to in Article 19 (1) (a) to (e) in an appropriate form to any person on request. Member States may provide that this provision does not apply to processing whose sole purpose is the keeping of a register which according to laws or regulations is intended to provide information to the public and which is open to consultation either by the public in general or by any person who can provide proof of a legitimate interest.

CHAPTER III: JUDICIAL REMEDIES, LIABILITY AND SANCTIONS

Article 22 - Remedies

Without prejudice to any administrative remedy for which provision may be made, inter alia before the supervisory authority referred to in Article 28, prior to referral to the judicial authority, Member States shall provide for the right of every person to a judicial remedy for any breach of the rights guaranteed him by the national law applicable to the processing in question.

Article 23 - Liability

1. Member States shall provide that any person who has suffered damage as a result of an unlawful processing operation or of any act incompatible with the national provisions adopted pursuant to this Directive is entitled to receive compensation from the controller for the damage suffered.
2. The controller may be exempted from this liability, in whole or in part, if he proves that he is not responsible for the event giving rise to the damage.

Article 24 - Sanctions

The Member States shall adopt suitable measures to ensure the full implementation of the provisions of this Directive and shall in particular lay down the sanctions to be imposed in case of infringement of the provisions adopted pursuant to this Directive.

CHAPTER IV: TRANSFER OF PERSONAL DATA TO THIRD COUNTRIES

Article 25 - Principles

1. The Member States shall provide that the transfer to a third country of personal data which are undergoing processing or are intended for processing after transfer may take place only if, without prejudice to compliance with the national provisions adopted pursuant to the other provisions of this Directive, the third country in question ensures an adequate level of protection.

2. The adequacy of the level of protection afforded by a third country shall be assessed in the light of all the circumstances surrounding a data transfer operation or set of data transfer operations; particular consideration shall be given to the nature of the data, the purpose and duration of the proposed processing operation or operations, the country of origin and country of final destination, the rules of law, both general and sectoral, in force in the third country in question and the professional rules and security measures which are complied with in that country.
3. The Member States and the Commission shall inform each other of cases where they consider that a third country does not ensure an adequate level of protection within the meaning of paragraph 2.
4. Where the Commission finds, under the procedure provided for in Article 31 (2), that a third country does not ensure an adequate level of protection within the meaning of paragraph 2 of this Article, Member States shall take the measures necessary to prevent any transfer of data of the same type to the third country in question.
5. At the appropriate time, the Commission shall enter into negotiations with a view to remedying the situation resulting from the finding made pursuant to paragraph 4.
6. The Commission may find, in accordance with the procedure referred to in Article 31 (2), that a third country ensures an adequate level of protection within the meaning of paragraph 2 of this Article, by reason of its domestic law or of the international commitments it has entered into, particularly upon conclusion of the negotiations referred to in paragraph 5, for the protection of the private lives and basic freedoms and rights of individuals. Member States shall take the measures necessary to comply with the Commission's decision.

Article 26 - Derogations

1. By way of derogation from Article 25 and save where otherwise provided by domestic law governing particular cases, Member States shall provide that a transfer or a set of transfers of personal data to a third country which does not ensure an adequate level of protection within the meaning of Article 25 (2) may take place on condition that:
(a) the data subject has given his consent unambiguously to the proposed transfer; or
(b) the transfer is necessary for the performance of a contract between the data subject and the controller or the implementation of precontractual measures taken in response to the data subject's request; or
(c) the transfer is necessary for the conclusion or performance of a contract concluded in the interest of the data subject between the controller and a third party; or
(d) the transfer is necessary or legally required on important public interest grounds, or for the establishment, exercise or defence of legal claims; or
(e) the transfer is necessary in order to protect the vital interests of the data subject; or
(f) the transfer is made from a register which according to laws or regulations is intended to provide information to the public and which is open to consultation either by the public in general or by any person who can demonstrate legitimate interest, to the extent that the conditions laid down in law for consultation are fulfilled in the particular case.
2. Without prejudice to paragraph 1, a Member State may authorize a transfer or a set of transfers of personal data to a third country which does not ensure an adequate level of protection within the meaning of Article 25 (2), where the controller adduces adequate safeguards with respect to the protection of the privacy and fundamental rights and freedoms of individuals and as regards the exercise of the corresponding rights; such safeguards may in particular result from appropriate contractual clauses.
3. The Member State shall inform the Commission and the other Member States of the authorizations it grants pursuant to paragraph 2. If a Member State or the Commission objects on justified grounds involving the protection of the privacy and fundamental rights and freedoms of individuals, the Commission shall take appropriate measures in accordance

with the procedure laid down in Article 31 (2). Member States shall take the necessary measures to comply with the Commission's decision.
4. Where the Commission decides, in accordance with the procedure referred to in Article 31 (2), that certain standard contractual clauses offer sufficient safeguards as required by paragraph 2, Member States shall take the necessary measures to comply with the Commission's decision.

CHAPTER V: CODES OF CONDUCT

Article 27

1. The Member States and the Commission shall encourage the drawing up of codes of conduct intended to contribute to the proper implementation of the national provisions adopted by the Member States pursuant to this Directive, taking account of the specific features of the various sectors.
2. Member States shall make provision for trade associations and other bodies representing other categories of controllers which have drawn up draft national codes or which have the intention of amending or extending existing national codes to be able to submit them to the opinion of the national authority. Member States shall make provision for this authority to ascertain, among other things, whether the drafts submitted to it are in accordance with the national provisions adopted pursuant to this Directive. If it sees fit, the authority shall seek the views of data subjects or their representatives.
3. Draft Community codes, and amendments or extensions to existing Community codes, may be submitted to the Working Party referred to in Article 29. This Working Party shall determine, among other things, whether the drafts submitted to it are in accordance with the national provisions adopted pursuant to this Directive. If it sees fit, the authority shall seek the views of data subjects or their representatives. The Commission may ensure appropriate publicity for the codes which have been approved by the Working Party.

CHAPTER VI: SUPERVISORY AUTHORITY AND WORKING PARTY ON THE PROTECTION OF INDIVIDUALS WITH REGARD TO THE PROCESSING OF PERSONAL DATA

Article 28 - Supervisory authority

1. Each Member State shall provide that one or more public authorities are responsible for monitoring the application within its territory of the provisions adopted by the Member States pursuant to this Directive. These authorities shall act with complete independence in exercising the functions entrusted to them.
2. Each Member State shall provide that the supervisory authorities are consulted when drawing up administrative measures or regulations relating to the protection of individuals' rights and freedoms with regard to the processing of personal data.
3. Each authority shall in particular be endowed with:
- investigative powers, such as powers of access to data forming the subject-matter of processing operations and powers to collect all the information necessary for the performance of its supervisory duties,
- effective powers of intervention, such as, for example, that of delivering opinions before processing operations are carried out, in accordance with Article 20, and ensuring appropriate publication of such opinions, of ordering the blocking, erasure or destruction of data, of imposing a temporary or definitive ban on processing, of warning or admonishing

the controller, or that of referring the matter to national parliaments or other political institutions,
- the power to engage in legal proceedings where the national provisions adopted pursuant to this Directive have been violated or to bring these violations to the attention of the judicial authorities. Decisions by the supervisory authority which give rise to complaints may be appealed against through the courts.
4. Each supervisory authority shall hear claims lodged by any person, or by an association representing that person, concerning the protection of his rights and freedoms in regard to the processing of personal data. The person concerned shall be informed of the outcome of the claim. Each supervisory authority shall, in particular, hear claims for checks on the lawfulness of data processing lodged by any person when the national provisions adopted pursuant to Article 13 of this Directive apply. The person shall at any rate be informed that a check has taken place.
5. Each supervisory authority shall draw up a report on its activities at regular intervals. The report shall be made public.
6. Each supervisory authority is competent, whatever the national law applicable to the processing in question, to exercise, on the territory of its own Member State, the powers conferred on it in accordance with paragraph 3. Each authority may be requested to exercise its powers by an authority of another Member State. The supervisory authorities shall cooperate with one another to the extent necessary for the performance of their duties, in particular by exchanging all useful information.
7. Member States shall provide that the members and staff of the supervisory authority, even after their employment has ended, are to be subject to a duty of professional secrecy with regard to confidential information to which they have access.

Article 29 - Working Party on the Protection of Individuals with regard to the Processing of Personal Data

1. A Working Party on the Protection of Individuals with regard to the Processing of Personal Data, hereinafter referred to as 'the Working Party', is hereby set up. It shall have advisory status and act independently.
2. The Working Party shall be composed of a representative of the supervisory authority or authorities designated by each Member State and of a representative of the authority or authorities established for the Community institutions and bodies, and of a representative of the Commission. Each member of the Working Party shall be designated by the institution, authority or authorities which he represents. Where a Member State has designated more than one supervisory authority, they shall nominate a joint representative. The same shall apply to the authorities established for Community institutions and bodies.
3. The Working Party shall take decisions by a simple majority of the representatives of the supervisory authorities.
4. The Working Party shall elect its chairman. The chairman's term of office shall be two years. His appointment shall be renewable.
5. The Working Party's secretariat shall be provided by the Commission.
6. The Working Party shall adopt its own rules of procedure.
7. The Working Party shall consider items placed on its agenda by its chairman, either on his own initiative or at the request of a representative of the supervisory authorities or at the Commission's request.

Article 30

1. The Working Party shall:
(a) examine any question covering the application of the national measures adopted under this Directive in order to contribute to the uniform application of such measures;

(b) give the Commission an opinion on the level of protection in the Community and in third countries;
(c) advise the Commission on any proposed amendment of this Directive, on any additional or specific measures to safeguard the rights and freedoms of natural persons with regard to the processing of personal data and on any other proposed Community measures affecting such rights and freedoms;
(d) give an opinion on codes of conduct drawn up at Community level.
2. If the Working Party finds that divergences likely to affect the equivalence of protection for persons with regard to the processing of personal data in the Community are arising between the laws or practices of Member States, it shall inform the Commission accordingly.
3. The Working Party may, on its own initiative, make recommendations on all matters relating to the protection of persons with regard to the processing of personal data in the Community.
4. The Working Party's opinions and recommendations shall be forwarded to the Commission and to the committee referred to in Article 31.
5. The Commission shall inform the Working Party of the action it has taken in response to its opinions and recommendations. It shall do so in a report which shall also be forwarded to the European Parliament and the Council. The report shall be made public.
6. The Working Party shall draw up an annual report on the situation regarding the protection of natural persons with regard to the processing of personal data in the Community and in third countries, which it shall transmit to the Commission, the European Parliament and the Council. The report shall be made public.

CHAPTER VII: COMMUNITY IMPLEMENTING MEASURES

Article 31 - The Committee

1. The Commission shall be assisted by a committee composed of the representatives of the Member States and chaired by the representative of the Commission.
2. The representative of the Commission shall submit to the committee a draft of the measures to be taken. The committee shall deliver its opinion on the draft within a time limit which the chairman may lay down according to the urgency of the matter. The opinion shall be delivered by the majority laid down in Article 148 (2) of the Treaty. The votes of the representatives of the Member States within the committee shall be weighted in the manner set out in that Article. The chairman shall not vote. The Commission shall adopt measures which shall apply immediately. However, if these measures are not in accordance with the opinion of the committee, they shall be communicated by the Commission to the Council forthwith. It that event:
- the Commission shall defer application of the measures which it has decided for a period of three months from the date of communication,
- the Council, acting by a qualified majority, may take a different decision within the time limit referred to in the first indent.

FINAL PROVISIONS

Article 32

1. Member States shall bring into force the laws, regulations and administrative provisions necessary to comply with this Directive at the latest at the end of a period of three years from the date of its adoption. When Member States adopt these measures, they shall contain a reference to this Directive or be accompanied by such reference on the occasion of their

official publication. The methods of making such reference shall be laid down by the Member States.
2. Member States shall ensure that processing already under way on the date the national provisions adopted pursuant to this Directive enter into force, is brought into conformity with these provisions within three years of this date. By way of derogation from the preceding subparagraph, Member States may provide that the processing of data already held in manual filing systems on the date of entry into force of the national provisions adopted in implementation of this Directive shall be brought into conformity with Articles 6, 7 and 8 of this Directive within 12 years of the date on which it is adopted. Member States shall, however, grant the data subject the right to obtain, at his request and in particular at the time of exercising his right of access, the rectification, erasure or blocking of data which are incomplete, inaccurate or stored in a way incompatible with the legitimate purposes pursued by the controller.
3. By way of derogation from paragraph 2, Member States may provide, subject to suitable safeguards, that data kept for the sole purpose of historical research need not be brought into conformity with Articles 6, 7 and 8 of this Directive.
4. Member States shall communicate to the Commission the text of the provisions of domestic law which they adopt in the field covered by this Directive.

Article 33

The Commission shall report to the Council and the European Parliament at regular intervals, starting not later than three years after the date referred to in Article 32 (1), on the implementation of this Directive, attaching to its report, if necessary, suitable proposals for amendments. The report shall be made public. The Commission shall examine, in particular, the application of this Directive to the data processing of sound and image data relating to natural persons and shall submit any appropriate proposals which prove to be necessary, taking account of developments in information technology and in the light of the state of progress in the information society.

Article 34

This Directive is addressed to the Member States.

DIRECTIVE 97/66/EC OF THE EUROPEAN PARLIAMENT AND OF THE COUNCIL OF 15 DECEMBER 1997 CONCERNING THE PROCESSING OF PERSONAL DATA AND THE PROTECTION OF PRIVACY IN THE TELECOMMUNICATIONS SECTOR

(Official Journal L 024, 30/01/1998, p. 0001)

THE EUROPEAN PARLIAMENT AND THE COUNCIL OF THE EUROPEAN UNION,

Having regard to the Treaty establishing the European Community, and in particular Article 100a thereof,
Having regard to the proposal from the Commission[1],
Having regard to the opinion of the Economic and Social Committee[2],

Acting in accordance with the procedure laid down in Article 189b of the Treaty[3], in the light of the joint text approved by the Conciliation Committee on 6 November 1997,

(1) Whereas Directive 95/46/EC of the European Parliament and of the Council of 24 October 1995 on the protection of individuals with regard to the processing of personal data and on the free movement of such data[4] requires Member States to ensure the rights and freedoms of natural persons with regard to the processing of personal data, and in particular their right to privacy, in order to ensure the free flow of personal data in the Community;

(2) Whereas confidentiality of communications is guaranteed in accordance with the international instruments relating to human rights (in particular the European Convention for the Protection of Human Rights and Fundamental Freedoms) and the constitutions of the Member States;

(3) Whereas currently in the Community new advanced digital technologies are introduced in public telecommunications networks, which give rise to specific requirements concerning the protection of personal data and privacy of the user; whereas the development of the information society is characterised by the introduction of new telecommunications services; whereas the successful cross-border development of these services, such as video-on-demand, interactive television, is partly dependent on the confidence of the users that their privacy will not be at risk;

(4) Whereas this is the case, in particular, with the introduction of the Integrated Services Digital Network (ISDN) and digital mobile networks;

(5) Whereas the Council, in its Resolution of 30 June 1988 on the development of the common market for telecommunications services and equipment up to 1992[5], called for steps to be taken to protect personal data, in order to create an appropriate environment for the future development of telecommunications in the Community; whereas the Council re-emphasised the importance of the protection of personal data and privacy in its Resolution of 18 July 1989

---

[1] OJ C 200, 22.7.1994, p. 4.
[2] OJ C 159, 17.6.1991, p. 38.
[3] Opinion of the European Parliament of 11 March 1992 (OJ C 94, 13.4.1992, p. 198). Council Common Position of 12 September 1996 (OJ C 315, 24.10.1996, p. 30) and Decision of the European Parliament of 16 January 1997 (OJ C 33, 3.2.1997, p. 78). Decision of the European Parliament of 20 November 1997 (OJ C 371, 8.12.1997). Council Decision of 1 December 1997.
[4] OJ L 281, 23.11.1995, p. 31.
[5] OJ C 257, 4.10.1988, p. 1.

on the strengthening of the coordination for the introduction of the Integrated Services Digital Network (ISDN) in the European Community up to 1992[6];
(6) Whereas the European Parliament has underlined the importance of the protection of personal data and privacy in the telecommunications networks, in particular with regard to the introduction of the Integrated Services Digital Network (ISDN);
(7) Whereas, in the case of public telecommunications networks, specific legal, regulatory, and technical provisions must be made in order to protect fundamental rights and freedoms of natural persons and legitimate interests of legal persons, in particular with regard to the increasing risk connected with automated storage and processing of data relating to subscribers and users;
(8) Whereas legal, regulatory, and technical provisions adopted by the Member States concerning the protection of personal data, privacy and the legitimate interest of legal persons, in the telecommunications sector, must be harmonised in order to avoid obstacles to the internal market for telecommunications in conformity with the objective set out in Article 7a of the Treaty; whereas the harmonisation is limited to requirements that are necessary to guarantee that the promotion and development of new telecommunications services and networks between Member States will not be hindered;
(9) Whereas the Member States, providers and users concerned, together with the competent Community bodies, should cooperate in introducing and developing the relevant technologies where this is necessary to apply the guarantees provided for by the provisions of this Directive.
(10) Whereas these new services include interactive television and video on demand;
(11) Whereas, in the telecommunications sector, in particular for all matters concerning protection of fundamental rights and freedoms, which are not specifically covered by the provisions of this Directive, including the obligations on the controller and the rights of individuals, Directive 95/46/EC applies; whereas Directive 95/46/EC applies to non-publicly available telecommunications services;
(12) Whereas this Directive, similarly to what is provided for by Article 3 of Directive 95/46/EC, does not address issues of protection of fundamental rights and freedoms related to activities which are not governed by Community law; whereas it is for Member States to take such measures as they consider necessary for the protection of public security, defence, State security (including the economic well-being of the State when the activities relate to State security matters) and the enforcement of criminal law; whereas this Directive shall not affect the ability of Member States to carry out lawful interception of telecommunications, for any of these purposes;
(13) Whereas subscribers of a publicly available telecommunications service may be natural or legal persons; whereas the provisions of this Directive are aimed to protect, by supplementing Directive 95/46/EC, the fundamental rights of natural persons and particularly their right to privacy, as well as the legitimate interests of legal persons; whereas these provisions may in no case entail an obligation for Member States to extend the application of Directive 95/46/EC to the protection of the legitimate interests of legal persons; whereas this protection is ensured within the framework of the applicable Community and national legislation;
(14) Whereas the application of certain requirements relating to presentation and restriction of calling and connected line identification and to automatic call forwarding to subscriber lines connected to analogue exchanges must not be made mandatory in specific cases where such application would prove to be technically impossible or would require a disproportionate economic effort; whereas it is important for interested parties to be informed of such cases and the Member States should therefore notify them to the Commission;
(15) Whereas service providers must take appropriate measures to safeguard the security of their services, if necessary in conjunction with the provider of the network, and inform

---

[6] OJ C 196, 1.8.1989, p. 4.

subscribers of any special risks of a breach of the security of the network; whereas security is appraised in the light of the provision of Article 17 of Directive 95/46/EC;
(16) Whereas measures must be taken to prevent the unauthorised access to communications in order to protect the confidentiality of communications by means of public telecommunications networks and publicly available telecommunications services; whereas national legislation in some Member States only prohibits intentional unauthorized access to communications;
(17) Whereas the data relating to subscribers processed to establish calls contain information on the private life of natural persons and concern the right to respect for their correspondence or concern the legitimate interests of legal persons; whereas such data may only be stored to the extent that is necessary for the provision of the service for the purpose of billing and for interconnection payments, and for a limited time; whereas any further processing which the provider of the publicly available telecommunications services may want to perform for the marketing of its own telecommunications services may only be allowed if the subscriber has agreed to this on the basis of accurate and full information given by the provider of the publicly available telecommunications services about the types of further processing he intends to perform;
(18) Whereas the introduction of itemized bills has improved the possibilities for the subscriber to verify the correctness of the fees charged by the service provider; whereas, at the same time, it may jeopardise the privacy of the users of publicly available telecommunications services; whereas therefore, in order to preserve the privacy of the user, Member States must encourage the development of telecommunications service options such as alternative payment facilities which allow anonymous or strictly private access to publicly available telecommunications services, for example calling cards and facilities for payment by credit card; whereas, alternatively, Member States may, for the same purpose, require the deletion of a certain number of digits from the called numbers mentioned in itemized bills;
(19) Whereas it is necessary, as regards calling line identification, to protect the right of the calling party to withhold the presentation of the identification of the line from which the call is being made and the right of the called party to reject calls from unidentified lines; whereas it is justified to override the elimination of calling line identification presentation in specific cases; whereas certain subscribers, in particular helplines and similar organizations, have an interest in guaranteeing the anonymity of their callers; whereas it is necessary, as regards connected line identification, to protect the right and the legitimate interest of the called party to withhold the presentation of the identification of the line to which the calling party is actually connected, in particular in the case of forwarded calls; whereas the providers of publicly available telecommunications services must inform their subscribers of the existence of calling and connected line identification in the network and of all services which are offered on the basis of calling and connected line identification and about the privacy options which are available; whereas this will allow the subscribers to make an informed choice about the privacy facilities they may want to use; whereas the privacy options which are offered on a per-line basis do not necessarily have to be available as an automatic network service but may be obtainable through a simple request to the provider of the publicly available telecommunications service;
(20) Whereas safeguards must be provided for subscribers against the nuisance which may be caused by automatic call forwarding by others; whereas, in such cases, it must be possible for subscribers to stop the forwarded calls being passed on to their terminals by simple request to the provider of the publicly available telecommunications service;
(21) Whereas directories are widely distributed and publicly available; whereas the right to privacy of natural persons and the legitimate interest of legal persons require that subscribers are able to determine the extent to which their personal data are published in a directory; whereas Member States may limit this possibility to subscribers who are natural persons;

(22) Whereas safeguards must be provided for subscribers against intrusion into their privacy by means of unsolicited calls and telefaxes; whereas Member States may limit such safeguards to subscribers who are natural persons;

(23) Whereas it is necessary to ensure that the introduction of technical features of telecommunications equipment for data protection purposes is harmonised in order to be compatible with the implementation of the internal market;

(24) Whereas in particular, similarly to what is provided for by Article 13 of Directive 95/46/EC, Member States can restrict the scope of subscribers' obligations and rights in certain circumstances, for example by ensuring that the provider of a publicly available telecommunications service may override the elimination of the presentation of calling line identification in conformity with national legislation for the purpose of prevention or detection of criminal offences or State security;

(25) Whereas where the rights of the users and subscribers are not respected, national legislation must provide for judicial remedy; whereas sanctions must be imposed on any person, whether governed by private or public law, who fails to comply with the national measures taken under this Directive;

(26) Whereas it is useful in the field of application of this Directive to draw on the experience of the Working Party on the protection of individuals with regard to the processing of personal data composed of representatives of the supervisory authorities of the Member States, set up by Article 29 of Directive 95/46/EC;

(27) Whereas, given the technological developments and the attendant evolution of the services on offer, it will be necessary technically to specify the categories of data listed in the Annex to this Directive for the application of Article 6 of this Directive with the assistance of the Committee composed of representatives of the Member States set up in Article 31 of Directive 95/46/EC in order to ensure a coherent application of the requirements set out in this Directive regardless of changes in technology; whereas this procedure applies solely to specifications necessary to adapt the Annex to new technological developments, taking into consideration changes in market and consumer demand; whereas the Commission must duly inform the European Parliament of its intention to apply this procedure and whereas, otherwise, the procedure laid down in Article 100a of the Treaty shall apply;

(28) Whereas, to facilitate compliance with the provisions of this Directive, certain specific arrangements are needed for processing of data already under way on the date that national implementing legislation pursuant to this Directive enters into force,

HAVE ADOPTED THIS DIRECTIVE:

Article 1 - Object and scope

1. This Directive provides for the harmonisation of the provisions of the Member States required to ensure an equivalent level of protection of fundamental rights and freedoms, and in particular the right to privacy, with respect to the processing of personal data in the telecommunications sector and to ensure the free movement of such data and of telecommunications equipment and services in the Community.
2. The provisions of this Directive particularise and complement Directive 95/46/EC for the purposes mentioned in paragraph 1. Moreover, they provide for protection of legitimate interests of subscribers who are legal persons.
3. This Directive shall not apply to the activities which fall outside the scope of Community law, such as those provided for by Titles V and VI of the Treaty on European Union, and in any case to activities concerning public security, defence, State security (including the economic well-being of the State when the activities relate to State security matters) and the activities of the State in areas of criminal law.

Article 2 - Definitions

In addition to the definitions given in Directive 95/46/EC, for the purposes of this Directive:
(a) 'subscriber' shall mean any natural or legal person who or which is party to a contract with the provider of publicly available telecommunications services for the supply of such services;
(b) 'user' shall mean any natural person using a publicly available telecommunications service, for private or business purposes, without necessarily having subscribed to this service;
(c) 'public telecommunications network' shall mean transmission systems and, where applicable, switching equipment and other resources which permit the conveyance of signals between defined termination points by wire, by radio, by optical or by other electromagnetic means, which are used, in whole or in part, for the provision of publicly available telecommunications services;
(d) 'telecommunications service' shall mean services whose provision consists wholly or partly in the transmission and routing of signals on telecommunications networks, with the exception of radio- and television broadcasting.

Article 3 - Services concerned

1. This Directive shall apply to the processing of personal data in connection with the provision of publicly available telecommunications services in public telecommunications networks in the Community, in particular via the Integrated Services Digital Network (ISDN) and public digital mobile networks.
2. Articles 8, 9 and 10 shall apply to subscriber lines connected to digital exchanges and, where technically possible and if it does not require a disproportionate economic effort, to subscriber lines connected to analogue exchanges.
3. Cases where it would be technically impossible or require a disproportionate investment to fulfil the requirements of Articles 8, 9 and 10 shall be notified to the Commission by the Member States.

Article 4 - Security

1. The provider of a publicly available telecommunications service must take appropriate technical and organisational measures to safeguard security of its services, if necessary in conjunction with the provider of the public telecommunications network with respect to network security. Having regard to the state of the art and the cost of their implementation, these measures shall ensure a level of security appropriate to the risk presented.
2. In case of a particular risk of a breach of the security of the network, the provider of a publicly available telecommunications service must inform the subscribers concerning such risk and any possible remedies, including the costs involved.

Article 5 - Confidentiality of the communications

1. Member States shall ensure via national regulations the confidentiality of communications by means of a public telecommunications network and publicly available telecommunications services. In particular, they shall prohibit listening, tapping, storage or other kinds of interception or surveillance of communications, by others than users, without the consent of the users concerned, except when legally authorised, in accordance with Article 14 (1).
2. Paragraph 1 shall not affect any legally authorised recording of communications in the course of lawful business practice for the purpose of providing evidence of a commercial transaction or of any other business communication.

Article 6 - Traffic and billing data

1. Traffic data relating to subscribers and users processed to establish calls and stored by the provider of a public telecommunications network and/or publicly available telecommunications service must be erased or made anonymous upon termination of the call without prejudice to the provisions of paragraphs 2, 3 and 4.
2. For the purpose of subscriber billing and interconnection payments, data indicated in the Annex may be processed. Such processing is permissible only up to the end of the period during which the bill may lawfully be challenged or payment may be pursued.
3. For the purpose of marketing its own telecommunications services, the provider of a publicly available telecommunications service may process the data referred to in paragraph 2, if the subscriber has given his consent.
4. Processing of traffic and billing data must be restricted to persons acting under the authority of providers of the public telecommunications networks and/or publicly available telecommunications services handling billing or traffic management, customer enquiries, fraud detection and marketing the provider's own telecommunications services and it must be restricted to what is necessary for the purposes of such activities.
5. Paragraphs 1, 2, 3 and 4 shall apply without prejudice to the possibility for competent authorities to be informed of billing or traffic data in conformity with applicable legislation in view of settling disputes, in particular interconnection or billing disputes.

Article 7 - Itemized billing

1. Subscribers shall have the right to receive non-itemized bills.
2. Member States shall apply national provisions in order to reconcile the rights of subscribers receiving itemised bills with the right to privacy of calling users and called subscribers, for example by ensuring that sufficient alternative modalities for communications or payments are available to such users and subscribers.

Article 8 - Presentation and restriction of calling and connected line identification

1. Where presentation of calling-line identification is offered, the calling user must have the possibility via a simple means, free of charge, to eliminate the presentation of the calling-line identification on a per-call basis. The calling subscriber must have this possibility on a per-line basis.
2. Where presentation of calling-line identification is offered, the called subscriber must have the possibility via a simple means, free of charge for reasonable use of this function, to prevent the presentation of the calling line identification of incoming calls.
3. Where presentation of calling line identification is offered and where the calling line identification is presented prior to the call being established, the called subscriber must have the possibility via a simple means to reject incoming calls where the presentation of the calling line identification has been eliminated by the calling user or subscriber.
4. Where presentation of connected line identification is offered, the called subscriber must have the possibility via a simple means, free of charge, to eliminate the presentation of the connected line identification to the calling user.
5. The provisions set out in paragraph 1 shall also apply with regard to calls to third countries originating in the Community; the provisions set out in paragraphs 2, 3 and 4 shall also apply to incoming calls originating in third countries.
6. Member States shall ensure that where presentation of calling and/or connected line identification is offered, the providers of publicly available telecommunications services inform the public thereof and of the possibilities set out in paragraphs 1, 2, 3 and 4.

Article 9 - Exceptions

Member States shall ensure that there are transparent procedures governing the way in which a provider of a public telecommunications network and/or a publicly available telecommunications service may override the elimination of the presentation of calling line identification:
(a) on a temporary basis, upon application of a subscriber requesting the tracing of malicious or nuisance calls; in this case, in accordance with national law, the data containing the identification of the calling subscriber will be stored and be made available by the provider of a public telecommunications network and/or publicly available telecommunications service;
(b) on a per-line basis for organisations dealing with emergency calls and recognized as such by a Member State, including law enforcement agencies, ambulance services and fire brigades, for the purpose of answering such calls.

Article 10 - Automatic call forwarding

Member States shall ensure that any subscriber is provided, free of charge and via a simple means, with the possibility to stop automatic call forwarding by a third party to the subscriber's terminal.

Article 11 - Directories of subscribers

1. Personal data contained in printed or electronic directories of subscribers available to the public or obtainable through directory enquiry services should be limited to what is necessary to identify a particular subscriber, unless the subscriber has given his unambiguous consent to the publication of additional personal data. The subscriber shall be entitled, free of charge, to be omitted from a printed or electronic directory at his or her request, to indicate that his or her personal data may not be used for the purpose of direct marketing, to have his or her address omitted in part and not to have a reference revealing his or her sex, where this is applicable linguistically.
2. Notwithstanding paragraph 1, Member States may allow operators to require a payment from subscribers wishing to ensure that their particulars are not entered in a directory, provided that the sum involved does not act as a disincentive to the exercise of this right, and that, taking account of the quality requirements of the public directory in the light of the universal service, it is limited to the actual costs incurred by the operator for the adaptation and updating of the list of subscribers not to be included in the public directory.
3. The rights conferred by paragraph 1 shall apply to subscribers who are natural persons. Member States shall also guarantee, in the framework of Community law and applicable national legislation, that the legitimate interests of subscribers other than natural persons with regard to their entry in public directories are sufficiently protected.

Article 12 - Unsolicited calls

1. The use of automated calling systems without human intervention (automatic calling machine) or facsimile machines (fax) for the purposes of direct marketing may only be allowed in respect of subscribers who have given their prior consent.
2. Member States shall take appropriate measures to ensure that, free of charge, unsolicited calls for purposes of direct marketing, by means other than those referred to in paragraph 1, are not allowed either without the consent of the subscribers concerned or in respect of subscribers who do not wish to receive these calls, the choice between these options to be determined by national legislation.
3. The rights conferred by paragraphs 1 and 2 shall apply to subscribers who are natural persons. Member States shall also guarantee, in the framework of Community law and applicable national legislation, that the legitimate interests of subscribers other than natural persons with regard to unsolicited calls are sufficiently protected.

Article 13 - Technical features and standardisation

1. In implementing the provisions of this Directive, Member States shall ensure, subject to paragraphs 2 and 3, that no mandatory requirements for specific technical features are imposed on terminal or other telecommunications equipment which could impede the placing of equipment on the market and the free circulation of such equipment in and between Member States.
2. Where provisions of this Directive can be implemented only by requiring specific technical features, Member States shall inform the Commission according to the procedures provided for by Directive 83/189/EEC[7] which lays down a procedure for the provision of information in the field of technical standards and regulations.
3. Where required, the Commission will ensure the drawing up of common European standards for the implementation of specific technical features, in accordance with Community legislation on the approximation of the laws of the Member States concerning telecommunications terminal equipment, including the mutual recognition of their conformity, and Council Decision 87/95/EEC of 22 December 1986 on standardisation in the field of information technology and telecommunications.[8]

Article 14 - Extension of the scope of application of certain provisions of Directive 95/46/EC

1. Member States may adopt legislative measures to restrict the scope of the obligations and rights provided for in Articles 5, 6 and Article 8(1), (2), (3) and (4), when such restriction constitutes a necessary measure to safeguard national security, defence, public security, the prevention, investigation, detection and prosecution of criminal offences or of unauthorised use of the telecommunications system, as referred to in Article 13(1) of Directive 95/46/EC.
2. The provisions of Chapter III on judicial remedies, liability and sanctions of Directive 95/46/EC shall apply with regard to national provisions adopted pursuant to this Directive and with regard to the individual rights derived from this Directive.
3. The Working Party on the Protection of Individuals with regard to the Processing of Personal Data established according to Article 29 of Directive 95/46/EC shall carry out the tasks laid down in Article 30 of the abovementioned Directive also with regard to the protection of fundamental rights and freedoms and of legitimate interests in the telecommunications sector, which is the subject of this Directive.
4. The Commission, assisted by the Committee established by Article 31 of Directive 95/46/EC, shall technically specify the Annex according to the procedure mentioned in this Article. The aforesaid Committee shall be convened specifically for the subjects covered by this Directive.

Article 15 - Implementation of the Directive

1. Member States shall bring into force the laws, regulations and administrative provisions necessary for them to comply with this Directive not later than 24 October 1998.By way of derogation from the first subparagraph, Member States shall bring into force the laws, regulations and administrative provisions necessary for them to comply with Article 5 of this Directive not later than 24 October 2000.When Member States adopt these measures, they shall contain a reference to this Directive or shall be accompanied by such a reference at the time of their official publication. The procedure for such reference shall be adopted by Member States.
2. By way of derogation from Article 6(3), consent is not required with respect to processing already under way on the date the national provisions adopted pursuant to this Directive

---

[7] OJ L 109, 26.4.1983, p. 8. Directive as last amended by Directive 94/10/EC (OJ L 100, 19.4.1994, p. 30).

[8] OJ L 36, 7.2.1987, p. 31. Decision as last amended by the 1994 Act of Accession.

enter into force. In those cases the subscribers shall be informed of this processing and if they do not express their dissent within a period to be determined by the Member State, they shall be deemed to have given their consent.
3. Article 11 shall not apply to editions of directories which have been published before the national provisions adopted pursuant to this Directive enter into force.
4. Member States shall communicate to the Commission the text of the provisions of national law which they adopt in the field governed by this Directive.

Article 16 - Addressees

This Directive is addressed to the Member States.

ANNEX

List of data

For the purpose referred to in Article 6(2) the following data may be processed:
Data containing the:
- number or identification of the subscriber station,
- address of the subscriber and the type of station,
- total number of units to be charged for the accounting period,
- called subscriber number,
- type, starting time and duration of the calls made and/or the data volume transmitted,
- date of the call/service, other information concerning payments such as advance payment, payments by instalments, disconnection and reminders.

7. Other Regulations

DIRECTIVE 98/84/EC OF THE EUROPEAN PARLIAMENT AND OF THE COUNCIL
OF 20 NOVEMBER 1998
ON THE LEGAL PROTECTION OF SERVICES BASED ON, OR CONSISTING OF, CONDITIONAL ACCESS

(Official Journal L 320, 28/11/1998, p. 0054)

THE EUROPEAN PARLIAMENT AND THE COUNCIL OF THE EUROPEAN UNION,

Having regard to the Treaty establishing the European Community, and in particular Articles 57(2), 66 and 100a thereof,
Having regard to the proposal from the Commission,[1]
Having regard to the opinion of the Economic and Social Committee,[2]

Acting in accordance with the procedure laid down in Article 189b of the Treaty,[3]

(1) Whereas the objectives of the Community as laid down in the Treaty include creating an ever closer union among the peoples of Europe and ensuring economic and social progress, by eliminating the barriers which divide them;

(2) Whereas the cross-border provision of broadcasting and information society services may contribute, from the individual point of view, to the full effectiveness of freedom of expression as a fundamental right and, from the collective point of view, to the achievement of the objectives laid down in the Treaty;

(3) Whereas the Treaty provides for the free movement of all services which are normally provided for remuneration; whereas this right, as applied to broadcasting and information society services, is also a specific manifestation in Community law of a more general principle, namely freedom of expression as enshrined in Article 10 of the European Convention for the Protection of Human Rights and Fundamental Freedoms; whereas that Article explicitly recognizes the right of citizens to receive and impart information regardless of frontiers and whereas any restriction of that right must be based on due consideration of other legitimate interests deserving of legal protection;

(4) Whereas the Commission undertook a wide-ranging consultation based on the Green Paper 'Legal Protection of Encrypted Services in the Internal Market'; whereas the results of that consultation confirmed the need for a Community legal instrument ensuring the legal protection of all those services whose remuneration relies on conditional access;

(5) Whereas the European Parliament, in its Resolution of 13 May 1997 on the Green Paper[4], called on the Commission to present a proposal for a Directive covering all encoded services in respect of which encoding is used to ensure payment of a fee, and agreed that this should

---

[1] OJ C 314, 16. 10. 1997, p. 7 and OJ C 203, 30. 6. 1998, p. 12.
[2] OJ C 129, 27. 4. 1998, p. 16.
[3] Opinion of the European Parliament of 30 April 1998 (OJ C 152, 18. 5. 1998, p. 59), Council Common Position of 29 June 1998 (OJ C 262, 19. 8. 1998, p. 34) and Decision of the European Parliament of 8 October 1998 (OJ C 328, 26. 10. 1998). Council Decision of 9 November 1998.
[4] OJ C 167, 2. 6. 1997, p. 31.

include information society services provided at a distance by electronic means and at the individual request of a service receiver, as well as broadcasting services;
(6) Whereas the opportunities offered by digital technologies provide the potential for increasing consumer choice and contributing to cultural pluralism, by developing an even wider range of services within the meaning of Articles 59 and 60 of the Treaty; whereas the viability of those services will often depend on the use of conditional access in order to obtain the remuneration of the service provider; whereas, accordingly, the legal protection of service providers against illicit devices which allow access to these services free of charge seems necessary in order to ensure the economic viability of the services;
(7) Whereas the importance of this issue was recognized by the Commission Communication on 'A European Initiative in Electronic Commerce';
(8) Whereas, in accordance with Article 7a of the Treaty, the internal market is to comprise an area without internal frontiers in which the free movement of services and goods is ensured; whereas Article 128(4) of the Treaty requires the Community to take cultural aspects into account in its action under other provisions of the Treaty; whereas by virtue of Article 130(3) of the Treaty, the Community must, through the policies and activities it pursues, contribute to creating the conditions necessary for the competitiveness of its industry;
(9) Whereas this Directive is without prejudice to possible future Community or national provisions meant to ensure that a number of broadcasting services, recognized as being of public interest, are not based on conditional access;
(10) Whereas this Directive is without prejudice to the cultural aspects of any further Community action concerning new services;
(11) Whereas the disparity between national rules concerning the legal protection of services based on, or consisting of, conditional access is liable to create obstacles to the free movement of services and goods;
(12) Whereas the application of the Treaty is not sufficient to remove these internal market obstacles; whereas those obstacles should therefore be removed by providing for an equivalent level of protection between Member States; whereas this implies an approximation of the national rules relating to the commercial activities which concern illicit devices;
(13) Whereas it seems necessary to ensure that Member States provide appropriate legal protection against the placing on the market, for direct or indirect financial gain, of an illicit device which enables or facilitates without authority the circumvention of any technological measures designed to protect the remuneration of a legally provided service;
(14) Whereas those commercial activities which concern illicit devices include commercial communications covering all forms of advertising, direct marketing, sponsorship, sales promotion and public relations promoting such products and services;
(15) Whereas those commercial activities are detrimental to consumers who are misled about the origin of illicit devices; whereas a high level of consumer protection is needed in order to fight against this kind of consumer fraud; whereas Article 129a(1) of the Treaty provides that the Community should contribute to the achievement of a high level of consumer protection by the measures it adopts pursuant to Article 100a thereof;
(16) Whereas, therefore, the legal framework for the creation of a single audiovisual area laid down in Council Directive 89/552/EEC of 3 October 1989 on the coordination of certain provisions laid down by law, regulation or administrative action in Member States concerning the pursuit of television broadcasting activities[5] should be supplemented with reference to conditional access techniques as laid down in this Directive, in order, not least, to ensure equal treatment of the suppliers of cross-border broadcasts, regardless of their place of establishment;

---

[5] OJ L 298, 17. 10. 1989, p. 23. Directive as amended by Directive 97/36/EC of the European Parliament and of the Council (OJ L 202, 30. 7. 1997, p. 60).

(17) Whereas, in accordance with the Council Resolution of 29 June 1995 on the effective uniform application of Community law and on the penalties applicable for breaches of Community law in the internal market,[6] Member States are required to take action to ensure that Community law is duly applied with the same effectiveness and thoroughness as national law;
(18) Whereas, in accordance with Article 5 of the Treaty, Member States are required to take all appropriate measures to guarantee the application and effectiveness of Community law, in particular by ensuring that the sanctions chosen are effective, dissuasive and proportionate and the remedies appropriate;
(19) Whereas the approximation of the laws, regulations and administrative provisions of the Member States should be limited to what is needed in order to achieve the objectives of the internal market, in accordance with the principle of proportionality as set out in the third paragraph of Article 3b of the Treaty;
(20) Whereas the distribution of illicit devices includes transfer by any means and putting such devices on the market for circulation inside or outside the Community;
(21) Whereas this Directive is without prejudice to the application of any national provisions which may prohibit the private possession of illicit devices, to the application of Community competition rules and to the application of Community rules concerning intellectual property rights;
(22) Whereas national law concerning sanctions and remedies for infringing commercial activities may provide that the activities have to be carried out in the knowledge or with reasonable grounds for knowing that the devices in question were illicit;
(23) Whereas the sanctions and remedies provided for under this Directive are without prejudice to any other sanction or remedy for which provision may be made under national law, such as preventive measures in general or seizure of illicit devices; whereas Member States are not obliged to provide criminal sanctions for infringing activities covered by this Directive; whereas Member States' provisions for actions for damages are to be in conformity with their national legislative and judicial systems;
(24) Whereas this Directive is without prejudice to the application of national rules which do not fall within the field herein coordinated, such as those adopted for the protection of minors, including those in compliance with Directive 89/552/EEC, or national provisions concerned with public policy or public security,

HAVE ADOPTED THIS DIRECTIVE:

Article 1 - Scope

The objective of this Directive is to approximate provisions in the Member States concerning measures against illicit devices which give unauthorised access to protected services.

Article 2 - Definitions

For the purposes of this Directive:
(a) protected service shall mean any of the following services, where provided against remuneration and on the basis of conditional access:
- television broadcasting, as defined in Article 1(a) of Directive 89/552/EEC,
- radio broadcasting, meaning any transmission by wire or over the air, including by satellite, of radio programmes intended for reception by the public,
- information society services within the meaning of Article 1(2) of Directive 98/34/EC of the European Parliament and of the Council of 22 June 1998 laying down a procedure for the

---

[6] OJ C 188, 22. 7. 1995, p. 1.

(b) conditional access shall mean any technical measure and/or arrangement whereby access to the protected service in an intelligible form is made conditional upon prior individual authorisation;
(c) conditional access device shall mean any equipment or software designed or adapted to give access to a protected service in an intelligible form;
(d) associated service shall mean the installation, maintenance or replacement of conditional access devices, as well as the provision of commercial communication services in relation to them or to protected services;
(e) illicit device shall mean any equipment or software designed or adapted to give access to a protected service in an intelligible form without the authorisation of the service provider;
(f) field coordinated by this Directive shall mean any provision relating to the infringing activities specified in Article 4.

Article 3 - Internal market principles

1. Each Member State shall take the measures necessary to prohibit on its territory the activities listed in Article 4, and to provide for the sanctions and remedies laid down in Article 5.
2. Without prejudice to paragraph 1, Member States may not:
(a) restrict the provision of protected services, or associated services, which originate in another Member State; or
(b) restrict the free movement of conditional access devices; for reasons falling within the field coordinated by this Directive.

Article 4 - Infringing activities

Member States shall prohibit on their territory all of the following activities:
(a) the manufacture, import, distribution, sale, rental or possession for commercial purposes of illicit devices;
(b) the installation, maintenance or replacement for commercial purposes of an illicit device;
(c) the use of commercial communications to promote illicit devices.

Article 5 - Sanctions and remedies

1. The sanctions shall be effective, dissuasive and proportionate to the potential impact of the infringing activity.
2. Member States shall take the necessary measures to ensure that providers of protected services whose interests are affected by an infringing activity as specified in Article 4, carried out on their territory, have access to appropriate remedies, including bringing an action for damages and obtaining an injunction or other preventive measure, and where appropriate, applying for disposal outside commercial channels of illicit devices.

Article 6 - Implementation

1. Member States shall bring into force the laws, regulations and administrative provisions necessary to comply with this Directive by 28 May 2000. They shall notify them to the Commission forthwith. When Member States adopt such measures, they shall contain a reference to this Directive or shall be accompanied by such reference at the time of their

---

[7] OJ L 204, 21. 7. 1998, p. 37. Directive as amended by Directive 98/48/EC (OJ L 217, 5. 8. 1998, p. 18).

official publication. The methods of making such reference shall be laid down by Member States.
2. Member States shall communicate to the Commission the text of the provisions of national law which they adopt in the field coordinated by this Directive.

Article 7 - Reports

Not later than three years after the entry into force of this Directive, and every two years thereafter, the Commission shall present a report to the European Parliament, the Council and the Economic and Social Committee concerning the implementation of this Directive accompanied, where appropriate, by proposals, in particular as regards the definitions under Article 2, for adapting it in light of technical and economic developments and of the consultations carried out by the Commission.

Article 8 - Entry into force

This Directive shall enter into force on the day of its publication in the Official Journal of the European Communities.

Article 9 - Addressees

This Directive is addressed to the Member States.

COUNCIL REGULATION (EC) NO 44/2001
OF 22 DECEMBER 2000
ON JURISDICTION AND THE RECOGNITION AND ENFORCEMENT OF JUDGMENTS IN CIVIL AND COMMERCIAL MATTERS

(Official Journal L 012, 16/01/2001, p. 0001)

THE COUNCIL OF THE EUROPEAN UNION,

Having regard to the Treaty establishing the European Community, and in particular Article 61(c) and Article 67(1) thereof,
Having regard to the proposal from the Commission[1],
Having regard to the opinion of the European Parliament[2],
Having regard to the opinion of the Economic and Social Committee[3],

Whereas:
(1) The Community has set itself the objective of maintaining and developing an area of freedom, security and justice, in which the free movement of persons is ensured. In order to establish progressively such an area, the Community should adopt, amongst other things, the measures relating to judicial cooperation in civil matters which are necessary for the sound operation of the internal market.
(2) Certain differences between national rules governing jurisdiction and recognition of judgments hamper the sound operation of the internal market. Provisions to unify the rules of conflict of jurisdiction in civil and commercial matters and to simplify the formalities with a view to rapid and simple recognition and enforcement of judgments from Member States bound by this Regulation are essential.
(3) This area is within the field of judicial cooperation in civil matters within the meaning of Article 65 of the Treaty.
(4) In accordance with the principles of subsidiarity and proportionality as set out in Article 5 of the Treaty, the objectives of this Regulation cannot be sufficiently achieved by the Member States and can therefore be better achieved by the Community. This Regulation confines itself to the minimum required in order to achieve those objectives and does not go beyond what is necessary for that purpose.
(5) On 27 September 1968 the Member States, acting under Article 293, fourth indent, of the Treaty, concluded the Brussels Convention on Jurisdiction and the Enforcement of Judgments in Civil and Commercial Matters, as amended by Conventions on the Accession of the New Member States to that Convention (hereinafter referred to as the 'Brussels Convention')[4]. On 16 September 1988 Member States and EFTA States concluded the Lugano Convention on Jurisdiction and the Enforcement of Judgments in Civil and Commercial Matters, which is a parallel Convention to the 1968 Brussels Convention. Work has been undertaken for the

---

[1] OJ C 376, 28.12.1999, p. 1.
[2] Opinion delivered on 21 September 2000 (not yet published in the Official Journal).
[3] OJ C 117, 26.4.2000, p. 6.
[4] OJ L 299, 31.12.1972, p. 32.
OJ L 304, 30.10.1978, p. 1.
OJ L 388, 31.12.1982, p. 1.
OJ L 285, 3.10.1989, p. 1.
OJ C 15, 15.1.1997, p. 1.
For a consolidated text, see OJ C 27, 26.1.1998, p. 1.

revision of those Conventions, and the Council has approved the content of the revised texts. Continuity in the results achieved in that revision should be ensured.

(6) In order to attain the objective of free movement of judgments in civil and commercial matters, it is necessary and appropriate that the rules governing jurisdiction and the recognition and enforcement of judgments be governed by a Community legal instrument which is binding and directly applicable.

(7) The scope of this Regulation must cover all the main civil and commercial matters apart from certain well-defined matters.

(8) There must be a link between proceedings to which this Regulation applies and the territory of the Member States bound by this Regulation. Accordingly common rules on jurisdiction should, in principle, apply when the defendant is domiciled in one of those Member States.

(9) A defendant not domiciled in a Member State is in general subject to national rules of jurisdiction applicable in the territory of the Member State of the court seised, and a defendant domiciled in a Member State not bound by this Regulation must remain subject to the Brussels Convention.

(10) For the purposes of the free movement of judgments, judgments given in a Member State bound by this Regulation should be recognised and enforced in another Member State bound by this Regulation, even if the judgment debtor is domiciled in a third State.

(11) The rules of jurisdiction must be highly predictable and founded on the principle that jurisdiction is generally based on the defendant's domicile and jurisdiction must always be available on this ground save in a few well-defined situations in which the subject-matter of the litigation or the autonomy of the parties warrants a different linking factor. The domicile of a legal person must be defined autonomously so as to make the common rules more transparent and avoid conflicts of jurisdiction.

(12) In addition to the defendant's domicile, there should be alternative grounds of jurisdiction based on a close link between the court and the action or in order to facilitate the sound administration of justice.

(13) In relation to insurance, consumer contracts and employment, the weaker party should be protected by rules of jurisdiction more favourable to his interests than the general rules provide for.

(14) The autonomy of the parties to a contract, other than an insurance, consumer or employment contract, where only limited autonomy to determine the courts having jurisdiction is allowed, must be respected subject to the exclusive grounds of jurisdiction laid down in this Regulation.

(15) In the interests of the harmonious administration of justice it is necessary to minimise the possibility of concurrent proceedings and to ensure that irreconcilable judgments will not be given in two Member States. There must be a clear and effective mechanism for resolving cases of lis pendens and related actions and for obviating problems flowing from national differences as to the determination of the time when a case is regarded as pending. For the purposes of this Regulation that time should be defined autonomously.

(16) Mutual trust in the administration of justice in the Community justifies judgments given in a Member State being recognised automatically without the need for any procedure except in cases of dispute.

(17) By virtue of the same principle of mutual trust, the procedure for making enforceable in one Member State a judgment given in another must be efficient and rapid. To that end, the declaration that a judgment is enforceable should be issued virtually automatically after purely formal checks of the documents supplied, without there being any possibility for the court to raise of its own motion any of the grounds for non-enforcement provided for by this Regulation.

(18) However, respect for the rights of the defence means that the defendant should be able to appeal in an adversarial procedure, against the declaration of enforceability, if he considers one of the grounds for non-enforcement to be present. Redress procedures should also be available to the claimant where his application for a declaration of enforceability has been rejected.

(19) Continuity between the Brussels Convention and this Regulation should be ensured, and transitional provisions should be laid down to that end. The same need for continuity applies as regards the interpretation of the Brussels Convention by the Court of Justice of the European Communities and the 1971 Protocol[5] should remain applicable also to cases already pending when this Regulation enters into force.

(20) The United Kingdom and Ireland, in accordance with Article 3 of the Protocol on the position of the United Kingdom and Ireland annexed to the Treaty on European Union and to the Treaty establishing the European Community, have given notice of their wish to take part in the adoption and application of this Regulation.

(21) Denmark, in accordance with Articles 1 and 2 of the Protocol on the position of Denmark annexed to the Treaty on European Union and to the Treaty establishing the European Community, is not participating in the adoption of this Regulation, and is therefore not bound by it nor subject to its application.

(22) Since the Brussels Convention remains in force in relations between Denmark and the Member States that are bound by this Regulation, both the Convention and the 1971 Protocol continue to apply between Denmark and the Member States bound by this Regulation.

(23) The Brussels Convention also continues to apply to the territories of the Member States which fall within the territorial scope of that Convention and which are excluded from this Regulation pursuant to Article 299 of the Treaty.

(24) Likewise for the sake of consistency, this Regulation should not affect rules governing jurisdiction and the recognition of judgments contained in specific Community instruments.

(25) Respect for international commitments entered into by the Member States means that this Regulation should not affect conventions relating to specific matters to which the Member States are parties.

(26) The necessary flexibility should be provided for in the basic rules of this Regulation in order to take account of the specific procedural rules of certain Member States. Certain provisions of the Protocol annexed to the Brussels Convention should accordingly be incorporated in this Regulation.

(27) In order to allow a harmonious transition in certain areas which were the subject of special provisions in the Protocol annexed to the Brussels Convention, this Regulation lays down, for a transitional period, provisions taking into consideration the specific situation in certain Member States.

(28) No later than five years after entry into force of this Regulation the Commission will present a report on its application and, if need be, submit proposals for adaptations.

(29) The Commission will have to adjust Annexes I to IV on the rules of national jurisdiction, the courts or competent authorities and redress procedures available on the basis of the amendments forwarded by the Member State concerned; amendments made to Annexes V and VI should be adopted in accordance with Council Decision 1999/468/EC of 28 June 1999

---

[5] OJ L 204, 2.8.1975, p. 28.
OJ L 304, 30.10.1978, p. 1.
OJ L 388, 31.12.1982, p. 1.
OJ L 285, 3.10.1989, p. 1.
OJ C 15, 15.1.1997, p. 1.
For a consolidated text see OJ C 27, 26.1.1998, p. 28.

laying down the procedures for the exercise of implementing powers conferred on the Commission[6],

HAS ADOPTED THIS REGULATION:

CHAPTER I: SCOPE

Article 1

1. This Regulation shall apply in civil and commercial matters whatever the nature of the court or tribunal. It shall not extend, in particular, to revenue, customs or administrative matters.
2. The Regulation shall not apply to:
(a) the status or legal capacity of natural persons, rights in property arising out of a matrimonial relationship, wills and succession;
(b) bankruptcy, proceedings relating to the winding-up of insolvent companies or other legal persons, judicial arrangements, compositions and analogous proceedings;
(c) social security;
(d) arbitration.
3. In this Regulation, the term ‚Member State™ shall mean Member States with the exception of Denmark.

CHAPTER II: JURISDICTION

SECTION 1: GENERAL PROVISIONS

Article 2

1. Subject to this Regulation, persons domiciled in a Member State shall, whatever their nationality, be sued in the courts of that Member State.
2. Persons who are not nationals of the Member State in which they are domiciled shall be governed by the rules of jurisdiction applicable to nationals of that State.

Article 3

1. Persons domiciled in a Member State may be sued in the courts of another Member State only by virtue of the rules set out in Sections 2 to 7 of this Chapter.
2. In particular the rules of national jurisdiction set out in Annex I shall not be applicable as against them.

Article 4

1. If the defendant is not domiciled in a Member State, the jurisdiction of the courts of each Member State shall, subject to Articles 22 and 23, be determined by the law of that Member State.
2. As against such a defendant, any person domiciled in a Member State may, whatever his nationality, avail himself in that State of the rules of jurisdiction there in force, and in particular those specified in Annex I, in the same way as the nationals of that State.

---

[6] OJ L 184, 17.7.1999, p. 23.

SECTION 2: SPECIAL JURISDICTION

Article 5

A person domiciled in a Member State may, in another Member State, be sued:
1.
(a) in matters relating to a contract, in the courts for the place of performance of the obligation in question;
(b) for the purpose of this provision and unless otherwise agreed, the place of performance of the obligation in question shall be:
- in the case of the sale of goods, the place in a Member State where, under the contract, the goods were delivered or should have been delivered,
- in the case of the provision of services, the place in a Member State where, under the contract, the services were provided or should have been provided,
(c) if subparagraph (b) does not apply then subparagraph (a) applies;
2. in matters relating to maintenance, in the courts for the place where the maintenance creditor is domiciled or habitually resident or, if the matter is ancillary to proceedings concerning the status of a person, in the court which, according to its own law, has jurisdiction to entertain those proceedings, unless that jurisdiction is based solely on the nationality of one of the parties;
3. in matters relating to tort, delict or quasi-delict, in the courts for the place where the harmful event occurred or may occur;
4. as regards a civil claim for damages or restitution which is based on an act giving rise to criminal proceedings, in the court seised of those proceedings, to the extent that that court has jurisdiction under its own law to entertain civil proceedings;
5. as regards a dispute arising out of the operations of a branch, agency or other establishment, in the courts for the place in which the branch, agency or other establishment is situated;
6. as settlor, trustee or beneficiary of a trust created by the operation of a statute, or by a written instrument, or created orally and evidenced in writing, in the courts of the Member State in which the trust is domiciled;
7. as regards a dispute concerning the payment of remuneration claimed in respect of the salvage of a cargo or freight, in the court under the authority of which the cargo or freight in question:
(a) has been arrested to secure such payment, or
(b) could have been so arrested, but bail or other security has been given; provided that this provision shall apply only if it is claimed that the defendant has an interest in the cargo or freight or had such an interest at the time of salvage.

Article 6

A person domiciled in a Member State may also be sued:
where he is one of a number of defendants, in the courts for the place where any one of them is
1. domiciled, provided the claims are so closely connected that it is expedient to hear and determine them together to avoid the risk of irreconcilable judgments resulting from separate proceedings;
2. as a third party in an action on a warranty or guarantee or in any other third party proceedings, in the court seised of the original proceedings, unless these were instituted solely with the object of removing him from the jurisdiction of the court which would be competent in his case;
3. on a counter-claim arising from the same contract or facts on which the original claim was based, in the court in which the original claim is pending;

4. in matters relating to a contract, if the action may be combined with an action against the same defendant in matters relating to rights in rem in immovable property, in the court of the Member State in which the property is situated.

Article 7

Where by virtue of this Regulation a court of a Member State has jurisdiction in actions relating to liability from the use or operation of a ship, that court, or any other court substituted for this purpose by the internal law of that Member State, shall also have jurisdiction over claims for limitation of such liability.

SECTION 3: JURISDICTION IN MATTERS RELATING TO INSURANCE

Article 8

In matters relating to insurance, jurisdiction shall be determined by this Section, without prejudice to Article 4 and point 5 of Article 5.

Article 9

1. An insurer domiciled in a Member State may be sued:
(a) in the courts of the Member State where he is domiciled, or
(b) in another Member State, in the case of actions brought by the policyholder, the insured or a beneficiary, in the courts for the place where the plaintiff is domiciled,
(c) if he is a co-insurer, in the courts of a Member State in which proceedings are brought against the leading insurer.
2. An insurer who is not domiciled in a Member State but has a branch, agency or other establishment in one of the Member States shall, in disputes arising out of the operations of the branch, agency or establishment, be deemed to be domiciled in that Member State.

Article 10

In respect of liability insurance or insurance of immovable property, the insurer may in addition be sued in the courts for the place where the harmful event occurred. The same applies if movable and immovable property are covered by the same insurance policy and both are adversely affected by the same contingency.

Article 11

1. In respect of liability insurance, the insurer may also, if the law of the court permits it, be joined in proceedings which the injured party has brought against the insured.
2. Articles 8, 9 and 10 shall apply to actions brought by the injured party directly against the insurer, where such direct actions are permitted.
3. If the law governing such direct actions provides that the policyholder or the insured may be joined as a party to the action, the same court shall have jurisdiction over them.

Article 12

1. Without prejudice to Article 11(3), an insurer may bring proceedings only in the courts of the Member State in which the defendant is domiciled, irrespective of whether he is the policyholder, the insured or a beneficiary.
2. The provisions of this Section shall not affect the right to bring a counter-claim in the court in which, in accordance with this Section, the original claim is pending.

Article 13

The provisions of this Section may be departed from only by an agreement:
1. which is entered into after the dispute has arisen, or
2. which allows the policyholder, the insured or a beneficiary to bring proceedings in courts other than those indicated in this Section, or
3. which is concluded between a policyholder and an insurer, both of whom are at the time of conclusion of the contract domiciled or habitually resident in the same Member State, and which has the effect of conferring jurisdiction on the courts of that State even if the harmful event were to occur abroad, provided that such an agreement is not contrary to the law of that State, or
4. which is concluded with a policyholder who is not domiciled in a Member State, except in so far as the insurance is compulsory or relates to immovable property in a Member State, or
5. which relates to a contract of insurance in so far as it covers one or more of the risks set out in Article 14.

Article 14

The following are the risks referred to in Article 13(5):
1. any loss of or damage to:
(a) seagoing ships, installations situated offshore or on the high seas, or aircraft, arising from perils which relate to their use for commercial purposes;
(b) goods in transit other than passengers' baggage where the transit consists of or includes carriage by such ships or aircraft;
2. any liability, other than for bodily injury to passengers or loss of or damage to their baggage:
(a) arising out of the use or operation of ships, installations or aircraft as referred to in point 1(a) in so far as, in respect of the latter, the law of the Member State in which such aircraft are registered does not prohibit agreements on jurisdiction regarding insurance of such risks;
(b) for loss or damage caused by goods in transit as described in point 1(b);
3. any financial loss connected with the use or operation of ships, installations or aircraft as referred to in point 1(a), in particular loss of freight or charter-hire;
4. any risk or interest connected with any of those referred to in points 1 to 3;
5. notwithstanding points 1 to 4, all ‚large risks™ as defined in Council Directive 73/239/EEC[7], as amended by Council Directives 88/357/EEC[8] and 90/618/EEC[9], as they may be amended.

SECTION 4: JURISDICTION OVER CONSUMER CONTRACTS

Article 15

1. In matters relating to a contract concluded by a person, the consumer, for a purpose which can be regarded as being outside his trade or profession, jurisdiction shall be determined by this Section, without prejudice to Article 4 and point 5 of Article 5, if:
(a) it is a contract for the sale of goods on instalment credit terms; or
(b) it is a contract for a loan repayable by instalments, or for any other form of credit, made to finance the sale of goods; or

---

[7] OJ L 228, 16.8.1973, p. 3. Directive as last amended by Directive 2000/26/EC of the European Parliament and of the Council (OJ L 181, 20.7.2000, p. 65).
[8] OJ L 172, 4.7.1988, p. 1. Directive as last amended by Directive 2000/26/EC.
[9] OJ L 330, 29.11.1990, p. 44.

(c) in all other cases, the contract has been concluded with a person who pursues commercial or professional activities in the Member State of the consumer's domicile or, by any means, directs such activities to that Member State or to several States including that Member State, and the contract falls within the scope of such activities.
2. Where a consumer enters into a contract with a party who is not domiciled in the Member State but has a branch, agency or other establishment in one of the Member States, that party shall, in disputes arising out of the operations of the branch, agency or establishment, be deemed to be domiciled in that State.
3. This Section shall not apply to a contract of transport other than a contract which, for an inclusive price, provides for a combination of travel and accommodation.

Article 16

1. A consumer may bring proceedings against the other party to a contract either in the courts of the Member State in which that party is domiciled or in the courts for the place where the consumer is domiciled.
2. Proceedings may be brought against a consumer by the other party to the contract only in the courts of the Member State in which the consumer is domiciled.
3. This Article shall not affect the right to bring a counter-claim in the court in which, in accordance with this Section, the original claim is pending.

Article 17

The provisions of this Section may be departed from only by an agreement:
1. which is entered into after the dispute has arisen; or
2. which allows the consumer to bring proceedings in courts other than those indicated in this Section; or
3. which is entered into by the consumer and the other party to the contract, both of whom are at the time of conclusion of the contract domiciled or habitually resident in the same Member State, and which confers jurisdiction on the courts of that Member State, provided that such an agreement is not contrary to the law of that Member State.

SECTION 5: JURISDICTION OVER INDIVIDUAL CONTRACTS OF EMPLOYMENT

Article 18

1. In matters relating to individual contracts of employment, jurisdiction shall be determined by this Section, without prejudice to Article 4 and point 5 of Article 5.
2. Where an employee enters into an individual contract of employment with an employer who is not domiciled in a Member State but has a branch, agency or other establishment in one of the Member States, the employer shall, in disputes arising out of the operations of the branch, agency or establishment, be deemed to be domiciled in that Member State.

Article 19

An employer domiciled in a Member State may be sued:
1. in the courts of the Member State where he is domiciled; or
2. in another Member State:
(a) in the courts for the place where the employee habitually carries out his work or in the courts for the last place where he did so, or
(b) if the employee does not or did not habitually carry out his work in any one country, in the courts for the place where the business which engaged the employee is or was situated.

Article 20

1. An employer may bring proceedings only in the courts of the Member State in which the employee is domiciled.
2. The provisions of this Section shall not affect the right to bring a counter-claim in the court in which, in accordance with this Section, the original claim is pending.

Article 21

The provisions of this Section may be departed from only by an agreement on jurisdiction:
1. which is entered into after the dispute has arisen; or
2. which allows the employee to bring proceedings in courts other than those indicated in this Section.

SECTION 6: EXCLUSIVE JURISDICTION

Article 22

The following courts shall have exclusive jurisdiction, regardless of domicile:
1. in proceedings which have as their object rights in rem in immovable property or tenancies of immovable property, the courts of the Member State in which the property is situated. However, in proceedings which have as their object tenancies of immovable property concluded for temporary private use for a maximum period of six consecutive months, the courts of the Member State in which the defendant is domiciled shall also have jurisdiction, provided that the tenant is a natural person and that the landlord and the tenant are domiciled in the same Member State;
2. in proceedings which have as their object the validity of the constitution, the nullity or the dissolution of companies or other legal persons or associations of natural or legal persons, or of the validity of the decisions of their organs, the courts of the Member State in which the company, legal person or association has its seat. In order to determine that seat, the court shall apply its rules of private international law;
3. in proceedings which have as their object the validity of entries in public registers, the courts of the Member State in which the register is kept;
4. in proceedings concerned with the registration or validity of patents, trade marks, designs, or other similar rights required to be deposited or registered, the courts of the Member State in which the deposit or registration has been applied for, has taken place or is under the terms of a Community instrument or an international convention deemed to have taken place.

    Without prejudice to the jurisdiction of the European Patent Office under the Convention on the Grant of European Patents, signed at Munich on 5 October 1973, the courts of each Member State shall have exclusive jurisdiction, regardless of domicile, in proceedings concerned with the registration or validity of any European patent granted for that State;
5. in proceedings concerned with the enforcement of judgments, the courts of the Member State in which the judgment has been or is to be enforced.

SECTION 7: PROROGATION OF JURISDICTION

Article 23

1. If the parties, one or more of whom is domiciled in a Member State, have agreed that a court or the courts of a Member State are to have jurisdiction to settle any disputes which have arisen or which may arise in connection with a particular legal relationship, that court or

those courts shall have jurisdiction. Such jurisdiction shall be exclusive unless the parties have agreed otherwise. Such an agreement conferring jurisdiction shall be either:
(a) in writing or evidenced in writing; or
(b) in a form which accords with practices which the parties have established between themselves; or
(c) in international trade or commerce, in a form which accords with a usage of which the parties are or ought to have been aware and which in such trade or commerce is widely known to, and regularly observed by, parties to contracts of the type involved in the particular trade or commerce concerned.
2. Any communication by electronic means which provides a durable record of the agreement shall be equivalent to 'writing'
3. Where such an agreement is concluded by parties, none of whom is domiciled in a Member State, the courts of other Member States shall have no jurisdiction over their disputes unless the court or courts chosen have declined jurisdiction.
4. The court or courts of a Member State on which a trust instrument has conferred jurisdiction shall have exclusive jurisdiction in any proceedings brought against a settlor, trustee or beneficiary, if relations between these persons or their rights or obligations under the trust are involved.
5. Agreements or provisions of a trust instrument conferring jurisdiction shall have no legal force if they are contrary to Articles 13, 17 or 21, or if the courts whose jurisdiction they purport to exclude have exclusive jurisdiction by virtue of Article 22.

Article 24

Apart from jurisdiction derived from other provisions of this Regulation, a court of a Member State before which a defendant enters an appearance shall have jurisdiction. This rule shall not apply where appearance was entered to contest the jurisdiction, or where another court has exclusive jurisdiction by virtue of Article 22.

SECTION 8: EXAMINATION AS TO JURISDICTION AND ADMISSIBILITY

Article 25

Where a court of a Member State is seised of a claim which is principally concerned with a matter over which the courts of another Member State have exclusive jurisdiction by virtue of Article 22, it shall declare of its own motion that it has no jurisdiction.

Article 26

1. Where a defendant domiciled in one Member State is sued in a court of another Member State and does not enter an appearance, the court shall declare of its own motion that it has no jurisdiction unless its jurisdiction is derived from the provisions of this Regulation.
2. The court shall stay the proceedings so long as it is not shown that the defendant has been able to receive the document instituting the proceedings or an equivalent document in sufficient time to enable him to arrange for his defence, or that all necessary steps have been taken to this end.
3. Article 19 of Council Regulation (EC) No 1348/2000 of 29 May 2000 on the service in the Member States of judicial and extrajudicial documents in civil or commercial matters[10] shall apply instead of the provisions of paragraph 2 if the document instituting the proceedings or

---

[10] OJ L 160, 30.6.2000, p. 37.

an equivalent document had to be transmitted from one Member State to another pursuant to this Regulation.
4. Where the provisions of Regulation (EC) No 1348/2000 are not applicable, Article 15 of the Hague Convention of 15 November 1965 on the Service Abroad of Judicial and Extrajudicial Documents in Civil or Commercial Matters shall apply if the document instituting the proceedings or an equivalent document had to be transmitted pursuant to that Convention.

SECTION 9: LIS PENDENS – RELATED ACTIONS

Article 27

1. Where proceedings involving the same cause of action and between the same parties are brought in the courts of different Member States, any court other than the court first seised shall of its own motion stay its proceedings until such time as the jurisdiction of the court first seised is established.
2. Where the jurisdiction of the court first seised is established, any court other than the court first seised shall decline jurisdiction in favour of that court.

Article 28

1. Where related actions are pending in the courts of different Member States, any court other than the court first seised may stay its proceedings.
2. Where these actions are pending at first instance, any court other than the court first seised may also, on the application of one of the parties, decline jurisdiction if the court first seised has jurisdiction over the actions in question and its law permits the consolidation thereof.
3. For the purposes of this Article, actions are deemed to be related where they are so closely connected that it is expedient to hear and determine them together to avoid the risk of irreconcilable judgments resulting from separate proceedings.

Article 29

Where actions come within the exclusive jurisdiction of several courts, any court other than the court first seised shall decline jurisdiction in favour of that court.

Article 30

For the purposes of this Section, a court shall be deemed to be seised:
1. at the time when the document instituting the proceedings or an equivalent document is lodged with the court, provided that the plaintiff has not subsequently failed to take the steps he was required to take to have service effected on the defendant, or
2. if the document has to be served before being lodged with the court, at the time when it is received by the authority responsible for service, provided that the plaintiff has not subsequently failed to take the steps he was required to take to have the document lodged with the court.

SECTION 10: PROVISIONAL, INCLDUING PROTECTIVE, MEASURES

Article 31

Application may be made to the courts of a Member State for such provisional, including protective, measures as may be available under the law of that State, even if, under this Regulation, the courts of another Member State have jurisdiction as to the substance of the matter.

CHAPTER III: RECOGNITION AND ENFORCEMENT

Article 32

For the purposes of this Regulation, 'judgment'means any judgment given by a court or tribunal of a Member State, whatever the judgment may be called, including a decree, order, decision or writ of execution, as well as the determination of costs or expenses by an officer of the court.

SECTION 1: RECOGNITION

Article 33

1. A judgment given in a Member State shall be recognised in the other Member States without any special procedure being required.
2. Any interested party who raises the recognition of a judgment as the principal issue in a dispute may, in accordance with the procedures provided for in Sections 2 and 3 of this Chapter, apply for a decision that the judgment be recognised.
3. If the outcome of proceedings in a court of a Member State depends on the determination of an incidental question of recognition that court shall have jurisdiction over that question.

Article 34

A judgment shall not be recognised:
1. if such recognition is manifestly contrary to public policy in the Member State in which recognition is sought;
2. where it was given in default of appearance, if the defendant was not served with the document which instituted the proceedings or with an equivalent document in sufficient time and in such a way as to enable him to arrange for his defence, unless the defendant failed to commence proceedings to challenge the judgment when it was possible for him to do so;
3. if it is irreconcilable with a judgment given in a dispute between the same parties in the Member State in which recognition is sought;
4. if it is irreconcilable with an earlier judgment given in another Member State or in a third State involving the same cause of action and between the same parties, provided that the earlier judgment fulfils the conditions necessary for its recognition in the Member State addressed.

Article 35

1. Moreover, a judgment shall not be recognised if it conflicts with Sections 3, 4 or 6 of Chapter II, or in a case provided for in Article 72.
2. In its examination of the grounds of jurisdiction referred to in the foregoing paragraph, the court or authority applied to shall be bound by the findings of fact on which the court of the Member State of origin based its jurisdiction.
3. Subject to the paragraph 1, the jurisdiction of the court of the Member State of origin may not be reviewed. The test of public policy referred to in point 1 of Article 34 may not be applied to the rules relating to jurisdiction.

Article 36

Under no circumstances may a foreign judgment be reviewed as to its substance.

Article 37

1. A court of a Member State in which recognition is sought of a judgment given in another Member State may stay the proceedings if an ordinary appeal against the judgment has been lodged.
2. A court of a Member State in which recognition is sought of a judgment given in Ireland or the United Kingdom may stay the proceedings if enforcement is suspended in the State of origin, by reason of an appeal.

SECTION 2: ENFORCEMENT

Article 38

1. A judgment given in a Member State and enforceable in that State shall be enforced in another Member State when, on the application of any interested party, it has been declared enforceable there.
2. However, in the United Kingdom, such a judgment shall be enforced in England and Wales, in Scotland, or in Northern Ireland when, on the application of any interested party, it has been registered for enforcement in that part of the United Kingdom.

Article 39

1. The application shall be submitted to the court or competent authority indicated in the list in Annex II.
2. The local jurisdiction shall be determined by reference to the place of domicile of the party against whom enforcement is sought, or to the place of enforcement.

Article 40

1. The procedure for making the application shall be governed by the law of the Member State in which enforcement is sought.
2. The applicant must give an address for service of process within the area of jurisdiction of the court applied to.
   However, if the law of the Member State in which enforcement is sought does not provide for the furnishing of such an address, the applicant shall appoint a representative ad litem.
3. The documents referred to in Article 53 shall be attached to the application.

Article 41

The judgment shall be declared enforceable immediately on completion of the formalities in Article 53 without any review under Articles 34 and 35. The party against whom enforcement is sought shall not at this stage of the proceedings be entitled to make any submissions on the application.

Article 42

1. The decision on the application for a declaration of enforceability shall forthwith be brought to the notice of the applicant in accordance with the procedure laid down by the law of the Member State in which enforcement is sought.
2. The declaration of enforceability shall be served on the party against whom enforcement is sought, accompanied by the judgment, if not already served on that party.

Article 43

1. The decision on the application for a declaration of enforceability may be appealed against by either party.
2. The appeal is to be lodged with the court indicated in the list in Annex III.
3. The appeal shall be dealt with in accordance with the rules governing procedure in contradictory matters.
4. If the party against whom enforcement is sought fails to appear before the appellate court in proceedings concerning an appeal brought by the applicant, Article 26(2) to (4) shall apply even where the party against whom enforcement is sought is not domiciled in any of the Member States.
5. An appeal against the declaration of enforceability is to be lodged within one month of service thereof. If the party against whom enforcement is sought is domiciled in a Member State other than that in which the declaration of enforceability was given, the time for appealing shall be two months and shall run from the date of service, either on him in person or at his residence. No extension of time may be granted on account of distance.

Article 44

The judgment given on the appeal may be contested only by the appeal referred to in Annex IV.

Article 45

1. The court with which an appeal is lodged under Article 43 or Article 44 shall refuse or revoke a declaration of enforceability only on one of the grounds specified in Articles 34 and 35. It shall give its decision without delay.
2. Under no circumstances may the foreign judgment be reviewed as to its substance.

Article 46

1. The court with which an appeal is lodged under Article 43 or Article 44 may, on the application of the party against whom enforcement is sought, stay the proceedings if an ordinary appeal has been lodged against the judgment in the Member State of origin or if the time for such an appeal has not yet expired; in the latter case, the court may specify the time within which such an appeal is to be lodged.
2. Where the judgment was given in Ireland or the United Kingdom, any form of appeal available in the Member State of origin shall be treated as an ordinary appeal for the purposes of paragraph 1.
3. The court may also make enforcement conditional on the provision of such security as it shall determine.

Article 47

1. When a judgment must be recognised in accordance with this Regulation, nothing shall prevent the applicant from availing himself of provisional, including protective, measures in accordance with the law of the Member State requested without a declaration of enforceability under Article 41 being required.
2. The declaration of enforceability shall carry with it the power to proceed to any protective measures.
3. During the time specified for an appeal pursuant to Article 43(5) against the declaration of enforceability and until any such appeal has been determined, no measures of enforcement may be taken other than protective measures against the property of the party against whom enforcement is sought.

Article 48

1. Where a foreign judgment has been given in respect of several matters and the declaration of enforceability cannot be given for all of them, the court or competent authority shall give it for one or more of them.
2. An applicant may request a declaration of enforceability limited to parts of a judgment.

Article 49

A foreign judgment which orders a periodic payment by way of a penalty shall be enforceable in the Member State in which enforcement is sought only if the amount of the payment has been finally determined by the courts of the Member State of origin.

Article 50

An applicant who, in the Member State of origin has benefited from complete or partial legal aid or exemption from costs or expenses, shall be entitled, in the procedure provided for in this Section, to benefit from the most favourable legal aid or the most extensive exemption from costs or expenses provided for by the law of the Member State addressed.

Article 51

No security, bond or deposit, however described, shall be required of a party who in one Member State applies for enforcement of a judgment given in another Member State on the ground that he is a foreign national or that he is not domiciled or resident in the State in which enforcement is sought.

Article 52

In proceedings for the issue of a declaration of enforceability, no charge, duty or fee calculated by reference to the value of the matter at issue may be levied in the Member State in which enforcement is sought.

SECTION 3: COMMON PROVISIONS

Article 53

1. A party seeking recognition or applying for a declaration of enforceability shall produce a copy of the judgment which satisfies the conditions necessary to establish its authenticity.
2. A party applying for a declaration of enforceability shall also produce the certificate referred to in Article 54, without prejudice to Article 55.

Article 54

The court or competent authority of a Member State where a judgment was given shall issue, at the request of any interested party, a certificate using the standard form in Annex V to this Regulation.

Article 55

1. If the certificate referred to in Article 54 is not produced, the court or competent authority may specify a time for its production or accept an equivalent document or, if it considers that it has sufficient information before it, dispense with its production.
2. If the court or competent authority so requires, a translation of the documents shall be produced. The translation shall be certified by a person qualified to do so in one of the Member States.

Article 56

No legalisation or other similar formality shall be required in respect of the documents referred to in Article 53 or Article 55(2), or in respect of a document appointing a representative ad litem.

CHAPTER IV: AUTHENTIC INSTRUMENTS AND COURT SETTLEMENTS

Article 57

1. A document which has been formally drawn up or registered as an authentic instrument and is enforceable in one Member State shall, in another Member State, be declared enforceable there, on application made in accordance with the procedures provided for in Articles 38, et seq. The court with which an appeal is lodged under Article 43 or Article 44 shall refuse or revoke a declaration of enforceability only if enforcement of the instrument is manifestly contrary to public policy in the Member State addressed.
2. Arrangements relating to maintenance obligations concluded with administrative authorities or authenticated by them shall also be regarded as authentic instruments within the meaning of paragraph 1.
3. The instrument produced must satisfy the conditions necessary to establish its authenticity in the Member State of origin.
4. Section 3 of Chapter III shall apply as appropriate. The competent authority of a Member State where an authentic instrument was drawn up or registered shall issue, at the request of any interested party, a certificate using the standard form in Annex VI to this Regulation.

Article 58

A settlement which has been approved by a court in the course of proceedings and is enforceable in the Member State in which it was concluded shall be enforceable in the State addressed under the same conditions as authentic instruments. The court or competent authority of a Member State where a court settlement was approved shall issue, at the request of any interested party, a certificate using the standard form in Annex V to this Regulation.

CHAPTER V: GENERAL PROVISIONS

Article 59

1. In order to determine whether a party is domiciled in the Member State whose courts are seised of a matter, the court shall apply its internal law.
2. If a party is not domiciled in the Member State whose courts are seised of the matter, then, in order to determine whether the party is domiciled in another Member State, the court shall apply the law of that Member State.

Article 60

1. For the purposes of this Regulation, a company or other legal person or association of natural or legal persons is domiciled at the place where it has its:
(a) statutory seat, or
(b) central administration, or
(c) principal place of business.
2. For the purposes of the United Kingdom and Ireland 'statutory seat' means the registered office or, where there is no such office anywhere, the place of incorporation or, where there is no such place anywhere, the place under the law of which the formation took place.

3. In order to determine whether a trust is domiciled in the Member State whose courts are seised of the matter, the court shall apply its rules of private international law.

Article 61

Without prejudice to any more favourable provisions of national laws, persons domiciled in a Member State who are being prosecuted in the criminal courts of another Member State of which they are not nationals for an offence which was not intentionally committed may be defended by persons qualified to do so, even if they do not appear in person. However, the court seised of the matter may order appearance in person; in the case of failure to appear, a judgment given in the civil action without the person concerned having had the opportunity to arrange for his defence need not be recognised or enforced in the other Member States.

Article 62

In Sweden, in summary proceedings concerning orders to pay (betalningsföreläggande) and assistance (handräckning), the expression 'court' includes the „Swedish enforcement 'service' (kronofogdemyndighet).

Article 63

1. A person domiciled in the territory of the Grand Duchy of Luxembourg and sued in the court of another Member State pursuant to Article 5(1) may refuse to submit to the jurisdiction of that court if the final place of delivery of the goods or provision of the services is in Luxembourg.
2. Where, under paragraph 1, the final place of delivery of the goods or provision of the services is in Luxembourg, any agreement conferring jurisdiction must, in order to be valid, be accepted in writing or evidenced in writing within the meaning of Article 23(1)(a).
3. The provisions of this Article shall not apply to contracts for the provision of financial services.
4. The provisions of this Article shall apply for a period of six years from entry into force of this Regulation.

Article 64

1. In proceedings involving a dispute between the master and a member of the crew of a seagoing ship registered in Greece or in Portugal, concerning remuneration or other conditions of service, a court in a Member State shall establish whether the diplomatic or consular officer responsible for the ship has been notified of the dispute. It may act as soon as that officer has been notified.
2. The provisions of this Article shall apply for a period of six years from entry into force of this Regulation.

Article 65

1. The jurisdiction specified in Article 6(2), and Article 11 in actions on a warranty of guarantee or in any other third party proceedings may not be resorted to in Germany and Austria. Any person domiciled in another Member State may be sued in the courts:
(a) of Germany, pursuant to Articles 68 and 72 to 74 of the Code of Civil Procedure (Zivilprozessordnung) concerning third-party notices,
(b) of Austria, pursuant to Article 21 of the Code of Civil Procedure (Zivilprozessordnung) concerning third-party notices.
2. Judgments given in other Member States by virtue of Article 6(2), or Article 11 shall be recognised and enforced in Germany and Austria in accordance with Chapter III. Any

effects which judgments given in these States may have on third parties by application of the provisions in paragraph 1 shall also be recognised in the other Member States.

CHAPTER VI: TRANSITIONAL PROVISIONS

Article 66

1. This Regulation shall apply only to legal proceedings instituted and to documents formally drawn up or registered as authentic instruments after the entry into force thereof.
2. However, if the proceedings in the Member State of origin were instituted before the entry into force of this Regulation, judgments given after that date shall be recognised and enforced in accordance with Chapter III,
(a) if the proceedings in the Member State of origin were instituted after the entry into force of the Brussels or the Lugano Convention both in the Member State or origin and in the Member State addressed;
(b) in all other cases, if jurisdiction was founded upon rules which accorded with those provided for either in Chapter II or in a convention concluded between the Member State of origin and the Member State addressed which was in force when the proceedings were instituted.

CHAPTER VII: RELATIONS WITH OTHER INSTRUMENTS

Article 67

This Regulation shall not prejudice the application of provisions governing jurisdiction and the recognition and enforcement of judgments in specific matters which are contained in Community instruments or in national legislation harmonised pursuant to such instruments.

Article 68

1. This Regulation shall, as between the Member States, supersede the Brussels Convention, except as regards the territories of the Member States which fall within the territorial scope of that Convention and which are excluded from this Regulation pursuant to Article 299 of the Treaty.
2. In so far as this Regulation replaces the provisions of the Brussels Convention between Member States, any reference to the Convention shall be understood as a reference to this Regulation.

Article 69

Subject to Article 66(2) and Article 70, this Regulation shall, as between Member States, supersede the following conventions and treaty concluded between two or more of them:
- the Convention between Belgium and France on Jurisdiction and the Validity and Enforcement of Judgments, Arbitration Awards and Authentic Instruments, signed at Paris on 8 July 1899,
- the Convention between Belgium and the Netherlands on Jurisdiction, Bankruptcy, and the Validity and Enforcement of Judgments, Arbitration Awards and Authentic Instruments, signed at Brussels on 28 March 1925,
- the Convention between France and Italy on the Enforcement of Judgments in Civil and Commercial Matters, signed at Rome on 3 June 1930,
- the Convention between Germany and Italy on the Recognition and Enforcement of Judgments in Civil and Commercial Matters, signed at Rome on 9 March 1936,
- the Convention between Belgium and Austria on the Reciprocal Recognition and Enforcement of Judgments and Authentic Instruments relating to Maintenance Obligations, signed at Vienna on 25 October 1957,

- the Convention between Germany and Belgium on the Mutual Recognition and Enforcement of Judgments, Arbitration Awards and Authentic Instruments in Civil and Commercial Matters, signed at Bonn on 30 June 1958,
- the Convention between the Netherlands and Italy on the Recognition and Enforcement of Judgments in Civil and Commercial Matters, signed at Rome on 17 April 1959,
- the Convention between Germany and Austria on the Reciprocal Recognition and Enforcement of Judgments, Settlements and Authentic Instruments in Civil and Commercial Matters, signed at Vienna on 6 June 1959,
- the Convention between Belgium and Austria on the Reciprocal Recognition and Enforcement of Judgments, Arbitral Awards and Authentic Instruments in Civil and Commercial Matters, signed at Vienna on 16 June 1959,
- the Convention between Greece and Germany for the Reciprocal Recognition and Enforcement of Judgments, Settlements and Authentic Instruments in Civil and Commercial Matters, signed in Athens on 4 November 1961,
- the Convention between Belgium and Italy on the Recognition and Enforcement of Judgments and other Enforceable Instruments in Civil and Commercial Matters, signed at Rome on 6 April 1962,
- the Convention between the Netherlands and Germany on the Mutual Recognition and Enforcement of Judgments and Other Enforceable Instruments in Civil and Commercial Matters, signed at The Hague on 30 August 1962,
- the Convention between the Netherlands and Austria on the Reciprocal Recognition and Enforcement of Judgments and Authentic Instruments in Civil and Commercial Matters, signed at The Hague on 6 February 1963,
- the Convention between France and Austria on the Recognition and Enforcement of Judgments and Authentic Instruments in Civil and Commercial Matters, signed at Vienna on 15 July 1966,
- the Convention between Spain and France on the Recognition and Enforcement of Judgment Arbitration Awards in Civil and Commercial Matters, signed at Paris on 28 May 1969,
- the Convention between Luxembourg and Austria on the Recognition and Enforcement of Judgments and Authentic Instruments in Civil and Commercial Matters, signed at Luxembourg on 29 July 1971,
- the Convention between Italy and Austria on the Recognition and Enforcement of Judgments in Civil and Commercial Matters, of Judicial Settlements and of Authentic Instruments, signed at Rome on 16 November 1971,
- the Convention between Spain and Italy regarding Legal Aid and the Recognition and Enforcement of Judgments in Civil and Commercial Matters, signed at Madrid on 22 May 1973,
- the Convention between Finland, Iceland, Norway, Sweden and Denmark on the Recognition and Enforcement of Judgments in Civil Matters, signed at Copenhagen on 11 October 1977,
- the Convention between Austria and Sweden on the Recognition and Enforcement of Judgments in Civil Matters, signed at Stockholm on 16 September 1982,
- the Convention between Spain and the Federal Republic of Germany on the Recognition and Enforcement of Judgments, Settlements and Enforceable Authentic Instruments in Civil and Commercial Matters, signed at Bonn on 14 November 1983,
- the Convention between Austria and Spain on the Recognition and Enforcement of Judgments, Settlements and Enforceable Authentic Instruments in Civil and Commercial Matters, signed at Vienna on 17 February 1984,
- the Convention between Finland and Austria on the Recognition and Enforcement of Judgments in Civil Matters, signed at Vienna on 17 November 1986, and

- the Treaty between Belgium, the Netherlands and Luxembourg in Jurisdiction, Bankruptcy, and the Validity and Enforcement of Judgments, Arbitration Awards and Authentic Instruments, signed at Brussels on 24 November 1961, in so far as it is in force.

Article 70

1. The Treaty and the Conventions referred to in Article 69 shall continue to have effect in relation to matters to which this Regulation does not apply.
2. They shall continue to have effect in respect of judgments given and documents formally drawn up or registered as authentic instruments before the entry into force of this Regulation.

Article 71

1. This Regulation shall not affect any conventions to which the Member States are parties and which in relation to particular matters, govern jurisdiction or the recognition or enforcement of judgments.
2. With a view to its uniform interpretation, paragraph 1 shall be applied in the following manner:
(a) this Regulation shall not prevent a court of a Member State, which is a party to a convention on a particular matter, from assuming jurisdiction in accordance with that convention, even where the defendant is domiciled in another Member State which is not a party to that convention. The court hearing the action shall, in any event, apply Article 26 of this Regulation;
(b) judgments given in a Member State by a court in the exercise of jurisdiction provided for in a convention on a particular matter shall be recognised and enforced in the other Member States in accordance with this Regulation. Where a convention on a particular matter to which both the Member State of origin and the Member State addressed are parties lays down conditions for the recognition or enforcement of judgments, those conditions shall apply. In any event, the provisions of this Regulation which concern the procedure for recognition and enforcement of judgments may be applied.

Article 72

This Regulation shall not affect agreements by which Member States undertook, prior to the entry into force of this Regulation pursuant to Article 59 of the Brussels Convention, not to recognise judgments given, in particular in other Contracting States to that Convention, against defendants domiciled or habitually resident in a third country where, in cases provided for in Article 4 of that Convention, the judgment could only be founded on a ground of jurisdiction specified in the second paragraph of Article 3 of that Convention.

CHAPTER VIII: FINAL PROVISIONS

Article 73

No later than five years after the entry into force of this Regulation, the Commission shall present to the European Parliament, the Council and the Economic and Social Committee a report on the application of this Regulation. The report shall be accompanied, if need be, by proposals for adaptations to this Regulation.

Article 74

1. The Member States shall notify the Commission of the texts amending the lists set out in Annexes I to IV. The Commission shall adapt the Annexes concerned accordingly.
2. The updating or technical adjustment of the forms, specimens of which appear in Annexes V and VI, shall be adopted in accordance with the advisory procedure referred to in Article 75(2).

Article 75

1. The Commission shall be assisted by a committee.
2. Where reference is made to this paragraph, Articles 3 and 7 of Decision 1999/468/EC shall apply.
3. The Committee shall adopt its rules of procedure.

Article 76

This Regulation shall enter into force on 1 March 2002.

This Regulation is binding in its entirety and directly applicable in the Member States in accordance with the Treaty establishing the European Community.

ANNEX I

Rules of jurisdiction referred to in Article 3(2) and Article 4(2)

The rules of jurisdiction referred to in Article 3(2) and Article 4(2) are the following:
- in Belgium: Article 15 of the Civil Code (Code civil/Burgerlijk Wetboek) and Article 638 of the Judicial Code (Code judiciaire/Gerechtelijk Wetboek);
- in Germany: Article 23 of the Code of Civil Procedure (Zivilprozessordnung),
- in Greece, Article 40 of the Code of Civil Procedure (Jþdijay PokisijÞy DijomolßaÞ),
- in France: Articles 14 and 15 of the Civil Code (Code civil),
- in Ireland: the rules which enable jurisdiction to be founded on the document instituting the proceedings having been served on the defendant during his temporary presence in Ireland,
- in Italy: Articles 3 and 4 of Act 218 of 31 May 1995,
- in Luxembourg: Articles 14 and 15 of the Civil Code (Code civil),
- in the Netherlands: Articles 126(3) and 127 of the Code of Civil Procedure (Wetboek van Burgerlijke Rechtsvordering),
- in Austria: Article 99 of the Court Jurisdiction Act (Jurisdiktionsnorm),
- in Portugal: Articles 65 and 65A of the Code of Civil Procedure (Código de Processo Civil) and Article 11 of the Code of Labour Procedure (Código de Processo de Trabalho),
- in Finland: the second, third and fourth sentences of the first paragraph of Section 1 of Chapter 10 of the Code of Judicial Procedure (oikeudenkäymiskaari/rättegångsbalken),
- in Sweden: the first sentence of the first paragraph of Section 3 of Chapter 10 of the Code of Judicial Procedure (rättegångsbalken),
- in the United Kingdom: rules which enable jurisdiction to be founded on:
(a) the document instituting the proceedings having been served on the defendant during his temporary presence in the United Kingdom; or
(b) the presence within the United Kingdom of property belonging to the defendant; or
(c) the seizure by the plaintiff of property situated in the United Kingdom.

ANNEX II

The courts or competent authorities to which the application referred to in Article 39 may be submitted are the following:
- in Belgium, the 'tribunal de première instance' or 'rechtbank van eerste aanleg' or 'erstinstanzliches Gericht',
- in Germany, the presiding judge of a chamber of the 'Landgericht',
- in Greece, the 'LomolekYy Pqxsodijeßo',
- in Spain, the 'Juzgado de Primera Instancia',
- in France, the presiding judge of the 'tribunal de grande instance',
- in Ireland, the High Court,
- in Italy, the 'Corte d'appello',
- in Luxembourg, the presiding judge of the 'tribunal d'arrondissement',
- in the Netherlands, the presiding judge of the 'arrondissementsrechtbank';
- in Austria, the 'Bezirksgericht',
- in Portugal, the 'Tribunal de Comarca',
- in Finland, the 'käräjäoikeus/tingsrätt',
- in Sweden, the 'Svea hovrätt',
- in the United Kingdom:
  (a) in England and Wales, the High Court of Justice, or in the case of a maintenance judgment, the Magistrate's Court on transmission by the Secretary of State;
  (b) in Scotland, the Court of Session, or in the case of a maintenance judgment, the Sheriff Court on transmission by the Secretary of State;
  (c) in Northern Ireland, the High Court of Justice, or in the case of a maintenance judgment, the Magistrate's Court on transmission by the Secretary of State;
  (d) in Gibraltar, the Supreme Court of Gibraltar, or in the case of a maintenance judgment, the Magistrates' Court on transmission by the Attorney General of Gibraltar.

ANNEX III

The courts with which appeals referred to in Article 43(2) may be lodged are the following:
- in Belgium,
(a) as regards appeal by the defendant: the 'tribunal de première instance' or 'rechtbank van eerste aanleg' or 'erstinstanzliches Gericht',
(b) as regards appeal by the applicant: the 'Cour d'appel' or 'hof van beroep',
- in the Federal Republic of Germany, the 'Oberlandesgericht',
- in Greece, the 'Eueseßo',
- in Spain, the 'Audiencia Provincial',
- in France, the 'cour d'appel',
- in Ireland, the High Court,
- in Italy, the 'corte d'appello',
- in Luxembourg, the 'Cour supérieure de Justice' sitting as a court of civil appeal,
- in the Netherlands:
(a) for the defendant: the 'arrondissementsrechtbank',
(b) for the applicant: the 'gerechtshof',
- in Austria, the 'Bezirksgericht',
- in Portugal, the ,Tribunal de Relação™,
- in Finland, the 'hovioikeus/hovrätt',
- in Sweden, the 'Svea hovrätt',
- in the United Kingdom:

(a) in England and Wales, the High Court of Justice, or in the case of a maintenance judgment, the Magistrate's Court;
(b) in Scotland, the Court of Session, or in the case of a maintenance judgment, the Sheriff Court;
(c) in Northern Ireland, the High Court of Justice, or in the case of a maintenance judgment, the Magistrate's Court;
(d) in Gibraltar, the Supreme Court of Gibraltar, or in the case of a maintenance judgment, the Magistrates' Court.

ANNEX IV

The appeals which may be lodged pursuant to Article 44 are the following
- in Belgium, Greece, Spain, France, Italy, Luxembourg and the Netherlands, an appeal in cassation,
- in Germany, a 'Rechtsbeschwerde',
- in Ireland, an appeal on a point of law to the Supreme Court,
- in Austria, a 'Revisionsrekurs',
- in Portugal, an appeal on a point of law,
- in Finland, an appeal to the 'korkein oikeus/högsta domstolen',
- in Sweden, an appeal to the 'Högsta domstolen',
- in the United Kingdom, a single further appeal on a point of law.

ANNEX V

Certificate referred to in Articles 54 and 58 of the Regulation on judgments and court settlements (English, inglés, anglais, inglese)
1. Member State of origin
2. Court or competent authority issuing the certificate
2.1. Name
2.2. Address
2.3. Tel./fax/e-mail
3. Court which delivered the judgment/approved the court settlement (*)
3.1. Type of court
3.2. Place of court
4. Judgment/court settlement (*)
4.1. Date
4.2. Reference number
4.3. The parties to the judgment/court settlement (*)
4.3.1. Name(s) of plaintiff(s)
4.3.2. Name(s) of defendant(s)
4.3.3. Name(s) of other party(ies), if any
4.4. Date of service of the document instituting the proceedings where judgment was given in default of appearance
4.5. Text of the judgment/court settlement (*) as annexed to this certificate
5. Names of parties to whom legal aid has been granted
The judgment/court settlement (*) is enforceable in the Member State of origin (Articles 38 and 58 of the Regulation) against:
Name:
Done at . . . . ,date . . . .
Signature and/or stamp . . . .

(*) Delete as appropriate.

ANNEX VI

Certificate referred to in Article 57(4) of the Regulation on authentic instruments (English, inglés, anglais, inglese)
1. Member State of origin
2. Competent authority issuing the certificate
2.1. Name
2.2. Address
2.3. Tel./fax/e-mail
3. Authority which has given authenticity to the instrument
3.1. Authority involved in the drawing up of the authentic instrument (if applicable)
3.1.1. Name and designation of authority
3.1.2. Place of authority
3.2. Authority which has registered the authentic instrument (if applicable)
3.2.1. Type of authority
3.2.2. Place of authority
4. Authentic instrument
4.1. Description of the instrument
4.2. Date
4.2.1. on which the instrument was drawn up
4.2.2. if different: on which the instrument was registered
4.3. Reference number
4.4. Parties to the instrument
4.4.1. Name of the creditor
4.4.2. Name of the debtor
5. Text of the enforceable obligation as annexed to this certificate
The authentic instrument is enforceable against the debtor in the Member State of origin (Article 57(1) of the Regulation)
Done at . . . ., date . . . .
Signature and/or stamp . . . .

CHILD ONLINE PROTECTION ACT

[H.R.3783] Child Online Protection Act (Engrossed in House)
(Source: http://thomas.loc.gov)

105th CONGRESS
2d Session
October 23, 1998

AN ACT

To amend the Communications Act of 1934 to require persons who are engaged in the business of distributing, by means of the World Wide Web, material that is harmful to minors to restrict access to such material by minors, and for other purposes.

SECTION 1. SHORT TITLE.

This Act may be cited as the 'Child Online Protection Act'.

TITLE I -- PROTECTION FROM MATERIAL THAT IS HARMFUL TO MINORS

SEC. 101. CONGRESSIONAL FINDINGS.

The Congress finds that--
(1)   while custody, care, and nurture of the child resides first with the parent, the widespread availability of the Internet presents opportunities for minors to access materials through the World Wide Web in a manner that can frustrate parental supervision or control;
(2)   the protection of the physical and psychological well-being of minors by shielding them from materials that are harmful to them is a compelling governmental interest;
(3)   to date, while the industry has developed innovative ways to help parents and educators restrict material that is harmful to minors through parental control protections and self-regulation, such efforts have not provided a national solution to the problem of minors accessing harmful material on the World Wide Web;
(4)   a prohibition on the distribution of material harmful to minors, combined with legitimate defenses, is currently the most effective and least restrictive means by which to satisfy the compelling government interest; and
(5)   notwithstanding the existence of protections that limit the distribution over the World Wide Web of material that is harmful to minors, parents, educators, and industry must continue efforts to find ways to protect children from being exposed to harmful material found on the Internet.

SEC. 102. REQUIREMENT TO RESTRICT ACCESS BY MINORS TO MATERIALS COMMERCIALLY DISTRIBUTED BY MEANS OF THE WORLD WIDE WEB THAT ARE HARMFUL TO MINORS.

Part I of title II of the Communications Act of 1934 (47 U.S.C. 201 et seq.) is amended by adding at the end the following new section:

"SEC. 231. RESTRICTION OF ACCESS BY MINORS TO MATERIALS COMMERCIALLY DISTRIBUTED BY MEANS OF WORLD WIDE WEB THAT ARE HARMFUL TO MINORS.

"(a) REQUIREMENT TO RESTRICT ACCESS-
"(1) PROHIBITED CONDUCT- Whoever knowingly and with knowledge of the character of the material, in interstate or foreign commerce by means of the World Wide Web, makes any communication for commercial purposes that is available to any minor and that includes any material that is harmful to minors shall be fined not more than $50,000, imprisoned not more than 6 months, or both.
"(2) INTENTIONAL VIOLATIONS- In addition to the penalties under paragraph (1), whoever intentionally violates such paragraph shall be subject to a fine of not more than $50,000 for each violation. For purposes of this paragraph, each day of violation shall constitute a separate violation.
"(3) CIVIL PENALTY- In addition to the penalties under paragraphs (1) and (2), whoever violates paragraph (1) shall be subject to a civil penalty of not more than $50,000 for each violation. For purposes of this paragraph, each day of violation shall constitute a separate violation.
"(b) INAPPLICABILITY OF CARRIERS AND OTHER SERVICE PROVIDERS- For purposes of subsection (a), a person shall not be considered to make any communication for commercial purposes to the extent that such person is--
"(1) a telecommunications carrier engaged in the provision of a telecommunications service;
"(2) a person engaged in the business of providing an Internet access service;
"(3) a person engaged in the business of providing an Internet information location tool; or
"(4) similarly engaged in the transmission, storage, retrieval, hosting, formatting, or translation (or any combination thereof) of a communication made by another person, without selection or alteration of the content of the communication, except that such person's deletion of a particular communication or material made by another person in a manner consistent with subsection (c) or section 230 shall not constitute such selection or alteration of the content of the communication.
"(c) AFFIRMATIVE DEFENSE-
"(1) DEFENSE- It is an affirmative defense to prosecution under this section that the defendant, in good faith, has restricted access by minors to material that is harmful to minors--
  "(A) by requiring use of a credit card, debit account, adult access code, or adult personal identification number;
  "(B) by accepting a digital certificate that verifies age; or
  "(C) by any other reasonable measures that are feasible under available technology.
"(2) PROTECTION FOR USE OF DEFENSES- No cause of action may be brought in any court or administrative agency against any person on account of any activity that is not in violation of any law punishable by criminal or civil penalty, and that the person has taken in good faith to implement a defense authorized under this subsection or otherwise to restrict or prevent the transmission of, or access to, a communication specified in this section.
"(d) PRIVACY PROTECTION REQUIREMENTS-
"(1) DISCLOSURE OF INFORMATION LIMITED- A person making a communication described in subsection (a)--
  "(A) shall not disclose any information collected for the purposes of restricting access to such communications to individuals 17 years of age or older without the prior written or electronic consent of--
    "(i) the individual concerned, if the individual is an adult; or
    "(ii) the individual's parent or guardian, if the individual is under 17 years of age; and

"(B) shall take such actions as are necessary to prevent unauthorized access to such information by a person other than the person making such communication and the recipient of such communication.
"(2) EXCEPTIONS- A person making a communication described in subsection (a) may disclose such information if the disclosure is--
"(A) necessary to make the communication or conduct a legitimate business activity related to making the communication; or
"(B) made pursuant to a court order authorizing such disclosure.
"(e) DEFINITIONS- For purposes of this subsection, the following definitions shall apply:
"(1) BY MEANS OF THE WORLD WIDE WEB- The term 'by means of the World Wide Web' means by placement of material in a computer server-based file archive so that it is publicly accessible, over the Internet, using hypertext transfer protocol or any successor protocol.
"(2) COMMERCIAL PURPOSES; ENGAGED IN THE BUSINESS-
"(A) COMMERCIAL PURPOSES- A person shall be considered to make a communication for commercial purposes only if such person is engaged in the business of making such communications.
" (B) ENGAGED IN THE BUSINESS- The term 'engaged in the business' means that the person who makes a communication, or offers to make a communication, by means of the World Wide Web, that includes any material that is harmful to minors, devotes time, attention, or labor to such activities, as a regular course of such person's trade or business, with the objective of earning a profit as a result of such activities (although it is not necessary that the person make a profit or that the making or offering to make such communications be the person's sole or principal business or source of income). A person may be considered to be engaged in the business of making, by means of the World Wide Web, communications for commercial purposes that include material that is harmful to minors, only if the person knowingly causes the material that is harmful to minors to be posted on the World Wide Web or knowingly solicits such material to be posted on the World Wide Web.
"(3) INTERNET- The term 'Internet' means the combination of computer facilities and electromagnetic transmission media, and related equipment and software, comprising the interconnected worldwide network of computer networks that employ the Transmission Control Protocol/Internet Protocol or any successor protocol to transmit information.
"(4) INTERNET ACCESS SERVICE- The term 'Internet access service' means a service that enables users to access content, information, electronic mail, or other services offered over the Internet, and may also include access to proprietary content, information, and other services as part of a package of services offered to consumers. Such term does not include telecommunications services.
"(5) INTERNET INFORMATION LOCATION TOOL- The term 'Internet information location tool' means a service that refers or links users to an online location on the World Wide Web. Such term includes directories, indices, references, pointers, and hypertext links.
"(6) MATERIAL THAT IS HARMFUL TO MINORS- The term 'material that is harmful to minors' means any communication, picture, image, graphic image file, article, recording, writing, or other matter of any kind that is obscene or that--
"(A) the average person, applying contemporary community standards, would find, taking the material as a whole and with respect to minors, is designed to appeal to, or is designed to pander to, the prurient interest;
"(B) depicts, describes, or represents, in a manner patently offensive with respect to minors, an actual or simulated sexual act or sexual contact, an actual or simulated normal or perverted sexual act , or a lewd exhibition of the genitals or post-pubescent female breast; and

"(C) taken as a whole, lacks serious literary, artistic, political, or scientific value for minors.
"(7) MINOR- The term 'minor' means any person under 17 years of age.'.

SEC. 103. NOTICE REQUIREMENT.

(a) NOTICE- Section 230 of the Communications Act of 1934 (47 U.S.C. 230) is amended--
(1) in subsection (d)(1), by inserting 'or 231' after 'section 223';
(2) by redesignating subsections (d) and (e) as subsections (e) and (f), respectively; and
(3) by inserting after subsection (c) the following new subsection:
"(d) OBLIGATIONS OF INTERACTIVE COMPUTER SERVICE- A provider of interactive computer service shall, at the time of entering an agreement with a customer for the provision of interactive computer service and in a manner deemed appropriate by the provider, notify such customer that parental control protections (such as computer hardware, software, or filtering services) are commercially available that may assist the customer in limiting access to material that is harmful to minors. Such notice shall identify, or provide the customer with access to information identifying, current providers of such protections.'.
(b) CONFORMING AMENDMENT- Section 223(h)(2) of the Communications Act of 1934 (47 U.S.C. 223(h)(2)) is amended by striking '230(e)(2)' and inserting "230(f)(2)".

SEC. 104. STUDY BY COMMISSION ON ONLINE CHILD PROTECTION .

(a) ESTABLISHMENT- There is hereby established a temporary Commission to be known as the Commission on Online Child Protection (in this section referred to as the 'Commission') for the purpose of conducting a study under this section regarding methods to help reduce access by minors to material that is harmful to minors on the Internet.
(b) MEMBERSHIP- The Commission shall be composed of 19 members, as follows:
(1) INDUSTRY MEMBERS- The Commission shall include--
    (A) 2 members who are engaged in the business of providing Internet filtering or blocking services or software;
    (B) 2 members who are engaged in the business of providing Internet access services;
    (C) 2 members who are engaged in the business of providing labeling or ratings services;
    (D) 2 members who are engaged in the business of providing Internet portal or search services;
    (E) 2 members who are engaged in the business of providing domain name registration services;
    (F) 2 members who are academic experts in the field of technology; and
    (G) 4 members who are engaged in the business of making content available over the Internet.
Of the members of the Commission by reason of each subparagraph of this paragraph, an equal number shall be appointed by the Speaker of the House of Representatives and by the Majority Leader of the Senate.
(2) EX OFFICIO MEMBERS- The Commission shall include the following officials:
    (A) The Assistant Secretary (or the Assistant Secretary's designee).
    (B) The Attorney General (or the Attorney General's designee).
    (C) The Chairman of the Federal Trade Commission (or the Chairman's designee).
(c) STUDY-
(1) IN GENERAL- The Commission shall conduct a study to identify technological or other methods that--
    (A) will help reduce access by minors to material that is harmful to minors on the Internet; and

(B) may meet the requirements for use as affirmative defenses for purposes of section 231(c) of the Communications Act of 1934 (as added by this Act).
Any methods so identified shall be used as the basis for making legislative recommendations to the Congress under subsection (d)(3).
(2) SPECIFIC METHODS- In carrying out the study, the Commission shall identify and analyze various technological tools and methods for protecting minors from material that is harmful to minors, which shall include (without limitation)--
　(A) a common resource for parents to use to help protect minors (such as a 'one-click-away' resource);
　(B) filtering or blocking software or services;
　(C) labeling or rating systems;
　(D) age verification systems;
　(E) the establishment of a domain name for posting of any material that is harmful to minors; and
　(F) any other existing or proposed technologies or methods for reducing access by minors to such material.
(3) ANALYSIS- In analyzing technologies and other methods identified pursuant to paragraph (2), the Commission shall examine--
　(A) the cost of such technologies and methods;
　(B) the effects of such technologies and methods on law enforcement entities;
　(C) the effects of such technologies and methods on privacy;
　(D) the extent to which material that is harmful to minors is globally distributed and the effect of such technologies and methods on such distribution;
　(E) the accessibility of such technologies and methods to parents; and
　(F) such other factors and issues as the Commission considers relevant and appropriate.
(d) REPORT- Not later than 1 year after the enactment of this Act, the Commission shall submit a report to the Congress containing the results of the study under this section, which shall include--
(1) a description of the technologies and methods identified by the study and the results of the analysis of each such technology and method;
(2) the conclusions and recommendations of the Commission regarding each such technology or method;
(3) recommendations for legislative or administrative actions to implement the conclusions of the committee; and
(4) a description of the technologies or methods identified by the study that may meet the requirements for use as affirmative defenses for purposes of section 231(c) of the Communications Act of 1934 (as added by this Act).
(e) STAFF AND RESOURCES- The Assistant Secretary for Communication and Information of the Department of Commerce shall provide to the Commission such staff and resources as the Assistant Secretary determines necessary for the Commission to perform its duty efficiently and in accordance with this section.
(f) TERMINATION- The Commission shall terminate 30 days after the submission of the report under subsection (d).
(g) INAPPLICABILITY OF FEDERAL ADVISORY COMMITTEE ACT - The Federal Advisory Committee Act (5 U.S.C. App.) shall not apply to the Commission.

SEC. 105. EFFECTIVE DATE.

This title and the amendments made by this title shall take effect 30 days after the date of enactment of this Act.

TITLE II--CHILDREN'S ONLINE PRIVACY PROTECTION

SEC. 201. DEFINITIONS.

In this title:

(1) CHILD - The term 'child' means an individual under the age of 13.

(2) OPERATOR- The term 'operator' means any person operating a website on the World Wide Web or any online service for commercial purposes, including any person offering products or services for sale through that website or online service, involving commerce--

    (A) among the several States or with 1 or more foreign nations;

    (B) in any territory of the United States or in the District of Columbia, or between any such territory and--

        (i) another such territory; or

        (ii) any State or foreign nation; or

    (C) between the District of Columbia and any State, territory, or foreign nation.

For purposes of this title, the term 'operator' does not include any non-profit entity that would otherwise be exempt from coverage under section 5 of the Federal Trade Commission Act (15 U.S.C. 45).

(3) COMMISSION- The term 'Commission' means the Federal Trade Commission.

(4) DISCLOSURE- The term 'disclosure' means, with respect to personal information--

    (A) the release of personal information collected from a child in identifiable form by an operator for any purpose, except where such information is provided to a person other than the operator who provides support for the internal operations of the website and does not disclose or use that information for any other purpose; and

    (B) making personal information collected from a child by a website or online service directed to children or with actual knowledge that such information was collected from a child , publicly available in identifiable form, by any means including by a public posting, through the Internet, or through--

        (i) a home page of a website;

        (ii) a pen pal service;

        (iii) an electronic mail service;

        (iv) a message board; or

        (v) a chat room.

(5) FEDERAL AGENCY- The term 'Federal agency' means an agency, as that term is defined in section 551(1) of title 5, United States Code.

(6) INTERNET- The term 'Internet' means collectively the myriad of computer and telecommunications facilities, including equipment and operating software, which comprise the interconnected world-wide network of networks that employ the Transmission Control Protocol/Internet Protocol, or any predecessor or successor protocols to such protocol, to communicate information of all kinds by wire or radio.

(7) PARENT- The term 'parent' includes a legal guardian.

(8) PERSONAL INFORMATION- The term 'personal information' means individually identifiable information about an individual collected online , including--

    (A) a first and last name;

    (B) a home or other physical address including street name and name of a city or town;

    (C) an e-mail address;

    (D) a telephone number;

    (E) a Social Security number;

(F) any other identifier that the Commission determines permits the physical or online contacting of a specific individual; or

(G) information concerning the child or the parents of that child that the website collects online from the child and combines with an identifier described in this paragraph.

(9) VERIFIABLE PARENTAL CONSENT- The term 'verifiable parental consent' means any reasonable effort (taking into consideration available technology), including a request for authorization for future collection, use, and disclosure described in the notice, to ensure that a parent of a child receives notice of the operator's personal information collection, use, and disclosure practices, and authorizes the collection, use, and disclosure, as applicable, of personal information and the subsequent use of that information before that information is collected from that child .

(10) WEBSITE OR ONLINE SERVICE DIRECTED TO CHILDREN-

(A) IN GENERAL- The term 'website or online service directed to children' means --

(i) a commercial website or online service that is targeted to children; or

(ii) that portion of a commercial website or online service that is targeted to children.

(B) LIMITATION- A commercial website or online service, or a portion of a commercial website or online service, shall not be deemed directed to children solely for referring or linking to a commercial website or online service directed to children by using information location tools, including a directory, index, reference, pointer, or hypertext link.

(11) PERSON- The term 'person' means any individual, partnership, corporation, trust, estate, cooperative, association, or other entity.

(12) ONLINE CONTACT INFORMATION- The term 'online contact information' means an e-mail address or another substantially similar identifier that permits direct contact with a person online .

SEC. 202. REGULATION OF UNFAIR AND DECEPTIVE ACTS AND PRACTICES IN CONNECTION WITH THE COLLECTION AND USE OF PERSONAL INFORMATION FROM AND ABOUT CHILDREN ON THE INTERNET.

(a) ACTS PROHIBITED-

(1) IN GENERAL- It is unlawful for an operator of a website or online service directed to children, or any operator that has actual knowledge that it is collecting personal information from a child , to collect personal information from a child in a manner that violates the regulations prescribed under subsection (b).

(2) DISCLOSURE TO PARENT PROTECTED- Notwithstanding paragraph (1), neither an operator of such a website or online service nor the operator's agent shall be held to be liable under any Federal or State law for any disclosure made in good faith and following reasonable procedures in responding to a request for disclosure of personal information under subsection (b)(1)(B)(iii) to the parent of a child .

(b) REGULATIONS-

(1) IN GENERAL- Not later than 1 year after the date of the enactment of this Act , the Commission shall promulgate under section 553 of title 5, United States Code, regulations that--

(A) require the operator of any website or online service directed to children that collects personal information from children or the operator of a website or online service that has actual knowledge that it is collecting personal information from a child --

(i) to provide notice on the website of what information is collected from children by the operator, how the operator uses such information, and the operator's disclosure practices for such information; and

(ii) to obtain verifiable parental consent for the collection, use, or disclosure of personal information from children;

(B) require the operator to provide, upon request of a parent whose child has provided personal information to that website or online service--
    (i) a description of the specific types of personal information collected from the child by that operator;
    (ii) notwithstanding any other provision of law, the opportunity at any time to refuse to permit the operator's further use or maintenance in retrievable form, or future online collection, of personal information on that child ; and
    (iii) a means that is reasonable under the circumstances for the parent to obtain any personal information collected from that child ;
(C) prohibit conditioning a child's participation in a game, the offering of a prize, or another activity on the child disclosing more personal information than is reasonably necessary to participate in such activity;
(D) require the operator of such a website or online service to establish and maintain reasonable procedures to protect the confidentiality, security, and integrity of personal information collected from children; and
(E) permit the operator of such a website or online service to collect, use, and disseminate such information as is necessary--
    (i) to protect the security or integrity of its website;
    (ii) to take precautions against liability;
    (iii) to respond to judicial process; and
    (iv) to provide information to law enforcement agencies or for an investigation on a matter related to public safety.

(2) WHEN CONSENT NOT REQUIRED- Verifiable parental consent under paragraph (1)(A)(ii) is not required in the case of--
(A) online contact information collected from a child that is used only to respond directly on a one-time basis to a specific request from the child and is not used to recontact the child and is not maintained in retrievable form by the operator;
(B) a request for the name or online contact information of a parent or child that is used for the sole purpose of obtaining parental consent or providing notice under this section and where such information is not maintained in retrievable form by the operator if parental consent is not obtained after a reasonable time;
(C) online contact information collected from a child that is used only to respond more than once directly to a specific request from the child and is not used to recontact the child beyond the scope of that request--
    (i) if, before any additional response after the initial response to the child , the operator uses reasonable efforts to provide a parent notice of the online contact information collected from the child , the purposes for which it is to be used, and an opportunity for the parent to request that the operator make no further use of the information and that it not be maintained in retrievable form; or
    (ii) without notice to the parent in such circumstances as the Commission may determine are appropriate, taking into consideration the benefits to the child of access to information and services, and risks to the security and privacy of the child, in regulations promulgated under this subsection; or
(D) the name of the child and online contact information (to the extent necessary to protect the safety of a child participant in the site)--
    (i) used only for the purpose of protecting such safety;
    (ii) not used to recontact the child or for any other purpose; and
    (iii) not disclosed on the site, if the operator uses reasonable efforts to provide a parent notice of the name and online contact information collected from the child, the purposes for which it is to be used, and an opportunity for the parent to request that the

operator make no further use of the information and that it not be maintained in retrievable form.

(c) ENFORCEMENT- Subject to sections 203 and 205, a violation of a regulation prescribed under subsection (a) shall be treated as a violation of a rule defining an unfair or deceptive act or practice prescribed under section 18(a)(1)(B) of the Federal Trade Commission Act (15 U.S.C. 57a(a)(1)(B)).

(d) INCONSISTENT STATE LAW- No State or local government may impose any liability for commercial activities or actions by operators in interstate or foreign commerce in connection with an activity or action described in this title that is inconsistent with the treatment of those activities or actions under this section.

SEC. 203. SAFE HARBORS.

(a) GUIDELINES- An operator may satisfy the requirements of regulations issued under section 202(b) by following a set of self-regulatory guidelines, issued by representatives of the marketing or online industries, or by other persons, approved under subsection (b).

(b) INCENTIVES-

(1) SELF-REGULATORY INCENTIVES- In prescribing regulations under section 202, the Commission shall provide incentives for self-regulation by operators to implement the protections afforded children under the regulatory requirements described in subsection (b) of that section.

(2) DEEMED COMPLIANCE- Such incentives shall include provisions for ensuring that a person will be deemed to be in compliance with the requirements of the regulations under section 202 if that person complies with guidelines that, after notice and comment, are approved by the Commission upon making a determination that the guidelines meet the requirements of the regulations issued under section 202.

(3) EXPEDITED RESPONSE TO REQUESTS- The Commission shall act upon requests for safe harbor treatment within 180 days of the filing of the request, and shall set forth in writing its conclusions with regard to such requests.

(c) APPEALS- Final action by the Commission on a request for approval of guidelines, or the failure to act within 180 days on a request for approval of guidelines, submitted under subsection (b) may be appealed to a district court of the United States of appropriate jurisdiction as provided for in section 706 of title 5, United States Code.

SEC. 204. ACTIONS BY STATES.

(a) IN GENERAL-

(1) CIVIL ACTIONS- In any case in which the attorney general of a State has reason to believe that an interest of the residents of that State has been or is threatened or adversely affected by the engagement of any person in a practice that violates any regulation of the Commission prescribed under section 202(b), the State, as parens patriae, may bring a civil action on behalf of the residents of the State in a district court of the United States of appropriate jurisdiction to--

    (A) enjoin that practice;

    (B) enforce compliance with the regulation;

    (C) obtain damage, restitution, or other compensation on behalf of residents of the State; or

    (D) obtain such other relief as the court may consider to be appropriate.

(2) NOTICE-

    (A) IN GENERAL- Before filing an action under paragraph (1), the attorney general of the State involved shall provide to the Commission--

        (i) written notice of that action; and

        (ii) a copy of the complaint for that action.

(B) EXEMPTION-
  (i) IN GENERAL- Subparagraph (A) shall not apply with respect to the filing of an action by an attorney general of a State under this subsection, if the attorney general determines that it is not feasible to provide the notice described in that subparagraph before the filing of the action.
  (ii) NOTIFICATION- In an action described in clause (i), the attorney general of a State shall provide notice and a copy of the complaint to the Commission at the same time as the attorney general files the action.
(b) INTERVENTION-
(1) IN GENERAL- On receiving notice under subsection (a)(2), the Commission shall have the right to intervene in the action that is the subject of the notice.
(2) EFFECT OF INTERVENTION- If the Commission intervenes in an action under subsection(a), it shall have the right--
  (A) to be heard with respect to any matter that arises in that action; and
  (B) to file a petition for appeal.
(3) AMICUS CURIAE- Upon application to the court, a person whose self-regulatory guidelines have been approved by the Commission and are relied upon as a defense by any defendant to a proceeding under this section may file amicus curiae in that proceeding.
(c) CONSTRUCTION- For purposes of bringing any civil action under subsection (a), nothing in this title shall be construed to prevent an attorney general of a State from exercising the powers conferred on the attorney general by the laws of that State to--
(1) conduct investigations;
(2) administer oaths or affirmations; or
(3) compel the attendance of witnesses or the production of documentary and other evidence.
(d) ACTIONS BY THE COMMISSION- In any case in which an action is instituted by or on behalf of the Commission for violation of any regulation prescribed under section 202, no State may, during the pendency of that action, institute an action under subsection (a) against any defendant named in the complaint in that action for violation of that regulation.
(e) VENUE; SERVICE OF PROCESS-
(1) VENUE- Any action brought under subsection (a) may be brought in the district court of the United States that meets applicable requirements relating to venue under section 1391 of title 28, United States Code.
(2) SERVICE OF PROCESS- In an action brought under subsection (a), process may be served in any district in which the defendant--
  (A) is an inhabitant; or
  (B) may be found.

SEC. 205. ADMINISTRATION AND APPLICABILITY OF ACT .

(a) IN GENERAL- Except as otherwise provided, this title shall be enforced by the Commission under the Federal Trade Commission Act (15 U.S.C. 41 et seq.).
(b) PROVISIONS- Compliance with the requirements imposed under this title shall be enforced under--
(1) section 8 of the Federal Deposit Insurance Act (12 U.S.C. 1818), in the case of--
  (A) national banks, and Federal branches and Federal agencies of foreign banks, by the Office of the Comptroller of the Currency;
  (B) member banks of the Federal Reserve System (other than national banks), branches and agencies of foreign banks (other than Federal branches, Federal agencies, and insured State branches of foreign banks), commercial lending companies owned or controlled by foreign

banks, and organizations operating under section 25 or 25(a) of the Federal Reserve Act (12 U.S.C. 601 et seq. and 611 et. seq.), by the Board; and

(C) banks insured by the Federal Deposit Insurance Corporation (other than members of the Federal Reserve System) and insured State branches of foreign banks, by the Board of Directors of the Federal Deposit Insurance Corporation;

(2) section 8 of the Federal Deposit Insurance Act (12 U.S.C. 1818), by the Director of the Office of Thrift Supervision, in the case of a savings association the deposits of which are insured by the Federal Deposit Insurance Corporation;

(3) the Federal Credit Union Act (12 U.S.C. 1751 et seq.) by the National Credit Union Administration Board with respect to any Federal credit union;

(4) part A of subtitle VII of title 49, United States Code, by the Secretary of Transportation with respect to any air carrier or foreign air carrier subject to that part;

(5) the Packers and Stockyards Act , 1921 (7 U.S.C. 181 et. seq.) (except as provided in section 406 of that Act (7 U.S.C. 226, 227)), by the Secretary of Agriculture with respect to any activities subject to that Act ; and

(6) the Farm Credit Act of 1971 (12 U.S.C. (2001 et seq.) by the Farm Credit Administration with respect to any Federal land bank, Federal land bank association, Federal intermediate credit bank, or production credit association.

(c) EXERCISE OF CERTAIN POWERS- For the purpose of the exercise by any agency referred to in subsection (a) of its powers under any Act referred to in that subsection, a violation of any requirement imposed under this title shall be deemed to be a violation of a requirement imposed under that Act . In addition to its powers under any provision of law specifically referred to in subsection (a), each of the agencies referred to in that subsection may exercise, for the purpose of enforcing compliance with any requirement imposed under this title, any other authority conferred on it by law.

(d) ACTIONS BY THE COMMISSION- The Commission shall prevent any person from violating a rule of the Commission under section 202 in the same manner, by the same means, and with the same jurisdiction, powers, and duties as though all applicable terms and provisions of the Federal Trade Commission Act (15 U.S.C. 41 et seq.) were incorporated into and made a part of this title. Any entity that violates such rule shall be subject to the penalties and entitled to the privileges and immunities provided in the Federal Trade Commission Act in the same manner, by the same means, and with the same jurisdiction, power, and duties as though all applicable terms and provisions of the Federal Trade Commission Act were incorporated into and made a part of this title.

(e) EFFECT ON OTHER LAWS- Nothing contained in this title shall be construed to limit the authority of the Commission under any other provisions of law.

SEC. 206. REVIEW.

Not later than 5 years after the effective date of the regulations initially issued under section 202, the Commission shall--

(1) review the implementation of this title, including the effect of the implementation of this title on practices relating to the collection and disclosure of information relating to children, children's ability to obtain access to information of their choice online, and on the availability of websites directed to children; and

(2) prepare and submit to Congress a report on the results of the review under paragraph (1).

SEC. 207. EFFECTIVE DATE.

Sections 202(a), 204, and 205 of this title take effect on the later of--

(1) the date that is 18 months after the date of enactment of this Act; or
(2) the date on which the Commission rules on the first application for safe harbor treatment under section 203 if the Commission does not rule on the first such application within one year after the date of enactment of this Act, but in no case later than the date that is 30 months after the date of enactment of this Act.